Principles of Business

8e

LES R. DLABAY

JAMES L. BURROW

BRAD A. KLEINDL

SOUTH-WESTERN
CENGAGE Learning™

Australia • Brazil • Japan • Korea • Mexico • Singapore • Spain • United Kingdom • United States

SOUTH-WESTERN
CENGAGE Learning™

**Principles of Business,
Eighth Edition**
Les Dlabay, James Burrow, Brad Kleindl

Vice President of Editorial, Business: Jack W. Calhoun

Vice President/Editor-in-Chief: Karen Schmohe

Executive Editor: Eve Lewis

Developmental Editor: Karen Caldwell

Editorial Assistant: Anne Kelly

Senior Marketing Communications Manager:
Sarah Greber

Senior Content Project Manager: Diane Bowdler

Senior Media Editor: Sally Nieman

Senior Website Project Manager: Ed Stubenrauch

Senior Frontlist Buyer: Kevin Kluck

Production Service: Integra Software Services Pvt. Ltd.

Senior Art Director: Tippy McIntosh

Cover and Internal Design: Liz Harasymczuk,
Liz Harasymczuk Design

Cover Image: ©Masterfile

Photo and Text Permissions Acquisitions Manager:
Deanna Ettinger

Photo Researcher: Darren Wright

For product information and technology assistance, contact us at
Cengage Learning Customer & Sales Support, 1-800-354-9706

For permission to use material from this text or product,
submit all requests online at **www.cengage.com/permissions**
Further permissions questions can be emailed to
permissionrequest@cengage.com

 The Career Clusters icons are being used with permission of the: States' Career Clusters Initiative, 2011, **www.careerclusters.org**

Exam*View*® is a registered trademark of eInstruction Corp. Windows is a registered trademark of the Microsoft Corporation used herein under license.

© 2012 Cengage Learning. All Rights Reserved.

All illustrations, tables, and figures are © Cengage Learning unless otherwise noted.

ISBN-13: 978-1-111-42694-1

ISBN-10: 1-111-42694-5

South-Western
5191 Natorp Boulevard
Mason, OH 45040
USA

Cengage Learning products are represented in Canada by Nelson Education, Ltd.

For your course and learning solutions, visit **www.cengage.com/school**
Visit our company website at **www.cengage.com**

About the Authors

Les R. Dlabay, Ed.D., is a Professor of Business in the Department of Economics and Business at Lake Forest College in Illinois. He has taught more than 30 different business courses in high school, community college, university, teacher preparation, and adult education programs. Dr. Dlabay has presented more than 300 teacher workshops and seminars emphasizing interactive learning strategies, including team projects and field research activities. His "hobbies" include a cereal package collection (from more than 100 countries) and banknotes from 200 countries; these are used to teach economic, cultural, and political aspects of global business. In an effort to prepare students to do business in varied economic settings, Professor Dlabay makes extensive use of class assignments related to world hunger, poverty, micro-finance, and micro-enterprise development.

James L. Burrow, Ph.D., has a background in marketing and human resource development. He works regularly with the business community and other organizations as a consultant on marketing and performance improvement strategies including the use of the Internet as an education and training resource. He recently retired from the faculty of North Carolina State University where he served as the coordinator of the graduate Training and Development Program for more than 15 years. Dr. Burrow received degrees from the University of Northern Iowa and the University of Nebraska in Marketing and Marketing Education.

Brad A. Kleindl, Ph.D., is dean of the School of Business at Park University in Kansas City, Missouri. He previously served as dean and professor of marketing of The Robert W. Plaster College of Business Administration at Missouri Southern State University. He has authored and co-authored six books and more than 60 articles and conference papers. Dr. Kleindl has served twice as a Senior Fulbright Scholar, during 2007 in Austria and 2003 in South Africa. He has taught courses in consumer behavior, marketing research, principles of marketing, Internet marketing, and international marketing, and has presented at conferences and industry meetings across the United States, Europe, Africa, and Asia.

Brief Contents

Contents

Digital Vision/Getty Images

Photodisc/Getty Images

UNIT 2
Business Organization and Management 96
Business Vision: From Start-up to Global Dominance 97

Digital Vision/Getty Images

Photodisc/Getty Images

CHAPTER 5
Business Organization 98

Features

Assessment and Review

CHAPTER 6
Entrepreneurship and Small Business Management 122

Features

Assessment and Review

Photodisc/Getty Images

Stockbyte/Getty Images

Blend Images/Getty Images

UNIT 3
Business Operations and Technology   228
Business Vision: Keeping Them in the Air   229

vm/iStockphoto.com

UNIT 4
Personal Financial Management 364
Business Vision: Financial Services Around the World   365

ilbusca/iStockphoto.com

CHAPTER 17

Banking and Financial Services 424

Photodisc/Getty Images

CHAPTER 18

Consumer Credit 452

Stockbyte/Getty Images

Photodisc/Getty Images

Reviewers

Debra Allen
Business and Information
Technology Teacher
Salem High School
Salem, Indiana

Herwin Auld
Business Instructor
Touro College
New York, New York

Toni Barrows
Business Teacher
Clay High School
Green Cove Spring, Florida

Vern T. Borrowman
Business Education Teacher
Mexico High School
Mexico, New York

Joseph G. Braccini
Business Teacher
Walpole High School
Walpole, Massachusetts

Dave Daubenspeck
Business Department Chair
Abington Sr. High School
Abington, Pennsylvania

Michelle V. Gonzalez
Sr. Business Process Analyst
Orange County Public Schools
Orlando, Florida

Nicholas Haug
Business and Marketing Teacher
St. Croix Central High School
Hammond, Wisconsin

Stephanie Hezekiah
Business Teacher
Lowndes High School
Valdosta, Georgia

Betsy Hudgins
Assistant Principal
Henry County High School
Paris, Tennessee

Dana Hurda
Business Teacher
Evansville High School
Evansville, Wisconsin

Karen Renfroe
Business Teacher
Washington County High School
Sandersville, Georgia

Amy Scroggs
Business Teacher
Jasper County Jr./Sr. High School
Monticello, Georgia

Kelli Lea Shill
Business Education Teacher
River Dell Regional High School
Oradell, New Jersey

Brooke Simmons
Business and Technology Teacher
Columbus City Schools
Columbus, Ohio

Your Building Blocks *for* Business Success!

Principles of Business 8e

Finance   Marketing   Operations   Management

DLABAY   BURROW   KLEINDL

Intro to Business is now *Principles of Business, 8e!*

This comprehensive introductory business text provides complete instruction in business concepts and skills students need in today's competitive environment. This market-leading text offers extensive coverage in major business concepts, such as Finance, Marketing, Operations, and Management. Students will gain valuable information and skills for the workplace, as well as preparation for success in competitive events.

Principles of Business is the foundations course for the following Career Clusters pathways:

- Business, Management & Administration
- Finance
- Marketing, Sales & Service

New Updates and Key Features help students better understand the business world.

Chapter 10 on Marketing includes **new content covering Retailing and Merchandising** to support important curriculum standards.

television, radio, newspapers, magazines, mass mailings, outdoor displays, and the Internet.

Consumers are exposed to hundreds of communications including promotional communications in the media each day. These messages are not developed for or delivered directly to individuals. For this reason, the advertisements must be designed to attract attention and focus the consumer on a small amount of specific information. Most advertisements do not result in an immediate sale. Rather, they attempt to influence prospects to take additional action such as visit a store, gather more information, or test the product.

Advertising campaigns direct communication efforts for both institutional ... the entire business and ...ising for the individual ...rtising campaigns and indi... ...ld be analyzed for effec... ...dual ads are often tested ... ...placed by using focus ...igns are evaluated during ...are completed to see if the ...unication has been received. ... of mass promotion are ...promotion, and public rela... ...is non-paid promotional ... presented by the media ...the business or organiza... ...g promoted. *Public...*

How can stores communicate effectively with customers through merchandising?

Merchandising

Retailers often attempt to obtain action from their customers by engaging in merchandising. **Merchandising** includes a set of promotional activities designed to generate sales in the retail setting. There are a number of retail merchandising strategies. *Visual merchandising* uses visual signals to communicate in a retail settin...

16-3 Taxes in Your Life

Goals

1 Identify the types of taxes paid by consumers.

2 Describe the steps when filing a federal income tax return.

3 Explain tax assistance sources.

4 Identify common tax-planning strategies.

Key Terms

tax 405
earned income 407
investment income 407
tax deduction 407
exemption 408
taxable income 408
tax credit 408

Focus on REAL LIFE

"I just got my first paycheck and was I surprised," commented Nick. "I earned more than $200, but my check was for less than $160. What's the deal with that?"

"I guess you didn't pay attention in business class about income taxes and Social Security taxes," suggested Margie.

"Well, I do know that some of my pay has to go for roads, parks, and protecting our country," responded Nick. "And that I must file a tax return to get my refund or to pay an additional amount. Also, my tax return must be filed each year by..."

"OK—it sounds like you did learn a few things about taxes in our business class," acknowledged Margie.

TYPES OF TAXES

Each day, without thinking about it, people pay taxes. Many people pay taxes through paycheck deductions. Depending where you live and shop, you might pay taxes when you make purchases. Wise tax planning starts with knowing the types of taxes you pay.

A **tax** is a charge imposed by a government to finance public services. Federal, state, and local governments levy taxes. Most people pay taxes in four major categories: purchases, property, wealth, and earning. Common taxes on purchases are sales tax and excise tax. Real estate property tax and personal property taxes are examples of taxes on property. Taxes on wealth include estate tax, inheritance tax, and gift tax. Social Security tax and income ... examples of ta...

When and Where You Pay Taxes

Some taxes are paid as part of everyday living. Other taxes are due on specific dates. And some taxes, such as estate taxes, are triggered by an event—the death of a person.

Sales tax is collected at the time of purchase. If you buy a jacket for $80 you might pay more than $80. If your state has a 5 percent sales tax and you are shopping in a county with a 1 percent sales tax, you will pay the seller $84.80 for your coat. The seller will pay $4 to the state and $0.80 to the county. In recent years, five states did not have a state sales tax: Alaska, Delaware, Montana, New Hampshire, and Oregon.

Goal 1

Identify the types of taxes paid by consumers.

A new Lesson on **Taxes in Your Life** covers types of taxes, federal income tax basics, completing Form 1040, and tax planning strategies.

Business Insight for the 21st Century

Online Micropayments

In the early years of the Internet, users expected information to be available free to anyone. Over time, Internet consumers started to accept that many websites restricted access to content through the use of registrations, passwords, or, in some cases, annual or monthly membership fees. Today, due to the quality and variety of online content, consumers are more willing to pay for the types of products and services they otherwise would have to purchase elsewhere—songs, movies, video games, event tickets, and magazines. The digital content business generated $36 billion in 2009 and is growing rapidly.

In 2008, more than 1.4 billion songs were purchased for download. While that number sounds impressive, there is a major gap between online digital content sales of very low-cost products and services and that of higher priced ones. Peo...

to pay a small amount to use an online game, download a song, view a new music video, or watch a sporting event online but they want a quick and easy payment method. Businesses will make those products available if they can collect the small fees in an efficient and profitable way.

Micropayments are online payments too small to be affordably processed by credit card or other electronic payment methods. Most micropayments are under $5 and may be as low as a few cents per transaction. Because of the limitations in payment options, micropayments currently make up less than 3 percent of all online digital content purchases.

New companies as well as industry giants are looking at ways to solve the micropayments problem. One of the first micropayment processing com-

individual purchases into one larger transaction for processing so the cost and time required to process separate payments are reduced. With Microsoft Points system, consumers buy points in advance and redeem them at the Xbox Live Marketplace for game add-ons, new arcade games, and even HD movie and TV show downloads. It is certain that new technologies will soon solve the micropayment problem due to the almost unlimited potential for digital content sales.

Think Critically

1. Why have many consumers changed their views about the value of online content so they are now willing to pay small fees?

2. Research micropayments and identify unique ...

Business Insight for the 21st Century focuses on current technology and e-commerce issues in the business world.

21st Century Skills

Communication and Collaboration

Working in Teams

Each day, thousands of workers make decisions and apply business actions in team settings. The ability to work in a team is rated by most employers as one of the most important career skills. The combined skills of the people in a team are greater than that of individuals working alone. When working in a team in class or on the job, consider the following:

- Be prepared for minor conflicts in the first phase of a team project. Differences in opinions will surface. Be ready to adapt to the personalities, behaviors, and actions of others.
- Agree upon guidelines for project goals, meeting times, location, agenda, missed meetings, conflict resolution, and other procedures.
- Define leadership and other roles. Some team members will keep notes and bring needed materials. Others will conduct research or create visuals for a presentation.
- Determine methods for decision-making. Usually this will be done based on agreement among team members after discussion of various issues and opposing points of view.
- Keep focused on your goals. Avoid being distracted by minor issues and personality conflicts. Maintain a team-oriented environment by saying "we, us, ours." Avoid using "I, me, my, mine."
- Be courteous to others. Respect differences in opinions, personalities, and decision-making styles.

Working in teams is something...
throughout...

Why is it important to define roles when working in teams?

responsibility for its work and take pride in its accomplishments. Some team projects will be frustrating. It is important to maintain a positive attitude. Some of the best learning and most valuable experiences result from encounters with others with different backgrounds and diverse points of view.

Think Critically

1. What do you like about working in teams? Are the... any aspects about working in teams th... Describe them...

> **21st Century Skills** exposes students to important everyday soft skills, such as making effective presentations, resolving conflict, teamwork, interviewing, and problem solving.

Evaluate the Advantages and Disadvantages of Each Choice

You might find it helpful to write down your choices and then list the advantages

Write an essay that describes how you could use the decision-making process to select classes for next year that will help you achieve your life-span goals. In what other ways will the decision-making process benefit you in the future?

Act o...
Once...
is the...
have c...
spend...
with y...
self. T...
you ha...
your c...
after i...
activit...
choice...
will be...

> **Life-Span Plan activities** are now part of each lesson, located where they apply to the content.

1-1 Satisfying Needs and Wants

Goals

1. Explain the difference between needs and wants
2. Distinguish between goods and services
3. Describe the types of economic resources

Key Terms

needs 6
wants 7
goods 7
services 7
economic resources 9

Focus on REAL LIFE

Gina and Jermaine walked into an electronics store to look at a portable digital media player that had just been released. It has a 250GB super drive allowing the user to store and retrieve movies, photos, and music all on one small device.

As they stood in line, Jermaine said, "I don't know if the player is worth the $400 price. I hear you can get the older model for only $150."

Gina responded, "I know, but you can watch wide screen videos and movies on the new model."

Jermaine looked around and said, "With most of these things, if you wait a few months, the price will drop. I'm not sure I need it right now."

Jermaine's decision is one you often face. You see advertisements for exciting new products, but you do not need and cannot afford all of them. How do you decide which ones you should buy and how much to pay?

Goal 1

Explain the difference between needs and wants.

NEEDS AND WANTS

Hardly a day goes by that you don't see a product or service that you would like to have. You see them at the shopping mall, the grocery store, and school. Store displays and advertisements on television, radio, and the Internet attempt to convince you that you need whatever is new. How do you decide what to buy or even if you need to buy at all?

good education, a good job, and safety. Most people need transportation to and from school and work. People who have health problems need health care and medicines.

Needs Are Essential

You want many things, but do you really need them? Determining what is a need and what is a want i...

> **Focus on Real Life** is a short conversational scenario that relates to student life and gets them thinking about the topics in each lesson.

Planning a Career in ...
BUSINESS DEVELOPMENT

Agriculture, Food & Natural Resources

Providing food, water, health care, education, and financial services to the billions of people in need around the world is the basis for working in business and economic development. A career in this field could involve a variety of employment opportunities—some close to home and some far away. If you have the interest and obtain the required training, you could be an organization executive, a government research director, or a field training consultant. Each of these jobs contributes to economic growth.

As you study various business topics, your awareness of economic activities will expand. Many business development positions are related to employment in government, technology, research, engineering, health care, nutrition, marketing, and financial planning.

Every country in the world can benefit from efforts to enhance its economic development and improve the quality of life for its citizens. Your decision to pursue a career in business development will have you participating in activities that will help people plan, start, and operate small business enterprises in communities in your neighborhood and around the world.

Related Job Titles
- Economist
- Transportation Engineer
- Urban and Regional Planner
- Survey Researcher
- Statistician
- Budget Analyst
- Microloan Officer

Analyze Career Opportunities in ...
BUSINESS DEVELOPMENT

Use library and Internet resources to learn more about careers in business and economic development. Choose one of the job titles listed in the box above and answer the following questions.

1. Wh

What's it like to work as a ...
Field Business Consultant?

As the sun rises over the mountains, hundreds of farmers are already on the job. Their goal is to harvest enough crops to generate income to provide for the basic needs of their families. They use traditional farming methods that they learned from their ancestors.

In a nearby village, an international organization has helped some of the people obtain oxen and farm equipment. These items have allowed the workers to double and triple their daily harvests.

Many government and private agencies work to help people improve their labor productivity. The use of new growing methods, machinery, and other agricultural techniques can provide families with more money for food, housing, clothing, school fees, and health care.

Funding for these improvements is often uncertain. Money may come from private investors or government grants and loans. In recent years, many organizations have started providing microloans to help peo

Planning a Career in... features correlate to the 16 Career Clusters and present the education, work experience, and industry opportunities for a variety of business-related career paths.

Work as a Team allows students to experience dynamics that enhance the learning process and learn the benefits and concerns of shared decision-making.

WORK as a TEAM

Do you believe your needs are very similar to or quite different from those that your parents had when they were your age? As a team, prepare a list of five needs that you agree would be similar to those of your parents when they were young and a list of five needs that you agree would likely be different. Justify why those listed are needs and not wants.

Doing Business in...Ecuador

Vendors and shopkeepers in Ecuador are happy to take your U.S. dollars for purchases, but your change might not include the familiar quarters, dimes, nickels, and pennies you see in the United States. Although Ecuador adopted the U.S. dollar in 2000, they minted their own coins. Both U.S. and Ecuadorian coins are in circulation.

In the late 1990s, Ecuador faced many economic difficulties, including high inflation, increased poverty, and a declining value of the sucre (its previous currency). Actions to address these concerns included adoption of the U.S. dollar. Dollarization generally helps control inflation and makes the country more attractive to investors.

When doing business in Ecuador, you will be expected to wear conservative clothing for business settings. You are likely to greet others with a handshake. As you get to know your business contacts, an embrace is likely; women may give "air" kisses on both cheeks.

Business meetings will likely start with an exchange of pleasantries. The importance of family in Ecuador is often reflected in these conversations. Avoid discussion of politics and the country's relations with Peru.

You will be expected to be on time for a business meeting, but don't expect it to start on time. For social gatherings, plan to arrive approximately 30 minutes after the appointed time. Lunch is usually taken between 1 P.M. and 2 P.M. For dinner invitations, prepare to eat as late as 11 P.M.

A local agent for selling goods and services is vital. This representative is necessary to do business with the Ecuadorian government. The use of a local attorney will ease the difficulty of maneuvering the country's complex legal system.

Think Critically
1. What are the benefits and possible disadvantages of a country using the U.S. dollar as its official currency?
2. How do business customs in Ecuador differ from others with which you are familiar?
3. Conduct library or Internet research to obtain additional information about business activities and economic conditions in Ecuador.

What currency are shoppers at this open-air market in Ecuador most likely using?

GOODS AND SERVICES

You satisfy your needs and wants by purchasing and consuming goods and services. **Goods** are things that you can see and touch. They are the products you can purchase to meet your wants and needs. **Services** are activities provided for the cons

Goal 2

Distinguish between goods and services.

Doing Business In... highlights various countries and provides a basic knowledge of international business activities that are vital for living and working in the global economy.

Web Workout is an end-of-chapter activity that gets students online to research some of the latest business topics and trends.

Winning Edge activities prepare students for DECA, FBLA and BPA competitive events.

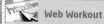

Web Workout

The U.S. government collects and reports information about the U.S. economy that is useful to businesses and individuals. The U.S. Census Bureau features economic data on its website, including economic indicators that provide important information about changes in the U.S. economy. Use your web browser to access the Census Bureau's website and locate the link to "Economic Indicators." Select one of the indicators and investigate how it has changed over the past 10 years.

Think Critically

1. Prepare a table to present the economic information you found. Use the data in your table to prepare a chart or graph.
2. Write a one-paragraph description of your findings. Include a statement explaining how the economic indicator helps people understand the U.S. economy. Also include information about how the indicator you selected might be used by businesses or individual citizens.

American Enterprise Project

The American enterprise system encourages individuals to take the risk of starting a business. Consumers play an important role in the American enterprise system because their demand for goods and services influences which businesses will be successful. Business success depends upon paying attention to consumer demand.

Your team of three has been challenged to design a presentation for middle school students that explains the power of consumers, the role of entrepreneurs, and the role of government in the American enterprise system. Your presentation should include an example of a real business, describe key elements of the free enterprise system, and define important terms. Your team is also responsible for developing a quiz based on your classroom presentation which will determine what the middle school students learn about the American enterprise system.

You will create a business report with supporting statements. Creativity through design and use of meaningful graphics is encouraged. The report should be a clear presentation about the American enterprise system and your strategy for teaching middle school students key concepts. The report should include the following parts:

- □e of project
- □h to determine business needs of selected
- □le
- □ion of project
- □ss of project
- □ion and results

spelling, and acceptable business style.

Performance Indicators Evaluated

- Understand the major concepts about the American enterprise system.
- Deliver an effective presentation to middle school students.
- Highlight measurable results through the use of a quiz about the American enterprise system
- Strengthen middle school students' understanding of the American enterprise system.

For more detailed information about performance indicators, go to the FBLA website.

Think Critically

1. Why is it important for young Americans to understand the American enterprise system?
2. List two strategies to use during the presentation that will hold the attention of middle school students.
3. List five major concepts that middle school students should understand about the American enterprise system.
4. Describe a joint project between FBLA members and middle school students that could be used to strengthen understanding about th□

Make Academic Connections

31. **Technology** Describe ways in which computers and other technology might affect a country's GDP.
32. **Geography** Select five countries. Create a map showing various economic statistics for each country. Explain reasons for differences among the countries.
33. **Science** Technology is often the basis for increased productivity. Prepare a poster or other visual presentation to demonstrate how the use of computers or other technology might make workers more productive.
34. **Culture** How might culture affect opportunities to increase productivity in different countries? Describe cultural and political factors that may enhance or limit actions to increase productivity.
35. **Math** Productivity for a small country was 25 units per worker hour in 2001. Productivity increased 20 percent between 2001 and 2006. What was the productivity figure for 2006? If the rate of increase is maintained, what will the figure be in 2011? In 2016?
36. **Math** Workers are paid a rate of $0.30 per unit. Using producti□

question, determine how much workers earned per hour in 2006. If their rate increases to $0.35 in 2011 and to $0.40 in 2016, how much would they earn per hour in those years?

37. **History** Research various phases of the business cycle in the United States during the past 200 years. Create a graph showing the ups and downs of the economy. What conclusions could be drawn from this research?
38. **Communication** Prepare a visual presentation to report (a) reasons government, businesses, and consumers borrow, and (b) potential problems that could occur for each group if credit is not used properly.
39. **Economics** Compare the use of stocks and bonds by companies to raise funds. Describe situations in which each would be most effective.
40. **Communication** Select two interest rates from the list on page 42. Conduct online research and create a chart showing these rates for the past four or five years. Explain possible reasons for □ in these rates.

Make Academic Connections connect business concepts with the four core academic areas of Language Arts, Math, Science, and Social Studies, to support integrated learning.

Develop Your Business Language offers a review of key terms to help students build a strong business vocabulary.

Develop Your Business Language

Match the terms listed with the definitions.

11. Process of choosing which wants, among several options, will be satisfied.
12. Individuals and organizations that determine what products and services will be available for sale.
13. The method a country uses to answer the three economic questions.
14. Means through which goods and services are produced.
15. Things that are required in order to live.
16. Not having enough resources to satisfy every need.
17. Quantity of a good or service that businesses are willing and able to provide.
18. Person who buys and uses goods and services.
19. Economy in which resources are owned and controlled by the government.
20. Things that you can see and touch.
21. Private ownership of resources by individuals rather than by the government.
22. □

27. Activities that are consumed at the same time they are produced.
28. Giving up on something to have something else.
29. Value of the alternative you did not choose.
30. Economy in which the resources are owned and controlled by the people of the country.

Key Terms
a. capitalism
b. command economy
c. consumer
d. demand
e. economic decision-making
f. economic resources
g. economic system
h. goods
i. market economy

Companion website at www.cengage.com/school/genbus/pob contains a wealth of online learning tools, including flashcards, quizzes, portfolio activities, and the Global Business Project, previously located at the end of each Unit.

Instructor Resources for *Principles of Business, 8e*

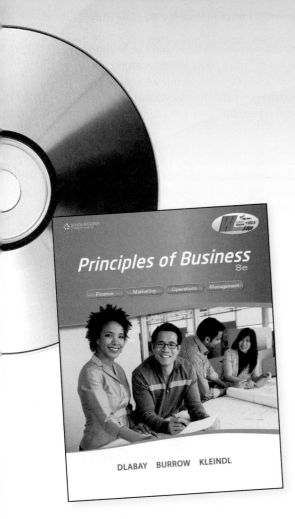

Activities and Study Guide
ISBN: 1111573689

Adoption Box
ISBN: 1111573735

Companion Website
ISBN: 1111474583

Competitive Events Guide
ISBN: 1111573727

eBook: Principles of Business
ISBN: 1111895244

ExamView® CD
ISBN: 1111430233

Instructor's Resource Box
ISBN: 1111573697

Instructor's Resource CD
Includes Lesson Plans, PowerPoint presentations, and Instructor's editions of the Activities & Study Guide, and Chapter and Unit Tests
ISBN: 1111573670

Instructor's Wraparound Edition
ISBN: 1111428212

Scans Activity Masters
ISBN: 1111573719

Spanish Resources
ISBN: 1111573883

Life-Span Plan Project

Goals

1. Explain how personal goals impact a life-span plan.

2. Name six areas of your life that should be part of your life-span plan.

3. Identify three life-span goals that can be used as the foundation for your own life-span plan.

Key Terms

personal goals xxii

life span xxiii

life-span goals xxiv

life-span plan xxiv

Focus on REAL LIFE

"What are you doing? It looks like homework," Emilee asked her older sister.

Kelly looked up and smiled, "I'm planning my life. See, this is my life-span plan."

"How can you be planning your life? You haven't even finished high school. You are planning to finish high school aren't you?

"Of course, but now's the time to think about what I want to do in the future—get a job, maybe own my own business, travel. I need to set some goals and figure out how I'm going to achieve them."

Emilee sat down and said, "I'm only two years behind you. I should probably be thinking about my future, too. Maybe you should tell me more about your life-span plan."

Goal 1

Explain how personal goals can impact a life-span plan.

LIFE-SPAN PLANNING

The Life-Span Plan Project will help you see how you can start planning for the rest of your life. The project consists of this six-page introduction, 33 activities that appear throughout this book, and creating your own life-span plan. Completing the project will help you develop skills you can use to make better decisions throughout your life.

Your Personal Goals

Personal goals are the things that people want most to achieve in their lives. They are the things that hold the greatest value to them. Most people have set a wide range of goals for themselves. Some are *short-term goals* that they hope to achieve within a year. Others are *long-term goals* that will take many years to attain. Individuals' goals are likely to

Besides graduating from high school, what is another one of your short-term goals?

Photodisc/Getty Images

involve family, living conditions, education, careers, community, and many other aspects of their lives. The goals you set for yourself are based on your personal values, your hopes, and your dreams. Although many people share common goals, most people also have unique goals that set them apart from others.

There is no way to judge most goals as right or wrong, or better or worse. Your most important goal may be to study law and become a judge while your best friend might want to own a farm and grow tomatoes. Your brother may want to start a family at a young age while you prefer to put off marriage and family responsibilities until well into the future. As long as a person's goals are based on what she or he really wants from life, there is no reason for them to be the same as other people's goals.

Almost every important goal you could set for yourself involves topics you will learn about while studying this textbook. Suppose, for example, your most important personal goal is to have a happy and secure family life. You might think that this goal has little to do with what you will learn about businesses during this course. But, if what you learn about businesses helps you make a better career choice, then you may be able to earn a greater income and be more satisfied with your life. This will also allow you to provide a better standard of living for a family. The same is true for almost any other personal goal you might set.

A Life-Span Plan

As you grow older you should expect the things you want most in your life to change. Today you might believe that owning a nice car is your most important goal. In ten years you may be more concerned with having a rewarding career, buying a home, or saving for your children's education. Even later you will

Although you might want to own a house in the future, what is your most important goal today?

want to have a satisfying retirement. Important events in your life, such as preparing for a career, raising a family or enjoying retirement are parts of your *life cycle*.

Your **life span** is the time from your birth to your death. It includes the events that make up your life cycle. When you are young, you will set long-term goals that you want to achieve over a period of years during your life span. Think of your life span as a straight line that contains the events of your life cycle.

The *life-span timeline* on the following page can help you understand the relationship between a life span and events in a person's life cycle. It shows a life span as a straight line along the top of the figure. Examples of events in the life cycle appear beneath the time in a person's life when they might happen. If you construct a figure like this for yourself, it is likely to have different events taking place at different times because your life will not be exactly the same as anyone else's.

Life-Span Timeline

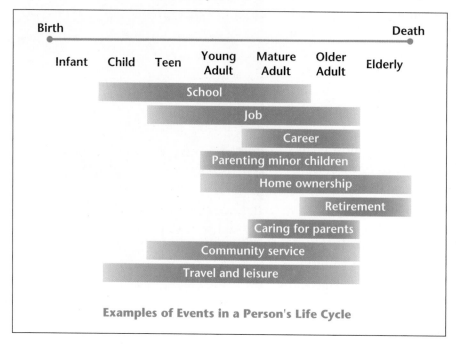

Examples of Events in a Person's Life Cycle

Life-span goals are long-term goals that you want most to reach during your life. They shape many of the most important decisions you will make. Examples of life-span goals include earning a college degree, owning a business, raising a family, or achieving financial security. For most people, life-span goals don't just happen. Successful people create long-term plans for how they can achieve their life-span goals. These plans are called **life-span plans**.

checkpoint ✓
How do personal goals impact your
career choice?

Goal 2

Name six areas of
your life that should
be part of your
life-span plan.

A LIFE-SPAN PLAN FOR KELLY

To help you prepare your own life-span plan, consider the example of Kelly. She is fifteen years old and a high school sophomore. Like most people her age, she is busy with school and social activities. However, she does think about her future including going to college, getting a job and living on her own. She hopes to have a career, a family, and a comfortable home.

Kelly's favorite subject in school is art. She has signed up for every art class that she could fit into her schedule. Kelly wants a career in the art world, but not as an artist. She likes the idea of working in an art museum or gallery, but she also thinks of herself as an entrepreneur. Kelly dreams of owning a gallery where she will showcase and sell the works of local artists.

In addition to continuing to develop her skills as an artist, Kelly knows that she will need to learn how to run a business. She also knows she needs to set short- and long-term goals. She needs a plan—a life-span plan.

First Things First

To begin her life-span plan, Kelly looked at six areas of her life: education, career, family, finances, community, and retirement. She then identified six central life-span goals that she most wants to achieve over the next 50 years. These goals fit in well with her values, interests, and personality.

1. Gain training and education needed to work in a retail art gallery.

2. Own and operate a successful retail art gallery.

3. Get married, have children, and own a house and a car.

4. Become financially secure.

5. Be active in community, church, and local government.

6. Be able to retire and take up other interests by the age of 65.

Kelly realizes that achieving these life-span goals will involve careful planning and many trade-offs. Almost all life-span goals people set require money. To pay for her education, a business of her own, a home, and a secure retirement, she will need to save and invest part of the income she receives during her working life. At times, she may need to borrow funds from others. She will need to construct and follow a budget that allows her to do this. At the present, Kelly may decide to limit the amount she spends on eating out, clothing, and entertainment so she can save more now to pay for college tuition later. Kelly will also need to identify related short-term goals that can help her achieve her more-important life-span goals in the future.

Related Goals

Kelly's central life-span goals are related to each other. Saving and investing to achieve financial security, for example, will help her pay for training and later to start a business. If her business is successful, she will be able to afford the house she wants to own. Financial security will also allow Kelly to enjoy a few luxuries. For example, Kelly would like to visit Ireland and see where her ancestors lived. If her business is a success, she will be able to take this trip.

Kelly wants to achieve many short- and long-term goals that are not central goals in her life. These include buying cars, furniture, and owning a sailboat. Although these goals are important, they aren't among the things Kelly cares most about in life, and so they are not listed in her life-span plan. In preparing her life-span plan, Kelly listed and evaluated her goals to decide which ones were the most important. The most important goals are part of her life-span plan.

How does Kelly's interest in art relate to her life-span plan?

Organizing Goals

Kelly organized her life-span goals in a table as shown below. Across the top she placed six categories to represent her six central life-span goals. On the left side she placed periods of time. These started with the next two years at the top and went fifty years into the future at the bottom. She then placed her goals according to when she would like to achieve them and how they contribute to her central life-span goals. In this way, she created a life-span plan that she believes will help her accomplish what she wants most in life.

Kelly feels a sense of satisfaction with her plan. She knows that she will almost surely revise it in the future, but she has a foundation on which to build. She can use her plan to help make decisions now. When she makes her class schedule for next year she will sign up for accounting, business management, and more art classes. She knows what type of work to look for and how to spend and save her income. Because she has definite goals, she is better able to make good spending decisions. Having goals makes it easier not to spend money for things she doesn't really need.

Kelly's life-span plan is right for her. It fits her values, personality, and family situation. Her plan, however, would not be right for most students, including you.

KELLY'S LIFE-SPAN PLAN						
TIME	EDUCATION	CAREER	FAMILY	FINANCES	COMMUNITY	RETIREMENT
Next 2 years	Complete high school. Apply to college.	Find a part-time job in an art gallery or museum.	Help parents with younger children.	Save $2,500 each year to help pay tuition.	Be an active member of my community.	No action is required at this time.
5 years from now	Graduate from college.	Work full time in an art gallery or museum.	Find a nice apartment in a good location.	Save and invest income to buy a home.	Teach art at the community center.	Open a retirement account.
10 years from now	Take classes in small business management.	Accept a managerial position at an art gallery.	Get married and buy a small home. Have one child.	Save and invest to buy an art gallery.	Continue teaching art classes.	Buy life insurance.
20 years from now	Travel to Ireland to see local artists' work.	Buy or start an art gallery.	Buy a larger house. Have another child.	Start a fund for children's education.	Continue teaching art classes.	Continue saving in retirement account.
35 years from now	Mentor young artists.	Build a successful business and look for a person to help run it.	Buy a vacation home at the beach.	Increase saving and investments now that children have moved out.	Run for town council or participate in government in some other way.	Investigate volunteer work I might enjoy.
50 years from now	Take classes in Irish cooking and history.	Sell business. Take part-time job in art store.	Buy a retirement home in a warm climate.	Manage investments carefully.	Volunteer to advise people who have small businesses.	Take at least one long trip each year and visit grandchildren.

▶ Figure 2

How old will Kelly be when she plans to buy life insurance?

You aren't Kelly. You have other values, abilities, and interests. Her personality is not your personality. Her family is not your family. You need to make your own life-span plan.

checkpoint ✓

What are the six areas of life that you should consider as you develop a life-span plan?

YOUR OWN LIFE-SPAN PLAN

Near the end of this class you will be asked to prepare a life-span plan for yourself. To do this, you should reflect on what you've leaned throughout this course. You will study numerous topics and finish many activities that you can use to help you complete this assignment.

The table on this page shows the locations of Life-Span Plan activities throughout this text. Look for the Life-Span Plan icon on these pages.

You will also want to consider things about yourself that were not directly covered in this course. The type and size of family you want to have is important, but will not be discussed in this course. The same is true of where you want to live and the role you wish to play in your community. Preparing your life-span plan will require you to consider all of your values and goals, not just those that are related to businesses and your career choice.

After you accumulate as many useful resources as you can, use these materials as references while you write a list of your goals. Base your goals on what you want from life for yourself, your family, and your community. Sort them according

LIFE-SPAN PLAN ACTIVITIES			
Chapter 1	p. 14	Chapter 11	pp. 263, 275
Chapter 2	p. 44	Chapter 12	pp. 295, 305
Chapter 3	p. 55	Chapter 13	p. 323
Chapter 4	pp. 77, 80, 90	Chapter 14	p. 348
Chapter 5	p. 106	Chapter 15	p. 373
Chapter 6	pp. 124, 136	Chapter 16	pp. 400, 413
Chapter 7	pp. 155, 163	Chapter 17	p. 426
Chapter 8	pp. 175, 187	Chapter 18	pp. 456, 463
Chapter 9	pp. 200, 208, 215	Chapter 19	pp. 487, 492, 502
Chapter 10	p. 249	Chapter 20	pp. 526, 531

to whether they are short- or long-term goals, and then classify them into overall life-span goals. Place your goals on a grid similar to Kelly's to construct your life-span plan.

When you have finished your life-span plan, it would be helpful to ask an experienced person to review your plan with you. A teacher, guidance counselor, or other adult you respect would be a good choice. Discuss your choices and the feasibility of your plan. This person can offer advice and encouragement for achieving your goals.

Making a life-span plan is an important first step. But, it is only a first step. Putting your life-span plan into action can make the difference between just thinking about your future and actually achieving the life-span goals that are most important to you. If you fail to act on your life-span plan, it will only a piece of paper.

Goal 3

Identify three life-span goals that can be used as the foundation for your own life-span plan.

checkpoint ✓

What three life-span goals can be used as the foundation for your own life-span plan?

Business in the Global Economic Environment

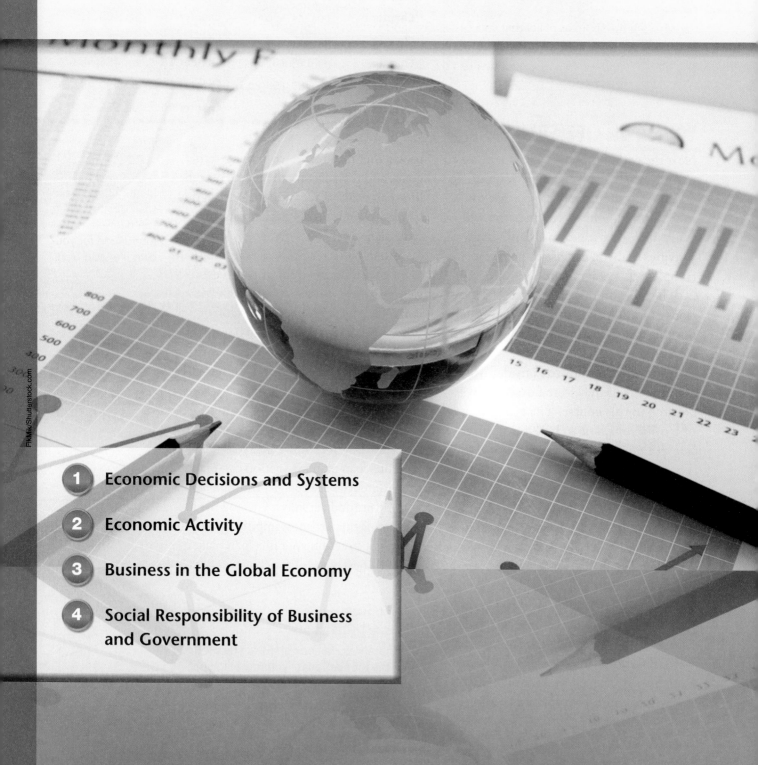

1 Economic Decisions and Systems

2 Economic Activity

3 Business in the Global Economy

4 Social Responsibility of Business and Government

FkMik/Shutterstock.com

The U.S. economy is the envy of people around the world. You and most other Americans have access to the latest products and services. Many families have the resources to purchase the products and services they need to maintain a good life. Yes, the U.S. economy takes downturns from time to time, people have a hard time finding jobs, businesses struggle and may even fail, and governments raise taxes to pay for the public services people demand. But year after year, the U.S. economy continues to grow offering people opportunities and advantages not seen in other countries.

In this unit you will learn about the U.S. economic system, how it compares to other economies, and how economic decisions are made. The United States operates in a global economy and so is affected by economic decisions made around the world. Decisions made by U.S. businesses can affect every other country as well as its own citizens. Businesses, consumers, and governments have responsibilities to make sure economic decisions are effective, fair, and contribute to the well-being of individuals and the environment.

Drinks for Developing Countries

Vitingo, an orange-flavored drink, not only provides refreshment but also health benefits. The Coca-Cola Company developed the new beverage, which is fortified with micronutrients, to provide a low-cost, healthy beverage for high poverty areas around the world. Vitingo contains important vitamins and minerals to help reduce the incidence of iron deficiency anemia, blindness related to vitamin A deficiency, and other health problems found particularly among children in developing economies.

Coca-Cola looks for ways to sell its products that fit the economic conditions in each country. In India, the company is partnering with 30 self-help groups that work to establish small businesses that offer job opportunities and increase the income of Indian families in high-poverty areas. The community groups are responsible for distributing and selling Vitingo and for educating families on ways to improve nutrition.

The goal is less poverty and better health across the country. While the effort is a way for Coca-Cola to demonstrate its social responsibility, it is also an effort to extend the company's reach into more countries and to increase sales of its products.

Think Critically

Why might someone object to Coca-Cola's efforts to sell products, even products with health benefits, to consumers who have limited resources?

Economic Decisions and Systems

CORPORATE ECONOMICS

Economists play an important role in the business world. They are often asked to be fortunetellers. They try to predict what economic changes are coming. This is a very important task, as businesses and government officials and even consumers use these predictions to make decisions that affect the economic future. Most economists work in government positions, for businesses and business associations, or as teachers and professors in colleges and universities.

Economists working for corporations forecast the size of markets, changes in consumer demand, and changes in sales and costs the businesses are likely to face. They analyze competitors' growth and market share and advise their company on how to plan. Today, economists pay attention to the international economy and the economic conditions in countries where the company currently operates or plans to expand.

Related Job Titles

- Actuary
- Commodities Broker
- Cost Estimator
- Economics Journalist
- Economics Teacher or Professor
- Forecasting Assistant
- Investment Analyst
- Quantitative Analyst

Analyze Career Opportunities in ...
CORPORATE ECONOMICS

Use library and Internet resources to learn more about careers in corporate economics. Choose one of the job titles listed in the box above and answer the following questions.

1. Identify the minimum educational requirements for the job. Explain other training or education that might be needed for advancement.

2. Is this a career that interests you? Describe how you might use your talents, abilities, and skills in this career.

What's it like to work as a ... *Corporate Economist?*

Pierre Latrobe is on his way to the office at 4 A.M. each morning. As an associate analyst, he helps prepare a morning briefing. He is responsible for tracking changes in the European economy.

Heading into the city on the commuter train, Pierre checks the Internet to get the latest information from the major stock markets. Then he checks the international news services for important stories that might affect the European economy. He updates forecast charts and enters notes so he will be ready for the team meeting as soon as he arrives at the office. His office work is usually finished by 2 P.M. each day, but he continues to check economic information even as he works out at the gym or completes other leisure activities.

What about you? What do you like and dislike about Pierre Latrobe's schedule and activities? What do you think happens in the team meetings as Pierre and his colleagues prepare the morning briefing?

1-1 Satisfying Needs and Wants

Goals

1 Explain the difference between needs and wants

2 Distinguish between goods and services

3 Describe the types of economic resources

Key Terms

needs 6

wants 7

goods 7

services 7

economic resources 9

Focus on REAL LIFE

Gina and Jermaine walked into an electronics store to look at a portable digital media player that had just been released. It has a 250GB super drive allowing the user to store and retrieve movies, photos, and music all on one small device.

As they stood in line, Jermaine said, "I don't know if the player is worth the $400 price. I hear you can get the older model for only $150."

Gina responded, "I know, but you can watch wide screen videos and movies on the new model."

Jermaine looked around and said, "With most of these things, if you wait a few months, the price will drop. I'm not sure I need it right now."

Jermaine's decision is one you often face. You see advertisements for exciting new products, but you do not need and cannot afford all of them. How do you decide which ones you should buy and how much to pay?

Goal 1

Explain the difference between needs and wants.

NEEDS AND WANTS

Hardly a day goes by that you don't see a product or service that you would like to have. You see them at the shopping mall, the grocery store, and school. Store displays and advertisements on television, radio, and the Internet attempt to convince you that you need whatever is new. How do you decide what to buy or even if you need to buy at all?

Needs Are Essential

You want many things, but do you really need them? Determining what is a need and what is a want is an important part of making good decisions.

Needs are things that are required in order to live. Everyone needs food, water, clean air, clothing, and shelter. Other needs in today's economy are a good education, a good job, and safety. Most people need transportation to and from school and work. People who have health problems need health care and medicines.

How easy is it for you to meet your basic needs?

Wants Add to the Quality of Life

Wants are things that add comfort and pleasure to your life. You may believe you can't live without name brand jeans and the latest cell phone technology, but you can, and many people do. A small apartment provides needed shelter, but many people want a large apartment or a house. Public transportation is available in many cities, but a late-model luxury car might provide a driver with an image of success.

It is not always easy to determine which products and services satisfy needs and which ones satisfy wants. The country in which you live, the economic status and lifestyle of your family, and the work you do help determine whether something is really necessary or not. Most purchases you make do more than meet your needs. They make your life easier and more comfortable.

Needs and Wants Are Unlimited

Your needs and wants never end. You are limited only by your imagination and by what businesses make available for sale. A new style convinces you your current backpack is no longer adequate. One purchase often leads to another. You purchase the latest model video game player and now you need a new set of games. Purchasing a new pair of shoes may mean you will want matching accessories.

Your wants can go on and on, and they change from day to day. A product you thought you couldn't live without two weeks ago doesn't seem as important now and is replaced by a new want. Everyone has unlimited want but those wants will not be the same for each person.

checkpoint ✓
What is the main difference between a need and a want?

WORK as a TEAM

Do you believe your needs are very similar to or quite different from those that your parents had when they were your age? As a team, prepare a list of five needs that you agree would be similar to those of your parents when they were young and a list of five needs that you agree would likely be different. Justify why those listed are needs and not wants.

GOODS AND SERVICES

You satisfy your needs and wants by purchasing and consuming goods and services. **Goods** are things that you can see and touch. They are the products you can purchase to meet your wants and needs. **Services** are activities provided for the satisfaction of others that are consumed at the same time they are produced. You purchase and use services to satisfy your wants and needs, but unlike goods, businesses must provide services to you at the time you want to consume them.

Goal 2

Distinguish between goods and services.

Photodisc/Getty Images

Do service businesses satisfy more of your needs or your wants?

What goods and services are represented in this photo?

Goods and Services for Businesses and Consumers

Goods and services are purchased by businesses as well as by individual consumers. Some goods and services are unique for business or consumer use. Others are similar but meet different needs and wants.

A business needs steel, plastic, gasoline, and computers in order to operate. It must have a constant supply of electricity, security for buildings and equipment, and accountants who maintain records and file tax returns.

Consumers buy furniture, televisions, cell phones, and books. They eat at restaurants, go on vacations, and take their car to the auto dealer for service and repairs. Businesses provide the goods and services that meet business and consumer needs and wants.

The U.S. Economy

The United States is the largest producer of goods and services in the world. It produces more than the next two largest producers, China and Japan, combined. The United States is also the world's largest consumer. For example, the United States ranks first in oil consumption. In 2009, it consumed almost 20 million barrels per day which was more than the combined consumption of the next four countries—China, Japan, Russia, and India.

America's lead in consuming goods and services increased throughout the twentieth century and continues today. The shift from an economy based on agriculture to an industrialized economy resulted in higher incomes and more choices of products and services for consumers. With more money to spend and more ways to spend it, consumer spending increased.

Increased consumer spending in a country results in more jobs and a higher standard of living. However, as consumption within a country increases, new challenges emerge for consumers. The ready availability of many products and services, along with frequent advertising, tempts consumers to buy things they may not need. With careful buying decisions, people can meet their basic needs, satisfy some of their wants, and still save and invest for the future.

Increased consumption also creates challenges for countries. Controlling pollution, preserving natural resources, and managing waste are all growing concerns worldwide. In addition to being the world's largest producer of goods and services, the United States is tops in another area—Americans produce more garbage per person per year than the residents of any other country.

> **checkpoint ✓**
> How do people satisfy their wants and needs?

ECONOMIC RESOURCES

How are the goods and services you need and want produced? Individuals no longer create most of the products and services they consume as people did many years ago. Businesses produce goods and services using economic

Goal 3

Describe the types of economic resources.

resources. **Economic resources** are the things available to be used to produce goods and services. Economic resources are also known as *factors of production*. The three types of economic resources are natural resources, human resources, and capital resources. Businesses and individuals must be able to obtain the needed economic resources to produce goods and services.

Natural Resources

Raw materials supplied by nature are *natural resources*. The earth contains oil, minerals, and the nutrients needed to grow crops and forests and to feed animals. Rivers, lakes, and oceans are the sources of both food and water. The air you breathe comes from the atmosphere that surrounds you. All products you consume begin with one or more natural resources.

Consider something as simple as a can of vegetable soup. What natural resources were used in its production? The vegetables and spices are produced using the resources found in rich farmland. The water comes from wells or reservoirs that were filled by rain. Aluminum was extracted from the ground and combined with other resources to produce the container.

While there is an abundance of many natural resources around the world, their supply is limited in many areas. Increased consumption as well as damage to the environment threatens the availability of many natural resources. Recycling and conservation practices as well as the design of more efficient products help to preserve resources.

Human Resources

The people who produce goods and services are known as *human resources*. In the example of the vegetable soup, many people are needed to complete the work required to produce that product. Farmers raise the livestock and crops.

Factory workers and managers use equipment designed by engineers and manufactured by the employees of other businesses to process the food. Truck drivers, salespeople, advertisers, and supermarket employees are also involved in making the soup available to consumers for purchase.

One type of human resource is an entrepreneur. An *entrepreneur* is the risk taker who uses resources to create a new product or service. Without the creative ideas of entrepreneurs and their belief that they can develop a successful business, there would be fewer choices of goods and services and fewer employment opportunities.

Stockbyte/Getty Images

In what ways does water contribute to the U.S. economy?

Capital Resources

People must have access to tools and equipment in order to convert natural resources into products. The products and money used in the production of goods and services are *capital resources*. Capital resources include buildings, equipment, and supplies. They also include the money needed to build a factory, buy or lease vehicles, pay employees, or purchase goods and services required to manufacture and distribute other goods and services.

Some people invest money in businesses so the business will have the capital needed to operate. Those people expect they will make money from the profits

What economic resources are needed for the construction of a house?

Business Insight for the 21st Century

Online Micropayments

In the early years of the Internet, users expected information to be available free to anyone. Over time, Internet consumers started to accept that many websites restricted access to content through the use of registrations, passwords, or, in some cases, annual or monthly membership fees. Today, due to the quality and variety of online content, consumers are more willing to pay for the types of products and services they otherwise would have to purchase elsewhere—songs, movies, video games, event tickets, and magazines. The digital content business generated $36 billion in 2009 and is growing rapidly.

In 2008, more than 1.4 billion songs were purchased for download. While that number sounds impressive, there is a major gap between online digital content sales of very low-cost products and services and that of higher priced ones. People are willing to pay a small amount to use an online game, download a song, view a new music video, or watch a sporting event online but they want a quick and easy payment method. Businesses will make those products available if they can collect the small fees in an efficient and profitable way.

Micropayments are online payments too small to be affordably processed by credit card or other electronic payment methods. Most micropayments are under $5 and may be as low as a few cents per transaction. Because of the limitations in payment options, micropayments currently make up less than 3 percent of all online digital content purchases.

New companies as well as industry giants are looking at ways to solve the micropayments problem. One of the first micropayment processing companies, Peppercoin, allowed online merchants to combine many small individual purchases into one larger transaction for processing so the cost and time required to process separate payments are reduced. With Microsoft Points system, consumers buy points in advance and redeem them at the Xbox Live Marketplace for game add-ons, new arcade games, and even HD movie and TV show downloads. It is certain that new technologies will soon solve the micropayment problem due to the almost unlimited potential for digital content sales.

Think Critically

1. Why have many consumers changed their views about the value of online content so they are now willing to pay small fees?

2. Research micropayments and identify unique methods being used by companies to accept and process these small payments.

earned by the business. Other people receive income by selling their knowledge and skills to businesses in the form of labor. Those with special skills or knowledge of important business processes often command higher incomes than those with knowledge and skills that are more common or in less demand.

Resources Are Limited

All economic resources have a limited supply. Most resources can be used to produce several different products and services. If resources are used to produce one type of product, they will not be available for the production of something else.

Individuals, businesses, and even countries compete for access to and ownership of economic resources. Those resources that are in very high demand or that have a limited supply will command high prices. Because there is a limited amount of natural resources, there will also be a limit to the amount of goods and services that can be produced.

> **checkpoint** ✓
> What are the three types of economic resources? Give an example of each type of resource.

Digital Vision/Getty Images

How can a country plan for future limits on its natural resources?

1-1 Assessment

Key Concepts

Determine the best answer.

1. True or False. It is not always easy to determine the products and services that satisfy needs and those that satisfy wants.

2. Which of the following would an economist most likely classify as a need?
   a. gasoline for a florist's delivery truck
   b. a college degree
   c. a flat-screen television
   d. a part-time job to earn extra money

3. An example of a natural resource is
   a. sunlight   b. a computer programmer
   c. a fishing net   d. money

Make Academic Connections

4. **Economics** List the three types of economic resources. Choose a product and describe how each type of economic resource is needed and used in its production. (Hint: refer to the vegetable soup example in the lesson.)

5. **Writing** Locate an article from a business publication or newspaper that illustrates the concepts of unlimited wants and needs and limited resources. Write a two-paragraph summary of the article that incorporates several of the key terms from the lesson.

Economic Choices

Steve Lovegrove/Shutterstock.com

Goals

1 Describe the basic economic problem.

2 Explain the steps in the decision-making process.

Key Terms

scarcity 12

economic decision-making 13

trade-off 13

opportunity cost 13

Focus on REAL LIFE

As soon as Tom answers the phone, Jacques says, "Tom, I just won two tickets to the concert and I want you to go with me. It's tomorrow at eight so we need to leave by five-thirty."

"Oh no!" Tom said. "My Dad's birthday is tomorrow and my family expects me to go out to dinner to celebrate tomorrow night."

Tom really wants to go to the concert but doesn't want to cause hard feelings with his family. What advice would you give Tom to help him resolve the dilemma he is facing?

Goal 1

Describe the basic economic problem.

THE BASIC ECONOMIC PROBLEM

Individuals and businesses have unlimited wants and needs. However, the economic resources that can be used to meet their needs are limited. The mismatch of unlimited wants and needs and limited economic resources is known as *the basic economic problem*. You may have identified several products you want to buy but you don't have enough money for all of them. Your school may be facing cutbacks on certain classes or extracurricular activities because operating costs are increasing faster than the annual budget. A business may want to expand in order to produce more products but does not have access to adequate land for a new larger building. A country may not be able to provide adequate health care for all of its citizens because it does not have enough doctors or hospitals.

The basic economic problem results from scarcity. **Scarcity** means not having enough resources to satisfy every need. Scarcity affects everyone, but some people are more affected than others. People with limited income have to carefully choose the best way to spend their money just to meet their basic needs. Countries with few natural resources or a poor education system may not be able to produce enough

How do you make personal choices between satisfying your wants and your needs?

Juanmonino/iStockphoto.com

products and services for their citizens. If roads, bridges, and railways are not well maintained, people may not be able to easily obtain the variety of products and services found in other areas.

Choices

Everyone has to make financial decisions based on scarcity. Individuals and families must decide how to spread their income among all of the things they want and need. City, state, and national governments must cope with the problem of providing the many services citizens demand using the tax dollars they collect. In each case, someone has to make the difficult choices.

Scarcity forces you to make *choices* or decisions among the alternatives. How do you decide which option is best? You usually choose the things you want the most or can afford. Suppose you earn $75 a week from a part-time job. If you spend the money you earned this week on a new pair of shoes, you will not have enough left over to spend on a movie and pizza with your friends on Saturday night. Due to the limited resources or amount of money you have, you cannot afford everything at the same time. You must make a choice by deciding which of your wants—the shoes or pizza and movie—you want the most. How do you determine which of these two options will satisfy you the most?

Following a logical process can help you make better decisions. It is a proven way to make many decisions, but is especially useful for making important economic decisions. **Economic decision-making** is the process of choosing which needs and wants will be satisfied. Once you learn the process, your decision-making will be easier and the process may lead to better choices.

Trade-offs and Opportunity Costs

Most of the choices you make result from considering a number of alternatives. When you decide on one alternative, you give up on the other alternatives you might have

NETBookmark

You need to have a source of income to pay for the things you want and need. And you need to consider carefully what to buy to make sure it is the best use of your money. Access the website shown below and click on the link for Chapter 1. Click on the Activities link to play a short game that shows you it is not always easy to balance your income and your expenses. Sometimes unexpected events or poor decisions keep you from achieving your goals. How did the game force you to think about choices and decisions?

www.cengage.com/school/genbus/pob

chosen. When you give up something to have something else, you are making a **trade-off**. You aren't able to buy a pair of shoes because you decided to spend your money on a movie and pizza with your friends.

The decision-making process helps you select the best and most satisfying alternative from among a set of choices. Economists recommend that you evaluate an alternative by considering the opportunity cost of the decision. The **opportunity cost** is the value of the next-best alternative that you were not able to choose. In making a decision, part of your choice will be what you are giving up by the choice you make. The benefit you get from your choice should be greater than the benefit from the next-best choice.

Businesses carefully calculate the opportunity costs of decisions before they make a decision about how they will invest their money. If they use money to purchase land for a new building, what choices must they give up? Would there be a greater value if they spent the money to purchase new equipment that is faster and more reliable? Part of the cost of the land is the missed opportunity to have better equipment.

checkpoint ✓
What is opportunity cost?

THE DECISION-MAKING PROCESS

You make better decisions when you use a thoughtful process rather than letting your emotions lead you to a quick choice. An effective decision-making process involves six steps. You will be asked to use the process shown in Figure 1-1 many times as you proceed through the chapters in this book. You can also use it when making everyday decisions. Businesses and individuals use the process as they choose the best uses for their limited resources.

Define the Problem

For every decision, the problem must be clearly defined in order to make a decision that will lead to a satisfying solution. If you only have two hours available to study for three tests, your problem is how to best use the limited amount of time to prepare for the tests.

Identify the Choices

It is common for you to face choices with many alternatives. Earlier we identified a problem deciding on the best use of $75. Along with spending money on shoes or the movies and pizza, some other choices you might face are covering your normal daily expenses and the need to save money for college. In fact, there are many ways you might choose to spend or save your $75. It is important to identify and then consider all of the alternatives when making a decision.

Evaluate the Advantages and Disadvantages of Each Choice

You might find it helpful to write down your choices and then list the advantages

THE DECISION-MAKING PROCESS
1. Define the problem.
2. Identify the choices.
3. Evaluate the advantages and disadvantages of each choice.
4. Choose the best alternative.
5. Act on your choice.
6. Review your decision.

▶ **Figure 1-1**

How does the decision-making process lead to better choices?

and disadvantages of each. If you buy the shoes, you will be able to wear them many times. It means you will miss the fun of pizza and a movie with friends on the weekend. If you choose to save some of the money, you may be able to make a larger purchase later. You and your friends may determine a less expensive way to spend your time on the weekend.

Choose the Best Alternative

Select the choice that you believe will be the best for you at this particular time. Even if you have done a good job with the first three steps, this is often a difficult step. Realize that choices have consequences both now and in the future. Remember that opportunity costs affect your decision.

Act on Your Choice

Once you have made what you believe is the best decision, do whatever you have chosen. If you have decided to spend your money on a movie and pizza with your friends, go and enjoy yourself. Try not to worry about the choices you have decided against. Rethinking your choices or regretting your decision after it is made can take away from the activity you decided upon. Life is full of choices. No matter what you do, there will be times when you will regret a

Write an essay that describes how you could use the decision-making process to select classes for next year that will help you achieve your life-span goals. In what other ways will the decision-making process benefit you in the future?

decision even if you carefully considered the alternatives. The next step will help you deal with those situations.

Review Your Decision

After you have had a chance to experience the results of your choice, it is important to review your choice. On a scale of one to ten, how would you rank your decision in terms of the level of satisfaction it provided? What was good and not so good about it? If you had to do it over again, would you make the same choice? Given what you know now, do you think there was a better alternative? Were there consequences you hadn't identified?

Based on your review of the decision, how well did you follow the steps of the decision-making process? This step gives you an opportunity to think about your decision and learn from it. Next time you face a similar decision, you may be more

comfortable with your choices or make a different decision based on what you learned.

Some decisions have to be made quickly and some with very little information available. But even in those situations, following the decision-making process will help you make wiser choices.

WORK as a TEAM You and some friends are meeting with city council members to ask them to build a skateboarding park that would cost $30,000. They ask you to identify the opportunity costs of other recreation alternatives for teenagers. As a team identify two other alternatives for the city and discuss how you would determine the opportunity cost of each.

> **checkpoint ✓**
> What are the six steps in the decision-making process?

1-2 Assessment

Key Concepts

Determine the best answer.

1. True or False. The basic economic problem is that consumers have too many products and services to choose from.

2. The decision-making process is best to use when
   a. you already know the choice you will make
   b. you are facing a decision with several good alternatives
   c. groups rather than individuals are making a choice
   d. you don't have enough money to pay for any of the choices

3. John has two hours before having to go to his part-time job. He is deciding between studying for a math exam and taking a nap. If John chooses to take a nap, the opportunity cost of his decision is
   a. the rest he is getting
   b. the score he will earn on the math exam
   c. the wages from his part-time job
   d. all of the above

4. The first step in the decision-making process involves
   a. defining the problem
   b. setting a goal
   c. identifying the choices
   d. evaluating alternatives

Make Academic Connections

5. **Writing** Write a one-page essay about a decision you made recently. Describe how you did or did not use the steps of the decision-making process. Discuss the outcome of your decision.

6. **Economics** Locate and read a news report describing a decision made by a business. Describe what you believe could be the opportunity cost of its choice. Justify your answer.

Information Literacy

Research Skills

Your abilities are more than just the sum of your experiences. Whether the goal is to improve a business or your own performance, you need to make sound decisions based on the best information available. Research skills are needed to improve decision-making.

Research is a systematic, objective study to establish facts and principles. The research process begins with a question or problem and results in a possible answer that can become the basis for further research.

Here are the steps to follow when conducting research.

Formulate a question. What is the problem you are facing or what is the issue you are trying to resolve? The question should be as specific as possible and relate to an important personal or business issue.

Gather and review information related to the question. Determine if others have studied the same problem and if they have reported on the results of their study. This step usually involves a careful search of library information, including books, magazines, and documents.

Separate fact from opinion. Effective research relies on objective data. The opinions of others may provide interesting ideas to consider but should not be relied on for answers to your question. Consider if the sources of information are credible and if the information provided is factual.

Propose a hypothesis. A hypothesis is a prediction about the answer to your research question. The hypothesis can be based on the information gathered, your experience, or your beliefs. You will conduct a study to gather information that will either support the hypothesis or determine that it is wrong.

Collect data to test the hypothesis. Researchers carefully design studies to gather information related to the question and hypothesis. The common methods of collecting data are the use of surveys, making observations, or conducting an experiment.

Analyze the data. After data has been collected, it is organized and then analyzed using statistical

Even with Internet access, why is it often necessary to use library resources to gather and review information related to your research question?

procedures. Careful review of the results of the data analysis will provide evidence to support or disprove the hypothesis.

Report the results. It is important that researchers document and report the results of their research. The report will help others understand the research and repeat it or improve upon it. It will also provide evidence that you were objective in the way you completed your research.

Put the research results into practice. You began the research process to answer a question or solve a problem. You need to apply what you learned and determine if what you learned makes a difference. No matter the results, you will want to continue to conduct research and study the research of others. It will help you make sound decisions and have confidence in your knowledge and abilities.

Think Critically

1. Why should you try to avoid basing your actions on opinions rather than facts?

2. Do you believe some questions can be answered by just gathering and reviewing existing information rather than collecting new data? Why or why not?

1-3 Economic Systems

Goals

1 Identify the three economic questions.

2 Differentiate among the main types of economic systems.

3 Describe the economic system of the United States.

Key Terms

economic system 19

command economy 19

market economy 19

traditional economy 20

mixed economy 20

capitalism 21

Focus on REAL LIFE

Jiang Liang is a resident of modern-day China, but he knows what it was like to grow up in a farming community in the Yangtze valley.

"The farmers still work the land with the same tools and methods they have used for generations, and the government tells them what they can and cannot grow," Liang explains to a colleague. Herlind asked, "What does your family think about you living in Hong Kong and working for a multinational company?"

Liang smiles and responds, "My parents were surprised when I told them that the company decides how many computers to produce and then sets the selling price."

Liang has experienced two very different economic systems. Which system seems most familiar to you?

THE THREE ECONOMIC QUESTIONS

Every country in the world must deal with the basic economic problem. No country has unlimited resources and each one has citizens with important basic needs for food, housing, education, and health care. As economies develop, people have a growing set of wants as well.

In order to determine how available resources will be used to meet the needs and wants, each country must answer three economic questions.

1. What goods and services will be produced?

2. How will the goods and services be produced?

3. What needs and wants will be satisfied with the goods and services produced?

How the questions are answered indicates the type of economic system that exists in each country.

What to Produce?

Countries have differing types and amounts of resources just as individuals differ in their skills and abilities. Some have rich soil and regular rains that yield large food supplies. Other nations have desert climates or long, cold winters that make farming difficult. Some countries have abundant supplies of oil, coal, and other energy sources, while many

What resources are necessary for farmers to obtain large yields of their crops?

Goal 1

Identify the three economic questions.

Joel Calheiros/Shutterstock.com

countries have only a limited supply. The resources of a country are very important in determining what goods can be produced. A country can decide to trade some of its resources with other countries to obtain those it needs.

Just as nations differ in the type and amount of resources, they also differ in what they determine to be their important needs and wants. One country may focus on manufacturing a variety of consumer products while another country builds roads and bridges. Some economies focus on improving agriculture while others build their militaries. Some nations have excellent colleges and universities while others have few schools and many unskilled workers.

Deciding how to use resources and what to produce is never an easy decision. If a country spends too much in one area or on one group of people there may not be enough resources to meet other needs. If most resources are used to produce consumer products, not enough attention may be paid to a country's infrastructure of roads, energy, and water systems.

How to Produce?

Countries must decide the best ways to use their resources to produce what is needed. As a country develops, tasks that were traditionally performed using human labor, such as farming and mining, are now performed with more efficient tools and equipment. Two centuries ago, more than 80 percent of U.S. citizens were involved in agriculture. Today, less than 3 percent of the U.S. population produces the food the country consumes.

The labor needs of the U.S. economy have changed. Today's complex economy requires highly specialized health care professionals, financial managers, computer specialists, and others who can design, produce, and distribute the goods and services that people want.

Each country decides how to use its resources to produce the goods and services it needs. It may rely on unskilled or skilled labor, on advanced or simple technology, on its own resources, or on those it obtains from other countries. Privately owned businesses may be responsible for production or a country may own and manage the resources and businesses.

What Needs and Wants to Satisfy?

Because wants and needs are unlimited, many will remain unmet no matter what goods and services a country decides to produce. Decision makers must determine which needs and wants are the most critical when deciding what to produce. Some countries may decide to invest in capital goods, while others produce more consumer goods. Some countries devote more resources to producing the goods and services important to government activities. Other economies respond to those citizens who have the most money or the most political power.

In the United States, goods and services are plentiful and many decisions are left to individual consumers. What wants and needs you satisfy largely depends on how much money you have and how you choose to spend or save it. The amount of money you have available to spend depends a great deal on your education and abilities as well as how you decide to use them to earn income.

> **checkpoint ✓**
> What are the three economic questions?

TYPES OF ECONOMIC SYSTEMS

An **economic system** is the method a country uses to answer the three economic questions. While each country makes decisions in different ways, there are three main types of economic systems. The level of government involvement in the marketplace differs among the three types.

Command Economy

In a **command economy**, the resources are owned and controlled by the government. Government officials decide what and how goods are produced and how they will be distributed and consumed. They decide how much of the resources will be used to produce goods and services for consumers, such as food, schools, vehicles, and houses. They also decide how much of the resources will be used to produce goods for business and government use including machines, equipment, and factories.

In a command economy, the government may decide to build a superior military or a world-class education system. They may decide to spend money to research new technologies or to build housing for the poor. Some command economies determine the work people do, the education they can obtain, and where and how they live. Personal economic choices are limited in a command economic system.

Market Economy

In a **market economy**, the resources are owned and controlled by the people of the country. The three economic questions are answered by individuals through buying and selling of goods and services in the marketplace. The *marketplace* is anywhere that goods and services exchange hands. This includes a supermarket, the Internet, a business office, or even a flea market.

When a business buys a new truck or orders several tons of steel, it is making an economic decision. An individual consumer who orders a movie on a pay-per-view channel, takes a vacation, or enrolls in college is also making an economic decision. No one directs consumers to make a particular purchase or tells businesses what they must produce. The government has limited involvement in a market economy.

Consumers and businesses make decisions based on their own self-interest. Every time consumers buy products in the marketplace, they "vote" with their dollars. They send a message to businesses regarding their buying preferences, helping to direct the use of resources. Businesses make decisions on what goods and services will be produced based on how they decide to use their resources. When they offer the products and services consumers want, they are rewarded with profits. By those independent decisions, individual producers and consumers answer the three economic questions.

Photodisc/Getty Images

What are some problems that might result from decisions made in a market economy?

Your team represents the citizens of a new country deciding on an economic system. You want to establish a successful economy that provides the greatest benefit to its citizens. What information about the country would you need in order to answer the three economic questions?

Traditional Economy

Before complex economic systems developed, simple economies operated according to tradition or custom. In a **traditional economy**, goods and services are produced the way it has always been done. The traditional economy is used in countries that are less developed and are not yet participating in the global economy.

In those countries, the answers to the three economic questions are still established by their traditions. Goods are produced the way they have always been produced, generation after generation. Children are taught to use the same methods to make the same goods their ancestors produced. They often use the natural resources readily available to them and the tools they make or can obtain in their communities. They will consume most of what they produce and sell or trade the rest with people who live close to them.

The traditional economy is usually centered on meeting the basic needs of people, such as food, clothing, and shelter. While the global economy has brought change and growth to the farthest corners of the world, there are still communities, and even some countries, that rely on a traditional economy. Because these economies lack the many formal structures found in more advanced systems, they usually have limited individual wealth and limited opportunities to improve their conditions.

Mixed Economies

Most nations of the world operate a mixed economy. A **mixed economy** combines elements of the command and market economies. While the end of the twentieth century saw a shift away from command economies and toward market economies, various degrees of government involvement in the marketplace exist.

The former Soviet Union disbanded and became 15 independent nations in the early 1990s. For more than 70 years, the Soviet Union operated under a command economic system called *communism*. Under communism, the Soviet Union developed a series of government-led plans to direct resources toward economic growth. This led to a limited choice and supply of consumer goods. Often, consumers found it difficult to

How is business ownership affected by different types of economic systems?

Vishal Shah/Shutterstock.com

find basic products such as bread or a hammer.

During the past decade, several of the Eastern European nations that had used a command economy have made major progress in changing over to a mixed economy. Some of these countries made such economic progress that they were granted membership into the European Union.

More than 1.3 billion Chinese citizens have a communist government that controls most of the resources and decisions. The economy of China is adopting elements of a market system for a growing number of economic decisions. Entire regions of the country, particularly the eastern cities bordering the ocean, are enjoying a booming consumer economy based on greater individual freedom of choice. China is fast becoming a world leader in goods and services produced. The country's developing education system is producing many skilled workers who are earning money to pay for the goods and services they want.

As many countries with traditional economies develop, they often adopt mixed economies. The government makes many of the decisions about how the country's resources will be used to develop schools, hospitals, roads, and utilities. As people become educated and develop new skills, they are able to obtain better jobs and earn more money. They then have the resources to purchase more goods and services. Often businesses from other countries will begin to sell products and services in the developing country or even open a business there, offering jobs and locally produced products to the citizens.

> **checkpoint** ✓
> What are the main difference among the three economic systems.

THE U.S. ECONOMIC SYSTEM

Goal 3

Describe the economic system of the United States.

From the descriptions provided, can you identify the economic system of the United States? Because individual businesses and consumers make most of the decisions about what will be produced and consumed, the U.S. system best fits the definition of the market economy.

Another name for the U.S. economic system is capitalism. **Capitalism** refers to the private ownership of economic resources by individuals, rather than by the government. Individual owners are free to decide what to produce with the resources they own. Individual consumers are also free to decide how they want to use their money to purchase products and services. This economic freedom lends itself to other names often associated with the U.S. economy—*free enterprise* or *private enterprise*. Individual choices and decisions are vital to the success of the U.S. economy.

The U.S. economic system is based on four important principles. They are private property, freedom of choice, profit, and competition.

Private Property

The right of *private property* means you can own, use, or dispose of things of value. In the United States, you can own anything you want and decide what you want to do with it, as long as it does not violate the law. If you invent something of value, you are protected from others taking your idea.

Freedom of Choice

Freedom of choice means that you can make economic decisions independently and must accept the consequences of those decisions. Business owners can decide where to open a business, what to sell, and how to operate the company. Consumers can decide where to shop, what to buy, and what they want to spend. Only when individual decisions unfairly harm others will there be restrictions on freedom of choice.

Profit

Businesses invest resources and take risks for one primary purpose—to earn a profit. *Profit* is the money left from sales after all of the costs of operating a business have been paid. Because businesses are not guaranteed a profit, investors may lose the money they have put into the business. They are challenged to plan carefully, invest wisely, and produce goods and services that customers want in order to make a profit.

While earning a profit is at the heart of the private enterprise system, it is not the only reason for investing money and operating a business. People enjoy the challenge and freedom of business ownership, as well as the satisfaction of providing goods and services that other people want.

Competition

The rivalry among businesses to sell their goods and services is known as *competition*. Consumers have many choices of products and services and will select the ones they believe will provide the greatest satisfaction for the money they must spend. Businesses work to improve their products and control their costs. If customers are not satisfied with one company's offerings, they will look for another choice. Competition encourages businesses to improve products, keep prices low, provide effective customer service, and improve business practices.

> **checkpoint ✓**
> Name the four principles on which the U.S. economic system is based.

1-3 Assessment

Study Tools

www.cengage.com/school/genbus/pob

Key Concepts

Determine the best answer.

1. Which of the following addresses the economic question of how to produce?
   a. growing corn instead of potatoes
   b. requiring individuals to complete specific types of work
   c. producing more capital goods and fewer consumer products
   d. selling natural resources to other countries

2. In which of the following economic systems is the government's role greatest?
   a. mixed
   b. traditional
   c. market
   d. command

3. The primary reason business owners make investments and take risks in a private enterprise economy is to
   a. make a profit
   b. satisfy customer needs
   c. develop new products
   d. meet government requirements

Make Academic Connections

4. **Research** Choose one of the following ten countries. Research that country and write a report describing its current economic system. Determine if the economic system has changed during the last 100 years and include your findings in the report.

Botswana	Hong Kong
Chile	Kazakhstan
Costa Rica	Latvia
Germany	Singapore
Greece	Zimbabwe

5. **Writing** Write a journal entry describing a typical school day in your life starting with waking up in the morning and ending at bed time. Include specific information about food, clothing, transportation, school, and activities. Write a second entry describing a typical day for someone your age living in a country with a traditional economy. Compare the journal entries and provide three examples of how the type of economy affects daily life.

1-4 Supply and Demand

Goals

1 Describe supply and demand orally and with graphs.

2 Discuss how supply and demand affect prices of products and services.

Key Terms

consumer 23

producers 23

demand 24

supply 24

market price 26

Focus on REAL LIFE

Jody and Dennis are both in the mood for Italian food. Their town has two Italian restaurants, Restaurant Italia and Mamma's Pizzeria. Both Jody and Dennis are on a limited budget, so they are always careful about how they spend their money. Mamma's Pizzeria is famous for its delicious pizza and has excellent service. Restaurant Italia has a broader menu including pizza, pasta, salads, and sandwiches. Jody and Dennis both feel the food is good but doesn't have that authentic Italian flavor. Often, the restaurant is crowded and the service is slow. Because Momma's is known for the best pizza in town, the pizza prices are quite a bit higher than at Restaurant Italia.

If you were going to eat with Jody and Dennis, how would you decide which restaurant to choose?

PARTICIPATING IN A MARKET ECONOMY

In a market economy, buyers and sellers use the marketplace to make economic decisions. Buying decisions are made by consumers—including individuals, businesses, and government. A **consumer** is a person who buys and uses goods and services. The individual buying decisions of consumers have a tremendous influence on a market economy. Consumers decide what to buy, where to buy, from whom to buy, and what price they are willing to pay.

Successful producers must pay close attention to the needs and experiences of consumers. **Producers** are individuals and organizations that determine what products and services will be available for sale. Producers invest resources and take risks in order to make a profit. They determine what products and services will be available in the economy, what needs and wants they will try to satisfy, and the prices they want to receive.

It may seem that the economy is a big, unorganized system in which everyone pursues his or her own self-interest. You may wonder how the system can work when each business makes its own decisions about what to produce and charge, while each consumer makes a decision about what and where to buy and how

Goal 1

Describe supply and demand orally and with graphs.

What are the advantages of being a consumer in a market economy?

much to pay. The system does work and works well based on the economic principles of supply and demand.

Consumers Set Demand

When consumers make decisions about what they will purchase, they determine the demand for goods and services. **Demand** is the quantity of a good or service that consumers are willing and able to buy. A business depends on demand for their products and services in order to make a profit. For example, if a new restaurant opens in your town, but the service is slow, the quality of the food is poor, and the noise level is high, will consumers continue to eat there? It is not likely. Suppose a new restaurant opens with terrific food as well as fast and friendly service. It will soon be packed with people who prefer that restaurant.

Producers Establish Supply

Understanding consumer demand helps businesses to determine what types and quantities of products to supply. **Supply** is the quantity of a good or service that businesses are willing and able to provide. If consumers want a popular product and are willing to pay a price that allows a business to make a profit, businesses will be willing to provide the product to meet the demand. On the other hand, if there is a greater supply of a product than consumers want or if customers are tiring of an older or poor quality product, businesses

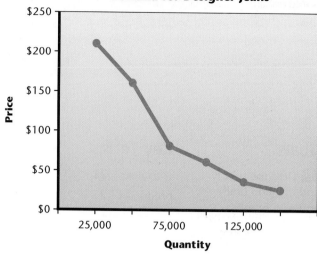

▶ **Figure 1-2**

The quantity of a product or service customers are willing to purchase at various prices can be illustrated with a graph known as a demand curve.

are less likely to continue to offer the product for sale.

A Graphic View

Demand and supply for a product or service can be illustrated using graphs known as demand curves and supply curves. The *demand curve* illustrates the relationship between the price of a product or service and the quantity demanded by consumers. As the price decreases, the number of consumers willing and able to

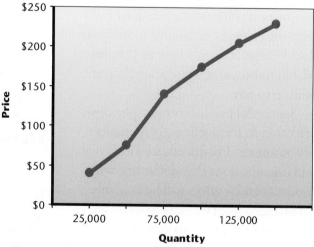

▶ **Figure 1-3**

The quantity of a product or service businesses are willing to supply at various prices can be illustrated with a graph known as a supply curve.

purchase the product and the quantity they will purchase increases. Figure 1-2 illustrates the possible customer demand for designer jeans at various prices in a specific market.

In the same way, the *supply curve* illustrates the relationship between the price of a product and the quantity businesses are willing to supply. At higher prices businesses will be willing to supply larger quantities of the product or service. Figure 1-3 illustrates the possible supply of designer jeans manufacturers are willing to provide to a market at various prices.

> **checkpoint ✓**
> How does the price of a product affect demand and supply?

DETERMINING PRICE

Why is the price of a hotel room in Phoenix, Arizona, higher in winter than summer? Why do the prices of many of the products sold by farmers remain quite low? Prices are affected by the relationship between supply and demand, plus other factors.

Factors Influencing Demand

If many consumers want (or demand) a particular good or service, its price will tend to go up. More people vacation in Phoenix in the winter than in the summer so demand and prices for hotel rooms rise. When fewer people visit that area during the hot summer, the supply of hotel rooms is greater than the demand. Therefore, prices will decline.

When customers see a number of products that they believe will satisfy a particular want or need, demand for any one of those products will not be as high. Customers will be willing to switch from one product to another if the price of one is much higher than the others. When customers cannot find a good substitute for a product they want, demand for that product will be high. Even if the price increases, they will be willing to pay the higher price because they are unwilling or unable to switch to another choice.

Factors Influencing Supply

The supply of a product can also affect the price. Because the supply of many of the crops and livestock raised on farms is large, prices remain low. If a drought cuts the quantity of corn grown by Midwest farmers one year, the price of corn will increase.

Competitors are businesses offering very similar products to the same customers. As the number of competitors increases, so does supply. A business will not be able to easily raise its prices. It will have to be much more sensitive to the prices charged by its competitors.

When competition is limited, consumers cannot find good alternatives. If you live in a part of town where there is only one supermarket, the prices at that store will often be higher due to a lack of competition. The prices of products featuring new technology will often be high because the company offering the new product seldom has direct competition.

Sometimes a natural disaster or other unforeseen circumstance affects supply. If the supply of oil, gasoline, or water is disrupted, their prices will increase. The supply of other products that use those resources in production may also be affected and their prices can increase as well. Sometimes businesses will try to restrict supply of products in order to

Goal 2

Discuss how supply and demand affect prices of products and services.

WORK *as a* **TEAM**	The prices of some products change a great deal in a short time, while the prices for other products remain quite stable. Work as a team to identify several products that experience regular price changes and several that do not. List the products and then discuss how supply and demand appear to affect the prices of each of the products.

obtain a higher price. That will only work if customer demand is high and if there are no good substitutes for the product.

Determining Market Price

Supply, demand, and competition determine the market price for a product or service. The **market price** is the point where supply and demand are equal. Figure 1-4 shows the market price for designer jeans. Look at the point where the demand curve and the supply curve intersect. This illustrates that consumers are willing to purchase nearly 65,000 pairs of jeans and businesses are willing to supply that same quantity if the retail price is about $110 per pair.

Market Price for Designer Jeans

▶ **Figure 1-4**

The market price for a product is the point where supply and demand are equal.

checkpoint ✓

How is the market price for a product determined?

1-4 Assessment

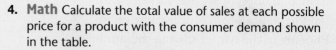

Study Tools

www.cengage.com/school/genbus/pob

Key Concepts

Determine the best answer.

1. True or False. Both individuals and organizations can be producers.

2. True or False. Supply is the quantity of a good or service that a consumer is willing and able to buy at a particular price.

3. As competition increases, prices
   a. usually increase as well
   b. are not affected so will usually not change
   c. usually will decrease
   d. There is no way to predict what will happen to prices due to competition.

Make Academic Connections

4. **Math** Calculate the total value of sales at each possible price for a product with the consumer demand shown in the table.

Price	Quantity demanded
$20.00	8,500
$22.50	7,800
$25.00	6,200
$27.50	5,900
$30.00	4,300

5. **Writing** Write an article for an online newsletter or blog about the importance of supply and demand in determining the prices to charge when opening a new restaurant. Be sure to include an explanation of how supply relates to competitors and demand relates to customers.

Business Improving Society

©Svetlana Prikhodko/iStock

Heifer International

Ending hunger and poverty around the world! It sounds like such a big dream that no one would undertake it. Nevertheless, since 1944, Heifer International has had that dream as its goal. Through a unique program of giving communities a source of food rather than just distributing food, the organization has reached millions of families in more than 115 countries.

Dan West was a Midwestern farmer serving as a relief worker during the Spanish Civil War. With a limited supply of milk and food, he had to decide who would receive the rations and who would not.

As a farmer, Mr. West realized that if people had livestock, farming tools, and some assistance in learning effective farming practices, they would have the capability to raise food for themselves and their families for a lifetime.

He returned to the United States and formed Heifers for Relief. He asked other farmers to donate a heifer. Dan delivered the first shipment of 17 heifers to Puerto Rico, giving them to families with malnourished children who had never tasted milk before. Why heifers? The young cows would give birth to a new calf. Each family that received a heifer and training in how to raise and maintain dairy animals was asked to "pass on the gift" by donating a calf to another family.

Photo courtesy of Heifer International/Jake Lyell

How might a family in Tanzania, where this young boy lives, benefit from having a cow?

For more than 65 years, Heifer International has been developing new projects around the world. Their mission is to work with communities to end hunger and poverty and to care for the earth. They envision a world of communities living together in peace and sharing the resources of a healthy planet. Today, hundreds of thousands of people continue to donate heifers, rabbits, goats, and chickens. Others make cash contributions to purchase livestock and supplies. Many people volunteer their time to travel to the rural communities with the animals to provide training and assistance so that the livestock will remain healthy, grow, and multiply for further distribution.

Recent projects of Heifer International include:

- Sending five rural veterinarians to Mongolia to work with animal herders to teach them improved animal management. These herders will then work with 500 additional herding families.
- Distributing 140 dairy cattle to 100 farm families in Kosovo who were victims of the war in their country in 1999.
- Placing 500 hives of bees in five Adaklu communities in Ghana, Africa. The communities will be taught hive management and honey harvesting techniques that do not harm the environment. Honey is a major source of nutrition in an area that suffers from illiteracy and high child mortality.

Think Critically

1. How does this approach to solving world hunger differ from other relief efforts that distribute food, milk, clothing, and health supplies?
2. Use the Internet to locate examples of other organizations that are working to reduce hunger around the world. How are they similar to or different from Heifer International?

Business Notes

1-1 Satisfying Needs and Wants

- Things that are necessary in order to live are needs. Things that add comfort and pleasure to life are wants.

- Goods are things that you can see and touch. Services are activities provided for others that are consumed at the same time they are provided.

- Economic resources are the things available to be used to produce goods and services. Economic resources are also known as factors of production. The three kinds of economic resources are natural resources, human resources, and capital resources.

1-2 Economic Choices

- Most choices result from considering a number of alternatives. When you give up something to have something else, you are making a trade-off. The opportunity cost is the value of the next best choice.

- The six steps in the decision-making process are: define the problem, identify the choices, evaluate each choice, choose the best alternative, act on the choice, and review your decision.

1-3 Economic Systems

- All economies must answer three economic questions: What goods and services will be produced? How will the goods and services be produced? What needs and wants will be satisfied with the goods and services produced?

- A nation's plan for answering the three economic questions is its economic system. In a command economy, most resources are owned and controlled by the government. In a market economy, resources are owned and controlled by the people of the country. In a traditional economy, goods and services are produced the way it has always been done. A mixed economy combines elements of command and market economies.

- Capitalism refers to the private ownership of resources by individuals rather than by the government. The U.S. economic system is based on the principles of private property, freedom of choice, profit, and competition.

1-4 Supply and Demand

- In a market economy, individual buyers and sellers use the marketplace to make economic decisions. Demand is the quantity of a good or service that consumers are willing and able to buy. Supply is the quantity of a good or service that businesses are willing and able to provide.

- If many consumers demand a particular good or service, its price will go up. If competition increases and therefore customers have more choices, businesses will not be able to easily raise their prices. The market price for a product or service is the point where supply and demand are equal.

Communicate Business Concepts

1. Identify five products or services that could be either a need or a want. Provide an example for each that illustrates when it would be considered a need and when it would be considered a want.

2. Select a business with which you are familiar. Describe factors of production used by the business that fit within each of the three kinds of economic resources.

3. Find a newspaper or magazine article that deals with scarcity of a product, service, or natural resource. Write a summary of the article in which you identify who is affected by the scarcity and the effect it is having on businesses and consumers.

4. Identify an important decision you will need to make in the near future, such as selecting a college or career or making a major purchase. Prepare a visual to illustrate how you would complete each step in the decision-making process for the problem.

5. Identify a possible opportunity cost for each of the following:

   a. Trying out for an athletic team
   b. Accepting a part-time job
   c. Studying for an important exam
   d. Saving money to buy a used car

6. Develop a table that compares the answers to the three economic questions for a command economy, a market economy, and a traditional economy.

7. Explain how freedom of choice can affect the availability of products and services for consumers. Now explain how it can also affect the profit a business might make on the products and services it sells.

8. Do you agree that the term "private enterprise" is a good description of the U.S. economy? Why or why not?

9. Select a product that is a regular purchase of many consumers. Use a graphing program to develop an illustration of a supply and demand curve for the product. Prepare a brief oral description of the illustration.

10. Review recent news reports of products and services where the price has been affected by supply and demand factors. Write a report using those examples that discusses the effect of supply and demand on prices.

Develop Your Business Language

Match the terms listed with the definitions.

11. Process of choosing which needs and wants will be satisfied.

12. Individuals and organizations that determine what products and services will be available for sale.

13. The method a country uses to answer the three economic questions.

14. Things available to be used to produce goods and services.

15. Things that are required in order to live.

16. Not having enough resources to satisfy every need.

17. Quantity of a good or service that businesses are willing and able to provide.

18. Person who buys and uses goods and services.

19. Economy in which resources are owned and controlled by the government.

20. Things that you can see and touch.

21. Private ownership of resources by individuals rather than by the government.

22. Economy in which goods and services are produced the way it has always been done.

23. Economy that combines elements of the command and market economies.

24. Quantity of a good or service that consumers are willing and able to buy.

25. Point where supply and demand are equal.

26. Things that add comfort and pleasure to your life.

27. Activities provided for the satisfaction of others that are consumed at the same time they are produced.

28. Giving up on something to have something else.

29. Value of the next-best alternative that you were not able to choose.

30. Economy in which the resources are owned and controlled by the people of the country.

Key Terms

   a. capitalism
   b. command economy
   c. consumer
   d. demand
   e. economic decision-making
   f. economic resources
   g. economic system
   h. goods
   i. market economy
   j. market price
   k. mixed economy
   l. needs
   m. opportunity cost
   n. producers
   o. scarcity
   p. services
   q. supply
   r. trade-off
   s. traditional economy
   t. wants

Make Academic Connections

31. Research Identify a product for which you believe there is a great deal of competition and one that you believe has very little competition. Use the Internet, newspapers, or personal shopping to identify the prices charged by three companies offering the product. Prepare a table to show the information you collected. Based on that information, do you believe you were correct in your original decision about the amount of competition for each product? How does the information support your belief?

32. Communication Your community has received a gift of 100 acres of land from a long-time citizen. A community group is encouraging the city council to use the land to develop a park. Another group would prefer that it be developed as an area for new small businesses. Prepare a one-page report for the city council comparing the two choices based on the opportunity costs of each.

33. Math The table below shows the average number of working hours it takes a worker in three cities in different countries to earn enough money to purchase several products and services. Use the information to answer the following questions:

a. How much longer than the worker in Country 1 must a worker in Country 3 work to earn enough to buy food for a family of four for a total of four weeks? Than a worker in Country 2?

b. How many eight-hour days would a worker in each country have to work to buy a large-screen TV?

c. What is the total amount of time a worker in each country would have to work to purchase each of the products and services listed?

	COUNTRY 1	COUNTRY 2	COUNTRY 3
1 lb. of ground beef	17.0 min.	29.0 min.	56.0 min.
Large-screen TV	65.0 hr.	132.0 hr.	701.0 hr.
1 tube of toothpaste	16.0 min.	13.0 min.	27.0 min.
City bus fare	7.0 min.	11.0 min.	3.0 min.
1 pair of men's shoes	8.0 hr.	7.0 hr.	25.0 hr.
1 week of food for a family of 4	18.6 hr.	24.7 hr.	53.5 hr.

Decision-Making Strategies

34. Countries that use modern technology and equipment can produce more with fewer people in a shorter time than countries in which many workers perform the work by manual labor. Study the figures below for farm workers and their yearly output in two different kinds of economic systems, and then answer the questions that follow.

a. How many more people were working in agricultural jobs in the traditional economy than in the market economy?

b. In which system was each farm worker more productive?

c. In terms of people supplied from the output of each farm worker, how much more productive was the worker in (b)?

	TRADITIONAL ECONOMY	MARKET ECONOMY
Size of the agriculture labor force	34,350,000	4,380,000
Number of people supplied with food from the labor of each agriculture worker	7	49

Linking School and Community

Interview the manager of a local grocery store or specialty retail store to learn more about how supply and demand work to establish the market price for products and services. Find one example where there appears to be evidence of high consumer demand, another with evidence of a great deal of competition among businesses, and a third where other factors seem to be influencing the market price of a product or service. Prepare an oral report to describe what you learned about supply, demand, and price to other students in your class.

Web Workout

The U.S. government collects and reports information about the U.S. economy that is useful to businesses and individuals. The U.S. Census Bureau features economic data on its website, including economic indicators that provide important information about changes in the U.S. economy. Use your web browser to access the Census Bureau's website and locate the link to "Economic Indicators." Select one of the indicators and investigate how it has changed over the past 10 years.

Think Critically

1. Prepare a table to present the economic information you found. Use the data in your table to prepare a chart or graph.

2. Write a one-paragraph description of your findings. Include a statement explaining how the economic indicator helps people understand the U.S. economy. Also include information about how the indicator you selected might be used by businesses or individual citizens.

American Enterprise Project

The American enterprise system encourages individuals to take the risk of starting a business. Consumers play an important role in the American enterprise system because their demand for goods and services influences which businesses will be successful. Business success depends upon paying attention to consumer demand.

Your team of three has been challenged to design a presentation for middle school students that explains the power of consumers, the role of entrepreneurs, and the role of government in the American enterprise system. Your presentation should include an example of a real business, describe key elements of the free enterprise system, and define important terms. Your team is also responsible for developing a quiz based on your classroom presentation which will determine what the middle school students learn about the American enterprise system.

You will create a business report with supporting statements. Creativity through design and use of meaningful graphics is encouraged. The report should be a clear presentation about the American enterprise system and your strategy for teaching middle school students key concepts. The report should include the following parts:

- purpose of project
- research to determine business needs of selected example
- description of project
- uniqueness of project
- evaluation and results

The format of your report will be evaluated for its clear, concise and logical presentation, creativity, correct use of grammar, punctuation, and spelling, and acceptable business style.

Performance Indicators Evaluated

- Understand the major concepts about the American enterprise system.
- Deliver an effective presentation to middle school students.
- Highlight measurable results through the use of a quiz about the American enterprise system
- Strengthen middle school students' understanding of the American enterprise system.

For more detailed information about performance indicators, go to the FBLA website.

Think Critically

1. Why is it important for young Americans to understand the American enterprise system?

2. List two strategies to use during the presentation that will hold the attention of middle school students.

3. List five major concepts that middle school students should understand about the American enterprise system.

4. Describe a joint project between FBLA members and middle school students that could be used to strengthen understanding about the American enterprise system.

www.fbla-pbl.org

2 Economic Activity

Agriculture, Food & Natural Resources

Providing food, water, health care, education, and financial services to the billions of people in need around the world is the basis for working in business and economic development. A career in this field could involve a variety of employment opportunities—some close to home and some far away. If you have the interest and obtain the required training, you could be an organization executive, a government research director, or a field training consultant. Each of these jobs contributes to economic growth.

As you study various business topics, your awareness of economic activities will expand. Many business development positions are related to employment in government, technology, research, engineering, health care, nutrition, marketing, and financial planning.

Every country in the world can benefit from efforts to enhance its economic development and improve the quality of life for its citizens. Your decision to pursue a career in business development will have you participating in activities that will help people plan, start, and operate small business enterprises in communities in your neighborhood and around the world.

Related Job Titles

- Economist
- Transportation Engineer
- Urban and Regional Planner
- Survey Researcher
- Statistician
- Budget Analyst
- Microloan Officer

Analyze Career Opportunities in ...

BUSINESS DEVELOPMENT

Use library and Internet resources to learn more about careers in business and economic development. Choose one of the job titles listed in the box above and answer the following questions.

1. What is the employment outlook for careers in this field?

2. Is this a career that interests you? What can you do now to help prepare yourself for this career?

What's it like to work as a ... Field Business Consultant?

As the sun rises over the mountains, hundreds of farmers are already on the job. Their goal is to harvest enough crops to generate income to provide for the basic needs of their families. They use traditional farming methods that they learned from their ancestors.

In a nearby village, an international organization has helped some of the people obtain oxen and farm equipment. These items have allowed the workers to double and triple their daily harvests.

Many government and private agencies work to help people improve their labor productivity. The use of new growing methods, machinery, and other agricultural techniques can provide families with more money for food, housing, clothing, school fees, and health care.

Funding for these improvements is often uncertain. Money may come from private investors or government grants and loans. In recent years, many organizations have started providing microloans to help people in poverty start and expand their businesses.

What about you? What aspects of working in business development interest you?

Stephen Coburn/Shutterstock.com

2-1 Measuring Economic Activity

Goals

1 Define gross domestic product.

2 Describe economic measures of labor.

3 Identify economic indicators for consumer spending.

Key Terms

gross domestic product (GDP) 34

GDP per capita 35

unemployment rate 36

productivity 36

personal income 37

retail sales 37

Focus on REAL LIFE

Measuring performance is common in many aspects of life. In a recent basketball game, Rosa Rivera of Middletown High School scored 19 points, pulled down 8 rebounds, and had 7 assists.

Later that day, the school's marching band was in competition and received a score of 88.3. By most standards, this was a good performance.

How about you? How much have you grown in the past 10 years? You can say, "I am 10 years older." Or, "I am 50 pounds heavier." Or, "I now wear shoe size 10C."

Several ways can be used to measure personal growth. In a similar manner, business and economic activity are measured to determine progress.

Goal 1

Define gross domestic product.

GROSS DOMESTIC PRODUCT (GDP)

Economic growth refers to a steady increase in the production of goods and services in an economic system. Just as you use different ways to measure your own growth, different methods can be used to measure the growth of an economy.

One way to find out how well an economy is doing is to compare output from year to year. Governments collect information from producers and estimate national output. The most widely used measure is gross domestic product. **Gross domestic product** or **GDP** is the total value of all final goods and services produced in a country during one year. Figure 2-1 reports the GDP of various countries in a recent year.

COMPARISON OF GDP IN SELECTED COUNTRIES					
COUNTRY	**TOTAL GDP (U.S. $)**	**GDP PER CAPITA (U.S. $)**	**COUNTRY**	**TOTAL GDP (U.S. $)**	**GDP PER CAPITA (U.S. $)**
United States	14.3 trillion	46,400	Canada	1.3 trillion	38,400
China	8.8 trillion	6,600	Poland	690.1 billion	17,900
Japan	4.1 trillion	32,600	Saudi Arabia	585.8 billion	20,400
Germany	2.8 trillion	34,100	South Africa	495.1 billion	10,100
India	3.6 trillion	3,100	Nigeria	357.2 billion	2,400
Brazil	2.0 trillion	10,200	Vietnam	258.1 billion	2,900
Mexico	1.5 trillion	13,500	Bolivia	45.1 billion	4,600

Source: CIA World Factbook

▶ **Figure 2-1**

Which country has the highest GDP per capita? The lowest?

Components of GDP

Gross domestic product includes four major categories of economic activity:

1. Consumer spending for food, clothing, housing, and other aspects

2. Business spending for buildings, equipment, and inventory items

3. Government spending to pay employees and to buy supplies and other goods and services

4. The exports of a country less the imports into the country

Some goods and services are not included. For example, GDP does not include the value of the work you do for yourself, such as cutting your own lawn or building a picnic table. If you buy the lawn service or the picnic table from a business, they would be included.

Only final goods, such as cars, are counted when you measure GDP. Intermediate goods used in manufacturing, such as steel and fabrics, are not included. If intermediate goods were counted, the value of these intermediate goods would be counted twice.

If the GDP increases from year to year, this usually signals that an economy is growing and is healthy.

WORK as a TEAM

The GDP of a country presents information about the economic output of a country. Work as a team to prepare a list of drawbacks resulting from only looking at GDP when evaluating the economic progress of a nation. What aspects of economic growth may not be reflected in the GDP of a country?

Comparing GDP

The more goods and services that are produced, the healthier an economy is considered to be. Just referring to the total monetary value of GDP as a measure of economic growth does not tell the whole story.

Another way to measure economic growth is **GDP per capita** or output per person. GDP per capita is calculated by dividing GDP by the total population (see Figures 2-1 and 2-2). For example, suppose that there is no change in GDP this year compared to last year. Suppose, also, that the population increases. The same output would have to be divided among more people.

An increase in GDP per capita means that an economy is growing. A decrease may mean that an economy is facing difficulties.

> **checkpoint ✓**
> What types of economic activities are not included in GDP?

COMPARING GROSS DOMESTIC PRODUCT			
	CANADA	**UNITED STATES**	**CHINA**
Area (sq km)	9,984,670	9,826,675	9,596,961
Population	33,212,696	303,824,640	1,330,044,544
GDP (U.S. $)	1,285,000,000,000	14,260,000,000,000	8,789,000,000,000
GDP per capita (U.S. $)	38,690	46,935	6,608

Source: CIA World Factbook

▶ **Figure 2-2**

How does this figure help you see how per capita output is measured?

LABOR ACTIVITIES

The workers of a country contribute to the economy in several ways. First, their labor activities create needed goods and services. In addition, the wages they receive are spent to create demand for various items.

Employment

Today, more than 155 million people work in the United States. These members of the *labor force* are employed in thousands of different jobs. They produce thousands of different products and services. The labor force consists of all people above age 16 who are actively working or seeking work. Students, retired people, and others who cannot or do not wish to work are not part of the labor force.

One economic statistic of concern is the **unemployment rate**. The unemployment rate is the portion of people in the labor force who are not working. People are considered to be "unemployed" if they are looking for work and willing to work but unable to find a job.

Unemployment rates vary from year to year and in different areas of the country.

The main cause of unemployment is reduced demand for the goods and services being provided by various workers. If fewer people travel by bus, for example, bus companies will need fewer workers.

Productivity

A vital source of economic growth is an increase in output per worker. **Productivity** is the production output in relation to a unit of input, such as a worker. Improvements in capital resources (equipment and technology), worker training, and management techniques can result in more output per worker.

Over time, the rate of growth in labor productivity has ups and downs. While increases in productivity occur in many years, the amount of the increase often becomes smaller. Sometimes, productivity may actually decrease.

If wages increase faster than gains in productivity, the cost of producing goods increases and prices rise. Even though workers earn more money, they are not able to improve their standard of living because of rising prices. For that reason, strong attention has been focused on ways of motivating workers to increase productivity. By doing so, workers will be contributing to a higher standard of living in the nation while also improving their own life situation.

An ability to produce more goods and services makes it possible to reduce the number of hours in a workweek. In the 1890s, the average worker in the United States put in about 60 hours a week. Today, the average workweek for many factory and union-contracted jobs has decreased to less than 40 hours. At the same

joyfull/Shutterstock.com

What motivates you to work harder and faster?

time, some people have decided to take positions that require working more than 40 hours a week.

In many industries, even though U.S. employees work fewer hours, more is produced and earned than ever before. More can be produced in less time because of technology and efficient work methods. The training and skill of workers also contribute to improved productivity.

> **checkpoint** ✓
> How can productivity be increased?

CONSUMER SPENDING

The money you earn and spend is one of the most important factors for economic growth.

Personal Income

Each day, people receive money from their participation in production. **Personal income** refers to salaries and wages as well as investment income and government payments to individuals.

These funds provide the foundation for buying needed goods and services.

Retail Sales

On a monthly basis, the U.S. Department of Commerce measures **retail sales**, or the sales of durable and nondurable goods bought by consumers. These retail sales are an indicator of general consumer spending patterns in the economy. Increasing retail sales usually points toward economic growth.

The main items whose sales are measured for estimating retail sales include automobiles, building materials, furniture, gasoline, and clothing, as well as purchases from restaurants, department stores, food stores, and drug stores.

> **Goal 3**
>
> Identify economic indicators for consumer spending.

> **checkpoint** ✓
> What are the main sources of personal income?

2-1   Assessment

Study Tools

www.cengage.com/school/genbus/pob

Key Concepts

Determine the best answer.

1. Which of the following would *not* be included in GDP?
   a. exports to other countries
   b. purchases of computers by government
   c. automobiles purchased
   d. dinner preparation for your family

2. Productivity would likely increase as a result of
   a. higher taxes
   b. expanded production technology
   c. decreased training programs
   d. lower interest rates

3. Retail sales include
   a. taxes collected
   b. companies buying new equipment
   c. borrowing by business
   d. school supplies bought by students

Make Academic Connections

4. **Technology** Using the data in Figure 2-1, create a graph with a spreadsheet program to compare the total GDP and GDP per capita for five countries you select.

5. **Visual Art** Create a collage or photo essay to illustrate one or more of the ideas presented in the lesson.

2-2 Economic Conditions Change

Goals

1 Describe the four phases of the business cycle.

2 Explain causes of inflation and deflation.

3 Identify the importance of interest rates.

Key Terms

business cycle 38

prosperity 38

recession 39

depression 39

recovery 40

inflation 40

price index 41

deflation 41

Focus on REAL LIFE

Do you have more knowledge than you had five years ago? Are you able to play a sport better than you did 10 years ago? As your skills and abilities increase, you will depend less on your family and begin to plan for your future. You might be concerned about earning and saving money. You will likely think about how your grades will affect plans for continuing your education. Various elements of your life change—both up and down. Your grades are likely to vary based on study skills and class efforts. The size of your savings account changes based on earning, saving, and spending.

Change is also true for the economy. Ups and downs occur for business activities. As economic conditions improve, quality of life in a country improves. In contrast, downward economic trends result in difficulties for workers and consumers.

Goal 1

Describe the four phases of the business cycle.

THE BUSINESS CYCLE

Economic and business activity tends to move in cycles. All nations experience economic good times and bad times. Fortunately, over time, bad conditions disappear and good conditions return.

Looking at the economic changes during the history of the United States shows a pattern of good times to bad times and back to good times. This movement of the economy from one condition to another and back again is called a **business cycle**.

Business cycles are the recurring ups and downs of GDP. Business cycles have four phases: prosperity, recession, depression, and recovery.

Prosperity

At the peak of the business cycle is prosperity.

Prosperity is a period in which most people who want to work are working, businesses produce goods and services in record numbers, wages are good, and the rate of GDP growth increases.

The demand for goods and services is high. This period is usually the high point of the business cycle. Prosperity, though, does not go on forever. The economy eventually cools off and activity slows down.

Think of ways in which spending habits change during a dramatic economic shift. How might this affect the small business owner?

Recession

When the economy slows down, a phase of the business cycle known as recession occurs. **Recession** is a period in which demand begins to decrease, businesses lower production, unemployment begins to rise, and GDP growth slows for two or more quarters of the calendar year.

This phase may not be too serious or last very long, but it often signals trouble for workers in related businesses. For example, if people buy fewer cars, a number of workers who make batteries, tires, and other parts may lose their jobs. This drop in related businesses is called the ripple effect.

Eventually, production weakens throughout the economy, and total output declines in the next quarter. Some recessions last for long periods as fewer factors of production are used and total demand falls.

The Bureau of Labor Statistics provides data on a variety of economic activities. Access the website shown below and click on the link for Chapter 2. Select one of the following topics: inflation, unemployment, or productivity. Obtain recent information for this economic statistic. Prepare a brief written summary, and describe how this information might affect consumers or businesses in your community.

www.cengage.com/school/genbus/pob

Depression

If a recession deepens and spreads throughout the entire economy, the nation may move into the third phase, depression. **Depression** is a phase marked by a prolonged period of high unemployment, weak consumer sales, and business failures.

©Andreas Prott/iStock

A Question of Ethics

Ethical Analysis Guidelines

Most business decisions are viewed in various ways. In some countries, people expect family members to be given jobs in a company before others. In other places, payments or gifts are expected before you are able to do business.

These and many other situations create ethical problems. Ethics are principles of right and wrong that guide personal and business decisions. When considering the ethics of business situations, consider using these three guidelines:

1. **Is the action legal?** Laws vary among states and in different countries. Most companies base international decisions on the laws in their home countries. When a conflict occurs, managers usually consider other factors, such as professional standards and the effect of the action on society.

2. **Does the action violate professional or company standards?** Professional or company standards will frequently exceed those required by the law. This helps to ensure that decisions will be in the best interest of both the company and the society in which it operates.

3. **Who is affected by the action and how?** An action may be legal and within professional or company standards. Decision-makers should also consider possible effects on employees, consumers, competitors, and the environment.

Think Critically

1. What are some examples of situations faced by workers and consumers that require ethical decisions?

2. Describe the effect on business activities if no ethical guidelines existed.

3. Research recent ethical situations that have been reported in the news. How have these situations affected workers, investors, and others?

GDP falls rapidly during a depression. Fortunately, our economy has not had a depression for more than 65 years. The period 1930–1940 in U.S. history is referred to as the Great Depression. Approximately 25 percent of the U.S. labor force was unemployed. Many people could not afford to satisfy even their basic needs.

Recovery

Economic downturns do not go on forever. A welcome phase of the business cycle, known as recovery, begins to appear. **Recovery** is the phase in which unemployment begins to decrease, demand for goods and services increases, and GDP begins to rise again.

People gain employment. Consumers regain confidence about their futures and begin buying again. Recovery may be slow or fast. As it continues, the nation moves back into prosperity.

> **checkpoint** ✓
> What are the four phases of the business cycle?

Goal 2

Explain causes of inflation and deflation.

CONSUMER PRICES

Have you ever noticed that packages of some items get smaller while the price stays the same? Have you bought new technology products that are less expensive than earlier ones? These are examples of changes in the buying power of your money.

Inflation

A problem with which most nations have to cope is inflation. **Inflation** is an increase in the general level of prices. In times of inflation, buying power decreases. For example, if prices increased 5 percent during the last year, items that cost $100 then would now cost $105. This means it now takes more money to buy the same amount of goods and services.

Inflation is most harmful to people living on fixed incomes. Due to inflation, retired people and others whose incomes do not change are able to afford fewer goods and services.

Causes of Inflation

One type of inflation occurs when the demand for goods and services is greater than the supply. When a large supply of money, earned or borrowed, is spent for goods that are in short supply, prices increase.

Even though wages (the price paid for labor) tend to increase during inflation, prices of goods and services usually rise so fast that the wage earner never seems to catch up.

Most people think inflation is harmful. Consumers have to pay higher prices for the things they buy. Therefore, as workers, they have to earn more money to maintain

Monkey Business Images/Shutterstock.com

Name something you regularly buy that has increased in price while decreasing in size. How does this affect your decision to purchase the item?

the same standard of living. Producers may receive higher prices for the goods and services they sell. If wages go up faster than prices, businesses tend to hire fewer workers and so unemployment worsens.

Measuring Inflation

Inflation rates vary. During the late 1950s and early 1960s, the annual inflation rate in the United States was in the 1 to 3 percent range. During the late 1970s and early 1980s, the cost of living increased 10 to 12 percent annually.

Mild inflation (perhaps 2 or 3 percent a year) can actually stimulate economic growth. During a mildly inflationary period, wages often rise more slowly than the prices of products. The prices of the products sold are high in relation to the cost of labor. The producer makes higher profits and tends to expand production and hire more people. The newly employed workers increase spending, and the total demand in an economy increases.

In the United States, one of the most watched measures of inflation is called the Consumer Price Index (CPI). A **price index** is a number that compares prices in one year with prices in some earlier base year. There are different types of price indexes.

Inflation rates can be deceptive because the Consumer Price Index is based on a group of selected items. Many people face hidden inflation given that they may not buy the exact items used to calculate the index. The cost of necessities (food, gas, health care) may increase faster than that of nonessential items, which could be dropping. This results in a reported inflation rate much lower than the actual cost-of-living increase being experienced by consumers.

Deflation

The opposite of inflation is called deflation. **Deflation** means a decrease in the general level of prices. It usually occurs in periods of recession and depression. Prices of products are lower, but people have less money to buy them.

Significant deflation occurred in the United States during the Great Depression of the 1930s. For example, between 1929 and 1933, prices declined about 25 percent. Deflation may occur for specific products. In recent years, the cost of computers and many other electronic products have declined mainly due to improved technology.

> **checkpoint ✓**
> What are the main causes of inflation?

INTEREST RATES

In simple terms, interest rates represent the cost of money. Like everything else, money has a price. Interest rates have a strong influence on business activities. Companies and governments that borrow money are affected by interest rates. Higher interest rates mean higher business costs.

As a consumer, you are affected by interest rates. The earnings you receive as

Goal 3

Identify the importance of interest rates.

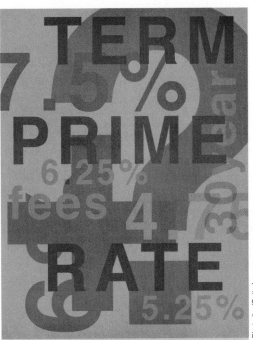

How do interest rates affect you and other consumers?

Photodisc/Getty Images

a saver or an investor reflect current interest rates. Consumers also borrow. People with poor credit ratings pay a higher interest rate than people with good credit ratings.

Types of Interest Rates

Many types of interest rates exist in every economy. These rates represent the cost of money for different groups in different settings. Some of the types of interest rates include the following:

- The *prime rate* is the rate banks make available to their best business customers, such as large corporations.

- The *discount rate* is the rate financial institutions are charged to borrow funds from Federal Reserve banks.

- The *T-bill rate* is the yield on short-term (13-week) U.S. government debt obligations.

- The *treasury bond rate* is the yield on long-term U.S. government debt obligations of up to 30 years.

- The *mortgage rate* is the amount individuals pay to borrow for the purchase of a new home.

- The *corporate bond rate* is the cost of borrowing for large U.S. corporations.

- The *certificate of deposit rate* is the rate for time deposits at savings institutions.

Changing Interest Rates

Each day, the cost of money (interest) changes because of various factors. The supply and demand for money is the major influence on the level of interest rates. As amounts saved increase, interest rates tend to decline. This occurs because more funds are available. When borrowing by consumers, businesses, and government increases, interest rates are likely to rise.

> **checkpoint** ✓
> How do interest rates affect business activities in our economy?

2-2 Assessment

Study Tools

www.cengage.com/school/genbus/pob

Key Concepts

Determine the best answer.

1. True or False. Deflation results in lower buying power of money.

2. True or False. When consumers increase their borrowing, interest rates tend to decline.

3. The phase of the business cycle in which unemployment is highest is
   a. recession
   b. recovery
   c. prosperity
   d. depression

Make Academic Connections

4. **Geography** Obtain information about business cycles in other countries. Do these other economies face similar changes in economic activities?

5. **History** Conduct research about *hyperinflation*. What caused high inflation in various countries? What actions were taken to solve this problem?

6. **Math** Over time, interest rates increase and decline. If the rate being paid on a savings account was previously 4.6 percent and is now 2.8 percent, what is the percentage of change for that interest rate?

Doing Business in...Ecuador

Vendors and shopkeepers in Ecuador are happy to take your U.S. dollars for purchases, but your change might not include the familiar quarters, dimes, nickels, and pennies you see in the United States. Although Ecuador adopted the U.S. dollar in 2000, they minted their own coins. Both U.S. and Ecuadorian coins are in circulation.

In the late 1990s, Ecuador faced many economic difficulties, including high inflation, increased poverty, and a declining value of the sucre (its previous currency). Actions to address these concerns included adoption of the U.S. dollar. Dollarization generally helps control inflation and makes the country more attractive to investors.

When doing business in Ecuador, you will be expected to wear conservative clothing for business settings. You are likely to greet others with a handshake. As you get to know your business contacts, an embrace is likely; women may give "air" kisses on both cheeks.

Business meetings will likely start with an exchange of pleasantries. The importance of family in Ecuador is often reflected in these conversations. Avoid discussion of politics and the country's relations with Peru.

You will be expected to be on time for a business meeting, but don't expect it to start on time. For social gatherings, plan to arrive approximately 30 minutes after the appointed time. Lunch is usually taken between 1 P.M. and 2 P.M. For dinner invitations, prepare to eat as late as 11 P.M.

A local agent for selling goods and services is vital. This representative is necessary to do business with the Ecuadorian government. The use of a local attorney will ease the difficulty of maneuvering the country's complex legal system.

Think Critically

1. What are the benefits and possible disadvantages of a country using the U.S. dollar as its official currency?

2. How do business customs in Ecuador differ from others with which you are familiar?

3. Conduct library or Internet research to obtain additional information about business activities and economic conditions in Ecuador.

What currency are shoppers at this open-air market in Ecuador most likely using?

Other Measures of Business Activity

Goals

1 Discuss investment activities that promote economic growth.

2 Explain borrowing activities by government, business, and consumers.

3 Describe future concerns of economic growth.

Key Terms

capital project 44

stock 45

bond 45

budget surplus 46

budget deficit 46

national debt 46

Focus on REAL LIFE

"Eddie, are those new boots?" asked Fritz.

"Yep," responded Eddie, "do you like them?"

"They're great, but I thought you were trying to sock away money to buy a car."

You can't expect to have enough money to buy a car in the future if you always spend everything you receive. Today's savings makes your future purchase possible. In a similar way, saving and investing is the foundation of a country's economic growth.

Governments, businesses, and consumers must save and invest for their futures. Government must have funds available for needed services desired by citizens. Companies must obtain equipment and other productive resources for a profitable future. Individuals must make choices that balance current spending with future financial security.

Goal 1

Discuss investment activities that promote economic growth.

INVESTMENT ACTIVITIES

Investing for the future can happen in several ways. Your time in school is an investment for your future. When companies buy buildings and equipment, they are also investing in their future.

Capital spending refers to money spent by a business for an item that will be used over a long period. **Capital projects** involve spending by businesses for items such as land, buildings, equipment, and new products. The money for capital projects comes from three main sources: personal savings, stock investments, and bonds.

Personal Savings

A major source of investment funds is personal savings. Companies use money you deposit in a bank or other financial institution. These funds provide the money necessary for buying expensive equipment or creating new products.

Name some long-term goals you might set for your savings account.

Calculate your savings rate (percent of your current income that you save). Do you believe you save enough of your income? Explain how saving is related to people achieving their life-span goals. Set a short-term saving goal that you could achieve now to help you eventually reach future life-span goals.

In return, savers are paid interest on the money they deposit.

The savings rate of a country is an important factor for economic growth. In recent years, the personal savings rate of the United States has been quite low, often below one percent. This situation can cause economic concerns in the future.

The Stock Market

Corporations are a major type of business organization. Many people invest by becoming part owners of a corporation. **Stock** represents ownership in a corporation. Stock ownership is commonly called *equity.* This term means "ownership."

The value of shares of stock is affected by many factors. Once again, supply and demand are the major influences. If a company has higher earnings, more people will want to buy its stock. This causes the value to increase.

The Bond Market

Another investment activity involves the sale of bonds. A **bond** represents *debt* for an organization.

If you purchase a corporate or government bond, you are a *creditor.* This means you have lent money to the organization. In return, bondholders are paid interest for the use of their money.

> **checkpoint ✓**
> Name some examples of capital projects.

BORROWING

"Buy now, pay later" commonly occurs in most economies of the world. Borrowing by governments, businesses, and consumers can have an important economic influence.

Goal 2

Explain borrowing activities by governments, businesses, and consumers.

Business Insight for the 21st Century

Cleantech: Energy Alternatives and Environmentally Friendly Products

The phrase *cleantech* refers to various goods and services that are environmentally friendly. It is also part of the name of an organization that promotes clean technology among investors, entrepreneurs, and service providers.

The Cleantech Venture Network provides a network of information, online services, and educational events to promote innovations that do not harm the environment. The emphasis of the group's efforts is to balance profit-making and environment-friendly business activities. Cleantech is not just interested in being socially responsible. It also recognizes the need for financial success.

Cleantech attempts to encourage and publicize investment and development for various *clean*, or environment-friendly, technologies. The companies in the Cleantech network are involved in a wide range of products, services, and processes designed to provide superior performance at lower costs. At the same time, these business activities must reduce or eliminate environmental concerns in an effort to improve the quality of life.

A concern for both companies and investors is that the "cleantech" label is often used for products and services that do meet the standards of the Cleantech Venture Network.

Many organizations attempt to attract investors by calling their enterprise "cleantech" even though their business activities are not improving the environment.

Think Critically

1. How do consumers, businesses, and the economy benefit by cleantech activities?

2. What concerns might be associated with cleantech companies?

3. Conduct library or Internet research to obtain examples of various environment-friendly products and services.

Getting involved in economic and social issues is a vital role for citizens. Working as a team, select a current topic that needs attention. Prepare a list of actions that governments, businesses, and consumers might take to address this concern.

Government Debt

People expect services from federal, state, and local governments. Those services cost money. Often, government uses borrowing to finance various projects. New schools, public buildings, highways, and parks are often financed by borrowing.

A government may spend less than it takes in. When this occurs, a **budget surplus** is the result. If a surplus exists, government may reduce taxes or increase spending on various programs.

In contrast, a government may spend more than it takes in. This situation is called a **budget deficit**. Over time, deficits build up. The total amount owed by the federal government is called the **national debt**.

Business Debt

Loans, bonds, and mortgages are common borrowing methods used by businesses. Most companies, large and small, use debt at some time.

Efficient use of borrowing can be helpful to companies. Using the funds of others can help expand sales and profits. Sometimes, when poor decisions are made, debt creates problems. Poor debt management can result in a company going out of business.

Consumer Debt

People commonly use credit cards, auto loans, and home mortgages to finance their purchases. The use of credit can be convenient. Often, however, overuse of credit results in financial difficulties for individuals and families.

Careful use of credit can be important for economic growth. In contrast, unwise borrowing can result in legal action and other trouble.

checkpoint ✓
What is the cause of a budget deficit?

ECONOMIC CHALLENGES AND ADAPTING TO CURRENT MARKETS

Expanded economic output results in more goods and services. Global business growth is occurring in *emerging markets*, places where consumer incomes and buying power are increasing because of economic expansion. With more jobs and more income for workers, quality of life improves.

However, many countries lack the technology, education, and business systems needed for economic success. Today, businesses and other organizations exist to help improve the situations in weak economies. By providing training, technology, loans, and other assistance, innovative solutions for various economic

Photodisc/Getty Images

What are some of the risks involved in a small business using credit?

problems such as hunger, disease, unsafe water, and poverty are being developed.

In order to adapt to various market needs, companies must be aware of consumer preferences and behaviors. Researching the culture, economic conditions, and political environment is the foundation for successful business activities. No one knows for sure what the future economic situation will be. To maintain or increase a country's standard of living and to prevent unemployment, government, businesses, workers, and consumers must coordinate their efforts. This cooperation can result in creating jobs and providing for the needs and wants of people.

checkpoint ✓
What economic challenges will countries face in the future?

thefinalmiracle/Shutterstock.com

How can business activities be used to solve various economic problems?

2-3 Assessment

www.cengage.com/school/genbus/pob

Key Concepts

Determine the best answer.

1. Equity refers to
   a. reduced spending by government
   b. ownership in a company
   c. borrowing to finance a capital project
   d. increased government taxes

2. Which of the following would most likely cause a budget surplus for government?
   a. higher spending
   b. lower spending
   c. higher borrowing
   d. lower taxes

3. In emerging markets, consumer incomes and buying power are
   a. decreasing
   b. fluctuating
   c. increasing
   d. stable

Make Academic Connections

4. **Economics** Taxes are a necessity. They provide necessary money for government services. What types of taxes do you believe would be best for a society?

5. **Social Studies** How might the future economic concerns of other countries differ from those of the United States?

Business Notes

2-1 Measuring Economic Activity

- Gross domestic product (GDP) is the total market value of all final goods and services produced in a country during one year. GDP per capita is calculated by dividing GDP by the total population.

- There are several economic measures of labor. The labor force of an economy consists of all people above age 16 who are actively working or seeking work. The unemployment rate is the portion of people in the labor force who are not working. People are considered to be unemployed if they are looking for work and willing to work but unable to find a job. Productivity is the production output in relation to a unit of input, such as a worker.

- There are several economic indicators for consumer spending. Personal income refers to salaries and wages, as well as investment income and government payments to individuals. Retail sales measure the sales of durable and nondurable goods bought by consumers.

2-2 Economic Conditions Change

- The movement of the economy from good times to bad and back again is called a business cycle. A business cycle has four phases: prosperity, recession, depression, and recovery.

- Inflation is a general rise in the level of prices. Inflation can occur when the demand for goods and services is greater than the supply. Deflation is a decrease in the general price level. Deflation can occur when prices of products are lower, but people have less money to buy them.

- Interest rates represent the cost of money. The level of interest rates in an economy is affected by the supply and demand for money. Interest rates affect both consumer and business activities.

2-3 Other Measures of Business Activity

- Investment activities that promote economic growth involve personal savings, buying stock as ownership in a corporation, and purchasing bonds from businesses and government.

- Governments, businesses, and consumers commonly use borrowing to finance various purchases. Careful borrowing can be important for economic growth. In contrast, unwise borrowing can result in legal action and other problems.

- Most economic growth is likely to occur in *emerging markets*, requiring improved technology, education, and business systems in those countries. Efforts will also be made to solve various economic problems such as hunger, disease, unsafe water, and poverty.

Communicate Business Concepts

1. "GDP is the best measurement of a country's economy." Explain why you agree or disagree with this statement.

2. The GDP of Country A is $400,000. The GDP of Country B is $800,000. Does this mean that the per capita output of Country B is about twice that of Country A? Explain.

3. Name three factors that can contribute to increased output of goods and services in a country. Explain how these factors can improve productivity.

4. What is the effect of increased productivity on a country's leisure time? How might increased productivity affect career opportunities?

5. Suppose that many auto and steel plants close in a country. Thousands of workers lose their jobs in a short period. If the country has been enjoying prosperous times, it may now be headed into what phase of the business cycle? Describe other conditions that might begin to occur.

6. Retail sales is a measure of durable and nondurable goods bought by consumers. What are some examples of durable and nondurable goods?

7. What actions might be taken by businesses and government in each phase of the business cycle?

8. Why is a high rate of inflation generally considered harmful to an economy?

9. Other than the economic indicators discussed in this chapter, what are some other data items that might be used to measure business and economic activities?

10. What are some economic concerns that may need to be addressed in the future?

Develop your Business Language

Match the terms listed with the definitions.

11. A decrease in the general price level.

12. The movement of an economy from one condition to another and back again.

13. Spending by businesses for items such as land, buildings, and equipment.

14. The total value of all final goods and services produced in a country in one year.

15. Government spends less than it takes in.

16. A phase marked by a long period of high unemployment, weak consumer sales, and business failures.

17. Represents debt for an organization.

18. Salaries and wages as well as investment income and government payments to individuals.

19. The GDP divided by the total population of a country.

20. Production output in relation to a unit of input, such as a worker.

21. The phase in which unemployment decreases, demand for goods and services increases, and GDP begins to rise.

22. An increase in the general price level.

23. Represents ownership in a corporation.

24. Government spends more than it takes in.

25. The portion of people in the labor force who are not working.

26. The sales of durable and nondurable goods bought by consumers.

27. A period in which unemployment is low, businesses produce many goods and services, and wages are good.

28. A number that compares prices in one year with prices in some earlier base year.

29. A period in which demand, production, and GDP growth decrease and unemployment begins to rise.

30. The total amount owed by the federal government.

Key Terms
a. bond
b. budget deficit
c. budget surplus
d. business cycle
e. capital project
f. deflation
g. depression
h. GDP per capita
i. gross domestic product (GDP)
j. inflation
k. national debt
l. personal income
m. price index
n. productivity
o. prosperity
p. recession
q. recovery
r. retail sales
s. stock
t. unemployment rate

Make Academic Connections

31. **Technology** Describe ways in which computers and other technology might affect a country's GDP.

32. **Geography** Select five countries. Create a map showing various economic statistics for each country. Explain reasons for differences among the countries.

33. **Science** Technology is often the basis for increased productivity. Prepare a poster or other visual presentation to demonstrate how the use of computers or other technology might make workers more productive.

34. **Culture** How might culture affect opportunities to increase productivity in different countries? Describe cultural and political factors that may enhance or limit actions to increase productivity.

35. **Math** Productivity for a small country was 25 units per worker hour in 2001. Productivity increased 20 percent between 2001 and 2006. What was the productivity figure for 2006? If the rate of increase is maintained, what will the figure be in 2011? In 2016?

36. **Math** Workers are paid a rate of $0.30 per unit. Using productivity figures from the previous question, determine how much workers earned per hour in 2006. If their rate increases to $0.35 in 2011 and to $0.40 in 2016, how much would they earn per hour in those years?

37. **History** Research various phases of the business cycle in the United States during the past 200 years. Create a graph showing the ups and downs of the economy. What conclusions could be drawn from this research?

38. **Communication** Prepare a visual presentation to report (a) reasons government, businesses, and consumers borrow, and (b) potential problems that could occur for each group if credit is not used properly.

39. **Economics** Compare the use of stocks and bonds by companies to raise funds. Describe situations in which each would be most effective.

40. **Communication** Select two interest rates from the list on page 42. Conduct online research and create a chart showing these rates for the past four or five years. Explain possible reasons for changes in these rates.

Decision-Making Strategies

In determining GDP, only final goods and services are included. This avoids having some items counted more than once. For example, a mining company sells iron ore to a steel-producing firm. That firm sells the steel to an auto manufacturer who uses it to produce a car. The iron ore, converted to steel, is counted once—in the price paid for the car, the final product. Read carefully the following list of goods and services produced in our economy and then answer the questions.

a. Electric toaster oven bought as a gift
b. Telephone service installed in a government office
c. Fiberglass sold to a company for use in making boats
d. Grooming services for your pet
e. Paper sold to a newspaper publishing company
f. Computer paid for by a city government
g. Computer bought for your family's use
h. Broccoli bought by a food-processing firm

41. Which of these items should be listed as a good and counted in GDP? Give reasons for your answer.

42. Which of these items should be listed as a service and counted in GDP? Give reasons for your answer.

Linking School and Community

Locate two or three people in your community who work in various jobs. Ask them about changes that have occurred in their work situation over the years. Did any of these changes occur in an attempt to increase productivity? Are there other changes that might be made to increase productivity? Prepare a short report to summarize your findings.

©sweetym/iStock

Web Workout

Blogs provide comments, news, and observations. These online journals communicate experiences along with other thoughts and information. Blogs are available on every business topic. The sources of blog postings can range from an economist at the Tax Foundation to a dissatisfied consumer. You should be cautious before believing or acting on information from a blog. Always confirm the information with other sources.

Think Critically

1. Locate a blog that relates to current economic conditions. Describe some recent postings.

2. What actions might you take to make sure the information on this blog is accurate?

3. Without actually posting it, write a comment that you would like to post on this blog.

Quick-Serve Restaurant Management Series Event Role Play

The DECA Series Event challenges participants to develop a plan of action for a business role play. You will have 10 minutes to develop a solution that covers the performance indicators associated with the role play. Participants have five minutes to explain their plan of action to the judge. The judge has an additional two minutes to ask questions about the plan of action.

Pearl's is a diner that has been in operation for five years. It is located along a major highway in a community that has a population of 5,000 people. The restaurant was built during an economic boom and business has grown steadily during the first five years of operation. The current economic recession has dramatically changed the business environment. Unemployment has grown to 12% and business for Pearl's is down 25% from last year. The prices of menu items at the diner range from $3.50 to $8.00; the restaurant accepts cash and local checks for payment. Pearl's has advertised in the local newspaper and counted heavily on word-of-mouth advertising. The diner is open daily from 7 A.M. until 9 P.M. You have been hired as a consultant to help Pearl's increase business during the recession. You are challenged to describe the marketing strategy for the restaurant considering its location, menu items and prices, hours of operation, and promotion. Your plan must cover all performance indicators.

Performance Indicators Evaluated

- Describe the economic impact of a recession on business.
- Explain customer buying behavior.
- Identify a company's unique selling proposition.
- Identify product opportunities.
- Explain the types of promotion.

For more detailed information about performance indicators, go to the DECA website.

Think Critically

1. How does a recession affect the spending habits of consumers?

2. How can the location for Pearl's be used to increase business beyond the town's population?

3. What promotional activities might bring more customers to Pearl's during the recession?

4. What are some advertising strategies that Pearl's should consider to increase business?

www.deca.org

Digital Vision/Getty Images

Planning a Career in ...

INTERNATIONAL BUSINESS

Transportation, Distribution & Logistics

Global business activities create many employment opportunities. Jobs could include directing foreign sales, negotiating with foreign distribution centers, arranging shipping, and planning conversion of products from American to foreign specifications. While the international business skills necessary to perform these tasks are increasingly important, job titles may not reflect them directly because a worker will often have other duties unrelated to importing and exporting. Transportation managers, for example, oversee both foreign and domestic shipping, including settlements between shippers. U.S. Customs Service agents investigate persons, common carriers, and merchandise arriving in or departing from the United States to prevent prohibited importing or exporting.

Related Job Titles

- Customs Inspector
- Interpreter or Translator
- Global Purchasing Manager
- Freight Inspector
- Cross-Cultural Trainer
- International Sales Representative
- International Marketing Manager
- Import-Export Coordinator

Analyze Career Opportunities in ...
INTERNATIONAL BUSINESS

Use library and Internet resources to learn more about careers in international business. Choose one of the job titles listed in the box and answer the following questions.

1. How would you describe the earnings potential for this field?

2. Is this a career that interests you? Describe a few things you could do to learn more about this career.

What's it like to work as a ... Freight Forwarder?

"I'm sorry, your shipment is being held at the Port of Hong Kong until the proper documentation is prepared."

These are words no exporter wants to hear. To avoid this type of situation, exporters turn to freight forwarding companies to help them ship their products around the world.

Freight forwarders specialize in shipping goods to customers in other countries. These global intermediaries also help companies selling around the world with other services. Areas of expertise include export regulations, costs for various shipping methods, and the customs process.

Most freight forwarders also serve as customs brokers, helping international companies pass inspections when goods enter another country. Customs brokers prepare needed documents and make sure the required tariffs are paid.

What about you? What are some aspects of international business that you might find of interest in the future?

3-1 International Business Basics

Goals

1 Describe importing and exporting activities.

2 Compare balance of trade and balance of payments.

3 List factors that affect the value of global currencies.

Key Terms

imports 55

exports 55

balance of trade 56

balance of payments 57

exchange rate 58

Focus on REAL LIFE

What did you and your family have for breakfast this morning? Coffee, cereal, and sliced bananas, perhaps? If it were not for trading with Brazil for coffee and with Honduras for the bananas, you might have had only cereal. The sugar on your table may have come from the Philippines. Even the morning newspaper was printed on paper that may have come from Canada.

As you look around your home, you will find many products made in other countries. For example, you may find a TV made in Japan or Korea, a music player made in Taiwan or China, clothing made in the Philippines or Honduras, kitchen appliances made in Hong Kong or Malaysia, and cocoa from Brazil or Colombia. Look around your classroom. Can you identify products made in other countries?

Goal 1

Describe importing and exporting activities.

TRADING AMONG NATIONS

Most business activities occur within a country's own borders. *Domestic business* is the making, buying, and selling of goods and services within a country. *International business* refers to business activities needed for creating, shipping, and selling goods and services across national borders. International business is frequently referred to as *foreign* or *world trade.* Evidence of foreign trade is everywhere.

Although the United States has many natural resources, a skilled labor force, and modern production facilities, American companies and consumers go beyond the U.S. borders to obtain many things. The United States conducts trade with more than 180 countries.

In the past, economies were viewed in terms of national borders. With international trade expanding every day, these boundaries are no longer fully valid in defining economies. Countries are interdependent and so are their economies. Consumers have come to expect goods and services from around the world.

Absolute Advantage

Two economic principles define buying and selling among companies in different countries. *Absolute advantage* exists when

What are some of the advantages and disadvantages of international trade?

a country can produce a good or service at a lower cost than other countries. This may result from an abundance of natural resources or raw materials in a country. For example, some South American countries have an absolute advantage in coffee production, and Saudi Arabia has an absolute advantage in oil production.

Comparative Advantage

A country may have an absolute advantage in more than one area. If so, it must decide how to maximize its economic wealth. A country may be able to produce both computers and clothing better than other countries. The world market for computers might be stronger than the market for clothing. This means it would be better for the country to produce computers but to buy clothing from other countries. *Comparative advantage* is a situation in which a country specializes in the production of a good or service at which it is relatively more efficient.

Importing

Imports are items bought from other countries. Did you know that imports account for the total supply of bananas, coffee, cocoa, spices, tea, silk, and crude rubber in the United States? The United States buys about half of its crude oil and fish from other countries. Imports also

Identify your special aptitudes or abilities that you believe could help you achieve your life-span goals. Explain how these aptitudes or abilities are similar to nations that have an absolute or comparative advantage in production and trade.

account for 20 to 50 percent of the supply of carpets, sugar, leather gloves, dishes, and sewing machines. U.S. companies must import tin, chromium, manganese, nickel, copper, zinc, and other metals to manufacture certain goods. Figure 3-1 shows how dependent the United States is on imported raw materials.

Without foreign trade, many things you buy would cost more or not be available. Other countries can produce some goods at a lower cost because they have the needed raw materials or have lower labor costs. Some consumers purchase foreign goods, even at higher prices, if they perceive the quality to be better than domestic goods. They may simply enjoy products made in other countries. French perfumes, Norwegian sweaters, and Swiss watches are examples.

Exporting

Goods and services sold to other countries are called **exports**. Just as imports benefit you, exports benefit consumers in other countries. Workers throughout

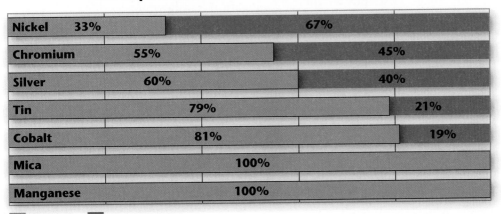

U.S. Import Reliance for Selected Raw Materials

Material	Import	U.S. Production
Nickel	33%	67%
Chromium	55%	45%
Silver	60%	40%
Tin	79%	21%
Cobalt	81%	19%
Mica	100%	
Manganese	100%	

■ Import   ■ U.S. Production

Source: United States Geological Survey Minerals Information

▶ **Figure 3-1**

How would U.S. manufacturing be affected if these imports were not available?

the world use factory and farm machinery made in the United States. They eat food made from U.S. agricultural products and use chemicals, fertilizers, medicines, and plastics from the United States. People in other countries like to view U.S. movies. They also watch CNN and ESPN. They read books, magazines, and newspapers published by U.S. companies. The goods and services exported by the United States create many jobs. One of every six jobs in the United States depends on international business. Figure 3-2 shows U.S. balance of trade with its top trading partners.

U.S. TRADE BALANCES WITH TOP TRADING PARTNERS (IN BILLIONS)

COUNTRY	GOODS EXPORTED	GOODS IMPORTED	U.S. TRADE BALANCE
All Countries	1056.9	1558.1	−501.2
1. Canada	204.7	224.9	−20.2
2. China	69.6	296.4	−226.8
3. Mexico	129.0	176.5	−47.5
4. Japan	51.2	95.9	−44.7
5. Germany	43.3	71.3	−28.0
6. United Kingdom	45.7	47.5	−1.8
7. South Korea	28.6	39.2	−10.6
8. France	26.5	34.0	−7.5
9. Netherlands	32.3	16.1	16.2

Source: U.S. Census Bureau

▶ **Figure 3-2**

Which country has the largest trade imbalance with the United States?

checkpoint ✓

How does importing differ from exporting?

Compare balance of trade and balance of payments.

MEASURING TRADE RELATIONS

A major reason people work is to earn money to buy things. First, they sell their labor for wages. They then spend the major part of those wages on goods and services. People usually try to keep their income and spending in balance. They know that if they spend more than they earn, they can experience financial problems. Nations are also concerned about balancing income with expenditures. When people buy more than their income allows,

they go into debt. In the same way, when a country has an unfavorable balance of trade it owes money to others. *Foreign debt* is the amount a country owes to other countries.

Balance of Trade

The difference between a country's total exports and total imports is called the **balance of trade**. If a country exports (sells) more than it imports (buys), it has a *trade surplus*. Its trade position is said to be favorable. If it imports more than it exports, it has a *trade deficit* and its trade position is unfavorable.

Possible Trade Positions

▶ **Figure 3-3**

Why is it better for a country to export more than it imports?

A country can have a trade surplus with one country and a trade deficit with another. Overall, a country tries to keep its international trade in balance. Figure 3-3 shows the two possible trade positions. After a long history of a favorable balance of trade, the United States has had a trade deficit in recent years.

Balance of Payments

In addition to exporting and importing goods and services, other forms of exchange take place among nations. Money goes from one country to another through investments and tourism. A citizen of one country might invest in a corporation in another country. A business may invest in a factory in another country. One government might give financial or military aid to another nation. Banks may deposit funds in foreign banks.

When tourists travel, they add to the flow of money from their country to the country they are visiting. Some countries

WORK *as a* **TEAM**

Countries attempt to have a favorable balance of payments. Create a list of actions a nation might take to improve its trade relations with other countries.

limit the amount of money their citizens can take out of the country when they travel.

The **balance of payments** is the difference between the amount of money that comes into a country and the amount that goes out of it. A *positive* or *favorable* balance of payments occurs when a nation receives more money in a year than it pays out. A *negative* balance of payments is *unfavorable*. It is the result of a country sending more money out than it brings in.

> **checkpoint ✓**
> How does balance of trade differ from balance of payments?

©Andreas Prott/iStock

A Question of Ethics

Bribery and Gift Giving

In the United States, it is considered unethical for a businessperson to pay bribes to government officials or to other businesspersons in exchange for favorable treatment, such as the awarding of well-paid contracts. In fact, it is against the law, whether the recipient is an American or someone in another country. The Foreign Corrupt Business Practices Act of 1977 outlawed the payment of bribes by Americans to foreign officials, companies, or individuals. At times, not doing so may put U.S. businesses at a competitive disadvantage. In some countries, paying and accepting bribes of various sorts is common, even expected. As more countries

recognize how harmful bribes are to economic progress, the practice is ending.

While it is relatively easy to outlaw bribes, it is much harder to define and identify what is a bribe and what is a gift given as a token of appreciation. Gift giving among businesspeople is relatively limited and infrequent in the United States and Canada. In other cultures, it is very common and regarded as entirely appropriate. Many organizations have policies that limit the monetary value and type of gifts that are acceptable. Policing intent is much more difficult because it is highly subjective. A social dinner invitation is usually meant to influence

the recipient's behavior, even if in a subtle way.

Think Critically

1. How can U.S. businesspeople handle situations in foreign countries where officials expect bribes to be paid as a condition for doing business there?

2. Suppose you work for a manufacturing company. A plastics supplier who is trying to get more business sends you a case of golf balls made with one of its high-tech composite materials. What would you do?

INTERNATIONAL CURRENCY

One challenge faced by businesses involved in international trade is the various currencies used around the world. Each nation has its own banking system and money. For instance, Russia uses the *ruble*; the European Union, the *euro*; Brazil, the *real*; India, the *rupee*; and Saudi Arabia, the *riyal*.

Why do many countries use a variety of colors in their currency?

Foreign Exchange Rates

The process of exchanging one currency for another occurs in the *foreign exchange market,* which consists of banks that buy and sell different currencies. Most large banks provide currency services for businesses and consumers. The **exchange rate** is the value of a currency in one country compared with the value in another. Supply and demand affect the value of currency. The approximate values of various currencies on a recent date in relation to the U.S. dollar (USD) are given in Figure 3-4.

Travelers and businesspeople must deal with currency exchanges as they go from one country to another. Travelers in another country can go to a currency exchange window and buy any amount of local currency they want. The amount of local currency they receive depends on the value of the two currencies at that time. Current rates are posted at exchange windows. Although locations vary throughout the world, exchange windows generally are found at airports, train stations, hotels, and local banks. Operators of exchange windows charge a fee for their services.

Factors Affecting Currency Values

Three main factors affect currency exchange rates among countries: the country's balance of payments, economic conditions, and political stability.

Balance of Payments When a country has a favorable balance of payments, the value of its currency is usually constant or

Figure 3-4

Which currency is worth the most in terms of U.S. dollars?

RECENT VALUES OF CURRENCIES			
COUNTRY	**CURRENCY**	**UNITS PER USD***	**VALUE IN USD***
Britain	pound	0.66 pounds	1.52
Brazil	real	1.73 reals	0.577
Canada	dollar	0.98 dollars	1.01
European Union	euro	0.76 euro	1.32
Japan	yen	94.6 yen	0.0106
Saudi Arabia	riyal	3.75 riyal	0.27
South Africa	rand	7.43 rand	0.135
South Korea	won	1117.67 won	0.0009
Venezuela	bolivar	4,300.00 bolivars	0.000232558

*United States Dollar

rising. An increased demand for both the nation's products and its currency causes this situation. When a nation has an unfavorable balance of payments, its currency usually declines in value.

Economic Conditions When prices increase and the buying power of the country's money declines, its currency is not as appealing. Inflation reduces the buying power of a currency. High inflation in Brazil, for example, would reduce the demand for the real.

Interest rates are the cost of using someone else's money. These rates can affect the value of a country's currency. Higher interest rates usually create lower consumer demand. This often results in a reduced demand for a nation's currency, causing a decline in its value.

Political Stability Companies and individuals want to avoid risk when they do business in other nations. If a government changes suddenly, this may create an unfriendly setting for foreign business. A

company could lose its building, equipment, or money on deposit in banks.

Political instability may also occur when new laws are put in place. These laws may not allow foreign businesses to operate as freely as they did under the old laws. Uncertainty in a country reduces the confidence that businesspeople have in its currency.

checkpoint ✓
What factors affect the value of a country's currency?

3-1 Assessment

Study Tools

www.cengage.com/school/genbus/pob

Key Concepts

Determine the best answer.

1. Which of the following would be an example of international business?
   a. A farmer in Iowa using equipment made in Indiana
   b. A sales staff in South Carolina representing a foreign producer
   c. A restaurant in Chicago offering Asian menu items
   d. A retail store in Oregon selling craft items from local artists

2. When a country's imports exceed its exports, there is a trade
   a. surplus
   b. deficit
   c. exchange
   d. balance

3. The value of a country's currency is likely to decline as a result of
   a. higher inflation
   b. lower interest rates
   c. a trade surplus
   d. a favorable balance of payments

Make Academic Connections

4. **Culture** While business knowledge is important, often cultural awareness in foreign markets is even more important. Interview someone who has lived in or visited another country about cultural factors that affect business activities in that country.

5. **Technology** Explain how the Internet and other technology help to expand international trade and global business activities.

3-2 The Global Marketplace

Goals

1 Describe the components of the international business environment.

2 Identify examples of formal trade barriers.

3 Explain actions to encourage international trade.

Key Terms

Infrastructure 61

trade barrier 62

quota 62

tariff 62

embargo 63

Focus on REAL LIFE

"Look, this shirt was made in El Salvador," Ross announced as he put the hanger back on the rack. "I want shirts made in the U.S.A."

Calinda touched the shirt and asked, "What's wrong with shirts from El Salvador?"

"I don't know, but wouldn't it be better if we bought things made here rather than giving our money to other countries?"

"Actually, trading with other countries can be good for us," Calinda explained. "When we buy goods from El Salvador it helps that country's economy and makes it possible for Salvadorans to buy goods and services from U.S. companies."

Ross picks up a shirt and says, "In that case, I'll buy this one."

Goal 1

Describe the components of the international business environment.

INTERNATIONAL BUSINESS ENVIRONMENT

Doing business in other countries requires knowledge of the differences that exist among people and places. As shown in Figure 3-5, businesses must consider four main factors—geography, cultural influences, economic development, and political and legal concerns.

Geography

The location, climate, terrain, seaports, and natural resources of a country influence business activity. Very hot weather will limit the types of crops that can be grown. A nation with many rivers or ocean seaports can easily ship products for foreign trade. Countries with few natural resources must depend on imports.

Cultural Influences

In some societies, hugging is an appropriate business greeting. In other societies, a handshake is the custom. These differences represent different cultures.

Culture is the accepted behaviors, customs, and values of a society. A society's culture has a strong influence on business activities. In Mexico, many businesses close in the afternoon by tradition while people enjoy lunch and a siesta (relaxing rest period).

The main cultural and social factors that affect international business are language, religion, values, customs, and social relationships. These relationships include interactions among families, labor unions, and other organizations.

Economic Development

Countries and individuals face the problem of limited resources to satisfy needs and wants. You continually make decisions about the use of your time, money, and energy. In a similar way, every country plans the use of its land, natural resources, workers, and wealth to best serve the needs of its people.

In some countries, people travel on a high-speed bullet train to manage a computer network in a high-rise building. In other countries, people go by oxcart to a grass hut to operate a hand loom to make cloth for people in their village. These differences in living and work environments reflect the level of economic development. The key factors that affect a country's level of economic development are:

- **Literacy Level** Countries with better education systems usually provide more and better goods and services for their citizens.

- **Technology** Automated production, distribution, and communications systems allow companies to create and deliver goods, services, and ideas quickly.

- **Agricultural Dependency** An economy that is largely involved in agriculture does not have the manufacturing base to provide citizens with great quantity and high quality of a product.

Another factor that supports international trade in industrialized countries is **infrastructure**. Infrastructure refers to a nation's transportation, communication, and utility systems. A country such as Germany—with its efficient rail system, high-speed highways, and computers—is better prepared for international business activities than other nations with a weaker infrastructure.

Political and Legal Concerns

Each day you come upon examples of government influence on business. Governments regulate fair advertising and enforce contracts. They require safety inspections of foods and medications. People in the United States have a great deal of freedom in their business activities. This is not true in all countries. In many places, the activities of consumers and business operators are restricted. The most common political and legal factors that affect international business activities

WORK as a TEAM

Knowledge of the international business environment is important for all global activities. As a team, create a list of items for each of the following categories: geography, cultural influences, economic development, and political-legal concerns. Explain how these items could affect a company when doing business in another country.

include the type of government, the stability of the government, and government policies toward business.

checkpoint ✓
List the four main elements of the international business environment.

GEOGRAPHIC FACTORS
- Location
- Climate
- Terrain
- Waterways
- Natural resources

ECONOMIC FACTORS
- Technology
- Education
- Inflation
- Exchange rate
- Infrastructure

INTERNATIONAL BUSINESS ENVIRONMENT

CULTURAL FACTORS
- Language
- Family
- Religion
- Customs
- Traditions
- Food

POLITICAL AND LEGAL FACTORS
- Government system
- Political stability
- Trade barriers
- Business regulations

▶ Figure 3-5

What are some specific examples of the four main factors of the international business environment?

INTERNATIONAL TRADE BARRIERS

Government actions can create **trade barriers**, which are restrictions to free trade. These political actions are *formal* trade barriers. Three common formal trade barriers are quotas, tariffs, and embargoes.

The culture, traditions, and religion of a country can create *informal* trade barriers. These situations are not based on formal government actions but they can restrict trade.

Quotas

To regulate international trade, governments set a limit on the quantity of a product that may be imported or exported within a given period. This limit is called a **quota**.

Quotas may be set for many reasons. Countries that export oil may put quotas on crude oil so that the supply will remain low and prices will stay at a certain level. Quotas may be set on imports from another country to express displeasure at the policies of that country.

Quotas can also be set by a country to protect one of its industries from too much competition from abroad. This often is done by a nation to shield its "infant industries," which need protection to get started. In the past, the U.S. government has imposed quotas on sugar, cattle, dairy products, and textiles.

Tariffs

Another device that governments use to control international trade is the tariff. A **tariff** is a tax that a government places on certain imported products. Suppose you want to buy an imported bicycle. The producer charges $140, but the government collects a 20 percent tariff ($28) on the bicycle when it is imported. Therefore, you will have to pay $168 plus shipping charges for the bike. The increased price may cause you to decide to buy a bike manufactured in the United States at a lower price.

Some tariffs are a set amount per pound, gallon, or other unit, while others are figured on the value of the good, as in the example of the bicycle. A tariff increases the price for an imported product. A high tariff tends to lower the demand for the product and reduce the quantity of that import. Many people believe that tariffs should be used to protect U.S. jobs from foreign competition.

Stockbyte/Getty Images

Do tariffs on imported goods help consumers or hurt them?

Embargoes

If a government wishes to do so, it can stop the export or import of a product completely. This action is called an **embargo**. Governments may impose an embargo for many reasons. They may wish to protect their own industries from international competition more than either the quota or the tariff will achieve. The government may wish to prevent sensitive products, especially those vital to the nation's defense, from falling into the hands of unfriendly groups or nations. A government sometimes imposes an embargo to express its disapproval of the actions or policies of another country.

> ### checkpoint ✓
> What are three formal trade barriers?

ENCOURAGING INTERNATIONAL TRADE

Specific actions by governments can promote international business activities. Governments view exporting as an effective way to create jobs and foster economic prosperity. Common efforts to encourage international trade include free-trade zones, free-trade agreements, and common markets.

Free-Trade Zones

To promote international business, governments often create free-trade zones in their countries. A *free-trade zone* is a selected area where products can be imported duty-free and then stored, assembled, and/or used in manufacturing. A free-trade zone is usually located around a seaport or airport. The importer pays duty only when the product leaves the zone.

©Jacob Wackerhausen/iStock

Business Insight for the 21st Century

Mobile Phone Financial Services in Developing Economies

In many rural areas of Africa, cell phones are changing the way farmers do business and improving economic development. From Senegal to Kenya, mobile phones provide access to financial services such as savings accounts, payment accounts, and loans. These services are especially needed in rural areas because banks are rare. Farmers can use cell phones to pay for livestock, agricultural equipment, seeds for crops, and other business expenses.

Organizations such as the Grameen Bank and Opportunity International have created mobile phone banking systems to serve farmers, business owners, and entrepreneurs in Africa and Asia. Customers use their phones to check account balances, pay bills, maintain savings accounts with debit cards, and obtain small loans. These loans are often used to start a community-based business.

In some cases the banks lease phones to help people set up a grocery shop, open a café, or start a weaving business. The loan funds are accessed by phone to pay workers and other business expenses. As farmers and entrepreneurs have business success, they create jobs which provide money to families for food, clean water, health care, and education.

Think Critically

1. What are the benefits of mobile phone banking services for people in poor and rural areas?

2. Use the Internet to find additional information about cell phone banking in developing economies.

Why do you think U.S. businesses would be interested in exporting?

Brand X Pictures/Getty Images

This pact does away with tariffs on goods traded among the three countries and eases the movement of goods. NAFTA is designed to enlarge the markets and economic bases of the countries involved.

Common Markets

In a *common market*, members do away with duties and other trade barriers. They allow companies to invest freely in each member's country. They allow workers to move freely across borders. A common market is also called an *economic community*. Common market members have a common external duty on products being imported from nonmember countries. Examples of common markets include the European Union (EU) and the Latin American Integration Association (LAIA). The goals are to expand trade among member nations and promote regional economic integration.

Free-Trade Agreements

Many countries set up free-trade agreements with other nations. Under a *free-trade agreement,* member countries agree to remove duties, also called import taxes, and trade barriers on products traded among them. This results in increased trade between the members. For example, the United States, Canada, and Mexico began implementing the North American Free Trade Agreement (NAFTA) in 1994.

> **checkpoint** ✓
> What actions could be taken to encourage international trade?

3-2 Assessment

Study Tools
www.cengage.com/school/genbus/pob

Key Concepts

Determine the best answer.

1. True or False. Infrastructure is a significant factor that affects the economic development of a country.

2. True or False. An informal trade barrier is created by government actions.

3. Religion is an element of the _?_ component of the international business environment.
   a. geographic
   b. economic
   c. cultural
   d. political

4. A country that wishes to enhance international trade activities would most likely use
   a. a tariff
   b. a common market
   c. an embargo
   d. a quota

Make Academic Connections

5. **Law** Use the Internet to locate information about laws in foreign countries that are different from those in the United States.

6. **Geography** Using library resources or the Internet, obtain copies of maps for various geographic regions. On your map, indicate how the terrain, climate, and waterways might influence international trade activities. Present a one- to two- minute summary of your findings.

7. **History** Conduct research on the history of a common market such as the EU or the LAIA. Describe some of the benefits the community provides to its member nations.

International Business Organizations

Goals

1 Discuss activities of multinational organizations.

2 Explain common international business entry modes.

3 Describe activities of international trade organizations and agencies.

Key Terms

multinational company (MNC) 65

joint venture 67

Focus on REAL LIFE

"How was Italy?" Cory asked as he settled into a chair across from a colleague who had just returned from a six-month assignment.

"I worked really hard, but I found time to soak up some Italian culture and eat some great food. Living and working in another country was a good experience and I would do it again. However, I must admit that I'm glad to be home," responded Duncan as he put a straw in his soft drink.

"What did you miss the most?"

Duncan held up his cup and said, "American soft drinks. It was easy to find my favorite brands, but they just weren't the same."

MULTINATIONAL COMPANIES

A **multinational company (MNC)** is an organization that does business in several countries. MNCs usually consist of a parent company in a *home country* and divisions or separate companies in one or more host countries. The country in which the MNC places business activities is called the *host country*.

MNC Strategies

Multinational corporations can use either a global or multinational strategy. A *global strategy* uses the same product and marketing strategy worldwide. The same product is sold in essentially the same manner throughout the world. One example with which you are probably familiar is Coca-Cola.

A *multinational strategy* treats each country market differently. Firms develop products and marketing strategies that adapt to the customs, tastes, and buying habits of a distinct national market. Many restaurant chains employ a multinational strategy when they modify their menus to local tastes.

MNC Benefits

Many benefits are associated with international business. Consumers have a large amount of goods available. Often, these goods are at lower prices than goods made domestically. Career opportunities also

Goal 1

Discuss activities of multinational organizations.

How does this image illustrate the following concepts: multinational company, home country, and host country?

expand as a company does business in a variety of countries.

Global business activities may also foster understanding, communication, and respect among people of different nations. Nations that are business partners usually try to maintain friendly relations for economic reasons.

Drawbacks of Multinational Companies

An MNC can become a major economic power in a host country. The workers of the host country may depend on the MNC for jobs. Consumers become dependent upon it for goods and services. The MNC may actually influence or control the political power of the country.

Good prices and extensive consumer choice are two advantages of international business.

> **checkpoint** ✓
> What are two strategies commonly used by multinational companies?

Goal 2

Explain common international business entry modes.

GLOBAL MARKET ENTRY MODES

As companies expand into other countries, several methods are available for their use.

Licensing

Some companies want to produce items in other countries without being actively involved. They may allow a foreign company to use a procedure they own.

Licensing is selling the right to use some intangible property (production process, trademark, or brand name) for a fee or royalty.

The Gerber Company started selling its baby food products in Japan by means of licensing. The use of television characters or sports team emblems on hats, shirts, jackets, notebooks, luggage, and other items also involves a licensing agreement. Licensing has a low financial investment, so the potential financial return is often low. The risk for the company is also low.

Franchising

Another method often used to expand into other countries is the *franchise*. A franchise is the right to use a company name or business process in a specific way. Organizations enter into contracts with people in other countries to set up a business that looks and runs like

WORK as a TEAM

International business success often increases when a company works with a local business partner in another country. Choose a company or product that could be sold in other countries. Identify the types of companies that you might consider as a partner in the other countries. Then identify information sources that you might contact to make sure these potential partners would be suitable companies with which to do business.

the parent company. The company obtaining the franchise will usually adapt a range of business elements. Marketing elements such as food products, packaging, and advertising messages must meet both cultural sensitivities and legal requirements.

Both franchising and licensing involve a royalty payment for the right to use a process or company name. Licensing usually involves a manufacturing process. Franchising commonly involves selling a product or service. Franchise agreements are popular with fast-food companies. McDonald's, Burger King, Wendy's, KFC, and Pizza Hut all have used franchising to increase their presence in foreign markets.

Joint Venture

Business partnerships can provide benefits to all parties involved. One type of global partnership is the joint venture. A **joint venture** is an agreement between two or more companies to share a business project.

The main benefit of a joint venture is the sharing of raw materials, shipping facilities, management activities, or production facilities. Concerns about this type of partnership include sharing of profits and not as much control because several companies are involved.

This arrangement is very popular for manufacturing. Joint ventures between Japanese and U.S. automobile manufacturers have been common. For example, the Ford Motor Company entered a joint venture with Mazda Motor Corporation. Ford used Mazda-produced parts for several of its cars. Mazda set up assembly plants for Ford vehicles.

checkpoint ✓
How does licensing differ from a franchise?

fyi *Cereal Partners Worldwide (CPW) is a joint venture between General Mills and Nestle to sell cereal in Latin America, Europe, the Middle East, and other areas of the world. General Mills brought popular products, such as Cheerios, Lucky Charms, and Trix, into the partnership. Nestle, well known all over the world, has a broad distribution system and is a well-known brand in most foreign countries.*

Joel Calheiros/Shutterstock.com

INTERNATIONAL TRADE ORGANIZATIONS

Goal 3

Describe activities of international trade organizations and agencies.

International business activities can be very complex. As a result, several organizations have been created to help companies with global trade activities.

World Trade Organization

The World Trade Organization (WTO) was created in 1995 to promote trade around the world. With more than 150 member countries, WTO settles trade disputes and enforces free-trade agreements between its members. Other goals of WTO include the following.

- Lowering tariffs that discourage free trade
- Eliminating import quotas
- Reducing barriers for banks, insurance companies, and other financial services
- Assisting poor countries with economic growth

International Monetary Fund

The International Monetary Fund (IMF), with more than 150 member nations, helps to promote economic cooperation. It maintains an orderly system of world trade and exchange rates. The IMF was established in 1946 when the economic interdependence among nations was growing at a greater pace than ever before in history.

NETBookmark

The U.S. Department of Commerce and other federal government agencies provide extensive help to companies involved in exporting. Access the website shown below and click on the link for Chapter 3. Review the various information sources available to exporters. Select one of the information links on this website. Describe how this information could be of value to companies that are starting or expanding their exporting activities.

www.cengage.com/school/genbus/pob

Before the International Monetary Fund was instituted, a country could often change the value of its legal tender to attract more foreign customers. As other countries lose business, they may impose trade restrictions or lower the value of their currency. As one nation tries to outdo another, a trade war may result. Today, cooperation among IMF nations makes trade wars less likely.

World Bank

The International Bank for Reconstruction and Development is commonly called the *World Bank*. It was created in 1944 to provide loans for rebuilding after World War II. Today, the bank's key function is to give economic aid to less-developed countries. These funds build communications systems, transportation networks, and energy plants.

The World Bank, with more than 180 member countries, has two main divisions: the International Development Association and the International Finance Corporation. The International Development Association (IDA) makes loans to help developing countries. The International Finance Corporation (IFC) provides capital and technical help to private businesses in nations with limited resources. The IFC promotes joint ventures between foreign companies and local companies to further capital investment in developing nations.

checkpoint ✓

How does the International Monetary Fund assist countries?

3-3 Assessment

Study Tools

www.cengage.com/school/genbus/pob

Key Concepts

Determine the best answer.

1. A company is planning to sell the rights to its brand name for use in other countries. This is an example of a
   a. joint venture
   b. trade agreement
   c. franchise
   d. licensing agreement

2. The international organization that settles trade disagreements and enforces free-trade agreements is the
   a. WTO
   b. United Nations
   c. IMF
   d. World Bank

Make Academic Connections

3. **Economics** Visit a store or online site that sells toys, sporting goods, or other merchandise printed with logos or images belonging to other companies. List the information given that indicates a licensing agreement.

4. **Communication** Create a visual presentation (using software, photos, or a poster) that communicates the purpose of the International Monetary Fund or the World Bank.

5. **Read** Find a news article that relates to a topic addressed in this lesson. Read the article and write a one-sentence summary of the main idea. Include a properly formatted citation for your source.

The Hunger Site

Each day, more than 1,000 tons of edible food is thrown away in the United States. Elsewhere, several million people go hungry. Around the world, more than 20,000 people die every day from hunger-related causes. But what can one person do to solve this problem?

Tim Kunin and Greg Hesterberg decided to take action with The Hunger Site.

On average, more than 200,000 people from around the world visit the website each day. Kunin and Hesterberg launched The Hunger Site in June 1999. The Hunger Site focuses the power of the Internet to address various social concerns, such as the elimination of world hunger, health care for children, and literacy. Since it started, more than 600 million visitors have given more than 700 million cups of staple food to the hungry all over the world. Site sponsors pay for the staple food, distributed to those in need by Mercy Corps, Feeding America, and other organizations.

When visitors to The Hunger Site press the Click Here to Give button, they view ads from various sponsoring organizations. Money from the advertising fees goes to the charity partners. Funds are divided among the organizations to help hungry people in more than 70 countries. Included are those in Africa, Asia, Eastern Europe, the

What actions can people take to reduce hunger in local and global settings?

Middle East, Latin America, and North America. Tim and Greg, long-time friends and social activists, are committed to using this online effort to end world hunger.

Sponsors on The Hunger Site benefit in several ways. First, they are able to reach well-educated, upper-income consumers who are a desired target audience for their goods and services. Also, advertising on The Hunger Site creates goodwill. Sponsorship builds customer loyalty. Research shows that at least three-fourths of adults are more likely to buy a product linked with a social cause about which they care. More than half would be willing to pay a higher price for the product if it benefits a charity in which they believe.

Think Critically

1. Locate another website that promotes awareness of and attempts to solve a social issue or concern facing society today. Write a brief description of the website, the issue, and the goals. Include your opinion about the likelihood of success.

2. Identify a social issue of interest to you and plan a website that might raise awareness of the situation and lead to a solution.

Business Notes

3-1 International Business Basics

- Domestic business is the making, buying, and selling of goods and services within a country. International business refers to the business activities needed for creating, shipping, and selling goods and services across national borders.

- A country is said to have an absolute advantage when it can produce a good or service at a lower cost than other countries. If a country specializes in the production of a good or service at which it is more efficient, it is said to have a comparative advantage.

- Imports are items bought from other countries. Exports are goods and services sold to other countries. Nations do business with each other to increase the variety of goods and services available to their consumers.

- Balance of trade is the difference between a country's exports and imports. The difference between a country's total payments to other countries and its total receipts from other countries is the balance of payments.

- The exchange rate is the value of a currency in one country compared with the value of a currency in another country.

- The value of global currencies is affected by three main factors: balance of payments, economic conditions, and political stability.

3-2 The Global Marketplace

- The international business environment involves four main components: geography, cultural influences, economic development, and political and legal concerns.

- Three formal barriers to international trade are quotas, tariffs, and embargoes. A quota is a limit set on the quantity of a product that may be imported or exported within a given period. A tariff is a tax placed on certain imported products. An embargo stops the import or export of a product completely.

- Actions to encourage international trade include free-trade zones, free-trade agreements, and common markets.

3-3 International Business Organizations

- Multinational companies conduct business activities in several countries and have management capable of doing business worldwide.

- Common methods used for global business include licensing, franchising, and joint ventures.

- The World Trade Organization was created to promote trade around the world. The International Monetary Fund helps to promote economic cooperation by maintaining a system of world trade and exchange rates. The World Bank provides economic assistance to less-developed countries.

Communicate Business Concepts

1. Describe how an absolute advantage might affect a country's imports and exports.

2. Explain why it is difficult for a community or a nation to be completely independent.

3. How does international business contribute to a better standard of living for many people in various countries?

4. What are some attitudes and behaviors that might make it difficult for a foreign-based company to do business in the United States?

5. For the following situations, decide whether this is an example of an *informal* or *formal* trade barrier.

   a. Law requiring that stores be closed on Sunday
   b. Beliefs about not eating certain foods
   c. Special tax on the sale of books
   d. Required nutritional information on food packaging
   e. Hiring family members when jobs are available in an organization

6. Describe situations in which a joint venture would benefit a company involved in international business.

7. A country sometimes uses high tariffs to protect its new and developing industries. What are two examples of new and developing industries either in the United States or in other countries? Do you think that such industries should be protected by high tariffs? If so, how long should they be protected?

8. Some people believe that the United States should place stiff controls on imports of goods that compete with U.S. businesses to prevent the "exporting of American jobs" to other countries. Give arguments for and against such a position.

Develop Your Business Language

Match the terms listed with the definitions.

9. Goods and services sold to another country.

10. A limit on the quantity of a product that may be imported and exported within a given period.

11. Government restrictions to reduce free trade.

12. An organization that conducts business in several countries.

13. The value of money of one country expressed in terms of the money of another country.

14. Goods and services bought from another country.

15. Stopping the importing or exporting of a certain product or service.

16. An agreement between two or more companies from different countries to share a business project.

17. The difference between a country's total exports and total imports of goods.

18. A tax that a government places on certain imported products.

19. The difference between a country's total payments to other countries and its total receipts from other countries.

20. A nation's transportation, communication, and utility systems.

Key Terms

a. balance of payments
b. balance of trade
c. embargo
d. exchange rate
e. exports
f. imports
g. infrastructure
h. joint venture
i. multinational company (MNC)
j. quota
k. tariff
l. trade barrier

Make Academic Connections

21. **Geography** Locate examples of multinational companies in different countries. Create a map showing where the companies are based and the other nations in which the companies operate.

22. **Economics** Go to the website of an economic community (common market) or a regional trade organization. Make a list of the countries involved and describe some of the organization's activities.

23. **History** Conduct research on the history of money systems that have been used in other countries. Find examples of the use of a country's currency in another country.

24. **Music** Very often, the music of a country reflects its history, culture, and religion. Find examples of music from other nations that reflect the past and current culture. What aspects of the music are distinctive to that country?

25. **Math** To make their exports suitable for use in other countries, U.S. manufacturers must produce goods that are measured in the metric system. For example, if a manufacturer wanted to export paint, which is sold in gallons in this country, it would probably export the paint in 4-liter cans (about 1.4 gallons). To what sizes would the items listed be converted for export to countries using the metric system? (See Appendix D.)

    a. A quart bottle of liquid detergent
    b. A 50-yard bolt of fabric
    c. An automobile engine measured in cubic inches
    d. A 12-inch ruler
    e. A bathroom scale that measures in pounds

26. **Technology** Using a spreadsheet program, create a table and graph to report the changing value of the U.S. dollar compared with currencies of three other countries.

27. **Math** Using the information in Figure 3-4, determine how many U.S. dollars someone could buy for these amounts of currencies from other countries.

    a. In Japan, 1,200 yen
    b. In Canada, 5 Canadian dollars
    c. In Saudi Arabia, 150 riyals

28. **Career Planning** Investigate what types of legal agreements a person would encounter when applying for a job to work for a multinational company in another country.

Decision-Making Strategies

Assume you have started a business that manufactures electric toasters that you want to sell to the people of China.

29. What are some potential difficulties that you might encounter when doing business in the Chinese market?

30. What actions could your company take to help improve your opportunities for success?

Linking School and Community

Visit a retail store in your community and select 10 clothing items you would like to own. Being careful not to damage the clothing, collect the following information about each item: description of garment, fiber content, and country of origin.

Use the data you collected to prepare a list or table of your findings. Review the following questions and be prepared to discuss your findings.

- Which countries are most often on your list?
- Are there several countries from the same geographic region?
- What are some possible similarities among these countries?
- What are possible economic advantages of these countries involved in clothing manufacturing?

Web Workout

Sold in more than 200 countries, Coca-Cola is one of the most recognized brand names in the world. A visit to the company's website provides some insight into how the company has tailored its products and image to address cultural differences around the globe.

Think Critically

1. Locate a website with information about the culture of a specific country. Write a paragraph describing an element of the culture that Coca-Cola might need to consider when doing business in that country.

2. Visit the website of a company that produces another popular American product and locate information about its international operations. Write a paragraph summarizing content that demonstrates the company's sensitivity to the cultural differences of customers around the world. Illustrate your work with several images from the website.

Emerging Business Issues Event

Each day people cross the U.S. border with Mexico hoping to find work in the United States. Some enter legally, but many enter illegally and stay in violation of federal laws. There are growing concerns about illegal immigration in the United States. Some of the concerns center on unfair competition for jobs, terrorism, and illegal drug activities. There are also concerns about the high cost of providing education and medical services for illegal immigrants.

Some states and cities affected by the entry of illegal immigrants are proposing laws to help control the entry of illegal workers and check the legal status of current residents. Research this issue and prepare to argue both sides of the issue—for and against state laws related to immigration.

Each team of two or three members must conduct research to gather facts to support their stand on the issue. Teams will be permitted to bring prepared materials written or printed on white 8½" by 11" paper or note cards. One 4" by 6" index card will be given to each participant and may be used during the preparation and presentation.

Fifteen minutes before presentation time, team members will draw to determine whether they will present an affirmative or negative argument. Teams will then have 15 minutes to finalize their preparations.

Each presentation may last no more than five minutes. Following each oral presentation, judges may conduct a five-minute question-and-answer period during which the presenters should be prepared to defend their affirmative or negative argument.

Performance Indicators Evaluated

● Demonstrate sound research with the information gathered.
● Present the case in a clear and logical manner.

You will be evaluated on

● Organization of your oral presentation.
● Rationale of your presentation.

For more detailed information about performance indicators, go to the FBLA website.

Think Critically

1. How is illegal labor from Mexico beneficial to the United States?

2. Do illegal workers from Mexico actually take away jobs from Americans?

www.fbla-pbl.org

4 Social Responsibility of Business and Government

Government & Public Administration

Accountants, interviewers, restaurant inspectors, and engineers are just a few of the many employment opportunities in government. Federal, state, and local agencies employ more than 18 million people. As you can see, government is a major employer in the U.S. economy.

About 60 percent of federal workers hold managerial, business, financial, and professional positions. While many business and government jobs require similar training, some government positions demand specialized training. Food production regulators and homeland security officials need academic and practical experiences related to their fields.

Increased job opportunity in some federal agencies is being offset by slow growth and declines in other federal sectors. Despite increased demand for services from state and local governments, employment levels will be affected by economic conditions and the availability of tax revenues. Staffing of government positions is directly affected by budget levels approved by legislative bodies and local governing boards.

Related Job Titles

- Purchasing Agent
- Conservation Scientist
- Correctional Officer
- Firefighter
- Highway Maintenance Engineer
- Municipal Clerk
- Social Worker

Analyze Career Opportunities in ...

GOVERNMENT

Use library and Internet resources to learn more about careers in government. Choose one of the job titles listed in the box above and answer the following questions.

1. How would you describe the nature of the work? Include examples of things that might happen in a typical work day.

2. Is this a career that interests you? Explain how careers in this field match up with your goals and interests.

What's it like to work as a ... Government Employee?

Kathleen works for her local school district, but her job lasts all year. She is the assistant accountant for the district. Her accounting job is just like an accounting job at a nonpublic business.

Kathleen is responsible for collecting expense and payment records. She must make sure that incoming bills are correct and that payments are made in a timely manner. Kathleen also works with the school district's head accountant to develop expense reports and budgets. Throughout the year, Kathleen helps the head accountant present reports to the school board.

Kathleen uses computer software for accounting records, report writing, and presentations. She could use her accounting skills in the private sector and perhaps earn more money. Although a higher salary would be nice, Kathleen enjoys working for the school district and is happy with her career choice.

What about you? What are some government jobs that might interest you? How would your state or city financial situation impact your desire to work in those jobs?

4-1 Social Responsibility and Business Ethics

Goals

1 Describe social responsibility issues.

2 Identify benefits and costs of social responsibility.

3 Explain the purpose of a code of ethics.

Key Terms

social responsibility 76

non-renewable resource 76

ethics 79

business ethics 79

code of ethics 79

Focus on REAL LIFE

"At JA Custom Kitchens, we take social responsibility seriously," Jo Ann Keck told an audience of business students.

"As a business owner, I know that this is good for my business, my community, my employees, and for me as a person," she continued.

Later in her speech, Jo Ann said, "The company encourages employees to be active in community affairs and to volunteer with a variety of organizations. In some cases, the company provides paid time off for volunteer commitments during work hours. Workers are likely to be more satisfied on the job if they believe their company actively contributes to community life."

<table>
<tr><td>

Goal 1

Define social responsibility issues.

</td></tr>
</table>

SOCIAL RESPONSIBILITY ISSUES

Social responsibility refers to the duty of a business to contribute to the well-being of a community. In considering its responsibility to society, a business must weigh the interests and concerns of many groups. A broadened view of social responsibility of business calls for more attention to social concern. This includes protection of the environment, inclusion of minorities and women in the workplace, employment of physically challenged and older workers, and a healthy and safe work environment.

Environmental Protection

Conservation is saving scarce natural resources. It is a goal of many companies. For example, lumber companies that consume trees have reforestation programs. Some natural resources cannot be replaced. A **non-renewable resource** is a natural resource that cannot be replaced when used up. Examples are gas, oil, and minerals, such as copper and iron ore.

Pollution occurs when the environment is tainted with the by-products of human actions. Some production methods cause pollution of lakes, rivers, and air. A socially responsible business takes action to improve or change operations that cause pollution. For example, engineers design new equipment for reducing pollution.

The federal government has set measurable standards for water and air quality. The Environmental Protection Agency

How does preserving the environment benefit business?

(EPA) monitors and enforces those standards. Businesses and the EPA work together to reduce pollution. They try to make the environment healthier.

Workplace Diversity

Businesses are more and more sensitive to the role of women, ethnic groups, and physically challenged and older workers. The workforce of a business should reflect the groups in a community. Members of these groups must have equal access to education, training, jobs, and career advancement. A major challenge facing businesses today involves learning how to manage a workforce made up of workers who represent the diverse cultures in society.

Another issue involves the removal of employment barriers for women. For example, employers are not allowed to exclude women applicants from a physically demanding job unless the business can prove the job requires physical skills that women do not have.

Employers also have taken steps to accommodate individuals who are physically challenged. Passage and enforcement of the Americans with Disabilities Act (ADA), along with other federal and state legislation, has resulted in major improvements in accommodating workers who are physically challenged. Buildings must have access for wheelchairs. People with sight or hearing limitations must be accommodated on the job.

Other laws have been passed to eliminate bias against older workers. The passage of the Age Discrimination in Employment Act bars employers from using age as a basis for employment decisions, including hiring, promotions, or termination from a job. The law protects persons aged 40 and older.

Job Safety

Having a safe place in which to work is important to all employees. They should be able to work in an office or factory free from risks that could cause accidents. The work environment should provide full protection from fire and other hazards. In addition to protection from physical harm, workers need to know how to manage the unexpected. Safety also involves employee training in how to work safely and what to do in case of an emergency.

To ensure the right to safety, most employers have put a variety of programs into practice to protect workers. Federal and state governments have also passed laws to make the workplace safer. Safety standards are regulated and enforced by agencies such as OSHA, the Occupational Safety and Health Administration.

Create a list of five social and environmental issues that might have an impact on your future. How well do you understand these issues? Explain how these issues might affect the life-span goals you set for yourself.

How has the Americans with Disabilities Act increased employment opportunities for people who are physically challenged?

Image Source/Getty Images

Employee Wellness

A healthy workforce is a productive workforce. Workers who have good physical health are valuable assets. Businesses today do a number of things to improve the health of their workforce. Among programs offered are stop-smoking seminars, counseling for employees with drug problems, and weight-loss sessions.

Your general well-being as an employee needs to be protected, too. Clauses that relate to employee well-being are often included in labor contracts and company policy manuals. These clauses are *conditions of work* that pertain to the health and safety of employees while on the job.

Many companies offer programs to promote good health. Seminars on eating a balanced diet, getting proper exercise, and maintaining a healthy lifestyle are a few examples. Some businesses sponsor sports teams and encourage employees to take part.

Monkey Business Images/Shutterstock.com

How do employees who are healthy benefit their employers?

Goal 2

Identify benefits and costs of social responsibility.

> **checkpoint** ✓
> What are four areas of social responsibility that may require the attention of business?

SOCIAL RESPONSIBILITY EVALUATION

Socially responsible actions can cause controversy. While a number of benefits exist, these actions also have various costs.

Benefits

Common benefits of socially responsible activities include the following:

- Expanded justice for groups of a society
- Enhanced company image
- Reduced need for government actions
- Improved quality of life in a community and around the world
- Increased awareness of social issues among workers, consumers, and others

Costs

There are costs involved when a business takes socially responsible actions. Money must be spent for new non-polluting or safer equipment, for building repairs to remove risks, for wellness and rehabilitation programs, and for social projects sponsored by a company.

A business must make a profit to stay open. If a business does not earn a profit, the business will close and employees will lose their jobs. Spending on social programs must be at a suitable level so a business can still earn a reasonable profit.

> **checkpoint** ✓
> What are the main benefits of social responsibility?

BUSINESS ETHICS

A socially responsible business engages in ethical business practices. **Ethics** are principles of morality or rules of conduct. **Business ethics** are rules about how businesses and their employees ought to behave. Ethical behavior involves conforming to these rules. Unethical behavior violates them. In dealing with business ethics, a code of ethics can help a business identify proper employee behavior.

Code of Ethics

A **code of ethics** is a set of rules for guiding the actions of employees or members of an organization. Codes of ethics address topics such as confidentiality of business information. Figure 4-1 lists topics to consider when developing a code of ethics. Once established, the code should be a guide for all employees within that company.

A code must be worded in terms of acceptable behavior rather than forbidden action. Even with a code of ethics, the choice of proper behavior can cause dilemmas for decision-makers within a business. Here are some examples of ethical dilemmas.

- Should a company expand into a profitable market in a country where doing business requires giving expensive gifts to government officials?

- Should a company continue to produce a popular product after it discovers a minor defect in it?

Ethical Conduct Guidelines

The ethical conduct of a business is greatly determined by its top management. Executives who show strong moral character and make ethical business decisions set the ethical standards for a business.

WORK as a TEAM

Using the three ethical conduct guidelines on this page, select a situation in a work setting that might be considered unethical. As a team use these three questions to assess the ethical aspects of the situation.

Companies concerned about ethical behavior in their employees have set up educational programs on ethical conduct. These programs are designed to promote employee honesty and integrity. Program topics range from making personal phone calls during work hours to taking supplies for personal use. Employees are also trained on how to make ethical decisions on the job.

When considering the ethics of business situations, you could follow these guidelines.

1. Is the action legal?

2. Does the action violate professional or company standards?

3. Who is affected by the action and how?

Goal 3

Explain the purpose of a code of ethics.

GUIDELINES FOR WRITING A CODE OF ETHICS
1. Determine the purpose of the code.
2. Tailor the code to the needs and values of the organization.
3. Consider involving employees from all levels of the company in writing the code.
4. Determine the rules or principles that all members of the organization will be expected to adhere to.
5. Include information about how the code will be enforced.
6. Determine how the code will be implemented and where it will be published or posted.
7. Determine how and when the code will be reviewed and revised.

▶ **Figure 4-1**

Do you think a code of ethics can increase a business' profits? How?

Photodisc/Getty Images

A common concern in ethical decision-making involves a *conflict of interest*. This can occur when an action by a company or individual results in an unfair benefit. For example, it would be a conflict of interest if a person serving on a company's board pressured the company to buy items only from businesses that the board member owns or controls.

In addition to workplace codes of ethics, many employees, including accountants and engineers, adhere to codes of professional conduct established by their professional associations. They also participate in continuing education related to ethical issues specific to their professions.

What are some costs to society of unethical behavior?

checkpoint ✓
What is the purpose of a code of ethics?

4-1 Assessment

Study Tools

www.cengage.com/school/genbus/pob

Key Concepts

Determine the best answer.

1. An example of a non-renewable resource would be
   a. solar energy
   b. gold
   c. agricultural products
   d. a library book

2. The Americans with Disabilities Act (ADA) requires that a company
   a. provide training to people with disabilities
   b. find ways to help workers who are physically challenged
   c. hire a certain number of people with special needs
   d. adapt products manufactured for special-needs customers

3. A code of ethics is designed to
   a. meet government regulations
   b. reduce operating costs of a company
   c. provide guidelines for proper behavior
   d. improve employee productivity

Make Academic Connections

4. **Science** List a variety of natural resources and agricultural products used in the production of goods and services. What actions might be taken by companies to improve the efficient use of these resources?

5. **Technology** Search the Internet to locate an example of a code of ethics. Describe the benefits of this code of ethics for the organization.

21st Century Skills

Communication and Collaboration

Working in Teams

Each day, thousands of workers make decisions and apply business actions in team settings. The ability to work in a team is rated by most employers as one of the most important career skills. The combined skills of the people in a team are greater than that of individuals working alone. When working in a team in class or on the job, consider the following:

Why is it important to define roles when working in teams?

- Be prepared for minor conflicts in the first phase of a team project. Differences in opinions will surface. Be ready to adapt to the personalities, behaviors, and actions of others.

- Agree upon guidelines for project goals, meeting times, location, agenda, missed meetings, conflict resolution, and other procedures.

- Define leadership and other roles. Some team members will keep notes and bring needed materials. Others will conduct research or create visuals for a presentation.

- Determine methods for decision-making. Usually this will be done based on agreement among team members after discussion of various issues and opposing points of view.

- Keep focused on your goals. Avoid being distracted by minor issues and personality conflicts. Maintain a team-oriented environment by saying "we, us, ours." Avoid using "I, me, my, mine."

- Be courteous to others. Respect differences in opinions, personalities, and decision-making styles.

Working in teams is something you are likely to do throughout your life. These experiences can be enjoyable and productive. Members of an effective team take responsibility for its work and take pride in its accomplishments. Some team projects will be frustrating. It is important to maintain a positive attitude. Some of the best learning and most valuable experiences result from encounters with others with different backgrounds and diverse points of view.

Think Critically

1. What do you like about working in teams? Are there any aspects about working in teams that you dislike? Describe them.

2. Describe a problem that might occur when working in teams. Explain how this situation might be resolved.

Government Protection Activities

Goals

1 Identify the roles and levels of government.

2 Explain the role of government protection and the legal system in business.

3 Describe types of intellectual property.

Key Terms

contract 83

patent 84

copyright 85

trademark 85

Focus on REAL LIFE

Brenda Hiam was concerned about the deteriorating road she drove to work. She believed that it was becoming dangerous and could lead to someone losing control.

Brenda wanted to contact a government agency to notify them of this potentially dangerous driving hazard. She asked her neighbor, Kevin, if he knew whether the city, county, state, or federal highway department was responsible for the road.

"I think we should contact the county highway department and ask that question," he answered. "The county highway office keeps records on roads in this area."

"Let's call." said Brenda. "If they can't help us, we can call our county commissioner."

Goal 1

Identify the roles and levels of government.

GOVERNMENT IN SOCIETY

Government plays a role in all economic systems. Your role as a citizen and voter has an effect on the decisions and actions taken by government. In a private enterprise system, government's role is much less extensive than in other economic systems. It is still a vital one. The role of government in the economy often changes as newly elected officials take office.

Roles of Government

As issues facing society change, so must government change. There are some basic roles of government.

Government is mainly concerned with these areas:

- Providing services for members of society

- Protecting citizens, consumers, businesses, and workers

- Regulating utilities and promoting competition

- Providing information and support to businesses

- Buying goods and services

- Hiring public employees

- Raising revenue

Each of these roles has either a direct or indirect impact on business expansion, consumer affairs, and economic growth in the economy.

Levels of Government

The main goal of the federal government is to oversee the activities that involve

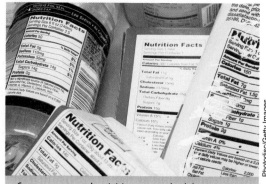

Can governmental activities support both businesses and consumers?

two or more states or other countries. In general, the Constitution gives the federal government the power to regulate foreign and interstate commerce.

Interstate commerce is business dealings involving companies in more than one state. The federal government would regulate a trucking company that ships products to several states.

State governments regulate business actions within their own borders. *Intrastate commerce* refers to business dealings involving companies that do business in only one state. A trucking company that hauls products only within a state's boundaries would be regulated by that state and not the federal government.

All states have assigned some of their legislative power to local governments. Local governments include county boards and city or town councils. Local governments provide services needed for an orderly society, such as police and fire protection.

How does government regulate commerce?

Digital Vision/Getty Images

> **checkpoint** ✓
> What are the three levels of government?

GOVERNMENT PROTECTION ACTIVITIES

Government protects your rights in a number of ways. Citizens are protected through police and fire-fighting services. The armed forces provide for national defense. National security is a chief concern of the federal government.

Worker Protection

Laws have been established to help provide a safe work environment. As a worker, you have a basic right to safe working conditions. Safety standards for buildings, machines, and chemicals are set by government agencies.

Government inspection and regulation of work areas help reduce the number of job-related accidents.

More government regulations result from the need to protect the basic human rights of workers. For example, you cannot be denied work because of your race, religion, sex, or age. Selection of someone for a job must be based on job requirements, training, and experience. Prejudices and personal biases must not affect a hiring decision.

Contract Enforcement

Contracts are another example of government protection. A **contract** is an agreement to exchange goods or services for something of value, usually money. It is a basic part of doing business. A contract may be written or unwritten. Certain elements must be included for the contract to be enforceable. Figure 4-2 highlights the main provisions of every enforceable contract.

> **Goal 2**
>
> Explain the role of government protection and the legal system in business.

> **fyi** *It is important to read and understand a contract before signing it. The court system does not protect you from your own lack of common sense.*

Joel Calheiros/Shutterstock.com

CONTRACT BASICS	
Valid, enforceable contracts must contain:	
Agreement	An offer must be made, and an acceptance must occur.
Competent Parties	Those entering into the contract must be of legal age and must be mentally competent.
Consideration	Something of measurable value must be exchanged by the parties involved.
Legality	The contract must be for a product or service that may be legally sold; also, no fraud or deception exists in the agreement.

▶ **Figure 4-2**

Provide examples of contracts you might encounter in the future.

These four elements—agreement, competent parties, consideration, and legality—are the basis for many legal disputes. An item seen as having different values (*consideration*) by different people can result in a legal dispute. Examples of contracts include a lease to rent an apartment, a credit card agreement, and documents that state the terms of a purchase.

Both consumers and businesses benefit from government enforcement of contracts. If you agree to have repairs made on your car for $65, the business firm must do the work as agreed upon. You must pay for the work when it is finished. If work is not done correctly or if you fail to pay, legal action can be taken to force the work to be corrected or force you to pay.

Legal System

Without enforcement, dishonest consumers or business owners could refuse to

Goal 3

Describe types of intellectual property.

WORK *as a* **TEAM**

Intellectual properties are also called intangible assets. As a team, prepare a list of various patents, copyrights, and trademarks owned by companies and nonprofit organizations. Explain how these assets contribute to the success of the organization. Why is protection of intellectual property important?

honor their agreements. Daily business activities would be very difficult.

The legal system enforces laws and government regulations. There are typically two types of cases that move through our legal systems, criminal cases and civil cases.

A *criminal case* is brought for violations of criminal laws. A business could be involved in a criminal case if it pressed charges against a customer or employee engaged in shoplifting. If a business violates criminal or regulatory laws, it could be a defendant in a criminal case.

Civil cases typically have a plaintiff who asks the courts to take action against a defendant. Businesses can both sue and be sued for a breach, or violation, of contract; liable, or damage caused by someone's action; or unauthorized use of copyrights, trademarks, or patents.

Unethical behavior can violate either criminal laws or government regulations. A business can be held responsible for products that that cause harm, unsafe working conditions, or failure to pay taxes.

checkpoint ✓

What are the main elements of a contract?

PROTECTION OF INTELLECTUAL PROPERTY

Intellectual property is purely intangible, with no physical characteristics—a person cannot touch it. Intellectual property includes patents, copyrights, and trademarks.

Patents

When individuals or companies create new products, they may obtain a patent. A **patent** gives the inventor the sole right to make, use, or sell the item for 20 years. A company that creates a new means to record programs from television could get a patent for this process. It would prevent other companies from making or selling recorders using this process.

Copyrights

A **copyright** protects the creative work of authors, composers, and artists. Copyright protection lasts for the life of the person receiving the copyright. It also extends for 70 years after the person's death. Examples of copyright statements can be found on the front pages of most books. Copyrights are identified with the symbol ©.

Trademarks

A **trademark** is a word, letter, or symbol linked with a specific company or product. Businesses register company names, team emblems, and label designs with the government. A trademark can be very valuable. Many are famous all over the world and are often identified

What are some examples of creative work that can be copyrighted?

with a symbol, called a *logo*. Can you think of some logos that you see frequently?

> **checkpoint ✓**
> What are three types of intellectual property?

4-2 Assessment

Key Concepts

Determine the best answer.

1. True or False. International trade with other countries is the responsibility of state and local governments.

2. True or False. An oral contract can be legally binding.

3. Fire and police protection is the main responsibility of
   a. local government
   b. state government
   c. federal government
   d. all levels of government

4. A _?_ would protect the composer's musical score.
   a. patent   c. copyright
   b. trademark   d. contract

Make Academic Connections

5. **Math** A city government spends $186,000 a month on public services. Of that amount, 46 percent is used for fire and police protection.
   a. How much is spent each month for fire and police protection?
   b. How much is spent by the city in a year for fire and police protection?

6. **Math** In a city in which there are 90,000 employed workers, 18,000 are public employees. Of this number, the federal government employs 6,000; the state, 8,000; and the city, 4,000.
   a. What percentage of all workers are public employees?
   b. What percentage of the public employees does the federal government employ?

7. **Law** Prepare a list of possible problems that could occur in a contract situation.

Doing Business in... Vietnam

One minute you see peaceful villages with carts pulled by animals. A moment later, you see busy city streets in which seven of ten Vietnamese families use a motorcycle as their main method of transportation.

Vietnam is a country of contrasts, combining traditional production methods with modern business activities. The nation is moving from decades of strong central planning to emerging capitalism.

Even as Vietnam transitions to a modern market economy, the Vietnamese people continue to place a high value on traditions and family relationships. Several generations may live together in the same home. Children show great respect for the elders of the family, even their older brothers and sisters.

Vietnam's business environment is rapidly evolving as it moves from a command to a more capitalistic business environment. Vietnam is attempting to put in place rules and regulations that comply with the Word Trade Organization (WTO) and the U.S.–Vietnam Bilateral Trade Agreement (BTA). This should lead to more government transparency, stronger commercial laws, and lowered trade barriers.

At the start of a business meeting in Vietnam, the exchange of business cards occurs. Cards should be presented and received with both hands. If your card is printed in both English and Vietnamese, it is polite to have the Vietnamese side facing up. You may be asked how old you are. This classifies you as either older or younger than the Vietnamese person in order to determine the correct form of address.

The business meal is likely to include tea and perhaps some exotic foods. You may be served bat meat, stir-fried baby birds, dog, or snake, as well as many types of seafood. It is polite to taste and drink small amounts of all items you are offered.

The conversation will slowly lead to business negotiations. Take care to not move too quickly through the agenda because this is considered rude. Use a low-pitched voice and low-key gestures. Do not allow your hosts to see the soles of your shoes.

Think Critically

1. What cultural factors affect business activities in Vietnam?

2. How do business activities in Vietnam differ from those in other countries?

3. Conduct library or Internet research to obtain additional information about business and economic activities in Vietnam.

What impact might the use of motorcycles in Vietnam have on a company's efforts to sell products to Vietnamese consumers?

Photobank/Shutterstock.com

4-3 Government Regulation and Assistance

Goals

1. Explain actions by government to regulate business.

2. Discuss efforts of government to assist businesses.

3. Identify methods used by government to raise money.

Key Terms

public utility 87

monopoly 88

antitrust laws 88

Focus on REAL LIFE

The riverfront skateboard park is one of the most popular areas in the city. Kent Walling recently noticed that due to extensive use, the ramps, jumps, and tracks are wearing out.

Kent mentioned the condition of the park to his dad and asked, "Why doesn't the city spend some money to improve the skate park?"

His dad responded, "The city has many financial needs. The skate park might not be a priority. Maybe the city should charge a fee for using the park."

"Or, they could raise your taxes, Dad!," Kent said with a smile.

REGULATORY ACTIVITIES

Business activity in the United States is structured as a private enterprise or free market system. Private organizations own the factors of production. They choose efficient methods of production in order to earn a profit. Price and output decisions are made not by the government, but by businesses and consumers acting under varying economic conditions.

Government does get involved in some areas of business activities. These include regulating utilities and preventing unfair business practices.

Regulation of Utilities

Most goods and services you use come from private businesses. These businesses are for the most part free of government regulation. A **public utility** is an organization that supplies a service or product vital to all people. These include companies that provide local telephone service, water, and electricity. A public utility is chosen

to serve a community. If your city had six different electric companies, each might have its own utility poles, lines, and expensive equipment. The service you would get would be more expensive and less

Is it better for consumers if utilities are offered by competing businesses?

Goal 1

Explain actions by government to regulate business.

Companies can take actions that reduce competition and give consumers fewer choices. Describe some advertising, pricing, or branding actions that could result in unfair competition.

efficient. The extra poles and wires would create an unattractive environment.

While many utility companies are privately owned, usually government closely regulates them. The rates they can charge for things such as electricity, water, or natural gas have to be approved by government agencies. In recent years, there has been a trend toward deregulation of prices where competition can be introduced.

Prevent Unfair Business Practices

Most businesspeople are fair and honest. A few may try to take advantage of their customers or competitors. Government attempts to promote fair competition. If a company charges different prices to different people for the same product, it is treating its customers unfairly. If one business receives lower rates for the same quality and quantity of supplies than other businesses receive, it has an advantage. Such action may result in unfair competition.

Goal 2

Discuss efforts of government to assist businesses.

A **monopoly** exists when a business has control of the market for a product or service. A public utility monopoly may benefit consumers by making sure they receive a needed service at a fair price. Other monopolies may not be good for the economy. If the same company owned all food stores in your city, consumers might not be treated fairly. This business could charge high prices and sell poor-quality products. When competition is present, consumers get the best values at the fairest prices.

One government action meant to promote competition and fairness and to avoid monopolies was the passage of **antitrust laws**. Antitrust laws prevent other unfair business practices such as false advertising, deceptive pricing, and misleading labeling. Each of these unfair practices hurts competition and reduces consumer choice.

checkpoint ✓
Why does government regulate utilities?

GOVERNMENT ASSISTS BUSINESS

Government helps businesses by collecting and reporting valuable information. Data gathered by the government can help with planning. Information about incomes, prices, worker availability, and business failures can help a businessperson make wiser choices. For example, census information can help a business decide where a majority of potential customers live. The Bureau of Labor Statistics, the Department of Agriculture, and the Department of Commerce are a few of the government agencies that provide information.

The federal government, through the Small Business Administration (SBA), helps new businesses get started by guaranteeing private bank loans. The new

NETBookmark

With hundreds of agencies, the U.S. federal government has created a website to assist citizens. Access the website shown below and click on the link for Chapter 4. This website offers information about everything from Amtrak to zoos. Select a topic area of interest to you. Obtain information on the topic and prepare a written summary of how this information might be used by consumers or business.

www.cengage.com/school/genbus/pob

businesses must develop an acceptable business plan. Farmers and others may receive financial help in times of great hardship, such as during a drought, flooding, or other natural disasters. Destruction of home and property by a tornado may make a person eligible for a low-interest government loan. These programs are designed to promote the financial well-being of society.

Government Buys Goods and Services

Government spends a great deal of money each day to buy an array of products and services. Total federal, state, and local government spending make up about 20 percent of all the goods and services produced in the United States.

Governments buy everything from file cabinets to buildings to military jet aircraft. In this role, government is a key economic force. Many businesses depend on government contracts for their survival. For instance, government pays businesses to construct highways and build schools.

Government Employs Workers

Government is the single largest employer in the U.S. economy. About 16 percent of workers are public employees. Most people think only of police officers, firefighters, and sanitation workers as government workers. Government also employs the same types of workers as private businesses. Administrative assistants, lawyers, teachers, meat inspectors, and data analysts are all employed by government. Although the number of employees has grown slowly in recent years, good employment opportunities in government continue—in spite of efforts to eliminate or reduce the size of some agencies.

> **checkpoint** ✓
> How does government assist business?

Why do you think a company would want to perform work for the government?

Stockbyte/Getty Images

GOVERNMENT RAISES MONEY

> **Goal 3**
>
> Describe how the government raises money.

Government must have a way to raise money to fund operations and pay wages to workers. Government income is called *revenue*. Governments can obtain revenue through taxes and borrowing. In addition, governments can raise revenue in other ways. Fines for traffic violations and other violations of the law provide revenue for government. Fees and licenses are a source of income. Certain types of ventures require a business license. For example, insurance and real estate agents pay a fee for the privilege of running a business. Governments

also charge fees for such things as driver's licenses and fishing privileges.

Taxes

A government creates tax policies to pay for the services it provides. Taxes are levied on earnings, the value of property, and on the sale price of goods and services. Your earnings as an individual are subject to an income tax. *Income taxes* are levied on the income of individuals. The individual income tax is the largest source of revenue for the federal government. Corporate income taxes also provide government revenue. The corporate income tax is based on business profits.

A major source of revenue for local governments is the real estate *property tax*. This tax is based on the value of land and buildings. Most property tax revenue is used to pay for schools and

Business Insight for the 21st Century

Expanding E-Government

Computers have a major impact on the way government operates. More than 80 percent of adults who use the Internet have been to a government website within the last 12 months. Rather than going to a government office to pick up a form, apply for a license, or make a payment, people can complete many of these activities online.

In a study of the development of e-government services around the world, the United Nations has identified the following five stages:

● *Emerging* Official government online presence established

● *Enhanced* Number of sites increases; sites become more interesting and useful

● *Interactive* Users can download forms, e-mail officials, and interact through the Internet

● *Transactional* Users can complete transactions and pay for services online

● *Connected* Responds to the needs of its citizens by developing integrated back-office operations

The U.S. government has an online portal to all of the information and services offered online. USA.gov links to more than 10,000 federal, state, and local web pages. The site receives over 4 million hits per month. In addition to computer-based access, cell phone apps are opening new avenues for contact.

The federal government spends more than $80 billion per year for information technology services. Moving government services online saves more than 1 billion dollars each year.

Two major barriers stand in the way of e-government expansion. Most important is the privacy and security of the personal information contained in government records and submitted by citizens. That information includes tax records and personal information such as driver's license and social security numbers. The second barrier is the unequal access to technology. Thousands of citizens do not have secure high-speed Internet connections. Others do not have the literacy or computer skills to use online government services.

Think Critically

1. Search the Web and identify government services provided by your local and state governments. What stage of development is demonstrated by the websites you visited?

2. What can governments do to reduce the barriers of privacy, security, and citizen access to e-government services?

other local government services, such as police protection and community parks. Businesses also pay a property tax.

The cost of buying things is increased by a sales tax. A *sales tax* is a state or local tax on goods and services that is collected by the seller. If you buy a can of paint for $15.00 and the state sales tax is 6 percent, the seller collects $15.90 from you. The seller then will pay 90 cents to the state. You were the one who provided the money for the tax.

Paying taxes is a duty of citizens and businesses. You should pay your taxes, but not more than your share. Tax laws and policies are set to help make the paying of taxes fair. Whether a particular tax or tax policy is fair is always subject to debate. Businesses, in spite of public misconceptions, pay a lot of taxes to all levels of government.

Borrowing

Government income from taxes and other sources may not always be enough to cover the costs of providing services. Borrowing is another activity of government. When a government wants to construct a building, such as a new courthouse or convention center, the funds needed are often raised through borrowing.

Government borrows money by selling bonds. When you buy a government bond, you are helping to fund the services provided by government. Banks, insurance companies, and other financial institutions help finance governments by purchasing bonds in large numbers.

By borrowing money, the government becomes a debtor and must pay interest on its debt. Bonds issued by the U.S. government are backed by the "full faith and credit" of the federal government. Bonds issued by the federal government are considered the least risky of all debt.

> **checkpoint** ✓
> What is the difference between tax revenue and borrowing by government?

4-3 Assessment

www.cengage.com/school/genbus/pob

Key Concepts

Determine the best answer.

1. Antitrust laws are designed to
   a. reduce utility rates
   b. lower taxes
   c. create more jobs
   d. maintain competition

2. A(n) _?_ tax is a common source of revenue for state and local governments.
   a. sales
   b. import
   c. gift
   d. unemployment

3. True or False. A monopoly is never a benefit to consumers.

Make Academic Connections

4. **History** Conduct research about various antitrust laws. What situations caused the creation of these laws?

5. **Communication** Conduct a survey of people to obtain their opinions about which types of taxes are most appropriate to raise government revenue. Prepare a summary data table with your findings.

6. **Economics** Describe government actions to raise money that might have a positive or negative influence on business activities.

Business Notes

4-1 Social Responsibility and Business Ethics

- Socially responsible businesses care about their communities. They help make them better places in which to live. Social responsibility concerns relate to environmental protection, workplace diversity, safety on the job, and employee wellness.

- Benefits of social responsibility include expanded justice for societal groups, enhanced company image, reduced need for government action, improved quality of life, and increased awareness of social issues. Costs of social responsibility are that money must be spent for new or safer equipment, for building renovations to remove hazards, for wellness and rehabilitation programs, and for social projects sponsored by a company. These costs must be balanced with profits to make sure the business stays viable.

- A code of business ethics is a guide for behavior within an organization.

4-2 Government Protection Activities

- The primary roles of government are to provide services to society; protect citizens, consumers, businesses, and workers; regulate utilities and promote competition; provide information and help to businesses; buy goods and services; hire public employees; and raise revenue. The levels of government are federal, state, and local.

- Government protects citizens through police and fire services, protects consumers and business owners by enforcing contracts and intellectual property rights, and protects workers through laws that require safe working conditions.

- The three types of intellectual property are patents, copyrights, and trademarks.

4-3 Government Regulation and Assistance

- Government regulates utilities and prevents unfair business practices.

- Government buys a wide range of goods and services and employs workers. Governments also collect and report valuable information and provide loans to help businesses get started or overcome natural disasters.

- Governments raise needed funds through taxes and borrowing.

Communicate Business Concepts

1. What are some natural resources that you use every day? Which of those natural resources need to be protected? What can you as an individual do to avoid using up non-renewable resources?

2. Safety is often a matter of individuals being careful about where they place things and how they conduct their own business. Name some ways in which you and others can help make a workplace safe.

3. What does the term "discrimination" mean to you? What examples of discrimination in the workplace are you aware of?

4. Why do you think employers are willing to spend money to help employees improve their general health? Be specific about how a company might benefit.

5. Make a list of public utilities that serve your community. What services do they provide? Do you think it would be better for these services to be offered by several competing businesses? Explain your answer.

6. Here is a list of some of the public services provided by government. For each item, tell whether the federal, state, or local government would most likely have the responsibility for the service. (Some services may be provided by more than one level of government.)

    a. Fire protection
    b. Education
    c. Parks and recreation
    d. Water supply

e. Highways between cities
f. Assistance to low-income families
g. Sewage and trash disposal
h. Public buses
i. Police protection
j. Public libraries
k. Street maintenance
l. National defense

7. Each day people enter into many contracts, both written and unwritten.

   a. Give examples of contracts between a consumer and a business, between two businesses, and between a worker and a business.
   b. What services does government provide to enforce contracts?

8. Two students are discussing the topic "Government Is Our Biggest Business." Dan believes that some government activities are in direct competition with private businesses. He thinks that this is unfair. He believes that government should limit its activities to those that private businesses cannot or will not take on. Brian thinks that government should undertake any business activities that it can perform better or at a lower cost than private business. What do you think? Give some examples of business activities undertaken by both private businesses and by government.

9. Why do you suppose government raises revenue through bonds that create debt and require interest payments when government could raise the revenue through an increase in taxes?

Develop Your Business Language

Match the terms listed with the definitions.

10. Principles of morality or rules of conduct.

11. The obligation of a business to contribute to the well-being of a community.

12. Rules about how businesses and their employees ought to behave.

13. A natural resource, such as gas, coal, copper, or iron ore, that cannot be replaced once it is used up.

14. A statement of values and rules that guides the behavior of employees or members of an organization.

15. A business that supplies a service or product vital to all people; the price charged for the service (or product) is determined by government regulation rather than by competition.

16. Laws designed to promote competition and fairness and to prevent monopolies.

17. Protection of the work of authors, composers, and artists.

18. An agreement to exchange goods or services for something of value.

19. The exclusive right given to a person to make, use, or sell an invention for a period of 20 years.

20. A word, letter, or symbol associated with a specific product or company.

21. A business that has complete control of the market for a product or service.

Key Terms

a. antitrust laws
b. business ethics
c. code of ethics
d. contract
e. copyright
f. ethics
g. monopoly
h. non-renewable resource
i. patent
j. public utility
k. social responsibility
l. trademark

Make Academic Connections

22. **Communication** Interview various people to ask them for a definition and an example of "conflict of interest." Prepare a summary report of two to three paragraphs.

23. **Math** The Johnson Manufacturing Co. has an annual operating budget of $750,000. Each year it budgets for the following expenses: pollution control equipment, $37,500; contributions to community projects, $22,500; employee fitness/sports programs, $7,500.

    a. What percentage of the annual budget is allocated to each socially responsible action (pollution control, community projects, fitness/sports)? What is the total spent?
    b. What will be the amount budgeted for each expense category next year if there is a 15 percent increase? What will be the total spent?

24. **Technology** Explain how new technology is making it more difficult to protect intellectual property rights.

25. **Visual Art** Look for examples of trademarks and logos of products from companies based inside and outside of the United States. Design a brand name or trademark that might be effective in several countries around the world.

26. **Culture** Research different systems of government. Explain how history and culture can affect business regulations in various countries.

27. **Science** Research a patent on a product. Identify the inventor, the year the patent was granted, and the product's function. Prepare a summary report of your findings.

28. **Career Planning** Investigate various legal restrictions that might be encountered when applying for a job position.

Decision-Making Strategies

Centerville wants to build a new sports complex near the center of town. The complex will cost $250,000. There are two financing proposals:

Proposal A Issue $250,000 worth of bonds at an interest rate of 4 percent. The town will pay $10,000 per year in interest for 15 years. The total interest would be $150,000. The amount borrowed ($250,000) would have to be paid off in 15 years. Fees charged to users of the complex would pay the interest each year and the amount due bondholders ($250,000). Construction could begin right away.

Proposal B Establish a 1/4 percent city sales tax on all purchases. The revenue needed could be raised in about five years. There would be no user fee charged to residents of Centerville. Construction would be delayed a few years.

29. What are the advantages and disadvantages of the two proposals?

30. Which proposal do you favor, and why?

Linking School and Community

Interview someone in your community who owns a business or works for a large company or organization. Obtain information about actions that need to be considered when hiring people, designing products, and making other business decisions. Ask them how ethics might affect their daily lives and the lives of others. Based on their answers, create a short code of ethics that might be used to guide the decisions made by managers and employees in a company.

Web Workout

Global warming is a hot topic. There is strong consensus that the world is getting warmer. Eleven of the last 12 years have been the warmest on record.

Although the warming trend is well documented, there is considerable debate about the cause. Could it be part of a natural cycle? Or, is it due to human activity? Scientists, environmentalists, and policymakers who believe that human activity is the cause of global warming point to the reduction of carbon emissions as part of the solution.

Think Critically

1. Use the Internet to learn more about global warming and get some different perspectives on the issue. Visit at least one website for each of the following categories: government agency, environmental advocacy organization, large manufacturer, and energy company. In a short report, summarize what you find and offer an opinion about what should be done to combat global warming.

2. Use the Internet to identify actions and strategies that businesses, governments, and individuals could adopt to limit greenhouse gases. Report your findings in a table.

3. Choose three actions or strategies that could help reduce greenhouse gases and write a short explanation of how they might impact business practices.

Prepared Speech Event

Every day, in companies around the world, employees are spending part of their workday making personal phone calls and using their work computers for shopping online, playing games, sending personal e-mails, and visiting social networking sites. This unethical behavior results in decreased productivity. Today's technology focus has many people thinking about personal interests over dedication to their employer. Business leaders are challenged to monitor employees in the workplace for ethical use of their time.

You will prepare a speech that identifies current ethical challenges and offers strategies to encourage respect and ethical conduct in the workplace. Your speech must emphasize the expectation of employee productivity in the work world and how attention must be shifted from personal interest of employees to customer service and ethical use of work time.

You will have three to five minutes to present your plan to improve ethical conduct in the workplace. Audiovisual equipment and visual aids may be used in this presentation.

Performance Indicators Evaluated

- Define ethical conduct in the workplace.
- Explain the relationship between the employee's commitment to the workplace and productivity.
- Describe strategies to improve ethical conduct in the workplace.
- Explain how ethical standards will be implemented and monitored in the workplace.
- Describe a work environment that requires and rewards sound ethical behavior.

You will be evaluated for your

- Knowledge of the topic
- Organization of the presentation
- Confidence, quality of voice, and eye contact
- Presentation of the business strategy

For more detailed information about performance indicators, go to the BPA website.

Think Critically

1. Why must businesses have standards and rules for employees?

2. Why are many ethical issues associated with technology in the workplace?

3. How can businesses increase employee dedication?

4. What has contributed to the lack of productivity in the workplace?

5. What should happen to employees who have demonstrated unethical behavior in the workplace?

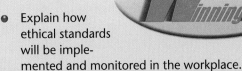
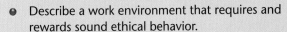

www.bpa.org

UNIT 2

Business Organization and Management

Digital Vision/Getty Images

Business Vision

There are three factors of production: economic resources, natural resources, and human resources. This unit looks at how a business organizes and manages human resources.

Each chapter in this unit includes some aspect of organizing and managing a business. These include different forms of ownership. Some businesses are entrepreneurial start-ups; others are large corporations. Some small businesses need to manage only a few workers; others may have thousands of employees. In all cases, businesses are challenged with finding qualified human resources.

From Start-up to Global Dominance

In the late 1960s, two friends had a hobby of writing software. In 1975 they wrote a BASIC programming language for the first personal computer, the Altair 8800. The entrepreneurs, Bill Gates and Paul Allen, named their new partnership Micro-Soft. Revenue for the first year in business was $16,000.

In 1980, the computer company IBM introduced a new personal computer and needed an operating system. They chose Microsoft's MS-DOS. Microsoft grew as its DOS became the standard for all PC manufacturers. Microsoft incorporated in 1981 to become Microsoft, Inc.

In 1986, Microsoft moved to Redmond, Washington. The company built a 40-acre campus for its employees. Buildings were designed in an X pattern to allow workers to have offices with windows. The goal was to develop a culture where Microsoft employees could sit and think. Microsoft tried to hire the "smartest" people and then give them the freedom to think and develop products. By 1995, Microsoft's

revenue exceeded $6 billion and it had more than 17,000 employees.

Perhaps Microsoft's greatest challenge was underestimating how the World Wide Web could replace Microsoft's software dominance. Microsoft was able to tap into its human resources to turn the company around. Microsoft employees camped out by sleeping at their headquarters to change the design of their products to support the Internet.

By 2009 Microsoft's revenue was more than $58 billion and it had grown to 90,000 employees. Today, some people think that Microsoft has become too large and less entrepreneurial. Microsoft is facing competition from a number of start-up companies. One was started by two friends, Larry Page and Sergey Brin. This company is called Google.

Think Critically

Explain why Microsoft's growth over time would affect how it was organized and how it would manage employees.

CHAPTER

5

Business Organization

5-1   Business in the U.S. Economy

5-2   Forms of Business Ownership

5-3   Organizational Structure for Businesses

Planning a Career in ...

CORPORATE LEADERSHIP

Business, Management & Administration

Rising to the top of one of the world's largest corporations seems like the dream job in business. The chief executive officer (CEO) of a corporation may make several million dollars a year in salary and bonuses, have a large office with dozens of support staff, travel worldwide on a corporate jet, and make daily decisions that directly influence the success of the company. Corporate executives also work long hours and face the competing expectations of stockholders, the board of directors, employees, and customers. While they receive many perks and benefits, their success or failure may be determined more by economic conditions, government regulations, and the stock market than their own decisions and abilities.

A corporation's goals and policies are established by the top executives. The executives meet frequently to set direction, review company performance, and establish policy. They then delegate work to the organization's managers and employees. They know that they are ultimately responsible and accountable for the performance of the company.

Related Job Titles

- Chief Executive Officer
- Chief Operating Officer
- President

Analyze Career Opportunities in ...
CORPORATE LEADERSHIP

Use library and Internet resources to learn more about careers in corporate leadership. Choose one of the job titles listed in the box above and answer the following questions.

1. How would you describe the physical work environment for jobs in this field?

2. Is this a career that interests you? Describe how you might use your talents, abilities, and skills in this career.

What's it like to work as a ...
Corporate Executive?
The schedule of a CEO is packed most days. It may start with an hour of reading before attending a conference with the heads of other companies and government officials. Lunch is with the management team to review the company's financial performance, followed by a press conference. Two hours are spent on the telephone talking to a senator about a telecommunications law, discussing labor contract negotiations with the vice president of human resources, and speaking with a manufacturer in Japan about a proposed joint venture. After a workout at the executive gym and a quick dinner, it is off to the airport for a flight to Brazil to oversee the opening of a new manufacturing facility. The flight will be spent studying reports, completing correspondence, and watching a video briefing on Brazil's economy.

What about you? How would you prepare for the stress of being a corporate executive? Do you believe that the work justifies the high salary and benefits?

5-1 Business in the U.S. Economy

Goals

1 Describe the changing status of U.S. employment.

2 Discuss the role of business in the U.S. economy.

3 Describe three major types of businesses.

Key Terms

contingent worker 101

intermediaries 105

service business 105

Focus on REAL LIFE

Sami Rehm loves digital photography. Last year she turned her hobby into a professional photography business. She uses photo editing software to produce digital images. Sami has started to wonder if she might be able to expand her business. Sami has a friend who can help sell the images to newspapers, magazines, advertising agencies, and other businesses.

Sami isn't sure if her friend should be an employee or a partner. To expand, the business will need to purchase new equipment and develop sales brochures.

Sami expressed her feelings to her mother. "I love my photography business. Would I like it as much if I had to share control with a partner? I wonder if I can afford to purchase new equipment by myself?"

Goal 1

Describe the changing status of U.S. employment.

THE CHANGING U.S. JOB MARKET

The first decade of the twenty-first century has seen periods of growth and decline in overall employment. Part of this change was due to careers shifting from traditionally important jobs in manufacturing and agriculture to service jobs. Periods of job decline were due to recessions.

Employment Data

Following the 9/11/2001 terrorist attacks, a recession resulted in a loss of jobs through 2003. From 2003 to 2008 total employment grew by nearly 6 percent. In 2008, 138 million people held non-farm jobs. A recession in 2009 resulted in a loss of more than 775 thousand jobs.

A wave of retirements started in 2011 as the first group of *baby boomers*, the people born between 1946 and 1964, turned 65. Although retirements will continue, the average age of U.S. workers in 2020 will be over 50. At the same time,

a mini-boom of younger workers will cause the 20- to 30-year-old age group to grow faster than the overall labor force for the first time in 25 years. Other groups that will go through higher employment growth rates are Asian-, Hispanic-, and African-American workers. Currently, white non-Hispanic workers make

How will the demographics of U.S. workers change over the next decade?

up 68 percent of the labor force. That number will drop to 64 percent by 2018. Over the last 50 years, one of the most striking trends in employment has been the participation of women. In the early 1960s, 35 percent of women were working outside the home. The number of working women doubled by 2000. By 2018 nearly one half of all jobs (47 percent) in the United States will be held by women.

Pressures on Employees

At one time, it was thought that technology would allow people to work fewer hours. This has not occurred. Economic stress has led to downsizing of the number of people employed by many companies. Companies streamlined production and implemented other cost-cutting procedures. Businesses required employees to take on new tasks and work extra hours. Some full-time jobs were reduced to part-time. Wage rates decreased. Many people were forced to find second jobs to meet their economic needs.

A recent survey reported that 7 of 10 parents felt they were not able to spend enough time with their children. At the same time, children see their parents changing jobs, taking on more responsibility, completing additional education to improve career opportunities, and making important decisions to balance work and family life. Those experiences will likely shape the career and family decisions of the next generation.

Economic pressures also resulted in the increased use of contingent workers. A **contingent worker** is one who has no explicit or implicit contract for long-term employment. About 5 percent of the U.S. workforce (nearly 6 million people) is made up of contingent workers. Some estimates project that number will double in 10 years. Some people take contingent work because they cannot find permanent employment. Others choose contingent work because they like the flexibility it offers.

NETBookmark

The U.S. Bureau of Labor Statistics collects and reports detailed information on the status of the work force nationwide. Access the website shown below and click on the link for Chapter 5. Locate the Economic and Employment Projections. Identify and study tables that describe how employment is projected to change for people of your age and race and for an industry in which you might be interested in working. How can you use that information to help you make education and career decisions in the next several years?

www.cengage.com/school/genbus/pob

checkpoint ✓
List several groups that will increase as a percentage of the total U.S. workforce in the next decade.

BUSINESS AND THE ECONOMY

Businesses make the goods and services you use each day. That includes the products and services used by other businesses as well as those needed by individual consumers. In 2009, all businesses worldwide produced more than $70 trillion of goods and services. U.S. businesses were responsible for almost 20 percent of that production. Nearly 25 million full- and part-time businesses produce those goods and services.

Goal 2

Discuss the role of business in the U.S. economy.

Size of U.S. Businesses

Most U.S. businesses are quite small. The largest number, nearly 19.5 million businesses, have no employees other than the owner. About 6.5 million companies employ fewer than 20 people. Just over 886,000 employ 20–100 people. About 182,000 large U.S. businesses employ 100 or more workers. Of those large companies, 890 employ more than 10,000 people. Figure 5-1 shows the distribution of U.S. businesses by employment size.

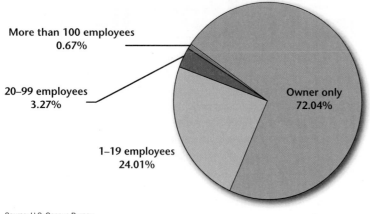

Percent of Businesses by Employment Size

More than 100 employees
0.67%

20–99 employees
3.27%

1–19 employees
24.01%

Owner only
72.04%

Source: U.S. Census Bureau

▶ **Figure 5-1**

Would you prefer to work in a large or small business? Explain your answer.

Roles of Business

Businesses play several key roles in the U.S. economy. The most important role of businesses is to make and distribute products and services needed by consumers, government, and other businesses. Businesses make the clothing, movies, music, food, and other items you use every day.

Businesses provide employment for millions of people. Employee wages are used to purchase goods and services. Profits earned by businesses are used to compensate owners and investors. Most businesses pay taxes to federal, state, and local governments. Governments spend these taxes to provide services such as clean water, well-maintained streets, police and fire protection, hospitals, and schools.

Impact on a Community

A business can have an important impact on the community in which it operates. When a new business opens, it pays wages to its workers. It also buys goods and services from other businesses in the area. This money has not been in the community before. Employees and businesses in turn spend much of the money to purchase things they need.

The money spent may result in the need for more employees in the community. They will need housing, automobiles, food, and entertainment. They will pay taxes to the community to support needed community services.

When a large business opens in an area, other businesses will often locate there to support the larger business. Small businesses may be started to meet the needs of the residents and other businesses. Successful businesses contribute to more jobs, more income, and a thriving economy in the communities where they operate.

Business Activities

Businesses may be large or small, simple or complex. A business might operate in only one community. It may have many locations across the nation or around the world. Although there are many types and sizes of businesses, all firms perform six basic activities.

Generating Ideas A business begins with a new idea. Someone must have an idea for a new product or service or a new way to carry out a business process. A business must continue to improve and develop new ideas in order to remain successful. Businesses must remain competitive with other firms that sell similar goods and services. Many companies have a research and development department that works full-time to discover new product, service, and operating ideas.

Raising Capital Businesses need financial resources to operate. They use these financial resources to buy buildings and equipment, hire and train workers, and complete day-to-day business operations. A large amount of capital is needed to start most businesses. Some capital comes from owners. Most is obtained through loans from financial institutions or from investors.

A business needs more capital as it develops and grows. Some of that capital will come from reinvested profits. A business will need to continue to work with banks and attract additional investors to have enough money for ongoing operations.

Employing and Training Personnel
Businesses need human resources. Even businesses that begin with no employees other than the owner will add part- and full-time employees as they grow. Businesses have procedures for recruiting, hiring, and training employees. They pay wages, benefits, and employment taxes. New employees receive training in order to perform their jobs correctly. Further training will be necessary when procedures change, new tasks are added, or technology is introduced.

Buying Goods and Services All businesses buy goods and services. Businesses use many of the purchases for their own operations. Other purchases are resold. Manufacturers of automobiles must buy steel, aluminum, and plastics to be used to form the frame and body of new cars. They will also purchase tires, batteries, airbags, and air conditioning units that will be installed on the production line.

Business Insight for the 21st Century

Mass Customization

When the automobile was first mass-produced in the early 1900s, Henry Ford would tell potential customers, "You can have any color car you want as long as it's black!"

Since then, businesses have continually tried to make items that meet the distinct needs and wants of consumers. Today, companies with millions of customers are making products designed for the individual. *Mass customization* is production of personalized products at mass market prices.

If you are downloading music and creating personalized play lists you already know something about mass customization. Instead of buying a CD with 10 to 15 tracks, you choose only the songs you want.

Many products have the potential for mass customization. Cosmetics can be mixed to match skin tones and types. Financial services companies offer computerized investment advice based on a person's income, age, and household situation.

Mass customization benefits customers and businesses. The customer gets a product that is individualized and the company makes products customers want. Dell Computer only builds personal computers that have actually been ordered. This approach keeps profit margin up by keeping inventory costs down.

Many automotive companies allow you to design a car online. You can do this just for fun, or design the car you want to buy. Because automotive manufacturing is highly mechanized, assembly lines can easily customize your vehicle with the options you want. Henry Ford might be surprised that you can pick a color other than black.

Think Critically

1. Locate a website or local business that would provide another example of customized products or services. How does technology make this situation possible?

2. Describe an idea to offer a customized product or service online or in your community.

A retailer buys an assortment of products to sell to customers. It must also buy the display equipment, computers, and cleaning supplies used to operate the business. Businesses purchase an array of services from other companies. These include advertising, legal and accounting services, lawn care and building maintenance, and security.

Marketing Goods and Services
Marketing refers to the activities directed at providing the goods and services wanted by a business's customers. Without marketing, even the best products and services may remain unsold. Businesses need to understand and perform many marketing activities. They must satisfy customers who usually can choose to buy from competitors offering similar products and services.

Maintaining Business Records All businesses must have some type of record-keeping system. Owners and managers need records to track performance and make decisions. Customers need information about orders and payments. Businesses are required by government to keep records and submit information. Today, technology is available to make record keeping easy and accurate. With computer technology, business owners and employees can quickly access information needed to understand business performance and solve problems.

checkpoint ✓
What are the six basic activities completed by all businesses?

TYPES OF BUSINESSES

You, your family, and your friends use a variety of businesses to buy the things you want and need. You recognize other businesses but never use them. And, you don't even know about many others. There are three major categories—producers, intermediaries, and service businesses.

Producers

Producers create the products and services used by individuals and other businesses. They are responsible for using resources to make something that is needed by others. A business that takes resources from nature for direct consumption or for use in developing other products is an *extractor*. Extractors pump oil, mine coal, or cut timber. *Farmers* cultivate land and use other natural resources to grow crops and raise livestock for consumption. *Manufacturers* get supplies from other producers and convert them into products. They sell their products to consumers and other businesses.

Business activities start with producers. A builder obtains lumber, cement, shingles, carpet, and paint to construct a house, factory, or office building. A cereal manufacturer buys wheat and oats, sugar, and dried fruit as well as cardboard, glue, and ink to process and package your favorite breakfast food.

How does marketing affect a consumer's decision to purchase a product?

Digital Vision/Getty Images

Goal 3

Describe three major types of businesses.

Intermediaries

Intermediaries are businesses involved in selling the goods and services of producers to consumers and other businesses. The most common types of intermediaries are retailers and wholesalers. Many other businesses focus on one or a few activities that assist in distributing and selling products and services. Specialized intermediaries include transportation companies, advertising agencies, storage centers, sales offices, and data processing centers.

Service Businesses

Many businesses do not make products. They offer something that is intangible, meaning it has no physical qualities. A **service business** carries out activities that are consumed by its customers. It does not offer products for sale. Service businesses include dentists, physicians, and lawyers as well as pet sitters, painters, and furniture movers. New types of service businesses

are Internet service providers, web designers, and online travel agents. Businesses as well as final consumers use services. A business might contact an international trade specialist to help it set up a sale to a new customer in Africa. A communications firm could design and install a new phone system for large telemarketing businesses.

Service businesses are the fastest growing part of the economy. More than 60 percent of all U.S. employment is now in service-producing businesses. While you often hear about low-pay and low-skill service jobs, there are many new businesses offering professional and technical services requiring highly educated employees.

> **checkpoint** ✓
> How does a manufacturer differ from an extractor?

5-1 Assessment

Study Tools
www.cengage.com/school/genbus/pob

Key Concepts

Determine the best answer.

1. The largest number of U.S. businesses employ
   a. more than 100 people
   b. between 50 and 100 people
   c. between 10 and 20 people
   d. no employees other than the owner

2. Which of the following is not one of the common activities of all businesses?
   a. producing goods and services
   b. employing and training personnel
   c. marketing goods and services
   d. maintaining business records

3. A retailer is an example of a(n)
   a. extractor
   b. producer
   c. intermediary
   d. service business

Make Academic Connections

4. **Math** If 42 percent of all people working in the United States are baby boomers, how many were working in 2008? If 15 percent of the baby boomers retire in 10 years, how many jobs will this represent from 2008 employment? Use employment information from the lesson to make the calculations.

5. **Visual Arts** Select a product that involves all of the types of businesses in its production and marketing. Draw an illustration that shows each business and its role in the successful production and sale of the product. Title your illustration and label the component parts.

Forms of Business Ownership

Goals

1 Understand the three major forms of business ownership.

2 Determine when each form of business ownership is most appropriate.

3 Recognize other specialized business ownership forms.

Key Terms

proprietorship 106

partnership 107

corporation 107

partnership agreement 108

articles of incorporation 109

franchise 111

Focus on REAL LIFE

Jaden keyed in the ticker symbol APPL at his favorite financial website. He was checking the listing of the stock he owned—Apple.

Jaden's grandparents had given him five shares of stock in Apple when he was born. He didn't get interested in it until recently when he learned more about the stock market. Now he knew he was an owner of the technology company. The success of the company determined the value of his ownership. While the stock price had gone up and down, it was now at its highest point since he began following the stock price.

Goal 1

Understand the three major forms of business ownership.

BUSINESS OWNERSHIP

Many people think they would like to own a business. The chance to be in control, make decisions, and invest money to make a profit is challenging and exciting. Thousands of people are business owners. The amount of control they have, how decisions are made, the sources of money for the business, and control over profits is not the same for every business owner. The form of ownership affects each of those aspects of the business.

There are three major forms of business ownership—proprietorship, partnership, and corporation. There are also several other specialized forms of ownership.

Proprietorship

A **proprietorship** is a business owned and run by just one person. It is the easiest

What are the advantages and disadvantages of owning your own business?

Is owning a business something you might want to explore as you plan your future? What kind of businesses might you consider? What steps do you need to take now to make owning a business part of your life-span plan?

U.S. BUSINESS COMPARISON BY FORM OF OWNERSHIP				
FORM OF OWNERSHIP	NUMBER OF BUSINESSES (2006)	TOTAL REVENUE (THOUSANDS)	PERCENT OF ALL BUSINESSES	PERCENT OF TOTAL REVENUE
Proprietorship	22,075,000	1,278,000,000	71.53%	4.06%
Corporation	5,841,000	26,070,000,000	18.93%	82.82%
Partnership	2,947,000	4,131,000,000	9.55%	13.12%
Total	30,863,000	31,479,000,000	100.00%	100.00%

Source: U.S. Census

▶ **Figure 5-2**

Why are there so many proprietorships?

form of business to start and end. There are very few legal requirements regarding the business ownership or capital needs that must be met.

Many individuals like the proprietorship form of ownership. It gives them sole control over all business decisions. The owner receives all profits made by the business. He or she can determine how those profits are used. The owner is also responsible for all debts of the business. If the business fails, the owner has almost no shelter from creditors. Any money and other assets owned by the proprietor, whether used in the business or not, can be claimed by creditors to pay the business debts.

Partnership

A **partnership** is a business owned and controlled by two or more people who have entered into an agreement. A partnership is very similar to the proprietorship in several ways. It is quite easy to start. The owners are both responsible for key business decisions and functions. The partners share both investments and profits based on the terms of the partnership agreement. Each partner is liable for all of the debts of the business should it fail.

Corporation

A **corporation** is a separate legal entity formed by documents filed with a state. It is owned by one or more shareholders

and managed by a board of directors. Most corporations have several owners who invest in the business by purchasing shares of stock. Corporations are more difficult to form than either proprietorships or partnerships. They must also meet more legal requirements. Not all owners have direct involvement in decision-making about business functions. They will not have access to profits unless the board of directors approves it. Corporations protect the liability of stockholders to only the amount of money they have invested.

Most U.S. businesses are organized as proprietorships. However, as shown in Figure 5-2, proprietorships have a very small percentage of business revenues.

> **checkpoint** ✓
> What are the differences between the three main forms of business ownership?

CHOOSING A FORM OF BUSINESS OWNERSHIP

When a new business is started, the owner should carefully consider the form of ownership. While it is possible to change the form of ownership for an existing business, it is best to decide which form to use both for the long-term future of the business as well as for its first few years.

Goal 2

Determine when each form of business ownership is most appropriate.

Compare the unique interests and skills of each member of your team. Identify possible businesses that could be formed as a partnership by combining the talents of two or more team members.

Choosing a Proprietorship

Most businesses begin as a proprietorship. They remain in that form as long as the sole owner operates the business. Often people choose to start a business because they prefer the freedom of working for themselves rather than for another person. They want to be in total control of the business. Many new business owners have limited knowledge of the forms of ownership and want to begin the business as easily as possible. Some people form a business from a hobby or operate a business on a part-time basis. They may expand the business over a few years and spend little time thinking about other ways the business could be organized.

Starting a proprietorship is easy. You just have to begin buying and selling as a business. You don't even need a business name. You do need to obtain any required government licenses and permits. You will need to account for income and expenses and pay taxes on the profits of the business. If operating the business for several years will be your primary job, it is best to choose a name for the business. You will need to register the name with local, state, and federal governments.

A proprietorship provides a tax advantage for the owner. All income is taxed as a part of your personal income. Many business expenses can be used to reduce the income. That benefit also carries the most significant disadvantage of a proprietorship. In the eyes of the law, the owner is the same as the business. Any debts of the business are the responsibility of the owner. Personal assets not connected to the business will need to be used to pay business debts if the business assets are not adequate to cover those debts. In that way, a failed business may result in the owner losing almost everything.

For people who want total independence, do not want to be exposed to significant government regulation, want to be in control of all business decisions, and are willing to take on the entire risk of a business, the proprietorship offers an effective form of ownership. For a person who wants to expand the business, is willing to share control and decision-making in return for additional resources and reduced risk, and wants some protection for money invested, other forms of ownership are better.

Choosing a Partnership

A partnership is a bit more complex and formal than a proprietorship. In many states, a partnership can be formed by the verbal agreement of two or more people. It is usually better to have a written partnership agreement. The **partnership agreement** is a written agreement among all owners. It details the rules

How might a partnership be more advantageous than a proprietorship?

and procedures that guide ownership and operations. It typically identifies the business name, the investments, and other contributions of each partner. The agreement shows how profits and losses will be divided among the partners. It defines the authority and responsibilities granted to each person and how the partnership can be dissolved. Most states require that partnerships register a business name as well as the name of each person in the partnership.

The advantage of a partnership is that two or more people can contribute to the investment needed to start the business as well as the expertise required to run a business. At the same time, each partner is responsible for decisions made by all other partners. There is no protection for the personal assets of any partner. If the business fails, each person can lose much more than the amount of the original investment. If a partner chooses to leave the partnership or dies, the partnership normally must be dissolved.

A partnership is a good ownership form for people who share an idea for a business. They want to cooperate in managing and investing in the business. It is the easiest form for people who work well together and want to share the risks and rewards of the business. It has the same liability of a proprietorship and presents problems if other people want to join the partnership or if it needs to be dissolved.

Choosing a Corporation

Most people think of corporations as very large businesses. It is the most popular form of ownership for large businesses. It is becoming increasingly popular for new and small businesses as well. Corporations are subject to many more laws and are more difficult to form than either proprietorships or partnerships. They offer a number of advantages to the owners as well.

fyi Proprietors must pay self-employment taxes in addition to their income tax. Self-employment taxes are contributions to Medicare and Social Security. People employed by another business have those payments deducted from their paychecks, and employers contribute half of the required payments.

Joel Calheiros/Shutterstock.com

Corporations are treated as an "individual" by governments. They must follow the laws of the state in which they are organized. To form a corporation, you must file articles of incorporation with the appropriate state government office. The **articles of incorporation** is a written legal document that defines ownership and operating procedures and conditions for the business. Each state has specific information that must be included. States usually provide a form that can be filled out. The business must create *corporate bylaws* that are the operating procedures for the corporation. It must name a *board of directors*, the people who will make the major policy and financial decisions for the business. The corporation also issues shares of stock to the investors and details how more investments can be made.

Even though a corporation is more difficult to form and is subject to more government rules, it offers several advantages to owners. The liability of any owner is limited to the amount of money invested. The amount of debt of the business does not matter. People can invest in the business and receive some of the profit without having to take part in the day-to-day management and operations. The business can be easily expanded and ownership can be changed by the sale of stock.

Disadvantages of corporate ownership are that decision-making is shared among managers, the board of directors, and shareholders. Many more records are required and more laws regulate operations than for other forms of ownership. Because corporations are treated as individuals by governments, they must pay corporate taxes on profits earned. Then the investors also pay taxes on their individual earnings from the business.

checkpoint ✓
Which form of business ownership is the most complex and difficult to form?

Goal 3

Recognize other specialized business ownership forms.

OTHER FORMS OF OWNERSHIP

Most businesses are organized as one of the three common forms just discussed. There are other choices of ownership. Some are specialized forms of partnerships and corporations. Others are totally unique forms.

Specialized Partnerships and Corporations

In a general partnership, all partners take part in ownership and operation of the business. A *limited liability partnership* identifies some investors who cannot lose more than the amount of their investment, but they are not allowed to participate in the day-to-day management of the business. This type of partnership is difficult and costly to set up. A *joint venture* is a unique business organized by two or more other businesses to operate for a limited time and for a specific project. It is a type of partnership.

A corporate form that is favored by many small businesses is the S corporation. An *S corporation* offers the limited liability of a corporation. All income is passed through to the owners based on their investment and is taxed on their individual tax returns. A newer ownership form is the limited liability company (LLC). It combines the best features of a partnership and a corporation. A *limited liability company* provides liability protection for owners. It has a simpler set of organizing and operating requirements than a corporation. No articles of incorporation or bylaws are needed. A simple document much like a partnership agreement must be developed.

A *nonprofit corporation* is a group of people who join to do some activity that benefits the public. They work in areas such as education, health care, charity, or the arts. Nonprofit corporations are free from corporate income taxes. They can raise funds by receiving grants and donations from individuals and businesses. As with other corporations, they must organize as a corporation. The government must approve their purpose and operations.

Cooperatives and Franchises

Sometimes a group of people forms a cooperative to provide goods and services that they all need. A *cooperative* is owned by members, serves their needs, and is managed in their interest. Members form a consumer cooperative so that they can purchase goods and

What forms of corporate business ownership exist in your community?

services more cheaply as a group than they could individually. A business cooperative forms to market the products produced by members or to purchase products needed by the members. Large numbers of small businesses will have greater bargaining power than the individual businesses.

A **franchise** is a written contract granting permission to operate a business to sell products and services in a set way. The company that owns the product or service and grants the rights to another business is known as the *franchiser*. The company purchasing the rights to run the business is the *franchisee*. A franchise is a way to expand a business using the investments of others while maintaining control over the name, product quality, and operating procedures.

The franchisee maintains day-to-day operations and receives the profits of the business. It pays a fee and percentage of the profits to the franchiser in return for operating assistance. Some popular and successful franchises include Jiffy Lube, Century 21 real estate offices, Mail Boxes Etc., Wild Birds Unlimited, Merry Maids, Dunkin' Donuts, MAACO Collision Repair and Auto Painting, and New York NY Fresh Deli.

> **checkpoint ✓**
> What are the other specialized forms of business ownership?

5-2 Assessment

Study Tools

www.cengage.com/school/genbus/pob

Key Concepts

Determine the best answer.

1. The form of ownership that gives one person sole control over all business decisions is the
   a. proprietorship
   b. partnership
   c. corporation
   d. franchise

2. True or False. All investors in a general partnership have full liability for the debts of the business.

3. The people who make the major policy and financial decisions in a corporation are the
   a. investors
   b. board of directors
   c. managers
   d. owners

4. A special form of business organization that combines advantages of a corporation and a partnership is a
   a. franchise
   b. nonprofit corporation
   c. cooperative
   d. limited liability company

Make Academic Connections

5. **Communication** Two friends who want to open a store to sell the work of local artists ask you to explain the advantages and disadvantages of the three common forms of business ownership. Write a memo outlining the advantages and disadvantages. Include a list of questions that might help your friends make a decision.

6. **Research** Use the Internet to find information on a franchise opportunity related to a current career interest. Prepare a table that describes the franchise, the products or services, the investment requirements, and the benefits of becoming a franchisee.

7. **Read** Find a news article about cooperatives or a specific cooperative. Read the article and write a reaction. Respond as if you were posting an online comment for other readers to see. Prepare a properly formatted citation for the article. Possible sources include printed and online versions of newspapers or magazines. You should also consider independent online sources that produce original content.

Critical Thinking and Problem Solving

Understanding Stock Tables

STOCK TABLE EXAMPLE								
52 WK HI-LO	SYM	DIV	VOL	YLD	PE	HI-LO	CLOSE	NET CHG
28-13	LZD	1.1	228	4.58	10.53	25-23.5	24	0.5

Knowing how to read a stock table is an important life skill. People who own stock or are interested in buying stock must be able to read a stock table. It provides information on the performance of the stock each day and over an extended period of time. By understanding stock tables, investors can determine how well the company is performing. They can decide whether to maintain their investment, buy additional stock, or sell and move their money to another investment.

Stock tables are available in most daily newspapers. They can also be accessed online. They report on the performance of publicly traded stocks on all of the major stock exchanges. Tables may be organized a bit differently, but they will contain the same information shown in the example above. On weekends, many newspapers report stock performance for the entire week.

52 WK HI-LO is the highest and lowest prices at which the stock was sold in the past year (52 weeks). In the example, the highest price was $28 and the lowest was $13.

SYM is the company symbol or abbreviation that identifies the firm issuing the stock. This symbol is sometimes referred to as the company's "ticker symbol." The fictitious symbol in the example is LZD.

DIV represents dividends, which are the amount of money approved by the board of directors of the company to be paid to stockholders. The column shows the most recent dividend paid per share—$1.10. Dividends are a measure of the health of the business. They are one way that stockholders earn a return on their investment in addition to gains in the value of the stock.

VOL shows the volume of shares (in 100s) traded on the date of the table. In the example, 22,800 shares were traded by LZD. Volume gives information on the change in demand for the company's shares.

YLD approximates the yield of the dividend paid. The dividend yield is the current rate of return on all capital invested in the company. This allows easier comparison of the performance of companies with different stock prices. The yield is calculated by dividing the current dividend by the closing stock price.

$$\frac{\text{Dividend}}{\text{Price}} = \frac{\$1.10}{\$24.00} = 4.58\% \text{ yield}$$

PE is the comparison of the price per share to the earnings per share. It is called the price/earnings ratio. It shows how much an investor is willing to pay for $1 of current earnings by one share of stock. The ratio is calculated by dividing the price by the earnings per share (EPS). In the example, LZD stock is selling for more than 10 times the current earnings.

$$\frac{\text{Price}}{\text{Eps}} = \frac{\$24.00}{\$2.28} = 10.53 \text{ PE}$$

HI-LO represents the highest and lowest prices of all trades made during the date of the table. In the example, the high was at $25.00 and the low was $23.50.

CLOSE is the last price at which a trade was made during the trading day. In the example, $24.00 is the close.

NET CHG is the difference between the closing price for the previous day and the current day. Because the net change listed is 0.5, the price of the stock on the previous day was $23.50.

Think Critically

1. What information from the stock table do you think is most important for a stock owner to watch on a regular basis? What is the least important?

2. How do stock tables help in comparing the performance of two stocks with very different prices?

5-3 Organizational Structure for Businesses

Goals

1 Understand important principles in designing an effective organization.

2 Compare alternative organizational structures for businesses.

Key Terms

mission statement 113

goal 113

policies 114

procedures 114

organization chart 115

Focus on REAL LIFE

Mary Jo's company has just approved a policy that allowed some employees to telecommute. This means employees can work from home and complete their work using a computer and other technology. Mary Jo is interested in the idea but isn't sure if she should apply.

She is afraid she might not be as motivated to complete her work every day if she doesn't have to go to the office and keep a regular schedule. She also is concerned that it may be much more difficult to communicate with coworkers and get feedback from her manager using the technology. Mary Jo also wonders if she will be viewed as a productive and valued employee if people don't see her at work every day.

DESIGNING AN EFFECTIVE BUSINESS ORGANIZATION

It is not easy to create a successful business. Many new businesses fail in the first few years. Few businesses maintain their success for the lifetime of the owner. Successful businesses need more than a good product or service. Skilled managers, well-prepared and motivated employees, adequate resources, and effective procedures add to business success. A business needs to be well organized to help people do their work properly. An effective business begins with a clear purpose and the application of key principles for organizing work.

Setting Direction

The direction for a business comes from its **mission statement**. A mission statement is a short, specific written statement of the reason a business exists and what it wants to achieve. Here is an example from Starbucks: *To inspire and nurture the human spirit—one person, one cup and one neighborhood at a time.*

After a mission statement is developed, the business sets goals. A **goal** is a precise statement of results the business expects

Goal 1

Understand important principles in designing an effective organization.

How does effective organization help a business "hit the mark"?

to achieve. Goals are used to define what needs to be accomplished and to determine if the business is successful. An example of a goal for an automobile manufacturer is "to produce the top-rated brand for quality and customer satisfaction."

Finally, the business sets policies and procedures for the organization. **Policies** are guidelines used in making consistent decisions. **Procedures** are descriptions of the way work is to be done. Effective policies and procedures provide guidance and direction to people working in the organization.

Principles of Effective Organization

When several people work together, their work needs to be organized so they work together well and achieve their tasks. Several principles guide the effective organization of work.

Responsibility, Authority, and Accountability *Responsibility* is the obligation to complete specific work. *Authority* is the right to make decisions about how responsibilities should be accomplished. *Accountability* is taking responsibility for the results achieved. In an effective organization, all managers and employees have a set of responsibilities as a part of their jobs. With every job assignment, they know they have the authority to make the decisions and obtain the resources needed to complete the assignment. They know they will be recognized and rewarded if they are successful. They will be held accountable if the work is not completed well.

In an organization, every member has a specific role to fill. Describe some roles.

Matthew Jacque/Shutterstock.com

Unity of Command A key organizing principle is to provide unity of command. *Unity of command* means there is a clear reporting relationship for all staff of a business. If there is confusion in assignments and unclear relationships among people who are working together, it will be hard for people to know what to do or where to go for help. For each work assignment, people need to know who is the leader and how decisions will be made.

Span of Control The last organizing principle is span of control. *Span of control* is the number of employees who are assigned to a particular work task and manager. A large number of people working with little support from their manager cannot be effective. In the same way, a manager with only a very small number of people may provide too much control. Organizations need to make sure that workers have a balance of supervision and freedom to do their work. The span of control for well trained, experienced, and motivated employees can be much greater than for new and inexperienced employees who are not enthused about their work.

checkpoint ✓
What is the difference between a mission statement and a goal?

TYPES OF ORGANIZATIONAL STRUCTURES

Goal 2

Compare alternative organizational structures for businesses.

When only one person works in a business, there is little need for an organizational structure. The sole employee is responsible for all of the work. When more people are hired, there will need to be an agreement on what work each person will do and if one person has authority over the work of others. An **organization chart** is a diagram that shows the structure of an organization, classifications of work and jobs, and the relationships among those classifications. You can see a simple organization chart for a business in Figure 5-3.

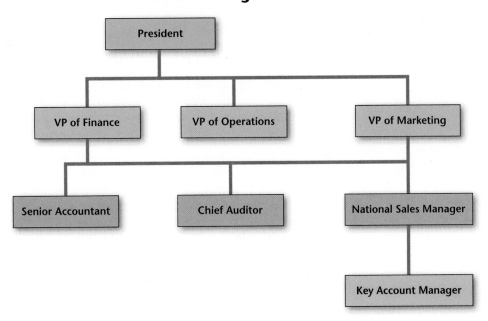

Business Organization Chart

▶ **Figure 5-3**

Why is it important for employees to understand the structure of the company where they work?

Your class is responsible for selling advertising for the school's yearbook. Work as a team to identify the tasks that will need to be completed to sell 50 ads in the next three weeks. Describe how a project team can be organized to achieve that goal.

Functional Organization Structure Most businesses use a *functional organizational structure.* In this type of organization, work is arranged within main business functions such as production, operations, marketing, and human resources. All of the people with jobs related to one of the functions will work together. They report to managers who are responsible for that function. The advantage of a functional organization is that people work with others who have the same skills. A drawback is that people become more focused on their specific function than on the success of the whole business. Often, people working in one function have little interaction with people in other parts of the business.

Matrix Organizational Structure

A newer organizational structure designed to overcome the drawbacks of the functional structure is the matrix organization. In a *matrix organizational structure,* work is structured around specific projects, products, or customer groups. People with varied backgrounds are assigned together because their expertise is required for the project or to serve the customer. The assignment may be temporary or long-term.

A matrix organization can be interesting and motivating to employees. They work with many different people. They are focused on a specific project or task. However, it can be confusing and inefficient without effective leadership and communication.

checkpoint ✓

What problems can result from the use of a functional organizational structure?

5-3 Assessment

Study Tools
www.cengage.com/school/genbus/pob

Key Concepts

Determine the best answer.

1. True or False. The direction for a business comes from its policies and procedures.

2. The obligation to complete specific work is
   a. responsibility
   b. authority
   c. accountability
   d. recognition

3. Which of the following is not shown on an organizational chart?
   a. the structure of an organization
   b. work relationships
   c. job descriptions
   d. classifications of jobs

Make Academic Connections

4. **Technology** Use the Internet to collect examples of the mission statements of five businesses. Rate each mission statement in terms of how effectively it communicates the purpose and direction of the company.

5. **Critical Thinking** Many schools are organized using a functional organizational structure. Teachers are organized into departments such as English, Mathematics, Science, and Business. How could a school be organized using a matrix structure? Design an organizational chart that illustrates a matrix structure for your school. Describe the advantages and disadvantages of the matrix structure as applied to a school.

Electricity Where There Was None

More than 25 percent of the world's population does not have electricity. No electricity means no water pumps, no lights, no refrigerators, and no real chance for a better life. Knowing that electricity is the key to improving the standard of living, some young innovators have devised strategies to help bring electricity to their communities.

At 22, Fabio Rosa was named secretary of agriculture for a city in rural Brazil and he faced a challenge. People were leaving their farms and moving to Palmeras because it was hard to earn a living in agriculture without electricity. This population shift put stress on city services and created the likelihood that there would be few farms in the future.

Fabio had an idea. He thought a dependable supply of low-cost solar energy would result in higher levels of food production. At the same time, improved health and education services could be provided, pollution levels would be reduced, and people could go back to their farms. He envisioned small business communities powered by solar energy springing up to serve the local farmers.

Fabio knew that farm families spent at least $11 per month on kerosene, candles, and batteries. This was about the same amount that would be needed to rent a simple solar energy system that would provide enough electricity for one farm. With that knowledge, he set out to electrify the rural areas of his country with solar energy kits. These kits came in three sizes. The smallest one rented for $10 per month. It came complete with a 60-watt solar panel, high-performance battery, all the wiring, plus a number of 12-volt fluorescent lights and electrical outlets for appliances. The system provided, on average per day, six to seven hours of light and several hours for running appliances, equipment, and a water

How did Fabio Rosa's ideas about a dependable supply of low-cost solar energy change rural Brazil while allowing some things to remain the same?

pump. Two larger kits rented for $16 and $24 per month, respectively, and came with more lights, outlets, and wattage. The installation cost for a kit, about $150, could be paid off over 12 months. When Rosa distributed the solar kits to farmers, he included materials about how to develop an irrigation system and build electric fences to protect farm animals as well as information on modern farming practices. Before long, power tools and appliances were humming and people were enjoying warm showers.

Around the same time Fabio was working to improve life in Brazil, William Kamkwamba also had a powerful idea. He was 14 when he decided to make a windmill to help grow crops in his village in Malawi, Africa. During a famine in 2002, William was forced to drop out of school, but he continued to read and study how to build a windmill. He collected scrap metal and tractor parts, and he built wind blades by heating and hammering PVC pipe.

His first working windmill created enough electricity to power four light bulbs and two radios for his family. His next accomplishment was building a solar-powered water pump to supply the first drinking water in his village.

Collaborating with journalist Bryan Mealer, William wrote a book about his life. *The Boy Who Harnessed the Wind* was published in 2009. William also inspired the Moving Windmills Project, a not-for-profit organization that raises money for windmills, books for libraries, and other support activities for Malawi.

Think Critically

1. In what ways might the standard of living improve when people have access to electricity?

2. Locate additional information about the work of Fabio Rosa or William Kamkwamba.

Business Notes

5-1 Business in the U.S. Economy

- The employment status of the United States is changing. Recessions have resulted in periods of lower employment. The labor pool is currently getting older, but that will begin to change as baby boomers retire. Minority groups make up a larger percentage of the workforce.

- Businesses play several key roles in the U.S. economy. They make and distribute products and services needed by consumers, government, and businesses. They provide employment for millions of people. They compensate owners and investors. They pay taxes to federal, state, and local governments.

- The three major categories of businesses are producers, intermediaries, and service businesses. Producers create the products and services used by individuals and other businesses. Intermediaries sell goods and services. A service business carries out activities that are consumed by its customers.

5-2 Forms of Business Ownership

- Most businesses are organized as proprietorships, partnerships, and corporations. A proprietorship is a business owned and run by one person. A partnership is a business owned and controlled by two or more people. A corporation is a separate legal entity owned by one or more shareholders and managed by a board of directors.

- For people who want to work and make decisions independently, do not want to be exposed to significant regulation, and are willing to take on the risk of a business, the proprietorship is an effective form of ownership. A partnership is good for people who share an idea for a business, want to cooperate in managing and investing, and want to share the risks and rewards of the business. A corporation is more difficult to form and is subject to more regulations. Investors' liability is limited to the amount invested, and they can invest without taking part in the day-to-day management.

- Other forms of ownership include limited liability partnership, joint venture, S corporation, limited liability company, nonprofit corporation, cooperative, and franchise.

5-3 Organizational Structure for Businesses

- Successful businesses have an effective organizational structure. A mission statement, goals, policies, and procedures guide them.

- The specific structure of a business can be illustrated with an organizational chart. Traditionally, businesses have used a functional structure but now many are using a matrix organizational structure.

Communicate Business Concepts

1. What are some rapidly growing employment opportunities? What types of jobs are declining in numbers? How can you predict what job categories may grow or decline in the future?

2. Why do most businesses have no employees other than the owner? Do you believe most of those business owners earn their entire income from that business? Why or why not?

3. Identify several businesses from your community that fit within each of the three categories of businesses listed in Lesson 5-1. Do you believe your community has more producers, intermediaries, or service businesses? Justify your answer.

4. Would you like to start and own your own business? Why or why not? What do you believe are the risks and benefits you would face if you decided to start a business?

5. Julie states that she wants to be her own boss. If she starts a business, it will be a proprietorship rather than a partnership or corporation. Explain to Julie why she might want to consider another ownership form. Is it possible for her to be her own boss and yet not use the proprietorship form of ownership?

6. Use a business directory to identify several non-profit corporations in your area. What public service is each providing? Why do you think each is a public rather than a private corporation?

7. "An effective organizational structure is as important to a business as the quality of its products and services." Do you agree or disagree with that statement? Discuss your beliefs with another student who has the opposing view.

8. You are starting a shopping service for elderly people in your community who cannot leave their homes. Write a mission statement that clearly communicates the purpose of your business.

9. How will the appearance of an organizational chart for a business using a functional organizational structure be different from one using a matrix organizational structure? What should you be able to learn about a business by studying its organizational chart?

Develop Your Business Language

Match the terms listed with the definitions.

10. A business owned and controlled by two or more people who have entered into a written agreement.

11. A short, specific written statement of the reason a business exists and what it wants to accomplish.

12. One who has no explicit or implicit contract for long-term employment.

13. Descriptions of the way work is to be done.

14. A specific statement of results the business expects to achieve.

15. A written legal document that identifies ownership and operating procedures and conditions for the business.

16. Businesses involved in selling the goods and services of producers to consumers and other businesses.

17. A separate legal entity, formed by documents filed with the state, which is owned by one or more shareholders and managed by a board of directors.

18. A written contract granting permission to operate a business to sell products and services in a prescribed way.

19. Businesses that complete activities that are consumed by customers rather than offering products for sale.

20. A business owned and controlled by just one person.

21. A written agreement among all owners that specifies the rules and procedures that guide ownership and operations.

22. Guidelines used in making consistent decisions.

23. A diagram that shows the structure of an organization, classifications of jobs, and the relationships among those classifications.

Key Terms

a. articles of incorporation
b. contingent worker
c. corporation
d. franchise
e. goal
f. intermediaries
g. mission statement
h. organization chart
i. partnership
j. partnership agreement
k. proprietorship
l. policies
m. procedures
n. service business

Make Academic Connections

24. **Math** To provide additional employment and add to its tax base from businesses, Yorketowne's city council opened a business park on the edge of the city. After five years, they had attracted two new manufacturers and four supporting service businesses to the park. The total value of the property of all six businesses was $15,825,500. The companies paid $0.78 per $1,000 of property value each year as property tax. In addition, the businesses employed 328 people at an average salary of $36,000. Each person paid a 1 percent city income tax each year.

    a. What is the total amount of taxes the city collected as a result of opening the business park?
    b. In addition to the tax dollars, what other benefits might the city receive from opening the business park?

25. **Technology** Use a spreadsheet and graphics program to make a chart or graph showing one of the following sets of data: (a) the five largest employers in the world and the number of employees for each, (b) the composition of the U.S. workforce by the age of employees, (c) the average size of U.S. business by annual sales revenues.

26. **Communication** The DECA chapter in your school is planning to open a school store to sell school supplies, school-related apparel, and spirit items before and after school. Prepare a mission statement for the store. Write one goal that identifies a specific result the store should achieve. Write a policy statement for accepting returns of merchandise purchased by customers.

27. **Science** Identify five types of natural resources that are extracted in the United States for use in manufacturing. For each, identify the leading states where the natural resources are extracted and important products for which the natural resource is needed.

28. **Public Service** Most communities have nonprofit corporations that support education. Find out if one or more organizations is working to support your school. If so, contact a leader of the organization. Determine how the organization is structured, if it is has articles of incorporation and bylaws, and its purpose. Find out how students in your school can support the organization through volunteer activities.

Decision-Making Strategies

Sonja Bartholomew started a lawn mowing service. She could not charge as much as she needed to make the profit she desired. Her competitors only charged $15 per lawn while she charged $20, but she did a superior job cutting lawns. Still, potential customers did not want to pay the extra $5.

A friend, Eduardo Guadalupe, suggested that they work together. He was good at trimming shrubs and had ideas for improving landscapes with flowers and lawn ornaments. They would offer a unique service when they combined their businesses. They could charge an amount that would result in a good profit for both of them. They would seek out homes in neighborhoods with above-average income levels.

29. What will be special about the services that Sonja and Eduardo can offer together? What other services might they include?

30. Why would they target above-average income levels?

31. Should Sonja continue to run her business as a proprietorship and hire Eduardo as an employee? If not, what other form of business ownership would you recommend? Justify your choice.

Linking School and Community

Interview a stockbroker or financial advisor in your community about the process of selecting and purchasing stock. Ask the professional to share information about how people decide which stock to purchase and how a stockholder can track the stock's performance. Ask the broker or advisor if he or she has any general advice for young investors.

Web Workout

The U.S. government provides support to small businesses through the Small Business Administration (SBA). Visit the SBA website to learn more about this resource. Browse or search for information about forms of ownership that small businesses might consider. Be sure to read the advantages and disadvantages of each form or ownership.

Think Critically

1. Use information from your textbook and the SBA website to identify and make a list of factors that influence the form of ownership choice.

2. Provide an example of business that might benefit from choosing the proprietorship form of ownership. Provide an example for each of these other types of ownership: partnership and corporation.

3. Based on one of your examples from above, write a short scenario describing the advantages and disadvantages of the chosen form of ownership. Describe how the business plans to use the form of ownership to its advantage and how it plans to deal with the disadvantages.

Small Business Management Team Event

Starting a business involves financial investment and risk. Individuals must decide the best form of business ownership for the business that they want to open. Your team has expertise in working at quick-serve and full-serve restaurants. Team members have college degrees in finance, hospitality marketing, and culinary arts. Your team is very excited about opening an Italian restaurant in a growing city with a population of 75,000 people. Currently there are two Italian restaurants associated with national franchises located in the community. Your team must describe the advantages associated with operating the restaurant as a sole proprietorship, partnership, corporation, and franchise. Then your team must decide upon the best type of ownership for your proposed restaurant and explain the rationale for your decision.

The Small Business Management Team Event involves a 90-minute test and a 10-minute oral presentation followed by a five minute question and answer session with the judges. A team of two to four members must present a solution for a Management Case Study. Your team may use one laptop/notebook computer, posters, flip charts, or graphs for the presentation.

Performance Indicators Evaluated

- Evaluate, prioritize, interpret, and communicate analysis of data.
- Negotiate business solutions with the team.
- Organize ideas and communicate orally in a group presentation.

- Apply an understanding of forms of business ownership.

Your team will be evaluated for

- Equality of responsibilities among team members of required tasks

- Demonstration of teamwork skills needed to function in a business setting

- Demonstration of self-esteem, self- and team-management, and integrity

- Demonstration of a working knowledge of business management/ownership concepts

- Demonstration of critical thinking skills to make decisions and solve problems

For more detailed information about performance indicators, go to the BPA website.

Think Critically

1. What advantages are offered by choosing to operate the restaurant as a partnership?

2. What advantages are offered by choosing the franchise form of business?

3. Why should tax laws be considered when deciding on the form of business ownership?

www.bpa.org

Assessment   **121**

6 Entrepreneurship and Small Business Management

Business, Management & Administration

When businesses face unique problems or undertake major changes, they often turn to consultants for advice and help. Consultants are not long-term employees of a company, but are hired to complete a specific task or to focus on an important challenge facing the business. Consultants may be self-employed and work independently, or they may be part of a large consulting business that employs many specialists. Large companies often form teams of specialists to work with a client.

Consultants bring expertise to a business that may not exist among its employees and that would be difficult to develop quickly enough to solve a current problem. Consultants also may be more objective about the business than people who are working there. The primary work of consultants is to conduct research and complete other types of analysis that help businesses address important challenges they are facing. Consultants often prepare written reports and plans, provide advice to decision-makers, and may even offer help in reorganizing the company and redirecting its efforts.

Related Job Titles
- Business Analyst
- Management Consultant
- Performance Consultant
- Quality Control Consultant
- Security Consultant
- Training Consultant

Analyze Career Opportunities in ...
CONSULTING

Use library and Internet resources to learn more about careers in consulting. Choose one of the job titles listed in the box above and answer the following questions.

1. Identify the minimum educational requirements for the job. Explain other training or education that might be needed for advancement.

2. Is this a career that interests you? What can you do now to help prepare yourself for this career?

What's it like to work as a ... Consultant?

Erin Gerrard works as a small business consultant for Security Savings Bank. The bank is committed to strengthening its services to small businesses. Security employs a 10-person team to support its small business customers.

Erin has a degree in accounting, worked five years for a major accounting business, and then operated her own accounting service for five years. The bank hired her as a small business consultant because of her accounting expertise and reputation in the community. She decided the consulting opportunity would be an interesting challenge.

This morning, Erin is meeting with Dawn Perrot, who is planning to open a florist shop. Dawn has submitted a business plan, but the financial plan is incomplete. Erin is looking forward to helping Dawn gather information and develop a complete picture of the financial needs of her business.

What about you? How do you believe Erin's work as a consultant is similar to and different from the work she did as the owner of a small accounting business?

Becoming an Entrepreneur

Goals

1 Identify characteristics of successful entrepreneurs.

2 Recognize the importance of entrepreneurship in the economy.

3 Describe opportunities and risks of entrepreneurship.

Key Terms

entrepreneur 124

entrepreneurship 124

venture capital 127

innovation 128

improvement 128

Focus on REAL LIFE

Jerelyn Frank has been working as an aerobics instructor for the Phase 4 Fitness Center for the past six years. Jerelyn enjoys her work because she has always been active and athletic. Since high school, she has taken wellness, first aid, and nutrition classes at the local adult education center. She has completed a number of certification courses in aerobics instruction and yoga. In her spare time, she has developed fitness programs for some of her friends and members of the fitness center where she works.

Jerelyn is seriously thinking about starting a personal fitness service. She wants to go to people's homes and offices to help them plan and maintain a fitness schedule and offer half-hour to one-hour workouts. She already has a number of contacts to help her get underway. Jerelyn is single with no family responsibilities, and she has no debts. She has been able to save more than $15,000 in her bank account.

Jerelyn decides to go forward with the plan just as thousands of other entrepreneurs do each year. Those that become new business owners are willing to contribute a great deal of time and energy and risk personal economic resources for their venture. They hold the hope of a successful business and a reasonable profit.

Goal 1

Identify characteristics of successful entrepreneurs.

CHARACTERISTICS OF ENTREPRENEURS

An **entrepreneur** is someone who takes a risk in starting a business to earn a profit. Some key factors in starting your own business are having a real desire to be your own boss and developing a good initial plan. Having special skills and abilities and coming up with innovative ideas are also important.

What personal characteristics do you have that could help you become a successful entrepreneur? What characteristics would you need to develop to be a successful entrepreneur? Describe how these characteristics may affect the life-span goals you set for your future.

Can you think of some service or product that is not being offered at this time but that could be in demand? Is there some service or product that you could offer more efficiently than others are doing now? Is there some special talent you have that could become the starting point for a business of your own? If so, you have the basis for a new business enterprise. There are good opportunities for entrepreneurship through small business ownership. **Entrepreneurship** is the process of starting, organizing, managing, and assuming the responsibility for a business. Here are some real-life examples of young entrepreneurs.

Entrepreneurs in Action

Joshua Moore was a high school student and brother to four-year-old Sophie

---

when he developed an idea for a baby stroller braking system. To fund work on his invention, Josh started Personal Affections, selling key chains, picture frames, mirrors, and personalized stickers at his Walhalla, South Carolina, high school. He received an Entrepreneur of the Year award for an operational business from the National Foundation for Teaching Entrepreneurship. At age 15, he was on his way to his dream of becoming an inventor and business owner.

Ben Cathers was not a typical student. At age 12 he started a web marketing and advertising business. His business grew to 10 employees and a network of more than 300 million advertisements per month. By age 17, Ben started a syndicated radio show called Teen America. Not content with just his own entrepreneurship, at age 19 Ben wrote *Conversations with Teen Entrepreneurs*. By 19, he cofounded Search Rate Technologies and Klick-TV. By the age of 25, Ben had turned his talent to working with the next generation of young entrepreneurs.

Rich Stachowski of Moraga, California, is an avid scuba diver. While enjoying his hobby, he recognized that he was unable to talk to others who were snorkeling with him. He put his imagination to work and invented Water Talkies™ at the age of 11. These walkie-talkies can be used under water. Rich worked with a family friend who developed the manufacturing process. He then opened a business to make and sell his product before he was even a teenager. Rich moved on to invent and patent seven more products including underwater binoculars and an underwater periscope.

Sometimes ideas for new products come from problems in daily life. Abbey Fleck was watching her father use a microwave oven to cook bacon one morning in their White Bear Lake, Minnesota, home. The bacon came out soaked in grease. Abbey had an idea to develop a pan that would cook the bacon while letting the

Do you have ideas or skills that you could use to start a small business?

grease drain out below. She and her father tested several designs that resulted in the Makin Bacon® microwave bacon tray. They were able to convince the producers of Armour brand bacon to sell the tray with an advertisement and order form printed

NETBookmark

The U.S. government provides a variety of services and programs for individuals who own their own businesses. One resource is a website dedicated to providing information for specific types of businesses and entrepreneurs. For example, the site has information about women-owned businesses, nonprofit organizations, and home-based businesses for women. Access the website shown below and click on the link for Chapter 6. Review the types of resources that can be accessed through the website. Choose one of the options and write a short summary about the information available.

www.cengage.com/school/genbus/pob

What are some advantages and disadvantages of turning a hobby into a business?

on each package of bacon. The product was an instant hit. Abbey's company currently sells Makin Bacon® trays at Kmart, Walmart, Target, and Le Gourmet Chef.

The experiences of these entrepreneurs are examples of the thousands of young people who have creative ideas and turn them into businesses each year. Not all ideas lead to successful businesses, but each provides evidence of the opportunities that exist for people who believe they can turn their idea into a profitable business.

What Does It Take?

Not all people who own or manage a business are entrepreneurs. It takes unique skills and personal characteristics to develop a new idea for a product or service. A person must also have both the confidence and capability to turn an idea into a business.

Entrepreneurs come from all age categories and racial and ethnic groups. They represent both genders as well as varied amounts and types of education. Many entrepreneurs own their first business while in their teens. Others do not take the step until retirement. More business owners are male, but young entrepreneurs are more equally divided between male and female.

It is important to have an understanding of business operations and management. This understanding does not always come from getting a business degree in college. People learn how to run a business in many ways. They may work in a business or ask for help and advice from an experienced business owner. They may read and study on their own as well as in school.

There are personal traits that are common to successful entrepreneurs, as shown in Figure 6-1. While some people already have many of these qualities, others do not. If you have a desire to become an entrepreneur, you can work to develop these characteristics.

▶ **Figure 6-1**

Which characteristics of successful entrepreneurs do you possess? Which ones would you like to develop?

PERSONAL CHARACTERISTICS OF SUCCESSFUL ENTREPRENEURS	
ENTREPRENEURS ARE	**ENTREPRENEURS HAVE**
• competitive	• ability to partner
• creative	• ability to secure resources
• energetic	• ability to spot opportunity
• goal oriented	• capability to learn from failure
• independent	• personal initiative
• inquisitive	• problem-solving skills
• persistent	• strong integrity
• reliable	• tolerance for ambiguity
• self-confident	• willingness to work hard

ENTREPRENEURSHIP AND THE ECONOMY

Entrepreneurship is a key part of the U.S. economy. Nearly one in ten of all Americans 18–64 years old is involved in some type of entrepreneurship activity. More than 625,000 new businesses are created annually. Entrepreneurship is also risky. Nearly as many small businesses close as begin each year.

Employment

Small businesses are responsible for most new employment. Figure 6-2 shows employment growth by firm size between 1990 and 2005. Over 60 percent of new jobs were created by businesses with fewer than 500 employees.

Financing

Most new businesses start on $10,000 or less. High tech firms are more likely to obtain funding from outside sources. A nationwide study found that 75 percent of startup capital comes from owner savings, bank loans, and credit card debt. Funding also comes from the entrepreneur's family and friends. One in ten Americans has invested in a business of someone they know well. Obtaining funding from family and friends can be risky for both the entrepreneur and the investors. If the business fails and the investment is lost, hurt feelings and resentment are common.

Another source of money for some new businesses is venture capital. **Venture capital** is money provided by large investors to finance new products and new businesses that have a good chance to be very profitable. In the late 1990s, many venture capital companies were formed.

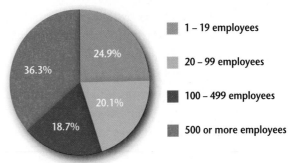

Employment Growth by Business Size 1990 – 2005

- 1 – 19 employees
- 20 – 99 employees
- 100 – 499 employees
- 500 or more employees

24.9%
36.3%
20.1%
18.7%

Source: U.S. Bureau of Labor Statistics

▶ **Figure 6-2**

What percentage of job growth came from businesses with fewer than 100 employees?

They supplied more than $100 billion each year to new businesses. Many of the businesses receiving those funds were e-commerce and high-tech start-ups. When many of those businesses failed, the amount of venture capital declined to less than $16 billion in 2009. More than 2,400 companies receive venture capital each year. That shows that many people think new businesses provide a good investment opportunity. The other sources of financing for new businesses are loans from banks and financial institutions and credit given by businesses that sell products and services to the new business.

Productivity

New and small businesses produce a large volume of goods and services for the economy. Businesses with just a single owner and no staff account for more than $770 billion in sales annually. Small businesses are responsible for more than half of the U.S. gross domestic product each year. They account for more than half of all innovative products and services developed.

Goal 2

Recognize the importance of entrepreneurship in the economy.

checkpoint ✓
What are the sources of financing that entrepreneurs use for their new businesses?

OPPORTUNITIES AND RISKS

When Jerelyn Frank was deciding whether she would open her own personal fitness business, she had to think about both the opportunities and the risks. Giving up a regular job and stable income is a difficult choice. As benefits, she will have personal control over her own business. She can take personal satisfaction if her idea develops into a successful, profitable company.

New Business Opportunities

The American private enterprise economy promotes innovation and new business development. Individuals are able to take the risk to start a new business. They can compete with other businesses to sell their products and services and make a profit. Consumers are always looking for new and better choices to meet their wants and needs.

Many opportunities are open to prospective entrepreneurs. The opportunities begin with the creation of new or improved products and services. An **innovation** is an invention or creation that is brand new. An **improvement** is a designed change that increases the usefulness of a product, service, or process.

Inventors often develop innovations. Those inventions may become the basis for a new business. The inventor may sell them to another company for development and sale. Examples of well-known innovations include the Apple personal computer developed by Steven Jobs and Stephen Wozniak and Post-it Notes created by Arthur Fry and Spencer Silver. Recent innovations that may become successful products include a miniaturized artificial heart, a virtual computer

What do innovation, invention, and improvement have to do with entrepreneurship opportunities?

©Corbis

keyboard, and an optical camouflage system that allows people wearing a special reflective material to seem to disappear.

In addition to inventions, innovators create new services that become the basis for a business. Frederick Smith envisioned an economical worldwide system for quickly and efficiently shipping packages. The creation of FedEx was the result. Mary Kay Ash founded Mary Kay Cosmetics and has helped more than 1.8 million business women worldwide. When the Internal Revenue Service no longer prepared individual tax returns for free, two brothers, Henry and Richard Bloch, created the H & R Block Company. They trained people to provide efficient, low-cost tax preparation services to individual taxpayers.

Not all entrepreneurship opportunities emerge from those types of inventions and innovations. Many come from an improved design, more effective procedures, or greater attention to quality. Entrepreneurs are creative problem-solvers. Those traits lead to ideas for improved products and services.

Recognizing Risks

Many successful entrepreneurs and their businesses are well known. Their success

WORK *as a* **TEAM**

New businesses usually need investments from other people. As a team, develop a list of questions you would ask an entrepreneur to determine if the new business would be one in which you would want to invest some of your money.

encourages others to think about starting a new business. Developing a successful new business is not easy. Many more new businesses fail than succeed. The time and energy required of new business owners is much higher than most people expect.

The National Federation of Independent Business reports that of all new businesses, about one-third are profitable, one-third do not make a profit but continue to operate, and the remaining third lose money. Over a 10-year period, more than 50 percent of all new businesses are discontinued. The primary reasons that businesses started by entrepreneurs close are

- Lack of adequate capital
- Low sales
- Higher than expected expenses

- Competitive pressure
- An owner unprepared to manage a growing business
- Operations requiring more time than the owner is willing to commit

Entrepreneurs need to be aware of the many risks they may face and prepare for them. Most entrepreneurs are willing to take risks. They will work hard to make their businesses succeed. However, many entrepreneurs have seen one or more of their business ideas fail before they are able to grow a successful company.

checkpoint ✓
Where do entrepreneurship opportunities begin?

6-1 Assessment

Key Concepts

Determine the best answer.

1. True or False. Everyone who owns or manages a business is an entrepreneur.

2. Which of the following is *not* a characteristic of entrepreneurship in the United States?
   a. About 3 percent of people aged 18–64 are involved in entrepreneurship activity.
   b. About 625,000 new businesses are created each year.
   c. About 25 percent of job growth comes from businesses with less than 20 employees.
   d. One in every five Americans has invested in a business of someone who they know well.

3. Money provided by large investors to finance new products and new businesses that have a good chance to be very profitable is known as
   a. a loan
   b. credit
   c. venture capital
   d. start-up funding

Make Academic Connections

4. **Math** Ronaldo Jacarda is opening a manufacturing business. It will produce a new type of USB flash storage card for cell phones and digital cameras. He has several sources for the money needed to start his business. Those sources and amounts are personal savings, $56,500; loans from family and friends, $38,000; venture capital investment, $128,000; bank loan, $22,500. Determine the total amount of capital he has accumulated and the percentage of that total from each of the sources. Prepare a pie chart that illustrates the answers.

5. **History** Use the Internet to identify important inventions and innovations developed in the past 50 years. Select the five you believe have had the greatest business success. Now select the five you believe have been most important in improving society. Prepare a short report in which you identify and briefly describe each of the inventions and innovations you selected and justifications for your choices.

6-2 Small Business Basics

Goals

1 Identify important characteristics of small businesses.

2 Recognize the competitive advantages of small businesses.

3 Identify problems faced by many small businesses.

Key Terms

small business 130

Small Business Administration (SBA) 134

Focus on REAL LIFE

During dinner, Jasmine excitedly told her family what happened in her Principles of Business class. The class had spent the time thinking about opportunities for owning a small business. Jasmine knew that is what she wanted to do.

Jasmine's grandfather said, "Did you know I ran a small business for almost 10 years when I was young? I was as excited as you are about starting a business when I graduated from high school. I went to work for the owner of a small hardware store. I hoped that I could save enough money to open my own store. Luckily, after eight years, he decided to retire. We worked out an arrangement where I could buy the store from him over a number of years."

"What happened to the business?" Jasmine asked.

"Being a small business owner is exciting, but it is a difficult life," explained her grandfather. "As the bigger stores moved in, I found it more and more difficult to attract customers. I decided to sell the business. I'm excited for you, but I want you to know that achieving your goals will be challenging."

> **Goal 1**
>
> Identify important characteristics of small businesses.

SMALL BUSINESS OWNERSHIP

Business is often viewed as very large corporations. These companies employ thousands of people with locations all over the country and the world. That is not the true picture of most businesses. By far the greatest percentage of businesses in the United States is small businesses. Small businesses employ more than 60 percent of all private sector employees.

You may be surprised by the definition of small business used by the federal government. According to the Small Business Administration (SBA), a **small business** is an independent business with fewer than 500 employees. Using that standard, 99.9 percent of the roughly 26 million U.S. businesses are small businesses.

A more specific description of a small business includes the following points.

- The owner is usually the manager.
- It operates in one or very few locations.
- It typically serves a small market.
- It is not dominant in its field.

Most people would probably not consider businesses with 500 employees to be small. Even if you use a standard of fewer than 100 employees, 25 million businesses fit that description. Nearly 19.5 million businesses have no staff other than the owner. Many of those businesses are run on a part-time basis from the owner's home. Twenty-two million businesses are set up as proprietorships. No matter how you identify small businesses, they are by far the greatest number of businesses operating today.

Small Business Employment

On average, small businesses are responsible for creating 60–80 percent of all new jobs. Figure 6-3 shows some of the common types of small business. It is not surprising that there are a large number of service businesses. Many small business services are professional and technical. Many construction companies operate as small businesses.

Ownership Diversity

Women own more than one-fourth of all small businesses. More than 17 percent of small businesses have African-American, Asian-American, or Hispanic-American ownership. The majority of small business owners are over 35 years old, but nearly 14 percent are under 35.

fyi *Small business owners report that the Internet is having a positive impact on their companies. In a recent survey, 51 percent said the Internet helped increase their profits and 49 percent said its use resulted in reduced operating costs.*

Today, almost all people starting small businesses have at least a high school diploma. Nearly 64 percent have finished some college work.

Half of all small businesses are home-based businesses. Because many businesses are part-time ventures or service businesses, the owners report that on average they needed $5,000 or less to start that type of business. Full-time businesses with buildings, equipment, and employees may require more than $100,000 of initial capital.

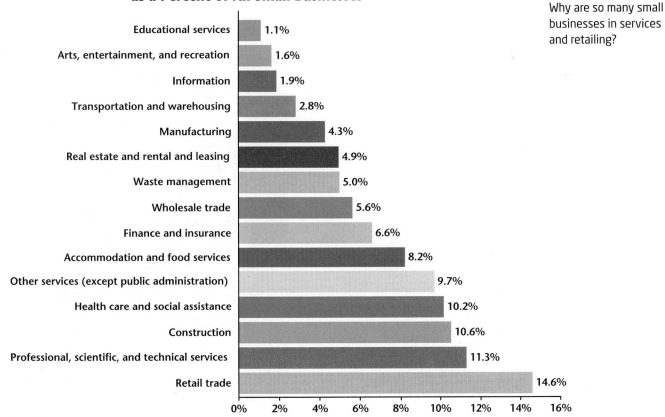

Common Types of Small Businesses as a Percent of All Small Businesses

Type	Percent
Educational services	1.1%
Arts, entertainment, and recreation	1.6%
Information	1.9%
Transportation and warehousing	2.8%
Manufacturing	4.3%
Real estate and rental and leasing	4.9%
Waste management	5.0%
Wholesale trade	5.6%
Finance and insurance	6.6%
Accommodation and food services	8.2%
Other services (except public administration)	9.7%
Health care and social assistance	10.2%
Construction	10.6%
Professional, scientific, and technical services	11.3%
Retail trade	14.6%

Source: U.S. Census Bureau

▶ **Figure 6-3**

Why are so many small businesses in services and retailing?

checkpoint ✓
Beyond the formal definition of a small business, what four points can be used to describe a small business?

Goal 2

Recognize the competitive advantages of small businesses.

SMALL BUSINESS ADVANTAGES

You need someone to mow your lawn, make a gourmet meal in your home for a few close friends, build a custom display case for a model train, or repair hardware on your home computer. Where would you turn for help? It's not likely that you will find a large business for any of those services.

Meeting Customer Needs

Small businesses play a vital role in the economy. They often serve customers where the number of products and services needed is small or the requirements are too specialized for large businesses to make a profit. It is easier for a small business to meet the precise needs of customers than a large business. Even though a large business has more resources, to operate efficiently it must focus on products and services that meet the needs of a large group of customers. That makes it harder to satisfy the unique needs of single customers.

Small businesses often are not able to match the lower operating costs of larger businesses. They can compete by paying attention to their customers. Small businesses serve fewer customers and usually have more frequent contact with those customers than large businesses. They are more likely to be located close to the customer. They depend less on other businesses to distribute or service their products.

Large businesses often rely on consumer research to gather information. Small businesses usually get direct information from their customers about what they like and dislike.

Providing Unique Services

Small businesses are especially suited to provide unique services for customers. They may plan a wedding or design a customized sound system for your home. Providing those types of services means that business representatives must take a special interest in the customer. They spend time determining needs and discussing alternatives. They have the expertise to plan and deliver the services that satisfy the customer. Large businesses may not find it profitable to spend that much time with each customer. Each employee that works with customers may not have the expertise to design the needed service.

Big business has a clear advantage when a large number of customers are

How do small businesses provide unique services that large businesses cannot?

CandyBoxPhoto/Shutterstock.com

willing to buy standard products and prefer low cost and efficient delivery. Small businesses gain an advantage when customers have unique needs, want more individual attention, and are willing to pay a bit more for the product or service to obtain what they really want. When asked, "What businesses do you believe are most concerned about you as a customer?" the majority of consumers identify small businesses.

> **checkpoint** ✓
> How can small businesses compete successfully with larger businesses?

COMMON SMALL BUSINESS PROBLEMS

Not all small businesses succeed. In fact, their failure rate is much higher than larger businesses. Many failures result from the inability to pay expenses. The business is then forced to close. Some companies quietly go out of business when the owner believes that he or she is not doing well enough to continue. The owner may also get tired of the long hours and hard work.

Reasons for Failure

The following are the most common reasons for small business failure:

- Not keeping adequate records
- Not having enough start-up money
- Lack of management experience
- Lack of experience with the type of business
- Not controlling operating expenses
- Poor location for the business
- Failure to manage credit offered to customers

WORK *as a* **TEAM**

Identify two or three small businesses in your community that have been successful for many years. As a team, discuss what you think these businesses do that allows them to compete successfully with other small and large businesses.

Small Business Assistance

With the right kind of assistance, small businesses can overcome each of the causes of failure listed above. Small business owners can get help from a number of sources. Universities and colleges

> **Goal 3**
> Identify problems faced by many small businesses.

What do you think would be the hardest part of managing a small business?

Where can small businesses find assistance?

The **Small Business Administration (SBA)** is a government agency that helps small business owners develop business plans and obtain financing and other support for their companies. Information about the SBA and its services can be obtained by visiting www.sba.gov.

The SBA offers information, publications, counseling, and many other forms of support. The SBA sponsors the Service Corps of Retired Executives (SCORE). Members of SCORE are retired local businesspeople who volunteer their services to counsel and mentor new business owners.

often have faculty members who can give advice and support to people who are starting or have started their own businesses. Local groups of businesspeople, such as Chambers of Commerce, have members who can help others with business problems.

checkpoint ✓
List common reasons for small business failure.

6-2 Assessment

Study Tools
www.cengage.com/school/genbus/pob

Key Concepts

Determine the best answer.

1. The Small Business Administration considers a business small if it employs fewer than _?_ employees.
   a. 5
   b. 20
   c. 100
   d. 500

2. A competitive advantage that small businesses have over larger businesses is
   a. lower costs
   b. more consumer research
   c. lower prices
   d. attention to unique customer needs

3. Which of the following is not one of the reasons small business fail?
   a. poor customer credit practices
   b. the owner does not have adequate experience
   c. a poor business location
   d. not enough employees to do the work

Make Academic Connections

4. **Technology** eBay has become the home of many small businesses. Thousands of small business owners earn an excellent income by selling their products using the online auction services provided by eBay. Visit the eBay website and identify three ways a small business can use the website to support its operations.

5. **Communication** Interview a small business owner who has operated his or her business for at least three years. Determine the factors that have contributed to success as well as the major challenges that have been faced. Prepare an audio or video presentation based on your interview.

6. **Research** Interview 10 people who have recently purchased products or services from a small business. Ask them to list the top three reasons they made the purchase from a small business rather than a large business. Summarize the results from your interviews and present your findings in a table or chart.

Information, Communications, and Technology Literacy

Writing with Technology

Today's technology allows written communication to be exchanged at a much faster pace. Traditional forms of written communication, including letters, reports, and brochures, have not changed. However, when composed and completed, they can be sent to recipients in minutes using the Internet.

Many uses of traditional written communication have been replaced by instantaneous informal communications including e-mail, texting, and other new media. The immediate nature of the technology as well as the informal approach to composing those messages often result in poor communication or even miscommunication. When you use technology for written communication, especially in business, a few basic rules will demonstrate to your recipients that they are important and you want to communicate effectively.

The two primary types of communication used in business are memos and e-mail messages. Memos are formal and are used to convey more complex information. Send a memo when there is a need for a more permanent record of your correspondence or there is a need for formal language, or if the information included would make an e-mail too long. E-mail is more informal and used for direct and brief communication. Here are some important guidelines.

When Composing a Memo

1. *Know your audience.* Direct your memo to one person or a small group of people. Who needs the information? What do they need to know?

2. *Focus on one specific subject.* Make sure the subject is important to the audience. Specifically identify the subject of the memo. Do not stray into other topics.

3. *Select your words carefully.* Use language appropriate for the organization and understandable to your audience. Be clear, direct, and objective.

4. *Start strong.* Have an attention-getting first sentence. Focus the attention of the reader and get to the point.

5. *Provide only needed information.* Keep the memo brief, usually no more than one page, so it can be read in a few minutes. Before you end, be sure the information is complete.

6. *End effectively.* Identify any action needed and emphasize the importance of the information.

When Composing an E-mail Message

1. *Send only to the people who need the information.* Do not "reply to all" or use a mass e-mail list. Use e-mail for more individualized and specific messages.

2. *Use a specific subject line.* People get many e-mails. They can read and respond more efficiently if they can identify a clear subject.

3. *Provide a context.* If you are responding to an e-mail, briefly identify the information to which you are responding. Provide any information needed by the reader to understand your message.

4. *Don't get caught up in the technology.* Avoid "flaming" with all caps or inserting emoticons, flashing text, or other gimmicks that detract from the information.

5. *Keep the message short.* An e-mail should be read in about a minute. If the message is longer, send it in a different format or add an attachment or link.

6. *Don't write in haste.* You may regret an emotional message sent in haste. Consider the effect your message may have on the recipient.

7. *Even when informal, use effective writing skills.* Write in complete, active sentences, organize using paragraphs, and check your spelling.

8. *Use e-mail to create a record.* E-mail servers hold records of your files, even after you think they are deleted. If you need a record of a memo, use e-mail.

Think Critically

1. When should you send a memo rather than an e-mail?

2. What are the communication problems that are most likely to occur when using instant communication methods?

Starting a Small Business

Goals

1 Recognize important factors to be considered when starting a business.

2 Describe the elements of a business plan.

3 Identify types and sources of financing for a small business.

Key Terms

business plan 138

start-up financing 139

short-term financing 140

long-term financing 140

Focus on REAL LIFE

Quinn turned his baseball card hobby into a business. He had a small store where he bought and sold baseball cards and memorabilia. Quinn began his business with a small bank loan and money saved from working while in college.

The business grew steadily and Quinn prepared a specific budget at the start of each year. He was able to spend his money on inventory, advertising, and improvements to his store.

This year he used the same budgeting process that he had for the past four years. Based on last year's results, he estimated a sales increase of 8 percent. Even with the increased expenses, the budget projected another nice profit.

The first two months of the year went well. Then the economy faltered and customers cut back on spending. Quinn's sales declined while his expenses continued to increase. Quinn studied his budget to determine why he had problems in the fifth year when his planning had been so successful in the past.

Goal 1

Recognize important factors to be considered when starting a business.

THE BUSINESS DECISION

Many people think about starting a business. Few actually do. The procedures followed to start a business often determine whether it will be successful. The process begins with an idea and concludes with a careful study of information to establish whether the idea can be successful.

An Idea Plus Experience

Business ideas come from many sources. Hobbies, interests, and business experiences often give people ideas for new businesses. Books and magazines suggest new business opportunities, including available franchises. Few people should think about starting a business without working for some time in a small business. Several years of training in a range of business operations will prepare you for the role of owner. Having responsibility for decisions and opportunities to manage people is a key part of that experience.

Right Place and Time

Putting your business idea into action means finding the right place to open the business. Most retail businesses need good customer traffic. If the business is not easy to find or requires a great deal of travel time, many potential customers will stay away. A wholesaler needs easy

What hobbies, interests, and experiences do you have that could help you achieve your life-span goals? Describe steps you could take now that would expand your experiences and opportunities for achieving your life-span goals.

---

access to manufacturers where products are obtained for resale to other businesses. Manufacturers must be located in an area with access to the raw materials used in manufacturing. Transportation systems must also be easy to reach for distributing finished products. Timing is another key factor in starting a business. Most successful businesses start during a period when customer demand for certain products or services is high.

Team Approach

Many small business owners are quite independent. They started their businesses because they do not want to take direction from other people. A business is not easy to run without the help of others. Even the smallest businesses need a few full- or part-time employees to grow or cover extended hours. The employees must be chosen carefully for their ability to work as a team. Choosing the "team" members becomes one of the most important initial business decisions.

In addition to employees, small business owners will need assistance from people with specialized business knowledge. These include bankers, lawyers, and accountants. If possible, the new owner should identify business professionals who focus on working with small businesses.

Preparation and Research

The most important step in starting a business is preparation. Preparation includes having enough information to make good decisions about the business. Time spent gathering and studying information before the

WORK as a TEAM

You are planning to open a small business that will rent bicycles, rollerblades, push scooters, and electric scooters by the hour for people to use for relaxation and exercise. As a team, identify three possible business locations in your community and discuss which location would be best for the business. Prepare a presentation that compares and contrasts the locations. Use visuals such as maps, photos, and drawings to help illustrate your presentation.

business is started will save time and avoid later problems.

Information is needed about customers, competitors, important operations, government regulations, and many other topics. This information is available through libraries, colleges or universities, and small business assistance centers. At times, the new business owner will have to do further research to gather more current data. Information will help to make sure that decisions are made objectively.

Is there a small business assistance center in your neighborhood? What resources can you use to locate the closest center?

Photodisc/Getty Images

checkpoint ✓

Why is it important to use a team approach when starting a new business?

DEVELOPING A BUSINESS PLAN

When successful businesses are compared with those that fail, one factor stands out as the most important difference. The owners of successful businesses develop and follow a business plan. The owners of businesses that fail often do not have a business plan.

What Is a Business Plan?

A **business plan** is a written description of the business idea and how it will be carried out, including all major business activities. Key features of a business plan are a general description of the company, the credentials of the owner(s), a description of the product or service, an analysis of the market (demand, customers, and competition), and a financial plan. Most business plans are developed for one year and then updated for the next year. If the business owner needs help from others, especially for financing the new business, a business plan will usually be required. Figure 6-4 is an outline of the sections of a business plan.

Even if help is not needed, a business plan should be developed. By developing a plan, the owner is forced to think about important activities, the amount of time they will take, and their cost. This process may identify potential problems. The plan also serves as a guide to keep the business on track.

Steps in Developing the Business Plan

The business owner is in charge of developing the business plan. The most popular use of business plans is to persuade lenders and investors to finance the venture. A well-developed plan will lay out an idea and will require an owner to analyze his or her concept and make decisions about key business activities such as production, marketing, staffing, and financing.

Some owners hire someone to write the plan. Others get help from a bank or a local office of the Small Business Administration. Even if others are involved in developing the plan, the owner must be familiar with all of the information and make the major decisions for the plan.

The first step in developing the business plan is to gather and review information. If possible, the owner should review other business plans and study information on the activities and financial

---

ELEMENTS OF A BUSINESS PLAN

Description of the Business
- the business idea
- major products and services
- ownership structure
- strengths/weaknesses
- long- and short-term goals

Customer Analysis
- description of customers
- location, number, and resources of customers
- sales forecasts

Operations Plan
- organization of the company
- description of major operations
- analysis of resources needed
- human resource plans

Marketing Plan
- description of major marketing activities
- description of resources needed
- schedule of marketing activities

Financial Plans
- start-up costs
- short- and long-term financial needs
- sources of financing
- budgets and financial statements

▶ **Figure 6-4**

Why are each of these elements important when planning a new business?

Where can the entrepreneur find help in creating a business plan?

Digital Vison/Getty Images

performance of similar businesses, especially potential competitors.

Next, the owner should develop strategic alternatives. Alternative plans for production, marketing, staffing, and financing should be studied and identified. The owner can select the best choices from the alternatives.

Finally, each section of the business plan should be written. A plan devotes several sections to a general description of the business. These sections include the basic legal form of the organization and major products or services. Other sections detail the competition, potential customers, operations, marketing, and finances. Before the plan is completed, the owner should have business experts review the plan and offer their advice about its strengths and weaknesses.

> **checkpoint ✓**
> What are "strategic alternatives" in a business plan?

FINANCING THE SMALL BUSINESS

A new business with a good product or service may run out of money before it can become profitable. Several years of operation are required before most new businesses earn a profit. Finding adequate financing is a key step in starting and running a new business.

Types of Financing

Three types of financing must be considered. **Start-up financing** is the amount

> **Goal 3**
>
> Identify types and sources of financing for a small business.

Joel Calheiros/Shutterstock.com

of money needed to open the business. It includes the cost of buildings, equipment, *inventory* (products or raw materials on hand), supplies, licenses, and the like. **Short-term financing** is the money needed to pay for the current operating activities of a business. Short-term financing is obtained for a period of less than a year and often for one or two months.

Long-term financing is money needed for the main resources of a business (such as land, buildings, and equipment) that will last for many years. These resources usually require large amounts of money and will be paid over many years.

Sources of Financing

Finding the needed money may be the most difficult part of starting a business. The money required to start and operate a new business usually comes from a mixture of owner-supplied and borrowed funds.

The source of owner-supplied money depends on the ownership structure. In a proprietorship, one person will supply the money. In most partnerships each

Business Insight for the 21st Century

Global Social Responsibility

Many Europeans are concerned about their personal health and the health of their environment. In part, this concern is based on Europe's high population density. There are 3.6 times as many people per square mile in Europe as there are in the United States. Europe's high population density has led to concerns about waste disposal, air quality, and the availability of natural resources such as fresh water.

Some businesses based in the United States and doing business in Europe are working hard to address the concerns of European customers and governments, including that of the European Union. McDonald's wants to be seen as a socially responsible company and is developing

policies and practices to address concerns about the nutritional value of its products and the impact of its operations on the environment.

Throughout Europe, McDonald's prints nutrition information directly on food containers and wrappers. This means consumers can see information about calories, fat, and sodium as they pluck fries out of the cardboard pouch.

McDonald's has launched an environmental initiative in southern England to convert used cooking oil into biodiesel. The fuel is used to power the company's delivery vehicles. This program removes cooking oil from the waste stream and reduces the consumption of gasoline.

Think Critically

1. What motivates U.S. companies to tailor their policies and practices to address the social concerns of global customers?

2. Research another company's efforts to be socially responsible and address social concerns around the world. Develop a short presentation about your findings.

3. Use the Internet to locate McDonald's Worldwide Corporate Values in Action website. Write a summary of one of the programs mentioned on the website.

partner will be expected to contribute. A corporation is owned and financed by the shareholders.

Borrowed funds are obtained through loans from banks and other financial institutions or through funding provided by other people, such as family and friends. Often companies that sell equipment, materials, or inventory to a business will offer credit if the business does not have financial problems. A new business owner should be careful about accepting credit. The owner must take into account the cost of the credit and when payments are due.

MichaelDeLeon/iStockphoto.com

Why would a lending institution insist that the money required for starting a business be a mixture of owner-supplied and borrowed funds?

checkpoint ✓

In addition to owner-supplied capital, what are several other sources of financing for a small business?

6-3 Assessment

Study Tools
www.cengage.com/school/genbus/pob

Key Concepts

Determine the best answer.

1. Every business begins with a(n)
   a. customer
   b. profit
   c. idea
   d. invention

2. True or False. Most small business owners enjoy being part of a team.

3. True or False. A business plan does not have to be written because the business owner is well aware of the information in the plan.

4. Money needed for the important resources of a business (such as land, buildings, and equipment) that will last for many years is called
   a. start-up financing
   b. short-term financing
   c. long-term financing
   d. credit

Make Academic Connections

5. **Technology** Locate an outline for a business plan on the Internet. Compare the sections of the plan you found with those in Figure 6-4. Develop a final outline using both resources. Write a two-sentence statement for each section of the outline describing why that section is important to a successful small business.

6. **Math** Gwen Osterhaus and Portia Juarez have formed a partnership to open a garden coffee cafe in Central Park. Gwen invests $23,000 and Portia invests $31,000. They get a micro loan from the Small Business Administration for $18,500. They have $9,000 of credit from the Bean Machine Company that sold them some of their equipment. Calculate the total amount of start-up financing available to the partnership. Make a pie chart that shows the percentage of total financing that is provided from each source. How much of the financing is owner supplied and how much is borrowed?

Business Notes

6-1 Becoming an Entrepreneur

- Successful entrepreneurs have a real desire to be their own boss. They use special skills and abilities to come up with innovative ideas and then develop a good initial plan for a business. Entrepreneurs come from all age categories, racial and ethnic groups, and both genders, as well as varied educational levels.

- Entrepreneurship is a key part of the U.S. economy. Money needed to start a new business may come from the owner, family, friends, or venture capital. Other sources of financing are loans from banks and financial institutions and credit given by other businesses. Small businesses are responsible for nearly half of the U.S. gross domestic product each year and more than half of all innovative products and services developed.

- Opportunities open to entrepreneurs include the creation of new or improved products and services, an improved design, more effective procedures, or greater attention to quality. Risks include lack of adequate capital, low sales, higher than expected expenses, competitive pressure, an owner unprepared to manage a growing business, and operations that require more time than the owner is willing to commit.

6-2 Small Business Basics

- In a small business, the owner is usually the manager, it operates in one or very few locations, it typically serves a small market, and it is not dominant in its field of operation.

- Small businesses play an important role in the economy. They often serve customers where the number of products and services needed is small or the requirements are too specialized for large businesses to be profitable.

- The most common reasons for small business failure are not keeping adequate records, not having enough start-up money, lack of management experience, lack of experience with the type of business, not controlling operating expenses, poor location for the business, and failure to manage customer credit.

6-3 Starting a Small Business

- Factors that lead to a successful new business are an idea plus experience, the right time and place, a team approach, and preparation and research.

- By developing a written business plan, the owner will think about important activities, the amount of time they will take, and their cost. The plan also serves as a guide to keep the business on track.

- Obtaining adequate financing is an important step in starting and operating a new business. Three types of financing to be considered are start-up, short-term, and long-term financing. The money required to start and operate a new business usually comes from a mixture of owner-supplied and borrowed funds.

Communicate Business Concepts

1. What is a new product or service that could become the basis for a new business that fits your interests, hobbies, or special skills and abilities? What are some reasons you would be interested or not interested in becoming an entrepreneur?

2. Why do you believe that small businesses contribute more of the new jobs to the economy than large established businesses?

3. What are factors that you believe contributed to the success of the young entrepreneurs described in Lesson 6-1? Do you believe the idea for their product or service was more or less important than their personal characteristics?

4. How is the Internet changing the characteristics of small businesses? Do you believe the Internet can make small businesses more competitive with large businesses? Why?

5. Freddie is thinking about starting a small business and has come to you for advice. Using the reasons why most small businesses fail as listed in Lesson 6-2, what would you tell Freddie that will help him increase his chances for being successful?

6. In most communities, there are several locations where retail businesses locate but soon fail. They are followed by other businesses that also fail. People say the pattern of failure is because of a poor location. Do you agree that the location is the most likely reason that the businesses fail? Why would a new business consider a location where a previous business has already failed?

7. Identify the three types of people you believe would be the most important to assist a new small business owner. Justify each of your choices.

8. If you were a banker reviewing a business plan to determine if you will provide financing, what information would be most important in determining if you would support the small business or not?

9. What are the advantages and disadvantages of hiring another experienced person to develop and write the business plan for the owner of a new business?

Develop Your Business Language

Match the terms listed with the definitions.

10. A government agency that helps small business owners develop business plans and obtain financing and other support for their companies.

11. Money provided by large investors to finance new products and new businesses that have a good chance to be very profitable.

12. The money needed to pay for the current operating activities of a business.

13. The amount of money needed to open the business.

14. An invention or creation that is brand new.

15. Someone who takes a risk in starting a business to earn a profit.

16. A written description of the business idea and how it will be carried out, including all major business activities.

17. Money needed for the important resources of a business (such as land, buildings, and equipment) that will last for many years.

18. An independent business with fewer than 500 employees.

19. A designed change that increases the usefulness of a product, service, or process.

20. The process of starting, organizing, managing, and assuming the responsibility for a business.

> ### Key Terms
> a. business plan
> b. entrepreneur
> c. entrepreneurship
> d. improvement
> e. innovation
> f. long-term financing
> g. short-term financing
> h. small business
> i. Small Business Administration (SBA)
> j. start-up financing
> k. venture capital

Make Academic Connections

21. Communication Many small business owners obtain some of their start-up financing from family members and friends. Assume you are starting a small Internet business that will develop and maintain low-cost websites for local organizations, clubs, and nonprofit groups. You have $2,500 of your own money to invest and need to raise an additional $5,000. Develop a letter or one-page brochure that you can use to interest family and friends in investing $500 or more in your new business. Make sure it is persuasive and tells them what benefits they will receive from their investment.

22. Government The federal government and most state governments provide many resources as well as financial support for small businesses. Use the Internet to locate two agencies of the federal government that provide services developed specifically for small businesses. Then search the website for your state's government and locate one state agency that provides small business services. Prepare a three-paragraph report on each of the agencies you identified in which you describe the agency, the services provided, and how a new business can qualify for the services.

23. Economics The U.S. Census Bureau maintains information on the number of businesses and amount of business activity in every county of each state. Access the U.S. Census Bureau website and then search for "County Business Patterns." Choose your state and then choose the county where you live. Find data on the number of businesses with one to four employees in your county. List the total number of businesses of that size, the five industries with the most businesses employing fewer than five employees, and the total number of establishments in each of those industries.

24. Technology Use the Internet to identify the number of small business owners by age. Then enter the information in a spreadsheet program and calculate the percentage of all small business owners represented by each age classification. Then use the graphing function to create a chart or graph illustrating the results.

Decision-Making Strategies

David Obolski completed a community college program in Small Business Management. He now wanted to own his own floral business. He had worked for Flower-a-Bunda during high school and college. In addition, he was able to save almost $20,000 toward starting his own business. However, he knew that he would need more than $20,000 to buy a florist shop. He would need almost double that amount to qualify for the necessary loans to start up the business. David studied three ways he might start his business.

    a. He could find a partner to provide the additional cash.

b. He could work for the owner of Flower-a-Bunda until she retired in seven years and buy the business with his accumulated savings.

c. He could purchase a franchise for an investment of $20,000. However, David would have to pay a franchise fee of 6 percent of total sales each year to the franchisor.

25. What are the advantages and disadvantages of each route to small business ownership for David?

26. If you were David, which choice would you make? Why?

Linking School and Community

Survey at least 10 people in your community about their experiences as consumers with small businesses and large businesses. Ask them to describe the reasons they prefer to buy from small businesses and the reasons they prefer to buy from large businesses. Then ask them to describe the disadvantages of each. Summarize the results of your discussions in a chart or short written report.

Web Workout

The Internet is the ultimate niche small business platform. The Internet can bring together sellers and individual buyers at a very low cost. Many small businesses, including home-based businesses, use portals such as Amazon.com and eBay to sell their products. This way, the small business owners do not need to set up their own website or e-commerce system.

Think Critically

1. Use the Internet to find a niche seller (a product with a very narrow appeal). Determine if the seller uses a sales portal (like Amazon.com or eBay) or if the business has its own website.

2. Identify a niche product that you would like to sell. Develop a short business plan to determine if it would be better to sell through a sales portal or by developing your own website.

Desktop Publishing Event

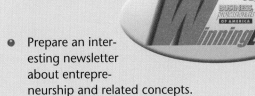

You and a partner have been hired to create, design, and produce a business publication using desktop publishing software. You have two hours of class time to prepare a newsletter that focuses attention on entrepreneurship, small business management, time management tips, professional networking, and successful entrepreneurs. The target audience for your newsletter includes entrepreneurs, student business leaders, and community leaders. Content of the newsletter must be up-to-date and relevant. The newsletter should provide solid tips for successful entrepreneurs. Your team is allowed to use two computers, a scanner, and clip art. No other equipment may be used. The finished product may be submitted in black and white or in color on plain paper. Word division manuals and dictionaries may be used as reference materials. The second part of this competition includes a one-hour written objective test to determine your knowledge of desktop publishing. The score received on the test will equal 15 percent of the final event score.

Performance Indicators Evaluated

- Understand graphics, text creation, layout, creativity, and selection of appropriate fonts and type sizes for desktop publishing.

- Prepare an interesting newsletter about entrepreneurship and related concepts.
- Incorporate graphics and layout that are visually appealing.
- Use correct punctuation, grammar, and sentence structure.
- Demonstrate creativity throughout the publication.

For more detailed information about performance indicators, go to the FBLA website.

Think Critically

1. What characteristics make a great publication?
2. What can be done to make a publication reader-friendly?
3. Who should be considered when producing a publication?
4. Give two examples of items in a newsletter that might be distracting to readers.

www.fbla-pbl.org

Management and Leadership

The career choice you make will likely be driven by your interests and abilities. People who are focused on a specific field such as accounting, sales, nursing, or biomedical engineering may or may not have aspirations to become managers. However, many people start their business careers with the goal of becoming a manager some day. They view the chance to move up and contribute to major decisions as a challenging goal.

Managers are key to the success of a company. Management opportunities exist in all companies and in every part of a business. Whether your interests are in finance, marketing, information management, engineering, or human resources, you can become a manager.

You can take the first step by accepting a role such as a team leader. You can then advance to a position as a supervisor or assistant manager after only a few years of experience. With additional experience, and perhaps some additional education, you can become a mid- or top-level manager. Your career advancement will be based on how well you perform management duties and your contribution to the overall success of the business.

Related Job Titles

- Administrator
- Assistant Manager
- Coordinator
- Department Head
- Project Manager
- Supervisor

Analyze Career Opportunities in ...

MANAGEMENT

Use library and Internet resources to learn more about careers in management. Choose one of the job titles listed in the box above and answer the following questions.

1. What is the employment outlook for careers in this field?

2. Is this a career that interests you? Describe a few things you could do to learn more about this career.

What's it like to work as a ... Supervisor?

Although Frank enjoys his job as the supervisor of a production line at the Emprex Corporation, today will be challenging. This morning, Frank needs to interview nine people to fill three full-time positions and one part-time position. This afternoon he is meeting with his team to talk about overtime and budgets.

Frank needs to let his work group know that they will have to work at least 10 hours of overtime each week for the next two months to meet their quota. Some team members will be happy about the extra money but others will complain about giving up their free time.

He also needs to talk to his group about the budget. He doesn't have full authority over the budget, but his manager has asked him to help find ways to reduce expenses.

Finally, Frank has to complete one of his least favorite duties—terminating an employee. A new employee has not been able to meet the job expectations and has to be let go. Frank has a meeting scheduled at 3 P.M. with the employee to break the news.

What about you? What would you find the most and least enjoyable about Frank's work?

7-1 Management Functions and Styles

Goals

1 Define the five functions of management.

2 Describe the levels of management in businesses and organizations.

3 Discuss how and when to use the two management styles.

Key Terms

management 148

planning 148

organizing 148

staffing 149

implementing 149

controlling 149

management style 151

Focus on REAL LIFE

Have you considered a career in management? Do you realize that you might already have experience with activities that are similar in some aspects to those of a managers' work? You manage your time and your money. You might be a leader of a team or organization. Maybe you have taken a leadership role in a group activity. As a leader you probably took responsibility, gave directions, and solved problems.

While not the same as leading a business, these activities give you a taste of the work of managers. Consider what it would be like to be responsible for a million-dollar budget, directing the work of hundreds of people, or making sure an important project involving several parts of a business is completed on schedule.

Do you think you have what it takes to be a manager? Would you find working as a manager exciting as well as challenging? If so, what can you do now to begin to prepare for a management career?

Goal 1

Define the five functions of management.

ROLE AND WORK OF MANAGERS

Managers are responsible for the success or failure of businesses and organizations. Managers receive recognition and other rewards when a business meets its goals. They also are held accountable when goals are not met. People who want to experience the risks and rewards of leading a business often become managers.

Who Is a Manager?

Management is the process of accomplishing the goals of an organization through the effective use of people and other resources. Managers make things happen in businesses. The entrepreneur who develops the idea for a new business is a manager. The top executive of a multi-million dollar business who must make the final decision on a plan to enter

a new international market is a manager. Supervisors with responsibility for the work of a small number of employees are managers, as are vice presidents with hundreds of employees reporting to them.

What Do Managers Do?

Every manager has specific job duties, but all managers must complete similar activities no matter what the size or type of organization. Managers' work can be organized within five functions: planning, organizing, staffing, implementing, and controlling.

- **Planning** involves analyzing information, setting goals, and making decisions about what needs to be done.

- **Organizing** means identifying and arranging the work and resources needed to achieve the goals that have been set.

- **Staffing** includes all of the activities involved in obtaining, preparing, and compensating the people who work for a business.

- **Implementing** is the effort to direct and lead people to accomplish the planned work of the organization.

- **Controlling** determines to what extent the business is accomplishing the goals it set out to reach in the planning stage.

Large businesses and organizations have many managers. Responsibilities for specific management functions are assigned to each manager. Often, due to the size of a business, several managers may have responsibilities within just one of the functions. If a business is owned by more than one person, the management functions are usually divided among the owners based on the type of work each enjoys and does well. In a new small business, the owner usually is responsible for all of the management functions. As the business grows, other employees will be

WORK as a TEAM

Your class is responsible for picking up litter on a highway on the edge of your town. Your team has responsibility for managing that project. For each of the five management functions, identify two or three management activities that your team must complete in order for the project to be successful.

moved into management positions. They will be assigned one or more of the management functions to complete.

Managing a business or even a part of a business can be a very complex process. Managers must make decisions, solve problems, respond to competition, and develop new strategies. Decisions made to complete one management function often affect other functions. The efforts of each manager impact the work of others. Effective managers motivate employees to do their best work. They also use the money and other resources of the business wisely. Successful businesses must have managers who are able to complete each of the management functions well.

> **checkpoint ✓**
> What are the five management functions?

Think of a business in your neighborhood. What levels of management do you think exist there?

Creatas/Getty Images

MANAGEMENT LEVELS

Unless a business is very small, there will be several managers with responsibilities for the success of the business. Every manager devotes some time to each of the management functions and has authority over other people and their work. Not every manager gives the same amount of attention and time to each of the functions. Most organizations have three levels of managers—executives, middle managers and supervisors.

Goal 2

Describe the levels of management in businesses and organizations.

Top Management

Executives are top-level managers with responsibilities for the direction and success of the entire business. They set long-term direction and plans. They are held accountable for the profitability and success of the business. Job titles of executives include chief executive officer, president, chief operating officer, and vice president.

Executives spend most of their time on planning and controlling activities. They study the economy and competition. They approve all major business decisions and expenditures. Executives are responsible for the work of all other managers and employees.

Middle Management

Middle managers are specialists with responsibilities for specific parts of a company's operations. Examples of middle management jobs are marketing manager, information technology manager, customer service manager, operations manager, and human resources manager. Middle managers work with the company's business plan once it has been approved by executives and develop specific plans for their part of the business. They must coordinate their work with other managers. Much of their time is devoted to the organizing, staffing, and implementing functions.

Supervisors

Supervisors are the first level of management in a business. They are responsible for the day-to-day work of a small group of employees. They help employees plan

their work and monitor their activities and results. They make sure that needed resources are available and used wisely. Supervisors must evaluate the quality of the work of their employees and help to solve problems that occur in their area. Supervisors spend most of their time implementing the plans of executives and middle managers. They may have non-management duties in addition to their management work.

Management by Others

Employees who are not managers may complete work that seems to be a part of one of the management functions. Employees plan and organize their work. They might take part in hiring and training new employees. They may evaluate the quality of the work they complete. However, managers are responsible for the work of others and have authority over those employees. Without that authority and responsibility, the work of an employee is not considered management.

Some experienced employees are asked to serve as leaders in their work group. They may lead a project or oversee the work of a new employee.

Many companies organize employees into work teams. Those teams have both authority and responsibility for much of their work. The team meets to make plans, determine how work will be completed, and divide the work among the team members. The team is responsible for meeting objectives and may even have some say about their budget. Work teams still report to a manager and can ask for assistance when needed.

Both work group leaders and employee teams complete a limited number of management activities. Both situations are effective ways for employees to develop experience with management activities. They can help to develop the skills needed by managers and increase their interest in a management career.

checkpoint ✓

What are the differences among the three levels of management?

MANAGEMENT STYLES

Managing a group of people can be a difficult job. Mangers must often get people with different backgrounds, personalities, and experience to work well together. Have you been a part of an athletic team or musical group? If so, you can remember how hard it was at first to coordinate the talents of each group member so the team or group performed well.

Managers approach the task of directing a group in different ways based on their management style. **Management style** is the way a manager works with and involves employees. Two very different styles often used by managers are tactical management and strategic management.

Sometimes a management style is chosen based on the characteristics of the employees being managed. At other times, the choice is based on the work assignment. Figure 7-1 describes situations where each style will be more effective. Experienced and effective managers can change their management style. It should

As an employee, which management style would you prefer from your supervisor?

be based on the urgency of the work to be done and the confidence the manager has in the employees.

Tactical Management Sometimes managers are faced with a crisis. They feel they don't have time to let the group decide how to complete the task. In other situations, a manager may be working with a group of new employees or may have work for which the members have no previous experience. In those situations, the manager should use tactical management. *Tactical management* is a style in which the manager is more directive and

Goal 3

Discuss how and when to use the two management styles.

CHOOSING A MANAGEMENT STYLE	
A MANAGER SHOULD USE TACTICAL MANAGEMENT WHEN	**A MANAGER SHOULD USE STRATEGIC MANAGEMENT WHEN**
• Working with part-time or temporary employees	• Employees are skilled and experienced
• Working with employees who lack motivation for a new task	• The work is routine with few new challenges
• Working under tight time pressures	• Employees are doing work they enjoy
• Assigning a new task for which employees are not experienced	• The manager wants to improve group relationships
• Employees prefer not to be involved in decision-making	• Employees are willing to take responsibility for planning their work

▶ **Figure 7-1**

Why is tactical management appropriate when assigning a new task that must be completed quickly?

controlling. The manager will make the major decisions and stay in close contact with employees while they work to make sure the work is done well.

Strategic Management When a group of employees is experienced and works well together, a manager does not have to be as directive and controlling. If there is enough time to bring a team together to help plan a work assignment, team members will often prefer being involved in the decision-making process. These are examples of the use of strategic management. *Strategic management* is a style in which managers are more collaborative and involve employees in decision making. A manager using a strategic style expects employees to work without direct supervision and will seek their input on important decisions.

Mixed Management Which of the two management styles would you prefer if you were an employee? If you were a manager, which of the styles would you use? Everyone will not answer these two questions the same way. In the past, many managers believed they needed to use the tactical style of management. They believed they needed to be directive and controlling in order to make sure that work was completed. Some employees became frustrated when they felt their manager did not trust them. Some employees prefer that the manager make day-to-day decisions. Other employees are not experienced enough to work without close supervision. As a result, effective managers are prepared to use both styles. The combined use of tactical and strategic management is known as *mixed management*.

> **checkpoint** ✓
> How is tactical management different from strategic management?

www.cengage.com/school/genbus/pob

Study Tools

7-1 Assessment

Key Concepts

Determine the best answer.

1. True or False. An entrepreneur who starts a new business is not considered to be a manager.

2. Which of the following is not one of the five functions of management?
   a. planning
   b. implementing
   c. producing
   d. controlling

3. Which level of management spends most of its time completing planning and controlling activities?
   a. top management
   b. middle management
   c. supervisors
   d. team management

4. True or False. Effective managers should use strategic management rather than tactical management.

Make Academic Connections

5. **Research** Use the Internet or library to gather information on the top executive of a large corporation or an entrepreneur. Prepare a written report on the manager, describing the person's career path to his or her current position. Identify the important responsibilities of the executive in leading the company.

6. **Careers** Use an employment website to identify job listings for a top management position, a middle management position, and a supervisor position. Develop a table that lists the main duties the person in each position needs to perform. Classify those duties within the five management functions.

7. **Critical Thinking** Imagine you are managing a team of students that is running the concession stand at a basketball game to raise money for your DECA chapter. List two situations that could occur for which a tactical management style would be most appropriate and two other situations when a strategic style would be most appropriate. Discuss the situations with other students and see whether they agree with your decisions.

Doing Business in... South Africa

In 1994, South Africa celebrated the arrival of democracy. After decades of apartheid, the government policy that segregated blacks and other non-whites from the dominant whites, voting rights were extended to all citizens. Today, the country is often seen as a model for developing economies and emerging markets.

South Africa has developed an effective transportation system and has implemented advanced mobile communications technology countrywide. However, its aging electrical, water, and sewage infrastructure serves only limited parts of the country making life difficult for many citizens.

With an abundance of natural resources and a progressive government, South Africa has become a prime location for foreign investment and trade. However, the government is under growing pressure to extend basic services, improve education, and offer more job opportunities to all of its citizens. About half the population lives below the poverty rate and unemployment is over 20 percent The Black Economic Empowerment program has been instituted to overcome continuing inequalities in employment, business management, and business ownership.

South Africa has two economies. The major economy is dominated by large international businesses including finance and manufacturing. The second economy is the cash economy operated by small traders who serve middle- and low-income South Africans.

South Africa has eleven official languages reflecting many cultures. English is most widely used in business. Relationships develop over time with relaxed conversation including the exchange of personal information.

Business meals are often a sociable and shared occasion. The foods are influenced by the many local, European, and Asian cultures that are part of the country's heritage. *Bredie* is traditional stew of vegetables and mutton. *Frikkadels* are little nutmeg flavored hamburgers wrapped in cabbage and served with yellow rice. European-influenced foods include Boer chicken pie and *bobotie*—curry flavored beef mixed with raisins, nuts, and apples topped with custard.

Think Critically

1. What makes South Africa an attractive location for foreign investment?

2. How might the two different economies affect business?

3. Use library or Internet resources to obtain additional information about the history and economic activities of South Africa.

What do you see in this photograph that illustrates South Africa's economy?

Goals

1 Describe the need for leadership skills and the characteristics of an effective leader.

2 Identify the human relations skills needed by managers and leaders.

3 Recognize four types of leadership influence.

Key Terms

leadership 155

human relations 156

influence 159

informal influence 160

formal influence 160

Focus on REAL LIFE

The Downtown Business Council's Leadership Award committee is meeting to identify possible nominees for the award.

Janice offered the first suggestion, "We should find out which businesses have been the most profitable during the past year and each company's top manager should be nominated."

"I think there is more to leadership than being the top manager of a profitable company. There are other things that demonstrate outstanding leadership," Franklin offered.

"We shouldn't limit it to the top manager. Often the managers who work with employees every day are as responsible for a company's success as the top manager," Jack pointed out.

Felicia asked, "Does the award have to go to a manager? Many employees provide leadership in their organizations."

Janice looked around the table and said, "Before we go any further, we need to agree on what leadership is."

Goal 1

Describe the need for leadership skills and the characteristics of an effective leader.

WHAT IS LEADERSHIP?

A business uses many resources to accomplish its work and make a profit. Those resources include buildings, equipment, money, materials, supplies, and people. The ability to manage resources, including people, is critical to the success of any business. Some managers are effective at managing other resources but not as good at managing people. Because employees are so important, managers who can effectively manage people are in high demand.

Need for Leadership

Ideas about the effective management of people have changed in recent years. In the past, it was acceptable for managers to decide what needed to be done and how it was to be done without consulting the people who would be asked to do the work. Employees were expected to do what they were told. Although workers might have done what was asked of them, they might not have been doing their best.

Most businesses cannot afford to have employees who are not doing their best. The cost of hiring, training, and paying

Name an organization or group in which you have been involved. Do you feel there was effective leadership? Why or why not?

employees is usually one of the largest expenses for a business. Employees who do not feel their contributions are valued may not perform well. They might not produce the quantity or quality of work that is required. Other employees who do not feel appreciated might look for other jobs. Companies pay a high cost for these kinds of problems.

Today, managers are expected to do more than just give orders. They are expected to find ways to meet employee needs as well as business needs. Managers must be effective leaders.

Leadership is the ability to motivate individuals and groups to accomplish important goals. When a manager can get individual employees and groups to work well together to accomplish objectives, she or he is an effective leader.

Leadership Characteristics

Leadership is much more than just being friendly with employees. It takes skill to get people with different characteristics, needs, and interests to work well together and do the work needed by the business.

Identify and evaluate your own leadership abilities. List things you have done and activities you have completed that you believe contribute to your leadership skills. Explain how your leadership skills may affect the life-span goals you set for yourself. Identify possible leadership roles in your school and community that can help you achieve your life-span goals.

The characteristics of effective leaders are listed and described in Figure 7-2.

You may have heard, "Leaders are born and not made." Most leaders will say that they did not always have the characteristics needed for success. Rather, they worked hard over many years to develop them.

It is harder for some people to develop leadership skills. You may be shy and find it hard to assume leadership roles. You may prefer to let others make decisions while you work to make those decisions successful. You may believe other students seem to be natural leaders or already have mastered many of the leadership characteristics. They are the ones who seem

CHARACTERISTICS OF EFFECTIVE LEADERS	
CHARACTERISTIC	**DESCRIPTION**
Understanding	Respecting the feelings and needs of the people they work with.
Initiative	Having the ambition and motivation to get work done without being asked.
Dependability	Following through on commitments.
Judgment	Making decisions carefully.
Objectivity	Looking at all sides of an issue before making a decision.
Confidence	Being willing to make decisions and take responsibility for the results.
Stability	Not being too emotional or unpredictable.
Cooperation	Working well with others, recognizing others' strengths, and helping to develop effective group relationships.
Honesty	Being honest and sincere in decision-making and treatment of others.
Courage	Willing to take reasonable risks and make unpopular decisions.
Communication	Able to listen, speak, and write effectively.
Intelligence	Having the knowledge and understanding needed to perform well.

▶ **Figure 7-2**

Identify people who you believe have most of these leadership characteristics. How do they demonstrate their leadership?

to be willing to take control, take a risk, or make a hard decision. Others look to them for direction and ideas.

Preparing to Be a Leader

You do not have to be a manager to be a leader. You shouldn't wait until you become a manager to begin developing leadership skills. There are several ways you can develop them right now, including:

- *Study leadership.* Many books on the subject of leadership and leadership skills can help you understand what it takes to be a leader. You can also take courses to develop specific leadership skills.

- *Participate in organizations and activities.* Clubs, teams, and organizations need leaders and offer a variety of opportunities to develop leadership skills.

- *Practice leadership at work.* If you have a part-time job, you can develop leadership skills as you help customers, complete work assignments, take initiative to solve problems, and demonstrate dependability and honesty.

- *Observe leaders.* Every day you can observe people in leadership positions in your school and community. You also can see and read media reports

about people in leadership positions in business and government. Some are effective, while others are not.

- *Work with a mentor.* An older brother or sister, a trusted adult, a teacher or coach, or your supervisor at work may be willing to help you learn about leadership skills and offer direction and feedback on your progress.

- *Do a self-analysis and ask for feedback.* Find opportunities to demonstrate leadership characteristics. Review the results to identify what you did well and what you can improve. Ask others for constructive feedback.

> **checkpoint** ✓
> What are several ways to develop leadership skills?

IMPORTANCE OF HUMAN RELATIONS

Managers and leaders must be able to work well with other people. Most managers spend a majority of their time interacting with people. They work with employees, customers, people from other businesses, and other managers in their own organizations. The ability to get along with other people largely determines whether a manager is successful or not. **Human relations** is the way people get along with each other.

Human Relations Skills

Effective managers and leaders must be able to get along well with all of the people with whom they work. In addition, they must help their employees develop effective human relations skills. The important human relations skills needed by leaders and managers are (1) self-understanding, (2) understanding others, (3) communication, (4) team building, and (5) developing job satisfaction.

Goal 2

Identify the human relations skills needed by managers and leaders.

Which leadership qualities do you possess? Which qualities do you most need to develop? Are there others that you think you could develop?

AVAVA/Shutterstock.com

Self-Understanding To be able to meet the expectations of others, leaders must first understand their own strengths and weaknesses. A manager cannot always do exactly what employees would prefer or make decisions with which every employee agrees. In addition, a manager cannot be viewed as either unpredictable or unfair. To gain a better understanding of yourself, you can study how you get along with others. Try to recognize the ways you communicate and work with others individually and in groups. It is important to recognize how you make decisions. You must learn which decisions were effective and which were not so you can improve your decision-making ability over time.

Understanding Others Leaders recognize that people they work with often are more alike than different. Recognizing those similarities will help develop a stronger team. Differences can also improve a work team. If everyone thought and acted the same, there would seldom be new ideas or anyone to question a decision in order to improve it. An effective leader

Business Insight for the 21st Century

Assistive Technology In the Workplace

People with physical disabilities face special challenges when completing many personal and job functions. Today, assistive technologies are making many tasks possible that previously were difficult or impossible to complete. *Assistive technology* is any unique equipment, modification, or special design used to increase, maintain, or improve the capabilities of persons with disabilities. Companies benefit when providing assistive technology for disabled employees. The technology allows the employee to be productive, often at a level equal to non disabled employees.

The computer industry has developed unique applications so that individuals with disabilities can use computers. For blind persons, software is available that gives audio signals for on-screen images such as windows, menus, icons, and cursor location. A computer can also become a translator for the blind by converting printed pages to speech or Braille. Touch-sensitive Braille displays mechanically lift small rounded plastic or metal pins as needed to form Braille characters. The user reads a line of Braille letters with his or her fingers and then refreshes the display to read the next line. In the same way, a device can monitor computer sounds and alert a deaf computer user with light signals.

Special applications have been designed for people with other physical disabilities. Low-pressure, touch-sensitive keyboards can make typing easier, and special seven-key keyboards are designed primarily for one-handed typists. Special keyboard designs can customize each key's size, position, and function. Touch-screen keyboards and menus allow computer use with almost any part of the body. In addition, joysticks, writing pads, and alternative pointing devices can facilitate the use of most computer software when the physical disability requires it.

Think Critically

1. In what ways does a company benefit when it provides assistive technologies for employees with disabilities?

2. What other uses can you see for the technologies described in addition to benefiting physically disabled employees?

Name some problems that might occur if a business lost communications, computer, and Internet services for a day.

communications move across the organization at the same level—employee to employee or manager to manager.

● *Oral or written* Oral communications are spoken directly or using technology. Written communications include notes, letters, reports, and text or graphics sent via technology.

Managers need to recognize and effectively use many methods of communication. The message must include specific words that are understandable and meaningful to the people receiving the communications. An effective communicator must be a good listener as well as skilled at providing information. Listening helps managers understand employees and demonstrate respect for their ideas.

Team Building Businesses are organized into groups and teams. The combined skills of the people in an effective team are greater than that of individuals working alone. On the other hand, if there are problems in the team and members cannot get along, the team will not be effective. Managers need team-building skills to help people understand each other and their responsibilities. Managers should be able to identify any problems developing within the group and help resolve issues quickly.

Developing Job Satisfaction Most people are more satisfied than dissatisfied with their work because they have jobs that use their skills and interests. The jobs also provide needed income and benefits. Managers can influence how employees feel about their jobs on a daily basis. Sources of dissatisfaction include assignments employees do not like, difficult working conditions, ineffective communication, and lack of recognition. Daily difficulties can lead to long-term dissatisfaction. On the other hand, employees appreciate it when a manager pays attention to the needs and concerns of individual employees.

gets to know each person's skills and abilities as well as strengths and weaknesses. The leader will not treat everyone alike, but will attempt to involve each person in the way that is most beneficial to the business and that employee.

Communication Communication is essential in business. Managers must have effective communication skills. Communication can be classified in several ways.

● *Formal or informal* Formal communications methods are the established and approved ways for information to move between managers, employees, customers and others in the business. Informal communications are commonly used but unofficial ways that information moves in an organization.

● *Internal or external* Internal communications occur between managers, employees, and work groups. External communications occur between people inside the organization and people outside the organization such as customers, suppliers, and other businesses.

● *Vertical or horizontal* Vertical communications move up or down in an organization between management and employees. Horizontal

checkpoint ✓
Why do managers and leaders need
effective human relations skills?

INFLUENCING PEOPLE

Have you been a part of a group that often disagrees on how things should be done and takes a long time making decisions? It is interesting to see what the leader of a group does when the group is not working well. Some leaders will complain and criticize group members. Others will give up on the group and attempt to do the work themselves. Neither of those responses improves the group's effectiveness. Effective leaders must be able to influence team members and others in positive ways. **Influence** enables a person to affect the actions of others.

Kinds of Influence

There are several kinds of influence a leader may be able to use.

Position influence is the ability to get others to accomplish tasks because of the position the leader holds. If the leader is a manager with authority over an employee it is likely that the employee will feel obligated to respond to the leader's requests.

Reward influence results from the leader's ability to give or withhold rewards. Rewards may be monetary such as wages or job benefits. Rewards can also be non-monetary, such as recognition and praise. Rewards are usually positive but can be used in a negative way by requiring people to work overtime or by criticizing rather than praising employees.

Expert influence exists when group members recognize and appreciate a leader's expertise in a specific area. For example, a group of inexperienced sales representatives with a manager who has years of successful selling experience will likely look to the manager for guidance.

Identity influence stems from the personal trust and respect members have for the leader. If the leader is well liked and appears to have the best interests of the group in mind, members are likely to support the leader.

The influence of leaders is not always positive. It may not be effective for a long period. If a manager is not viewed as an expert and is not well liked, he or she will have to rely on position and reward influence. It is not easy to continue to get people to do things for you just because you are their manager. They will probably do just enough to get by, get a reward, or avoid punishment. Most leaders try to develop expert and identity influence to gain the respect and support of the group.

Formal and Informal Influence

How does a person influence a group to accomplish important goals? Groups can be affected by formal and informal influence. It may depend on the person's role within the organization. Managers have formal influence. Others can have informal influence as a result of their personal characteristics rather than their role in the organization.

Goal 3

Recognize four types of leadership influence.

moodboard/Jupiter Images

Think of a manager, coach, or teacher you've enjoyed working with. What characteristics made it easy to follow his or her lead?

What happens when your teacher assigns a group project and the team members get together for the first time? Usually one or two people emerge as leaders to help get the group focused and organized using informal influence. **Informal influence** is power resulting from the personal characteristics of a leader rather than the formal structure of an organization. Consider another situation where members of the student council meet for the first time. There are bylaws that call for the election of officers. The person elected president has formal influence. **Formal influence** is power based on a leader's position within the formal structure of an organization.

Often in organizations, both formal and informal influence will operate at the same time. One person will be the manager and have formal influence. There may be a well-liked and respected employee in the group who will have informal influence. If there is a conflict between the formal and informal influence, the group will probably not work effectively. Group members will have difficulty deciding whose influence to follow. Effective managers recognize informal influence and work closely with the informal leaders to gain their support and avoid conflicts.

> **checkpoint ✓**
> What is the difference between formal and informal influence?

7-2 Assessment

Study Tools
www.cengage.com/school/genbus/pob

Key Concepts

Determine the best answer.

1. The ability to motivate individuals and groups to accomplish important goals is
   a. influence
   b. power
   c. management
   d. leadership

2. True or False. Research has proven that effective leaders are born and not made.

3. The way people get along with each other is known as
   a. human relations
   b. influence
   c. management style
   d. communications

4. A person who is not a manager but is still able to get a group focused and organized is using
   a. tactical management
   b. strategic management
   c. formal influence
   d. informal influence

Make Academic Connections

5. **Technology** Virtual teams are groups that complete a project by communicating using technology rather than meeting face to face. Complete Internet research on virtual teams. Prepare a report that describes a business project completed by a virtual team. Discuss how technology was used to support communication among team members and successful completion of the project.

6. **Communication** You are the supervisor of a new employee having difficulty completing some tasks. You believe the new employee may be reluctant to ask questions of experienced employees. You encourage your employees to help each other when asked. You want to meet with the new employee to discuss the situation and want the discussion to be positive and result in improved performance. Role-play the discussion with another student using effective oral communication.

7. **Math** A survey of one company's employees asked them to identify which type of influence their managers used most often. Seven hundred employees responded with the following results: Position influence, 305 responses; reward influence, 80 responses; expert influence, 120 responses; identity influence, 195 responses. Prepare a chart that illustrates the percentage of managers using each of the types of influence most frequently.

Ethical Management

Goals

1 Justify the need for ethical management.

2 Identify the role of leaders in increasing ethical behavior.

Key Terms

ethical business practices 162

core values 163

Focus on REAL LIFE

"Did you hear about the people who got fired for taking kickbacks from one of the suppliers?" Nadia asked as she walked to the parking lot with her co-workers.

"Yeah, I heard some of them got tickets to ball games and concerts, island vacations, and even cash. What were they thinking?" Gilbert added.

"The employee handbook is pretty clear—no gifts worth more than $25. It's obvious that stuff cost more than twenty-five bucks!" Sandrine exclaimed.

"They were wrong to take the stuff, but how about the suppliers who offered it to them?" Nadia asked.

Most people, including corporate executives, employees, and consumers, are honest and behave ethically. Unfortunately, there are plenty of people who don't think the rules apply to them. This includes businesspeople who exaggerate the effectiveness of their products and job seekers who embellish their resumes. It also includes employees who spend hours conducting personal business during work hours and students who plagiarize the work of others.

IMPORTANCE OF ETHICAL BEHAVIOR

Would you copy a paper from the Internet and submit it to your teacher as your own work? Would you cheat on a test to ensure a higher grade? Is it okay for an employee to call in sick to justify a day off from work or to take office supplies from the company for use at home? Do you believe a manager should ever lie to an employee or ignore unsafe working conditions in order to save money or speed production?

Each of those situations describes an ethical decision you and others may face in your personal life and in business. Not everyone will have the same belief about what is ethical and what is not ethical. It is important for each business and those who work in the business to develop

Goal 1

Justify the need for ethical management.

What affect could the unethical behavior of one employee have on a work team?

Since 1996, the Center for the Study of Ethics in the Professions has developed a collection of Codes of Ethics representing nearly 1,000 organizations, professions, and businesses. Access the website shown below and click on the link for Chapter 7. Select and review several of the ethics codes. Identify principles and values that are common to most of the codes. Develop a sample code of ethics for a business containing 8–10 statements.

www.cengage.com/school/genbus/pob

agreement on behaviors that are acceptable and unacceptable.

Individuals and organizations develop reputations based on their actions and the decisions they make. You can identify people who are not trustworthy and companies that do not compete fairly. When an individual or a company develops that reputation, others will not trust them or want to work with them. Once a good reputation is lost, it will be difficult to rebuild. It is important for an organization to develop and enforce a climate of acceptable and ethical business behavior for all employees.

What Is Ethical Behavior?

Ethics are the principles of conduct governing an individual or a group. **Ethical business practices** ensure that appropriate standards of conduct are maintained by everyone who is a part of the business and with anyone affected by the business. Ethical behavior is not just the responsibility of a company's executives and managers. It is expected for all decisions and actions of every employee.

Ethical behavior is made up of two parts: the decisions and actions of individuals and groups and the results of those actions. Ethical behavior meets several standards:

- It is lawful.

- It is consistent with company values and policies.

- It is not intended to harm some so that others can benefit.

- If the actions and results become public, it will not embarrass the company.

Ethical Management

Managers are ultimately responsible for the success of a business. Success or failure is not just determined by financial results, such as sales and profits or losses. It is also determined by the actions and activities of the business. Are the actions legal, honest, and ethical? Are people and other companies treated fairly? Does the work of the company improve the communities and countries in which it operates? Are resources used efficiently with consideration of the effect on people and the environment? In order to say "yes" to all of these questions, managers must make sure that the decisions and actions of employees are honest, responsible, and ethical.

Are all unethical activities illegal? Explain your answer.

Prepare a personal statement of core values. Develop one or more statements to guide your actions for each of the following situations: (1) relationships with family members, (2) interacting with peers, (3) commitment to school, (4) improving community, (5) preparing for a career.

INCREASING ETHICAL BEHAVIOR THROUGH LEADERSHIP

Most people want to do what is right. When they are under time pressures or facing a major problem, some people act unethically. That unethical behavior ends up harming the business and its relationships with customers and the community. Leaders must take actions to prevent unethical behavior.

Preparing the Organization

It is easier for employees to make poor choices when they do not view ethics as important. The day-to-day atmosphere of a business will usually suggest to employees whether ethical behavior is important or not. If employees see managers cutting corners, overlooking improper employee behavior, and approving activities that may be illegal, they will soon recognize that ethical behavior is not a priority. On the other hand, managers can create an atmosphere in which all employees know they are expected to act ethically. Employees must know they will be supported when they make ethical choices. Leaders also must demonstrate that unethical behavior is unacceptable and will be punished if it occurs. Managers can take several steps to develop an ethical environment.

Most organizations have a mission statement. A *mission statement* describes the reason a business exists and what it wants to accomplish. To make ethical behavior a part of a company's mission, many businesses develop a statement of core values. **Core values** are the important principles that will guide decisions and actions in the company. Figure 7-3

shows the core values of the Rite Aid Corporation. There is no standard form for communicating core values. Some companies use simple statements similar to those shown in Figure 7-3. Other companies convey their core values by using a list of single words such as integrity, leadership, passion, humility, and trust. In most cases, companies provide descriptions and examples to help employees see how the core values can be incorporated throughout the company. As a part of the planning process, managers should work with employees to develop core values that emphasize ethical behavior.

The staffing function offers another chance for managers to emphasize the importance of ethical behavior. The company's commitment to ethical behavior should be made clear when each

Goal 2

Identify the role of leaders in increasing ethical behavior.

RITE AID CORPORATION'S CORE VALUES
Passion for our customers
Encouragement for our associates
Winning through teamwork
Commitment to diversity and respect for the individual
Accountability for our actions and results
Integrity in all we do
Value for our shareholders
Caring neighbors

Reprinted by permission of Rite Aid Corporation.

▶ **Figure 7-3**

Can you think of other core values that are important to a business?

new employee is hired. In employment interviews, prospective employees should be questioned about ethics and asked to describe how they would handle situations involving ethical behavior. New employee training should include information about the company's commitment to ethics and values.

In the day-to-day operations of the business, managers and supervisors should often stress the importance of ethics. They should look for situations that might encourage employees to act unethically and take preventive action before problems occur. Individual employees and work teams should be encouraged to develop ethical solutions to problems. Employees should also be encouraged to speak up when they become aware of any behavior or decision they believe may be unethical.

Ethical behavior should be a part of employee evaluations and promotions. Managers and supervisors should recognize and reward employees who

A Question of Ethics

©Andreas Prott/iStock

What Happened to the Jobs?

Many important business decisions have both positive and negative results. The move toward international outsourcing of jobs by many companies has been viewed as both good and bad for the U.S. economy. International outsourcing is a business decision to transfer jobs from the United States to other countries. In an era of international business and the implementation of new trade agreements among many countries, the concept of outsourcing seems to make sense. U.S. companies want to expand their international business and at the same time reduce costs wherever possible. By shifting jobs from the United States to countries where wage rates are much lower, companies can greatly reduce their costs, providing a higher profit for shareholders.

A negative result of outsourcing decisions is that U.S. workers are displaced from their jobs. Forrester

Research, Inc., estimates that nearly 1.6 million jobs have already been lost to outsourcing and that, by 2015, up to 3.3 million U.S. workers will be affected by outsourcing. Lost jobs are found in almost all job categories, particularly manufacturing and service jobs, but also high-tech computer and data management jobs. Some suggest that other problems result from outsourcing. Companies are often not held to the same strict regulations as when they operate in the United States. That can mean lower environmental standards and poorer working conditions for employees. One of the major issues being raised is the privacy and security of personal customer data that is transferred from a U.S. company to be handled by employees in other countries.

Those who are in favor of outsourcing argue that in the long run, the movement of jobs to other countries will increase the standard

of living for those countries, making them better markets for U.S. products. Opponents say that unless all countries have the same rules and regulations for business operations, U.S. employees do not have a fair playing field and cannot be competitive. The loss of higher paying jobs by many U.S. employees combined with increasing profits for many companies has only made the debate more intense.

Think Critically

1. How should companies balance the issue of increasing profits available from outsourcing and the resulting loss of jobs for U.S. employees?

2. Should the U.S. government take action to protect U.S. jobs even if it means that international trade and business profits may be affected? Why or why not?

display high ethical standards. They also need to be quick to identify and correct ethical problems if they occur.

Modeling Ethical Behavior

The most important action leaders can take to emphasize the importance of ethical behavior in an organization is to always act ethically. If employees read the core values of a company but do not see managers living up to those values, it will be clear that ethics are not that important. On the other hand, if employees see their manager acting in ways that demonstrate the company's values, they will be encouraged to act ethically as well.

When managers show respect for each employee, it demonstrates that everyone in the organization is valued. When a manager forcefully rejects a decision that is illegal or damaging to the company's reputation even though it would be profitable, employees know that ethical behavior is a core value of the organization.

Supri Suharjoto/Shutterstock.com

Think of a time when you were faced with an ethical dilemma. How did you handle it?

Being an ethical role model inspires others to do the same.

> **checkpoint** ✓
> What are the core values of an organization?

Study Tools

www.cengage.com/school/genbus/pob

Key Concepts

Determine the best answer.

1. Which of the following is *not* a standard of ethical behavior?
   a. It should be lawful.
   b. It should not harm some so others benefit.
   c. It should not give the company a competitive advantage.
   d. It should not result in embarrassment for the company.

2. True or False. Managers are responsible for the ethical actions of a business.

3. Important principles that guide decisions and actions in a company are known as
   a. a mission statement
   b. a business plan
   c. ethical behavior
   d. core values

Make Academic Connections

4. **Writing** Use the Internet to locate a news report on a business charged with unethical or illegal activities. Gather information to identify the unethical actions taken, the impact of those actions on individuals inside and outside of the company, and the effect of the actions on the image of the company. Prepare a written report on what you learned.

5. **Debate** Form two debate teams. Assign each team the pro or con position on the following statement: "Managers must be responsible for the ethical behavior of every employee." Each team will have five minutes to present their arguments and then two minutes of rebuttal time. At the end of the debate, have class members vote on which team made the most convincing argument.

Business Notes

7-1 Management Functions and Styles

- Managers' work can be organized within five functions: planning, organizing, staffing, implementing, and controlling. Not every manager devotes the same amount of attention and time to each of the functions.

- Most organizations have three levels of managers. Executives are top-level managers with responsibilities for the direction and success of the entire business. Middle managers are specialists with responsibilities for specific parts of a company's operations. Supervisors are the first level of management in a business and are responsible for the day-to-day work of a small group of employees.

- A manager might choose tactical management when working with employees who are inexperienced, unmotivated, or uncomfortable being involved in decision-making. Tactical management might also be a good choice when operating under tight time pressures or assigning a new task. A manager should use strategic management when employees are skilled and experienced, the work is routine with few new challenges, employees are doing work they enjoy, the manager wants to improve group relationships, or employees are willing to take responsibility for the results of their work.

7-2 Leadership

- Leadership gets people with different backgrounds and personalities to work well together and do the work needed by the business. The characteristics of an effective leader are understanding, initiative, dependability, judgment, objectivity, confidence, stability, cooperation, honesty, courage, communication, and intelligence.

- The important human relations skills needed by leaders and managers are (1) self-understanding, (2) understanding others, (3) communication, (4) team building, and (5) developing job satisfaction.

- Position influence is the ability to get others to accomplish tasks because of the position the leader holds. Reward influence results from the leader's ability to give or withhold rewards. Expert influence arises when group members recognize a leader's expertise. Identity influence stems from the personal trust and respect members have for the leader.

7-3 Ethical Management

- When an individual or a company develops an unethical reputation, others will be reluctant to trust them or work with them. It is important for an organization to develop a clear view of what is acceptable business behavior and what is not.

- It is the responsibility of managers to establish an atmosphere in which all employees know they are expected to act ethically and believe they will be supported when they make the right decision. Managers demonstrate their commitment to ethical behavior with their actions.

Communicate Business Concepts

1. How are the managing activities of an entrepreneur starting a new business and the top executive of a large corporation similar and different? What are the most important management skills both types of managers need for their companies to be successful?

2. Describe an important management activity that illustrates each of the five management functions.

3. The number of middle managers has been declining in many businesses as companies cut personnel and give employees more responsibilities. In your opinion, what are the advantages and disadvantages of that change for businesses? How will the skills needed by employees change when there are fewer middle managers?

4. Which type of management style would you personally prefer a manager you work for to have? Why? What would you have to do to work effectively for a manager who used another style?

5. You have been assigned to be the team leader of a work group that must complete a very important project. What are the first things you would do to prepare and motivate the individuals to work well as a team to complete the assignment?

6. Review the list of leadership characteristics in Figure 7-2. Which three characteristics do you believe are the most important to managers? Which three do you believe are least important? Justify your choices. Compare your decisions with those of other students.

7. To demonstrate your self-understanding, what do you believe are your human relations strengths? What are your current weaknesses? Describe some examples of situations where you get along well with others.

8. In your school or another organization, identify a person that illustrates each of the four kinds of influence. Prepare an example of how each person uses his or her influence to accomplish the work of the organization.

9. Do you believe the ethical behavior that a person demonstrates in his or her personal life will be the same as the person's ethical behavior in business? Why or why not?

10. As an employee, what would you do if you saw the following individuals behaving unethically: a co-worker, a customer, a competitor, the top executive of your company?

Develop Your Business Language

Match the terms listed with the definitions.

11. Power based on a leader's position within the formal structure of an organization.

12. The important principles that will guide decisions and actions in the company.

13. The effort to direct and lead people to accomplish the planned work of the organization.

14. All of the activities involved in obtaining, preparing, and compensating the employees of a business.

15. Enables a person to affect the actions of others.

16. Ensure that appropriate standards of conduct are maintained by everyone who is a part of the business and with anyone affected by the business.

17. The process of accomplishing the goals of an organization through the effective use of people and other resources.

18. The way people get along with each other.

19. The ability to motivate individuals and groups to accomplish important goals.

20. Determines to what extent the business is accomplishing the goals it set out to reach in the planning stage.

21. Analyzing information, setting goals, and making decisions about what needs to be done.

22. The way a manager works with and involves employees.

23. Identifying and arranging the work and resources needed to achieve the goals that have been set.

24. Power resulting from the personal characteristics of a leader rather than the formal structure of an organization.

KEY TERMS

a. controlling
b. core values
c. ethical business practices
d. formal influence
e. human relations
f. implementing
g. influence
h. informal influence
i. leadership
j. management
k. management style
l. organizing
m. planning
n. staffing

Make Academic Connections

25. **Speech** Managers are responsible for reinforcing the importance of ethical behavior in a business. You are the CEO of a company that has a reputation of being a very ethical business. Prepare a two-minute speech that you will give to a group of newly hired employees that focuses on the importance of that reputation and encourages each person to act ethically in all they do.

26. **Personal Development** The characteristics of effective leaders are shown in Figure 7-2. Create a three-column table. In the first column, list the characteristics from the figure. In the middle column, describe things you have done (hobbies, work, projects) that give evidence of each leadership characteristic. In the final column, list other things you can do in the next two years to further develop your capabilities as a leader.

27. **Economics** Some people believe that ethical behavior and a company's profitability do not go hand in hand. Use the Internet to locate research on the relationship between ethics and profits. Develop a one-page report on your findings. In the report, indicate whether you believe an ethical company can be profitable.

28. **Math** The three levels of management spend different amounts of time on the five management functions. The records of one company show the average amount of time their managers spent on each function in a week. The results are shown in the table below. Calculate the total time spent per week by all levels of management for each of the five functions. Develop a graph that shows the percentage of the total hours each group devotes to each of the management functions during their workweek.

WEEKLY AVERAGE HOURS DEVOTED TO MANAGEMENT FUNCTIONS			
	EXECUTIVES	**MIDDLE MANAGERS**	**SUPERVISORS**
Planning	22	10	5
Organizing	6	12	8
Staffing	2	7	3
Implementing	4	14	20
Controlling	18	7	6

Decision-Making Strategies

Valencia Price has just become a supervisor in the Roxbury Manufacturing Company, where she has worked for 11 years. She had often heard employees complain that their supervisors were not interested in employees' ideas and did not involve them in decision-making. As a result, Valencia felt it was important to avoid using position and reward influence and to try to adopt a strategic leadership style. From the first day of work as a supervisor, Valencia asked employees to discuss how the work could be improved. She knew that the other employees respected Manny, a long-time member of the work team. She would often ask Manny to lead the discussion when she wanted the team to make a decision so the employees would not think she was trying to influence them. After a month, Valencia started to hear that employees believed she could not make a decision on her own and wasted too much time in meetings. Several even suggested that maybe Manny should be the supervisor. They said that if Valencia had to ask Manny to run her meetings, she must not have any confidence in her own supervisory skills.

29. What principles of effective leadership was Valencia demonstrating as a supervisor?

30. Why were the employees not satisfied with the way Valencia was leading?

31. What would you recommend she do?

Linking School and Community

There are many opportunities in your community to develop skills that will help you become an effective business leader. Select five of the leadership characteristics shown in Figure 7-2 that you would like to develop. For each characteristic selected, identify a community activity in which you can participate that will help you develop the characteristic. List the community group or organization that offers the activity and the requirements to participate in the activity. Determine the procedures and requirements for volunteering at one of the groups or organizations.

Web Workout

Leadership and leadership development are important issues in business today. Many business executives maintain personal blogs to discuss their ideas, beliefs, and leadership experiences. Most of the leadership blogs encourage feedback and discussion of leadership from blog readers both inside and outside of the executive's company.

Think Critically

1. Locate two blogs written by business executives on the topic of leadership. Read several postings by the executive and responses from blog readers.

Write a one-paragraph description of each blog, including the blogger's name and job title, company, the purpose of the blog, and the types of topics or discussions included.

2. Identify and write a brief description of one blog posting that discusses an aspect of leadership that you studied in this chapter. Identify and briefly describe another blog posting that provides information on leadership you did not study in the chapter.

3. How can reading blogs of business executives help develop your leadership skills?

Travel and Tourism Team Decision-Making Event

During the DECA Team Decision-Making Event, each team of two has 30 minutes to develop a plan of action for the specific situation described. Your team will present a 10-minute detailed strategy to the state director of economic development.

The economies of the states that border the Gulf of Mexico depend heavily on tourism dollars. Their semi-tropical climate and sandy beaches make them ideal vacation spots. Your team works for the governor and the director of travel and tourism for a Gulf Coast state. Your team is concerned about the negative economic impact of a recent natural disaster on travel and tourism. The national media has focused on the disaster and many tourists have changed their travel plans due to the images they have seen in the news.

Although your state has made great strides in repairing damage following the disaster, tourism is down 40 percent this year compared to last year. Your team must do the following:

- Develop a marketing campaign to counter the negative images in the media.
- Describe a plan to restore your state's image and increase travel and tourism.
- Describe a marketing campaign that generates more tourism dollars for your state.
- Include promotions and advertisements as part of the marketing campaign.

Performance Indicators Evaluated

- Demonstrate understanding of the economic impact of a natural disaster.
- Explain the impact that media has on consumer perception.
- Describe an advertising campaign to meet the challenge.
- Explain the best advertising media to communicate a message.
- Describe a promotional campaign to meet specific goals.
- Explain how to measure the effectiveness of an advertising campaign.

For more detailed information about performance indicators, go to the DECA website.

Think Critically

1. How are consumer decisions influenced by the media?
2. What are the best methods for promoting travel and tourism?
3. Why should the advertising campaign avoid mentioning the national disaster?

www.deca.org

Human Resources, Culture, and Diversity

Stockbyte/Getty Images

8-1   Human Resources Basics

8-2   Managing Human Resources

8-3   Organizational Culture and Workforce Diversity

HUMAN RESOURCES

Today's businesses recognize the importance of their employees. A highly skilled, motivated workforce provides a competitive edge. Companies often spend more money on their personnel than on any other resource. With that large investment, they need professional human resources personnel to recruit, train, motivate, and compensate employees.

The goal of human resources is to have the right people in the right jobs at the right time. This is accomplished by hiring the best people, maintaining a work environment that encourages productivity and satisfaction, and offering programs that allow employees to develop skills to meet rapidly changing job requirements.

Large human resources departments are made up of a number of specialists. They work closely with managers and employees to ensure that employees are available, capable, and willing to work. They also make sure employees are paid and recognized for their contributions.

Related Job Titles

- Director of Human Resources
- Benefits Specialist
- Employment Recruiter
- Employee Relations Manager
- Organizational Development Consultant
- Training Specialist
- EEO/Affirmative Action Representative
- Labor Contracts Negotiator
- Job Analyst

Analyze Career Opportunities in ...
HUMAN RESOURCES

Use library and Internet resource to learn more about careers in human resources. Choose one of the job titles listed in the box above and answer the following questions.

1. How would you describe the earnings potential for this field?

2. Is this that interests you? Explain how careers in this field match up with your goals and interests.

What's it like to work as a ... Corporate Trainer?

Emiko is a lead trainer for the Orbis Company. She has had an interesting career path, starting as a high school science teacher, followed by five years as a laboratory specialist in industry. Six months ago, she applied for a training position in the company. In this new job, Emiko combines her passions for teaching, science, and helping her co-workers.

As a lead trainer, Emiko meets with managers to identify training needs. Those needs might be helping new employees learn their jobs, preparing experienced employees for new processes, or developing a teamwork course. Emiko works with instructional designers and media specialists to prepare training materials. She must stay up to date with the latest educational technology in order to deliver training to employees located at sites all over the world.

What about you? What aspects of a career as a corporate trainer do you think you would you find interesting?

8-1 Human Resources Basics

Goals

1 Describe the nature of today's workforce.

2 Identify important goals and activities of human resources.

Key Terms

workforce 172

downsizing 175

outsourcing 175

Focus on REAL LIFE

"Do you think we'll ever see the time when people don't have jobs because robots do all the work?" Indee asked Alex as they left the theater after enjoying the latest sci-fi thriller.

"It would be fun to think about never having to work but I think I'd get bored after awhile," replied Alex. "Besides, I want to be an industrial designer. That will require creativity and I don't think robots can be creative."

Indee laughed and said, "There are probably lots of things computers can't do. Plus, even if computers and robots are able to complete even more complex tasks in the future, people will still be responsible for planning and programming the work."

"The creativity, personalities, and skills of employees are what really make a business," Alex responded.

"So I guess we won't be replaced by robots," said Indee. "We'll just have to learn how to get along with them."

Goal 1

Describe the nature of today's workforce.

THE CHANGING WORKFORCE

The **workforce** is made up of all the people 16 years and older who are employed or who are looking for a job. In 2010 the size of the U.S. workforce was more than 150 million people. That includes everyone holding a full- or part-time job and those seeking employment. It does not include the nearly 1.5 million people serving in the active military.

The days when you could get a good job if you had basic skills and a willingness to work hard are gone. Most jobs today require at least a high school education. For many jobs you need specialized training beyond high school or a college degree. Today's jobs offer a variety of working conditions and different wages and benefits. Some involve working mainly with machines and technology. Others deal mainly with people and information.

Types of Jobs

The business world consists of hundreds of thousands of companies offering a wide variety of jobs. The federal government, as well as state governments, provides useful information about the jobs available to the workforce. The Bureau of Labor Statistics(BLS), part of the U.S. Department of Labor, researches thousands of different jobs. It offers up-to-date information about the U.S. workforce through publications and websites including the *Occupational Outlook Handbook*.

There are two major types of industries analyzed in the *Occupational Outlook Handbook*. The *service-providing industries* include businesses that perform services that satisfy the needs of other businesses and consumers. Service companies include health care facilities, insurance companies, retail stores,

INDUSTRY CATEGORIES	
SERVICE-PROVIDING INDUSTRIES	**GOODS-PRODUCING INDUSTRIES**
• Trade, Transportation and Utilities • Information • Financial Activities • Professional and Business Services • Education and Health Services • Leisure and Hospitality • Other Services	• Natural Resources and Mining • Construction • Manufacturing

Source: U.S. Bureau of Labor Statistics

▶ **Figure 8-1**

In your opinion, which category, service-providing or goods-producing, accounts for more jobs in your community?

and transportation businesses. *Goods-producing industries* include businesses that produce or manufacture products used by other businesses or purchased by final consumers. These companies are involved in construction, manufacturing, mining, and agriculture. Figure 8-1 highlights the industry categories from the *Occupational Outlook Handbook*.

The U.S. economy has experienced a change. It has moved from an emphasis on goods-providing businesses to service-providing businesses. The BLS estimates that the economy will add more than 15 million new jobs over the next 10 years.

Almost all of that job growth will be in service-providing industries. However, due to the number of retirements and the growing economy, job opportunities will exist in all occupational categories. It is estimated that more than 50 million job openings will be available from now until 2018.

Another way of looking at the changing workforce is to think about groups of occupations. Occupations are affected by short- and long-term changes in industries, technology, and the overall economy. BLS estimates of future employment trends for ten major occupational groups are shown in Figure 8-2.

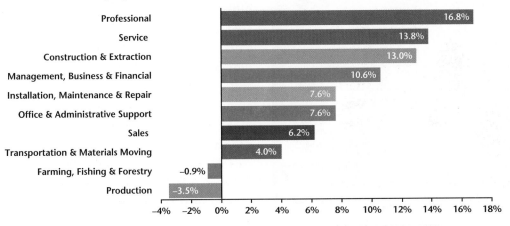

Employment Projections for Occupational Categories

Occupational Category	Percentage Change in Employment, 2008–2018
Professional	16.8%
Service	13.8%
Construction & Extraction	13.0%
Management, Business & Financial	10.6%
Installation, Maintenance & Repair	7.6%
Office & Administrative Support	7.6%
Sales	6.2%
Transportation & Materials Moving	4.0%
Farming, Fishing & Forestry	−0.9%
Production	−3.5%

Source: U.S. Bureau of Labor Statistics

▶ **Figure 8-2**

What factors other than the rate of employment growth would you consider when choosing an industry in which to work?

Occupations also are referred to in terms of two very broad types of workers: white-collar and blue-collar. A *white-collar worker* is one whose work is more mental than physical and involves the handling and processing of information. Most white-collar workers are employed in offices, stores, and professional services businesses. They include professional, managerial, and clerical workers. A *blue-collar worker* is one whose job involves a great deal of physical work, including the operation of machinery and equipment or other production activities. Blue-collar workers are employed in factories, on construction sites, on farms, and in the delivery of many basic services.

Changing Job Requirements

White-collar and blue-collar workers are equally important and needed in the workforce. Increased use of computers and information technology in factories, on farms, and in construction is changing the nature of both types of work. It is resulting in a need for higher levels of education and training. Nearly half of all new job openings in the next ten years will require education beyond high school.

The jobs in the workforce are subject to a variety of factors that can cause the need for these jobs to change. Some of these influences may cause jobs to be eliminated. Others will cause the work to be modified. Changes may require employees to develop new skills and get different training. Consumer preferences, economic conditions, new technology, and business competition are strong influences on the workforce.

Consumer Preferences Consumers regularly cast their "dollar votes" in the marketplace. Preferences by consumers have an effect on available jobs. Jobs are affected by consumer demand for a product or service. Sometimes new products entering the market make those already available obsolete. Workers making the old products may find that their jobs will be eliminated. New jobs would be created by the demand for the new products.

Business Cycles Stages of the business cycle affect job opportunities. When businesses expand because consumers buy more goods and services, new jobs are created to meet the growing demand. More workers are employed and earn more money. In turn, they spend more on goods and services that they need and want. The growing demand continues.

High prices cause consumers to decrease their buying. When interest rates increase, both businesses and consumers find it difficult to borrow money. Demand for goods and services decreases. As a result, jobs may be eliminated or the number of workers reduced.

Benis Arapovic/Shutterstock.com

Name ways in which computer technology changes the way manufacturing businesses operate.

Consumer spending and demand is decreased even more.

New Technologies *Technology* refers to the use of automated machinery, electronic equipment, and integrated computer systems to help increase the efficiency of producing goods and services. Technology is important in the workplace. It improves efficiency so that businesses may stay competitive in international markets. Computerized systems and robots have greatly reduced the need for production workers in many manufacturing industries. These include steel, autos, tires, and consumer electronics. Sophisticated computer and communications systems have also reduced the need for office employees such as bookkeepers and clerks. New technology continues to change the types of jobs in production and manufacturing. It has also changed how office workers and professionals perform their jobs.

Business Competition Companies must be competitive to stay in business. Costs are a major factor. The cost of running a business affects jobs and workers. When costs begin to increase, the business must look for ways to stay profitable. Installing new equipment and streamlining processes make workers more productive. Businesses may also decide to downsize. **Downsizing** is a planned reduction in the number of employees needed in a firm in order to reduce costs and make the business more efficient. **Outsourcing** removes work from one company and sends it to another company that can complete it at a lower cost. In recent years, many U.S. jobs have been outsourced to companies in other countries.

> **checkpoint** ✓
> What are several strong influences on changes in the workforce?

Why might it not make sense to set a life-span goal of becoming a telephone switchboard operator? Explain why it is necessary to understand changes that are taking place in the workplace when you set your life-span goals.

HUMAN RESOURCES OVERVIEW

Goal 2

Identify important goals and activities of human resources.

The work of every company is completed by the people who work for the organization. Employees who have the knowledge and skills needed, who are motivated to work efficiently, and who complete their jobs with quality contribute to the success of the business. Companies that have difficulty finding qualified employees, have a poor work environment, and suffer from quality issues, waste, and employee errors

Photodisc/Getty Images

Think of the places you frequent regularly. What types of workers are visible? Are there "behind the scenes" employees?

Meeting the ongoing need for training and retraining employees is one of the many challenges a human resources manager might encounter. What are some others?

Digital Vision/Getty Images

will have difficulty remaining competitive or meeting customer needs.

Human resources are the people who work for a business. Human resources include management and employees, full-time and part-time workers. People hired to fill temporary positions as well as those who have worked for the company for many years are human resources. Managing human resources is one of the most important responsibilities of a business. Most medium- to large-sized businesses have a department devoted to human resources management and activities. The owner of a small business will be responsible for managing human resources or will hire others to complete the work.

Human Resources Goals

Human resources are different from almost every other resource needed by businesses. Each person is different. They bring varied knowledge, skills, experience, and motivation to their jobs. People are used in different ways in a company. Some will be required to do hard, physical labor. Others will operate complex equipment. Some employees

will work in groups where they must have effective interpersonal skills and demonstrate teamwork. Others will work independently, relying on their own abilities. Managers will direct the work of others and make long-term plans that affect the entire company. New employees must be willing to follow directions and may have few decision-making responsibilities at first.

Human resources must be able to work with the vast differences and unique capabilities of each employee and develop a workforce that is productive and efficient. There are seven major human resources goals.

1. Identify the personnel needs of the company.

2. Maintain an adequate supply of people to fill those needs.

3. Match abilities and interests with specific jobs.

4. Provide training and development to prepare people for their jobs and to improve their capabilities as job requirements change.

5. Develop plans to compensate personnel for their work.

6. Protect the health and well-being of employees.

7. Maintain a productive and satisfying work environment.

Human Resources Activities

Managing human resources involves four broad categories of activities. The categories are planning and staffing, performance management, compensation and benefits, and employee relations. Specific human resources activities for each of the categories are listed in Figure 8-3.

Planning and staffing activities are directed at identifying and filling all of the jobs in the company with qualified

HUMAN RESOURCES ACTIVITIES			
PLANNING & STAFFING	**PERFORMANCE MANAGEMENT**	**COMPENSATION & BENEFITS**	**EMPLOYEE RELATIONS**
• Job analysis • Recruitment and selection • Job placement	• Performance assessment • Performance improvement • Managing promotions, transfers, and terminations	• Wage and salary planning • Benefits planning • Payroll, benefits, and personnel records management	• Health and safety planning • Labor relations • Employment law and policy enforcement • Organizational development

▶ **Figure 8-3**

Which activities do you think are the most important to the success of the business? Explain your answer.

people. *Performance management* involves evaluating the work of employees and improving performance through training and development. *Compensation and benefits* is responsible for planning and managing payroll, personnel records, and benefits programs. *Employee relations* is responsible for maintaining a safe, healthy, and productive work environment for all employees.

checkpoint ✓
What are the seven major goals of human resources?

8-1 Assessment

Study Tools
www.cengage.com/school/genbus/pob

Key Concepts

Determine the best answer.

1. The U.S. workforce is made up of about_?_ people.
   a. 80 million
   b. 100 million
   c. 150 million
   d. 190 million

2. The Bureau of Labor Statistics publication that provides detailed and up-to-date information about the U.S. workforce is the
   a. *Occupational Outlook Handbook*
   b. *IRS Publication 15*
   c. *Congressional Record*
   d. *Business Report*

3. A person whose work is more mental than physical and involves the handling and processing of information is a
   a. blue-collar worker
   b. human resources manager
   c. white-collar worker
   d. service employee

4. Which of the following would *not* be a part of a company's human resources?
   a. managers
   b. full-time employees
   c. temporary employees
   d. All could be included in human resources.

Make Academic Connections

5. **Math** The population of the United States is approximately 309,300,000. If 150,000,000 people are not employed, what percentage of the total population is not currently working? What accounts for the difference in that percentage and the approximate 5 percent unemployment rate that is typically reported by the Bureau of Labor Statistics?

6. **Art** Create a collage on poster board that illustrates the many activities that are a part of human resources. Clip pictures from newspapers and magazines that represent the four broad categories of activities. Show your collage to other students and describe the activities you have illustrated.

Managing Human Resources

Goals

1 Identify important planning and staffing activities.

2 Describe compensation and benefits plans.

3 Recognize the goals of performance management.

Key Terms

job analysis 179

compensation 181

salary and wages 181

benefits 181

incentive systems 181

promotion 183

transfer 184

termination 184

Focus on REAL LIFE

"How was your day?" Jacqueline asked her business partner as she dropped into a chair after a busy day.

"It was fine until Esme came to see me," Leo responded as he looked up from the report he was reading. "She is going to work for a competitor."

"That's a shame," said Jacqueline, "She is great with customers and her work is terrific. Did she say why she is leaving?"

"The usual reasons: better benefits and more opportunities for advancement," Leo replied.

"We need to look for a replacement right away," Jacqueline said. "I'll call the staffing agency tomorrow."

"Maybe we should take our time and think about our needs. It might be time to plan a better hiring strategy rather than just quickly replacing people when they leave," Leo said.

"Leo, you're right. We should turn this in to an opportunity for reviewing the way we manage our human resources. I bet there are things we can do to be more competitive. And, we especially need to focus on ways to retain our talented employees."

Goal 1

Identify important planning and staffing activities.

HUMAN RESOURCES PLANNING AND STAFFING

Human resources management ensures that needed employees are available, productive, paid, and satisfied with their work. If human resources management does its job well, the company will have employees who do their jobs well. This contributes to a successful, profitable business.

Planning and Job Analysis

Human resources management begins by analyzing where the business currently is in terms of its personnel and where it wants to be. The decision to hire people must be made carefully. Once an employee is hired, the person's salary must be paid whether the company is profitable or not. An employee should be hired when the

work of that employee will add more to the company's profitability than it will cost.

Classifying Employees The company must decide whether the person to be hired will be permanent or temporary. A *permanent employee* is one to whom the company makes a long-term commitment. It is expected that the employee will work for the business as long as the business is profitable and the employee's performance is satisfactory. A *temporary employee* is one hired for a specific time or to complete a specific assignment.

Because permanent employees feel that they are a part of the business, they are often more productive than temporary employees. On the other hand, there is more control over the company's resources when temporary employees are hired. The employee is paid only until the temporary assignment ends. Temporary employees are usually hired during a busy time for the business or when a special task needs to be done.

Whether permanent or temporary, employees can be hired full-time or part-time. A *full-time employee* regularly works a schedule of 30 hours or more a week. A *part-time employee* has a shorter work schedule with either fewer hours each day or fewer days each week.

Determining Job Requirements Before starting the hiring process, human resources staff studies the work that must be done in the job. Specific information about each job is needed in order to hire people with the right skills. That information is often collected by completing a job analysis. A **job analysis** is a specific study of a job to identify in detail the job duties and skill requirements.

First, human resources staff reviews the current job in detail by observing the work and talking with employees and managers. They identify all important job duties, as well as the knowledge and skills required to successfully complete the job. Next, they add any new activities planned for that job to the analysis. The job analysis will help determine if the needs of the business can best be met with temporary, permanent, part-time, or full-time employees.

Recruiting and Hiring

Once the specific need and skill requirements are determined, prospective

Why would a business choose not to advertise a job opening outside the company?

employees meeting the requirements must be located. If this search is not done carefully, an employer may spend a great deal of time and expense and an appropriate employee may still not be found. Several good sources of prospective employees exist and are identified in Figure 8-4. Businesses should use sources that will provide an adequate number of candidates for the position. The candidates must have the skills required for the job and an interest in working for the business.

The Application Process Most companies ask prospective applicants to fill out an employment application. The application gathers personal information, information on education, and work experience history. It may also ask for specific

EFFECTIVE SOURCES FOR RECRUITING PROSPECTIVE EMPLOYEES	
Company employment office	Job and career fairs
Company websites	Newspaper advertising, online and print
Employment agencies, public and private	Placement offices, school and college
Executive recruiters	Radio and television advertising
Industry publications	Referrals by employees
Job search and career websites	Social networking

▶ **Figure 8-4**

Why do employers often use multiple sources when recruiting new employees?

skills related to the job and contact information for people who can serve as references. For career-level jobs, the applicant may be asked to submit an application letter and a resume as well. Applications are used to eliminate people who are clearly not qualified for the job and to identify those who appear to be especially qualified.

Once applications have been reviewed, the remaining applicants are studied more carefully. Information is checked for accuracy. References are contacted. The employer selects a few applicants to interview. These applicants may be asked to complete special tests related to needed job knowledge and skills. During the interview, the applicant will be introduced to the work area, managers, and co-workers. The applicant will be given more detailed information about the company and the job. Finally, the applicant whose qualifications best match the job requirements will be offered the job.

New Employee Orientation The final step in the hiring process is to help the new employee get a good start in the company. As a part of the orientation, the new employee will meet with human resources specialists to complete all of the paperwork needed to receive pay and benefits. In turn, the company will have a complete employee record. There will usually be at least several days of training. The employee may be paired with an experienced co-worker, or mentor.

Business Insight for the 21st Century

Temp-To-Hire

Companies are continually challenged to maintain an effective work force while controlling costs. Payroll expenses typically account for 30 to 50 percent of company expenses with some companies spending much more. Human resources managers are challenged to find ways to hire qualified, productive personnel while keeping costs down.

In difficult economic times the challenge is even greater. Companies must be cautious about hiring new employees when sales and profits are declining. On the other hand, the company must function in the present and be prepared when the economy improves.

Today, human resources managers often use hiring practices to help create a flexible work force. Hiring temporary employees is a way to meet urgent, short-term needs. Temps are hired for a limited time, a specific project, or when a company does not want to risk committing to a new permanent employee. Another approach, known as temp-to-hire, adds the possibility of full-time employment for temporary employees. Sometimes called "try it before you buy it," the temporary employee is offered a trial period. If the company determines it needs a permanent employee and the temp likes the work and the company, the temp becomes a permanent employee.

The American Staffing Association, a trade association, reported that in a recent year nearly 2.5 million people worked in temporary or non-employee positions each day. That is nearly two percent of the total workforce. To place that many temporary employees, staffing companies had to recruit more than 11 million prospective employees during the year.

Think Critically

1. How do the temporary employment options discussed help a company control costs if they are actually hiring people to do the work?

2. Why might temp-to-hire be used by companies in good economic times?

The mentor answers questions and helps the new employee solve problems and build confidence for the new job. The company may have a probationary period of several weeks to several months. At the end of that time, the new employee is evaluated to be sure job performance is meeting the company's expectations.

checkpoint ✓
Why do human resources personnel need to study jobs before beginning the hiring process?

COMPENSATION AND BENEFITS

One of the reasons people work is to earn money. **Compensation** is the amount of money paid to an employee for work performed. Compensation is made up of two parts. **Salary and wages** are direct payment of money to an employee for work completed. Compensation in forms other than direct payment is known as **benefits**. Examples of benefits are insurance, vacations, retirement plans, and health and fitness programs.

Compensation Methods

A *time wage* pays the employee a specific amount of money for each hour worked. A *straight salary* pays a specific amount of money for each week or month worked. Neither of these types of compensation are based directly on the amount or quality of work done, but are determined by the amount of time spent on the job. For that reason, it is a simple system to manage. The business just has to keep records on the amount of time each employee works.

Incentive systems connect the amount of compensation to the quality or quantity of an employee's performance. Some businesses pay a *commission* in which an

WORK as a TEAM Automobile dealerships have traditionally paid their salespeople with a straight commission. Some dealerships now pay each salesperson a salary and add a bonus based on customer satisfaction surveys. As a team, discuss how this change might affect the performance of the salespeople and why the dealerships may have chosen to make the change.

employee is paid a percentage of sales for which he or she is responsible. Salespeople are often compensated with commissions. Another pay-for-performance plan is known as a *piece rate*. An employee receives a specific amount for each unit of work produced. Piece rates are commonly used in manufacturing, agriculture, and service centers. For example, workers might be paid a piece rate for each seam they sew, each pound of grapes they pick, each call they answer, or each claim they process.

Some companies use a *base plus incentive* compensation system. This system combines a wage or salary with an additional amount based on the employee's performance. One type of base plus incentive plan is profit sharing. With profit sharing, employees receive their regular

Goal 2

Describe compensation and benefits plans.

If you were a telemarketer, would you rather be paid commission on your sales or an hourly wage rate? Explain your answer.

Sean Prior/Shutterstock.com

compensation plus a share of the profits earned by a company. This system encourages commitment, teamwork, and effective job performance so that profits will be high.

Employee Benefits

Employee benefits can be an expensive addition to the cost of compensation. On average for all businesses, an additional 20 to 40 percent of an employee's wages is spent on benefits. If an employee earns $11.00 an hour, 30 percent added for benefits increases the hourly cost to $14.30. If the employee works 40 hours a week, the additional cost is $6,864 per year.

State and federal laws require some benefits. Most businesses must offer and pay the cost of these required benefits. Benefits include compensation for overtime hours worked, social security, Medicare, and contributions to funds for injured employees and for unemployed workers. Full-time employees may expect companies to offer insurance plans including health, life, dental, and disability insurance. Many companies, especially small businesses, cannot afford the cost of all of those types of insurance. The rapidly rising cost of health insurance has been particularly difficult for businesses to handle. As a result, many companies are reducing health insurance benefits or require employees to pay a larger part of insurance premiums.

Time off for vacations is another popular benefit for employees. Paid vacations are a costly benefit because employees are paid for time when they are not working. On the other hand, the time off may result in a more satisfied and productive employee. Other benefits offered by businesses include retirement programs, employee savings plans, personal or sick days, and flexible work schedules.

The costs of benefits programs are very high and continue to increase. Each employee may prefer different benefits. As a result, human resources departments have developed cafeteria plans. A *cafeteria plan* allocates a certain amount of money to each employee that can be spent on benefits. The employee selects the preferred benefits. If the cost of the benefits does not use all of the allocated money, the employee can receive the difference in additional pay. If the costs are higher, the employee has to pay the difference.

Photodisc/Getty Images

What kinds of benefits are important to you?

checkpoint ✓
List three types of incentive systems for employee compensation.

PERFORMANCE MANAGEMENT

Managers work closely with their employees to make sure work goals are being accomplished as planned. Every employee is expected to meet quality standards as well as work efficiently. In addition, employees must demonstrate effective working relationships with co-workers, managers, and customers. As jobs change, new equipment and procedures will be introduced. Employees must upgrade their skills to meet the changing job requirements. Most companies offer training and development programs to help employees perform their work well.

Employee Evaluation

Managers evaluate the work of each of their employees on a regular basis. The human resources department is in charge of developing the evaluation procedures and forms. Managers will be trained to complete objective evaluations and hold effective evaluation conferences with employees. Human resources maintains the records of employee evaluations in the employee's personnel file.

The Evaluation Process Performance evaluations focus on the specific job duties of each employee. They also review the important work qualities expected of all employees. Those qualities include factors such as communication, interpersonal relationships, quality and quantity of work, and ethical behavior.

Managers are given evaluation forms to complete. Evaluation decisions are based on observations of the employee's performance and evaluation of the quantity and quality of the work. Some companies ask co-workers to provide feedback that is considered in the evaluation process. Using the evaluation form, the manager identifies each employee's strengths and areas that need improvement.

The Evaluation Conference After the manager completes the evaluation form, a conference is scheduled with the employee. The purpose of the conference is to review and discuss the results of the evaluation and to plan for any needed performance improvement. Often, both the manager and employee are concerned about the conference. They might not be comfortable with a specific discussion of performance. Human resources personnel should work with all employees to help them prepare for evaluation conferences. The conference should be meaningful and positive. The conference should result in reasonable agreement on the employee's performance, goals, and plans for the future. It should identify the support the employee can expect from the manager and the company in order to improve performance.

Promotions, Transfers, and Terminations

Employees expect that if they work for a company for a long time and perform well, they should be rewarded with increased pay and the chance of promotion. A **promotion** is the advancement of an employee to a position with greater responsibility. Companies want

Goal 3
Recognize the goals of performance management.

Is earning a good wage or salary enough for you to be satisfied with your work? What else do you expect?

Digital Vision/Getty Images

to keep good employees. They want to place good employees in positions where they can provide the most benefit to the company. When possible, companies should fill open positions with current employees. Those employees are familiar with the company and will view the promotion as a reward. They will be motivated to continue to work for the company and continue to work effectively.

In some cases, promotional opportunities do not exist, but employees want to change jobs. It is not unusual for some jobs in a company to be eliminated while other jobs are created. In that case, employees may accept a job transfer. A **transfer** is the assignment of an employee to another job in the company with a similar level of responsibility. The job may provide a new challenge for the employee or may be a better match with the person's skills.

If performance does not meet the company's expectations or if jobs are being reduced, the company may have to terminate the employee. A **termination** ends the employment relationship between a company and an employee. The termination may be a *discharge* that ends employment due to inappropriate work behavior. Another type of termination is a *layoff*, which is a temporary or permanent reduction in the number of employees due to changing business conditions. The company should complete all terminations carefully. The terminations must meet legal requirements and be as helpful as possible to the employee who is asked to leave the business.

> **checkpoint ✓**
> What is the purpose of an evaluation conference?

8-2 Assessment

Study Tools
www.cengage.com/school/genbus/pob

Key Concepts

Determine the best answer.

1. An employee to whom a company makes a long-term commitment is considered to be
   a. full-time
   b. part-time
   c. permanent
   d. temporary

2. True or False. Companies should interview all prospective employees who apply for a job.

3. On average, the percentage of employees' wages spent on benefits is
   a. less than 5%
   b. 10%–20%
   c. 20%–40%
   d. more than 50%

4. The employment relationship between a company and an employee is ended with a (an)
   a. termination
   b. interview
   c. evaluation
   d. lawsuit

Make Academic Connections

5. **Math** Augusta is paid $3,100 a month and a commission of 2 percent on all sales. She also is given a yearly bonus of $4,500. If Augusta's sales for the year are $186,200, what is her total compensation for the year?

6. **Research** Use the Internet to locate four different sources of current job opportunities. Develop a table that compares the sites in terms of their effectiveness in providing information about the job, the company, and the procedure applicants should follow in applying for a job.

7. **Critical Thinking** You are a human resources specialist giving advice to a new supervisor on how to conduct a performance evaluation conference with an employee. List three recommendations you would make to the supervisor that will contribute to an effective conference.

8-3 Organizational Culture and Workforce Diversity

Goals

1 Recognize factors that contribute to an effective organizational culture.

2 Describe the benefits of diversity to an organization, individuals, and society.

Key Terms

organizational culture 185

work environment 186

labor union 188

diversity 190

glass ceiling 191

Focus on REAL LIFE

Three years of related employment experience required. Josh, a recent graduate, reads this line in a job description and decides he is not qualified even though he has all the skills the job requires. Josh doesn't think the employer will recognize the skills he has developed through leadership activities and community service.

Must be energetic and eager. Madeline, who is 58, sees this phrase as she views job postings on a career website. She doesn't bother to apply for the job because she believes the employer must be looking for young people.

Requires heavy lifting. Kamala is surprised to see this requirement listed in a job description because her friend Ed, who told her about the job, said she might have to lift boxes occasionally, but never anything over 50 pounds. She wonders if this qualification was included in the job description to discourage women from applying.

Can employment advertisements intentionally or unintentionally discourage otherwise well-qualified people from applying? To build the best workforce, job recruitment should focus on the skills and abilities needed to do the work, not on the type of person the manager believes would be best for the job. How can companies eliminate these types of intentional or unintentional hiring practices?

DEVELOPING AN EFFECTIVE CULTURE

The ways businesses are organized and operate have changed a great deal in the past few decades. Some of the changes that have occurred are obvious. Technology has reduced the need for low-skilled employees and demanded that current workers have much greater skills. The Internet has changed the way consumers and businesses communicate, share information, buy and sell. Globalization of business has resulted in greater competition. It has also resulted in more opportunities for every business to reach many new customers.

Other changes are just as important but not as clear. The workforce is more diverse, with growth among both younger and older workers. Jobs are changing, with a larger temporary and part-time workforce and a rise in the number of successful small businesses. Jobs are being shifted to other countries in an effort by businesses to cut costs. The number of manufacturing jobs is declining while service jobs are growing at a rapid pace. Some of the service jobs are low skill. Others are complex jobs requiring technical knowledge, creativity, and decision-making skills.

Businesses have to respond to all of the changes and maintain a positive organizational culture. An **organizational culture**

Goal 1

Recognize factors that contribute to an effective organizational culture.

is the environment in which people work, made up of the atmosphere, behaviors, beliefs, and relationships. An organizational culture shows people how they will be treated and how they are expected to treat others. It identifies what is acceptable behavior and what is not. If a company has a positive organizational culture, employees enjoy going to work. They have positive working relations with co-workers and managers. They believe the company values them and their work. They are motivated to do a good job for the company.

Work Environment

The **work environment** is the physical conditions and the psychological atmosphere in which employees work. The physical conditions are the work area, offices, break rooms, storage areas, and all other spaces where employees spend time while at work. Tools and equipment, lighting, temperature, and air quality are also a part of the physical work environment. The physical conditions must be safe and healthy. That is certainly a legal requirement of businesses. It is also important in assuring employees that the company has their interests at heart. If employees believe the physical environment is unsafe or unhealthy, they will likely look for another job.

In addition to the physical conditions, companies need to provide a positive psychological atmosphere. Employees do not want to work in a place where they feel they are mistreated or where their work and ideas are not valued. An atmosphere of mistrust or fear is likely to result in low

morale and poor performance among employees.

Not all jobs can be physically comfortable. Some require people to work outside in very hot or cold conditions. Other jobs require a great deal of physical effort or can be quite hazardous. Even in those jobs, the business needs to find ways to provide as much physical comfort and safety as possible. The business should offer protective clothing and equipment, allow needed breaks, and ensure that every employee receives adequate safety training.

Offering a positive psychological environment means that managers are trained in effective communications and interpersonal skills. They are honest, fair, and ethical in their treatment of each employee. Employees get important information from their managers rather than from rumors through the grapevine. They believe their work is important and valued. They are recognized and rewarded for their contributions to the company.

Work–Life Relationships

People seem to be working more days and longer days. Some people hold two

Would you rather work inside or outside? Alone or in a group?

Brand X Pictures/Getty Images

jobs. There are many two-career families. Balancing work and personal life is a very important issue for most employees. A recent survey revealed that a majority of people would give up additional income from overtime work to be able to spend more time with their families.

A positive organizational culture is one that respects the pressures on employees from outside of the job. It offers ways for employees to meet those demands while also fulfilling the requirements of the job. Some of those ways include personal time, family leave, flextime, job sharing, and flexplace.

Many companies now offer personal time for employees to complete non-job activities that can only be done on work time. It is hard to schedule a dental or medical appointment, visit a child's school, or renew a driver's license while working. *Personal time* is a few hours each month that can be scheduled for non-job activities. Some companies even offer paid time for employees to volunteer at schools or other community organizations.

Family leave policies allow employees to take a leave from work for the birth or adoption of a child, to care for a sick family member, or for other personal emergencies. In 1993, the U.S. Congress passed the Family and Medical Leave Act. It requires companies employing 50 or more people to provide up to 12 weeks of unpaid leave for employees who face specific family or personal circumstances.

Flextime allows employees some choice in how their work days and work hours are arranged. Some employees may start and end their work day earlier or later than normal. They may be able to work a longer day and thereby work fewer days each week. *Job sharing* offers one job to two people. Each person works a part-time schedule. They share the work space and duties of the job. *Flexplace* means that some employees can complete part or all

How important do you believe family leave policies, flextime, or job sharing would be to you in choosing a career? Explain why work–life relationships are important when people set their life-span goals.

of their work away from the business site. Telecommuting is becoming increasingly popular. Employees who primarily use computers and other personal technologies may be able to work from home. They communicate with managers, co-workers, and customers using the Internet, telephone, and fax.

Some of the strategies for improving work–life relationships cost companies very little. Others do have a cost but often result in reduced absenteeism, lower employee turnover, and happier and more productive employees.

Which work–life program might allow a parent to take time off to take a child to a medical appointment in the middle of the day?

Employer–Employee Relations

Both managers and employees want their business to succeed. Unprofitable businesses have to reduce the number of employees they hire. They must limit salary and benefit increases. If everyone can work together to make the business successful, all should benefit. Managers and employees do not always have the same immediate goals. Managers must make sure that a company makes a profit. They try to get more work done at a lower cost. Employees are most concerned about compensation, working conditions, and job security.

Photodisc/Getty Images

What are the advantages a manager might experience by gaining employee input?

Many years ago, a boss made all of the important decisions and told employees what to do. This characterized employer–employee relations. Employees had little input as to what they did or how they did it. Each person was assigned a specific job. They often had little interaction with other employees while they worked.

That approach often left employees thinking that their ideas were not welcomed or appreciated. They believed they knew a great deal about their jobs and the business and could offer suggestions to improve the way work was done. Those differences led to disagreements and conflicts between many employers and their employees.

Much is often made of the differences between management and employees. Still, there may be more things that are alike than different between the two groups. Managers and employees have discovered that as they work together, they find ways to accomplish the goals of both the organization and the individuals who work for it. Managers who involve employees in decision-making find that better decisions are made. Employees are more likely to support those decisions. Employees discover that when they cooperate with management, managers have a better understanding of their needs and expectations. Both groups benefit through cooperation.

Labor Unions

Early in the twentieth century, as industries were growing rapidly, many employers did not treat their employees well. Low wages, long hours and unsafe working conditions caused employees to band together and form labor unions. A **labor union** is an organized group of employees who negotiate with employers about issues, such as wages and working conditions. Unions can be effective because they represent large numbers of employees. The popularity of labor unions peaked in the 1940s and 1950s when more than one-third of the U.S. labor force was unionized. Unions, particularly in the goods-producing industries, had been successful in achieving higher wages and benefits. At the same time federal and state governments were regulating unsafe working conditions. Beginning in the 1970s, the U.S. economy moved from a goods-producing to a service-providing economy. Employment in heavily unionized industries has declined. The percentage of U.S. workers who belong to a union has been steadily declining during that same time and is now about 12 percent.

As union participation in traditional industries has declined, membership in service-providing industries has grown. Some of the largest unionized occupations today are government, education, public safety, health care, and hospitality.

Unions and management resolve issues through *collective bargaining*, which is formal negotiation between members of both groups. When agreement is reached, both groups sign a written labor contract. There are also federal and state laws that regulate the relationships of businesses and unions.

Relationships between many companies and their unions are much more positive today than in the past. They work together on issues that affect the success of the business and the work life of employees. Examples include job training to keep employee skills up to date, employee assistance if a business site closes, and improving product quality to make businesses more competitive.

How might human resources managers help increase diversity in the workplace?

Photodisc/Getty Images

checkpoint ✓
What are some ways that companies help employees meet personal demands outside the job?

WORKFORCE DIVERSITY

Goal 2

Describe the benefits of diversity to an organization, individuals, and society.

Imagine a world where everyone looked, thought, and acted alike. The world is diverse, and the United States is the most diverse country in the world. That diversity continues to grow. Not all businesses reflect that diversity. Even in companies with a diverse workforce, that diversity is not always reflected in various job categories or in management positions.

Prospective employees and customers are attracted to work and shop in businesses where the employees are similar to themselves. When people with diverse backgrounds and characteristics are promoted into leadership and management positions, it will encourage others like them to work hard to achieve that same success.

Benefits of Diversity

"Workplace diversity" has many definitions. The basic definition of **diversity**, as it applies to the workplace is the comprehensive inclusion of people with differences in personal characteristics and attributes. The federal government has recognized important personal characteristics in equal employment legislation. The key laws are identified in Figure 8-5. Today, businesses working to build a diverse workforce use a much broader view of diversity. They try to build a broad workforce that reflects the communities in which they operate and the markets they want to serve. Diversity includes race, ethnicity, gender, age, and disability. It also includes socio-economic status, culture, religion, and even personal interests, abilities, and values.

When people in an organization are more alike than different, there is often reduced creativity and innovation. There will be limited understanding of people who are different including their attitudes, experiences, and needs. It will be difficult to recognize and plan for those differences when developing products and services for customers who are different from the people in the company. Companies that build a diverse workforce see several benefits. The benefits can be classified as organizational, individual, and societal.

Organizational Benefits *Prospective employees and managers are drawn from the broadest possible employment pool.* The greatest increase in the labor force in the future will be women, ethnic and racial minorities, and older workers. If people from those groups are not considered,

---

FEDERAL LAWS REGULATING DISCRIMINATION

- **The Equal Pay Act of 1963** disallows pay discrimination based on gender for jobs requiring equal skill, effort, and responsibility.

- The **Civil Rights Act of 1964** prohibits job discrimination based on race, color, religion, gender, and national origin.

- The **Age Discrimination in Employment Act of 1967** protects individuals who are 40 years of age or older.

- The **Americans with Disabilities Act of 1990,** which was amended in 2008, prohibits discrimination against qualified disabled workers and requires employers to make reasonable work accommodations.

▶ **Figure 8-5**

How have these laws increased employment opportunities for most Americans?

---

the company will have a much smaller pool from which to choose.

The company will have a broader base of knowledge and understanding when making decisions. People with different backgrounds, experiences, and even ways of thinking and planning will be a part of the organization. They will bring new ideas on how to design processes, plan products, work and communicate with others, and provide leadership.

Prospective customers will have a more positive image of the company. Customers with diverse characteristics will see a company that values diversity. They will have a greater level of respect and trust for the company and its products. They will see their own views and interests represented within the company.

The company will be better at serving diverse markets. The company will understand similarities and differences in needs, decision-making processes, and communication strategies among diverse customer groups. Traditional stereotypes that may have upset consumers in the past will no longer be used.

WORK *as a* **TEAM**

Many companies and organizations have developed diversity statements to reflect their beliefs about the importance of diversity. As a team, use the Internet to identify and study examples of those statements from several companies. Select one that your team agrees is the best statement. Justify your choice.

Global business strategies will improve. The United States is the most diverse country in the world and a country of immigrants. That offers American businesses a unique advantage to recognize and understand global needs and differences. They can do this much easier than companies from countries with limited diversity.

Individual Benefits
All employees will have the opportunity to develop to their full ability. In the past, women and other minority employees have faced a glass ceiling.

A **glass ceiling** is an artificial limit placed on minority groups moving into positions of authority and decision-making. Businesses that value diversity remove those obstacles so everyone has an opportunity to advance based on ability and performance.

Individuals will feel they are respected and supported despite their differences. Employees who are different from the typical employee do not have to hide those differences. They do not have to be uncomfortable because they are different. Individual differences will be expected and viewed as a valuable part of the organization. Employees can comfortably represent their uniqueness when participating in planning and decision-making.

Societal Benefits *Prejudice and discrimination will be reduced as a societal problem*. People involved in diverse

How does a new small business benefit from a commitment to diversity?

track5/iStockphoto.com

organizations learn to recognize and value diversity. This is true for neighborhoods, schools, and businesses alike. They lose their stereotypes and recognize the strength that comes from the full participation of every person.

The country has a more talented, experienced, economically successful workforce. Diversity opens more job opportunities for everyone. It allows people to develop and use all of their abilities. It increases access to higher-paying jobs for more people. Diversity in business leads to greater opportunities in society.

Developing a Diverse Organization

An organization's culture develops over many years. Employees and managers become comfortable with the way things have always been done. It may be hard to recognize all of the ways that an organization makes it difficult for people from diverse backgrounds to be successful in the organization. The whole organization will need to be committed to diversity in order for the necessary changes to occur.

The following steps have been used successfully in a number of businesses and other organizations to increase diversity.

1. **Develop a written commitment to diversity.** Prepare a mission statement that clearly communicates the company's values.

2. **Have the full support of top executives.** The top managers in the business must make diversity a priority in their written and oral communications and in their actions.

3. **Review evidence of diversity in the company.** Gather data on the diverse characteristics of all employees, managers, and customers. If any part of the organization does not reflect the diversity expectations, determine what is standing in the way and make changes.

4. **Update policies and procedures.** Make sure that recruiting, hiring, performance evaluation, and promotion practices encourage diversity.

5. **Provide continuing diversity education.** Managers and employees benefit from increased understanding of inclusion and diversity. Participating in classes and workshops prepares employees to work more effectively in a diverse organization.

6. **Recognize and celebrate diversity.** Make diversity a part of the organization's culture. Have visible evidence of the variety of languages, music, art, celebrations, and customs of employees and customers.

> **checkpoint ✓**
> Identify several organizational, individual, and societal benefits of diversity.

8-3 Assessment

Study Tools
www.cengage.com/school/genbus/pob

Key Concepts

Determine the best answer.

1. True or False. There are greater numbers of both younger and older employees in the workforce today than in the past.

2. Some employees can complete part or all of their work away from the business site under
   a. flextime
   b. flexplace
   c. job sharing
   d. personal time

3. The term most closely related to diversity is
   a. affirmative action
   b. discrimination
   c. minority
   d. inclusion

Make Academic Connections

4. **Social Studies** Use the Internet to identify data that describe the changing characteristics of the U.S. population in terms of age, gender, race, religion, and immigration status. Develop a written report of your findings. Include at least three tables and charts to support your written report.

5. **Art** Working with other students in your class, create a bulletin board, exhibit, or display that illustrates the diversity in your school and community.

6. **Journalism** Select a business in your community and contact a company manager to schedule an interview. Prepare several questions on the steps the company has taken to increase diversity and the results of those steps. Record your interview. Use the information to prepare an 500–750 word feature for an online news service or business blog site.

Coffee and a Conscience

In 1981, while on a skiing trip in Vermont, Robert Stiller stopped at a coffee shop for a cup of coffee. He liked the coffee so much that he decided to buy the business. Green Mountain Coffee Roasters is no longer a small-town coffee shop. It has expanded to become a major wholesaler of specialty coffees with a large direct-mail and Internet business. The company has been recognized by *Forbes* magazine as one of the best 200 small companies in America, by *Fortune* as one of the 100 fastest-growing companies in the world, and by *Corporate Responsibility* magazine as one of the 100 best corporate citizens.

Mr. Stiller was not only interested in developing a successful business. He had a belief that a company can be profitable and still have a social conscience. He wanted to operate a company that demonstrated a concern for the environment, for the people who grow and supply the coffee, and for the local and global community. Green Mountain Coffee is a partner and advocate in Businesses for Social Responsibility and the Fair Trade Partners.

Most coffee growers are small family farmers who are at the mercy of large coffee companies. Those companies had pushed the price paid for coffee beans to less than 70 cents a pound. The result was a drop in the income of small farmers to a level that didn't allow them to maintain their families' nutrition, health care, or education. Fair Trade Partners guarantee a minimum fair price when they purchase a farmer's coffee beans, as much as $1.40 per pound. In return, they ask the farmers to use farming practices that result in high-quality products and that protect the environment.

Another program supported by Green Mountain is Coffee Kids, a nonprofit international organization. It is committed to improving the lives

How do coffee companies benefit from paying small coffee growers a fair minimum price for their coffee beans?

of children and families in the small mountain towns of coffee-growing regions around the world. The organization offers health care, nutrition training, educational scholarships, and money for local schools to improve the lives of children living in poverty. Green Mountain and its employees have donated more than a million dollars to Coffee Kids.

Through the Community Action For Employees (CAFÉ) program, Green Mountain encourages employees to perform volunteer work while on company time. Every employee is allowed up to 52 hours each year in paid time off to volunteer for nonprofit organizations in their communities.

Social responsibility is an ongoing focus and commitment of the company. The following are examples of Green Mountain's principles.

Ethics Do the right thing. Integrity is the foundation of all our decisions, actions, and relationships.

Sustainability Pathway to our future. We use resources wisely and make decisions that take into account the well-being of people, profit, and the planet.

World Benefit Creating positive change. We are a force for good in the world. We celebrate and support the power of businesses and individuals to bring about positive changes, locally and globally.

Think Critically

1. Why would Green Mountain be willing to pay farmers almost twice as much for their coffee beans than the large coffee companies pay?

2. How do you believe social programs, such as those supported by Green Mountain Coffee, affect customers' views of the company? Do you believe it affects the sales of their products? Why or why not?

Business Notes

8-1 Human Resources Basics

- There are more than 150 million people who have full-time or part-time jobs in the United States workforce. Changes in the economy may require employees to develop new skills and get additional training. Consumer preferences, economic conditions, new technology, and business competition are strong influences on the workforce.

- Human resources are the people who work for a business. The major goals of human resources are to (1) identify the personnel needs, (2) maintain a supply of people to fill needs, (3) match abilities and interests with specific jobs, (4) provide training and development, (5) develop compensation plans, (6) protect the health and well-being of employees, and (7) maintain a satisfying work environment. The activities of human resources are planning and staffing, performance management, compensation and benefits, and employee relations.

8-2 Managing Human Resources

- Human resources management ensures that needed employees are available and that they are productive, paid, and satisfied with their work. If human resources management does its job well, the company will have productive and motivated employees who do their jobs well, contributing to a successful, profitable business.

- Compensation is the amount of money paid to an employee for work performed. Compensation is made up of two parts. Salary and wages are direct payment to an employee for work completed. Compensation in forms other than direct payment for work is known as benefits.

- The manager regularly evaluates the work of all employees. Performance evaluations focus on the specific job duties of each employee as well as the important work qualities expected of all employees.

8-3 Organizational Culture and Workforce Diversity

- An organizational culture is the environment in which people work, made up of the atmosphere, behaviors, beliefs, and relationships. An organizational culture shows people how they will be treated and how they are expected to treat others. A positive organizational culture respects the demands on employees from outside of the job.

- Prospective employees and customers are attracted to work and shop in businesses where people like them work. Companies that build a diverse workforce see several benefits. The benefits can be classified as organizational, individual, and societal.

Communicate Business Concepts

1. Why are service-providing industries growing more rapidly than goods-producing industries? What effect will this trend have on the skills people need for careers in the next 10 years?

2. Provide several examples of the effect of consumer "dollar votes" on jobs. What are some jobs that have increased and decreased in importance due to those consumer demands?

3. Small businesses usually cannot offer the same levels of wages and benefits to employees as large businesses. In what other ways can small

businesses compete to hire and retain highly qualified employees?

4. In addition to offering insurance benefits, what types of activities should businesses undertake to protect and improve the health and safety of their employees?

5. What are the advantages and disadvantages for a company in hiring part-time and temporary employees rather than full-time and permanent employees?

6. You are the economic development director for your community. Identify three service-providing companies that you believe could be successful in your community and offer the potential for many new jobs. Develop a short computer slide presentation for your Board of Directors introducing your selections and justifying your choices.

7. You are the human resources manager for a company and want to hire an accountant. List three good recruiting sources and justify your choices. If you wanted to hire a web designer, would your sources change? Why or why not?

8. Make a list of three benefits you would personally like to see a company offer its employees. How do you believe your list might change as your life situation changes?

9. Do you believe the physical conditions or psychological atmosphere of a business are more important to maintaining an effective work environment? Justify your choice.

Develop Your Business Language

Match the terms listed with the definitions.

10. Ends the employment relationship between a company and an employee.

11. Removes work from one company and sends it to another company that can complete it at a lower cost.

12. Amount of money paid to an employee for work performed.

13. Environment in which people work, made up of the atmosphere, behaviors, beliefs, and relationships.

14. Compensation in forms other than direct payment for work.

15. The assignment of an employee to another job in the company with a similar level of responsibility.

16. The comprehensive inclusion of people with differences in personal characteristics and attributes.

17. An organized group of employees who negotiate with employers about issues, such as wages and working conditions.

18. All the people 16 years and older who are employed or who are looking for a job.

19. Physical conditions and psychological atmosphere in which employees work.

20. The advancement of an employee to a position with greater responsibility.

21. Connect the amount of compensation to the quality or quantity of an employee's performance.

22. Direct payment to an employee for work completed.

23. A planned reduction in the number of employees needed in a firm in order to reduce costs and make the business more efficient.

24. A study of a job to identify in detail the specific job duties and skill requirements.

25. An artificial limit placed on minority groups moving into positions of authority and decision-making.

Key Terms

a. benefits
b. compensation
c. diversity
d. downsizing
e. glass ceiling
f. incentive systems
g. job analysis
h. labor union
i. organizational culture
j. outsourcing
k. promotion
l. salary and wages
m. termination
n. transfer
o. work environment
p. workforce

Make Academic Connections

26. **Math** A small business budgets $80 per employee per year for training costs. An additional $50 is provided for the first year of training for each new employee. Last year the firm started with 35 employees and added 6 new employees. Both parts of the training budget have been increased by 10 percent for this year.

  a. What was the total cost of training for last year?
  b. What percentage of that amount was spent on new employee training?
  c. With the proposed increase, how much will be spent for training each experienced employee and each new employee this year?
  d. What will be the total cost of training for all employees if four new employees are hired this year?

27. **Technology** Use a spreadsheet and graphics program to make a chart or graph showing current data for the U.S. workforce using the following characteristics: (a) part-time versus full-time employees; (b) gender of employees; (c) racial classification of employees.

28. **Read** Companies participate in community activities to demonstrate that they value diversity. Find a news article that relates to a community activity or service project completed by a company in your state. Read the article and outline the major concepts presented in the article using bullet points. Include a properly formatted citation for your source. Possible sources include printed and online versions of newspapers, magazines, and business or organization websites.

29. **Advertising** Use the Internet or a newspaper to locate classified advertising for employment opportunities. Select a job of interest to you and find detailed listings from three different companies for that type of job. Develop a table that compares the three opportunities based on job duties, wages or salary and benefits, and work environment of the company.

30. **Math** Nicole works for a store that pays her an hourly wage of $7 plus a commission of 2 percent on all sales over $500 per day. Her hours worked and daily sales for the past week are shown in the table.

  a. How much did Nicole earn in base salary and commission for each of the days she worked?
  b. How much was the total of her base salary for the week?
  c. How much was the total of her commissions for the week?
  d. What were Nicole's total earnings for the week?

Monday	6 hrs	$735 total sales
Tuesday	4 hrs	$320 total sales
Wednesday	5 hrs	$570 total sales
Thursday	3 hrs	$450 total sales
Friday	0 hrs	$0 total sales
Saturday	8 hrs	$1,050 total sales

Decision-Making Strategies

Arte Malik has operated a lawn care business for many years. The business offers landscaping services including seeding and sodding lawns, applying chemicals and fertilizer, and regular lawn mowing. Mr. Malik has 25 employees. Many of them have worked for him for 5 to 10 years. He usually hires two or three new employees each year. In the past, Arte was not concerned about the skills of new employees. He prefers to find people who are interested in the work and want to learn. Yet the machinery he uses is getting more complex, and employees must know a great deal about safe handling of chemicals, detecting plant diseases, and effective lawn care. The local community college has a two-year degree program in lawn care management. Arte is deciding whether to continue his present hiring procedure of allowing new employees to learn on the job, develop a training program to be offered to all employees, or hire only people who have completed the community college program.

31. What are the advantages and disadvantages of each of the choices Mr. Malik is considering?

32. If you were Mr. Malik's human resources manager, what choice would you recommend? Why?

Linking School and Community

Identify several people from your community who work full time. Ask them their views on the importance of maintaining a balance between their work life and their personal life. Have them identify ways they believe the company they work for supports or does not support a balance in work–life relationships. Based on your discussions, do you believe most of the companies are or are not sensitive to work–life relationships?

Web Workout

Each year *Fortune* magazine publishes a list of the "100 Best Companies to Work For." This is not the only list that ranks employers. Several organizations, magazines, and websites publish lists of outstanding employers in specific industries or for particular types of workers. Because each set of rankings is based on different criteria, the companies appearing on each list may be different.

Looking at the lists and the criteria used to rank employers can provide insight into these businesses for consumers, investors, and potential employees. They give particular insight into companies that appear to be working hard to develop and maintain a positive organizational climate and work environment.

Think Critically

1. Think about the criteria you might use to rank companies as the best places to work. Compare and discuss your ideas with your classmates.

2. Locate the website of an organization or magazine that provides an annual ranking of the best places to work. Review the rankings, the criteria, and the companies included in the list. Write a short summary of your findings. Include the official name of the list and your source.

3. Choose a company from the list you found and visit the company's website. Locate information about organizational culture, work environment, and work–life relationships. Describe your findings and offer your opinion about this company as a great place to work.

International Business Plan Event

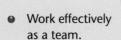

Opening a business in another part of the world presents a unique challenge that requires a detailed business plan. The business plan is used to convince potential investors to financially support the international business idea.

This event may be completed by one to three students. Participants will conduct research for a specific international location, determine a business/product/service needed for the selected country, and prepare a business plan to convince investors about the soundness of the international plan.

Participants will prepare a business plan limited to 30 pages that includes an introduction for the business plan, trade area and cultural analysis, planned operation, and planned financing for the international business. The body of the business plan must be typed following the sequence outlined. Participants may bring a copy of the written entry or note cards and appropriate visual aids to use during the presentation. Participants have 10 minutes to present their international business plan. Five additional minutes are allotted for the judges or audience members to ask questions about the business plan.

Performance Indicators Evaluated

● Demonstrate critical thinking and problem solving skills associated with starting an international business.

● Work effectively as a team.

● Demonstrate an understanding of the basic steps involved in starting a business in an international setting.

● Analyze information to derive data necessary for a convincing business plan.

● Present facts that support the rationale for locating a business in another part of the world.

For more detailed information about performance indicators, go to the DECA website.

Think Critically

1. Why is it important to research the culture of the location for a potential international business?

2. Why is it more difficult to obtain domestic funding for an international business idea?

3. What demographics should be considered when locating a business in another part of the world?

4. What sources can be used to locate solid financial information when developing an international business?

5. Why might investors be reluctant to support an international business idea during a recession?

www.deca.org

Career Planning and Development

Blend Images/Getty Images

EMPLOYMENT ASSISTANCE

Education & Training

While most jobs involve planning, creating, or distributing goods and services, some careers may help people obtain employment and guide them to advance in their careers. The field of employment assistance includes a variety of career development activities. Some workers are employed by schools and companies to help people explore career options. Others assist people with preparing a resume, writing a cover letter, or practicing interview skills.

Every state has an employment bureau to help workers who have lost their jobs or who require retraining if they are injured on the job. Employment assistance workers are available to help identify, encourage, and plan advanced training for persons who have jobs. In addition to schools, businesses, and government agencies, some career professionals provide fee-based services for individuals. The field of career counseling is especially important as employment opportunities change due to technology, global competition, and demographic trends.

Related Job Titles

- Career Counselor
- Career Placement Advisor
- Career Planning Instructor
- Career Coach
- Resume Writer
- Interviewing Trainer
- Vocational Testing Center Manager

Analyze Career Opportunities in ...
CAREER COUNSELING

Use library and Internet resources to learn more about careers in employment assistance. Choose one of the job titles listed in the box above and answer the following questions.

1. How would you describe the nature of the work? Include examples of things that might happen in a typical work day.

2. Is this a career that interests you? Describe how you might use your talents, abilities, and skills in this career.

What's it like to work as a ... Career Counselor?

"You are very capable in science, mathematics, and computer technology. However, your interests seem to lie in working with people." Comments like this from a career counselor can help people better understand what they do well and what they enjoy doing.

In the next stage of the career search process, a career counselor will provide assistance with developing the content and format for a resume. Then, sample interviews will take place to help the person present a confident and competent appearance.

The counselor's work doesn't end when a person obtains a job. A desire to advance in a career field can result in additional interaction with a counselor. Or, if a desire exists to change careers, the counselor can direct you to needed resources for education and training.

What about you? Have you ever helped someone with finding a job or preparing for an interview? Is this something you enjoy?

Career Opportunities

Goals

1 Describe the steps in the career planning process.

2 Identify the main sources of career information.

3 Discuss career fields with the most growth potential.

Key Terms

career 200

informational interview 202

mobility 204

Focus on REAL LIFE

"How did Uncle Ted prepare for his job as a regional sales manager?" Dan Capparus asked his mother.

"You should talk to him about that," she responded. "Your Uncle Ted could give you some very helpful information for your career planning activities."

Later on the phone, Dan asked, "Uncle Ted, how did you become a regional sales manager? What experience and training was most important? What computer software do I need to know? What classes should I take in school to help me prepare for a similar job? How can I get some work experience while in school?"

"Wait a minute, one question at a time," Uncle Ted responded. "Let's start by talking about the classes that you find most interesting and those in which you receive high grades."

Goal 1

Describe the steps in the career planning process.

THE CAREER PLANNING PROCESS

An *occupation* is a task or series of tasks that is performed to provide a good or service. People are hired to fill occupations, and they are paid for the work they perform.

A **career** is a goal for work that is fulfilled through an occupation or series of occupations. You actually have a kind of career goal now: "to complete your schooling and get ready for your future."

Career planning is the process of studying careers, assessing yourself in terms of careers, and making decisions about a future career. As shown in Figure 9-1 on the next page, this process begins by carry-ing out a personal assessment. Your interests, values, talents, and abilities provide the basis for a career choice as you develop new interests and abilities.

Your search for the right career could continue for a long time. In the years ahead, some of your values and goals will change. You will develop new interests and abilities.

Do you want a career or an occupation? Explain your answer.

Describe a career planning activity you might complete to help you achieve your life-span goals. Consider talking to people you know about their work activities and careers. You might also observe various work situations to determine if those jobs would be of interest to you.

Your Study of Careers

The study of careers is a continuous process. New career opportunities occur all the time. You do not just decide to study careers for one day or one week. It is important to view learning about careers as a lifelong activity. This process is something that continues even after you begin your career.

Your first decision will likely be a *tentative career decision*—a decision that is subject to change as new information is received. A tentative decision is much better than no decision at all. Your career decision will give you a direction that is needed.

Making initial career decisions while you are in school has many advantages. One is that, in school, you have a lot of information readily on hand. More importantly, early career planning will help you choose the right courses. An early career decision can also encourage you to become involved with organizations such as Future Business Leaders of America (FBLA), DECA, and Business Professionals of America (BPA). These organizations teach you about business and careers.

Career Training

Many careers require education and training beyond high school. These educational alternatives include:

- Two-year schools, often called community colleges or junior colleges, offer training in many areas.

- Four-year colleges and universities, both public and private, provide education for many careers and professions.

- Private business schools and other institutions specialize in training students for specific occupations such as court reporter, computer technician, barber, or medical assistant.

Consider the cost for further schooling as an investment in your future that will help

THE CAREER PLANNING PROCESS
Step 1 Personal Assessment
• Determine interests and values
• Identify talents and abilities
Step 2 Employment Market Analysis
• Geographic influences
• Business and economic trends
Step 3 Application Process
• Application form
• Resume and cover letter
Step 4 Interview Process
• Prepare for interview
• Follow-up activities
Step 5 Employment Acceptance
• Salary and financial factors
• Organizational environment
Step 6 Career Development and Advancement
• Practice career success behaviors
• Develop strong work relationships

▶ **Figure 9-1**
What are some resources you can use in planning your career?

you earn higher wages and expand your potential. Many ways exist to help finance additional schooling. Most schools have financial aid programs including scholarships, student loans, and work-study opportunities.

Some financial aid programs are based on your academic record. Others are based on financial need. You should assess these methods for financing an education as you continue your career planning and decision-making.

How can you be sure that you are making the best career decision? There is no way to guarantee a perfect decision. Those who follow the right steps generally make good decisions.

checkpoint ✓
List the six steps in the career planning process.

The Riley Guide offers information and links on various career-planning topics. Access the website shown below and click on the link for Chapter 9. Click on one of the Riley Guide links and obtain information from two different sources. Is the information provided similar or are conflicting findings evident?

www.cengage.com/school/genbus/pob

Goal 2

Identify the main sources of career information.

CAREER INFORMATION SOURCES

Many information sources for career planning are easily available. Your school may have a career resource center with magazines, books, videos, and other material related to careers. Some information covers careers in general. Other sources provide specific coverage about occupations and careers in your area.

Print and Media Sources

The *Occupational Outlook Quarterly* or other print publications from the

Digital Vision/Getty Images

What are some ways you can get career information?

Bureau of Labor Statistics can be helpful. The *Occupational Outlook Handbook* gives in-depth information on hundreds of occupations including job duties, working conditions, education and training requirements, advancement possibilities, employment outlook, and earnings. These resources are also available online.

Career World magazine publishes information about a variety of careers. It often looks at careers of the future. *The Encyclopedia of Careers and Vocational Guidance* can give you basic information about many occupations.

Newspapers, including online versions, are valuable sources of career information. Articles about business trends, local companies, and career topics are published in the career and business sections. Help-wanted ads, which appear in the classified advertising section and online, provide insight into the kinds of career opportunities available. These ads also tell you what training and skills are in demand in the current job market.

Online Sources

Many websites are available to help you with career planning. These sites offer information about career opportunities, resumes, effective interviewing, and creating a career portfolio.

Informational Interviews

A very useful method to get career information is with an informational interview. An **informational interview** is a planned discussion with a worker who is willing to help you find out about the work that a person does, the preparation needed for that career, and the person's feelings about the career. Informational interviews will help you gain insight into what actually happens in a specific career area.

You will find that most workers like to talk about their career experiences. Be sure to plan your questions for a career information interview. Some suggested questions might include:

- How did you get your current job?

- In what ways do you find your work most satisfying? What are your main frustrations?

- What tasks and activities are required in your work?

- What are the most important qualifications for working in this field?

- What advice would you give a young person who is thinking about this type of work?

Keep notes on what you learn in your informational interviews. The experiences of others can provide key career planning information.

If a specific career interests you, ask your teacher or guidance counselor about the possibility of becoming a *job shadow* at a company employing workers that reflect your career interest. Job shadowing allows you to spend time with a worker

WORK *as a* **TEAM**

Using Figure 9-2, select three of the career areas listed. For each career area: (1) create a list of additional jobs, and (2) describe various skills that would be necessary to work in this career area.

for a day or a week to learn about a certain occupation.

Business Contacts

The process of talking to other people about their jobs is called *networking*. The advantage of networking is that your contacts are not limited to the people you know personally. Every person you meet is a potential contact for career information. The contacts in your network can provide support when you start work as well as later in life.

> **checkpoint** ✓
> What are the main sources of career information?

CAREER AREAS WITH GREATEST GROWTH POTENTIAL		
Business services • data analysts • employee benefits managers • language translators • web consultants	**Financial services** • actuaries • e-commerce accountants • investment consultants • risk assessment managers	**Management and human resources** • employee benefits administrators • interviewers • supervisors
Computer technology • computer operators • service technicians • systems analysts • website developers	**Health care** • health care administrators • home health workers • lab technicians • physical therapists	**Sales and retailing** • electronics marketing representatives • financial services representatives • medical products sales managers
Education • corporate trainers • educational administrators • special education teachers	**Hospitality and food service** • customer service representatives • food service managers • meeting planners • resort and hotel administrators	**Social services** • child care workers • elder care coordinators • family counselors • social service agency administrators

▶ **Figure 9-2**

Which of the career areas shown above interest you? Do you think you should limit your career exploration to these career areas?

GROWTH CAREER AREAS

The life work you choose could be affected by the careers available in a field. Future employment opportunities are influenced by geography and business trends.

Geographic Influences

You may have to decide whether you want to work in the geographic area in which you now live or whether you are willing to move to where the job you really want is located. There may be reasons why you would prefer to live and work near your home. People who successfully pursue the careers of their choice often have mobility. **Mobility** is the willingness and ability of a person to move to where jobs are located.

The lack of mobility can lead to *locational unemployment*. This occurs when jobs are available in one place but go unfilled because those who are qualified to fill those jobs live elsewhere and are not willing to relocate.

Economic and Industry Trends

Career areas with the most potential are influenced by economic trends and current business activities. Consumer demand, changing demographic trends, and new technology are factors that often affect career opportunities. As shown in Figure 9-2 on the previous page, service industries are expected to have the greatest employment potential.

While these are fields with strong future demand, do not limit yourself. Every career area will need new employees. Think about your personal interests and abilities in addition to economic and business trends.

> **checkpoint** ✓
> What factors affect the career areas that will be in demand in the future?

9-1 Assessment

Study Tools

www.cengage.com/school/genbus/pob

Key Concepts

Determine the best answer.

1. The first step of the career planning process is to
   a. prepare a resume and cover letter
   b. interview for a job
   c. determine your interests and abilities
   d. obtain career training

2. The purpose of an informational interview is to
   a. obtain information about a career area
   b. apply for a job with a nonprofit organization
   c. research salaries for starting employees
   d. gain career training experience

3. Spending time with a worker on the job to learn about a career is called
   a. networking
   b. personal assessment
   c. career training
   d. job shadowing

Make Academic Connections

4. **Geography** Conduct research to identify areas of the country with strong demand for various careers. What factors have affected job opportunities in these geographic regions?

5. **Science** Identify recent scientific developments. Explain how these discoveries might affect (a) the type of career opportunities available in the future and (b) how people work in organizations.

6. **Math** A survey in a major city revealed that 32,000 people used personal contacts for obtaining a job, while 18,000 others obtained their jobs through the Internet. In this survey, what percentage of jobs were obtained through personal contacts.

Doing Business in... Ukraine

As the country of Ukraine moved from using the Russian ruble to its current currency, the hryvnia, something rather unusual occurred. To prevent a shortage of money, the government issued coupons to use when buying some of the limited food and other products. While the coupons were not intended to become currency, their acceptance grew as the ruble became less attractive. The people of Ukraine desired to separate themselves from their past as a Russian state.

Today, the hryvnia is a fairly strong currency, reflecting an expanding economy and encouraging business investment from around the world. Ukraine's strategic location, between Europe and Asia, is also attractive. More than 300 U.S. companies have business operations there. Ukraine's economy benefits from fertile farmland, rich natural resources, a well-developed industrial base, and a highly trained labor force.

Ukraine has seen extremes in its history. The country was the major political and cultural center in Eastern Europe until conquered in 1240. More recently, Ukraine was part of the Soviet Union for 70 years. It became independent in 1991 and has expressed interest in being considered for membership in the European Union.

Visitors to the country often comment on the friendliness and generosity of the Ukrainian people. In business, however, be sure to use formal titles, such as Mr., Mrs., Miss, Ms., or Dr., until you are told to use a first name. When conducting business negotiations, don't accept the first "no." This initial "no" may be quick and automatic. Instead, be pleasant and ask again using a different phrasing. In addition, "final offers" may not be final. Be prepared to wait. Ukrainian businesspeople may walk out or shout. While responding in a similar dramatic way might be useful, patience will usually be more effective.

Social events are important in the business process. As you develop trust, acceptance of you will develop. Meetings will usually include highly sweetened coffee or tea along with chocolates or cookies. Some of the most popular dinner foods of Ukrainians include pork, chicken, seafood, potatoes, and many types of bread—white, brown, rolls, bagels, pita, and flat bread.

Think Critically

1. How does Ukraine's history affect current business and economic activities?

2. What aspects of Ukrainian culture might create difficulties for international companies?

3. Conduct library or Internet research to obtain additional information about business and economic activities in Ukraine.

How does a country's weather affect business activities including tourism?

Gleb Garanich/Reuters/Landov

Planning Your Career

Goals

1 Describe factors of a personal assessment for career planning.

2 Discuss methods for obtaining career experience.

3 Identify information sources for available jobs.

Key Terms

values 207

talent 207

ability 207

Focus on REAL LIFE

"Brianna, what things have you done to develop a better understanding of careers that you are considering?" asked the guidance counselor.

"I prepared a career study on becoming a corporate lawyer for one of my classes," Brianna responded. "I also interviewed two local lawyers. One of them works in private practice and the other one is legal counsel for a local company."

The counselor nodded and followed up by asking, "Anything else?"

"I took a marketing course last year and found it interesting." Brianna replied. "Then I got a part-time job as a marketing assistant last summer. It was a great experience. I learned tons about marketing activities. But the best part was getting to talk to sales and marketing people about their careers. Since then, I have decided to take more courses related to marketing."

"OK, let's review your class schedule."

Goal 1

Describe factors of a personal assessment for career planning.

PERSONAL ASSESSMENT

How can you make sure you select a job you will enjoy and that fits your life situation? Your career planning activities should start with a self-assessment of your interests, values, and abilities. These three areas will help you better understand the careers that will be the best for you. With a thorough self-assessment, you will be more likely to have a satisfying and successful career.

Interests

Many resources are available in print and online to determine the activities that give you satisfaction. Your *interests* provide a basis for your employment goals and possible career paths.

People with strong social tendencies may be best suited for work interacting with people. If you enjoy investigating situations, a career in some type of research should be considered. What are some topics or activities of interest to you?

What interests and values will influence your choice of career?

Values

Your **values** are things that are important to you. You can learn about your values with exercises or activities. These exercises show how you rank items such as prestige, money, power, achievement, independence, security, belonging, or serving others. Each of these may influence you, directly or indirectly, when you select your life's work.

You can begin to look at your values by answering some questions. Your answers will help you understand what you consider important. Examples of questions include:

- Is it important for me to earn a lot of money?

- Am I mainly interested in work that provides a service for others?

- Is it important for me to have an occupation that others think is important even if I do not really care for it?

- Do I want an occupation that is very challenging and may require additional schooling?

- Would I be willing to start in a job that pays a lower salary than another if that job was more challenging and offered better opportunities for future advancement?

- Do I consider investing money in education or occupational training as important as spending for other things?

Another question to better understand your values is: "What would you do if someone gave you a large sum of money to be used in any way you desire?" Would you start your own business? Would you hire a jet and travel around the world? Would you set up a foundation to support athletics for underprivileged children? Would you buy the trendiest wardrobe ever? Would you use the money to finance an expensive education? Your answers will reveal something about your personal values.

WORK as a TEAM

Prepare a list of common values of people in our society. For each item on your list, describe career situations that would be appropriate for people with this value. Identify the career situations on your list that represent a type of work you might enjoy.

Talents and Abilities

Each of you has certain talents and abilities. A **talent** is a natural, inborn aptitude to do certain things. People often say someone has a "natural talent." **Ability** is the quality of being able to perform a mental or physical task. Your talents and abilities, along with your career goals and interests, are important in career planning.

You can learn about your abilities in a number of ways. Think about the courses you have taken and the grades you have received in school. What kinds of courses have you taken? In which ones have you done your best work? Which

How can your natural abilities help you get a job?

Life-Span Plan

Complete a personal assessment of yourself. It should include listings of your interests, values, talents, and abilities. Explain how these lists may help you create your own life-span plan. Describe some work situations that reflect your current interests, values, talents, and abilities.

courses have been easiest for you? Which have been the most difficult? Which do you like the best? Answers to questions such as these will identify your talents and abilities.

Abilities can be developed, and that is important to keep in mind. If you are weak in a certain area, you may want to take courses that will improve that area. For instance, employers continually report that writing, reading, and computing skills are very important.

If you are not strong in preparing reports, take extra courses in English and Business Communication. If reading is a concern, get help in that area. If working with fractions and decimals is not easy for you, more courses in math, including business math, would be desirable. Work to strengthen your weak areas *before* you go into full-time work. You can plan your courses and future activities to help you grow toward your chosen career.

Goal 2

Discuss methods for obtaining career experience.

checkpoint ✓

What is the difference between an interest and a talent?

EMPLOYMENT EXPERIENCE

Most people have more career skills than they realize. Your involvement in a range of school and community activities provides the basis for employment experiences. You can obtain further career-oriented abilities in four main ways: work-study programs, part-time employment, volunteering, and school activities.

A Question of Ethics

Discriminatory Hiring Practices

Tomas Novak applied for a position as a regional sales manager for a technology company. Tomas was born and educated in Prague, located in what is now the Czech Republic. He has lived and worked in the United States for eight years and recently became an American citizen. He has more than 10 years of computer sales experience.

After the interview, Tomas was told that other applicants were more qualified. He did not receive a job offer. Tomas feels he was a victim of discrimination due to his slight Czech accent. He believes his ability and skills were comparable to others who were hired.

According to the Civil Rights Act and the Americans with Disabilities Act (ADA), it is illegal for employers to make hiring decisions based on personal characteristics such as age, marital status, ethnicity, race, and gender.

You can help reduce illegal hiring practices. Be cautious when deciding what kinds of personal information you include in a resume or cover letter. Most potential employers do not want to see this personal information related to characteristics that might be a basis for hiring bias. Instead, only offer personal information that is related to the job and your career skills, such as hobbies, community activities, memberships, or personal interests.

Think Critically

1. Describe other situations in which a person might be discriminated against when applying for a job.

2. What actions can companies and workers take to eliminate discriminatory hiring practices?

Work-Study Programs

Cooperative education combines school with work-related experience. These programs provide an occasion to develop a variety of on-the-job skills. You will not only learn about technical aspects of the job, but will also learn to interact in work settings.

In a similar way, *internships* involve work experience in organizations while learning about a career field. Internships for careers in accounting, finance, marketing, and communications are available with many companies and nonprofit organizations.

Applying for an internship is similar to applying for a job. First, identify potential positions. Then prepare a resume and cover letter to communicate your background and interest in participating in an internship.

Part-Time Employment

Summer and part-time work can provide valuable experience. In addition, these work situations will allow you the chance to see if you enjoy a particular career field. Your part-time work experience also helps you make contacts. These people will be able to guide you and offer support throughout your working life.

Volunteer Activities

Involvement in community service can result in gaining career experiences and improving work habits. Volunteering in community organizations also helps you develop organizational skills while making future career contacts.

Name some volunteer and part-time activities that could help in a career search.

Brand X Pictures/Getty Images

School Activities

Class assignments can provide work-related experiences. For example, research and communication skills are developed when you prepare reports and oral presentations. Working on team projects offers you a chance to interact with others, a skill vital in every career.

School clubs and organizations can result in a range of valuable skills. Goal setting, planning, supervising, and delegating responsibility are activities needed in many employment settings.

> **checkpoint ✓**
> What are methods for obtaining employment experience?

SOURCES OF AVAILABLE JOBS

Finding available positions is a common concern for job hunters. Several sources are often used to obtain leads. Your ability to find job openings is a key part of career planning activities.

> **Goal 3**
>
> Identify information sources for available jobs.

Joel Calheiros/Shutterstock.com

The Media

Some of the same sources that provide career planning information are also valuable for identifying potential employment positions. Help-wanted ads can be a starting point. Newspapers post employment ads on their websites and job-search websites have searchable databases of currently advertised positions. Be aware that most available positions are not advertised to the general public. Therefore, other job search actions are very important.

Personal Contacts

You need to let as many people as possible know that you are looking for a job. Your school counselors and business teachers can be helpful. If your school has a placement office, be sure to register with that office. Your relatives, friends, neighbors, and others can be valuable sources of job leads.

Business Contacts

You should visit businesses and ask about their openings. Some businesses post help-wanted signs in their windows. Some retail businesses, including restaurants, accept applications continuously. They make it easy for prospective employees to pick up and turn in applications. Employment kiosks, where you can apply for a job online, are common in large stores. Getting a job means going out and looking around. During a visit, you will be able to observe the types of activities performed by employees. You may also be able to make contacts for future career information.

Use phone books, business directories, and websites to find names of organizations that may have unadvertised jobs. Communicating with these companies can produce business contacts that can result in current or future employment opportunities.

Career Fairs

Career fairs are often held at schools or community centers. These events allow a chance to contact several prospective employers in a short time. You will be asked a few questions to determine if you qualify for a longer interview.

Get ready for job fairs by being prepared to quickly communicate your potential contributions to an organization. Knowing something about the company will help set you apart from other applicants.

Government Employment Offices

Local and state government employment offices are another source for

Stockbyte/Getty Images

Name some ways you can find out about job openings.

information about available jobs. These tax-supported agencies help people find jobs and provide career information, and work with employers to find qualified workers.

Employment offices can provide up-to-date information about the job market in your area. They can help you look for part-time, summer, or full-time work.

When seeking employment, use a variety of sources. Be sure to talk to as many people as possible about potential jobs and job search strategies. Use this information to create a plan that will make you a strong job candidate.

> **checkpoint** ✓
> What are the main sources of information about available jobs?

Stockbyte/Getty Images

What do you think would be the most reliable source of job information?

9-2 Assessment

Study Tools
www.cengage.com/school/genbus/pob

Key Concepts

Determine the best answer.

1. True or False. A person's values are also called natural talents.

2. True or False. Volunteering experience can result in obtaining career skills.

3. A desire to assist others in your job is an example of your
   a. talents
   b. interests
   c. abilities
   d. values

4. A(n) _?_ is an event that allows a person to contact several prospective employers in a short time.
   a. career fair
   b. informational interview
   c. network
   d. career resource center

Make Academic Connections

5. **Research** Use library research or an Internet search to locate a career assessment tool. After answering the questions, describe what you learned about yourself in relation to potential future careers.

6. **Communication** Look at the classified advertising section in your Sunday newspaper or online. Find three jobs that include an international factor. Prepare a paragraph summary explaining actions a person might take to prepare for these jobs.

7. **Read** Locate an article that relates to obtaining employment experience or locating available job positions. Read the article and outline the major ideas presented in the article using bullet points. Include a properly formatted citation for your source. Possible sources include printed and online versions of newspapers or magazines. Also consider independent online sources that produce original content.

Media Literacy

Effective Presentations

"Please prepare a presentation about the recent changes in our product line for the executive committee meeting."

This request and others point out your need to be able to make oral presentations. Your ability to communicate orally is a vital skill that can be enhanced by considering these actions.

Plan Your Presentation

- Clearly define your purpose. Organize the main sections. Conduct research to get needed information.
- Plan a creative introduction. Use a story, quote, statistic, or involvement activity to get the audience's attention and to communicate your main theme.
- Consider using a handout with key ideas, graphs, tables, maps, or other visuals.
- Develop a clear conclusion. Summarize the main ideas and key findings.

Practice Your Presentation

- Prepare an outline of key ideas and main phrases. Do not memorize or read your entire presentation.
- Present your complete presentation several times. Record your presentation to determine areas for improvement.

Make Your Presentation

- Talk to the audience, don't read to them. Don't read from your visuals—posters, slides, or other items.
- Use effective voice projection, expression, and enthusiasm. Avoid repetitious phrases such as "OK," "you know," and "like."
- Look and talk professionally—dress appropriately and stand up straight.

You are likely to make many presentations throughout your life. At first it may seem difficult. As you prepare, practice, and present more talks, your ability and comfort level will increase.

How might you benefit from practicing a presentation in front of a colleague or classmate?

Think Critically

1. What are the main suggestions you should follow for making an effective presentation?
2. Describe some situations in which you may make presentations during your life.

9-3 Applying for Employment

Goals

1 Prepare an application form and a resume.

2 Identify the parts of an application cover letter.

3 Discuss the online application process.

Key Terms

application form 213

resume 214

career portfolio 216

cover letter 216

Focus on REAL LIFE

"Congratulations, Fran!" said Maria as she hugged her niece. "What are you going to do now that you've graduated?"

"Get a job," responded Francisca. "My resume is ready and I've already created profiles on some of the job search websites."

"What kind of job are you looking for?" asked Maria as they posed for a photo.

"I've got a plan, Aunt Maria. I'm looking for an accounting position where I can use the skills I learned in high school. In the fall, I want to take an accounting class at the community college. Eventually, I want to transfer to the university. For now, I want to earn some money and get some experience."

Maria smiled and said, "There might be some openings where I work. I'll check the website."

APPLICATION ACTIVITIES

The application process may start in several ways. You might fill out an application form provided by the employer. The application might be a printed form, but online applications are also common. You may also apply by submitting a resume and cover letter. As an alternative to mailing these documents, you might send them via e-mail or post them to a website.

Personal Data Sheet

Before you fill out an application form, you need to prepare a *personal data sheet*. A personal data sheet is a summary of your important job-related information. It should list your education and work experience, as well as your references. Preparing your personal data sheet will ensure you have all the necessary information to fill out the application form.

Application Form

An employer often has each applicant complete an application form. An **application form** asks for information related to employment. The form gives the employer standard information about each job applicant. The form will likely ask for your name, address, education,

Goal 1

Prepare an application form and a resume.

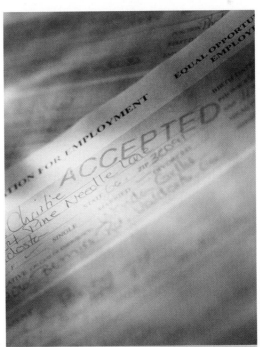

How can letters and forms provide insight into your personal attributes?

► **Figure 9-3**

How might your completion of an online application form reflect how you would approach your work?

Online Employment Application

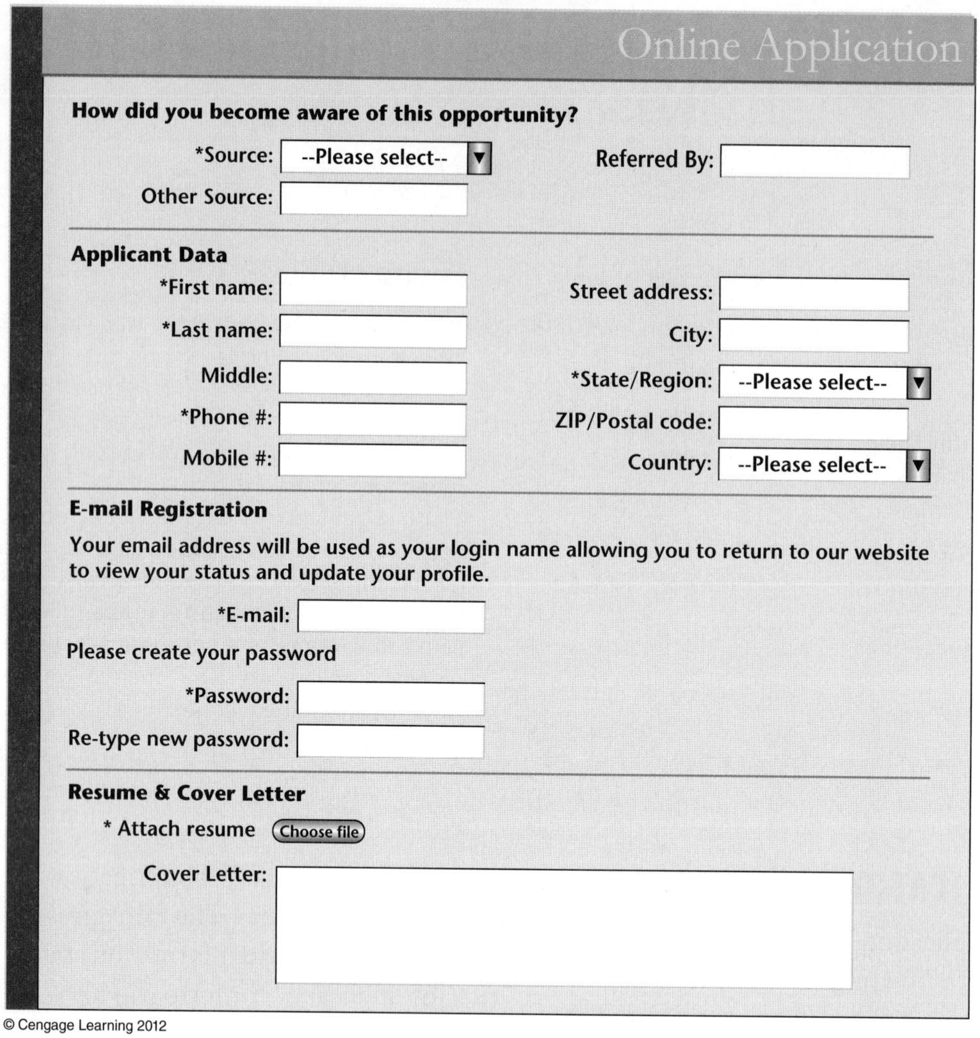

Online Application

How did you become aware of this opportunity?

*Source: --Please select--   Referred By: [   ]

Other Source: [   ]

Applicant Data

*First name: [   ]   Street address: [   ]

*Last name: [   ]   City: [   ]

Middle: [   ]   *State/Region: --Please select--

*Phone #: [   ]   ZIP/Postal code: [   ]

Mobile #: [   ]   Country: --Please select--

E-mail Registration

Your email address will be used as your login name allowing you to return to our website to view your status and update your profile.

*E-mail: [   ]

Please create your password

*Password: [   ]

Re-type new password: [   ]

Resume & Cover Letter

* Attach resume (Choose file)

Cover Letter: [   ]

© Cengage Learning 2012

work experience, the job for which you are applying, and references.

Filling out the application form should be viewed as your first job task. Follow directions carefully. Print answers neatly if you are using a paper application form. If you are completing an online application form, key carefully. Answer all questions completely. Figure 9-3 shows a portion of an online application form.

Resume

A **resume** is a tool that provides information about you to a potential employer. Two of the most popular types of resumes are *experience-based* and *qualifications-based*. In an experience-based resume, experiences are usually listed in order of work

history. In a qualifications-based resume, your abilities and experiences related to the job for which you are applying are highlighted.

As shown in Figure 9-4, a resume usually includes the following sections:

- **Personal information** Name, address, phone, e-mail

- **Career objective** A focused, specific, personal employment goal

- **Education** Schools attended, dates, degrees, programs of study

- **Experience** Work and volunteer activities with dates and responsibilities

- **Career-related honors and other activities** Awards, school and community involvement

► Figure 9-4

How will the information in this resume help an employer who wants to hire the best person possible?

Francisca Negalo

1602 Collegewood Drive
Madison, WI 53711-2821

(608) 555-0308

fnegalo@badgernet.com

CAREER OBJECTIVE

To use my accounting, computer, and business skills in an organization with an opportunity for advancement

EDUCATION

Four Lakes High School, Madison, Wisconsin
- Emphasis in Business Education
- Graduated June 10, 20--

EXPERIENCE

Records Clerk, Tempest Tea Pot Company, Houghton, Wisconsin
- Created and updated database of customer contact information for promotional mailings
- Maintained sales records for online and mail order shipments
- Designed promotional materials for mailings and website content

General Clerk, City Assessor's Office, Cambridge, Wisconsin
- Updated Excel spreadsheets with listings of homeowners tax assessments
- Researched government programs to assist delinquent taxpayers

HONORS AND ACTIVITIES

- Markley Leadership Award, Four Lakes Alumni Association
- Honor Roll, Four Lakes High School
- Treasurer, Future Business Leaders of America
- Program Planning Committee, Dane County Youth Council
- Publicity Coordinator, Four Lakes Pep Club
- Co-captain, Lakeside Recreation Center swim team
- Volunteer, Lakeside Library Young Readers Club

© Cengage Learning 2012

Be sure your resume is presented in a professional manner—clean, organized, with no errors. Limit your resume to one page. Use a format that highlights how your skills will contribute to the company's needs.

Remember that resumes are usually skimmed quickly. Some companies even use scanners to check for keywords. Be sure to connect your experiences to the requirements of the job, such as: fluent in Japanese, proficient with Adobe Illustrator, Cisco network certification, research

Complete a resume for yourself. Identify steps you could take over the next year that would improve your resume and increase your chances of being hired. Explain how these short-term steps might help you achieve your life-span goals.

ability, team projects, leadership skills, overseas study, and international experience.

Use action words that demonstrate what you have achieved. See Figure 9-5 for examples of strong action words.

When preparing your resume, be completely honest about your qualifications. Remember that employers check resume information. Providing false information can cause you to lose a job. False information, found after you have been hired, can lead to your dismissal and long-term career problems.

Many career experts suggest not including a career objective on the resume. Often, a career objective is too vague or too general. Instead, this goal is better addressed in the cover letter when you connect your abilities to the organization's needs.

References are not usually included on the resume. Have this information on hand when requested by a prospective employer. Prepare a list of people who can give a report about your character, education, and work habits. These individuals may be teachers, previous employers, supervisors, or co-workers. Be sure to obtain permission from the people you plan to use as references.

Goal 2

Identify the parts of an application cover letter.

Career Portfolio

Many job applicants prepare a career portfolio. A **career portfolio** provides tangible evidence of your ability and skills. A career portfolio may include the following items:

- Resume, cover letter, and answers to sample interview questions

- Sample reports, presentation materials, and research findings from school projects

- Website designs, creative works from school activities or previous employment such as ads, packages, and promotions

- News articles of community activities or other experiences in which you have participated

- Letters of recommendation

ACTION VERBS FOR RESUMES AND COVER LETTERS		
Achieved	Directed	Organized
Accomplished	Edited	Planned
Administered	Facilitated	Produced
Coordinated	Initiated	Researched
Created	Implemented	Supervised
Designed	Managed	Trained
Developed	Monitored	Updated

▶ **Figure 9-5**

What are some other action verbs that might be used on a resume or in a cover letter?

A career portfolio can show your abilities in a tangible manner to prospective employers. In addition, these materials will communicate your initiative and uniqueness.

checkpoint ✓
What are the main sections of a resume?

APPLICATION COVER LETTER

The application **cover letter** expresses your interest in a specific job. Think of this as a sales letter for the purpose of obtaining an interview. Like any good sales letter, a cover letter should draw attention and interest. It should build a desire to meet you. Your letter should urge the reader to invite you to come for an interview. Figure 9-6 on the next page shows a cover letter that is neat, courteous, and to the point. A carelessly written letter may cause the employer to think that you will be a careless worker. A cover letter usually involves three main sections: introduction, development, and conclusion.

Introduction

Your cover letter should start by getting the reader's attention. Next, indicate the reason for writing. Refer to the job or type of employment in which you are interested. Give a brief summary of your experience and qualifications. If applicable, mention the name of the person who referred you to this organization.

Development

This section should highlight your background and experiences that specifically qualify you for the job. Refer the employer to your resume for more details. At this point, summarize information about your experiences and training. Connect your skills and background to specific organizational needs.

Conclusion

The final section is designed to request action—ask for the opportunity to discuss your qualifications in more detail. In other words, request an interview! Include your contact information, telephone numbers, times when you are available, and e-mail address. Make sure your e-mail address is professional. Close the letter with a summary of how you could benefit the organization. Create a personalized cover letter for each position for which you apply.

Targeted Letter

In recent years, some job applicants are using a *targeted application letter* instead of a resume and cover letter. This letter provides a quick summary of your ability to meet the needs of an organization. A target letter will usually include a list of major skills and competencies. Once again, your goal is to emphasize achievements and skills so you will be invited for an interview.

1602 Collegewood Drive
Madison, WI 53711-2821
June 25, 20--

David Haugen, Ph.D.
Vice President of Finance
Lakeview College
Madison, WI 53706-3692

Dear Dr. Haugen

This is to express my interest in the accounting clerk position available with Lakeview College. My academic training and previous work experiences qualify me for this position.

While attending Four Lakes High School, I achieved a strong academic record and developed many business skills that would be of value to your organization. My part-time employment experiences provide evidence of skills and competencies required for the available position.

In a work experience program during my senior year, I was employed ten hours a week at the Tempest Tea Pot Company. In that position, I was involved with various recordkeeping and marketing activities. In addition, I worked on projects related to online sales and website development.

During my summer job in the city assessor's office, I was part of an office team responsible for maintaining spreadsheets and conducting research. The skills I developed in this position will allow me to effectively contribute to the needs of your organization.

Enclosed is my resume with additional information about my experiences. Please contact me to set up an interview. My telephone number is (608) 555-0308, and my e-mail address is fnegalo@badgernet.com. I look forward to the opportunity to meet with you to discuss my qualifications and learn more about the accounting clerk position.

Sincerely

Francisca Negalo

Francisca Negalo

▶ **Figure 9-6**

What aspects of this letter would cause a reader to want to meet the applicant in person?

© Cengage Learning 2012

> **checkpoint** ✓
> What is the purpose of a cover letter?

WORK as a TEAM

Plan an online portfolio. Design a website that could serve as a career portfolio. Describe the format, elements, graphics, and links of this electronic portfolio. Talk about how an online portfolio could be used when applying for various types of careers.

ONLINE APPLICATION PROCESS

Many people use the Internet, social media, and phone apps for career planning activities. While researching potential employment is the most common use, job seekers also apply and interview online. Because an Internet resume is less personal, do not overlook other job search methods—phone calls, ads, job fairs, and personal contacts.

Online Applications

Many organizations allow you to apply online. In addition to the basic application, you may also be asked some preliminary questions to determine your suitability for the position available. When posting your resume online or sending it by e-mail, consider the following:

- Use a simple format. Avoid bold, underline, italics, and tabs.

- Do not attach files that may be difficult to open.

Cyber resumes are posted on various websites. They are scanned for keywords to identify candidates with the necessary job qualifications. The words and phrases that might make you an attractive job candidate vary depending on the company and the position. One company might search for words such as *leader*, *interpersonal*, and *team* and another might scan for *word processing*, *database*, and *spreadsheet*.

Cyber Interviewing

Many organizations hold screening interviews using video conferencing. Others require that you post preliminary interview responses online. These "e-interviews" may involve questions such as: "Would you rather have structure or flexibility in your work?" and "What approach do you use to solve difficult problems?"

Online interviewing may also be used to test a person's ability in job-related situations. For example, an applicant may be asked to respond to tasks such as those that a bank teller or retail clerk might encounter.

---

checkpoint ✓

How is the Internet used in the job application process?

9-3 Assessment

Study Tools

www.cengage.com/school/genbus/pob

Key Concepts

Determine the best answer.

1. The item *least* likely to be included on a resume is
   a. a school award
   b. your references
   c. schools attended
   d. your work experience

2. The main purpose of a cover letter is to
   a. request an interview
   b. obtain career information
   c. ask a person to be a reference
   d. apply for a government job

Make Academic Connections

3. **Law** Conduct library or online research to obtain information on laws that protect people during the hiring process. What actions are illegal when selecting among various people for a job?

4. **Technology** Locate an online application form. What types of questions are asked? Are you prepared to answer these questions? How?

5. **Math** A person who makes $54,000 at work in a small city is considering taking a new job in a larger city that has an 8 percent higher cost of living. What would be a comparable salary in the new city?

Goals

1 Describe activities involved in the interview process.

2 Compare factors to consider when accepting a job offer.

3 Identify attitudes and actions for success on the job.

Key Terms

employment interview 219

mentor 222

exit interview 223

Focus on REAL LIFE

"Hello Barda, this is Mr. Yang from the Child Development Care Facility calling about the part-time job to assist our program director. Would you be available to come in for an interview at noon on Thursday?"

Barda is able to attend the interview as scheduled. As she gets ready, she asks her aunt, "How should I respond to the questions they might ask?"

"Be ready to tell them about your volunteer work with children at the park district, such as helping to coach soccer," her aunt reminded Barda. "Also, explain why you are interested in working with children."

"Finally," Barda's aunt added, "be ready to ask questions about the organization and your job responsibilities."

THE INTERVIEW PROCESS

"We want to meet with you in person." This is your goal after submitting an application or resume. An **employment interview** is a two-way conversation in which the interviewer learns about you and you learn about the job and the company.

Before You Interview

Prepare for an interview by obtaining more information about your prospective employer and the job for which you are applying. Prepare questions to ask in the interview. These might include

● What training opportunities are available to employees?

● What qualities do your most successful employees possess?

● What new opportunities are your company considering in the next few years?

Successful interviewing requires practice. Record yourself so you will answer questions in a smooth and complete manner. Prepare concise answers for specific questions you might be asked. Ask friends to help you practice your interview skills. Attend workshops on interviewing skills. Work to organize your ideas. Speak clearly and calmly. Be sure to communicate enthusiasm.

As part of your interview preparation you should plan to make a good

Goal 1

Describe activities involved in the interview process.

What kinds of information can you learn about a position in an interview?

first impression. It is important to arrive on time for your appointment and dress appropriately. Make sure you know how to get to the interview location and give yourself plenty of time to get there. You should go alone to the interview even if someone else is providing transportation. Wear the type of clothing that is appropriate for the company and the job for which you are applying.

During the Interview

The person who interviews you wants to find out such things as your appearance, manners, use of language, and general ability for the job. An interviewer may take a number of different approaches. Most interviewers will try to put you at ease when your interview begins. Interviews may include situations or questions to determine how you react under pressure. Answer clearly in a controlled manner. Use of *behavioral interviewing* is expanding to better evaluate an applicant's on-the-job potential. Questions typically begin with "describe" or "tell me about..." Some common interview questions are shown in Figure 9-7.

Some employers use pre-employment tests to screen applicants for skills and abilities needed on the job. Examples of pre-employment tests include keyboarding, word processing,

calculating, and other skills. The interviewer may review your test results and discuss specific job requirements with you.

Avoid talking too much, but answer each question completely using good eye contact. Stay calm during the interview. Remember, you are being asked questions on a subject about which you are the world's expert—you! Finally, thank the interviewer for the opportunity to discuss the job and your qualifications.

After the Interview

Within a day or two, send a *follow-up letter* to express your appreciation for the opportunity to interview. Even if you don't get the job, this thank-you letter will make a positive impression for future consideration.

COMMON INTERVIEW QUESTIONS

Education and Training Questions
- What qualifies you for this job?
- Why are you interested in this company?
- What activities have helped you to expand your interests and knowledge?

Work and Other Experience Questions
- In what situations have you done your best work?
- Describe the supervisors who motivated you most.
- Which of your past accomplishments are you most proud of?
- Describe people with whom you have found it difficult to work.

Personal Qualities Questions
- What are your major strengths?
- What are your major weaknesses? What have you done to overcome these?
- What do you plan to be doing 5 or 10 years from now?
- Which individuals have had the greatest influence on you?

▶ **Figure 9-7**

Think of answers to each question and write them down.

Next, evaluate your interview performance. Try to remember questions that you were not expecting or not prepared to answer. Write notes about areas in which you need improvement. The more interviews you have, the better you will present yourself. More interviews will also increase the chance of being offered a job.

Be patient after the interview. It may take several weeks for the company to complete all of its interviews and make its selection.

> **checkpoint ✓**
> What actions should be taken when preparing for an employment interview?

JOB OFFERS

"We'd like you to work for us." When you hear those words, remember to consider several factors before accepting or declining the position. The financial aspects of a job should be assessed along with some organizational factors.

Salary and Financial Factors

The type of work and your experience will affect your rate of pay. The position may include *employee benefits*. Insurance, vacation time, and retirement programs are examples of common employee benefits. Some companies offer free parking, on-site fitness centers, discount gym memberships, and other programs and services. Ask what benefits, services, and programs will be available to you and how much you will be expected to pay for them. Part-time and seasonal employees may or may not be offered benefits.

Organizational Environment

While the financial elements of a job are very important, also consider the working environment. Leadership style, dress code, the physical workspace, and the social atmosphere should be explored.

Advancement potential and training programs should be assessed. Some companies take pride in promoting from within and work hard to provide career and personal growth opportunities for workers.

> **checkpoint ✓**
> What factors should a person consider when accepting a job?

WORK as a TEAM

Work in teams of three to practice answering the common interview questions that appear in Figure 9-7. Take turns playing the roles of interviewer, job applicant, and observer. The team member acting as the interviewer should create follow-up questions based on responses from the job applicant. Both the interviewer and observer should comment on the strong aspects of answers and make suggestions for improvement.

Goal 2

Compare factors to consider when accepting a job offer.

How would you describe a work environment that appeals to you?

Stockbyte/Getty Images

ON-THE-JOB BEHAVIOR

Attitude can make a big difference in your career success. A positive attitude helps you learn and cooperate with others. Always think, speak, dress, and act in ways that project a positive image. Then, you will likely find your job more satisfying and enjoyable.

Job Success Strategies

As you prepare for your first day of work, remember the following:

- **Ask questions.** If you do not understand directions, have them repeated and listen carefully. You probably will make mistakes when learning your job. Be sure to learn from each mistake and avoid repeating it.

- **Avoid complaining.** If you seem to have more work to do than you can handle, talk with your supervisor.

- **Honor the time for breaks.** Don't abuse rest periods and lunch breaks by extending the time limit.

- **Consider your appearance.** Dress neatly and be well groomed. Employers often observe that sloppy appearance reflects sloppy work habits.

- **Be on time.** Arriving late or leaving early is a poor practice.

- **Be friendly with everyone.** Respect your co-workers and learn to get along. Each person in an organization is important. Any co-worker may be of help to you in the future.

- **Show you are dependable.** Do quality work that is completed on time. Sloppy work or work turned in late affects others. You are part of a team—take pride in that. Pay attention to details. Return phone calls and e-mails promptly to show that you care about your work.

What aspect of a job do you think contributes the most to employee satisfaction?

Digital Vision/Getty Images

- **Follow the rules.** If a rule seems unfair or unreasonable, discuss it with others and find out why it was created.

Many successful people get assistance from a person with more experience. A **mentor** is an experienced employee who serves as counselor to a person with less experience. Mentors frequently offer specific advice related to work assignments as well as general career guidance. For example, your mentor might help you develop skills needed in your current position and provide insight about future opportunities.

Leaving a Job

When the time comes to leave a job, it is important to depart on good terms. The following tips can help you leave a job in an appropriate manner.

- Give at least a two-week notice. Write a short, polite letter of resignation; include the date of the last day you will be working.

- Try to finish all of your current projects. If they are not completed, leave a note explaining to the next person where to begin.

- If there is an **exit interview**, in which your employer asks questions about

Is it possible that your new job may bring you back in contact with a former employer?

Stockbyte/Getty Images

your work, be constructive and cooperative.

- Let co-workers know that you appreciated the opportunity to work with them.

Leaving on a positive note is good for you and for those you are leaving.

> **checkpoint ✓**
> How does a mentor assist less experienced employees?

Study Tools
www.cengage.com/school/genbus/pob

9-4 Assessment

Key Concepts

Determine the best answer.

1. A commonly suggested action to take after an interview is to
   a. contact the organization about the salary
   b. evaluate your performance in the interview
   c. revise your resume
   d. estimate the cost of career training for the job

2. The _?_ interview occurs when leaving a job.
   a. informational
   b. exit
   c. employment
   d. coaching

Make Academic Connections

3. **Communication** Work with another person to improve your interview skills. Ask each other some of the questions in Figure 9-7. Describe strengths and needed improvements to each other.

4. **Culture** Describe questions and actions that might occur in the interview process in different countries. How could body language be interpreted differently in various cultures?

Business Notes

9-1 Career Opportunities

- The career planning process involves a self-assessment, an analysis of the employment market, application activities, the interview process, a comparison of job offers, and career development activities.

- Important sources of career information include print and media sources, online sources, informational interviews, and business contacts.

- Career fields with the most growth potential include computer technology, health care, business services, social services, sales and retailing, education, hospitality and food service, financial services, management, and human resources. Service industries are expected to have the greatest employment potential in the future.

9-2 Planning Your Career

- Your interests, values, talents, and abilities should be assessed when making a career decision.

- Employment experience may be obtained through work-study programs, part-time employment, volunteer activities, and school activities.

- Information sources about available jobs include the media, personal contacts, business contacts, career fairs, and employment agencies.

9-3 Applying for Employment

- The application process may start with completing an application form or with the use of a resume and cover letter.

- There are three main parts to an application letter. The introduction gets the reader's attention. The development highlights your background and the skills that qualify you for the job. The conclusion asks for an interview.

- Online application activities include the application process, e-resumes, and cyber interviewing.

9-4 Securing a Job

- The interview process involves preparing for the interview, participating in the interview, and follow-up activities.

- Factors to consider when accepting a job offer are salary, benefits, leadership style, dress code, social atmosphere, and advancement potential.

- A positive attitude is the foundation of success on the job. Other success strategies include asking questions, avoiding complaints, giving attention to your appearance, following the rules, and being on time, dependable, and friendly.

Communicate Business Concepts

1. Who are some people you know that you might consider for an informational interview?

2. Give examples of how consumer demand, changing demographic trends, and new technology might affect career opportunities.

3. Make a list of your talents and abilities. Specify whether you believe each one is strong or weak. Indicate how you might use your strengths in career planning. Also indicate what actions you might take to improve your weak areas.

4. What actions might a person take when preparing to attend a career fair?

5. Your personal data sheet should list several references. Application forms also ask references to be listed. Make a list of three or more references you could use right now. Then note the type of information each reference could give that would be of help to a potential employer.

6. Prepare a list of items that you might include in a career portfolio when applying for a job.

7. If you were in charge of hiring people, what information would you want to obtain from applicants? How would you go about getting this information? What are some specific questions you would ask if you were to interview the applicants?

8. Job applicants may encounter role-playing situations in an interview. What types of situations may be used to assess the skills and abilities of prospective employees?

9. Information has been received about three job openings in your community. Each is quite different. Assume that you are qualified for only one position. Make up whatever qualifications you think you would like to present to a prospective employer. Then write a letter of application for the position.

   a. Reliable person is needed to handle a variety of responsibilities in a small business office. Must be able to work without supervision and communicate effectively with people who call for information. Word processing and other office skills are desirable. Salary is better than average in this community.

   b. Salespeople are needed for the auto parts and cosmetics departments of a large retail store. Applicants should have some familiarity and/or experience with selling. Hours are flexible, although some evening and weekend work will be required. Benefits are especially attractive; incentive bonus policy can provide a good income for the right person.

   c. Ours is a leading bank in this region. We are in need of capable people who want to begin a career in banking. Our training program starts at the bottom, but provides a great opportunity to learn about the banking industry. Salary is competitive.

10. What kinds of questions would you ask in an exit interview if you were the supervisor interviewing a sales clerk who is leaving?

Develop Your Business Language

Match the terms listed with the definitions.

11. A planned discussion with a worker to find out about the work that person does, the preparation necessary for the career, and the person's feelings about the career.

12. The willingness and ability of a person to move to where jobs are located.

13. The things that are important to you in life.

14. A natural, inborn aptitude to do certain things.

15. A goal in life that is fulfilled through a job or a series of occupations.

16. The quality of being able to perform mental or physical tasks.

17. A sales letter about an applicant written for the purpose of getting an interview.

18. A summary of job-related information about yourself.

19. An experienced employee who serves as counselor to a person with less experience.

20. A document used by employers that asks for information related to employment.

21. A two-way conversation in which the interviewer learns about you and you learn about the job and the company.

22. An interview in which an employer asks questions about how an employee liked his/her work and inquires about job improvements that might be made.

23. Tangible evidence of your ability and skills provided when applying for a job.

KEY TERMS

a. ability
b. application form
c. career
d. career portfolio
e. cover letter
f. employment interview
g. exit interview
h. informational interview
i. mentor
j. mobility
k. resume
l. talent
m. values

Make Academic Connections

24. **Economics** The website for the Bureau of Labor Statistics presents a wide variety of data on employment and wages. Select a topic area and present a two-paragraph summary. Explain how this information could be useful in your career planning activities.

25. **Culture** Talk to someone who has worked in another country. Obtain information about the application process and hiring activities in a different culture.

26. **Math** Nancy's college tuition and fees come to $9,500 per year. She spends $1,200 each year on books and supplies. In addition, she has living expenses of $11,600 per year. She has three sources of income: financial aid of $3,500 per year, a scholarship that pays one-half of her tuition, and a work-study job from which she earns $5,300 per year.

   a. How much income does Nancy receive each year from her three sources of income?
   b. How much does it cost Nancy to go to this college each year?
   c. What percentage of her annual college costs is covered by her three sources of income? (Round off your answer.)
   d. How much money does Nancy need to borrow each year?

27. **Communication** Prepare an in-class presentation or video with examples of strong and weak interview behaviors.

28. **Technology** Visit a website that allows people to post their resumes. Prepare a summary of the procedure, cost (if any), and other information from the website.

29. **Math** Emilie Antoine is a personnel interviewer. On Monday, she interviewed seven job applicants; on Tuesday, six applicants; on Wednesday, nine applicants; on Thursday, five applicants; and on Friday, eight applicants.

   a. How many applicants did Emilie interview that week? What was the average number per day?
   b. On Wednesday, the first interview took 50 minutes; the next two each took 40 minutes; the next four took 35 minutes each; and the last two took 45 minutes each. How many total hours did Emilie spend in these interviews? What was the average length of the interviews?

30. **Geography** Obtain information about salaries in different geographic regions of the United States. What factors affect the differences that exist?

31. **History** Research a significant world event. Explain how this event affected the location and types of careers available around the world.

Decision-Making Strategies

Jeff Barbson is looking to his future and wondering what kind of career he should prepare for. His father is the city's civil engineer. His mother is a buyer for a major department store. Both of his parents are successful and enjoy their careers. Both of them have talked with Jeff about their work. He has visited his father's office and has worked as a sales clerk in his mother's store. Jeff's favorite subjects are computers, economics, and art. His least favorites are history, English, business law, and math. He earns his best grades in computers and art.

Jeff's father wants him to be an engineer because there is a need for engineers in their state. His mother wants him to go into retailing. Jeff would like to go to medical school and become a heart specialist.

32. Based on his school record, which of the three career areas do you think he should choose?

33. What advice would you give Jeff regarding career planning?

Linking School and Community

Talk to two or three people in your community to obtain information about their job search and interviewing experiences. Use the following questions in your discussion with these people:

● What are some ways that you have learned about available jobs?

● What actions did you take to improve your chances of being selected for a job?

● How did you prepare for job interviews?

Prepare a one-page summary of your findings. Which of these ideas did you find most interesting and potentially useful in the future?

Web Workout

The Internet can be a very useful source of career planning information. Select a career topic and compare the advice given on two different career websites. Choose a career topic such as preparing a resume, identifying job opportunities, networking, or effective interviewing.

Think Critically

1. Prepare a summary of the main ideas from each website.

2. What are the similarities and differences between the advice presented on the two websites?

3. How might the information obtained be of value to you in the future?

Job Interview Event

You are applying for a an entry-level management position at ABC Corporation in Charlotte, North Carolina. Company benefits include paid holidays and vacations, sick leave, a retirement plan, and health insurance. Salary will be based upon experience and education. The event consists of three parts:

- Letter of application and resume
- Job application form
- Interviews

You are required to prepare a one-page letter of application. Your resume should not exceed two pages in length. The resume, letter of application, and job application should be put together in a file folder with your name on the tab of the folder. You will be required to complete a job application form with the use of your resume and a one-page reference sheet. No other reference materials may be used. Your initial interview with a member from the business community (representing ABC Corporation) will last 10 minutes. Finalists from the first round of interviews will have a 15-minute second interview. Total scores will be calculated for the letter of application, resume, job application, and interview to determine which students will be hired.

Performance Indicators Evaluated

- Understand the importance of a professional portfolio that includes a resume and letter of application.

- Demonstrate strong interviewing skills necessary to earn a job.
- Prepare a business resume and letter of application that generate results.

You will be evaluated for

- Organization of your professional portfolio
- Performance during the interview
- Quality of participation in the interview

For more detailed information about performance indicators, go to the FBLA website.

Think Critically

1. Why is the letter of application important?

2. Why should you research a company before going on the interview?

3. Give two good examples of questions a candidate can ask the interviewer.

4. List the major sections of the resume.

www.fbla-pbl.org

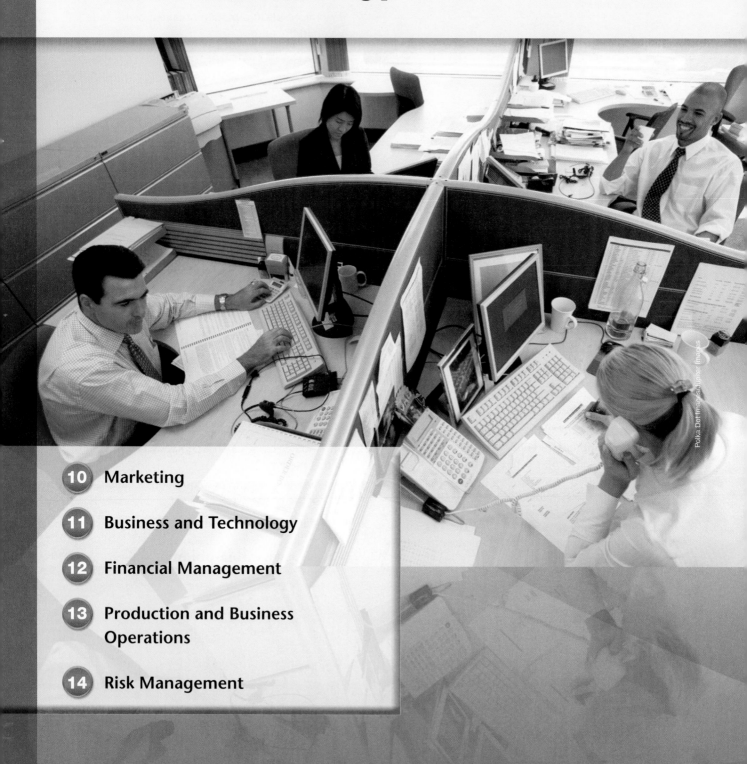

UNIT

3

Business Operations and Technology

Polka Dot Images/Jupiter Images

Business Vision

Businesses perform many functions to produce goods and services. Regardless of the size of the organization, similar business functions are carried out by extractors, manufacturers, wholesalers, retailers, service providers, government agencies, and nonprofit organizations. Businesses use marketing to communicate with and deliver value to customers. Financial planning and management ensure adequate resources are available and used efficiently. Computers and other technology increase the speed and accuracy of ever more complex business activities.

In this unit you will study some of the most important functions of business and the activities that managers and employees complete for each. Most medium and large-sized businesses employ workers skilled in a particular type of work. Engineers, maintenance and service personnel, adverting and marketing specialists, accountants, computer technicians, and others complete the day-to-day operations of businesses. All parts of the business must operate effectively and in coordination with each other. Today's employees need to know how to do their specific work, how to use the technology that is a part of that work, and how their work interfaces with and supports the other activities in the business.

Keeping Them in the Air

The operation of a major airline is a complex business filled with unpredictable problems. A mechanical problem discovered shortly before takeoff has passengers waiting in Baltimore as a replacement aircraft is located. Thunderstorms in Dallas result in flight delays and missed connections. A security issue in Chicago means planes must be held at the gate. A flight delay, even a short one, can affect many other operations not only in the airport where the problem occurred but all across the country and possibly around the world. These problems affect almost all areas of airline operations, ground and gate personnel, flight crews, ticketing, and customer service. Rescheduling a flight and rebooking passengers costs thousands of dollars.

When a problem occurs, managers immediately involve other personnel in resolving the problem as quickly and effectively as possible. Dispatchers, customer service agents, ground and flight crew managers are all called upon to contribute to solutions. Technology allows instantaneous communication and access to complete information about aircraft, personnel, and costs. In order to resolve the problem, managers need to identify the problem, evaluate options, choose the best course of action, and resolve the issue. The goal is to keep customers happy and keep the planes in the air.

Think Critically

Why is it important for airlines to involve managers from so many areas of the company in resolving problems?

CHAPTER

10 Marketing

vm/iStockphoto.com

Planning a Career in ...

MARKETING

Marketing is a career area that offers a great variety of job opportunities. Corporate positions range from entry level to top management and everything in between. There are career opportunities in all industries, including technology, health care, manufacturing, and entertainment. If you want to work in marketing, you might find a job in your hometown, in a different state, or halfway around the globe.

The work of marketers is diverse and exciting. A marketing researcher conducts focus group interviews in a mall or for a political candidate. A marketing team designs a multi-million dollar advertising campaign for a new product. An international sales representative for a pharmaceutical company travels the world to introduce a life-saving drug. A distribution center manager develops a plan to reduce shipping costs. Not only are marketing careers available to people with a wide range of interests, talents, and education, they also include some of the highest-paying business careers.

Related Job Titles

- Sales Agent
- Merchant Wholesaler
- Marketing Consultant
- Manager of Corporate Brands
- Trade Show and Special Events Coordinator
- Marketing Database Manager
- Media Relations Specialist

Analyze Career Opportunities in ...

MARKETING

Use library and Internet resources to learn more about careers in marketing. Choose one of the job titles listed in the box above and answer the following questions.

1. How would you describe the physical work environment for jobs in this field?

2. Is this a career that interests you? What can you do now to help prepare yourself for this career?

What's it like to work as a ... Sales Manager?

Before Kerri Snodgrass boards a flight to Cairo, she returns a call to Ferris Joachum, one of her sales representatives. Kerri knows Ferris is in negotiations with a customer for a $1.5-million order of environmental monitoring equipment.

Ferris says, "If we can get the order shipped within two weeks and spread the payments over two years, I think I can make the sale."

Kerri calls her company's production manager and the loan officer of the international bank they use for customer financing. After several discussions, they get approval on the shipping date and are able to offer free financing for one year. As she gets off the plane, Kerri receives a text message—the sale has been completed and the order has been placed.

As a sales manager, Kerri needs to understand all aspects of her business, gather information, and make quick but effective decisions to support her salespeople and satisfy the customers. Salespeople and sales managers are the face of the company to its customers.

What about you? What skills and personal qualities do you believe make Kerri Snodgrass a successful sales manager?

10-1 Marketing Basics

Goals

1 Define important marketing concepts.

2 Identify the steps in a marketing strategy.

3 Describe the consumer decision-making process.

Key Terms

marketing 232

marketing strategy 235

target market 235

marketing mix 235

marketing orientation 236

final consumers 237

business consumers 237

consumer decision-making process 237

buying motives 238

Focus on REAL LIFE

"MJ Support Solutions provides two main services. We help small businesses clients communicate through targeted e-mail and we provide fulfillment services," Malcolm explains to a new employee.

"Okay, I understand targeted e-mail. I get e-mail ads from an online bookseller with recommendations based on what I have bought in the past. What do you mean by fulfillment services?" Janice asks.

Malcolm replies, "We develop distribution strategies. Online retailers contract with us to warehouse their products and ship them to customers as the orders come in. Some clients batch their orders and transfer the data to us electronically every night."

"Then why do you have such a big call center?"

"Well Janice, for other clients, we actually function as the customer service department."

"Exactly what kinds of products are we talking about?" inquires Janice.

"Come on, I'll show you the warehouse. You'll be surprised what we have out there."

Goal 1

Define important marketing concepts.

UNDERSTAND MARKETING

Marketing may be the most visible set of business activities to consumers. Yet it may also be the most misunderstood business function. When asked to define marketing, people often use terms such as advertising or selling. While both of these are important, many other activities are a part of effective marketing.

The American Marketing Association's definition of marketing shows how complex it is: "**Marketing** is the activity, set of institutions, and processes for creating, communicating, delivering, and exchanging offerings that have value for customers, clients, partners, and society at large." These words describe a complex but key part of every business. Marketing includes a range of activities and a number of businesses in the U.S. economy.

Marketing Activities

As a consumer you are exposed to marketing activities all of the time. You take part in many of these activities. You see or hear advertisements for products and services. You see the brand names on the packages of foods you eat and on the clothes that you and your friends wear. You read product descriptions on a company's website. You interact with salespeople in your favorite retail store. These are all examples of marketing.

There are less obvious but equally important marketing activities. These include storing products in warehouses and distribution centers and moving the products to the places where they will be sold or used. Establishing and accepting credit and arranging means of online payment are marketing activities. Businesses use marketing when they gather data on consumer needs, use that information to improve products, and test new products before they are sold.

A great deal of marketing is not even aimed at final consumers. Businesses market products and services to other businesses. These businesses then use the products and services in their own business processes or sell them to final consumers. More time and money is spent in business-to-business marketing than in marketing products and services to final consumers.

Marketing Businesses

All businesses must complete some marketing activities even if that is not their focus. Many businesses are directly involved in marketing. Marketing businesses include advertising agencies and marketing research firms. Transportation companies such as trucking, railroad, and air freight move products from producers to consumers. Shipping and delivery companies provide express pickup and delivery of documents and packages. Financial services companies issue and manage credit cards. They can also provide loans to businesses for purchasing raw materials and finished goods. Wholesalers and retailers participate in the distribution, storage, and sale of products to connect manufacturers and their customers. Marketing activities, marketing businesses, and marketing careers are an important part of the U.S. economy.

Marketing Functions

Marketing activities can be organized into seven functions as shown in Figure 10-1. Each function occurs every time a product or service is developed and sold. Businesses provide many of the marketing functions. Consumers often take part in one or more of the marketing functions when they make purchases.

WORK as a TEAM

A company in Ft. Lauderdale, Florida, meets fishing boats when they dock. They buy fresh fish caught that day. Have each member of your team identify a marketing activity that must be completed by the company to purchase and then resell the fish to restaurants and supermarkets.

Product and service management is designing, developing, maintaining, improving, and acquiring products and services that meet consumer needs. Producers and manufacturers develop new products. Other businesses are also involved in product/service management when they obtain products for resale. Services are created and provided by the employees of service businesses.

Distribution involves determining the best ways for customers to locate, obtain, and use the products and services of an organization. Careful shipping, handling, and storing of products are needed for effective distribution.

▶ **Figure 10-1**

Why is each marketing function needed whenever a product or service is sold?

Selling is communicating directly with potential customers to determine and satisfy their needs. Selling can be face to face, such as when a customer visits a business or when a salesperson goes to the home or business of a potential customer. Selling is also performed using a telephone or other technology such as instant messaging or videoconferencing to communicate directly with a customer.

Marketing-information management is obtaining, managing, and using market information to improve business decision-making and the performance of marketing activities. Marketing-information management includes marketing research and the development of databases with information about products, customers, and competitors.

Financial analysis is budgeting for marketing activities, obtaining the necessary funds needed for operations, and providing financial assistance to customers so

they can purchase the business' products and services. Customers must have the resources and methods to pay for their purchases. Businesses must receive timely payments so they can continue to operate.

Pricing is setting and communicating the value of products and services. Customers must be able to easily identify the price of items that interest them or they will move on to another choice. Consumers want to know that they are getting a fair value for the money they are spending. Prices must be set low enough that customers are willing to pay but high enough that the business makes a profit.

Promotion is communicating information about products and services to potential customers. Advertising and other promotional methods are used to encourage consumers to buy. Advertising may occur in a variety of ways—television, newspapers, magazines, radio, direct mail, and the Internet. Other methods include

Business Insight for the 21st Century

Marketing Ethics

Some people may think that the term "marketing ethics" is an oxymoron, or a contradiction in terms. Many people have a low opinion of marketers. Individuals receive unsolicited sales calls, junk mail, and spam. They watch advertisements that don't tell the whole story on products. They encounter salespeople who only seem to be interested in their own commissions.

Marketers, however, play a very important role in society. They deliver a standard of living. They identify

new products. They find ways to get those products into customers' hands through convenient distribution and at low costs. If marketers did not work within a society, customer's choices would be very limited.

Ethical marketers abide by a set of standards outlined by the American Marketing Association. These standards require that marketers must do no harm and adhere to all applicable laws and regulations. Marketers must make products that work and advertising should not be intentionally

deceptive or misleading. Marketers also must be honest, responsible, fair, have respect, be open, and be good corporate citizens.

Think Critically

1. Describe why individuals may have a low opinion of marketers.

2. Explain why marketers play an important role in society.

3. Describe ethical standards that marketers should follow.

contests, product displays, sponsorships, and public relations activities.

checkpoint ✓

Define marketing and the seven marketing functions.

MARKETING STRATEGY

Marketing is an important and costly part of business operations. Marketing activities often cost 50 percent or more of the selling price of a product or service. In order for a company to make a profit, marketing must be carefully planned. It must be done well, yet at a low cost. Consumers usually have many choices of products and services. If they are not satisfied with the offering of one company, they will look to a competitor to meet their needs. Careful marketing will aid a company in understanding and meeting customer needs. Successful marketing results in satisfying exchanges between businesses and consumers. Businesses offer products and services that satisfy their customers' needs. Customers pay for those products and services, providing the businesses with revenues and profit.

Marketing Planning

Marketing planning is aimed at satisfying customer needs better than competitors do, resulting in sales and profits. A company's plan that identifies how it will use marketing to achieve its goals is called a **marketing strategy**.

Developing a marketing strategy is a two-step process. The first step is to identify a target market. A **target market** is a specific group of consumers who have similar wants and needs. Many companies try to promote their products to a wide audience whose wants and needs are quite varied. It is not easy for the company to meet all of those needs. The result is that many people will not want the company's

products or will be dissatisfied with them. Focusing on a target market makes it easier to develop products and services that specific groups of customers want.

The second step in developing a marketing strategy is to create a marketing mix. A **marketing mix** is the blending of four marketing elements—product, distribution, price, and promotion. A successful marketing mix satisfies the wants and needs of the target market. It also provides a profit for the company.

Goal 2

Identify the steps in a marketing strategy.

Develop a Successful Marketing Strategy

Many businesspeople believe they know what consumers want. They produce a product and then begin to plan how they will market it to consumers. This approach to marketing typically results in an emphasis on advertising and promotion in order to attract the attention of potential customers and convince them to buy the company's product. If the product does not appeal to consumers, the business will be forced to cut the price. Lower profits or even losses may be the result.

To increase the chances of developing a product or service that meets customer needs and can be sold at a profit,

How would the elements of a marketing mix be used for a new apparel line?

companies adopt a marketing orientation. A **marketing orientation** considers the needs of customers when developing a marketing mix. With a marketing orientation, businesspeople don't assume they know what customers want. They use research to study customers and their needs. The results of the research are used to plan a marketing mix designed to satisfy those needs.

A company that owns a fleet of cruise ships gathers information on people who might consider a cruise as a vacation choice. Families with young children, young singles, and retirement-age adults usually will want different kinds of vacation experiences. First-time cruisers will need different information than experienced cruisers. Menu items, entertainment, travel arrangements to and from the port, and payment options all must be planned to appeal to potential customers.

The company will first study possible customers and the similarities and differences in vacation wants and needs. Then it will select the target market that presents the best opportunity for planning a successful cruise. Using the information gathered about the target market, the company then develops the marketing mix. The product will be an exciting and relaxing cruise experience. There will be enjoyable onboard activities and interesting onshore excursions at cities on the ship's schedule. Distribution will include providing all of the documents needed by travelers, arranging customer travel to and from the port city, handling baggage, and ensuring effective customer service throughout the process. Pricing decisions provide an affordable cruise with payment options to meet the budgets of the target customers. Promotion offers information to interest prospective customers in the cruise and persuade them to decide it is the best vacation choice.

The cruise company will make each of these marketing mix decisions to meet the specific needs and expectations of their target market. The decisions will be different in many ways than if the cruise was planned for a different group of consumers.

> ### checkpoint ✓
> What are the two steps in developing a marketing strategy?

Goal 3

Describe the consumer decision-making process.

What information would you need before you decide to purchase tickets for a cruise?

Photodisc/Getty Images

UNDERSTAND CUSTOMERS

Effective marketing begins with customers. Think of a recent product or service you purchased and why you made the choice you did. You likely had several products that would generally meet your needs. You considered those choices and selected the one that you believed would provide the most satisfaction for the money you had to pay.

Many new businesses fail because the owners have an idea for a product but fail to consider customers and their needs. If a product appeals to a group of customers with unsatisfied needs, it has a real chance to succeed. If customers do not see a need for a product or believe they have other choices that are better or less costly, the product will likely not succeed.

Businesses can develop products for two types of consumers. **Final consumers** are persons who buy products and services mostly for their own use. **Business consumers** are persons, companies, and organizations that buy products for the operation of a business, for incorporation into other products and services, or for resale to their customers.

Consumer Decision-Making

The specific sequence of steps consumers follow to make a purchase is known as the **consumer decision-making process**. Both the steps and the sequence of decisions are the same for all consumers. The length of time taken to complete the process and the information used to complete each step might be quite different from one consumer to the next. The five steps in the consumer decision-making process are shown in Figure 10-2.

Decision-making begins with a need. You may be hungry or thirsty, or you may want to plan an evening's entertainment with friends. Maybe you need a summer job or are trying to choose a college to attend. If the need is urgent, you will try to satisfy it right away. If it is less important you may put it off or even ignore it. If the need is one that is familiar to you and you have satisfied it before, you will often use that past experience to help make a decision. If it is a new need, you may have a hard time deciding how to make the best choice because you have no similar experience.

People use information to make decisions. You may talk to friends or a trusted adult. An advertisement, magazine article, or Internet site may catch your attention because it provides information related to an important need. You choose sources that you trust and that provide information you understand. Using this information, you will select a very few products

STEPS IN THE CONSUMER DECISION-MAKING PROCESS
1. Recognize a need.
2. Gather information.
3. Select and evaluate alternatives.
4. Make a purchase decision.
5. Determine the effectiveness of the decision.

▶ **Figure 10-2**
How might you use these steps to help you make your next consumer decision?

that seem to meet your needs. Once the choices are narrowed, you will compare them to determine if one appears to be a better choice or a greater value than the others.

Based on the information you have obtained and the urgency and importance of the need, you will make a decision. The decision is usually to buy the product you have decided is best for you. The decision may be not to buy because you have not found a satisfying choice or you do not have the money you need at the time. You may

Photodisc/Getty Images

How do you decide which products to purchase when you visit a supermarket?

Joel Calheiros/Shutterstock.com

then go back to a previous step and look at other choices or gather more information.

If you decide to purchase a product, you will complete the purchase and use the product you chose. Based on that experience you will decide if you made a good choice. If you liked the product, you will probably make the same decision the next time you have the same need. You may also make the decision more quickly and easily. If the product was not what you expected, you will be unlikely to purchase that product again.

Buying Motives

Why do you shop in a certain store or choose one brand of a product over another? The reasons consumers decide what products and services to purchase are called **buying motives**. Understanding the motives of consumers helps businesses plan a marketing mix.

Some purchases are guided by emotions. *Emotional buying motives* are reasons to purchase based on feelings, beliefs, and attitudes. If you are concerned about protecting your family and possessions, you may decide to buy a home security system. Purchases of gifts and cards for holidays and occasions are triggered by feelings of love and affection.

Rational buying motives are guided by facts and logic. You may want the most cost-effective car, so you consider fuel use and repair costs of various models. When choosing a college to attend, you can compare the costs of tuition and the reputation of the college in the major you plan to study.

> **checkpoint ✓**
> What are the steps in the consumer decision-making process?

10-1 Assessment

Key Concepts

Determine the best answer.

1. The best definition of marketing is
   a. promotion and selling
   b. producing and distributing products and services to customers
   c. finding customers and convincing them to buy your products
   d. None of the above is correct.

2. The two steps in a marketing strategy are
   a. developing a product and promoting it to consumers
   b. identifying a target market and developing a marketing mix
   c. conducting marketing research and planning production
   d. pricing a product and distributing it to customers

3. Which of the following is an example of a rational buying motive?
   a. love
   b. fear
   c. economy
   d. self-image

Make Academic Connections

4. **Marketing** List the seven marketing functions. Using a business directory or a telephone book, identify a business that specializes in providing each service for final consumers or other businesses. Briefly describe what the business does and the types of customers it serves.

5. **Technical Writing** Select one of your recent purchases. Using computer software, develop a chart or illustration that identifies the steps in the decision-making process and how you completed each step to make the purchase decision.

10-2 Develop Effective Products and Services

Goals

1. Justify the importance of marketing research.

2. Identify the components of a product.

3. Describe how services differ from products.

Key Terms

marketing research 239

product 241

services 242

intangible 242

inseparable 243

perishable 243

heterogeneous 243

Focus on REAL LIFE

Eli and Tedra wanted to start a new custom hat design store and sell online. They knew that they would have a lot of competition with other companies selling online.

"We need to decide what will make our products different from those offered by other companies," Tedra said. "I think we need to develop a brand name for our products."

Eli had his own thoughts, "I think we need to find differences in the way we design our products and the features we offer. We can also offer a number of options on our design."

"We don't want to make our ordering process too complex," Tedra replied. "We need to help consumers sort through their choices. We should offer additional services to help customers find a design that meets their needs. Maybe we should do some research on how customers make these choices."

CREATE AND IMPROVE PRODUCTS

How do businesses develop new products? In many cases, products that are identified as new in a company's advertising are not new at all. Some type of change has been made in the product that may be a major improvement. The change may also be a minor one that provides little benefit to the customer. The business calls the product new to attract the attention of customers and encourage them to buy.

Totally new products that have never been seen before by customers are not often introduced. What new products can you recall having been introduced during your lifetime? The Internet, airbags in automobiles, scanning equipment used in retail stores, and artificial hearts did not have similar substitutes before they were introduced. They were the result of research by engineers and scientists seeking to find solutions to important problems. Most products you use today are minor or major improvements in existing products. New cell phone technologies that store and replay music, take pictures or video, or have computer applications are improved versions of older wireless telephones, MP3 players, and digital video cameras. These and many other product improvements occur through the development of new technology or redesign of current products.

Scientists and other researchers often develop product improvements. Many ideas for product improvements result from the ideas of consumers and from their experience in using current products. Finding solutions to problems through carefully designed studies involving consumers is known as **marketing research**.

Goal 1

Justify the importance of marketing research.

Plan Marketing Research

Many types of research procedures can be used to solve marketing problems. Each type of research follows the scientific problem solving process outlined in Figure 10-3.

All marketing research studies involve gathering and analyzing information. A great deal of information about consumers and competitors is available to businesses without doing new studies. Analyzing existing information gathered for another purpose but used to solve a current problem is known as *secondary research*. Studies carried out to gather new information specifically directed at a current problem is *primary research*.

Types of Research Studies

The most common type of marketing research study involves consumer surveys. *Surveys* gather information from people using a carefully planned set of questions. The surveys are often sent to consumers through the mail or using the Internet. They can also be conducted over the telephone.

Another less structured way of gathering the ideas, experiences, and opinions of consumers is through *focus groups*. In this research method, a small number of consumers take part in a group discussion.

STEPS IN MARKETING RESEARCH
1. Define the marketing problem.
2. Study the situation.
3. Develop a data collection procedure.
4. Gather and analyze information.
5. Propose a solution.

▶ **Figure 10-3**

Why is defining the problem the first step in marketing research?

A focus group leader acts to identify areas of agreement and disagreement and to develop new ideas. Focus group members might discuss their experiences with a product, react to new product ideas, or make suggestions for product improvements.

Observations of consumers provide useful information for marketing researchers. *Observations* collect information by recording the actions of consumers rather than asking them questions. A store may be interested in how customers study and choose products in a display case or the routes they take through a store when shopping. A product design team may observe any problems consumers have using a product to make design improvements.

A final method of marketing research is conducting experiments. An *experiment* presents two carefully controlled alternatives to subjects in order to determine which is preferred or has better results. A marketing experiment may compare two sizes of packages to see if one size results in more sales than the other. A study could determine the effect of offering a 50-cent coupon to grocery shoppers on their choice of cereal brands.

checkpoint ✓

List the steps in a marketing research study.

PRODUCT PLANNING

Each part of the marketing mix is important when you decide to buy a product. The product must be available through effective distribution and must have an affordable and fair price. You must be aware of the product through effective promotion and know how it will meet your needs better than other choices. However, one mix element is more critical than the other three. If the product itself is not what you want, the effectiveness of the other mix elements does not matter. A business must carefully plan each of its products to make sure it meets the needs of the target market better than similar products offered by competitors.

Parts of a Product

A **product** is everything a business offers to satisfy a customer's needs. A product is made up of several components. It starts with the *basic product*, which is the simplest form of a product. The basic product is not unique and is usually available from several companies. Additions and improvements to the basic product are known as *product features*. One model of cellular telephone offers a built-in digital camera, voice dialing, and a web browser as features. When customers are offered choices of features, the choices are known as *options*. When buying an automobile, customers can choose options such as color, engine size, and manual or automatic transmission.

A *brand name* provides a unique identification for a company's products. Companies try to develop a memorable brand name with an appealing image.

Packaging is a part of many products. *Packaging* provides protection and security for the product before it is used. It also may make product storage and use easier. A new container for ground coffee is created with indentations that allow customers to pick it up easily with one hand. Some customers struggled with handling the original round container. The package is a convenient way to provide information to customers that help them make a purchase decision or explain how to use the product.

A way to build customer confidence in a company's products is by offering a *guarantee* or *warranty*. If the product breaks or does not meet customer expectations, the company will repair, replace, or provide a refund.

Product Planning

New product planning is a costly and time-consuming process. It is not unusual for a company to invest several million dollars and spend years to develop a new product. Many people are involved in creating the product idea, determining how it will be produced and marketed, analyzing costs, and predicting sales. When that much money is at stake, companies need a procedure that results in products customers want and that can make a profit for the company for several years. The planning process involves multiple stages.

Idea Development Generating new product ideas is a creative process. Ideas come from the work of scientists, from the suggestions of salespeople and other employees, and from consumer surveys

Digital Vision/Getty Images

What risks do businesses take if they do not follow a careful product planning procedure?

and focus groups. Most ideas are for improvements to existing products.

Idea Screening Companies encourage the development of a large number of new product ideas. Then they evaluate the ideas to determine which have the best chance to be successful. Ideas are screened to determine if a demand exists for the new product. Do other companies offer similar products? Can the product be produced at a reasonable cost? Is the product legal and safe?

Strategy Development If a product idea appears to be workable, the next step is to develop a full marketing strategy. The target market for the product is studied carefully. There must be a strong need for the new product. Alternative marketing mixes are developed and tested with potential customers. The costs of the alternatives are compared to determine which provide the greatest value.

Production and Financial Planning Next, the company develops a production procedure and identifies the facilities, equipment, and people that will be needed to produce the product. The costs of production and marketing are determined and a financial plan is developed to be sure the product will make a profit.

Limited Production and Test Marketing If a new product idea makes its way through the planning process, a company may produce a limited quantity of the product and test it in a small part of the market. This step allows the company to make sure the product can be produced and marketed as planned before a large investment is made for full production.

Goal 3

Describe how services differ from products.

Full-Scale Production If each of the preceding steps is completed successfully, the new product will move into full-scale production and marketing. The company will continue to gather information on production and sales to be sure financial projections are being met. Competitors will also be watched because they will likely introduce competitive products if the new product is successful. Few unsuccessful products should make it through. Products that are fully screened have a much greater chance of being successful than new products that do not go through a planning procedure.

> **checkpoint** ✓
> What are the components of a product?

SERVICES

Products are tangible items you can see and examine such as books, boats, and hamburgers. Marketing is used for both products and services, but services are more difficult to market. **Services** are activities that are consumed at the same time they are produced.

Services are **intangible**, meaning that they have no physical form. Because services are intangible, it is more difficult to examine a service and determine if it will meet your needs. Marketers must find ways to describe the service in understandable ways to prospective customers.

Effective service marketing is done in much the same way as product marketing. Using the two-step marketing strategy, service marketers first identify target markets for services. They then develop a marketing mix that appeals to the market. In addition to the service itself, the market mix includes distribution, pricing, and promotion of the service. The nature of services compared to the nature of products requires a change in the way they are marketed.

WORK *as a* **TEAM**

The employees of a company that provides a service to consumers are responsible for the quality of the service. If your team owned a pet-sitting business, what would you do to make sure the employees provided high-quality service for each customer?

Photodisc/Getty Images

How can a server affect your perception of a restaurant?

A service cannot be stored for later consumption like many products. If all seats at a concert are filled, no more people will be able to hear that performance. If a hair-stylist does not have a client, the service goes unused.

Services are **heterogeneous**, meaning that there will be differences in the type and quality of service provided. Because people usually provide services at the time they are consumed, there is less control over quality than is possible with products. The skill, training, and motivation of the service provider affect service quality.

Services are **inseparable**, meaning that they are consumed at the same time they are produced. The person or technology producing the service must be available when and where the customer needs it. Marketers must determine where and when consumers want a service and must be able to provide it at that location and time.

Services are **perishable**, meaning that the availability of a service must match the demand for that service at a specific time.

> **checkpoint** ✓
> In what ways are services different from products?

Study Tools

www.cengage.com/school/genbus/pob

Key Concepts

Determine the best answer.

1. True or False. Most new products introduced by companies are not totally new, but are improvements on existing products.

2. True or False. The first step in marketing research is to develop a data collection procedure.

3. The availability of a service must match the demand for that service at a specific time because it is:
   a. heterogeneous
   b. perishable
   c. inseparable
   d. intangible

Make Academic Connections

4. **Critical Thinking** Use the Internet to locate an article describing a new product that failed. Review the information to determine the possible reasons for failure. Write a short memo to the company describing how using the new product planning process may have reduced the likelihood of failure for the product.

5. **Research** Identify a product that many of your classmates use regularly. Prepare a five-question survey to determine their feelings about the strengths and weaknesses of the product and possible ways the product could be improved. Give the survey to at least 10 students. Present the results in a short report including at least one table, graph, or chart.

Price and Distribute Products

Goals

1 Discuss how the selling price of a product is calculated.

2 Differentiate between a direct and an indirect channel of distribution.

Key Terms

price 245

distribution 246

channel of distribution 246

channel members 247

retailer 247

Focus on REAL LIFE

Max was beginning his summer employment at a shipper's local terminal. His new boss, John, explained his duties. "We help many companies fill orders for products purchased online. If a product isn't delivered when and where customers want it, if it is damaged in shipment, or if the costs of shipping are higher than customers want to pay, these companies can lose future sales."

Max said, "When I buy products online, I can track the shipment."

John replied, "We track everything. We have benchmarks that include how long a product stays in storage, how many times it is handled, the percentage of items damaged during distribution, and many other measures of performance. We are judged on these benchmarks."

Goal 1

Discuss how the selling price of a product is calculated.

VALUE AND PRICE

When you decide to purchase a product, how do you determine what to pay? Do you always pay the price that is marked on the product by the seller? Do you compare prices of several businesses to find the lowest price? Do you consider how much money you have available to spend in determining what price to pay? Are you concerned whether the seller is making a profit and whether that profit is low or high? Buyers usually want to pay the lowest price possible and sellers want to charge the highest price possible. Determining the best price for a product is a difficult marketing challenge.

Pricing Factors

Many factors go into a decision about a fair price. What you might consider an appropriate price may be different from the decision of other customers.

It probably is very different from the price the seller believes is appropriate. There are both general and specific factors that influence the price paid for a product.

Supply and Demand A product that has a ready supply will have a lower price than a product with a very limited supply. If demand for a product is high, prices will increase. Products with low levels of demand will have comparatively low prices.

Uniqueness When a product has few close competitors because it is unique, the price will be higher than products that are very similar to others.

Age When products are first introduced to the market, prices will be quite high. As products age, the price gradually decreases.

Season Many products are used at a particular time of the year. Winter apparel, air conditioners, and holiday decorations have high levels of sales for a short time and then almost no sales for the rest of the year. Prices will be highest just before and at the beginning of the season. Prices will be lower during other times of the year.

Complexity Highly complex and technical products have higher prices than simple products. Products with many features and options will also command higher prices.

Convenience People pay for convenience. If a product is easily available and the seller provides a high level of customer service, prices will go up. Customers expect to pay low prices if they shop at a large warehouse store that is not as conveniently located and offers little service.

Price a Product

Price is the money a customer must pay for a product or service. The price of a product changes as it moves from producer to consumer. The manufacturer sets a price that is paid by other businesses that will sell the product to the final customer. The price is set by the business by adding together the product costs, operating expenses, and profit. The formula for calculating the selling price is shown in Figure 10-4.

Selling price is the price paid by the customer for the product.

Product costs are the costs to the manufacturer of producing the product or the price paid by other businesses to buy the product.

Operating expenses are all expenses of operating the business that are associated with the product. They can include salaries, storage and display equipment, facilities, utilities, taxes, and many others.

Profit is the amount of money available to the business after all costs and expenses have been paid.

Gross margin is an important factor in product pricing. The *gross margin* is the difference between the

SELLING PRICE FORMULA
Product costs + Operating expenses + Profit = Selling price

▶ **Figure 10-4**
What is the selling price for a rocking chair if the company buys the chair from the supplier for $65, has operating expenses of $17, and makes a profit of $48?

selling price and the product costs. It represents the amount of money on hand to pay for operating expenses and provide a profit.

Markup A pricing concept related to gross margin is markup. A *markup* is the amount added to the cost of a product to set the selling price. The markup is equal to the expected gross margin. A markup is stated as a percentage of the product's cost or as a percentage of the product's selling price. If a product costs $15 and has a 100 percent markup on cost, the markup is $15 and the selling price is $30. That $30 product would have a markup on selling price of 50 percent. The formulas for calculating markup on cost and markup on selling are shown in Figure 10-5.

Markdown Businesses are not always able to sell products at the original price they set. If customer demand is not as high as projected, if the selling season is ending, or if there is a flaw in the product, the business may have to take a markdown. A *markdown* is a reduction from the original selling price.

MARKUP FORMULAS
Markup on Cost
Product costs × Percent markup = Markup on cost
Markup on Selling Price
Gross margin ÷ Selling price = Percent markup on selling price

▶ **Figure 10-5**
What is the relationship between markup and the expected gross margin?

A markdown should be thought of as a pricing mistake because it reduces the amount of money the business has to cover operating expenses and profits. However, the original selling price can be set high because the product is new and there is higher demand. Small markdowns result in most of the remaining products being sold while still making a profit. The leftover products may need to be sold at large mark downs that still provide some money to cover the product cost and expenses.

checkpoint ✓

What is the formula for calculating the selling price of a product?

Goal 2

Differentiate between a direct and indirect channel of distribution.

CHANNELS OF DISTRIBUTION

Do you own any products that were produced in India or New Zealand? If so, the process of getting the products from those countries to a store in your area was probably difficult and time consuming. In contrast, have you shopped at a farmers' market? Here, local producers sell fruits, vegetables, and other home-grown products. The products have to be transported only a short distance and may be harvested the same morning they are sold. Each situation describes a distribution process.

Distribution involves determining the best methods and procedures to use so customers can find, obtain, and use a product or service. As a marketing mix element, **distribution** is the locations and methods used to make a product or service available to the target market. The route a product follows and the businesses involved in moving a product from the producer to the final consumer are known as a **channel of distribution**.

Need for Distribution Channels

In the earliest economic exchanges, people often bartered to exchange goods and services. If two people each had something the other person wanted, they would agree on how much of each product would be exchanged and the trade would be made. For example, a bushel of apples might be traded for a yard of fabric. The distribution process was relatively simple. In complex economies, exchanges are much more difficult due to several differences that exist between producers and consumers.

- **Differences in Quantity** Businesses produce or sell large amounts of each product to many customers. Each consumer needs only a very small number of products at a given time.

- **Differences in Assortment** Businesses typically specialize in producing a specific type of product while consumers want to purchase a variety of products.

- **Differences in Location** In today's global economy, thousands of miles often separate producers and consumers. Businesses may need to distribute their products to customers in many countries.

How have parcel delivery services influenced the success of many e-commerce businesses?

Digital Vision/Getty Images

• **Differences in Timing** Businesses gain efficiency by producing large amounts of a product at one time. Some agricultural products can only be produced at a specific time of the year. Consumers may want to buy products at different times than when they are produced.

Distribution channels develop to make adjustments in these differences. An effective channel of distribution takes the large quantities produced and breaks them into quantities customers want to buy. The channel gathers products from many producers to offer customers the array of products they need in convenient locations. They move products efficiently from where they are produced to where they can be sold. Distribution channels store products from the time they are produced until customers want to buy them.

Channels and Channel Members

The businesses that take part in a channel of distribution are known as **channel members**. All marketing functions and activities are performed by a channel member or by the consumer. Businesses join a channel of distribution when either the producer or consumer does not want to perform one or more marketing activities or when the business can perform the activities better or at a lower cost.

Channels are either direct or indirect. In a *direct channel of distribution*, products move from the producer straight to the consumer with no other organizations participating. An *indirect channel of distribution* includes one or more other businesses between the producer and consumer. These

WORK as a TEAM

A movie rental store in your community is concerned that it is losing business to an e-commerce company that delivers movies by mail and to cable companies that offer movies on demand. While the prices of the competitors are higher, people seem to like the convenience. Brainstorm suggestions of ways the movie rental store can make renting movies more convenient for its customers.

other businesses provide one or more of the marketing functions.

Indirect distribution channels can include *wholesalers*. Wholesalers are intermediaries between manufacturers and retailers. They create an assortment by breaking larger bulks of producer's products into smaller units by repacking and redistributing in smaller lots for retailers and other industrial buyers. Wholesalers who take *title*, or ownership of goods, are called merchant wholesalers. Other types of wholesalers who don't take title include agents and brokers.

Retailing Retailers are a well-known and important part of distribution channels for consumer products. **Retailers** are the final business organization in an

Name several ways a distribution center improves the exchange process between businesses and consumers.

Photodisc/Getty Images

How can a knowledgeable salesperson increase customer confidence in their decision to purchase a product?

indirect channel of distribution for consumer products. Retailers offer a range of products at convenient locations for consumers. They help consumers to select the best products. They can provide financing and delivery services. They may even offer repairs and other customer services. Retailers assist manufacturers by storing, displaying, and advertising the products and often paying the manufacturer well before final consumers buy the products.

> **checkpoint ✓**
> What is the difference between a direct and an indirect channel of distribution?

10-3 Assessment

Key Concepts

Determine the best answer.

1. Which of the following conditions will result in a lower rather than a higher price?
   a. a high customer demand
   b. a large quantity of available products
   c. a product that has very few similar competing products
   d. All would result in lower prices.

2. When businesses specialize in producing a specific type of product, a channel of distribution will be needed to adjust differences in
   a. timing
   b. location
   c. assortment
   d. quantity

Make Academic Connections

3. **Math** Visit a department store or the online catalog of an Internet business. Identify five products that have been marked down and for which the original price and sale price are listed. Prepare a spreadsheet on which you list the product, the original price, and the sale price. Calculate the amount of the markdown and the markdown percentage. Determine the amount you would pay if you purchased all five items at the original price and if you purchased them at the sale price. What is the total savings in dollars and as a percentage of the original prices?

4. **Research** List the seven marketing functions. Use a business directory or the Internet to locate a business that specializes in the first function on your list. Choose a business that is part of an indirect channel of distribution. Do this for each function on your list.

10-4 Plan Promotion

Goals

1 Justify the importance of communication in marketing.

2 Identify and describe the common types of promotion.

Key Terms

promotion 249

effective communication 250

personal selling 251

advertising 252

merchandising 253

Focus on REAL LIFE

As an account representative for an advertising agency, Melody is trying to sell the agency's services to a new customer—Calista Whitford.

"The most powerful marketing tool influencing consumer behavior is promotion," Melody says.

"Really?" Calista asks.

"Yes, it can attract attention and remind customers of their needs. Advertising can tap their emotions and encourage them to buy."

"How does advertising influence emotions?" asks Calista.

"Advertising can create an image with a picture or other graphic, the language we use, even the colors of the headline, text, picture, or background. All of these things can establish feelings of pleasure, happiness, fear, or sadness," explains Melody. "We can create an advertisement that leaves your customers with a positive feeling toward your products."

COMMUNICATION AND PROMOTION

Promotional messages from businesses, organizations, government agencies, and political candidates bombard you on a regular basis. Each day newspapers, television and radio programs, and mailboxes are filled with advertisements. Sides of buses, tops of taxis, even posters in public restrooms contain promotional messages asking you to buy something, support a cause, or change an opinion. Every time you visit the World Wide Web, you are exposed to a variety of virtual promotions. It is apparent that businesses and organizations believe in the power of promotion, but is it always effective? What determines whether promotion is used well or not?

Promotion is any form of communication used to inform, persuade, or remind. Businesses, organizations, groups, or individuals use promotion. It is used to influence knowledge, beliefs, and actions about products, services, or ideas. To plan effective promotion, marketers must first understand the communication process. They then must apply effective communication to interact with consumers in a way that results in information, understanding, and action.

The Communication Process

Most of you have played the game where one person starts a message by whispering in the ear of a second person. That person

How easily are you able to communicate with other people? Explain how an ability to communicate with other people can affect the life-span goals you set and your ability to achieve them.

Components of Effective Communication

Encode message → **Communication Channel** → *Decode message*

Sender **INFORMATION** **Receiver**

Feedback

whispers to the next and so on until several people have heard the message. When the last person states what he or she heard, it is seldom the same as the initial message. The game makes the point that effective communication is not easy. **Effective communication** is the exchange of information so there is common understanding by all participants. Effective communication is illustrated in Figure 10-6.

Communication begins with a person or organization (*sender*) that has information to communicate to another person or organization (*receiver*). The sender chooses the way (*communication channel*) the information will be transmitted to the receiver. Before sending the message, the sender decides the form in which the information will be sent—text, spoken words, pictures. Preparing the information to be communicated is called *encoding*. The receiver obtains the information from the channel and interprets it for understanding (*decoding*). To be sure that the communication achieved the desired result, the sender needs to have a response from the receiver (*feedback*). If the receiver understood the information and responds in a way the sender wanted, communication was effective. If the receiver does not

respond or acts in an unexpected way, communication failed.

Communicating Through Promotion

Promotion is an important form of communication. A business needs to provide information to consumers in order to persuade them to make a purchase. As the sender, the business decides what information to provide. The consumer is the receiver. The information is encoded in the form of a promotional message such as an advertisement. The business chooses an information channel. Common promotional channels include advertising media, salespeople, and the Internet. If the customer sees or hears the message, it is decoded. The response of the consumer gives feedback to the business about the effectiveness of the promotion.

Choosing target markets and studying their needs and decision-making process can make promotion more effective. When the focus of a business is a target market, communication can be very specific to the needs of that group using media that are familiar to and trusted by those consumers. The business will understand where the customers are in the decision-making process. It will tailor promotional messages at that stage. Early messages get attention and give simple information about the product or service and the needs it satisfies. Later promotions can compare the product to competing brands. They may point out advantages that are important to the

Choose a newspaper, television, or magazine advertisement that is familiar to each person. Using that advertisement, identify each of the components of the communication channel. Discuss whether the advertiser seems to be demonstrating effective or ineffective communication.

target market. When customers purchase the product, promotions can switch to providing reinforcement of their decision and offering after-sale services.

TYPES OF PROMOTION

An inventor asks you for advice on how to promote a new type of cellular telephone that provides satellite TV reception. What types of promotion would you recommend? Would it be a glitzy television campaign or direct mail to cellular service subscribers? Maybe you would suggest text messaging delivered to cell phones. What about salespeople ready to demonstrate the new product to customers who visit shopping mall kiosks? There are many choices for promotional communications. The types of promotion are divided into personalized promotion and mass promotion. *Personalized promotion* communicates directly with each customer using information tailored to that person. *Mass promotion* communicates with many people at the same time with a common message.

Personalized Promotion

Personalized promotion is the most effective form of marketing communication. It is also the most expensive. The most well known type of personalized promotion is personal selling. **Personal selling** is direct, individualized communication with prospective customers to assess their needs and assist them in satisfying those needs with appropriate products and services. Personal selling usually is done face-to-face with each customer. The customer visits the business to meet with a salesperson or the salesperson goes to the home or

business of the customer. Personal selling also can be completed using telephone calls or live audio and video Internet connections. Because personal selling is often used for complex and expensive products and services, it may require several contacts between the salesperson and the customer to complete the sale.

To prepare for a sale, salespeople gather information on the prospective customer they will visit. They study product information. They need to be able to make the best match of products to customer needs. When a customer is qualified, meaning

What questions would help a salesperson determine the best clothing and jewelry to recommend for a particular consumer?

they appear to have the need for and resources to buy a product, the salesperson schedules a meeting with the customer. During the meeting, the salesperson asks questions, provides information, and demonstrates the product for the customer. If the product meets the customer's needs, the salesperson helps the customer make a decision to purchase. The salesperson may also arrange payment or financing as well as product delivery and any services the customer requires. After the customer has used the product, the salesperson contacts the customer to answer additional questions and determine that the customer is satisfied.

Mass Promotion

Mass promotion is directed to many people at the same time. If the people are from the same target market, they will have like needs. Because the promotional message is aimed at many people, it cannot be as individualized and specific as personalized promotion. However, reaching many people with the same message through mass media is much less expensive. While a large company may spend hundreds of thousands of dollars on a television advertisement, it reaches more than a million people. Therefore the cost of the message for each customer is quite low.

Advertising is the most known and used type of mass promotion. **Advertising** is any paid form of communication through mass media directed at identified consumers to provide information and influence their actions. The most common advertising media are

A Question of Ethics

The Price of Success

Should a successful company be penalized because it has developed a successful product? An important principle of private enterprise is that businesses and consumers benefit from competition. The belief is that competition increases the choices and quality of products and reduces prices for consumers. European courts recently stepped in to fine Microsoft for trying to reduce competition for several of its products.

Microsoft develops and sells the operating system used in most personal computers. Because computer manufacturers know that consumers expect to buy computers that have the Microsoft operating system installed, they must purchase the systems from Microsoft. Microsoft includes many features that are added

to the operating system such as an Internet browser, e-mail and productivity programs, and a media player. All of the added programs are owned and sold by Microsoft. It is not easy for consumers to uninstall the programs once they buy a computer and difficult for Microsoft's competitors to get computer manufacturers and consumers to purchase and use their programs because Microsoft has already included them in the system.

Microsoft argues that its programs are popular among consumers, the features improve the operating system, and when pre-installed are easier to use and cheaper for consumers than if they had to buy all of the added programs separately. Its competitors argue that Microsoft is monopolizing the market by forcing

computer manufacturers to include its products and reject the similar products of competitors.

Think Critically

1. Should courts step in to prevent Microsoft from requiring computer manufacturers to install the additional Microsoft software in order to buy its popular operating system?

2. Do you believe competition among businesses usually benefits consumers? Why or why not?

3. Use the Internet to gather the latest information on legal actions taken by governments and competitors against Microsoft designed to encourage greater competition.

television, radio, newspapers, magazines, mass mailings, outdoor displays, and the Internet.

Consumers are exposed to hundreds of communications including promotional communications in the media each day. These messages are not developed for or delivered directly to individuals. For this reason, the advertisements must be designed to attract attention and focus the consumer on a small amount of specific information. Most advertisements do not result in an immediate sale. Rather, they attempt to influence prospects to take additional action such as visit a store, gather more information, or test the product.

Advertising campaigns direct communication efforts for both institutional advertising for the entire business and product advertising for the individual product. Advertising campaigns and individual ads should be analyzed for effectiveness. Individual ads are often tested before they are placed by using focus groups. Campaigns are evaluated during and after they are completed to see if the desired communication has been received.

Other types of mass promotion are publicity, sales promotion, and public relations. *Publicity* is non-paid promotional communication presented by the media rather than by the business or organization that is being promoted. *Public relations* is an ongoing program of non-paid and paid communications. It is planned to favorably influence public opinion about an organization, marketing effort, idea, or issue. *Sales promotion* includes activities and materials designed to reinforce a company's brand and image. It is also a direct incentive to take an action likely to immediately increase sales of a product or service. Sales promotion includes contests and games as well as the many products companies give away to consumers or sell at a low cost that highlight a brand name or product.

How can stores communicate effectively with customers through merchandising?

Merchandising

Retailers often attempt to obtain action from their customers by engaging in merchandising. **Merchandising** includes a set of promotional activities designed to generate sales in the retail setting. There are a number of retail merchandising strategies. *Visual merchandising* uses visual signals to communicate in a retail setting. These include the use of shelf labels, signs, or displays. Visual merchandising allows a retailer to use visual signals to replace a salesperson for information.

Retailers will also set up a *display* to exhibit a product at the point of sale. For example, retailers will place product displays at the front of stores to entice customers into the store. Sale items may be displayed at the back of the store to bring customers past other merchandise to increase impulse purchasing.

Retailers should develop merchandising plans that identify strategies for price markdowns or markups, visual displays, and special events such as seasonal sales. For example, many stores start their holiday displays as early as Thanksgiving. The entire holiday season may have a specific merchandising plan. The merchandising plan may come from a corporate headquarters with specific instructions for each store in a chain. Stores that do not have a corporate merchandising staff need to develop their own merchandising plans.

Mass Personalization

Businesses can combine the advantages of personalized and mass promotion by using mass personalization promotion. Mass personalization begins with promotion through mass media such as newspapers, mass mailings, or the Internet. Prospective customers see the advertisement and become interested in the product or service. The company then provides an easy-to-use method for the consumer to gather more personalized information.

A customer who views an Internet advertisement or uses a search engine to gather information can be encouraged to complete an online survey. The questions provide the business with more specific information about the consumer, including their interests and needs. When the survey is submitted, the consumer is taken to a more specific website tailored to their profile or they are sent specific information via e-mail. They can even contact an online customer service representative who can answer detailed questions. A simpler form of mass personalization on the Internet is a set of links that take customers with specific questions to other web pages. The links can help them choose a specific product and complete an online purchase.

> **checkpoint** ✓
> Describe the advantages and disadvantages of the major types if promotion.

10-4 Assessment

www.cengage.com/school/genbus/pob

Key Concepts

Determine the best answer.

1. Which of the following is not a part of effective communication?
   a. the sender
   b. the receiver
   c. the advertisement
   d. information

2. The most expensive but also most effective type of promotion is
   a. personal selling
   b. advertising
   c. publicity
   d. public relations

Make Academic Connections

3. **Critical Thinking** Use Figure 10-6 to illustrate three different examples of business communications: a business-to-business communication, a business-to-final consumer communication, and a consumer-to-business communication.

4. **Research** Identify three different products or services you would consider buying. For each product, identify the information you need to help you make a purchase decision and what media or information source you would choose to gather the information. Describe how a business could use promotion to influence your decision.

Flexibility and Adaptability

Resolve Conflict

Conflict can be defined as competing differences between two or more people. These differences are often caused by struggles over goals, motives, values, ideas, and resources. Believe it or not, conflict can be both good and bad, depending upon the results of the conflict. The costs of negative, unresolved conflict include decreased productivity, low employee morale, and heightened workplace tensions. These all have the potential to damage the success of a business. But conflict of the right nature can be beneficial to business. For example, friendly conflict can encourage competition, diverse thinking, creativity, and a wider variety of solutions to business problems. Prevention is the solution to many problems, including workplace conflict. Some tips for preventing negative conflict in the workplace include the following:

How are the people in this photo demonstrating respect for each other?

- Be open to others' ideas. Listen before making up your mind.
- Avoid stereotyping your co-workers and superiors.
- Do not use language or expressions that may be offensive or demeaning to others.
- Disagree constructively. Offer alternative suggestions or solutions rather than simply rejecting others' ideas.
- Above all, treat your co-workers and superiors with the respect you want them to show you.

Unfortunately, conflict cannot always be avoided. All types of conflict can arise, from personality clashes to conflict over business ideas. The following strategies can be helpful in managing conflict with co-workers.

- **Intervention** Ask a co-worker or supervisor to provide a setting for conflict resolution between you and those with whom you are in conflict. A supervisor also might speak on your behalf to the co-worker with whom you are in conflict.
- **Confrontation** Approach the co-worker with whom you are having trouble. Both of you must recognize the problem and then work together toward a solution.

- **Compromise** If the conflict involves a disagreement over a particular business issue, you might work out a compromise solution. For example, you may agree to your co-worker's idea in exchange for similar treatment during the next conflict.
- **Avoidance** The avoidance technique should be your last solution, but in some situations it may be best. If you simply cannot solve a personality conflict, deal with the individual when you need to, but otherwise steer clear.

Conflict between a worker and a superior is acceptable, and in some cases even beneficial, if it leads to increased mutual respect. Conflict with superiors must be handled with care and should not be seen as a challenge to the superior's authority. Conflict with superiors should be kept professional and private.

Think Critically

1. What is conflict?
2. What are the consequences of negative conflict?

Business Notes

10-1 Marketing Basics

- Marketing is the activity, set of institutions, and processes for creating, communicating, delivering, and exchanging offerings that have value for customers, clients, partners, and society at large. The seven marketing functions are product and service management, distribution, selling, marketing-information management, financial analysis, pricing, and promotion.

- A marketing strategy is a two-step process used to plan and market products. The first step is to identify a target market and the second step is to develop a marketing mix.

- The steps in the consumer decision-making process are: recognize a need, gather information, select and evaluate alternatives, make a purchase decision, and determine the effectiveness of the decision.

10-2 Develop Effective Products and Services

- The steps in a marketing research study are: define the marketing problem, study the situation, develop a data collection procedure, gather and analyze information, and propose a solution.

- The components of a product are the basic product, product features, options, brand name, packaging, and a guarantee or warranty.

- Products are tangible items that you can see and examine. Services are intangible activities that are consumed at the same time they are produced.

10-3 Price and Distribute Products

- Businesses use the following formula for setting the price of a product: Selling price = Product costs + Operating expenses + Profit.

- A direct channel of distribution moves products from the producer directly to the consumer with no other organizations participating. An indirect channel of distribution includes one or more other businesses between the producer and consumer. These other businesses provide one or more of the marketing functions.

10-4 Plan Promotion

- When the focus of a business is a target market, communication can be very specific to the needs of that group using media that are familiar to and trusted by those consumers.

- There are two major types of promotion. Personalized promotion communicates directly with each customer using information tailored to that person. Mass promotion communicates with many people at the same time with a common message.

Communicate Business Concepts

1. Some companies are not marketing businesses, but complete marketing activities as a part of their business operations. Other businesses are marketing businesses because their primary activities are to complete marketing activities. Identify three businesses from your community that are not marketing businesses and three that are marketing businesses. Justify your choices.

2. Use the Yellow Pages of the telephone directory for your town or city. For each of the seven marketing functions, locate a business whose primary work relates to that function. Identify the work of the business to show how it relates to the marketing function.

3. You are planning the marketing strategy for a new portable printer that weighs less than two pounds and can fit in a backpack or briefcase. Identify one target market for the printer that is a business consumer and one that is a final consumer. Describe how the marketing mix would be similar and different for each target market.

4. Often it is believed that people will purchase the lowest-priced product available, but experience shows people will pay more for a product if they believe the higher-priced product is better than the lowest-priced products. Think of several products you purchase for which you know you pay more than you would have to. List the features of the products that cause you to pay a higher price. After you have developed the list, classify the reasons according to the four elements of the marketing mix: product, distribution, price, promotion.

5. The price charged for a product is affected by a number of factors. For each of the following situations, identify whether you believe it will result in a higher or lower price. Write one or two sentences to justify each answer.

a. One customer purchases a very large quantity of a product.
b. A business provides a high level of customer service.
c. The product is very fragile and requires special handling.
d. The product moves through many businesses in the channel of distribution before it reaches customers.

6. Internet services have the same traits as those provided by bricks and mortar businesses. Locate an Internet service business. Review the company's website and find information that describes how the service is intangible, inseparable, perishable, and heterogeneous.

Develop Your Business Language

Match the terms listed with the definitions.

7. Any paid form of communication through mass media directed at identified consumers to provide information and influence their actions.

8. The exchange of information so there is common understanding by all participants.

9. A specific group of consumers that have similar wants and needs.

10. The specific sequence of steps consumers follow to make a purchase.

11. The locations and methods used to make a product or service available to the target market.

12. The blending of the marketing elements.

13. Intangible activities that are consumed at the same time they are produced.

14. The activity, set of institutions, and processes for creating, communicating, delivering, and exchanging offerings that have value for customers, clients, partners, and society at large.

15. The route a product follows and the businesses involved in moving a product from the producer to the final consumer.

16. Finding solutions to problems through carefully designed studies involving consumers.

17. A company's plan that identifies how it will use marketing to achieve its goals.

18. The reasons consumers decide what products and services to purchase.

19. Direct individualized communication with prospective customers to assess their needs and assist them in satisfying those needs with appropriate products and services.

20. Any form of communication used to inform, persuade, or remind.

21. The money a customer must pay for a product or service.

22. The final business organization in an indirect channel of distribution for consumer products.

23. A set of promotional activities designed to obtain sales in the retail setting.

KEY TERMS

a. advertising
b. buying motives
c. channel of distribution
d. consumer decision-making process
e. distribution
f. effective communication
g. marketing
h. marketing mix
i. marketing research
j. marketing strategy
k. merchandising
l. personal selling
m. price
n. promotion
o. retailer
p. services
q. target market

Make Academic Connections

22. **Math** The use of intermediaries reduces the number of exchanges needed to distribute products from producers. Consider a situation where three manufacturers produce products that are purchased by 1,000 customers. Use the following information to determine the number of exchanges needed for each customer to purchase one product from each manufacturer.

    a. How many exchanges will be needed if each manufacturer sells one product to each of the 1,000 customers?

    b. How many exchanges will be needed if each manufacturer sells its products to 10 retailers and each of the retailers sells all three products to 100 customers?

23. **Research** Use the Internet, business magazines, or newspapers to locate a report on a marketing research study. Review the research and prepare a two-page analysis. The report should include the purpose of the research, the characteristics of the people studied, the data collection method, important findings, and the sponsor of the research. Describe how a business could use the research to improve its marketing strategy.

24. **Communication** Promotion is used for three purposes: to inform, to persuade, and to remind. Select a product or service with which you are familiar. Write three short radio advertisements for the product. Direct each advertisement at one of the three purposes of promotion.

25. **Math** Calculate the missing amounts in the table below for each product.

Product	Product Cost	Markup Percent	Markup Amount	Selling Price	Total Cost	Net Profit
A	$30	40	$12			$2
B		50	$50			$25
C	$60			$84	$72	

Decision-Making Strategies

DeeLites is a popular bakery in a small Iowa town. The bakery produces a variety of fresh pastries, cakes, pies, and other specialty desserts that have reduced calories. Loyal customers say that the low-calorie baked goods are better tasting than similar higher-calorie products they can purchase elsewhere. Customers have encouraged the owner of DeeLites to allow ordering over the Internet so their friends and relatives from other cities and states can purchase the products. The owner would like to increase sales, but is concerned whether the Internet is a good way to expand.

26. What would be the advantages of using the Internet to expand sales?

27. What changes in the marketing mix would have to be made to sell products using the Internet?

Linking School and Community

Interview three people from your community to learn more about the consumer decision-making process. One person should be approximately your age or younger, another at least 10 years older than you, and the third at least 20 years older than you. Ask each to identify a product they recently purchased. Then ask them questions about how they decided they needed to make the purchase, how they gathered information about choices, and how they made the decision, as well as their satisfaction following the decision. Ask them if they believe they made an effective decision or not and why. When you have completed all of the interviews, compare the procedures they followed with the steps of the consumer decision-making process.

©sweetym/iStock

Web Workout

The Internet is becoming a very strong tool for marketing research. Companies can place surveys online, run online focus groups, and deliver alternative web pages to see which ones are most effective. Harris Interactive has more than 6 million members from more than 125 different countries in its Harris Poll Online Panel. Visit the Harris Interactive website. Evaluate the benefits that this research service offers customers.

Think Critically

1. Read an article that appears under the "Headlines" banner. Describe how the information that Harris has collected could help a business.

2. Browse through the Harris site and list all the marketing functions where Harris provides marketing research services.

3. List three of the specialty groups that Harris Poll Online uses to collect information for companies. Why would companies be interested in these market segments?

Advertising Campaign

Successful businesses develop effective advertising campaigns that outline the schedule of all planned advertising and all sales promotion activities.

For this event, the advertising campaign may be completed by individuals or teams consisting of two or three members. Participants in the event must demonstrate critical thinking skills to develop an advertising campaign for an existing business. The advertising campaign must outline all planned advertising and sales promotion activities for an entire year. The advertising campaign should also include a budget for all activities.

The advertising campaign document must follow guidelines provided by DECA. Participants will have 10 minutes to present the advertising campaign to the judge or class. Visual aids and a copy of the advertising campaign may be used during the presentation. Five minutes are scheduled following the presentation for the judge or class to ask questions.

Performance Indicators Evaluated

- Conduct research to determine the most effective advertising strategies.
- Analyze facts about existing advertising campaigns to make the best choices.
- Demonstrate critical thinking and problem-solving skills.

- Work effectively as a team.
- Prioritize tasks and practice time management.
- Demonstrate oral and written communication skills.

You will be evaluated for:

- Quality of research findings and conclusions
- Credibility of the proposed advertising campaign
- Ability to present information in a convincing manner with factual information

For more detailed information about performance indicators, go to the DECA website.

Think Critically

1. Why must a business outline an advertising campaign for an entire year?

2. Why is it important to research the competition when developing an advertising campaign?

3. Why is the budget an important element of the advertising campaign?

4. How could a consumer panel's input strengthen the advertising campaign?

www.deca.org

CHAPTER

11

Business and Technology

Digital Vision/Getty Images

Planning a Career in ...

INFORMATION TECHNOLOGY

Almost every job in business is touched by technology. Technology supports core business functions such as communication through phones and e-mail, information storage and processing by computers, and reporting through printing, presentations, and conferencing.

Information technology workers use a variety of skills and educational backgrounds to help businesses function. These skills can be used to support hardware, such as computer or communication networks. Technology workers can also support software usage by installing, programming, or training others to use computer programs.

Most high schools offer a number of computer classes. Instruction is also available at computer training centers. Some employers will pay for employees to take computer courses. Self-paced and online programs are also available. Information technology training may be achieved through a specialized vocational program or a college degree program. Knowledge of computer systems, computer languages, application software, and other technology is required for specialized positions.

Related Job Titles

- Information Systems Manager
- Computer Programmer
- Software Engineer
- Computer Support Specialist
- Network Administrator
- Systems Analyst
- Computer Scientist
- Database Administrator

Analyze Career Opportunities in ...

INFORMATION TECHNOLOGY

Use library and Internet resources to learn more about careers in information technology. Choose one of the job titles listed in the box above and answer the following questions.

1. Identify the minimum educational requirements for job. Explain other training or education that might be needed for advancement.

2. Is this a career that interests you? Describe a few things you could do to learn more about this career.

What's it like to work as a ... Web Developer?

"Should we use a Flash intro? Will a banner heading be most appropriate? What functions are required to serve the needs of this new customer?" Kellye, a web developer, is in a morning brainstorming session with her team. The team plans to have some ideas ready in time for a meeting with the customer tomorrow.

Around the world, more than a billion people access the Internet for information, entertainment, and business activities. Websites are the basic element of the Internet. Web developers analyze, plan, design, implement, and support the websites of their organizations. Many businesses use outside vendors like Kellye's company to create and maintain their websites.

Knowledge of multimedia software is a key requirement for web developers. Graphics, digital imagery, audio, and video are vital to the appeal and effectiveness of a website. Web developers are often involved with creating websites for online selling and other e-commerce activities.

What about you? In what ways do you use computers and technology each day that might be the basis for a future career?

11-1 Computer Systems

Goals

1 Identify the main elements of a computer system.

2 Describe input devices and processing activities.

3 Explain computer storage media and output types.

Key Terms

computer system 263

hardware 263

software 263

computer network 263

central processing unit (CPU) 265

program 265

computer language 265

operating system software 265

application software 265

Focus on REAL LIFE

Ms. Jenkins announced to her class, "The French Club will meet today during sixth period. The topic for discussion will be computers and new technology."

Fran looked at Brenda and said, "That doesn't make sense! What do computers have to do with the French Club?"

"Recently our club decided to use a database program to keep track of our membership records," said Brenda. "In addition," she went on, "the club is using e-mail to talk to students in France. Then, we are planning a videoconference with other French clubs around the United States. We will also use our computer network to..."

"Wait a minute!" Fran exclaimed. "OK. OK. Computers do have a lot to do with the French Club."

"Well then, I guess you'll be coming to the meeting today after school," responded Brenda.

Goal 1
Identify the main elements of a computer system.

COMPUTERS IN SOCIETY

Computers are everywhere. These electronic devices process store receipts, test scores, and sports statistics. Computers in business are used to store, process, and report information. Computers are also used to design factories, control traffic patterns, and measure medical test results.

Nearly every business uses some type of computer. A company needs quick, efficient processing to control its operating costs, manage resources, and stay competitive. When you think about the billions of business transactions, checks, and school records that are processed each day, you realize the importance of computers.

Each day in banks, stores, offices, factories, homes, and nonprofit organizations, the use of computer systems is expanding. As managers plan and implement computerized activities, they must decide how best to use technology to serve the production and distribution needs of the organization.

How have computers changed records management in business?

Ximagination/Shutterstock.com

Elements of a Computer System

Video games, smart phones, and automated highway toll collection systems all have four basic components:

1. Input device
2. Processing unit
3. Memory and storage
4. Output device

As shown in Figure 11-1, these four basic components make up what is called a **computer system**. The physical elements of a computer system are called the **hardware**. Examples of computer hardware include keyboards, cameras, microphones, speakers, monitors (or screens), chips, and printers.

Hardware is constantly changing and expanding. For example, today most computers can handle sound, graphics, animation, and video. These features are being offered on smaller and more compact computers as well as other devices. Most smart phones offer some computer functions.

In contrast to hardware, **software** refers to the instructions that run the computer system. Businesses commonly use several types of software. These include word

Do you believe that you are *computer literate*—able to understand and use computers efficiently? Are you comfortable using computers? Describe how the computerization of our society and economy may affect your ability to achieve your life-span goals.

processing, spreadsheet, database, presentation, and communications programs.

Computer Networks

Computers in businesses and schools are commonly linked together in a **computer network**. Organizations link computers together so users can share hardware, software, and data.

The Internet is the largest and best-known computer network in the world. The Internet is most often used for two activities: exchanging e-mail and accessing the World Wide Web.

The World Wide Web (WWW) is also called the Web. It allows computer users to access information on almost every topic. The Web uses text, images, hyperlinks, graphics, frames, animation, video, and audio. It is an extensive information source. This global computer

Computer System

ABV/iStockphoto.com

▶ **Figure 11-1**

Which components of a computer system are represented in this illustration?

What do you think the next input device invented for use with a computer will be?

Digital Vision/Getty Images

Goal 2

Describe input devices and processing activities.

network provides access to information, facilitates e-commerce, and allows millions of people around the world to make connections. The World Wide Web is also an important source for handling business transactions.

A local computer network, sometimes called an *intranet,* is an organization's private computer network. It is based on the same communication standards as the Internet. An intranet is a smaller version of the Internet. Only members or employees can utilize an intranet. An intranet's website looks and functions just like a typical website, but it is private and only accessible to authorized users.

Like the Internet, an intranet is primarily used to share information. An intranet is an effective tool for saving time and money for companies. It can bring many benefits to an organization.

checkpoint ✓

List the four main elements of a computer system.

INPUT AND PROCESSING

Computer systems start with the entering of data or other input items. Operation of the system continues with the processing of the data.

Input: Getting Started

The first major component of a computer system is known as *input*. While people are mostly concerned with the results of computer operations, there has to be a starting point. Data is entered into a computer system with an input device.

The keyboard is a common input device. Keyboards are generally used to enter text and numbers. Another common input device is the mouse, a hand-controlled device used to point to commands or images on the computer screen.

Other input devices are often used for specific activities. The following list includes some common examples.

- Touchpads built into laptop computers allow the user to point and click just as you would with a mouse.

- Controllers and joysticks for video games allow players to direct the actions of game characters.

- Touch-sensitive screens allow users to use finger contact to enter data, give commands, and make selections.

- Laser devices use light to read bar codes to track sales, inventory, and shipping.

- Webcams allow for video conferencing anywhere in the world.

- Scanners translate words and images into computer-readable formats.

- Voice-activated systems allow words spoken into a microphone to be entered as data or to be translated into instructions or commands.

- Microphones and cameras allow input of audio and video.

Processing: Making Things Happen

How does data become meaningful information to be used by organizations and individuals? *Processing* is the second major component of a computer system. This activity takes place in the **central processing unit (CPU)**, which is the control center of the computer.

The CPU is the "brain" of a computer system. In a personal computer, the CPU consists of tiny wafers or chips. These chips carry instructions and data using electronic pulses.

The most common way to give instructions to a computer is with a program. A **program** is a series of detailed, step-by-step instructions that tell the computer what functions to complete.

Most powerful computer programs are in formats that are difficult to understand. The format of a computer program is a computer language. A **computer language** is a system of letters, words, numbers, and symbols used to communicate with a computer.

fyi *Biometric input devices are used to recognize fingerprints, facial features, voices, and eye patterns. These personal characteristics are scanned and processed to allow access to buildings, offices, and other secured areas. They are also used to authorize access to computers, files, and specific transactions, including purchases.*

The two main types of computer programs are operating system software and application software. **Operating system software** translates commands and allows application programs to interact with the computer's hardware. The most commonly used operating system is Windows®. **Application software** refers to programs that perform specific tasks such as word processing, database management, or accounting. Commonly used application software includes word processing, desktop publishing, database, spreadsheet, and presentation software.

Word Processing An organization's reports, correspondence, and other information are created with word processing software. This type of program allows the

What types of computer application software have you found most useful in your daily life?

user to enter, store, revise, and print text for letters, memos, reports, or standard business forms.

Desktop Publishing Word processing activities may be expanded to produce newsletters, brochures, and other publications. Desktop publishing usually includes graphics software to prepare charts, graphs, and other visual elements. Today, computer graphics are commonly used in television commercials, movies, training materials, and in other settings with a need for visuals.

Database Software "Create a list of employees who speak a language used in Asia." This type of request would involve the use of *database software*. A database is an organized collection of information with data items related to one another in some way.

In recent years, *database marketing* has become popular. Software is used to maintain, analyze, and combine customer information files. The information about customers is then used to increase sales by better serving customer needs. For example, a household with young children might receive advertising about educational software. Using a database increases the chance of reaching potential customers who are likely to buy the product.

Spreadsheet In the past, accountants used worksheet paper with many rows and columns. Such a worksheet is an example of a manually prepared spreadsheet. *Spreadsheet software* is a program that formats data in columns and rows in order to do calculations.

The location where a column and row intersect is called a *cell*. A spreadsheet is created with specific information, words, numbers, or formulas entered into the cells. Spreadsheets are used to prepare payroll records, financial statements, budgets, and other financial documents. An example of a spreadsheet screen appears in Figure 11-2.

▶ **Figure 11-2**

How can spreadsheet software improve accuracy?

	PROFIT & LOSS - ACTUAL VS. BUDGET			
		Actual	Budget	$ Over/(Under) Budget
Income				
	Product Sales	432,144	450,000	(17,856)
	Service Sales	471,866	500,000	(28,134)
	Total Income	904,010	950,000	(45,990)
Cost of Goods Sold				
	Payroll-Direct Labor	186,433	200,000	(13,567)
	Subcontractors	201,074	172,500	28,574
	Other Cost of Goods Sold	34,975	42,500	(7,525)
	Total Cost of Goods Sold	422,482	415,000	7,482
Gross Profit		481,528	535,000	(53,472)
	Overhead Expenses			
	Advertising	742	500	242
	Bad Debt	1,050	0	1,050
	Depreciation	17,433	17,500	(67)
	Employee Benefits	32,876	35,000	(2,124)
	Insurance	32,777	33,500	(723)
	Office Expenses	2,192	2,000	192
	Payroll-Administrative	153,044	175,000	(21,956)
	Professional Fees	12,125	11,750	375
	Rent	67,200	67,200	0
	Taxes-Business	16,433	17,000	(567)
	Taxes-Payroll	34,362	38,000	(3,638)
	Travel Expenses	15,273	12,200	3,073
	Utilities	8,924	9,475	(551)
	Total Expenses	394,431	419,125	(24,694)

Spreadsheet software may also be used to do a *what-if* analysis of a situation. For example, a manager may want to see the effect of different prices on profit. The spreadsheet automatically recalculates for each price.

Presentation Software Creating slide shows for educational and business seminars has become very common. The use of *presentation software* allows a speaker to show text, data, photos, and other visuals. These images may be accompanied by sound effects, music, or other audio. The use of multimedia elements adds to the value and enjoyment of presentations.

> **checkpoint** ✓
> What are common input devices?

MEMORY AND OUTPUT

Various programs must be stored for use in the computer system. Memory is also used for data processing activities.

Memory and Storage: Saving for Later

The third major component of a computer system is the *memory*. When in use, a program is stored in the computer's memory. This memory within the computer is also called *internal* (or *primary*) *storage*. During processing, both the program and any data entered with an input device are stored in memory.

As shown in Figure 11-3 memory capacity is measured using units such as *bit, nibble, byte,* and *kilobyte* (*K*). To give you an idea of a computer's internal storage capacity, it would take at least a 1K computer to store the information on an average page in this book.

Primary storage cannot hold all of the programs and all of the data needed by

computer users. Therefore, *external* (or *auxiliary*) *storage* that is not part of memory is available for storing both programs and data.

A hard disk is housed inside the computer allowing storage of billions of characters. CDs, DVDs, magnetic tapes, memory cards, and flash memory sticks are examples of commonly used auxiliary storage devices.

Output: Obtaining Results

The final component of a computer system is known as *output*. This element is of greatest interest to most people. Your score on a video game, the results of a test, or the sales for a new product are important outcomes of data processing activities.

> **Goal 3**
>
> Explain computer storage media and output types.

MEMORY CAPACITY	
Bit	smallest unit
Nibble	4 bits; a ½ byte
Byte	8 bits
Kilobyte	1,024 bytes
Megabyte	a million bytes
Gigabyte	a billion bytes
Terabyte	a thousand gigabytes

▶ **Figure 11-3**

Why is it important to know the number of bytes of memory capacity in a computer? How many kilobytes of memory are in a computer with 3 gigabytes of memory?

What types of data output do you expect to see on a company website? What types of data output are used routinely in the workplace? Give some examples.

1. Text output, which includes processing results displayed on a computer screen (monitor) or in a printed report

2. Graphics output, which might include company logos, photos, drawings, scrolling messages, and animated graphics

3. Audio output, which involves music and broadcast clips as well as presentations for training seminars

4. Video output, which may be in the form of a training film, television commercial, or news report

Quite often, a single output source, such as a website, includes more than one of these categories.

Output devices present data in a form that can be retrieved later or may be communicated immediately. There are four common types of output:

checkpoint ✓
How do internal and external memory differ?

11-1 Assessment

Study Tools

www.cengage.com/school/genbus/pob

Key Concepts

Determine the best answer.

1. An optical scanner is a device in the _?_ component of a computer system.
   a. input
   b. output
   c. memory
   d. processing

2. A list of potential customers for your new product would be created using _?_ software.
   a. desktop publishing
   b. word processing
   c. spreadsheet
   d. database

3. Which of the following is an example of auxiliary storage?
   a. CPU
   b. DVD
   c. monitor
   d. software

Make Academic Connections

4. **Technology** Prepare a visual presentation of a computer system and explain how each part works in the system.

5. **Economics** Describe how technology might affect the operating costs and profits of a company. What are possible effects of technology on the wages of workers?

Doing Business in... Egypt

Protected by deserts on both sides, Egypt has a tradition of architecture and culture. Today, the country is dependent on the fertile land along the Nile River. Cotton, fruits, and vegetables are some of the country's main exports. The Suez Canal provides a vital trade route between the Atlantic Ocean and the Indian Ocean.

As you enter a meeting in Egypt, several greetings may be used. The handshake is most common. Expect to see some traditional clothing, but foreign businesspeople should wear business suits. Clothing styles should always be modest and conservative. Even though it can be extremely hot, most of the body must remain covered. Even shirt collars are expected to be buttoned. You may be expected to take off your shoes, but only after following the lead of your host.

The workweek in Egypt runs from Saturday to Wednesday. Friday is the Muslim holy day, and most people also take off Thursday. In your negotiations, the pace will start slowly. Do not rush the situation. Because Egyptians must get to know you and like you before doing business, the decision process will take time. Also, be ready to compromise in your negotiations.

While the main language of Egypt is Arabic, many business discussions may be carried out in English or French. Business cards will be better received if one side is English and the other side is Arabic. Language meaning will not always be direct. A "yes" may in fact mean "possibly."

Be cautious of body language. The left hand is considered unclean in the Arab world. Always use your right hand unless both are needed, such as for lifting a heavy object. While Egyptians may gesture with their hands when speaking, pointing is considered very rude. The "thumbs up" sign is offensive.

Your conversations may include talk of soccer, basketball, and boxing. Avoid talking about political issues. In regard to food, many of the most popular Egyptian recipes are thousands of years old. Wheat and barley are the basis for many breads, pastries, and cakes. Peas, beans, lettuce, cucumbers, leeks, and other vegetables are often served with oil and vinegar dressing. Figs, dates, pomegranates, and grapes are important parts of the Egyptian diet, as are fish, poultry, lamb, and beef.

Think Critically

1. How does doing business in Egypt differ from business activities with which you are familiar?

2. What common mistakes might a person make when doing business in Egypt?

3. Conduct library or Internet research to find additional information about business and economic activities in Egypt.

How do climate and geography impact doing business in Egypt?

KHALED EL-FIQI/EPA/Landov

11-2 Business Applications of Technology

Goals

1 Describe the components of a management information system (MIS).

2 Identify computer applications in service industries.

3 Discuss e-commerce activities.

Key Terms

management information system (MIS) 270

computer-assisted instruction (CAI) 272

e-commerce 274

Focus on REAL LIFE

Josh Aki arrived on the first day of his new part-time job at NBI Distributors. This retailing company sells an array of products by mail, telephone orders, and via the Internet.

During orientation, Josh met the sales manager and learned that some of the firm's products were doing well and others were just sitting in the warehouse. After he got settled at his desk, Josh's supervisor said, "Josh, please outline a report with the sales results of the new products we have introduced over the past six months. Alicia will help you get started."

After some initial pleasantries, Alicia showed Josh how to check the database for sales results. She suggested that he summarize the data on the spreadsheet program and prepare his report with word processing software.

"Thanks, will you be around if I need more help?" Josh asked.

Alicia smiled and said, "Sure, Josh. Welcome to the NBI team."

Goal 1

Describe the components of a management information system (MIS).

MANAGEMENT INFORMATION SYSTEMS

Managers need information to make business decisions. A **management information system (MIS)** is a coordinated system of processing and reporting information in an organization. Computer systems and software are essential parts of management information systems.

A company may need a departmental budget that provides information on expected income and expenses for the next three months. Using an accounting program, past company data and future projections can be processed to create this budget. Budgets help with day-to-day decisions and planning for the future.

Components of an MIS

As shown in Figure 11-4 on the next page, the four main components of an MIS are gathering data, analyzing data, storing data, and reporting results. These activities allow an organization to obtain needed information in four main categories—financial, production and inventory, marketing and sales, and human resources.

Why are computer systems and software essential parts of an MIS?

Main Components of Management Information Systems

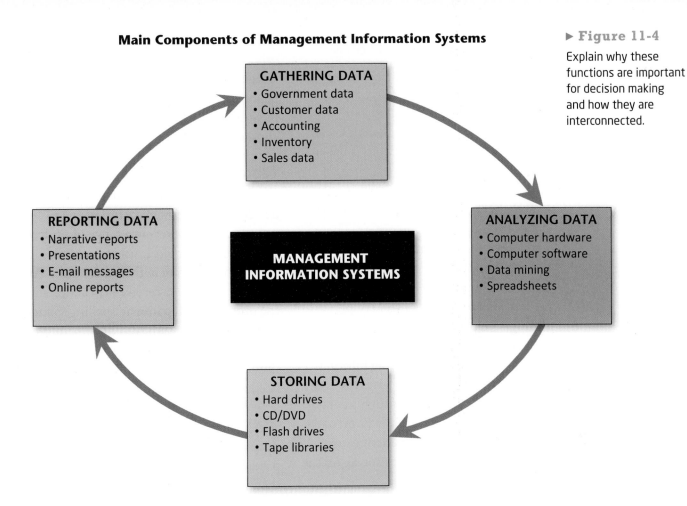

GATHERING DATA
- Government data
- Customer data
- Accounting
- Inventory
- Sales data

ANALYZING DATA
- Computer hardware
- Computer software
- Data mining
- Spreadsheets

MANAGEMENT INFORMATION SYSTEMS

STORING DATA
- Hard drives
- CD/DVD
- Flash drives
- Tape libraries

REPORTING DATA
- Narrative reports
- Presentations
- E-mail messages
- Online reports

▶ **Figure 11-4**
Explain why these functions are important for decision making and how they are interconnected.

1. *Financial information*, including budgets, sales reports, and financial statements
2. *Production and inventory information*, including production summaries, lists of tools and supplies, and finished goods reports
3. *Marketing and sales information*, including data on customer needs, current economic conditions, and actions of competitors
4. *Human resources information*, including salaries, employee benefit data, and employee evaluations

Data Sources

The information for an MIS comes from several sources. *External* data sources are outside an organization. Financial institutions, government agencies, and customers are examples of external data sources.

In contrast, *internal* data sources provide input from within the organization. Internal data includes accounting records, inventory information, and company sales figures. While gathering raw data may be an easy task, changing these facts and figures into meaningful information is the major goal of an MIS.

The MIS in Action

What activities are involved in a management information system? How is needed information communicated to managers? The operation of the MIS involves the following steps:

1. Identify the information needs of the organization.
2. Obtain facts, figures, and other data.
3. Process, analyze, and organize data in a useful manner.
4. Distribute information reports to those who make decisions.
5. Update data files as needed.

Computer networks are often used in an MIS to distribute information to managers, employees, and others. These networks connect computers, printers, and other equipment within a company or around the world.

Worldwide networks are set up through telephone lines, satellites, and other communication technology. Also important for communicating information is e-mail. E-mail gives users the ability to send data quickly through a computer system. After an employee prepares a letter or report, the document is sent electronically to another computer on the local or worldwide network.

checkpoint ✓
What are the four components of a management information system?

TECHNOLOGY IN SERVICE INDUSTRIES

More than 60 percent of workers in the United States are employed in service industries. The use of computers in these organizations is extensive.

Public Service

Government agencies use computers to keep records. For example, the federal government keeps social security records for all past and present workers in the United States and military records for people who have served in the armed forces.

Agencies are always expanding their use of computers. Medical information can be found within seconds to save lives. Police records can be sent to other locations minutes after a crime has occurred, helping to solve the crime. Schools and other agencies can transfer records easily when someone moves to another area of the country.

Education

Computers have become vital teaching devices. Computers make it possible to train and test workers in a range of professions. Office workers learn to use word processing software in their daily tasks. At the same time, they receive instruction on the proper use of grammar, spelling, punctuation, capitalization, and document formats. Airline pilots use computerized simulators to learn and improve skills needed for flying new types of aircraft.

Computer-assisted instruction (CAI) is the use of computers to help people learn or improve skills at their own pace. With CAI, students work at a speed that best serves their needs. The student does not have to go to a school building

How have computers changed the classroom in recent years?

for instruction. The student can learn at home on a computer network system connected to a central training location.

The demand for computer and *information technology* (IT) training in the workplace continues to grow. With the proper computer skills, you will be able to compete for some of the best-paying jobs in the business world.

Health Care

Computers are widely used in hospitals and other medical facilities. Uses range from keeping patient records to monitoring medications during surgery.

Medical professionals are also able to see to the healthcare needs of people in rural areas without leaving the city. The use of *telemedicine* with videoconference equipment allows diagnosis by a doctor in a different location, followed by treatment provided by a local healthcare professional. Technology of this type helps to expand the availability of health care in remote areas of less developed economies.

Financial Services

Paying bills online, checking your credit report, and selling stocks and bonds are just a few examples of computerized financial activities. Electronic banking and other financial services have made it possible for consumers to do business beyond usual banking hours. Each day, computers transfer billions of dollars. Payments to workers, businesses, and government flow through local and global computer networks.

Most people are familiar with credit cards and cash cards. You may not be aware of the existence of *smart cards*. These plastic cards with a silicon chip are used to store information. The chip within the card stores such data as your current account balance and credit history. It may even store medical information for emergencies.

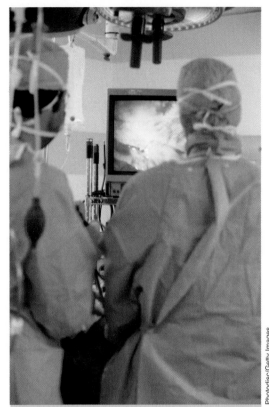

What are some of the benefits of computers in science?

Photodisc/Getty Images

The card could serve as a personal record keeper for travel and other expenses. In addition, a smart card can be used to prove you paid for merchandise you want to exchange, to gain admittance to your place of work, or to unlock and start your car without keys.

> **checkpoint** ✓
> What service industries make extensive use of computers?

fyi *The use of mobile phones and other wireless technology is sometimes called "m-commerce" (m for mobile). Various handheld devices are expanding and enhancing e-commerce activities. Instant messaging, stock trading, banking, online buying, music, and sports video clips are most common. Close to 70 percent of the world's population will be using wireless technology in the near future.*

Joel Calheiros/Shutterstock.com

E-COMMERCE

You are walking through the mall. As you pass a clothing store, a message appears on your cell phone screen. "Now on special for spring, waterproof jackets, $34.95." This targeted promotion is just one example of the fast, powerful capabilities of e-commerce and wireless technology.

E-commerce (*e* for *electronic*) refers to conducting business transactions using the Internet or other technology. These online business activities come in a range of forms. Almost every function of a company has been adapted to e-commerce. The most common e-commerce activities include:

- Providing product information
- Promoting a company
- Selling online
- Conducting market research
- Making payments
- Obtaining parts and supplies
- Tracking shipments

Types of E-Commerce

E-commerce opens up opportunities to companies previously limited by geographic, financial, or political restrictions. These online economic activities involve four basic models with two selling and buying parties: businesses (B) and consumers (C). See Figure 11-5.

The first and most familiar model is Business-to-Consumer, or B2C. Expanded sales of products in different geographic markets will create B2C

Do you think e-commerce provides more opportunities for the entrepreneur?

Supri Suharjoto/Shutterstock.com

growth. Examples are online companies such as Amazon.com and Dell.

The second e-commerce model is Business-to-Business, or B2B. These online exchanges are the largest and fastest-growing segment of e-commerce. They account for more than 90 percent of Internet transactions. Examples are Ford and General Motors buying parts online from their suppliers.

Consumer-to-Business (C2B) is the third e-commerce model. In C2B, consumers originate online transactions through price offers to businesses. The online company Priceline was one of the first companies in this category. Priceline allows shoppers to make bids for products and services such as airline tickets and hotels. The airline and hotel companies then decide whether to accept the offers. Although C2B activity is not a big part of e-commerce at this time, it could expand with new technologies and consumer initiatives.

▶ **Figure 11-5**

How does the Internet help each of these e-commerce models operate efficiently?

E-Commerce Matrix

	Business Seller	Consumer Seller
Business Buyer	B2B	C2B
Consumer Buyer	B2C	C2C

Finally, Consumer-to-Consumer (C2C) is the fourth e-commerce model. In the long economic tradition of bartering and auctions, buying and selling among consumers is growing in cyberspace. The ease and speed of transactions among online parties is encouraging more C2C exchanges. An example is the online company eBay.

Global E-Commerce

Internet-based computer systems, along with software that translates information from one language to another, make it possible to do business around the world without leaving your computer. Instant transmission of data with the use of satellites makes even the farthest point on earth as close as a button on your computer. Increased global business can have an important impact on world trade and international relations.

Importing and exporting can take place using a computer system. The goods are shipped from the closest location to save time and money. For example, you may order an item from a company in Italy using your computer. When the Italian marketers receive your order on their computer, they check a database and find there are five such items in stock in Canada.

Have you purchased products online? Conducted searches for product information online? Do you have ideas for products you would like to sell online? Explain how you believe the growth of e-commerce will affect the life-span goals you set or your ability to achieve them.

They instruct the Canadian importers through the Internet to ship the items to you. You receive them the next day.

You pay the Italian company. Later, the Italian and Canadian companies settle their accounts through the computerized banking system.

Another way of bringing people together to do business is *videoconferencing*. This system allows people in different geographic locations to meet "face-to-face" by satellite. It is used for sales presentations, training sessions, and other types of meetings. A sales staff in Peru can make a presentation to potential customers in Spain, South Africa, Pakistan, and the United States without leaving their offices in Lima.

> **checkpoint ✓**
> What do the notations B2C and B2B mean?

11-2 Assessment

Study Tools

www.cengage.com/school/genbus/pob

Key Concepts

Determine the best answer.

1. An example of external data would be
   a. a company sales report
   b. a list of employee qualifications
   c. a government economic forecast
   d. payroll records

2. CAI refers to
   a. paying bills online
   b. electronic inventory control
   c. providing health care to remote areas
   d. individualized instruction

3. When a packaged food producer sells items to a restaurant, this is considered to be a _?_ e-commerce transaction.
   a. B2C
   b. B2B
   c. C2B
   d. C2C

Make Academic Connections

4. **Visual Art** Create a visual presentation of a management information system for a specific information flow for a company of your choice.

5. **Culture** Research other cultures to determine how people in these societies might react to various aspects of e-commerce.

11-3 Other Technology Issues

Goals

1 Explain workplace uses of technology.

2 Identify home and personal applications of technology.

3 Discuss social concerns related to technology.

Key Terms

robotics 276

artificial intelligence (AI) 276

expert system 277

computer-aided design (CAD) 277

telecommuting 277

piracy 280

computer virus 280

Focus on REAL LIFE

Herb Cunningham is a talented worker, but he has seen demand for his skills as a bookkeeper declining. More and more, computerized accounting systems are keeping track of sales and expenses in companies.

"I guess it's time to upgrade my technology skills," Herb commented to his son, Joe. "I'm going to enroll in an online training class for accounting software."

"That's a good idea, but it might not be enough, Dad," responded Joe. "You should learn how to use spreadsheets, work with tax software, and learn about supporting computer-based accounting systems."

"I'm not sure I'll be able to learn how to do all of those things," was Herb's reply.

"But, Dad, I'll be here to help you," said Joe. "We are learning how to use this type of software in school. My teacher has also told us that the local college is using computer-assisted instruction to teach modern bookkeeping practices."

Goal 1

Explain workplace uses of technology.

WORKPLACE TECHNOLOGY

Computers are present in almost every business situation. They help improve efficiency and productivity. Computers can be found in oil fields, warehouses, retail stores, hospitals, offices, and factories.

Robotics

Most of you have seen robots and other computer systems in science fiction movies set in outer space and in the future. In real life, **robotics** involves mechanical devices programmed to do routine tasks, such as those in many factories. An example of work where robots are used is assembly line work that requires repetitive tasks.

Early robots did only simple tasks such as tightening a bolt on an automobile. Today, robots exist that can see, hear, smell, and feel. Robots are able to work 24 hours a day. These computerized workers can perform in dangerous situations such as in outer space, underwater, or underground. The use of domestic robots is growing in the home with robots that can clean floors, clean pools, mow lawns, or entertain.

Expert Systems

Have you ever wanted a quick answer to a question without having to find a book or person who knew the answer? **Artificial intelligence (AI)** is software that enables computers to reason, learn, and make decisions. It uses logical methods similar to the methods humans use. An example of artificial intelligence is computer programs that make decisions about complex topics. For example, software exists that asks people questions about their health in order to determine solutions for potential medical problems. This software allows people in areas without doctors to receive better medical care.

Computer programs that help people solve technical problems are called **expert systems**. They are now available for medical services, financial planning, and legal matters. Expert systems are based on the knowledge of human experts in many specialized areas. These systems provide intelligent answers as effectively as human experts in those subject matters. For example, employees of the Internal Revenue Service use an expert system to quickly answer questions from taxpayers.

Computer-Aided Design

Computers created many of the products you use each day. **Computer-aided design (CAD)** refers to the use of technology to create product styles and designs. CAD allows you to try different sizes, shapes, and materials for a new machine, automobile, or food package. This process can be used to experiment with many variations before spending time and money building a model or going into production.

Telecommuting

Each morning, more than 20 million Americans travel to their offices—in another room of their homes! These people do all or part of their work at home. **Telecommuting** involves the activities of a worker using a computer at home to do a job. Telecommuting saves travel time and costs. It results in less traffic along with reduced noise and air pollution.

Each year more and more people become telecommuters. This working arrangement is especially attractive to people who have a hard time leaving their home to go to work. These include workers who are disabled or parents who desire to be with their young children. A work-at-home arrangement is most common among workers such as writers and

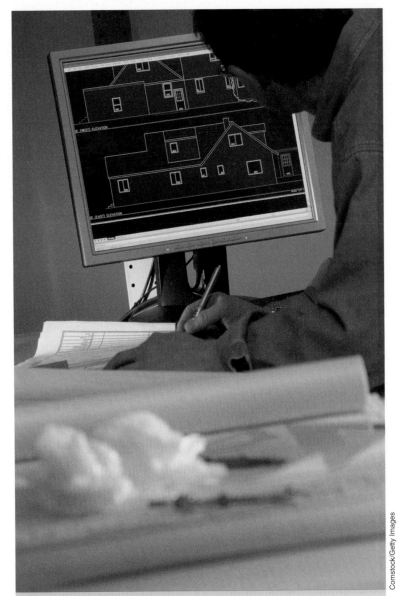

Comstock/Getty Images

What types of businesses might use computer-aided design?

editors, researchers, accounting clerks, sales representatives, computer programmers, and website designers.

These workers can easily send their reports, documents, and ideas to their employers by computer. Telecommuting is made possible with computers and other technology. E-mail and faxes allow a person to communicate with the company's main office.

checkpoint ✓
How is computer-aided design (CAD) used by businesses?

HOME AND PERSONAL TECHNOLOGY

Computers not only change the way you work, but technology also affects almost all aspects of life.

School and Homework

Internet studies reveal that computers are a key homework tool for students. For many students, more than one-third of homework time involves the computer. More than 80 percent of all students use the computer as an important homework resource.

Students today find many uses for the computer. Online information sources, presentation software, and other technology increase your ability to communicate and use ideas.

Home Robotics

Robots are no longer just in factories and businesses. Computerized systems now exist for repetitive chores such as vacuuming and mowing the lawn. Toys and other electronic devices for children can both entertain and educate. In the future, you can expect home robots to monitor household appliances, roll trash cans to the street, and assist the elderly with lifting heavy items.

What are some types of software that can make household activities easier?

Photodisc/Getty Images

Household Record Keeping

Computer systems are becoming information centers in people's homes. They are used for sending and receiving e-mail, shopping online, keeping financial records, completing homework assignments, and downloading music and videos.

Programs can keep a list of names and addresses of people to whom you send greeting cards. You may store your favorite recipes by categories. A family's medical history can be kept on file. You can have an inventory of household items for insurance records in case of theft or damage. In addition, computer programs may be used for personal financial record keeping, budgeting, writing checks, and preparing your income tax return.

NETBookmark

Businesses want to maximize the number and quality of visitors to their websites through search engine results. What can businesses do to use search engines to market their company? Access the website shown below and click on the link for Chapter 11. Obtain suggestions for businesses to maximize the number and quality of visitors.

www.cengage.com/school/genbus/pob

checkpoint ✓
What types of technology tools are available to students?

SOCIAL CONCERNS OF TECHNOLOGY

New technology will continue to expand the potential uses of computers in business. New software will eliminate some jobs while increasing job growth in others. It will also continue to change the way work is done.

Expanded computer use has resulted in concerns about health and safety, criminal activities, and privacy. While computers are beneficial to society, the wise person will not place complete faith in the reliability or safety of computer systems.

Employment Trends

Many people think computers are taking away their jobs. What is actually occurring is a shift in the job duties and skills needed to work in business and industry. When computers replace workers, companies need to retrain the workers with skills in programming, operating, or repairing computer systems.

Displaced workers are workers who are unemployed because of changing job conditions. They must adapt to the changing job market in order to have continued employment. What actions can companies and workers take to be ready for the new jobs of the future?

Computers and other technology are becoming more important in our lives each day. The ability to use this technology is vital to each person's economic survival. *Computer literacy* is the ability to use computers to process information or solve problems. You do not have to understand how to program a computer in order to use it. You do need to know how to enter, store, process, and retrieve information.

Health Concerns

Various products and substances can be dangerous. While little danger exists from using computers and other technology, some people have encountered discomfort resulting from on-the-job activities. For example, eyestrain and vision problems have been linked with prolonged work at computer screens. Muscle tension and nerve damage can occur from too many hours at a keyboard. These and other concerns have resulted in guidelines from labor organizations and government agencies for safe computer operation.

Computer Crime

Widespread use of computers has led to an increase in white-collar crime. *White-collar crime* is illegal acts carried out by office or professional workers while at work. Workers may steal money, information, or computer time through improper use of databases or illegal access to computer systems.

While the typical bank robbery results in a loss of $10,000, computer crimes involving bank records average hundreds of thousands of dollars. Theft of a physical

Goal 3

Discuss social concerns related to technology.

What concerns have resulted from the use of computer technology?

Yuri Arcurs/Shutterstock.com

item is obvious. Theft of computer time or information from a database is usually harder to detect.

Piracy is stealing or illegally copying software packages or information. It can be a significant problem. In some countries, between one-third and one-half of the software used is obtained illegally. Companies that develop software may lose more than half of their profits to information pirates who violate the law. Copyright laws apply to software as well as books and music.

Destructive efforts are also a concern to computer users. A **computer virus** is program code hidden in a system that can later do damage to software or stored data. The virus may be programmed to become active on a certain date or when certain data is accessed. Some computer viruses are harmless, only showing up as a funny message. Others have been known to destroy critical government records.

Privacy Concerns

One of the greatest challenges facing computer users is the need to guarantee privacy. Some dishonest people have learned how to illegally access computer databases. While some laws exist to protect your privacy, many concerned people believe these regulations are not strong enough. Some businesses are becoming stricter about who can access and use company information. Tighter security systems are being developed. Some organizations change the password needed to access information several times a day to protect their databases.

In recent years, *identity theft* has become a major concern for consumers and companies. Thieves obtain information online about a person. They apply for a credit card in the person's name or access the bank account of that person. According the Federal Trade Commission, 9 million people have their identities stolen in the United States each year. Con artists illegally obtain millions of dollars each year through identity theft.

> **checkpoint** ✓
> How do companies suffer from software piracy?

11-3 Assessment

Study Tools
www.cengage.com/school/genbus/pob

Key Concepts

Determine the best answer.

1. Telecommuting refers to
   a. the use of computers to design products
   b. working at home by computer
   c. difficulties from overusing computers
   d. illegal acts of office workers

2. Hidden software code that can damage computer operations is
   a. piracy
   b. a displaced worker
   c. a virus
   d. computer literacy

3. Illegal acts carried out by office or professional workers while at work are referred to as
   a. computer crime
   b. identity theft
   c. piracy
   d. white-collar crime

Make Academic Connections

4. **Communication** Prepare a memo that sets out the benefits of telecommuting for an organization. In your memo, present specific details of a job that would be appropriate for telecommuting.

5. **Music** Select three different types of music. Discuss how each might be appropriate or inappropriate for an office setting to reduce stress associated with working on computers.

Green America

Every time you spend or invest a dollar, it goes to work in the world.
—Green America website

Green America is an organization with a vision. The vision includes a world where:

- All people have enough
- All communities are healthy and safe
- The bounty of the earth is preserved for generations to come

The organization was founded on the belief that your purchases can support businesses that create jobs, care about their communities, engage in fair trade, and protect the environment. The mission is "to harness economic power—the strength of consumers, businesses and the marketplace—to create a socially just and environmentally sustainable society."

Green America was started in 1982 under the name Co-op America to provide practical tools to address today's social and environmental problems. While many environmental organizations fight political and legal battles, Green America educates people and business about making improvements through the economic system. Descriptions of some of their programs are shown below.

- **Climate Action Campaign** Encourages consumers and businesses to minimize their carbon footprint and offers strategies for pressuring corporate polluters to take climate change seriously.
- **Green Business** Provides resources for businesses interested in being socially and environmentally responsible.
- **Green Energy** Focuses on actions that will reduce energy consumption, reduce dependence on fossil fuels, and take advantage of renewable energy.

How is a farmer in a developing country helped when you purchase a fair trade cotton shirt?

- **Fair Trade** Encourages businesses and consumers to participate in fair trade to ensure that farmers and artisans around the world receive a fair price for their products.
- **Responsible Shopper** Profiles hundreds of companies and offers guidance for shopping decisions that promote corporate responsibility.
- **Social Investing** Suggests strategies for making socially and environmentally responsible investment decisions.

Green America publishes a variety of materials. The organization's National Green Pages is a directory of America's leading socially and environmentally responsible businesses.

Green America has 100,000 individual members and 4,000 member businesses that work together to achieve the goals of the organization. In addition, Green America manages the Social Investment Forum, a trade organization for socially responsible investing professionals.

Each day, Green America encourages consumers to rethink their buying habits. Your purchases should be with companies that are trying to become more socially and environmentally responsible. Investors are encouraged to support socially responsible companies. Most importantly, Green America wants consumers, investors, and businesses to demand change.

Think Critically

1. How does Green America serve consumers and businesses in our society?

2. What aspect of Green America do you believe is most valuable for people in your state or community?

3. Go to the website of Green America to obtain additional details about the activities of this organization.

Business Notes

11-1 Computer Systems

- Computer systems consist of four main components: the input device, the processing unit, the memory and storage facilities, and an output device.

- Commonly used input devices include the keyboard, mouse, video game controllers, touch-sensitive screens, scanners, and voice-activated mechanisms.

- The main types of storage devices are the internal memory in a computer and external memory such as disks, CDs, DVDs, magnetic tape, and flash memory sticks. Data processing results are reported as text output, graphics output, audio output, or video output.

11-2 Business Applications of Technology

- The four main components of a management information system (MIS) are gathering data, analyzing data, storing data, and reporting results. The goal of an MIS is to change raw data (facts and figures) into information that can be used by managers.

- Service industries that make extensive use of computers and technology include public service organizations, educational institutions, healthcare facilities, and financial service organizations.

- E-commerce involves the conducting of business transactions over the Internet or through other electronic technology.

11-3 Other Technology Issues

- Robotics, expert systems, computer-aided design (CAD), and telecommuting are used in a variety of business situations to help improve efficiency and productivity.

- Personal technology applications include schoolwork, home robotics, and household recordkeeping.

- Expanded technology and computer use can result in concerns about job loss, health and safety, criminal activities, privacy, and identity theft.

Communicate Business Concepts

1. Identify each of the following items as either *hardware* or *software*.

   a. monitor (screen)
   b. word processing program
   c. chips
   d. keyboard
   e. operating system program
   f. disk drive
   g. mouse
   h. printer

2. What are possible business activities currently performed by people that might be performed in the future using a computer system?

3. Identify whether word processing software, database software, spreadsheet software, or graphics software would be used to perform the following computer applications.

   a. Preparing a report of new equipment purchased for each office of a company
   b. Preparing a list of employees that is sorted by ZIP code
   c. Creating a form letter to go to new customers of a mail-order business
   d. Creating a pie chart showing the portion of sales of each product
   e. Preparing a document listing the total sales for each geographic area of the country
   f. Listing the employees who have not missed a day of work in five years
   g. Sending a letter to each employee who has not missed a day of work in five years

4. List examples of (a) external data and (b) internal data used by most companies.

5. Who would benefit from schools that would allow students to take classes at home by computer?

6. Describe the benefits to workers, employers, and society when an organization allows some of its employees to do all or part of their work at home.

7. How has e-commerce expanded global business in countries that previously had limited economic activity?

8. How is it possible for the increased use of computers to create more jobs than are lost?

9. How might expert systems be used in the future to help people solve medical, legal, financial, and other technical problems?

10. What are potential benefits from the use of smart cards in handling everyday transactions?

11. What actions could be taken by organizations to prevent computer crime?

Develop Your Business Language

Match the terms listed with the definitions.

12. Several computers linked into a single system.

13. Computer programs that perform specific tasks such as word processing, database management, or accounting.

14. Instructions that run a computer system.

15. The control center of the computer.

16. The combination of an input device, a processing unit, memory and storage facilities, and an output device.

17. Conducting business transactions over the Internet or using other technology.

18. Software that translates a computer user's commands and allows application programs to interact with the computer's hardware.

19. A system of letters, words, numbers, and symbols used to communicate with a computer.

20. The components or equipment of a computer system.

21. A series of detailed step-by-step instructions that tell the computer what functions to complete and when to complete them.

22. The use of computers to help people learn or improve skills at their own pace.

23. A term used to describe the activities of a worker using a computer at home to perform a job.

24. Mechanical devices programmed to do routine tasks.

25. Technological assistance used to create product styles and designs.

26. Stealing or illegally copying software packages or information.

27. Programs that assist people in solving technical problems.

28. An organized system of processing and reporting information in an organization.

29. A program code hidden in a system that can later do damage to software or stored data.

30. Programs that enable computers to reason, learn, and make decisions using logical methods similar to the methods humans use.

KEY TERMS

a. application software
b. artificial intelligence (AI)
c. central processing unit (CPU)
d. computer language
e. computer network
f. computer system
g. computer virus
h. computer-aided design (CAD)
i. computer-assisted instruction (CAI)
j. e-commerce
k. expert systems
l. hardware
m. management information system (MIS)
n. operating system software
o. piracy
p. program
q. robotics
r. software
s. telecommuting

Make Academic Connections

31. **Technology** Research types of input, output, and memory devices that have recently been developed for use by businesses and individuals. Find an example of each type of device and write a paragraph about each one.

32. **Communication** Talk to people who make online purchases. What types of products do they buy most frequently? What do they like best about shopping online? What concerns do they have about buying online? Prepare a table with a summary of your findings.

33. **Technology** Prepare a list of daily activities and information items that might be included in the processing and storage capabilities of a smart card. Using information from your list, provide an example of a situation where a smart card might be used.

34. **Science** Investigate various uses of telemedicine and telesurgery in the United States and in other areas of the world.

35. **Math** The Barkley Corporation usually sends about 3,800 pieces of mail per month at $0.42 each. If the firm switches to e-mail service at a cost of $1,250 per month, how much money would it save or lose? What other factors

should the company consider before making this change?

36. **Geography** Many nations around the world do not have reliable telephone service. As a result, cell phones and wireless communication has grown at a fast pace in these countries. Conduct research and prepare a map reporting the countries with a significant usage rate of wireless communication.

37. **Technology** Research recent computer viruses. What types of damage do various viruses do to computer systems? How can you protect your computer against virus attacks?

38. **Law** Conduct an Internet search to obtain information about avoiding identity theft. Make a list of 10 ways to protect your identity. Write a short explanation of how each of the protection strategies helps protect your identity.

39. **Read** Find a news article that relates to e-commerce. Read the article and outline the major concepts presented in the article using bullet points. Include a properly formatted citation for you source. Possible sources include printed and online versions of newspapers or magazines. You should also consider independent online sources that produce original content.

Decision-Making Strategies

The Kendall Manufacturing Company assembles electronic devices used in offices and homes. They employ about 600 people in various office, factory, and warehouse positions. Currently, all factory and warehouse jobs are done manually.

Managers at Kendall are considering replacing 150 assembly line workers with a computerized system. The

company can save $135,000 a year in operating costs by using this new technology.

40. What factors should the company consider before using the computerized assembly line system?

41. If the company uses this new system, what should the company do to help workers who are displaced by this technology?

Linking School and Community

Talk with a few members of your community about the computers and technology they use on the job. Ask them to describe technology changes they have seen in their jobs during the last year and during the last three

years. Also ask them to identify the computer skills they think are important for career success. Prepare a one-minute presentation that summarizes your findings.

©sweetym/iStock

Web Workout

The number and popularity of social networking sites on the Internet continue to grow. Social networking websites allow multiple users to communicate through an individual's website. There are a wide variety of social networking sites with many users. Facebook alone has over 500 million users worldwide. The enjoyment and convenience of a social networking site is tempered by concerns about illegal and unethical behavior. All users need to take precautions when using these sites.

Think Critically

1. Make a list of the activities that people participate in while using social networking sites.
2. Make a list of problems that might arise when using social networking sites.
3. Use the Internet or library resources to identify recommendations for safe social networking practices. Create a one-page flyer of tips for social network users.

Internet Marketing Plan

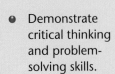
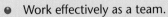

In the twenty-first century, business success depends on the ability to communicate ideas and concepts using the Internet and related technologies. The purpose of the Internet Marketing Plan Event is to provide an opportunity for the participants to research and design a plan to start an Internet marketing business or enhance a component of an existing Internet marketing business. This event challenges students to design a plan that will enhance recognition and increase sales. Students must follow the marketing plan format provided by DECA. This event can be completed by one person or teams of 2 or 3 members.

You must design a market research study to identify the potential for Internet marketing and prepare a business plan based on your research. Major sections for the Internet marketing plan include analysis of the business situation, proposed business outline, and a conclusion.

You will have 10 minutes to present your Internet marketing plan to the judge or class. Five minutes are scheduled following the presentation for the judge or class to ask questions. Your oral presentation must be supported by relevant research and demonstrate an understanding of the business for which the Internet marketing plan was developed.

Performance Indicators Evaluated

- Conduct business research.
- Prepare a business plan based on marketing research.
- Demonstrate critical thinking and problem-solving skills.
- Work effectively as a team.
- Prioritize tasks and practice time management.
- Demonstrate oral and written communication skills.

You will be evaluated for:

- Quality of research findings and conclusions
- Credibility of the proposed business outline
- Ability to present facts and information in a convincing manner

For more detailed information about performance indicators, go to the DECA website.

Think Critically

1. Why must the Internet marketing plan be based upon research?
2. Why are businesses using Internet marketing?
3. What is a disadvantage of using Internet marketing?
4. What product information needs to be included in an Internet marketing plan?

www.deca.org

12 Financial Management

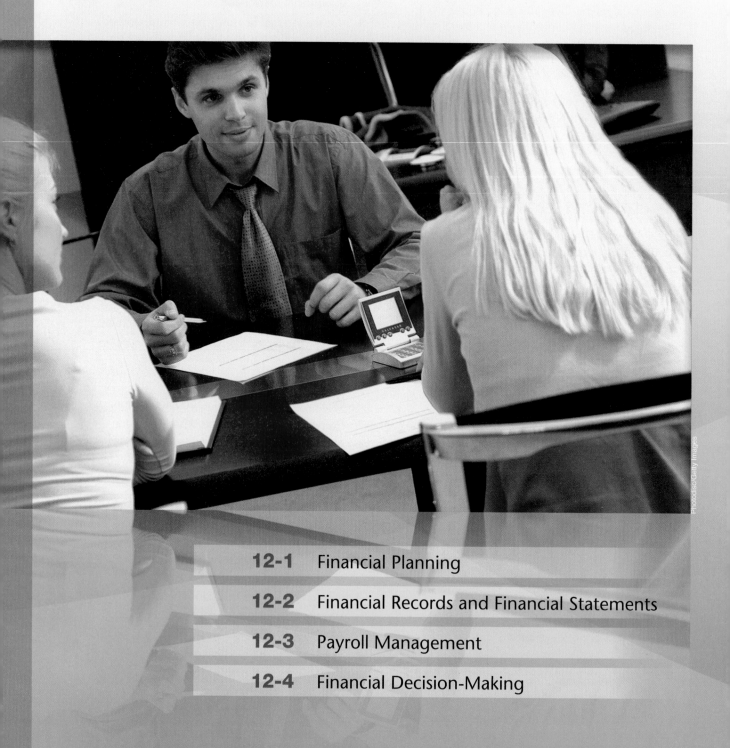

Planning a Career in ...

ACCOUNTING

Managing the financial records and decisions of a business is an important task. All income and expenses must be accurately identified and recorded. Financial records must be kept up to date and financial statements prepared. When requests are made for financial information, the necessary records must be retrieved, the information summarized, and reports prepared. All financial decisions of a company need to be evaluated to make sure they meet federal and state laws as well as ethical standards. Accountants and other financial personnel complete all of these activities.

Public accountants perform accounting, auditing, tax, and consulting activities for their clients. Management accountants record and analyze the financial information of the companies for which they work. They advise executives and other managers to help them make good business decisions. A unique and growing area is forensic accounting. Forensic accountants investigate crimes such as securities fraud, embezzlement, and money laundering. They often appear as expert witnesses in criminal and civil cases.

Related Job Titles

- Auditor
- Budget Analyst
- Chief Financial Officer
- Payroll Accountant
- Regulation and Control Manager
- Treasurer

Analyze Career Opportunities in ...

ACCOUNTING

Use library and Internet resources to learn more about careers in accounting. Choose one of the job titles listed in the box above and answer the following questions.

1. What is the employment outlook for careers in this field?

2. Is this a career that interests you? Explain how careers in this field match up with your goals and interests.

What's it like to work as an ... Accountant?

After graduating from the community college, Ali went to work as an accounting technician. She enjoyed her job but after a few years wanted more challenges and promotional opportunities. She decided to go back to school for a bachelor's degree in Accounting. She was hired by a public accounting firm as a junior staff accountant. She was assigned to work on several auditing projects of large companies. She and the audit team would usually spend several weeks at the offices of a client reviewing the financial records and statements and preparing audit reports. After several years, Ali felt she was ready for a new challenge. She prepared for and completed the rigorous requirements to become a Certified Public Accountant (CPA).

Today, Ali is employed as a managerial accountant for a midsize communications company. She is a part of a five-person department that oversees all company bookkeeping and accounting activities. Most days, Ali spends her time assigning work and reviewing the reports and records generated by her staff. She meets with company managers to prepare forecasts and budgets and to present and explain financial reports.

12-1 Financial Planning

Goals

1 Recognize important financial questions that must be answered in a business.

2 List the steps in budget preparation.

3 Describe three types of business budgets.

Key Terms

revenue 289

expenses 289

budget 290

start-up budget 292

operating budget 293

cash budget 293

Focus on REAL LIFE

Ernest enjoys everything about his job as a sales manager including the thing many of his colleagues do not—reviewing financial reports. Each day he receives a number of financial reports. Some describe the financial condition of the entire business and some are specific to his department. He sees the payroll expenses for his employees, the changing costs of materials and supplies, as well as all other expenses of his department. The reports show whether he is over or under budget for every expenditure.

At first, Ernest wasn't always sure what he should do with the information. But he was comfortable asking questions of other managers and the company's accountants. He knows that the financial decisions he makes are among the most important to the success of his department and his career. He is constantly seeking ways to improve his financial management skills.

Goal 1

Recognize important financial questions that must be answered in a business.

FINANCIAL PLANNING

Picture yourself as a business owner. One of the constant problems you face is the need to have adequate financial resources to operate the business. From the first day you begin planning the business and each day it operates, financing questions must be addressed. Financial questions never go away. Even the most successful businesses are continually active in financial planning.

Beginning a Business

The moment a decision is made to start a business, financial planning begins. How much money will be needed to start the business? Where will that financing come from? How will adequate funds be obtained to operate the business for the months or years until the business becomes profitable? What will be the best sources of sales and other income? What will be the major expenses? When must they be paid?

Many new businesses fail due to poor financial planning. Experts in business finance should be consulted to help the new business with its financial planning. The business owner needs to know the importance of financial planning and must develop financial management skills.

Why is the cost of leasing a building or office space important to financial planning for a new business?

Ongoing Operations

Finances are a key part of the operations of all businesses. Every business activity costs money. Without careful planning and management, those costs can grow to a level where the business income cannot cover the expenses. All income that a business receives over a period of time is called **revenue**. Businesses also have expenses. **Expenses** are the costs of operating a business. Every business is guided by the basic financial equation: revenue minus expenses equals profit or loss. The equation is illustrated in Figure 12-1.

The difference between revenue and expenses determines whether a business makes a profit or loss. If revenue is greater than expenses, the business will make a *profit*. If expenses exceed revenue, the business will suffer a *loss*.

All managers are responsible for the costs of the part of the business they manage. Each employee should also be concerned about those costs. The profitability of a business is directly linked to the number of employees and the wages they are paid.

While the costs of personnel are some of the highest expenses for most businesses, reducing those costs by employing fewer people or paying them less will not usually result in higher profits. Employees are needed to do the work of the business. Employees that are well trained, motivated, and efficient will be more productive than those that are not. A business that tries to save money by hiring fewer people, paying lower wages, or reducing the amount of training may find that costs increase due to waste, inefficiency, or poor-quality products.

Managers and employees should find ways to reduce waste and control expenses. They can also make suggestions about ways to increase sales and income through better products and services.

Ongoing operations require that employees be paid, supplies and materials ordered, and buildings maintained. Equipment must be repaired and technology updated. Each decision related to ongoing operations requires careful attention to costs.

Business Expansion

Successful businesses expand to be able to serve more customers, reach unserved markets, and sell new products. Yet expansion costs money. The hope is that the income generated by the expansion will be far greater than the cost. A more profitable business is the result.

Business expansion calls for research to develop new products and locate new markets. New factories and equipment may be needed to produce the products. Additional employees must be hired and trained. Marketing activities will be planned and implemented to distribute and promote the products. Most expansion plans occur over a long period and can cost thousands or even millions of dollars. Each time business expansion is anticipated, careful financial planning must be completed. The planning must anticipate the costs associated with the expansion, the source of the funds to pay for the expansion, and the expected income that will result from the new plans. If the planning is not correct and the expansion results in substantial losses rather than profits, the previously successful business may fail.

BASIC FINANCIAL EQUATION
Revenue − Expenses = Profit or Loss
Revenue > Expenses = Profit
Revenue < Expenses = Loss

▶ **Figure 12-1**
If a business has annual revenue of $5 million and expenses of $3 million, did the business make a profit or suffer a loss?

checkpoint ✓
What is the basic financial equation for businesses?

Goal 2

List the steps in budget preparation.

DEVELOPING BUSINESS BUDGETS

A **budget** provides detailed plans for the financial needs of individuals, families, and businesses. A *business budget* has two main purposes:

1. Anticipate sources and amounts of income for a business.

2. Predict the types and amounts of expenses for a specific business activity or the entire business.

The business must be able to identify and predict the amount of each source of income and each type of expense. In addition, the business will need to determine when each expense must be paid and when income will be received. For the business to succeed, enough revenue must be available to pay all expenses.

Sources of Budget Information

To develop an effective budget, information to predict income and expenses is needed. If a business has operated for several years, identifying sources of income and types of expenses will not be difficult. The main source of that information is the financial records of the business. Budgeting is much harder for a new business. No financial records exist to serve

Business Insight for the 21st Century

Cash or Accrual?

When you pay for something with cash you know you no longer have that amount of money to spend. But what about a credit card purchase? You may not receive a statement until several weeks after you made the purchase and then still have several weeks to pay the bill. When do you recognize that you no longer have the money you spent for that purchase?

Businesses face a similar issue when maintaining their financial records. When do they identify the income and expenses? Many small businesses use a cash method where income and expenses are recorded when money is actually received or a payment is made. Even though the business has billed a customer for a purchase, the associated income is not recognized until the customer actually pays. In the same way, if the business

purchases inventory from a supplier and owes money for the purchase, the amount of the purchase is not recognized in the financial records until a check has been issued.

Most businesses do not use the cash method; they use an accrual method. Accruals recognize income and expenses when they actually occur rather than when the associated payment is made or received. If a product is sold to a customer, the amount of the sale is recorded in the financial records of the seller at the time of sale rather than waiting for cash to be received. At the time a company makes a purchase, whether payment is made immediately or not, the financial records identify the expense.

Keeping track of what you actually owe and the income you have really earned gives you a much more

accurate picture of your financial situation than waiting until the money exchanges hands. Businesses have many financial transactions each day amounting to thousands of dollars. They might soon find themselves in financial difficulty if they only recorded cash receipts and expenditures.

Think Critically

1. Why might many small businesses use a cash rather than accrual method to maintain their financial records? Why are they at less risk than larger businesses when using the cash method?

2. Accounting rules and laws require many businesses to use the accrual method in their financial record keeping. Use the Internet to determine two situations where accrual accounting is required.

as a guide. Other sources of information must be used.

The Small Business Administration (SBA) provides many planning tools for new businesses. Among those tools are guides to developing a budget and financial information to help the new business owner predict income and expenses. Another source of information is private businesses that collect and publish financial information on similar businesses and industries. Examples of those companies are Dun and Bradstreet, Value Line, and Standard and Poor's. Some information is also available from business magazines and newspapers including *Fortune, Forbes, Entrepreneur, Black Enterprise, Hispanic Business,* and *The Wall Street Journal.*

Professional associations, such as the National Federation of Independent Business and the National Retail Merchants Association, offer resources to help with financial planning. A new franchise will typically receive assistance with financial planning from the franchisor. This help might include a complete beginning budget. A bank or other financial institution where a new business has established accounts is another source of financial planning. Franchisors and financial institutions want to see businesses succeed, so they typically require careful financial planning.

Budget Preparation

The most important step in financial planning is developing a budget. You can compare the use of a budget to the use of a road map when you are traveling to an unfamiliar location. Without the map, you will have little idea where you are going while you travel. If you take a wrong turn, you will have difficulty knowing your mistake. It will be hard to get back to the correct road without the map. In the same way, a budget identifies where a business is going. It allows the owner to determine if

the business is making progress toward its financial destination. By regularly comparing the business' financial performance to the budget, the owner can determine if the budget goals are being met. If not, the owner can make corrections before serious financial problems occur.

A business budget has the same basic goals as a personal or family budget developed to manage the household finances. The goals are to determine the sources and amounts of income, to identify the types of expenses and predict their costs, to determine how income will be distributed to cover those expenses, and to reward investors if there is a profit.

sjlocke/iStockphoto.com

What do you think are the most important personal and family budget categories for most people? How might they differ from a business budget?

Your team is developing a budget for a large land-scaping business that has operated for ten years. As a group, agree on three categories of income and five categories of expenses that will be a part of the budget. For each category, brainstorm several ways the business could accurately estimate the monthly amount of income or expense to include in the budget.

Goal 3

Describe three types of business budgets.

The budgeting process involves four fundamental steps.

1. Prepare a list of each type of income and expense that will be a part of the budget.

2. Gather accurate information from business records and other information sources for each type of income and expense.

3. Create the budget by calculating each type of income, expense, and the amount of net income or loss.

4. Explain the budget to people who need financial information to make decisions.

The people responsible for preparing business budgets need several skills. Budgeting requires an understanding of financial information, computer skills, mathematical abilities, and effective communications skills. New small business owners often seek the help of an accountant or banker when preparing a budget for the first time. Small and medium-sized businesses may hire an accounting firm to maintain financial records and to help with budget development. Larger businesses employ accountants and other financial planning experts to maintain the business' financial records. They also help with budgeting and using budget information.

checkpoint ✓

What are the four steps in preparing a business budget?

TYPES OF BUDGETS

A large business will have many specialized budgets. Each manager will be responsible for one or more budgets in his or her area of operations. For every business, three particular budgets are essential. They are the start-up budget, the operating budget, and the cash budget. The **start-up budget** plans income and expenses from the beginning of a new business or a major business expansion until it becomes profitable. Most start-ups require expenditures of thousands or even hundreds of thousands of dollars in order to open. Buildings and equipment must be purchased or leased. Inventory, supplies, and materials are needed. New employees will be hired or existing employees retrained. Expenses for utilities, licenses, advertising, and transportation will be incurred before the company can sell its new products and services. Sources of financing for these expenditures must be identified from either inside the company or from outside financial sources. The amount of start-up expenses must be

In addition to price, what other budget information would the owners of a company need to consider when buying a delivery van?

predicted correctly so that ample start-up financing is available until the new activities produce adequate income.

The **operating budget** describes the financial plan for ongoing operations of the business for a specific period. The operating budget is usually planned for three months, six months, or a year. An operating budget is prepared for the entire business. Each department and division of a large business will also develop and follow its own operating budget.

When planning an operating budget, income and expenses from prior budgets are reviewed. Planners look for possible changes that could increase or decrease income and expenses. Then the budget for the next period is prepared. It is used to manage the operations of the company for the period covered by the budget.

A **cash budget** is an estimate of the actual money received and paid out for a specific period. A cash budget anticipates that cash will come into a business and that cash will be paid out during each week or month of operation. Even though a new business might not be making a profit, it still must have adequate cash on hand to pay current expenses. Even profitable businesses may have times when adequate cash is not available due to high expenses or a delay in receiving payments from customers.

A cash budget will determine if a business has adequate financial resources on hand to pay bills as they become due or if they will need to borrow money. It will also show when there is so much cash on hand that some of it can be invested. Investing cash on hand provides another source of business income.

> **checkpoint** ✓
> Identify and describe the three types of budgets needed by all businesses.

12-1 Assessment

Study Tools
www.cengage.com/school/genbus/pob

Key Concepts

Determine the best answer.

1. True or False. Financial planning is needed by a small business only until it begins to make a profit.

2. The basic financial equation is
   a. revenue – profit = loss
   b. expenses + revenue = profit or loss
   c. profit – loss = revenue and expenses
   d. revenue – expenses = profit or loss

3. True or False. A cash budget is an estimate of the actual money received and paid out for a specific period.

Make Academic Connections

4. **Math** Use the basic financial equation to determine the profit or loss for each of the following:
   a. revenue $85,695; expenses $72,624
   b. revenue $1,824,300; expenses $2,183,680
   c. revenue $729,655; expenses $499,220

5. **Technology** Use the Internet to locate a sample business budget. Enter the entire budget into a spreadsheet program. Develop a new budget by adjusting each of the income and expense items in the budget with a 3 percent increase. Then develop another budget by adjusting the original income and expense items with a 1.5 percent decrease.

6. **Economics** Locate a newspaper or magazine article that describes an anticipated change in the economy that might result in higher or lower income or expenses for businesses. Write two paragraphs discussing how financial planners should use the information when developing an operating budget.

Financial Records and Financial Statements

Goals

1 Identify several types of financial records needed by businesses.

2 Describe the differences between an income statement and a balance sheet.

Key Terms

financial records 294

assets 296

liabilities 296

owner's equity 296

balance sheet 296

income statement 297

Focus on REAL LIFE

Paulette was closing the door on her bakery for the night when her accountant called.

"I was reviewing your accounts and wanted to alert you that you currently don't have enough cash to pay the quarterly loan payment that will be due in three weeks. I don't want to alarm you, I think you need a plan so you can keep your loan current and still have money to cover other expenses."

Pauline responded, "I appreciate your call. I try to make my loan payments on time but sometimes it's hard to have enough cash at the right time. I delivered two large orders for restaurant customers but I haven't yet been paid. They're big customers but they're slow payers. I hate to be too pushy about payment because I don't want them to take their business elsewhere."

Her accountant responded, "I know it's hard to always meet your cash needs and I know your bank appreciates how timely you have been in the past on your payments. Let's meet to talk about ways you might make sure you are building up a good cash balance in advance of your next loan payment."

Goal 1

Identify several types of financial records needed by businesses.

FINANCIAL RECORDS

Budgets reflect the financial plans of businesses. To determine if those plans have resulted in success, financial records are needed. **Financial records** are used to record and analyze the financial performance of a business. Several types of records are maintained. They provide detailed information about the financial activities of the company. Local, state, and federal governments require some records. Other records provide information

needed by owners and managers to aid their decision-making.

Types of Records

The following records are commonly maintained to document the performance of a business.

- *Asset records* identify the buildings and equipment owned by the business, their original and current value, and the amount owed if money was borrowed to purchase the assets.

- *Depreciation records* identify the amount assets have decreased in value due to their age and use.

- *Inventory records* identify the type and quantity of resources and products on hand along with the current value of each. Accurate records are crucial to

WORK as a TEAM

Create a table with two headings: Things I Own and Things I Owe. Have each member of your team in turn add items to the list representing their personal assets and liabilities. After the lists are complete, review each list and divide them into current and long-term assets and liabilities.

determine if adequate resources are available to meet operating and production needs as well as customer demand.

- *Records of accounts* identify all purchases and sales made using credit. An *accounts payable record* identifies the companies from which credit purchases were made and the amounts purchased, paid, and owed. An *accounts receivable record* identifies customers that made purchases using credit and the status of each account.

- *Cash records* list all cash received and spent by the business.

- *Payroll records* contain information on all employees of the company, their compensation, and benefits.

- *Tax records* show all taxes collected, owed, and paid. As a part of payroll, employers must withhold a percentage of employees' salaries and wages for income taxes, Social Security and Medicare taxes, and, in some cases, unemployment compensation insurance. In addition to the taxes withheld from employees, businesses must pay the employer's share of Social Security and Medicare taxes, and other taxes that are calculated as a percentage of payroll. Depending on the type of business and the location, a company may have to collect and pay state and local sales taxes. Businesses may have to pay several types of taxes on their income and value of their assets. Adequate records must be maintained to accurately calculate any taxes owed and to file the necessary tax forms.

Maintaining Financial Records

Business records have to be accurate and should be kept up to date. In the past, the preparation and maintenance of financial records was an expensive and time-consuming process. It was often done manually using paper documents that had to be carefully completed, saved, and

Describe ways in which the financial planning activities of a business are similar to the financial planning that must be done by people to achieve their life-span goals. Evaluate the status of your own financial planning. How will you know what financial resources you will need to achieve your life-span goals?

protected. Then those documents were sent to the people responsible for preparing the company's financial records.

Technology is changing the way financial information is collected. Much of the information is now collected using point-of-production and point-of-sale technology such as scanners, touch screens, and personal digital assistants (PDAs). Data files are transferred from the places information is collected to the computers of the people who prepare the financial records. Technology is also changing the way financial records are prepared and maintained. Businesses use computerized financial systems that have templates for each financial record. The software completes the necessary mathematical calculations. It updates records and compares those records with budgets. The software can even complete what-if comparisons

What are the differences between keeping records manually and on a computer?

to help managers determine the impact of changes in budgets and financial performance.

> **checkpoint** ✓
> How has the process of maintaining financial records been affected by technology?

Goal 2

Describe the differences between an income statement and a balance sheet.

FINANCIAL STATEMENTS

The three most important elements of a company's financial strength are its assets, liabilities, and owner's equity. In simple terms, **assets** are what a company owns, **liabilities** are what a company owes, and **owner's equity** is the value of the owner's investment in the business.

Reports that sum up the financial performance of a business are *financial statements*. A company reports its assets, liabilities, and owner's equity on the *balance sheet*.

Three other key financial elements for a business are the amounts of *sales, expenses,* and *profits*. Sales, expenses, and profits (or losses) for a specific time period are reported on the company's *income statement*.

The Balance Sheet

The assets, liabilities, and owner's equity for a specific date are listed on the **balance sheet**. The balance sheet is often prepared every six months or once a year. Figure 12-2 shows a balance sheet.

The left side of the balance sheet lists all assets. *Assets* are anything of value owned by the business. There are two common divisions of assets. *Current assets* include cash and those items that can be readily converted to cash such as inventory and accounts receivable. *Long-term assets* (also known as *fixed assets*) are the assets with a life span of more than a year. Common fixed assets are land, buildings, equipment, and expensive technology.

The right side of the balance sheet is divided into two categories. *Liabilities* are amounts owed by the business to others. As with assets, there are two types of liabilities. *Current liabilities* are those that will be paid within a year. *Long-term*

> **Figure 12-2**
>
> What can you tell about the success of this business based on this balance sheet?

The Co-Operate Company
Balance Sheet
June 30, 20xx

Assets			Liabilities		
Current Assets			**Current Liabilities**		
Cash	$22,225		Accounts payable	$18,250	
Accounts receivable	42,200		Payroll taxes payable	1,900	
Inventory	98,200		Wages payable	23,525	
Prepaid expenses	5,340		Short-term bank loan payable	5,700	
Total Current Assets		$167,965	**Total Current Liabilities**		$49,375
Long-Term Assets			**Long-Term Liabilities**		
Vehicles	68,500		Long-term notes payable	85,200	
Furniture and fixtures	21,450		Mortgage payable	120,600	
Equipment	33,000		**Total Long-Term Liabilities**		$205,800
Buildings	320,000				
Land	82,500		**Total Liabilities**		$255,175
Total Long-Term Assets		$525,450			
			Owner's Equity		$438,240
Total Assets		$693,415	**Total Liabilities and Owner's Equity**		$693,415

liabilities are debts that will continue for longer than a year. Current liabilities include payments owed to banks and other financial institutions for short-term loans. Also included are payments due to suppliers for inventory purchases, supplies, and inexpensive equipment. Long-term liabilities are debts owed for land, buildings, and expensive equipment.

Finally, *owner's equity* is the value of the business after liabilities are subtracted from assets. It shows how much the business is worth on the date the balance sheet is prepared. Another way of looking at owner's equity is that it shows the value of the investments owners have made in the business.

The Income Statement

To report the revenue, expenses, and net income or loss from operations for a specific period, a business prepares an **income statement**. An income statement usually covers six months or a year, but may also encompass a shorter period such as a month. Figure 12-3 shows a sample income statement.

What must be considered when establishing a sales price for your product?

Revenue is all income received by the business during the period. Sources of income include the sale of products and

The Netinc Company Income Statement For the 6-month Period Ending December 31, 20xx			
Revenue			
Sales	$1,289,650		
Sales returns and allowances	−20,200		
Net sales		$1,269,450	
Cost of goods sold		−325,650	
Interest earned		80,263	
Total Revenue			$1,024,063
Expenses			
Selling expense		$32,050	
Marketing expense		282,954	
Administrative expense		52,445	
Rent expense		38,220	
Utilities expense		22,900	
Payroll expense		184,908	
Total Expenses			$613,477
Income taxes			−68,250
Net Income			$342,336

▶ **Figure 12-3**
What can you tell about the success of this business based on this income statement?

services, plus interest earned from investments. *Expenses* are all of the costs of operating the business during the period. Expenses include things such as rent, supplies, inventory, payroll, and utilities. The business has *net income* when revenue is greater than expenses. A *net loss* occurs when expenses are greater than income.

Business managers review financial statements carefully to determine how their businesses are performing. Because the statements summarize financial performance for a specific time, the owner can compare the performance of the current period with the performance of last month or last year. If the value of assets is increasing in relation to liabilities, the business is in a better financial position. It may be able to invest in new products, buildings, and equipment. A rapid rise in liabilities or decline in owner's equity

should cause concern. The business must carefully evaluate what is causing the change. If net income is increasing, the owner will want to maintain and improve that performance. On the other hand, if expenses are increasing but revenue is not, the owner will want to determine the reasons for the problem and make changes.

In addition to comparing financial performance from one time period to another, the owner will want to make comparisons with similar businesses. A business that is less profitable than similar businesses, or with lower sales or higher expenses, may have difficulty competing.

> **checkpoint ✓**
> What is the difference between a balance sheet and an income statement?

Study Tools

www.cengage.com/school/genbus/pob

12-2 Assessment

Key Concepts

Determine the best answer.

1. The value of the buildings and equipment owned by a business can be determined in the
   a. inventory records
   b. asset records
   c. records of accounts
   d. tax records

2. True or False. The two most common and important financial records for businesses are the income statement and the balance sheet.

3. Current liabilities are amounts owed that will be paid in less than
   a. one month   c. one year
   b. six months   d. five years

4. The current value of investments made by the owners of a business can be found in the
   a. income statement   c. tax records
   b. balance sheet   d. record of accounts

Make Academic Connections

5. **Government** A business is required to collect taxes and make payments to local, state, and federal governments for its employees. Use the Internet to gather information on payroll taxes (local, state, and federal) that must be collected by a business in your community. Prepare a table that identifies each type of payroll tax, how the amount of tax to be collected is determined, and when and to whom the payments must be made.

6. **Accounting** Using the examples in Figures 12-2 and 12-3, any records, and your best memory, create a personal balance sheet and income statement. The balance sheet should reflect your personal financial status as of the current date. The income statement should represent your income and expenditures for the past three months.

12-3 Payroll Management

Goals

1 Describe the components of a business payroll system.

2 Identify key information included in payroll records and paychecks.

Key Terms

payroll 299

payroll records 301

direct deposit 302

Focus on REAL LIFE

Zena picked up her paycheck from the human resources office on her way to the parking lot. She had finished a hard week of work and was looking forward to a meal and a movie with friends. She would stop by her bank on the way to the restaurant to deposit her paycheck in her savings account and get some cash for the weekend.

Zena ripped open the envelope and looked at her check and the earnings report. First she looked at the amount of the check to make sure she got paid for the overtime hours she had worked. Then she looked to see how many vacation days and sick days she had earned. She had nine vacation days—more than enough to cover the week of camping she had planned for the end of the month.

She continued to look at the check and noticed that the cost of all of her benefits, including health and dental insurance, reduced her take-home pay by $62 each pay period. She also saw that the required withholding and other payments to federal and state governments totaled $143. Halfway through the year, Zena's deductions and withholding already had topped $3,500.

PAYROLL SYSTEMS

One of the most important financial duties of a business is maintaining a payroll. A **payroll** is the financial record of employee compensation, deductions, and net pay. A *payroll system* maintains information on each employee to be able to calculate the company's payroll and to make the necessary payments to each employee.

Most businesses pay every employee on a weekly, bi-weekly, or monthly basis. A majority of employees in most businesses receive an hourly wage, but the wage rate may be different for each employee. Some employees work part time while others work 40 hours or more a week. The rest of the employees, especially managers and others in professional positions, receive a weekly or monthly salary. Again, the amount of salary for each person may be different. Some may earn additional payments in the form of commissions, bonuses, and profit sharing.

As a part of the compensation system, most businesses provide employees a range of benefits. Benefits include such things as insurance options, paid or unpaid

Goal 1

Describe the components of a business payroll system.

Can you think of the various types of income people earn in addition to wages and salaries? For instance, waiters receive a large portion of their income from tips.

employee. These taxes consist of income taxes, Social Security, Medicare, and unemployment taxes and are commonly referred to as *payroll taxes*.

Income Taxes The federal government, most states, and some local governments require employers to withhold income tax from their employees' pay. The amount withheld is based on the wages or salary paid and the number of employee dependents.

Social Security and Medicare These payments are often referred to as FICA (Federal Insurance Contributions Act). The government requires employers to withhold and deposit these contributions from employees' paychecks along with matching contributions by the employer.

Unemployment Taxes Employers pay Federal Unemployment Tax (FUTA) to the unemployment insurance system. The amount owed is based on the

vacation, sick leave and personal time off, retirement plans, and education assistance. A business must keep records of employee benefits earned and used. The direct cost of benefits to the business and each employee is usually a part of the company's payroll system.

The final part of the payroll system is tax records and payments. Businesses are responsible for making required federal and state payments for each

---

A Question of Ethics

Disclosing Employee Performance Information

Following a three-month probationary period, a new employee was fired. The supervisor had heard from several employees that the new worker was hard to get along with and was not carrying her full share of the work. While two work evaluations completed by the supervisor rated her performance as above average, her performance was not outstanding so the decision was made to terminate her employment. When the employee was notified of the decision, she was shocked and asked why she was being fired. Not wanting to create problems for the current employees who had complained or to disclose that the evaluations had not shown

serious problems, the supervisor declined to provide reasons. Should the employee have a right to know why she was fired?

There are federal and state laws that regulate an employee's right to information. An employee generally can examine information in his or her personnel file that relates to work performance. That includes any written notes and formal performance evaluations. An employer should be careful about making judgments that are heavily influenced by the opinions of others without direct evidence. Also, providing regular feedback on evaluations and discussing any issues or concerns before they become major

problems are important management responsibilities.

Think Critically

1. Do you believe the supervisor was right in not disclosing the information gathered from the new employee's co-workers? Why or why not? Do you feel the same way about the results of the work evaluations?

2. What recommendations would you make to the supervisor to prevent the type of situation from occurring again? As a new employee, what would you do to make sure you have adequate feedback on how you are doing?

business' total employee wages. Many states also have their own unemployment taxes.

Employers must withhold taxes from employee wages and salaries as well as make their own required contributions. Businesses must prepare and maintain tax records. They also have to send required payments to the government on time.

Most payroll systems are part of a larger personnel records system. That system is a central location for all information the company maintains on all employees from the time they are hired until well after they no longer work for the business. Personnel records include personal information, employment history, performance evaluations, compensation records, and other information needed by the company. Most information in personnel files is confidential. Because of this, the businesses must carefully and securely maintain the records.

How do payroll records relate to employee vacations?

Photodisc/Getty Images

> **checkpoint** ✓
> What is the purpose of the payroll system?

PREPARING A PAYROLL

Maintaining payroll records and preparing paychecks is an ongoing and time-consuming task for businesses. In the past, each employee completed and submitted a time card. Payroll clerks entered the information into each employee's payroll record. When paychecks were to be issued at the end of each pay period, employee compensation and deductions had to be calculated, withholding and benefits records completed, and paychecks prepared. Today, computerized personnel records systems make the payroll process much more efficient and accurate. Easy-to-use software is available to manage simple or very complex payroll systems. Technology is used to collect employee time and production records each work period. When paychecks need to be prepared, information on benefits and deductions is determined and each employee's pay is calculated. All payroll records are updated and paychecks are printed or electronic deposits are transmitted to the employees' bank accounts.

Payroll Records

Payroll records are the documentation used to process earnings payments and record each employee's pay history. In some companies, payroll records are still maintained in paper form. Increasingly companies use computerized systems to maintain payroll records electronically.

The payroll records for each employee contain all the information an employer needs in order to pay the worker. This includes information about the worker's identity such

<table>
<tr><td>

WORK *as a* **TEAM**

</td><td>

Review the information in the Focus on Real Life at the beginning of the lesson. Discuss with your team what you could say to employees concerned with the amount of money taken from their paycheck each pay period to pay for benefits and taxes.

</td></tr>
</table>

as name, address, and Social Security number. An individual payroll record also has salary and wage rate data along with information about how vacation and sick days are earned. The tax filing status for the employee is included in order to calculate withholding for taxes. Additional information is required for payroll deductions such as health insurance payments and retirement plan contributions.

Each employee's pay history is maintained in the payroll records. This

includes the amount of gross pay, withholding and deductions, and net pay for each pay period. A year-to-date balance for each item is also maintained. Each time payroll is processed the payroll records are updated.

Preparing Paychecks

The information maintained in the payroll records is used to process payroll. For each pay period, the amounts for gross pay, withholding, deductions, and net pay are calculated and a paycheck is prepared for each person. The actual paycheck shows only the net pay amount—it is the amount of the check.

Employees want to know how the amount of pay they receive is determined and the type and amount of deductions made. Most businesses print an *earnings report* that is included with the employee's paycheck. It usually provides information for the current pay period as well as the cumulative amounts for the year. The earnings report is often attached to the paycheck and is sometimes called a *pay stub*.

Many businesses offer a direct deposit service for employees. With **direct deposit**, the employer transfers net pay electronically into the employee's bank account. The employee does not receive a printed paycheck but is given a receipt of the funds transfer. In addition to the receipt, sometimes called *advice of deposit,* the employee usually receives an earnings report.

The receipt and an earnings report may be posted to a secure area on the company's website where the employee can view it, save it electronically, or print a copy. An example of an employee earnings report and direct deposit receipt is shown in Figure 12-4.

Big Cheese Photo/Jupiter Images

What should an employee do with each earnings report and deposit receipt?

> **checkpoint** ✓
> What is the difference between a payroll record and an earnings report?

Sample Earnings Report and Direct Deposit Receipt

Employee Earnings Report

Marquese Co.	**Taylor Carson**	Date	05/21/20--
525 Liberty Street	**2346 Transport Dr.**	Document number	18925
Anchora, IN 46200	**Tollboard, IN 46299**	**Net pay**	**375.00**

SSN	XXX-XX-XXXX			
Employee ID	83-221		Pay period start	05/10/20--
Federal filing status	S	1	Pay period end	05/16/20--
State filing status	S	1	Pay frequency	Weekly

EARNINGS

Pay Type	Hours	Rate	Current	YTD
Regular Pay	40.00	12.00	480.00	8928.00
Overtime Pay	2.00	18.00	36.00	72.00
Holiday Pay	0.00			192.00
Vacation Pay	0.00			480.00
Sick Pay	0.00			
Total Hours	42.00			

SUMMARY

	Gross	Taxes	Deductions	Net Pay
Current	516.00	97.70	43.30	375.00
YTD	9672.00	1790.20	833.60	7048.20

DEDUCTIONS

Deduction	Current	YTD
401k (5.00%)	25.80	483.60
Health Insurance	17.50	350.00

TAXES

Tax Type	Current	YTD
Federal Income	41.34	734.46
Medicare	7.48	140.24
Social Security	31.99	599.66
IN State Income	16.89	315.84

NET PAY DISTRIBUTION

Account	Type	Amount
XXXX2077	Checking	355.00
XXXX1129	Savings	20.00
Check amount		0.00
Total net pay		375.00

▶ **Figure 12-4**

How is the employee's net pay determined?

12-3 Assessment

Key Concepts

Determine the best answer.

1. The financial record of employee compensation, deductions, and net pay is known as
   a. compensation
   b. payroll
   c. earnings report
   d. paycheck

2. True or False. Businesses are responsible for making required federal and state payments for each employee.

3. The electronic transfer of net pay into an employee's bank account is known as
   a. tax withholding
   b. FICA
   c. direct deposit
   d. an automated payroll system

4. True or False. Payroll records need to be maintained for all full-time employees, but not for part-time employees.

Make Academic Connections

5. **Math** Calculate the amount of employee withholding for Social Security (6.2%) and Medicare (1.45%) for each of the following employee's wages.
   Marjorie Elder: $865.00
   Antoine Fresher: $726.40
   Amelda Francois: $1,480.90

6. **Art** Create a poster or flowchart that illustrates the steps in the payroll process from the point that employees complete their work until their paychecks are issued.

Productivity and Accountability

Project Management

Success in the workplace requires the ability to function in complex and competitive environments. You need to be able to manage projects and produce results.

Managing Projects

Most people have some experience managing projects. Getting your chores finished in time to go out with friends, making a cake, or writing a term paper are all examples of projects that need to be managed. The ability to manage projects, big and small, complex and simple, is critical to success in today's workplace. In order to manage a project you must be able to:

- Set realistic goals
- Allocate resources including money, time, and energy
- Chart progress
- Overcome obstacles
- Meet goals

Producing Results

Producing results involves more than finishing the project on schedule and within budget. Although time and money are often the focus of attention, the quality of the results, the efficiency of the process, and a sense of satisfaction for all participants are also important.

In addition to managing a project to achieve the intended result, you need to demonstrate attributes that are associated with producing high quality products and services. These attributes are based on respect—respect for yourself and respect for others. Examples include:

- Positive attitude
- Ethical behavior
- Active participation
- Professional appearance
- Proper etiquette

Being Accountable

Accountability means being able to explain your actions and accept responsibility for the outcome. Workers are paid to produce goods and services. A baker is expected to produce baked goods such as bread and cookies. An auto mechanic is expected to provide automotive services

How is team management of a project different from individual project management?

such as oil changes and engine tune ups. In addition to producing goods and services, workers are expected to be accountable for the quantity and quality of their work, their personal behavior, their interactions with colleagues, customers, and vendors. You can demonstrate accountability by:

- Collaborating and cooperating with others
- Respecting and appreciating diversity
- Being punctual and reliable
- Being honest
- Owning up to mistakes
- Asking for help
- Working to improve skills

Think Critically

1. How does the ability to manage a project relate to productivity?
2. Provide a specific example of how you can demonstrate accountability at school, home, and another situation.

12-4 Financial Decision-Making

Goals

1. Recognize important financial information managers use to make decisions.

2. Identify the steps in making financial decisions in business.

Key Terms

financial performance ratios 305

discrepancies 308

Focus on REAL LIFE

John sat with his business partner, Anna, for their monthly meeting to review the company's financial statements.

"Once again our sales are up dramatically but our profit margins continue to hold steady or decline slightly," John noted. "We need to deal with this before it becomes a major problem."

"Well, we can see that the raw materials costs of our two top-selling products have gone up steadily over the past year and we are paying a lot more for utilities for our buildings and fuel for our vehicles," Anna responded.

"Yes, those two products are no longer really contributing much to profit even though they are by far our best sellers. Is it possible to reduce other expenses related to them or should we find ways to sell more of our currently profitable products?" John questioned.

Anna and John had a lot more work to do before making important decisions that would affect their company's future. They would need to study the financial reports long and hard to determine what needed to be done.

USING FINANCIAL INFORMATION

Financial statements are important management tools for business owners and managers. Financial statements present summaries of the financial activities of a business. Managers who understand the information in financial statements will be better able to make decisions that result in the wise use of the company's money.

Important Financial Information

As previously discussed, the three most important elements of a company's financial strength are its assets, liabilities, and owner's equity. Three other key financial elements for a business are the amount of sales, expenses, and profits. A company reports its assets, liabilities, and owner's equity on the balance sheet. Sales, expenses, and profits for a specific period are reported on the company's income statement.

Understanding Financial Performance Ratios

Managers use the financial elements found on the financial statements to calculate financial performance ratios. **Financial performance ratios** are

> ### Goal 1
> Recognize important financial information managers use to make decisions.

Explain why making good financial decisions is no less important to individuals than it is to businesses. How do you currently make important financial decisions? In what ways can you improve the process to help you achieve your life-span goals?

▶ **Figure 12-5**

Why do most banks
want to see a debt
to equity ratio no
higher than 2:1?

Financial Performance Ratios

Current Ratio	=	$\dfrac{\text{Current Assets}}{\text{Current Liabilities}}$
Debt to Equity Ratio	=	$\dfrac{\text{Total Liabilities}}{\text{Owner's Equity}}$
Return on Equity Ratio	=	$\dfrac{\text{Net Profit}}{\text{Owner's Equity}}$
Net Income Ratio	=	$\dfrac{\text{Total Sales}}{\text{Net Income}}$

comparisons of a company's financial elements that indicate how well the business is performing. Some important financial performance ratios are the current ratio, debt to equity ratio, return on equity ratio, and net income ratio. Figure 12-5 shows the formulas used to calculate each ratio.

Current Ratio Current assets compared to the current liabilities is the *current ratio*. Current assets are those that the business could convert to cash within one year. Current liabilities are all payments owed to creditors that must be made within one year. The current ratio tells you if the business can pay its debts as they become due. The current ratio should be at least 1:1 for a healthy business. A 1:1 ratio means that there are at least as many current assets as current liabilities.

Debt to Equity Ratio The company's liabilities divided by the owner's equity is the *debt to equity ratio*. This ratio tells you how much the business is relying on money borrowed from others that will have to be paid back rather than money provided by the owners. Most banks want to see a debt to equity ratio of about 1:1 but no higher than 2:1. Too little debt means a company

may not be using all of its resources effectively while too much debt puts a business at risk in meeting its obligations to lenders.

Return on Equity Ratio The net profit of the business compared to the amount of owner's equity is the *return on equity ratio*. The return on equity ratio shows the rate of return the owners are getting on the money they invested in the company. It should be compared to the return they could receive if they used their money in other ways such as savings, investing in other companies, or purchasing stocks and bonds.

Net Income Ratio The total sales compared to the net income for a period such as six months or a year is the *net income ratio*. The net income ratio shows how much profit is being made by each dollar of sales for the period being analyzed. You should compare the net income ratio to past periods and to competing companies. The ratio will show if additional sales are as effective in adding to the company's profit as those in the past.

checkpoint ✓

Identify four important financial performance ratios used by managers to determine how well the business is performing.

What does it mean if your company's net income ratio increases from one year to the next?

Digital Vision/Getty Images

MAKING FINANCIAL DECISIONS

Managers are responsible for the financial health of their company and for the specific areas of the company under their control. If adequate finances are not available, the work that is required will not be done as well or as quickly as needed. On the other hand, if more money than is needed is used for certain operations, there may not be enough for other parts of the company.

The first step in financial decision-making is preparing a budget. The budget identifies the amount of money needed for all parts of the business to complete planned activities. It also projects what types and amounts of income will be earned from the sale of the company's products, services, and other investments.

Once a budget is developed and approved, managers use the budget as

NETBookmark

Decision-making is an important skill for managers. It is also a skill that is needed by and useful for everyone. Access the website shown below and click on the link for Chapter 12. Study several of the decision-making techniques introduced on the website. Select one of the tools that would work well for an important individual decision and one that would be better for a decision made by a group. Compare your choices with other students.

www.cengage.com/school/genbus/pob

Goal 2

Identify the steps in making financial decisions in business.

Business Insight for the 21st Century

How Much Is Enough?

In 2009, the average compensation of the top executives of the largest 500 U.S. companies was $9.25 million. While that was down nearly 9 percent from the previous year, it came at a time of economic hardship for millions of Americans. In recent years, executive compensation has climbed much faster than employee pay. In 1968, the average corporate CEO made 20 times more than the average worker. Today the ratio is 400 to 1. As companies reduce the number of employees and make cutbacks to wage and benefit packages, many people are questioning the appropriateness of big paydays for executives. They are asking, "How much is enough?"

Corporate boards set executive compensation levels. Some critics, including shareholders, accuse board members of having close relationships with executives that result in the higher pay levels. Board members respond that managing a large corporation is extremely difficult and requires huge personal sacrifices. The compensation levels reflect those demands. They point out that total compensation for executives is a tiny percentage of overall company revenues and that successful management increases profits and financial returns to shareholders.

In response to concern about excessive executive compensation, regulations have been enacted that require more disclosure about compensation packages. The 2010 Restoring American Financial Stability Act requires public companies to submit executive pay plans to a non-binding shareholder vote to give them a "say on pay" in their companies.

Think Critically

1. If companies have annual revenues of tens or even hundreds of billions of dollars, is it appropriate for the top CEO to make $10 million or more in a year? Why or why not?

2. Do you believe there should be a relationship between compensation of a company's CEO and average employees' wages? Justify your answer.

WORK *as a* **TEAM**

Use the information from Figures 12-2 and 12-3 to calculate three of the financial performance ratios described in this lesson: current ratio, debt to equity ratio, and net income ratio. Use decimals to express your answers. Discuss what the results mean for the businesses.

a guide to operate the business. They regularly check to see if income and expenses are meeting budgeted amounts. Income should be as high as or higher than planned. Expenses should not exceed the budgeted amount. Managers get regular financial reports and examine them carefully, looking for discrepancies. **Discrepancies** are differences between actual and budgeted performance.

Discrepancies let managers identify problems before they become serious enough to harm the business. They might also see areas where financial performance is better than what was budgeted.

The final step is to make needed adjustments. If income and expenses are

similar to the budget, the manager will not need to take action. If there are financial problems, managers will take corrective action to try to bring performance back in line with the budget. That might include finding ways to improve revenue as well as seeking ways to cut expenses. In some cases, performance cannot be improved or factors outside the managers' control are responsible for the poor performance. The managers may have to adjust the budget. This should be done as a last resort because the budget was carefully planned.

At the end of the period covered by the budget, the business will prepare new financial statements. It will use the results to determine the financial success of the operations. The company will also use the results to improve the budgeting process in the future.

> **checkpoint ✓**
> List the three steps in financial decision-making.

12-4 Assessment

Study Tools

www.cengage.com/school/genbus/pob

Key Concepts

Determine the best answer.

1. Which of the following is not one of the three most important elements of a company's financial strength?
   a. assets
   b. owner's equity
   c. payroll
   d. liabilities

2. True or False. Sales and profits for a specific period are reported in a company's income statement.

3. True or False. Employees rather than managers are responsible for the financial health of a company.

4. Differences between actual and expected performance are
   a. ratios
   b. budgets
   c. profit or loss
   d. discrepancies

Make Academic Connections

5. **Communication** You are responsible for helping a new manager understand financial statements. Prepare and present a short presentation explaining the importance of the balance sheet and income statement. Use a computer and presentation software to develop several slides for your presentation.

6. **Critical Thinking** In comparing current operating costs with the budget, you see that payroll expenses are much higher than budgeted, but income has not increased. How would you attempt to identify the problem? What might be some reasons for the discrepancy?

7. **Math** At the end of the year, the financial statements of a small business showed total liabilities of $786,050; net profit of $27,293, and owner's equity of $326,927. Calculate the debt to equity and return on equity ratios for the company. Round your results to the nearest hundredth.

Doing Business in... Spain

Spain's economic and cultural history has shown several dramatic shifts in fortune. One of the European empires from the 1500s–1800s, Spain extended its economic and political reach throughout the Western Hemisphere. Spanish ships and conquistadors exerted ruthless control over people and land from South to North America, the Caribbean, Africa, and into Asia. The cost of maintaining the empire combined with a series of weak and inept monarchs led to the demise of the empire. While much of Europe was experiencing a social and economic awakening, Spain languished. A civil war in the early 1900s gave hope to its people but that was short-lived as a dictator, Francisco Franco seized control of the country and held power from 1936 until his death in 1975. Spain now is a parliamentary monarchy, a democracy with King Juan Carlos as the head of state, and a prime minister leading the country's government.

Spain was one of twelve countries that signed the Treaty on European Union in 1992. Since then it has been a leader of the European economy establishing itself as the eighth largest world economy. Its success has been propelled by its location on the Iberian Peninsula. Bordered on three sides by large bodies of water and sitting as the physical gateway to Europe, Africa, and the Middle East, Spain has attracted foreign investment and tourism resulting in a construction and real estate boom. The resulting increases in standard of living and personal income make Spain the fifteenth most developed country in the world. Recently however, affected by the global recession and real estate slump, Spain's economy has suffered a downturn.

In addition to attracting foreign investment, many Spanish companies are also multinational. Spain is the second biggest investor in Latin America after the United States. Spain is home to the world's largest renewable energy company, Iberdrola, and six of the largest infrastructure construction companies.

Although business in Spain might be conducted in English, all materials need a Spanish translation. Business cards are often printed in both English and Spanish, with the Spanish side up when presented. Business conversations often occur over lunch or dinner with dinner hours extending late into the evening. Spanish cuisine is characterized by homemade dishes incorporating fresh, local ingredients. People frequent street-side cafes to order tapas, churros, and cheese or fruit for dessert.

Think Critically

1. Why has Spain's geographic location been so important to recent economic success?

2. What advantages do Spain's major multinational businesses provide to Spain's economy?

3. Conduct library or Internet research to learn more about business and economic activities in Spain. Prepare a short report on your findings.

How does this photograph of a pedestrian bridge in Bilbao affect your view of Spain as a place you might want to do business?

Business Notes

12-1 Financial Planning

- The financial questions that must be answered in a business include: How much money is needed to start the business? From where will the financing come? How will funds be obtained to run the business for the months or years until it becomes profitable? What will be the best sources of sales and other income? What will be the expenses? When must they be paid?

- The four main steps in budget preparation are: prepare a list of the income and expenses that will be a part of the budget; gather accurate information for each income and expense; create the budget by calculating each type of income, expense, and amount of net income or loss; and show and explain the budget to people who need financial information to make decisions.

- There are three types of business budgets. The start-up budget plans income and expenses from the beginning of a new business or a major expansion until it becomes profitable. The operating budget describes the financial plan for ongoing operations of the business for a specific period. A cash budget is an estimate of the actual money received and paid out for a specific period.

12-2 Financial Records and Financial Statements

- Financial records are used to record and analyze the financial performance of a business. The types of records maintained include asset, depreciation, inventory, account, cash, payroll, and tax records.

- The two most common and important financial statements for businesses are the income statement and balance sheet. The business' assets, liabilities, and owner's equity for a specific date are listed on the balance sheet. An income statement reports the revenue, expenses, and net income or loss from operations for a specific period.

12-3 Payroll Management

- A payroll is the financial records of employee compensation, deductions, and net pay. A payroll system maintains information on each employee to be able to calculate the company's payroll and to make the necessary payments to each employee.

- Payroll records are the documentation used to process earnings payments and record each employee's pay history. An individual payroll record contains the employee's name, Social Security number, address, and other personal information, individual tax information, and a record of all benefits received. After all payroll records have been completed and pay amounts have been calculated, a paycheck is prepared for each person. An earnings report lists the employee's current and cumulative pay amounts and the type and amount of deductions.

12-4 Financial Decision-Making

- The three most important elements of a company's financial strength are assets, liabilities, and owner's equity. Two other key elements for a business are the amount of sales and profits. Managers use those financial elements to calculate financial performance ratios to make decisions that result in the wise use of the company's money.

- The first step in financial decision-making is preparing a budget. Second, managers use the budget as a guide to the operations of the business. The final step is to make needed adjustments.

Communicate Business Concepts

1. Identify several unique business expenses for three important times in a business' life: start-up, ongoing operations, and expansion.

2. What is the difference between a budget and a financial record? Why are both needed in a business?

3. Why is it important to maintain an accurate cash budget for a business? What happens to a business if it does not have access to cash even though it has other assets worth a lot of money?

4. What information is contained in a balance sheet that is not in an income statement?

5. Confidentiality of the personal information of employees is very important in businesses and other organizations. If you were the payroll manager of a large company and had several employees who had access to personnel and payroll records, what would you do to protect the confidentiality of the information that they could access as a part of their work?

6. The use of direct deposit for employee paychecks saves businesses and banks a large amount of time and money. Many employees are still reluctant to use it. What are some reasons people may not want to use this system? What could you say to a friend to convince them to use direct deposit?

7. Why are the assets, liabilities, and owner's equity more important to the financial strength of a business than the amount of profit they earned in a particular period?

8. If you were a stockholder in a business, which of the four financial performance ratios would be most important to you? Why? If you were a banker considering loaning money to a business, which ratios would be most important to you? Why?

9. Do you believe the financial performance of a business is a more important measure of a manager's effectiveness than other factors, such as customer satisfaction or employee satisfaction or turnover? Justify your answer.

Develop Your Business Language

Match the terms listed with the definitions.

10. Reports the revenue, expenses, and net income or loss from business operations for a specific period.

11. Provide detailed plans for the financial needs of individuals, families, and businesses.

12. The employer electronically transfers net pay into the employee's bank account.

13. Plans income and expenses from the beginning of a new business or a major business expansion until it becomes profitable.

14. Used to record and analyze the financial performance of a business.

15. All income that a business receives over a period of time.

16. Lists the business' assets, liabilities, and owner's equity for a specific date.

17. Differences between actual and budgeted performance.

18. Describes the financial plan for ongoing operations of the business for a specific period.

19. What a company owns.

20. The costs of operating a business.

21. An estimate of the actual money received and paid out for a specific period.

22. The documentation used to process earnings payments and record each employee's pay history.

23. Comparisons of a company's financial elements that indicate how well the business is performing.

24. The financial records of employee compensation, deductions, and net pay.

25. The value of the owners' investment in the business.

26. What a company owes.

KEY TERMS

a. assets
b. balance sheet
c. budget
d. cash budget
e. direct deposit
f. discrepancies
g. expenses
h. financial performance ratios
i. financial records
j. income statement
k. liabilities
l. operating budget
m. payroll
n. payroll records
o. owner's equity
p. revenue
q. start-up budget

Make Academic Connections

27. Math Lee Chan has owned a computer repair business for three years. The first year, Mr. Chan barely earned a profit. The next year's profit was more substantial. As shown in the table, he has just received the financial results from the third year and wants to compare them to those of the second year of operations.

a. How much money did Mr. Chan earn from sales each year?

b. What was his total cost of doing business each year?

c. What profit or loss did Mr. Chan earn this year? What is the dollar amount and percentage difference in the profit or loss from last year?

	LAST YEAR	THIS YEAR
Rent	$28,000	$28,000
Sales	78,250	80,725
Inventory	15,000	13,750
Payroll	17,850	18,210
Utilities	10,010	7,075
Supplies	1,020	2,020

28. Technology Use the Internet to identify two software programs that can be used by a small business to manage payroll. Evaluate the two programs and prepare a table that compares the features of the two programs. Prepare a written recommendation to a business owner on the software you believe would be the best choice with reasons for your decision.

29. Economics The budgets of a business are affected by events and changes outside the business, including the actions of competitors, and the strength and weakness of the local, national, and global economies. Review recent newspapers and business magazines. Find several articles that report on the economy and competition that could have a positive or negative effect on businesses in your community. Prepare a note card for each article on which you summarize the key points of the article and describe how the information could affect the financial decisions made by business managers.

30. Read Find a news article that relates to financial decision-making. Read the article and write a one-sentence summary of the main idea. Include a properly formatted citation for your source. Possible sources include printed and online versions of newspapers and magazines. You should also consider independent online sources that produce original content.

Decision-Making Strategies

Dominic sat at his office computer reviewing the financial statements for his three-year-old business. He had yet to make a profit. He was able to pay himself a small salary but still had to hold a part-time job to maintain his family's lifestyle. He had added a part-time employee and needed another, but didn't have the money to pay another person right now. Dominic studied the balance sheets and income statements side by side. The balance sheets showed that the value of assets was increasing. Liabilities had increased as well due to the need to continue to borrow money to purchase inventory as his sales increased. He had been able to make regular payments on his building and equipment loans, so long-term liabilities were decreasing. There had been no change in the value of the owner's equity, so his investment was not paying off. When he shifted his attention to the income statement, he could see that sales were up sharply, but so were the costs of his inventory and operating expenses. He did notice that he had more cash on hand to pay bills as they came due and that the losses were getting smaller and smaller.

31. Based on Dominic's review, which findings are positive? Which findings are negative?

32. Based on the financial information provided, do you believe Dominic's business is successful or not? Justify your answer.

Linking School and Community

Locate copies of the most recent year's financial statements for your local town or city. You should be able to find them on the government website or by visiting the administrative offices. Review the list of documents and identify those that are the same or similar as the balance sheet and income statement discussed in Lesson 12-2. Study each of those forms reflecting the financial condition of your town or city. What major similarities and differences do you notice between the two financial statements of your town or city and those shown in Figures 12-2 and 12-3? What other financial statements published by your town or city would be important in helping citizens understand its financial health?

Web Workout

Visit the website of the United States Internal Revenue Service. Locate information about the following tax forms related to business payroll:

Form W-2

Form W-4

Form 940

Form 941

Form 944

Think Critically

1. Prepare a brief description of the purpose of each form. Include answers to the following questions: Who is responsible for completing the form? When must it be completed? Where is it sent or distributed?

2. Other than sending checks, how can businesses make payroll tax payments to the federal government?

Entrepreneurship Event

In order to avoid the high failure rate experienced by many new businesses, successful entrepreneurs must conduct research, secure financing, and convince consumers to purchase the goods and services they offer. Developing a business plan is a good way to organize these activities.

For this event you must develop a business plan for a new restaurant to be located near a university campus that has 30,000 students during the regular school year. Your business plan must demonstrate how you will maintain favorable sales for the restaurant throughout the entire year. Currently the country is experiencing an economic recession.

Your business plan must include the products and services to be provided, market analysis, customer profile, competition, short-range operational goals, financial analysis (income statement, balance sheet, cash flow statement, and other analyses), and supporting research documents. The business plan must not exceed 10 single-spaced pages.

You will orally present your business plan to the judges or class members for 10 minutes. Following your presentation, they will have up to five minutes to ask questions about your business plan.

Performance Indicators Evaluated

- Develop a written business plan for a start-up business during a recession.
- Identify the customer base, including consumer and organizational markets, highlighting demographics.
- Analyze financial data.
- Demonstrate successful price selection methods.
- Identify and use internal and external resources.

You will be evaluated for your

- Knowledge and understanding of entrepreneurship
- Communication of research in a clear and concise manner both orally and in writing
- Demonstration of effective persuasive and informative communication and presentation skills

For more detailed information about performance indicators, go to the BPA website.

Think Critically

1. What is an apparent risk associated with opening a restaurant near a large university?

2. What are the strengths, weaknesses, opportunities, and threats with this business proposal?

3. What is the most effective means to advertise your business?

4. Who are the best external sources to finance your business? How will you convince these sources to invest in the business?

5. When do you plan on first making a profit with this business venture? How will the business survive until it makes its first profit?

www.bpa.org

13 Production and Business Operations

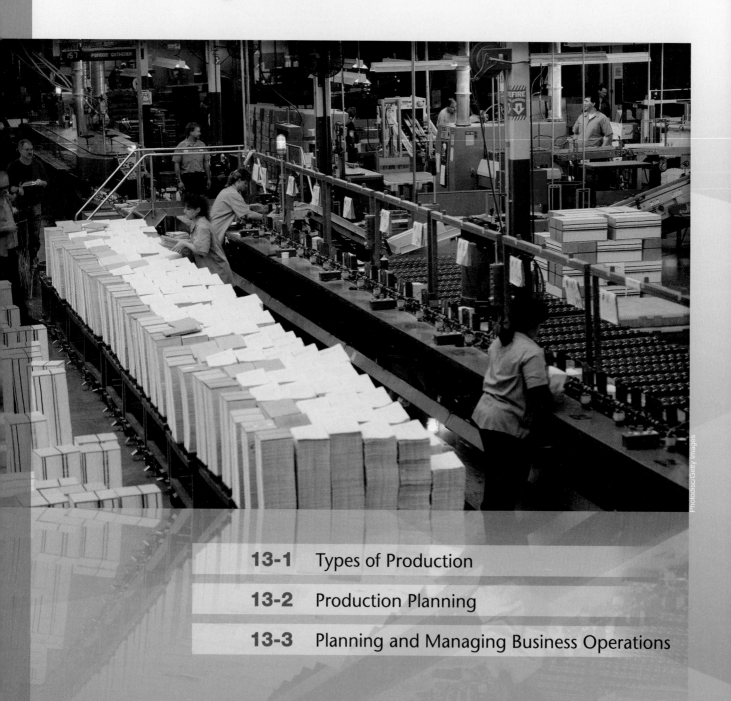

Photodisc/Getty Images

Planning a Career in ...

INDUSTRIAL ENGINEERING

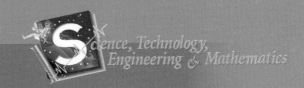
Science, Technology, Engineering & Mathematics

Industrial engineers work to improve the ways that businesses use the factors of production to develop products and services needed by businesses and consumers. They are involved in designing new products and improving the quality and usability of existing products. They help to improve the operations of businesses by introducing new technology, reorganizing work, and promoting the health and safety of workers.

Industrial engineers are highly educated scientists. They conduct research and apply mathematical and statistical models to problems. They work with managers and other experts in businesses to solve problems, reduce costs, and improve operations.

Even though the number of manufacturing companies and jobs is declining, the demand for industrial engineers is stable. Most industrial engineers work in manufacturing industries, they also work in health care, government, and higher education.

Related Job Titles

- Project Engineer
- Operations Analyst
- Quality Engineer
- Ergonomist
- Standards Engineer
- Systems Analyst
- Business Process Manager
- Supply Chain Engineer
- Industrial Engineering Leader

Analyze Career Opportunities in ...
INDUSTRIAL ENGINEERING

Use library and internet resources to learn more about careers in industrial engineering. Choose one of the job titles listed in the box above and answer the following questions.

1. How would you describe the earnings potential for this field?

2. Is this a career that interests you? Describe how you might use your talents, abilities, and skills in this career.

What's it like to work as an ... Industrial Engineer?

Four industrial engineers were gathered at the national conference of the Institute for Industrial Engineering. They had all graduated 10 years ago and were discussing their recent projects.

Rachel had just redesigned a work process in her company's metals recycling plant resulting in a reduction of worker injuries. Alistair was developing a prototype for a miniaturized GPS unit for use in search and rescue operations. Jacob had spent the last three years redesigning the emergency room layout, equipment, and procedures for a hospital in London. Frank had just started a new job where he would be developing and testing new materials to be used in high-speed rail systems.

They realized, as they talked about their work, that they were in an exciting, rapidly changing professional area. They were making important contributions to their organizations and to society. They agreed to meet again in a few years and see where their careers had taken them.

What about you? Why do you think industrial engineers are able to work in such varied types of businesses?

13-1 Types of Production

Goals

1 Describe the role of producers in the economy and the forms of production.

2 Differentiate among the various types of manufacturing.

Key Terms

extraction and cultivation 317

processing 317

manufacturing 317

mass production 319

custom manufacturing 319

materials processing 319

Focus on REAL LIFE

Lucy closed her web browser and turned to her mother. "I think I found the answer to the question you had while we were shopping the other day. Remember the jeans with the *Assembled in the USA* tag?"

"I've seen lots of labels that identify the country where a product is manufactured such as *Made in China* or *Made in Mexico*," her mom responded. "But, I'm not sure how *assembled* and *made* are different."

"According to the Federal Trade Commission," Lucy said, "for a product to be labeled *Made in the USA*, virtually all of the parts and materials used to produce it must come from the United States. And, it must be assembled in the United States. Jeans have denim, thread, zippers, buttons, and other materials. Only a small percentage of these things could be produced elsewhere for the jeans to carry a *Made in the USA* label."

"So that means much of the materials used in the jeans we saw must have come from other countries to a U.S. plant for final assembly. With all of the parts that go into many products, I can see why it is more and more difficult to find any that are completely made in just one country."

Goal 1

Describe the role of producers in the economy and the forms of production.

PRODUCTION AS AN ECONOMIC ACTIVITY

The economy begins with production. Consumers need products and services to satisfy their needs and wants. Businesses also need products and services. They incorporate products and services into the products they produce and use them in operations. They also resell them to their customers.

Role of Producers

The role of producers can be described by the categories of products produced and the types of businesses that make products. The three categories of products used by businesses and consumers are natural resources, agricultural products, and processed goods. *Natural resources* are raw materials supplied by nature. *Agricultural products* are crops and animals raised by farmers. *Processed goods* are products that have been changed in form to increase their value and usefulness.

There are four types of businesses that are responsible for production: producers, extractors, farmers, and manufacturers. *Producers* develop products to sell to other businesses or consumers. *Extractors* obtain natural resources, such as water, oil, coal, and timber, from the earth for processing and use. *Farmers* tend land and other resources to grow crops and livestock that are later sold and processed. *Manufacturers* obtain materials from other producers and convert them into products for sale to consumers and other businesses.

Forms of Production

The forms of production are extraction and cultivation, processing, and manufacturing. In **extraction and cultivation**, products are obtained from nature or grown using natural resources. Extraction and cultivation ensure that there is an available supply of natural resources and the crops, livestock, fish, and other agricultural products needed. This is the most basic form of production.

Processing involves changing and improving the form of another product. Few products are used exactly as they are found in nature or grown on farms. Most are processed in some way before they are used. Water must be filtered and treated before it can be consumed or used in the production of other products. Timber is cut and formed into lumber or processed into paper or other materials. Oil is pumped from deep in the earth. The oil is then sent to refineries to be converted into gasoline, heating oil, and petroleum-based products. They are then used in the production of other products such as plastics, cosmetics, medicines, and food. The crops and livestock raised by farmers are sent to processing plants. They are inspected, packed, and shipped to supermarkets or are processed and combined with other products. This gives you the variety of foods you prepare at home or order in a restaurant.

Manufacturing combines raw materials and processed goods into finished products. Either other businesses or final consumers use those finished products. Manufacturing can be as simple as a cabinetmaker using tools and materials to build an entertainment center. It also can

Describe a process that farmers and other producers must use to turn a crop into a saleable product.

be as complex as designing a microchip for a computer or building a high-speed rail system.

Each of these forms of production is needed to make all of the goods and services demanded by businesses and consumers. Each requires specialized tools and equipment, in addition to well-trained and often highly skilled personnel. The requirements to locate and pump oil from miles below the ocean floor, to design and build the equipment needed to create artificial diamonds, or the ability to plan and build a small spacecraft that can be piloted from the Earth's atmosphere into space and back are hard to comprehend. But they are no more important to your quality of life than the expertise of the production team on an assembly line installing airbags into automobiles or the capability of the person inspecting the prescription drugs as they are processed and packed for distribution to hospitals and pharmacies.

checkpoint ✓
What are the three forms of production?

WORK
as a
TEAM

In your team, create a table with three columns. Label each column with one of the types of manufacturing procedures. Agree on five products that would be manufactured using each procedure and list them in the column under the correct heading.

Goal 2

Differentiate among the various types of manufacturing.

MANUFACTURING

Manufacturers get products or raw materials from other businesses. They combine and change them into a form that their customers can use. One manufacturer might use steel, plastic, and other materials to make many parts into products such as skis or snowmobiles for winter sports. Another may purchase meat, vegetables, and fruit from farms to create frozen entrees you can heat in your microwave. A third takes timber from a forest and processes it into lumber and plywood. A construction company then purchases those building materials to build the houses for a new neighborhood.

A Manufacturing Process

Usually, several manufacturers are a part of the total activity needed to produce goods that are purchased by consumers or other businesses. Think about the jeans described in Focus on Real Life. The manufacturing process begins when a textile mill in Brazil buys cotton grown on a ranch in Paraguay. It spins the cotton into yarn which is sent to a fabric company in Canada. That company weaves, dyes, and processes many types of fabric including the denim used in jeans. A New York apparel manufacturer buys the denim as well as other materials needed. The fabric is finished and cut and sewers assemble the jeans before they are shipped to retailers.

While that entire process could have been completed by U.S. firms, increasingly manufacturing involves businesses from all over the world. Raw materials and processed goods often move long distances as they are produced, processed, and prepared for sale. Working together, producers each add unique processes that change the form of raw materials into products that fulfill consumers' needs.

Types of Manufacturing Procedures

Manufacturing businesses organize production in several ways to make their products. The number of products needed and the characteristics of the products will determine the type of manufacturing procedures.

Mass Production An assembly process that makes a large number of identical products using a continuous, efficient

What makes an assembly line a more efficient way of manufacturing?

Small Town Studio/Shutterstock.com

procedure is **mass production**. Mass production is sometimes called repetitive production. Automobile assemblies or beverage bottling plants often use this type of production. Mass production allows a business to assemble products in a very large quantity and at a low cost.

With mass production, employees usually have precise tasks. They use specialized tools and equipment as they work on product assembly. That allows training costs to be lower while maintaining quality. It can also result in monotonous work and worker boredom. Companies have been testing ways to improve the work environment in factories that use mass production. Computers and mechanized equipment now assist with or perform many of the procedures on an assembly line.

Custom Manufacturing Building a specific and unique product to meet the needs of each customer is done with **custom manufacturing**. Custom manufacturers make products ranging from stretch limousines to a concert hall to meet particular design standards. When each customer has quite different needs or someone is building the product for a specific use, it may require custom manufacturing.

A business using custom manufacturing works closely with the customer to plan and design the product. It may call for unique materials or a special assembly process. With products such as buildings, bridges, or landscaping, the construction takes place at a new site each time. In other situations, such as the design of a unique tool for the space program or a special running shoe for a professional athlete, the design and assembly of the unique product will occur at the manufacturer's site. Sometimes, a small team of designers, toolmakers, and assemblers take part in highly specialized custom manufacturing. This team works closely with the customer and each other to create

What kinds of everyday products are often custom made?

Comstock/Getty Images

a particularly unique product such as a musical instrument or race car.

Materials Processing Changing the form of raw materials so they can be consumed or used to make other products is **materials processing**. Oil companies refine crude oil to produce gasoline and other petroleum products. Mills process grain into flour, cereal, and feed for animals. Digital editors convert a variety of audio and image files into films, CDs, and other multimedia presentations.

There are two types of materials processing. With *continuous processing*, the raw materials constantly move through specially designed equipment.

fyi The U.S. manufacturing economy is the world's largest, according to the National Association of Manufacturers. Nearly 12 million people work in U.S. manufacturing jobs, producing 22 percent of all manufactured products. Manufacturing contributes more than $1.6 trillion to the U.S. economy annually.

Joel Calheiros/Shutterstock.com

This changes them into a specific product useable for consumption or for further manufacturing. Raw milk is sprayed into huge drying machines to produce powdered milk. Mills dry corn and then grind it for use in the production of feed for cattle or flakes for cereal.

Intermittent processing uses short production runs to produce a precise amount of a variation of a product. The machinery or materials are reconfigured each time to provide the required variation. A printer uses intermittent processing to complete a special order of stationary or to print and assemble a uniquely designed brochure. A baker resets the equipment to blend and bake wheat bread after making a batch of pumpernickel loaves.

What raw materials are used when making bread?

> **checkpoint** ✓
> What is the difference between custom manufacturing and materials processing?

13-1 Assessment

Study Tools

www.cengage.com/school/genbus/pob

Key Concepts

Determine the best answer.

1. Which of the following is *not* one of the categories of products used by consumers and businesses?
   a. natural resources
   b. agricultural production
   c. processed goods
   d. All of the answers are correct.

2. True or False. The most basic form of production is manufacturing.

3. Building a specific and unique product to meet the needs of one customer is known as
   a. materials processing
   b. mass production
   c. extraction
   d. custom manufacturing

4. Intermittent processing would most likely be used in the production of
   a. automobiles   c. textbooks
   b. customized houses   d. televisions

Make Academic Connections

5. **Writing** Conduct research on how automation has changed manufacturing procedures in an industry that interests you. Prepare a two-page report with a bibliography.

6. **Geography** Select an article of clothing or a popular food item. Conduct research to determine the major raw materials and natural resources that are used in the production of the product. Identify the country or countries that are the major sources of the production or supply of those materials.

13-2 Production Planning

Goals

1. Identify the activities involved in production planning.

2. Describe how manufacturing is organized.

Key Terms

applied research 321

pure research 321

production process 322

continuous process improvement 325

benchmarks 326

Focus on REAL LIFE

Yori sat with his partner, Ted, reviewing the latest production report. They were proud of their five-year-old business that produced beach shoes from recycled plastic.

"Our sales continue to grow at over 10 percent a year although profits are not keeping pace," said Yori. "I've noticed that as we have added new shoe designs our production errors have increased. Also, customer orders are not shipping as fast, resulting in more complaints."

Ted responded, "I'm not sure we should be using the same procedures we were using before we added five new products and 35 employees. Maybe there is more efficient technology we can use."

"It's clearly time we get help with our production planning," suggested Yori. "Improving our quality now will surely keep us from facing even greater problems in the future."

PRODUCTION ACTIVITIES

Production and manufacturing processes are very complex. They involve a number of activities and resources that businesses must carefully plan and coordinate. Before a company can manufacture a product, it must have the facilities and equipment needed to carry out the production activities. The company must obtain the materials needed for production. It must hire enough people with the required skills. It must check finished products for quality and store them until sold. The business must then distribute them to customers when and where they are needed.

Product Development

Before any production planning can occur, the company decides what products it will produce. A business cannot rely on selling the same products year after year. As customer needs and competition change, new products will have to be developed. Product planning involves two steps—product research and product design.

Product Research Companies devote a large amount of their resources to discovering new product ideas. For example, U.S. businesses spent more than $330 billion for research in 2008. Many scientists and engineers devote all of their work time to research and development activities. Their goals are to develop new products that will meet the needs of customers and improve the current products offered by the company and its competitors.

Companies carry out two types of research to discover new product ideas. **Applied research** studies existing products to develop design improvements or new product uses. Engineers working for an automobile manufacturer will study the current designs to improve the efficiency of engines or increase passenger safety. **Pure research** is research done

Goal 1

Identify the activities involved in production planning.

without a specific product in mind with the goal of discovering new solutions to problems. For example, scientists working for drug manufacturers study diseases and immune systems of the body. Their goal is to uncover treatments and cures.

Product Design When scientists develop a new product idea, businesses must turn that idea into a product that they can make and sell profitably. Design engineers create models and test them to come up with the best possible design. They select materials that make the product useable and durable.

After engineers build and test a model, the business determines all of the materials and parts needed for the final product. Financial experts calculate the cost of making the product. They will get information from customers and competitors to decide the price at which they can sell the new product. By comparing cost and pricing information,

the business can determine whether the product can be made and sold profitably.

Production Planning

If a company develops and tests a new product idea and concludes that it can sell the product at a profit, the company then develops plans to produce the product. Production planning includes three activities. First, the company develops a production process. Next, it obtains production resources. Finally, the company selects and prepares production personnel.

Production Process The activities, equipment, and resources needed to manufacture a product are part of the **production process**. If the business will make the product using mass production, it must organize the assembly line. Customized manufacturing requires that the company identify the changes in materials and assembly procedures that will be required for customizing each product.

Production Resources Next, the business orders or builds the machines, tools, and other equipment required for each step of the production process. Often, new products will call for customized equipment. The business must locate and organize adequate space to perform the needed production activities. This allows employees to complete work efficiently and safely. In some cases, a business will have to buy or construct a new building. In other situations, it can remodel current facilities from the production of older products that are being discontinued.

Another planning step is to determine the sources of the raw materials, parts, and supplies needed to make the product. Often the manufacturing company will not have all the needed resources. It will have to identify suppliers and negotiate agreements so an adequate and timely supply is available at an appropriate price. The company may decide it can produce some of the parts and materials needed.

PhotoStocker/Shutterstock.com

What are the benefits of making a model of a new product first?

Personnel Finally, the company focuses on personnel planning. It estimates the number of employees needed to complete all production activities. It determines the skills required of each employee. The company will check to see if there are enough employees in the company and if they have the needed abilities. If not, it must hire and train new employees. Another option is to find a separate company with the capability and employees needed to complete some or all of the production activities rather than using its own employees and facilities.

Inventory Management

Inventory is a detailed account of a company's materials, supplies, and finished products. *Inventory management* maintains the supply of all resources needed for production and the products produced. Inventory management is a vital manufacturing activity. Most products are assembled using many different parts and supplies. Each of the items needed to make a product must be available at the time and place needed

Business Insight for the 21st Century

Philips HomeLab

Can your home sense that you are too hot or cold and automatically adjust the temperature? As you get ready for school in the morning can you call up your favorite TV program as a digital image in your bathroom mirror? That is the vision guiding research in the Royal Philips electronics company. Their scientists created a laboratory called HomeLab in Eindhoven, The Netherlands. HomeLab is an actual house occupied by real consumers selected for the research. Their interactions with prototypes of products the company is designing are recorded with small cameras and microphones.

Philips calls the technology *ambient intelligence*. They believe that, in the home of the future, people

won't control products with knobs and switches. Instead technology will respond to the movements, sounds, gestures, and physical characteristics of the residents. They believe the unique research will result in innovative lighting, appliances, entertainment products, and even clothing that can interpret and respond to individual requests and actions.

While the HomeLab is a very expensive research investment, the company believes it provides an ideal setting to conceive, test, and improve new products in an environment that reflects the way consumers live. It speeds new product development because the products are tested at the same time they are being developed.

According to Philips' Chief Technology Officer, "Our innovation is centered around what consumers want. By observing them using our technology in their natural habitat—the home—we can better adapt that technology into real-world products."

Think Critically

1. What problems might the researchers encounter when observing people who know they are being observed? How might they overcome these problems?

2. Other than those listed, what types of products do you believe could benefit from study in this type of research laboratory?

Goal 2

Describe how manufacturing is organized.

for assembly. If an item is not on hand, the assembly process must be stopped. Conversely, if a supply of any of the items is larger than the business can use in a short time, inventory and storage costs will be too high.

Inventory managers keep records of the supply and cost of all resources used in production. They work to ensure that suppliers deliver orders on time and in the correct quantities and prices. The business maintains adequate storage space for parts and materials. In addition to being secure, the space needs to be organized so that parts and materials can be quickly and safely moved to production areas.

After the business completes product assembly and inspection, it moves the products into storage or distributes them to customers. The business must keep an accurate finished product inventory to make sure it can fill customer orders. Sales may be missed if products are not available. Although a business needs to have enough inventory to meet demand, it does not want to have too much inventory. Storing excess inventory can be costly and products might become outdated.

> **checkpoint √**
> Describe the three activities that are a part of production planning.

MANUFACTURING PROCEDURES

One of the biggest changes in manufacturing businesses is the production procedures used. Pictures of old factories show long assembly lines with employees located at workstations along the line. Employees are surrounded by tools and a supply of any parts they need to complete their part of the product assembly. Products moved slowly along the line and frequently stopped because additional time was needed to complete a procedure, correct a problem, or repair equipment.

Today, assembly is quite different. Employees often work in teams, completing many procedures together. Each employee is trained to be able to perform several assembly procedures. Supplies and parts move along conveyor belts or on robot-driven carts to arrive just as they are needed. Many products are customized to meet specific customer requirements as they are assembled. Managers, team leaders, and employees look at the screens of computers that monitor the assembly process and provide production information. Other employees quickly step in when needed to repair equipment or help to solve problems. Products move rapidly through the assembly process. Monitoring equipment checks products for quality at several points. When assembly is completed, the products are packaged, labeled, and moved to a loading area for immediate shipment to customers.

Organizing the Work Area

The type of product and production process will determine how the work area is organized. Mass production usually requires a large building. There must be space for the assembly line, equipment, tools, employee workstations, and storage for parts needed for assembly and finished products. If the company completes customized production of small products, such as framed artwork there will often be a larger workspace for each employee. They will have easy access to the variety of parts and materials needed for each product assembly. Often, as production of each customized product is planned, one employee will be assigned to collect the materials needed for an order. With the order in hand, the employee will wheel a cart through the room that stores the parts and quickly select those needed. Then the employee will move the cart to the work area of other employees who will complete the product assembly.

Building or assembling a product at the customer's location provides different challenges. Some examples are home construction, landscaping, and installing a business telephone system. In these activities, employees, equipment, and supplies must be moved to the customer's location. Transportation, storage, and security become major issues. Managers at the construction site must be able to communicate with inventory managers and with people responsible for transporting the supplies and materials needed. Often companies have an overall project manager who works in the company's office and visits the work sites from time to time. Other managers are located at the various work sites. They supervise the construction and are in regular communication with the project manager.

Improving Manufacturing

Manufacturers face challenges today as they cope with rising costs, greater competition in the global marketplace, and growing customer demands. The challenges include the need for faster production, increased quality, and reduced costs. Companies are responding with improved manufacturing procedures, better employee training, and more attention to quality.

Manufacturing is made up of a series of processes. One process follows another

until production is complete. In the past, if there was a problem within a process, managers and employees would try to identify the problem and attempt to correct it. This was time-consuming and it affected all of the processes that followed. Improvements were made only after problems were discovered.

Manufacturers have now adopted continuous process improvement detailed in Figure 13-1, as a way to make sure manufacturing processes are completed as effectively and efficiently as possible. **Continuous process improvement (CPI)** increases the quality of work by reducing errors, inefficiencies, and waste. Rather than waiting for a problem to occur, processes are continuously reviewed with the goal of finding ways to improve them and reduce defects and production errors.

CPI is designed to help an organization achieve its goals by improving the

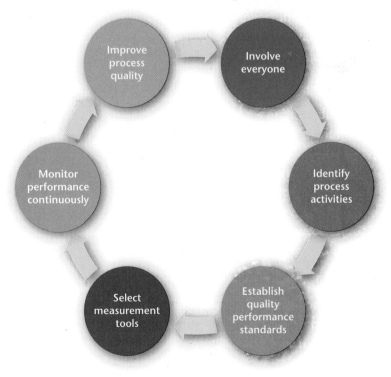

Continuous Process Improvement

- Improve process quality
- Involve everyone
- Identify process activities
- Establish quality performance standards
- Select measurement tools
- Monitor performance continuously

▶ **Figure 13-1**

How should continuous process improvement affect the prices that consumers pay for products?

quality of work. CPI should involve everyone linked to work processes. That includes employees, managers, other businesses involved in the process, and even customers. It begins by listing all of the activities involved in the process. Standards for quality performance are developed. Often the standards are based on **benchmarks**, or the best practices used by competitors. Measurement tools are chosen and measurements are taken to determine if activities are meeting the standards that have been set. Based on those results, the people involved look for ways to improve each procedure to meet and exceed the standards. They also consider ways to improve the overall process by changes in activities, equipment, and resources.

Some children's car seats have been recalled because they did not meet safety standards. Can you think of any other products that have recently been recalled?

checkpoint ✓

Why have manufacturers implemented continuous process improvement (CPI)?

www.cengage.com/school/genbus/pob

Study Tools

13-2 **Assessment**

Key Concepts

Determine the best answer.

1. True or False. Once a company has developed successful products, it should be able to continue to sell them year after year.

2. True or False. Pure research is done without a specific product in mind.

3. Inventory managers keep records of
   a. personnel
   b. customers
   c. production resources and finished products
   d. All of the answers are correct.

4. The best practices among all competitors are
   a. standards
   b. benchmarks
   c. CPI
   d. quality measures

Make Academic Connections

5. **Art** Choose a small household product that you or your family uses regularly. Evaluate the product and determine a design improvement for the product. Sketch a new design that illustrates the improvement. Show your sketch to other students and explain the product design.

6. **Math** A company keeps track of the number of defective products as part of its CPI program. For three months, the number of products and defects were

   January: 3,358 products, 31 defects
   February: 4,210 products, 38 defects
   March: 3,895 products, 28 defects

   a. Calculate the percent of defects for each month.
   b. Calculate the average production and defect rates for all three months.
   c. Create a graph or chart that illustrates and compares the three months of data.

13-3 Planning and Managing Business Operations

Goals

1. Discuss the importance of effective business operations.

2. Describe tools used to manage business operations.

Key Terms

logistics 328

just-in-time 329

operational plan 332

schedule 332

standard 333

Focus on REAL LIFE

Alton was clearly frustrated when his friend Kim picked him up in her car. "I can't believe my new laptop computer won't connect to my monitor with the cable I have always used. Now I have to go back to the store and buy a different one."

"I had a similar problem with the digital camera I bought last month," said Kim. "It takes a different type of media card. Not only did I need a new card, but I didn't have any way of viewing the pictures on my old card."

"What's going on?" asked Alton. "Why can't manufacturers get together and agree on standard designs, sizes, and formats for their products?"

THE IMPORTANCE OF BUSINESS OPERATIONS

The day-to-day operations of a business often determine its success or failure. The company may have products that meet customer needs. They may have competitive prices. Still, several things can go wrong in daily operations that result in problems. Work procedures may not be efficient. Security issues may result in product thefts or damage to buildings and equipment. Lack of maintenance can lead to costly repairs or safety hazards for employees and customers. A poor work environment can result in dissatisfied employees who are less productive than they could otherwise be. Businesspeople need to plan business operations as carefully as they work to satisfy their customers or plan for new products.

Types of Business Operations

Some business operations are specific to the type of business. The production activities of a manufacturer are different from the merchandise display and promotion activities of a retailer. They are different from the patient care activities of a hospital. Even among those very different types of businesses, there are some common types of business operations. They are facilities management, logistics, scheduling, and safety and security.

> **Goal 1**
>
> Discuss the importance of effective business operations.

What are some jobs where safety is a concern?

Facilities Management Buildings are one of the largest investments of a business. Buildings house the work and workers. They provide space for all of the business operations as well as storage of materials, supplies, and products. Facilities management protects the company's investment of thousands or even millions of dollars.

Facilities management begins with making economic decisions about the buildings needed. Some companies buy existing facilities. Others build new buildings to house their operations. It may be more cost-effective to rent some or all of the facilities needed. Facilities managers continually study the long-term plans of the company. They must determine if the current buildings are adequate, if more space is needed, or if some facilities are no longer needed or are out-of-date. It may be necessary to buy additional buildings or expand existing facilities. The expansion may require that expensive land be purchased. Some companies purchase land many years in advance at a cheaper price in anticipation of expansion.

Building maintenance and repair is another vital task of facilities management. A regular cleaning schedule is followed. From time to time, walls must be painted, carpets cleaned or replaced, and equipment updated. Exterior maintenance, including landscaping, is another ongoing task. A business must maintain a professional appearance for visitors and employees. It must also make repairs to facilities and equipment immediately so the problems don't affect operations. Failure to maintain and repair buildings and equipment on a regular basis will result in higher costs in the future.

Another key area of facilities management is energy and environmental management. Energy costs are a rapidly growing expense. Companies need a ready supply of electricity, gasoline, heating oil, and water. Yet they also need to keep utilities costs under control. Facilities managers study ways to conserve energy resources. They also monitor the quality of air, building temperature, and other environmental factors to maintain a healthy and productive workforce. Many businesses are actively involved in implementing green management practices. *Green management* is concerned with protecting the environment through conservation of natural resources, wise energy use, and reduction of emissions, waste, and pollution.

Logistics Large quantities of products and materials move in, around, and out of a business on a daily basis. **Logistics** is managing the acquisition, movement, and storage of supplies, materials, and finished products in a business. Logistics has become a very important part of business operations. A newer term for managing

Greg Henry/Shutterstock.com

Give an example of an improvement a business could make to its facility in order to attract more customers.

logistics is supply chain management. A *supply chain* is all of the businesses involved from the time raw materials are obtained until finished products are sold.

The major activities that make up logistics are locating sources of supplies, purchasing, transportation, and sales. In addition to the physical movement of resources, logistics is responsible for effective communication and information among all participants in the supply chain. One important logistics process is just-in-time. Using **just-in-time**, goods arrive when needed (just in time) for production, use, or sale rather than sitting in storage. Just-in-time logistics requires careful planning and coordination among supply chain members. It also requires an effective information system.

What are some complications that might occur when scheduling transportation of goods?

Brand X Pictures/Getty Images

Scheduling Even in small businesses, many activities occur at the same time. Scheduling involves determining the activities that need to be completed, the people who will perform the work, and the resources needed for the task. Consider a factory that produces a number of products to fill hundreds of customer orders. The factory must maintain the right inventory of products to fill each order. If customers have to wait too long, they may cancel their order. If too much time is spent producing one type of product, supplies of others may run low. If raw materials needed to produce a particular product arrive late, production of that product must be halted. Retail and service businesses find the same types of scheduling problems as they make sure they can match their resources with customer demand.

An important part of logistics planning is employee scheduling. Companies have a workforce made up of full-time, part-time, permanent, and temporary employees. The company assigns each employee to a work area. Each employee has a specific set of skills to meet job requirements. The company depends on having the right number of people available at any time to complete the scheduled work. The human resources department is responsible for making sure enough employees are available with the skills needed. They balance the workforce by determining the number of each type of employee needed. They may need to hire more employees at certain times or reduce the number of employees at other times. A key human resource activity is training. Training ensures employees have the skills needed for their job assignments.

Managers, supervisors, and team leaders are responsible for the weekly and daily work schedules. They determine the work that is required. They also prepare the work schedule. If a heavier than usual workload is expected, employees may be scheduled to work more hours. The schedule must anticipate employee vacations and the possibility that employees will be absent or leave the company. Most

managers have a specific wage and salary budget they are expected to meet. They must schedule carefully so as not to exceed the budget but still get the work finished.

Safety and Security Companies are responsible for protecting people and property. Many events and circumstances can result in injury to people or damage to property. Companies devote a great deal of effort to providing security and safety.

Security procedures and personnel protect both people and property. Damage and injury can occur because of crime, unintentional actions, or natural causes, such as tornados, hurricanes, and earthquakes. Security personnel study the resources and activities of a business to identify potential security problems. They then prepare security plans and procedures to prevent problems whenever possible. The plans also minimize the amount of loss if a security problem occurs.

Safety is another main business concern. The business wants to prevent accidents and injuries to employees and customers. Businesses work to maintain safe work areas and work procedures. They provide safety training and enforce rules and regulations designed to reduce accidents. Many businesses place safety posters around the workplace. They recognize work units that have a record of no accidents or injuries for a period of time.

Information Management

Effective business operations require the coordination of many activities, resources, and people throughout the business. It usually involves the activities of other businesses. For a growing number of businesses, operations in many locations and even in several countries need to be coordinated. *Information management* uses technology to access and exchange information to complete the work of an organization. Information management has four goals.

1. To collect, organize, and securely maintain all needed information.

2. To provide instantaneous access to information required to perform work and make decisions.

3. To prevent access to information by those unauthorized to use it.

4. To use technology to improve communication and information sharing.

What can retailers do to recover losses suffered from shoplifting?

Polka Dot/Jupiter Images

Can you think of other ways that technology has made communication in business easier?

There are many types of information used in businesses. They include text, data, graphics, pictures, and video. Businesses exchange information in a number of ways. Oral communications include telephone, voice mail, face-to-face meetings, and now voice-over-Internet. Written communications take the form of letters, memos, reports, brochures, product manuals, e-mail, text and instant messages, and many others.

Information managers are responsible for designing, purchasing, installing, and maintaining the many types of technology used in the business. They must develop procedures for collecting, storing, and using information. They make sure the information is accessible yet secure. They provide training and policies for all employees on the use of technology as well as on effective communications skills.

The Internet has become an important resource for communication and information management. Because most areas of the world are now connected via the Internet, businesses are able to provide continuous access to information by employees, customers, and business partners. Internet technology allows worldwide instantaneous voice, video, text and graphics communications. Businesses can replace many face-to-face meetings with Internet conferences, saving time and travel budgets. Digital communications are usually less expensive to produce, send, and store.

Those same technologies also present challenges. Information managers must deal with viruses, hackers, software glitches, and hardware failures. Digital records must be protected and stored securely. Upgrading to the latest most secure technology can be expensive. Businesses are working hard to find ways to meet those challenges.

checkpoint ✓
Identify four important types of business operations.

TOOLS FOR BUSINESS OPERATIONS

Several tools help people manage the day-to-day operations of a business. They include management tools and technology tools.

Management Tools

Operations activities require continuous management attention. The activities must be carefully planned, implemented, and controlled. Operations activities are the work completed to help a business achieve its goals. Operational plans are developed in each area of a business to identify necessary activities. An **operational plan** identifies how work will be done, who will do it, and what resources will be needed. An operational plan for the production area of a factory determines when each product will be produced. It assigns production activities and determines the number of employees needed. It also schedules adequate supplies of resources. In a marketing department, the operational plan will match salespeople to customer groups, outline the sales plan, and schedule promotional activities. The operational plan for marketing must be coordinated with the production operational plan. Together the plans must ensure that enough products are produced to meet customer demand and all inventory is sold.

Several management tools support the operational plans. An *operating budget* is a detailed financial plan for a specific area of the business. An operating budget is prepared for the production unit, the marketing department, and every other area of the business. The budgets help managers determine the amount of money needed for planned operations as well as how and when the money will be spent. The budgets will anticipate all types of operating expenses and areas of income, if any, for the specific area of the business.

A **schedule** is a time plan for completing activities. Schedules match people with resources to make sure activities are finished on time. A supervisor develops a weekly work schedule for employees. An inventory manager prepares a schedule of suppliers' deliveries of raw materials. An advertising manager makes up a schedule that coordinates television and newspaper advertising.

How can an ATM affect work schedules for a bank?

A *procedure* is a list of steps to be followed for performing a particular work activity. To maintain the quality of an activity and make sure it is completed as quickly as possible, a company may set up operating procedures. Employees are trained to follow those procedures. Following procedures and schedules helps employees coordinate their work with others.

A **standard** is a specific measurement against which an activity or result is judged. Businesses set standards for key activities to make sure an appropriate level of quality is maintained. The standard may state the number of products that should be finished on an assembly line. It may set the number of customers that should be served in a fast-food restaurant in a stated time period. It may also establish an acceptable number of product defects or customer complaints for those operations. Standards must be clear and realistic. By establishing standards and using them to measure performance, employees will know what is expected of

WORK *as a* TEAM

Work with your team to agree on the procedure that should be used to make a cash withdrawal at an ATM. Record the procedure by listing the steps on a sheet of paper. Share the procedure with another team and see if they agree with the steps.

them and the quality of operations should remain high.

Using Technology to Manage Operations

Using technology to help manage operations will make planning and decision-making more accurate, rapid, and timely. It also makes it easier to access and exchange information. The exchange may occur within a company, with other business partners, or with customers. Some of the most important software used in businesses to manage operations is described in Figure 13-2.

New types of software are now available to assist with supply chain management and support virtual collaboration

COMMON TYPES OF OPERATIONS SOFTWARE	
Project Management	Keeps track of project calendars, tasks, to-do lists, work assignments, and project resources.
Budgeting	Automates budget planning, compares budgets from one time period to another, and coordinates budgets among departments.
Scheduling	Manages employee, facility, resource, and production scheduling. Allows easy review of schedules by all participants as well as quick updating.
Inventory	Helps the management of sales, purchases, and payments; tracks production, usage, and sales levels; and even prints bar codes.
Computer Security	Provides access and restrictions, usage data, privacy, and virus protection for computers and networks.
Document Management	Controls the production, storage, management, and distribution of electronic documents.
Manufacturing Automation	Monitors and often controls manufacturing machines, checks for errors and defects, and reports on production levels.

▶ **Figure 13-2**

What are the advantages of using software designed for a specific purpose?

of team members. *Supply chain management* software allows cooperating companies to share ordering, production, and shipping information, track products, and exchange customer data. *Collaboration software* (also called *groupware*) provides real-time communications capabilities by voice, text, and video. It also allows team members working at their own computers from anywhere in the world to view the same documents on their computer screens and work on them as a team. Some companies are replacing software on individual computers with *cloud computing*. Needed software, resources, and work files are maintained on a common server and accessed by employees when needed.

How have advances in technology changed the coordination of supply chain activities?

Photodisc/Getty Images

checkpoint ✓

What are the benefits of using technology to help manage business operations?

13-3 Assessment

Study Tools

www.cengage.com/school/genbus/pob

Key Concepts

Determine the best answer.

1. Which of the following is a part of facilities management?
   a. personnel scheduling
   b. logistics
   c. energy and environmental management
   d. information management

2. A(n)_____?_____is a time plan for completing activities.
   a. budget
   b. schedule
   c. operating plan
   d. standard

3. True or False. Document management software keeps track of project calendars, tasks, to-do lists, work assignments, and project resources.

Make Academic Connections

4. **Math** Use the information that appears in the FYI feature in this lesson to calculate the amount lost to employee theft, shoplifting, administrative errors, and vendor fraud in the following situations:
   a. Assume that the total U.S. retail sales losses for last year were $38.6 billion. Calculate the losses in each category.
   b. Assume that one retailer had total sales of $128.6 million for the year and losses were 7 percent of sales. Calculate the total value of the losses and calculate the losses in each category.

5. **Writing** A small business owner has been using the Internet to communicate with customers and suppliers. The company will soon add a catalog to its website with purchasing capabilities. Write a one-page memo to the owner that discusses security issues that the business may encounter. Make three recommendations of ways to protect the business and customers.

Designs That Make a Difference

When the hostilities in Kosovo ended in 1999, nearly three-quarters of a million refugees came back from nearby countries where they had fled for safety. They found their homes destroyed. They had no place to live. They needed some form of shelter and protection while they rebuilt their houses.

In 2003, an earthquake hit southern Iran, killing thousands. It left cities in rubble and most of the people homeless. There seemed to be no solutions to rebuild homes rapidly and inexpensively or to provide needed services.

HIV/AIDS spread quickly through the continent of Africa during the 1990s. There were few local medical facilities. Without local health centers, it would be almost impossible for health workers to treat the disease and educate people about risks and prevention.

Architecture for Humanity took on those challenges by using the professional skills of the organization's members. It sponsored an open competition to design five-year transitional housing for the returning Kosovars. More than 200 architects and designers from 30 countries submitted plans. Architecture for Humanity worked with Relief International in Iran to raise funds and help with the design and construction of medical clinics, schools, and water supplies. To meet the HIV/AIDS crisis in Africa, the organization challenged architects and health care professionals to submit designs for a mobile HIV/AIDS health clinic that would be easy to deploy and maintain, be accepted by the communities in which they would be located, and not be expensive to build and operate.

When Hurricane Katrina devastated much of the Gulf coast of the United States in 2005, Architecture for Humanity quickly used its membership to connect displaced families and individuals with architects and designers. The group worked to help make difficult decisions about what could be salvaged and rebuilt and to plan new designs for homes and businesses that met more stringent building codes.

Architecture for Humanity was the brainchild of Cameron Sinclair, who was trained as an architect at the Bartlett School of Architecture in London. He has a long-term interest in building designs that meet social, cultural, and humanitarian goals. His postgraduate research focused on providing shelter to homeless people on the streets of New York. In 1999, he formed a nonprofit organization to encourage architects and designers from around the world to contribute their expertise to help communities in need. The organization sponsors competitions and educational programs. It solicits architects to donate time and effort to improve lives. Recently, the editor of the *Architectural Record* wrote, "Architecture for Humanity represents the finest of the new breed of architectural leadership, employing architectural skills and directing them for the larger good. Architecture for Humanity stands up for people in need."

What kinds of businesses might be involved in projects to help people rebuild their homes after a disaster?

Think Critically

1. Use the Internet to locate additional information about Architecture for Humanity and to view examples of its designs and projects. Write a short paragraph describing one of the current or completed projects.

2. Suggest other professions that could contribute to solving social and humanitarian problems and the types of skills and expertise each profession could contribute.

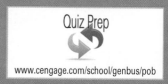

Business Notes

13-1 Types of Production

- Producers are businesses that develop products to be sold to other businesses or consumers. Consumers need products and services to satisfy their needs and wants. Businesses also need products and services to be incorporated into the products they produce, to be used in operations, and for resale to their customers. The three forms of production are extraction and cultivation, processing, and manufacturing.

- Manufacturing businesses can organize production in several ways to produce products. The types of manufacturing procedures are mass production, custom manufacturing, and materials processing.

13-2 Production Planning

- Production and manufacturing processes are very complex. They need to be carefully planned and coordinated. Product planning involves two steps—new product research and product design. Production planning includes three activities: a production process is developed, production resources are obtained, and production personnel

are identified and prepared. Inventory management maintains the supply of all of the resources needed for production and the products produced.

- The type of product and production process will determine how the work area is organized. Manufacturers face many challenges including the need for faster production, increased quality, and reduced costs.

13-3 Planning and Managing Business Operations

- The day-to-day operations of a business often determine its success or failure. Businesspeople need to plan business operations as carefully as they work to satisfy their customers or plan for new products. Common types of business operations are facilities management, logistics, scheduling, and safety and security.

- Several tools help people manage the day-to-day operations of a business. They include management tools and technology tools.

Communicate Business Concepts

1. Provide two examples for each of the three categories of products. For each example, identify one consumer use and one business use of the product.

2. What are the major differences between a processing business and a manufacturing business? What, if any, are the similarities between the two types of producers?

3. Why are several manufacturers usually a part of the total activity needed to produce a product? Why do you believe most manufacturers do not want to or are unable to complete the entire manufacturing process for a product?

4. How does the approach scientists use for pure research differ from the approach used for applied research? Why would a company choose to use one type of research over the other?

5. Identify three new products that appear to have been developed using applied research. Then identify three products that appear to have been developed based on results from pure research. What differences, if any, do you see in the types of products that result from each type of research?

6. What are the advantages for a company and for employees in using an employee team to assemble a product rather than the traditional assembly line where each employee completes a specific task?

7. Why should business partners and customers be involved in a continuous improvement process? What can they offer that managers and employees cannot?

8. For each of the following types of businesses, identify a business operation that would be unique to that business and not to the others:

   a. Hospital
   b. Law firm
   c. Dairy farm
   d. Internet service provider
   e. Taxi service

9. Make one recommendation to a retail business that would help reduce losses from each of the following sources: employee theft, shoplifting, administrative errors, vendor fraud.

10. In what ways has the Internet improved communications within a business and among businesses? What issues and problems have developed because of the use of the Internet for business communications?

Develop Your Business Language

Match the terms listed with the definitions.

11. The best practices used by competitors.

12. Managing the acquisition, movement, and storage of supplies, materials, and finished products in a business.

13. Changes the form of raw materials so they can be consumed or used to manufacture other products.

14. Studies existing products to develop design improvements or new product uses.

15. Products are obtained from nature or grown using natural resources.

16. Combines raw materials and processed goods into finished products.

17. Increases the quality of work by reducing errors, inefficiencies, and waste.

18. An assembly process that produces a large number of identical products using a continuous, efficient procedure.

19. A specific measurement against which an activity or result is judged.

20. Identifies how work will be done, who will do it, and what resources will be needed.

21. Goods arrive when needed for production, use, or sale rather than sitting in storage.

22. Changing and improving the form of another product.

23. Building a specific and unique product to meet the needs of each customer.

24. The activities, equipment, and resources needed to manufacture a product.

25. Time plans for completing activities.

26. Done without a specific product in mind with the goal of discovering new solutions to problems.

Key Terms

a. applied research
b. benchmarks
c. continuous process improvement (CPI)
d. custom manufacturing
e. extraction and cultivation
f. just-in-time
g. logistics
h. manufacturing
i. mass production
j. materials processing
k. operational plan
l. processing
m. production process
n. pure research
o. schedule
p. standard

Make Academic Connections

27. Science Identify several natural resources that are extracted and processed in your state. Using the Internet, print a map of your state. Mark and label the primary sources of those resources on the state map. List one company that is involved in the extraction or processing of each of the natural resources.

28. Economic Geography Some manufacturers locate their businesses very close to the sources of supply for the materials they need for production. Others locate closer to their main customers. Identify three manufacturers that fit each of those categories. Based on the types of products produced by the companies in each category, suggest reasons for the location decisions.

29. History Research the history of manufacturing in the United States from 1900 to the present. Prepare a visual timeline that identifies 15 events, products, and people that had a significant influence on manufacturing procedures during that time. To add perspective to the timeline, include 10 historical events such as presidential elections.

30. Reading Pure and applied research is an ongoing activity of businesses, universities, and government agencies. Use the Internet to locate a news report of a current research project that holds promise for a new product or product improvement. Based on your reading, write a short sidebar article that could be posted online describing the research and the potential future benefits of the research to consumers.

31. Math In 2010, *Fortune* magazine identified the top five U.S. manufacturers and processors. The companies and their 2009 sales and profits are shown in the table below.

COMPANY	TOTAL SALES (in millions)	PROFIT (in millions)
Exxon Mobil	$284,650	$19,280
Chevron	163,527	10,483
General Electric	156,779	11,025
ConocoPhillips	139,515	4,858
Ford Motor	118,308	2,717

a. Determine the total sales and net profit earned by all five companies combined.

b. What percentage of each company's sales is represented by its net profit?

Decision-Making Strategies

Eric Elongue has worked in construction his entire life. He worked part-time with a small contractor while completing his bachelor's degree in Construction Management at Eastern State University. Since then, he has been employed full-time for the past 15 years in increasingly responsible positions with a national homebuilder. He now wants to start his own home construction business. He is deciding between two options for his business.

OPTION A: Use a mass-production process in which he builds four models of homes. Customers can choose one of the four models, but cannot customize them. With this business model, Eric can build 20 homes a year. His work crews will not need to be as skilled. Materials and operating costs will be 10 percent lower than the industry average.

OPTION B: Build custom houses in which each home is specifically designed for the homebuyer. Eric's company will only be able to build 12 custom homes a year. It will require workers with much higher construction skills, and his costs will be 15 percent higher than the industry average. If he is able to maintain quality, he will be able to command premium prices for the custom homes.

32. What are the advantages and disadvantages of each option from the viewpoint of (a) managing business operations and (b) controlling quality and costs?

33. What option would you recommend to Eric? Why?

Linking School and Community

Safety and security has become an important issue for families, communities, and businesses. Interview several members of your community. Discuss their concerns about personal safety and security. Prepare a list of recommendations that could be followed in your community that address the safety and security concerns you heard. For each recommendation, identify who should be responsible for implementing the recommendation and the procedures that need to be followed.

©sweetym/iStock

Web Workout

Businesses and organizations are "going green" to protect the environment and reduce energy use and waste. Use the Internet to locate articles that describe the ways that green practices are being used in business. Look for specific examples related to building design, energy, the environment, and product design.

Think Critically

1. Develop a table that summarizes the green business practices you found using the following headings: Building Design, Energy and the Environment, Product Design.

2. Using the information from the table, prepare a poster that illustrates several important green business practices.

Buying and Merchandising Team Decision-Making Event

Teams consisting of two students will participate in this event. Each team will have 30 minutes to develop their plan of action based on the scenario presented. Teams have ten minutes to present a detailed strategy to the owners (judge or class).

Martin Furniture is a high-volume furniture store located in a large city in the United States. Last year the company developed a website and now sells merchandise throughout the country. The company offers free delivery to locations within a 50-mile radius of the store. Fees for delivery to points further away are determined by the distance between the store and the destination.

The Martin Furniture warehouse employs more than 200 workers to receive, prepare, and deliver furniture. The owners of the company count on a smooth, accident-free operation. Employees are expected to understand how to prevent damage to furniture and use safe procedures to avoid accidents and injuries.

The owners receive regular, detailed reports about the company's warehouse operation. The reports include quantity of damaged furniture, number of accidents in the warehouse, and unaccounted for furniture. Recent reports indicate a noticeable increase in warehouse accidents since Martin Furniture expanded delivery service throughout the country. These accidents have resulted in injuries to employees and damage to merchandise. The amount of damaged furniture has increased by 30 percent. When damaged, the furniture must be repaired and then resold at a 40 percent discount. The reports also indicate a 10 percent jump in the amount of merchandise that has disappeared. The owners are particularly concerned about this information because they believe that employee theft may be responsible for most of the missing furniture.

The owners of Martin Furniture have asked your operations and loss prevention team to develop a strategy that will reduce the amount of damaged furniture, injuries to warehouse employees, and the amount of missing furniture.

Performance Indicators Evaluated

- Recommend a plan to maintain a safe work environment.
- Develop a plan that will help enforce safety precautions.
- Analyze business systems and procedures.
- Explain how employees have a responsibility for the company's profitability.
- Explain security monitoring systems in a warehouse setting.
- Describe company strategies to strengthen employee commitment and honesty.
- Establish policies/procedures for preventing internal theft.

For more detailed information about performance indicators, go to the DECA website.

Think Critically

1. Why does business expansion sometimes result in operations problems and financial losses?

2. How can Martin Furniture monitor activity in the warehouse?

3. Why must all employees be involved with saving money for the business operation?

4. How can a company develop and maintain a workforce that demonstrates honesty and dependability?

www.deca.org

CHAPTER

14 Risk Management

shaunl/iStockphoto.com

Planning a Career in ...

RISK ANALYSIS

Consumers and businesses buy insurance for protection against risks. When people who have insurance are injured, need health care, or suffer property damage, insurance companies pay for some or all of the costs. Insurance companies rely on actuaries to determine the premiums needed to cover the costs. Actuaries determine the amount of risk insurance companies face and set the rates charged. They also evaluate investments to maximize the company's return.

Although actuaries work in all parts of the economy, many work in financial services businesses. Many actuaries work for insurance companies and consulting firms. Corporations and state and federal governments also employ actuaries. In order to demonstrate knowledge and skill to employers, colleagues, and clients, actuaries complete a series of professional exams. Since 1988, the *Jobs Rated Almanac* has rated the job of actuary as one of the five best jobs in the United States.

Related Job Titles

- Actuarial Assistant
- Pension Analyst
- Chief of Analytics
- Senior Actuary
- Chief Risk Officer
- Actuarial Consultant
- Risk Modeler
- Health Actuary

Analyze Career Opportunities in ...

RISK ANALYSIS

Use library and Internet resources to learn more about careers in risk analysis. Choose one of the job titles listed in the box above and answer the following questions.

1. How would you describe the nature of the work? Include examples of things that might happen in a typical work day.

2. Is this a career that interests you? What can you do now to help prepare yourself for this career?

What's it like to work as an ... Actuary?

After Janine graduated from college, she obtained her first job working for a large health insurance company as an actuarial assistant. During the first year, she worked on a project that will help employers reduce medical claims by emphasizing employee wellness and fitness. She worked with a team to develop a questionnaire to gather cost information from employers.

Janine was happy to learn her company encourages its actuaries to prepare for and pass the series of professional exams. New employees met twice a month with experienced actuaries for study sessions. Janine completed the first exam while in college. Since she started working, she has passed another exam and is preparing for the next one.

While her work is hectic, she enjoys the variety of the projects. "No day is like any other day," Janine stated. "You have to like pressure and tight deadlines." Eventually, she hopes to move into a management position and then maybe into consulting, with the goal of owning her own business.

What about you? What would you find interesting and rewarding about the work Janine is doing for her employer? Are there things you wouldn't like about being an actuary?

341

14-1 Overview of Risk Management

Goals

1 Identify the types of risks facing businesses.

2 Describe ways that businesses can deal with risks.

Key Terms

risk 342

economic risk 343

personal risk 343

property risk 343

liability risk 343

pure risk 343

controllable risk 343

insurance 343

Focus on REAL LIFE

As Jamie walked away from the cell phone kiosk, he was facing two important decisions. He had found a cell phone with all of the features he wanted. It was a bit more expensive than he anticipated, but he had enough money. The monthly plan was affordable with the services he wanted. The salesperson told Jamie he could save $100 on the price of the phone if he would sign a two-year contract with the wireless service provider. Yet if he cancelled the service during that time, he would have to pay the company up to $200. The service provider was a new company and Jamie wasn't sure he would like their service or the phone enough to commit to two years.

In addition, the salesperson offered Jamie a protection plan for an additional $4.95 a month that would provide a replacement if Jamie's phone is damaged or lost. Jamie had never lost his phone but knew of several friends who had. He knew he could not afford to replace the phone.

As Jamie walked away, he was thinking about the contract and the protection plan. He would have to think about the costs versus the risks before making a final decision.

Goal 1

Identify the types of risks facing businesses.

IDENTIFYING RISKS

Every day you face risks. **Risk** is the possibility of incurring a loss. You face many types of risks and possible losses. Some are very important to you and can have long-term effects. The risk of a serious illness or an accident that results in an injury would have a major impact on your life. A hurricane, tornado, or fire can leave homes, businesses, and even entire communities damaged or ruined.

Other risks are inconvenient but have little lasting effect. If you are caught in traffic, you risk being late for an appointment. When you buy a new product, you risk that it might go on sale in two weeks. Even if you are very careful, you cannot avoid all risks and losses. Still, individuals and businesses need to be aware of risks and try to reduce possible losses, especially for those

Can you think of reasons for buying an extended warranty on a product you just purchased?

risks that may result in physical or financial harm.

Types of Risks

There are many ways of viewing risks. Being able to identify the type of risk helps to determine how to plan for the risk. Planning for a risk may reduce the chance that it will occur or reduce its impact if it does occur.

Economic and Non-Economic Risks An **economic risk** can result in financial loss. There are three categories of economic risks. A **personal risk** can result in personal losses such as health and personal well-being. A **property risk** can lead to loss of personal or business property including money, vehicles, and buildings. A **liability risk** relates to harm or injury to other people or their property because of your actions.

Non-economic risks may result in inconvenience or discomfort but do not have a financial impact. A traffic accident is an economic risk. It can result in expenses such as medical care, automobile repairs, and higher insurance rates. Deciding with your friends to perform at the school talent show is a non-economic risk. You may be uncomfortable or embarrassed if the show does not go well, but you won't suffer financially.

Pure and Speculative Risks A **pure risk** presents the chance of loss but no opportunity for gain. Severe weather is an example of a pure risk. The storm may pass with no harm to a business. A heavy snowstorm that causes the business to close for a day or two will reduce sales. Wind and rain damage to a building will add to expenses because of the cost of repairs.

Speculative risks offer the chance either to gain or to lose. Suppose you invest your money in a new business. If it is successful,

What unexpected economic and non-economic issues may result from a traffic accident?

Photodisc/Getty Images

you will make a nice profit. On the other hand, if it fails you can lose all of the money you invested.

Controllable and Uncontrollable Risks A **controllable risk** can be reduced or eliminated by actions you take. To prevent loss from theft, businesses install security systems, hire guards, and train employees to be alert for possible problems. *Uncontrollable risks* cannot be reduced by your actions. A sudden hailstorm or prolonged drought can affect a farmer's crops and little can be done to reduce the losses suffered.

Insurable and Uninsurable Risks People look for ways to protect themselves from the negative effects of risks. A common form of protection is insurance. **Insurance** exchanges the uncertainty of a possible large financial loss for a certain smaller payment. If a large number of people face a given risk and the cost of possible losses can be predicted, it is an *insurable risk*. If a risk is not common or if it is impossible to predict the amount of loss that could be suffered, it is an *uninsurable risk*.

> **checkpoint** ✓
> What is risk?

Goal 2

Describe ways that businesses can deal with risks.

DEALING WITH RISKS

Suppose you and nine of your friends each have a new set of golf clubs. Each set is worth about $600. You all decide to form the GolfFriends Association (GFA). The purpose of GFA is to reduce the risk of a large financial loss should one member's clubs get stolen. To provide protection, each member agrees to share the cost of replacing a set of stolen clubs. You all agree on a replacement cost of $600. Therefore each member contributes $60 to a golf club replacement insurance fund. If you are not a member of the GFA and your clubs were stolen, you would have to pay the total cost of new clubs—$600. As a member, replacing your stolen clubs costs you only $60. Figure 14-1 illustrates the costs for members and non-members.

By contributing to the insurance fund, each member suffers only a relatively small economic loss. In that way, the members help one another by sharing the risk of economic loss.

Everyone faces risks. Many of these risks will result in financial damage or possible disaster if the loss is severe. Individuals and businesses must determine how they will deal with the risks and possible losses they face. Figure 14-2 on page 345 shows that there are four possible ways to deal with risks: avoid, transfer, insure, and assume.

Avoid the Risk

With thought and planning, you might be able to avoid some risks. If you don't believe you have enough experience or skill to start your own business, you can decide not to become an entrepreneur. If a snowstorm is in the forecast, you can choose not to drive your car to avoid a possible accident. If market research suggests there may not be enough demand for a new product to cover the costs, a business can choose not to make that product.

In order to avoid risks, decision-makers need to be aware of risks that can threaten a decision. They must determine the costs and possible rewards of their decisions. They must estimate the size of losses if anticipated problems occur. If the likelihood of risk or the amount of loss is too great, they may make the decision to avoid the action. This ensures that there will be no loss.

Transfer the Risk

Sometimes an activity must occur even though there is a risk that can have serious financial consequences. If a business is not in a position to assume the risk, it may choose to transfer it. When a business transfers a risk, someone else assumes the risk. A company may not be able to afford losses that it could suffer if the company offers customer credit and several credit customers do not pay their bills. In that situation, the company may transfer the risk of offering credit to a bank or credit card company. These businesses already have a credit operation. They are able to manage credit customers more effectively.

COST TO REPLACE ONE SET OF STOLEN GOLF CLUBS		
Total Cost ÷ Number of People	= Cost Per Person	
GFA members	$600 ÷ 10 = $60	
Non-members	$600 ÷ 1 = $600	

▶ **Figure 14-1**

Would you want to pay for someone else's clubs if you believed you could take care of your own clubs to make sure they were not stolen?

They are also in a position to handle larger credit losses. The bank or credit card company will be willing to accept the risk of credit sales with the likelihood that they can make a profit on fees paid by the company on credit sales and interest paid by credit customers.

A company can transfer the risk of product damage by using other channel members to store and distribute products. A manufacturer can transfer the risk of a costly or unsuccessful research process by forming a joint venture with an experienced research firm. The cost of the research will be shared with the other company that already employs experienced researchers. If the research is successful, the manufacturer will produce and sell the product. It will then share the profits with the research partner.

Insure the Risk

If a business faces the same type of risk also faced by others and the size of losses

FOUR POSSIBLE WAYS TO DEAL WITH RISK	
METHOD	**ACTIVITY**
Avoid	Choose not to complete the risky activity
Transfer	Find another business to complete the activity
Insure	Purchase insurance to pay for any losses
Assume	Complete the activity with full responsibility

► **Figure 14-2**
What method would you use to avoid the risk of your cell phone being stolen?

can be reasonably predicted, it is possible to purchase insurance. In the case of the GolFriends Association described earlier, each club owner insured the risk of stolen clubs by paying a small amount to the Association. In the same way, businesses that face the risk of fire damage to their buildings, equipment, and inventories can pool those risks with other businesses by purchasing fire insurance.

It is possible that a few businesses will have losses from fires during a specific period. Based on the history of fires in businesses, experts can reasonably estimate the total amount of fire damage among a number of businesses for that amount of time. Each business will pay a small amount for insurance that will cover the losses of the businesses that suffer a loss from fire.

Assume the Risk

Some companies decide that they are willing to assume certain risks. That means that if they suffer a loss, they will deal with the result. Typically, if a business decides to assume a risk, it means that the result of damage will not have serious negative consequences on the business. The company believes available funds can cover any financial loss.

A very large business may choose to set aside a small amount of money each month rather than purchasing insurance.

How can golfers deal with the possible risk of having their golf clubs stolen?

Work with your team to recognize several risks that could affect your school, students, staff, and visitors. Identify one or more risks that fit each of the following types: economic, non-economic, controllable, and uncontrollable. Discuss how the identified risks could be reduced.

They believe that if a financial loss occurs because of a risk, there will be enough money saved to cover the amount of the loss.

In other situations, it may not be possible to avoid, transfer, or insure a risk. If that is the case, the business will need to assume the risk. Once a business produces or purchases a product for resale, it must be able to sell the products at a reasonable price in order to cover its costs. If the sales goals are not met, the business suffers a loss. It assumes the risk of being able to sell its inventory at a profit.

Some risks are so unlikely that the company decides to do nothing. It assumes a problem will not occur. The company may be forced to take emergency actions if it is wrong. A company hires enough employees to operate the business. Company managers know a few extra employees are needed because at any time a certain number will be on vacation, sick, or absent for other reasons. If the company is suddenly hit with a major flu epidemic, there may not be enough employees available to run the business for a few days. Managers will have to decide whether to hire temporary employees, reduce some operations, or even close the business until employees recover.

> **checkpoint** ✓
> Identify four ways that a business can deal with risks.

14-1 Assessment

Study Tools

www.cengage.com/school/genbus/pob

Key Concepts

Determine the best answer.

1. True or False. Every risk you face results in a loss.

2. Which of the following is not a type of economic risk?
   a. personal risk
   b. property risk
   c. liability risk
   d. All are economic risks.

3. Using another business to complete a risky activity is known as _?_ the risk.
   a. assuming
   b. avoiding
   c. transferring
   d. insuring

4. True or False. To be insurable, the same type of risk must be shared by a large number of businesses or individuals.

Make Academic Connections

5. **Geography** Storms, earthquakes, and other natural disasters are often very costly to individuals, businesses, and communities. Millions of dollars in damages are suffered. It takes months and even years to recover. Use the Internet to identify the most costly natural disasters that have occurred in recent years. Identify the type of disaster, the country or region affected, and the estimated financial costs of each. Prepare a table to report your findings.

6. **Critical Thinking** Think carefully about the types of risks you and other family members face as a part of your daily lives. Make a list of 10 such risks. Classify each risk as controllable or uncontrollable and justify each of your classification decisions. For each of the controllable risks, describe actions you and your family members can take to reduce the risk or the possible damage that could occur.

21st Century Skills

Initiative and Self-Direction

Reducing Personal Risks with Lifestyle Choices

The decisions people make about lifestyles are by far the most important factors influencing their health. The U.S. Centers for Disease Control and Prevention report that several key factors influence a person's well-being.

- Quality of medical care, 10%
- Heredity, 18%
- Living and working environment, 19%
- Lifestyle choices, 53%

People want to live long, healthy, and happy lives. Even so, the day-to-day choices you make can result in poor physical and emotional health, accidents, and relationship problems. Your lifestyle reflects your activities, values, beliefs, and behaviors. Day-to-day choices also have an impact on your long-term health and happiness. Making risky choices or failing to be concerned about your physical and emotional health can have negative consequences. These consequences may be hard to overcome or even life-threatening.

Making positive lifestyle choices now and throughout your lifetime is key to reducing personal risks.

Nutrition Eat a balanced diet that includes a variety of foods. Select foods that promote energy and health. Don't overeat or eat too little. Avoid excessive snacking or foods and beverages filled with empty calories.

Physical Activity Maintain an active schedule involving enjoyable physical activities. Take part in activities that exercise your heart, strengthen muscles, and build flexibility. Develop skills in physical activities you can enjoy all of your life.

Medical Care Schedule regular visits with your doctor, dentist, and eye-care specialist. Actively participate in your medical care by providing accurate and complete information, asking questions, and following the advice of your health care providers.

Emotional Health Stay active mentally and emotionally. Develop friendships, but also take time for yourself. Take on creative activities. Develop positive emotional energy. Don't be afraid to discuss your feelings or seek help from counselors and mentors.

How can interpersonal relationships affect your emotional health?

Interpersonal Relationships Spend time with family and friends. Avoid using negative communications that others can easily misinterpret. Be open to people with different backgrounds and experiences. Resolve conflicts before they create problems or affect long-term relationships.

Personal Development Set personal, academic, and career goals and make plans to achieve them. Commit to lifelong learning.

Personal Safety Think about the short- and long-term consequences of your decisions and actions. Reject risky behaviors including the use of tobacco, alcohol, and drugs. Drive safely, wear your seat belt, and avoid distractions. Think before participating in activities that can lead to accidents or injuries to you or others.

Think Critically

1. How can decisions made today affect your lifestyle in the future?
2. What additional recommendations can you make for a healthy and happy lifestyle?

Goals

1 Recognize important insurance concepts.

2 Describe several types of business insurance.

Key Terms

insurer 348

insured 348

policyholder 348

insurance policy 348

premium 348

claim 348

Focus on REAL LIFE

Samuel looked on as the fire trucks pulled out of the parking lot of his wholesale produce business. As he watched, his insurance agent, Jake, walked up.

"I'm really sorry about the fire, Samuel," Jake said. "Luckily it looks like they were able to prevent extensive damage to the building."

"Yes, the fire marshal talked to me," replied Samuel. "Even though most of the damage is from smoke and water, all the inventory will have to be replaced, and some of the equipment needs to be repaired. It will probably take several weeks to get back in business."

"We'll get to work immediately getting your insurance claims filed." Jake vowed. "I know you will need cash and we should have your first insurance check tomorrow."

"I'm certainly glad you convinced me to spend a bit more on extended coverage, Jake. I want to be able to continue to pay my employees while we recover."

Goal 1

Recognize important insurance concepts.

PURCHASING INSURANCE

Most people and businesses cannot afford to pay for large economic losses. However, they can buy insurance to provide the financial protection they need in the event they suffer a financial loss. Insurance enables them to share the risk with other individuals or businesses. It brings peace of mind. In the event of an accident, injury, or other loss, they can concentrate on recovery rather than how to pay for the loss.

Insurance Basics

Insurance companies provide planned protection against economic losses. The company, called an **insurer**, agrees to take on certain economic risks and to pay for losses if they occur. The person or business for which the insurer assumes the risk is the **insured**. To show that it has taken on the risk, the company issues a written contract, or insurance policy. The person or company buying the policy is the **policyholder**. An **insurance policy** states the conditions to which the insurance company and the policyholder have agreed. The amount the policyholder must pay for insurance coverage is a **premium**. The policyholder makes payments monthly, quarterly, every six months, or once a year. A **claim** is a policyholder's request for payment for a loss that the insurance policy covers.

Describe several examples of losses you might suffer that would prevent you from achieving your life-span goals. Explain why taking measures to reduce risks, including buying adequate insurance, is an important part of every person's life-span plan.

Insurance Companies

In addition to offering financial protection for policyholders, insurance companies are also investment companies. The premiums collected from the policyholders make up the funds from which the insurance company pays for claims. The company invests these premiums. The additional amount earned from these investments allows the company to make a profit while covering the costs of claims.

Insurance protection can be obtained in several ways. Individuals can buy insurance directly from an insurance company. Employers may provide insurance as an employee benefit. Professional organizations and other groups may offer insurance coverage to members. Businesses often offer insurance for customers to provide protection for related risks. When using credit, customers may want credit insurance. Shippers may offer transportation insurance. Security companies may provide theft insurance.

Many people purchase insurance from an insurance agent. An *insurance agent* represents the insurance company and sells insurance policies to individuals and businesses. A key part of an insurance agent's job is to help each client choose the proper kind and amount of protection from possible economic losses. Based on the client's choices the agent submits information to the insurance company that will prepare the policy.

There are two basic types of insurance agents. One works for a large insurance company and sells only policies written by that company. The other is an independent agent who may sell many kinds of policies from a number of different companies. You can also purchase insurance directly from an insurance company or through an agent using the Internet.

Most people are concerned about the type and cost of insurance when choosing an insurance company. Any time you purchase insurance, the offerings of several companies should be compared for features and prices. Another key factor is the service provided by the company if a loss occurs. When a loss is suffered, policyholders want to be able to rely on the insurance company to act quickly in providing help. It should be easy to contact the company. Their response should be

WORK as a TEAM

Have team members locate the websites of several insurance agents in your community. Identify the insurance company or companies that the agent represents and the types of insurance sold by each for consumers and for businesses. The team should prepare a spreadsheet classifying the insurance products of each agent.

What other types of insurance might an employer purchase on an employee's behalf besides health insurance?

Brand X Pictures/Getty Images

Goal 2

Describe several types of business insurance.

prompt. The process used to file a claim needs to be easy and understandable. Full reimbursement for losses covered by the policy should be processed as quickly as possible.

Insured Losses

Both consumers and businesses can buy insurance to cover almost any kind of economic loss. Violinists can insure their fingers. Professional athletes can insure against injuries. Writers may insure their manuscripts. Businesses can insure against the loss of property damaged by fire, injury to consumers resulting from the use of the company's product, or theft by employees.

The kinds of insurance protection that will be important to most consumers are vehicle, property, health, and life insurance. Businesses also insure their vehicles and property. They may provide health and life insurance for some or all employees. They also need liability insurance. *Liability insurance* protects against losses from injury to people or property resulting from the products, services, or actions of a business.

> **checkpoint** ✓
> What information should be considered when selecting an insurance company?

BUSINESS INSURANCE

A company uses its financial resources to invest in land, buildings, operating equipment, inventory, and people. If the business suffers a serious loss of any of these resources, the business may have trouble replacing the resources and continuing to operate. Businesses buy many types of insurance to obtain financial protection for their assets. Figure 14-3 illustrates the three major business insurance categories of personnel, property, and business operations.

Insuring Personnel

The health and well-being of managers and employees are important to a business. If workers are sick or injured, they will not be able to work. The costs of medical care are high. Costs will need to be paid by either the employee or the company. If an accident occurs on the job, the business will often be responsible for the cost of medical care and lost wages while the employee recovers. Businesses can purchase or allow employees to buy several types of insurance to provide protection for the costs of those risks.

Health Insurance Many businesses offer *health insurance,* which provides assistance with the high costs of individual health care. Health insurance provides payments for routine costs of medical care as well as

▶ **Figure 14-3**

What types of losses might a business face if each of these categories is not properly insured?

BUSINESS INSURANCE	
MAIN CATEGORIES	**EXAMPLES**
Personnel	• Health insurance • Group insurance • Disability insurance • Workers' compensation • Life insurance
Property	• Commercial property insurance • Vehicle insurance
Business Operations	• Business interruption insurance • Liability insurance

costs for hospitalization or other needed medical treatments. Businesses often offer group health insurance. With *group insurance,* the employees of a business and their dependents can be covered under one policy. A group insurance policy covers a large number of people, and premiums are paid for all members of the group. Therefore, the cost of insurance can be less than if each person bought a separate policy. Some companies pay for the entire cost of employee health insurance. Most pay a percentage of the cost and employees pay the remainder of the premium.

Disability Insurance *Disability insurance* provides payments to employees who are not able to work for an extended period due to serious illness or injury. The amount of payment is usually 50 to 70 percent of the employee's income. There is usually a maximum amount of money or time period for payments. A special type of disability insurance is known as workers' compensation. *Workers' compensation* is a system of insurance set up by state law that pays employees who are injured on the job. Each business makes payments to the insurance fund based on the number of employees.

Life Insurance Many businesses also offer *life insurance,* which pays the amount of the insurance policy upon the death of the insured. The payment is made to people named in the policy known as beneficiaries. Beneficiaries are usually family members of the insured. Partnerships often purchase a life insurance policy on each partner with the company named as beneficiary. This provides money that will be used to maintain the business operations that the deceased partner performed. Corporations often insure the lives of key executives or employees because of their importance to the company's success. Businesses may offer a small amount of life insurance for each employee or allow employees to purchase low-cost life insurance as a benefit.

Insuring Property

Businesses buy various types of insurance policies to protect the company's assets from losses that may result from a variety of risks. Businesses want to protect buildings and their contents including all inventories and operating equipment. Businesses owning automobiles and other vehicles want to insure those assets as well.

Commercial Property Insurance Most businesses own one or more buildings that would be expensive to replace. In addition, the buildings contain company assets such as equipment, supplies, raw materials, component parts, and finished goods. *Commercial property insurance* covers property losses resulting from fire, storms, accidents, theft, and vandalism. Special policies can be purchased to provide coverage for hazards unique to a location or the type of business.

Vehicle Insurance Businesses own and operate all types of commercial vehicles including cars, vans, light and heavy duty trucks, trailers, and other business vehicles. By purchasing commercial *vehicle insurance,* damages to the vehicles and occupants resulting from accidents are covered. Vehicle insurance also pays the costs of damage to the property of others as well as medical costs for those injured if people driving a company vehicle cause an accident.

Insuring Business Operations

A business may suffer financial losses resulting from the actions of employees or business operations. Those actions or operations may result in accidents, injuries, property damage, or other types of losses. Insurance can be purchased to protect against those losses. Two common types of insurance for business operations are business interruption insurance and liability insurance.

Business Interruption Insurance Most businesses cannot afford to shut down for a few days or weeks without sustaining an economic loss. *Business interruption insurance* provides compensation for ongoing business expenses that occur if a business has a temporary shutdown due to a covered hazard.

Liability Insurance Many businesses purchase *liability insurance* to cover claims by others based on damages suffered because of business operations, employees, or products. A customer may be injured while visiting the business. The use of a product may result in physical injury, illness, or even death. An employee may be dishonest or take action that injures another person. The business may be held financially liable for any of these situations.

Which types of business insurance policies might cover damage related to a fire?

Photodisc/Getty Images

> **checkpoint** ✓
> What are the three major areas that can be covered by business insurance?

14-2 Assessment

Study Tools
www.cengage.com/school/genbus/pob

Key Concepts

Determine the best answer.

1. The reason businesses and individuals purchase insurance is to
   a. make a profit
   b. provide financial protection
   c. reduce taxes
   d. increase sales

2. True or False. Another term for an insurance company is the policyholder.

3. True or False. An insurance agent can work for only one insurance company or may represent several.

4. Insurance that provides coverage for claims by others based on damages suffered as a result of business operations, employees, or products is
   a. health insurance
   b. property insurance
   c. vehicle insurance
   d. liability insurance

Make Academic Connections

5. **Debate** Prepare a paragraph to support the following statement: The maximum amount of damages that a company should have to pay to one individual for any liability claim should be $1 million. Write a second paragraph in opposition.

6. **Math** Before being hired, a new employee had an individual health insurance policy that costs $280 per month plus $225 per month for his spouse and two children. The company offers a group policy that costs $165 a month for an individual or $386.50 for the entire family. The company contributes 20 percent of the cost of the individual policy toward either choice.
   a. How much does the group policy reduce the annual cost of health insurance for the entire family without the company's contribution?
   b. What will employees pay for family health insurance for an entire year? What is the annual savings compared to the previous policy?

14-3 Uninsurable Risks

Goals

1 Describe why some business risks are uninsurable.

2 List the strategies a company can use to reduce the risks of doing business internationally.

Key Terms

property rights 357
counterfeiting 358

Focus on REAL LIFE

Sophia looked up from her computer when Josh entered the room and asked what she was doing.

"Reading about software piracy. It says here that Microsoft products dominate the Chinese market but the company is not happy. Most of their software has been pirated. That means Microsoft doesn't get paid for those products."

"I know people who have tried to make copies of computer software here in the U.S.," said Josh, "but our laws are strict. The penalties are severe if people are caught."

"According to this article, more than 80 percent of software used in China has been pirated resulting in losses of more than $7 billion to the legitimate owners. By comparison, the U.S. piracy rate is 20 percent" Sophia reported.

"I guess some people don't worry about big companies like Microsoft, but billions of dollars lost each year means all of us pay more for our legal copies."

IDENTIFYING AND MANAGING RISKS

Businesses cannot insure many of the risks they face. To be insurable, the risk and amount of loss must be predictable. If the chance that a risk will occur cannot be reasonably predicted or the possible financial loss to the business cannot be calculated, it is not likely that an insurance company will provide coverage. The costs of some risks are so high that a business cannot afford the cost of insurance protection. In that case, the business must determine other ways to deal with those uninsurable risks.

Uninsurable Risk Factors

Several factors can lead to business risks that can be very costly to a company. The factors are economic conditions, consumer demand, competitors' actions, technology changes, local factors, and business operations.

What are the economic results of illegally downloading digital music and video files from the Internet?

Goal 1

Describe why some business risks are uninsurable.

Economic Conditions When the economy is strong, consumers and business customers are more willing to spend money. Sales will be strong and profits high. A downturn in the economy can quickly reduce sales and profits. If the company does not cut production and expenses, it can experience real problems. Managers need to study the economy carefully. They must be prepared to respond to improvements or declines in economic conditions.

Consumer Demand Companies produce products that they think will meet consumer demand. They study customer needs and preferences. If they can predict a change in demand, they may be able to take advantage of the need with new products. If consumer tastes change, the company may end up with products in inventory that they are unable to sell at a profit.

Competitors' Actions Businesses function in a competitive environment. The actions of competitors can affect the success of a business. If a competitor starts a major advertising campaign or decides to reduce prices, a business will have to decide whether it needs to respond or not. The wrong decision can result in lost sales and profits or additional unneeded expenses. A new competitor may enter the market or a current competitor may introduce a new product. If a company is not prepared for these types of competitive actions, its share of the market can quickly decline.

Technology Changes What happened to traditional businesses when other companies started to use the Internet? If a company is not prepared to accept debit cards as a form of payment, will customers

What can brick-and-mortar stores do to retain traditional customers who have turned to the Internet for shopping?

Photodisc/Getty Images

take their business elsewhere? When consumers can download music and movies from websites, are brick-and-mortar music and video stores affected? Anytime technology changes, there is a possible effect on a business. The cost of putting new technology in place is usually high, but if the business doesn't adopt the technology, it may lose sales.

Local Factors The highway that runs in front of a fast-food business closes for a month for repair. The utility company serving the city has a 5 percent rate increase for the cost of electricity. The county zoning board rejects a business'

request to expand its production facilities. The laws, regulations, taxes, and infrastructure of a local community can have an influence on the operations of a business. Some businesses decide to relocate from one state or country to another to get conditions that are more favorable. Businesses work with government officials and community organizations to keep a positive environment for business.

Business Operations The day-to-day operations of a business can have a major impact on its success or failure. A poorly run business will have higher costs, low morale, increased turnover, and a poor

Business Insight for the 21st Century

Businesses Respond to a Disaster

When Hurricane Katrina hit New Orleans and the gulf coast of the United States, federal, state, and local governments struggled to respond to the devastation. Faced with a growing crisis, businesses sprang into action with the same efficiency and effectiveness they use in their day-to-day operations to respond to emergencies in communities affected by the storm and its aftermath. Thousands of businesses, large and small, demonstrated their commitment to aiding people in need with donations of money, equipment, materials, and employee time.

Before Katrina made landfall, Walmart had 45 trucks loaded with supplies at its Brookhaven, Mississippi, distribution center and ready for delivery. With 34,000 of its own employees affected by the storm, Walmart immediately promised and delivered $20 million in cash donations, 1,500 truckloads of free merchandise, and food for 100,000 meals.

Two home improvement giants, Home Depot and Lowe's, saw some of their own stores heavily damaged or destroyed from high winds and flooding. All along the storm's path managers and dedicated employees opened less-damaged stores within hours to provide generators and emergency supplies for their neighbors. In addition, Home Depot pledged more than $11 million and worked with volunteer organizations to rebuild more than 100 playgrounds and athletic fields that had been damaged or destroyed. Lowe's teamed with designer Marianne Cusato to develop plans and materials for small, permanent homes called Katrina Cottages as affordable alternatives to FEMA trailers for displaced residents and emergency workers.

Marriott Corporation committed to help its 2,800 employees who worked at 15 New Orleans hotels as they faced the loss of their jobs and

in some cases their homes. Many employees were bused to Houston where they were housed and fed in the ballroom of the Houston Airport Marriott while the company helped them find temporary housing and jobs.

These are just a few examples of the efforts made by businesses following Hurricane Katrina. They illustrate ways businesses respond to disasters and how their efforts can help communities and individuals recover.

Think Critically

1. Why are businesses willing to commit resources to help deal with emergencies that affect other areas as well as their own communities?

2. How might the expertise of businesses be used by government agencies to improve responses to future disasters and emergencies?

Photodisc/Getty Images

What security measures are put in place by retail stores to deter theft?

Businesses need to implement measures to gather information and spot possible problems. They should continually study all of the risk areas. Managers need to be aware of changes in the economy, competitors' actions, and technology. The business should collect and review customer information, including complaints and requests. It should carefully watch sales to identify which product sales are increasing and which are decreasing. It should monitor all operating costs to make sure they do not get out of control.

Businesses should inspect facilities and equipment to make sure they are running properly and safely. Careful employee hiring and ongoing training will also add to effective and safe operations. Businesses should put security measures in place to prevent theft and vandalism and to protect employees and customers. Important information and company records should be protected from all forms of possible damage. Backup copies should be prepared and stored in safe locations.

Businesses should be active in their local communities. They should work to develop and maintain a positive image. They should build relationships with community organizations, consumer groups, and local, state, and national government officials. Businesses must be aware of any proposed changes in laws and regulations that could affect operations. Careful study and planning followed by positive actions will have the greatest effect on reducing business risks.

customer image. A lack of employee training and poor management can lead to production errors, safety problems that result in accidents and injuries, poorly maintained equipment and facilities, and labor relations problems. If managers and employees are not committed to the success of the company, they will miss opportunities to improve operations, increase customer satisfaction, and control expenses.

Managing Risks

Each of the situations just described poses a risk to businesses. Alone, any of the risks can cause serious financial problems. If several occur at the same time, the business may not be able to survive. Uninsurable risks present important challenges to managers and employees.

Everyone in a business needs to be aware that there are many uninsurable risks. The business must inform them of the types of risks that are particularly important to their part of the operations. All employees must be watchful for changes that can lead to problems.

checkpoint ✓
What are several things businesses can do to manage risks?

RISKS IN INTERNATIONAL BUSINESS

As an international business manager, would you be willing to ship automobiles to a company in another country before receiving the payment? Would you agree to take another country's currency for payment instead of U.S. dollars? These are examples of risks faced by every organization involved in international business.

Strategies for Reducing Risk

To reduce international business risk, management experts advise the use of four strategies. First, carry out business in many countries. This approach reduces the risk faced when doing business in only one country or a single region. If turmoil occurs in one nation, causing lost sales and profits, the global company is covered with profits from other markets.

Next, offer a range of products. When an organization broadens its product line, reduced sales of one item will not mean complete failure for the company. Successful global organizations continually create new products, seek new uses for existing products, and look for new markets for their products.

Third, involve local business partners in business decisions and activities. Joint ventures with local companies help to reduce political and social risks. An agreement between a global company and a local business can help both organizations. In addition, the citizens and government of the host nation will be more welcoming to outsiders if a company they are familiar with is involved.

Finally, employ local management in key positions. Executives and other managers who are native to a country or region better understand the cultural and social norms and the political environment. This knowledge can help the international company adapt its product and business activities to the needs of the market being served.

International Property Rights

In some South American countries, local companies not connected to the National Basketball Association make shirts celebrating the championship of an NBA team. In China, street vendors illegally duplicate and sell copies of popular movies, music videos, and books. These are both examples of violations of property rights.

Property rights are the exclusive rights to possess and use property and its profits. This excludes everyone else from interfering with the use of the item. *Intellectual property* refers to technical knowledge or creative work. It includes software, clothing designs, music, books, and movies. For many companies, their intellectual properties are valuable assets that generate sales and profits. A *patent* is the exclusive right of an inventor to make, sell, and use a product or process. An inventor may obtain a patent on a computer component, a new package design, or a prescription drug. These inventions can give a company a competitive advantage. Patents are designed to encourage innovation and progress.

A *trademark* is a distinctive name, symbol, word, picture, or combination of these that a company uses to identify products or services. Common trademarks known around the world include the McDonald's golden arches and Target's red circles. A *copyright* protects the original works of authors, composers, playwrights, artists, and publishers. In the United States, a new copyright gives originators sole rights to publish and exhibit their creative works for their lifetime plus 70 years.

Goal 2

List the strategies a company can use to reduce the risks of doing business internationally.

WORK *as a* TEAM   Work with your team members to describe a possible joint venture between companies in two different countries. Explain why the businesses might want to work together. What are possible benefits for each organization? How might the venture reduce risks facing each company?

Most other countries have similar laws. There may be differences in the definitions and type of protection. Some countries do little to enforce property rights laws, especially when the products of a foreign company are involved. **Counterfeiting** refers to illegal uses of intellectual property, patents, trademarks, and copyrights. For example, a company may make slight changes in a well-known product and sell it in other countries. They are using the product illegally so they don't have to pay for the development costs of their own products or pay the original company for the product. By using the actual product name or trademark illegally, they are trying to profit from the reputation of the famous company. When property rights laws are not enforced, companies lose profits. This discourages them from participating in international trade.

Pasticcio/iStockphoto.com

Who is hurt by the sale of counterfeit goods such as handbags and watches?

> **checkpoint** ✓
> Why do U.S. companies have difficulty enforcing intellectual property rights in some international markets?

14-3 Assessment

Study Tools
www.cengage.com/school/genbus/pob

Key Concepts

Determine the best answer.

1. True or False. Every risk a business faces can be insured.

2. The growing use of the Internet as a business tool is an example of what type of business risk?
   a. economic conditions
   b. technology change
   c. consumer demand
   d. business operations

3. True or False. To reduce the risks of international business, a company should conduct business in many countries.

4. The exclusive right of an inventor to make, sell, and use a product or process is a
   a. trademark
   b. copyright
   c. patent
   d. None of the above is correct.

Make Academic Connections

5. **Economics** Use the business section of newspapers and business magazines to gather information on predictions for changes in the economy for the next 6 to 12 months. Based on this information, prepare a two-page written report for small business owners in your community identifying how the changes might affect their businesses in a positive or negative way.

6. **Business Law** Use the Internet to gather information on the fraudulent use of the intellectual property of U.S. businesses in other countries. Develop a table that identifies the U.S. company, the product that has been misused, the country or countries in which the fraud has occurred, and any action taken by the company to protect its property rights. Present the information in your table to other class members. Discuss the effect of the fraud on businesses and consumers.

Doing Business in...Costa Rica

With more than 130 protected parks, refuges, and reserves, the natural beauty of Costa Rica is the foundation of this country's pride and its main tourist attraction. People come from all over the globe to enjoy Costa Rica's jungles, mountains, oceans, wildlife, and exotic birds. A growing part of the tourism industry is ecotourism—enjoying natural areas while having a minimum impact on the environment.

Costa Rica is an independent democratic republic with a representative government made up of three branches: executive, legislative and judiciary with an elected president. It is one of the most peaceful and stable democracies in Latin America and the world.

The stable political and economic environment of Costa Rica makes it an attractive Latin American location for foreign business investment. Unlike many countries, full ownership of real estate and businesses by foreigners is allowed. The high educational standards of Costa Rica also make it appealing to international companies. In recent years, many low-skilled workers have moved from surrounding countries to take advantage of job opportunities. High-tech businesses including microchip and medical products producers are adding to the economic base of the country. Even as technology exports increase, traditional agricultural products, including coffee, bananas, sugar, and beef, continue to contribute to the country's total trade.

Business attire is more formal than in some tropical climates. Being well groomed adds to your credibility and respect. Men usually dress in suits for important business meetings. Women often wear dresses or skirts, but pants are becoming more common. Personal relationships are important in business and are developed over time. Handshakes are important as is the use of correct titles and surnames.

Black beans and rice are foundations of the Costa Rican diet. Breakfast may consist of *gallo pinto* (a combination of rice and beans). At lunch, rice and beans might be mixed with salad, eggs, or meat. Then, for the evening meal, you may have rice with chicken and, of course, beans. Always be on time for a business meal and other meetings. These visits are usually prearranged. In rural areas of the country, life is less formal. Quite often, people visit unannounced. When you arrive at the door, don't knock. Instead, shout *"Upe!"* This greeting in Costa Rica means "let me in" or "anybody home?"

Think Critically

1. How does doing business in Costa Rica differ from other countries?

2. What elements of Costa Rican society help to enhance the country's economic development?

3. Conduct library or Internet research to find additional information about business and economic activities in Costa Rica.

How does this photo of a person using a rainforest canopy walkway represent ecotourism in Costa Rica?

Business Notes

14-1 Overview of Risk Management

- There are many types of risks and possible losses. The main types of risks are economic and non-economic, pure and speculative, controllable and uncontrollable, and insurable and uninsurable. Individuals and businesses need to be aware of risks and attempt to reduce possible losses, especially those that may result in physical or financial harm.

- Individuals and businesses must determine how they will deal with the risks and possible losses they face. There are four possible ways to deal with risks: avoid the risk, transfer the risk, insure the risk, or assume the risk.

14-2 Insurable Risks

- Most individuals and businesses cannot pay for large economic losses, so they share the risk with other individuals or businesses. They purchase insurance to provide the needed financial protection in the event they suffer a financial loss.

- Businesses purchase a variety of types of insurance to obtain financial protection for their assets. Business insurance can be categorized within three major areas: personnel, property, and business operations.

14-3 Uninsurable Risks

- If the chance that a risk will occur cannot be reasonably predicted or the possible financial loss to the business calculated, it will be unlikely that an insurance company will provide coverage. The costs of some risks are so high that a business cannot afford the cost of insurance protection.

- To reduce international business risks, companies should conduct business in many countries, offer a variety of products, involve local business partners, and employ local management.

Communicate Business Concepts

1. Identify one personal, property, and liability risk faced by a family. Identify one of each that is faced by a business. Now identify a non-economic risk for an individual and for a business.

2. What are several controllable risks you and your friends might face? What are some uncontrollable risks you and your friends might face? What makes the risks you identified controllable or uncontrollable?

3. People and businesses can deal with risks in four ways. Identify the four ways and describe the advantages and disadvantages of each.

4. Under what circumstances should you consider buying insurance? Are there circumstances where you are facing an insurable risk and you would choose not to buy insurance? Why would you make that decision?

5. List several questions you would want answered about an insurance company before you decided to purchase insurance from the company.

6. Use the Internet to find information on buying flood insurance for homeowners and business owners. How is purchasing flood insurance different from purchasing other forms of property insurance? Who is required to purchase flood insurance?

7. Visit the website of a large employer in your community or region. Locate information about the insurance benefits that the company offers its employees. Determine the types of insurance offered, who is eligible for the insurance benefits, and whether the company pays some or all of the costs for the insurance premiums.

8. Identify a type of business you would consider owning or managing. What are some specific risks the business could face that would be uninsurable because the chance of the risk or the amount of loss cannot be easily predicted? What are some risks facing the business that could be very expensive to insure?

9. What information sources are available that could be used by businesspeople to keep track of changes in economic conditions that could affect their companies? What are some current economic conditions that could have a positive or negative effect on U.S. businesses?

10. Suggest several ways that a retail business can improve security to prevent theft of merchandise by customers and employees. In what ways can operations be changed or improved to reduce the chances of theft?

11. You own a small business that produces computer games. You are considering selling the games in several foreign countries. What risks might you face as you begin international trade that you didn't face in the United States? Which of the risks are controllable and which are uncontrollable? Identify several steps you could take to reduce these risks.

Develop Your Business Language

Match the terms listed with the definitions.

12. Agrees to take on certain economic risks and to pay for losses if they occur.

13. Those that can be reduced or eliminated by actions you take.

14. Illegal uses of intellectual property, patents, trademarks, and copyrights.

15. The amount the policyholder must pay for insurance coverage.

16. The person or business for which the risk is assumed.

17. Those that can result in financial loss.

18. The possibility of incurring a loss.

19. A policyholder's request for payment for a loss that is covered by the insurance policy.

20. The person or company purchasing the policy.

21. Presents the chance of loss but no opportunity for gain.

22. The exclusive rights to possess and use property and its profits.

23. States the conditions to which the insurance company and the policyholder have agreed.

24. Exchanges the uncertainty of a possible large financial loss for a certain smaller payment.

25. Can result in losses, such as health and personal well-being.

26. Can lead to a loss of personal or business items such as money, vehicles, and buildings.

27. Related to harm or injury to other people or their property because of your actions.

KEY TERMS
a. claim
b. controllable risk
c. counterfeiting
d. economic risk
e. insurance
f. insurance policy
g. insured
h. insurer
i. liability risks
j. personal risks
k. policyholder
l. premium
m. property rights
n. property risks
o. pure risk
p. risk

Make Academic Connections

28. Economics Speculative risks offer the chance to gain or to lose. People invest their money hoping to get a good return on the investment. Still, most investments have some risk, which means the money can be lost. Common investments are savings accounts, stocks, and real estate. Identify two additional investments. Prepare a table that describes and compares each of the investments in terms of their risk and possible gain or loss.

29. Writing You have been asked by a business owner to give advice on how to deal with a risk the business is facing. During the winter after an ice storm, the parking lot and sidewalks are often very slippery. There is a risk that employees and visitors may slip on the ice and be injured. Prepare a memo to the business owner describing some ways the business might deal with the risk. Recommend the actions that should be taken and reasons for your recommendations.

30. Technology Identify five insurance agents that sell business insurance in your area. Use a computer to create a database of information about the agents. Include the agent's name, agency name, address, telephone number, e-mail address, insurance company represented, and types of business insurance sold.

31. Reading Health care practitioners face many risks. Malpractice insurance provides protection if there is a lawsuit for problems resulting from a medical procedure. However, the cost of malpractice insurance is affecting the cost and availability of many medical services. Locate an article in a magazine, newspaper, or on the Internet that addresses the affect of the cost of malpractice insurance on health care. Use a computer presentation program to outline the major concepts presented in the article using bullet points.

32. Art Businesses try to reduce the number of accidents and injuries in their buildings by continually reminding employees of the importance of safety. Prepare a poster with an attention-getting message about safety and accident prevention that is appropriate for display in a business setting.

33. Business Research Identify a retailer in your community that has recently gone out of business. Gather information about the business by reviewing newspaper articles and Internet information sources. Identify factors that contributed to the business failure. Write a one-page report on the major risks the business faced and why each contributed to the business failure.

34. International Business Several unique types of insurance are available for companies that participate in international commerce. Use the Internet to identify five types of insurance a company buying or selling products in another country might need. Prepare a table that identifies each type of insurance, its purpose, and a company or organization that offers the insurance for sale.

Decision-Making Strategies

The Chrismann Company is a manufacturer of lawn equipment that it sells through garden centers in a 10-state region of the upper Midwest. To distribute its products, it maintains a fleet of 25 trucks. It also has 18 cars driven by its salespeople. The company recently finished a review of its vehicle insurance costs. Records show that the average cost to insure each truck is $960 a year and $725 for each car. Insurance claims filed for the past eight years averaged $31,200 a year. When studied closely, data show that claims in two of those years were less than $10,000 and for three years exceeded $45,000. The company's executives are considering canceling their vehicle insurance. They want to set up a fund using the money they currently pay to the insurance company. This fund would be used to pay costs of repairs and injuries resulting from any vehicle accidents.

35. If the average costs related to repairs and injuries continue for the next five years, how much will the company save using their new plan?

36. Develop reasons for and against the new plan. If you were an executive, would you be in favor of or opposed to the plan?

Linking School and Community

Read, watch, and listen to local news reports and identify the types of risks that are currently affecting the quality of life in your community. Make a list of the risks you identify and determine if they are mainly controllable or uncontrollable, insurable or uninsurable. Determine what plans are being made by community leaders, including government, business, social service organizations, and others, to deal with the risks and reduce their potential impact on the citizens and visitors.

Web Workout

Insurance companies benefit when their policyholders work to reduce the risks that are covered by insurance policies. Many nonprofit organizations and government agencies also try to help individuals and businesses reduce the risks they face. Use an Internet search engine to identify websites that offer information on how to reduce a specific risk facing individuals or businesses.

Think Critically

1. Locate websites that provide information on reducing risks. Select one website for each of these categories: (a) insurance company, (b) government agency, and (c) nonprofit organization.

2. Prepare a table that identifies the sponsor of the website the type of risk discussed; whether it is a risk facing individuals, businesses, or both; and whether it is an economic or non-economic risk.

3. For each website selected, write one paragraph explaining why the business, agency, or organization is interested in reducing the particular risk or risks. What are their goals or how do they benefit if individuals or businesses follow their advice?

Retail Merchandising Series Event Role Play

In 2009, retail crimes such as shoplifting, employee theft, and supply chain fraud equaled 1.48% of sales in the United States or $42.3 billion. Employee theft accounted for more than 40 percent of these losses. Some cases involve taking merchandise without paying for it, but employees are also involved in other kinds of thefts. They facilitate shoplifting by friends and family members, they abuse their employee discount, and their actions cause retailers to charge higher prices for merchandise to cover the losses.

The manager of a retail store is upset with reports indicating that 12 percent, or $120,000, of the store's merchandise was stolen or shoplifted. The manager has determined that much of the stolen merchandise is related to employee activity. For this event, you must develop a strategy for reducing the losses related to theft and shoplifting. Your role play must address the following issues: loss of merchandise, basic insurance needs for the business, and stronger security systems.

Individual participants have 10 minutes to study the business situation described above and develop a plan of action for the role play. Participants are allowed to take notes regarding their response to the situation. Individual participants then have 10 minutes to present their role play to the judge or class. Five additional minutes are scheduled for the judge and class to ask questions.

Performance Indicators Evaluated

● Define business risk.

● Describe employee ethics with regard to shoplifting and employee theft.

● Describe strategies to reduce business risk and associated losses.

● Explain the purpose of purchasing insurance to cover losses due to employee theft and shoplifting.

● Describe a work environment that requires and rewards positive ethical behavior.

For more detailed information about performance indicators, go to the DECA website.

Think Critically

1. Why do many businesses purchase insurance to cover losses due to employee theft and shoplifting?

2. Why is it important to monitor employee behavior in retail businesses?

3. What are three specific strategies that can be used to deter theft and shoplifting?

4. How might shoplifting or employee theft present an ethical dilemma for a retail employee?

5. How does shoplifting affect prices charged for merchandise at a retail establishment?

www.deca.org

Financial planning activities are the foundation of business and personal decisions. Each year, poor money management in our society results in millions of personal bankruptcies and loss of billions of dollars from various frauds.

In this unit, you will study the components of personal financial management. Starting with wise consumer buying, your financial choices are based on daily money management skills. These include budgeting and wise use of credit. Your ability to select and use banking services is another skill that will help you achieve your financial goals. Finally, your knowledge of savings, investment, and insurance alternatives will help to provide for long-term financial security.

Financial Services Around the World

For your banking activities, you might go to an ATM while a person in India might go to the post office. Or, a person in Cameroon might go to a village lending group. Around the world people obtain financial services in varied settings.

Today, in the United States and other industrialized countries, more and more people are writing fewer and fewer checks. The use of electronic banking services through cash machines, home computers, and smart phones continues to expand.

In India, the postal service is a major provider of banking and other financial services. Since 1854, using the brand name "India Post," this government-operated enterprise offers savings accounts, money transfers, money orders, life insurance, and mutual funds through more than 150,000 offices. More recently, India Post allows customers to electronically transfer funds to pay bills at any postal service office.

People in developing economies lack access to formal financial institutions. As a result, rotating savings and credit associations (RoSCAs) exist in more than 70 countries so people can obtain loans. These community-based groups allow people to save or obtain credit to pay for household expenses or run a business. These informal lending groups involve members pooling their funds with each member taking a turn to use the funds.

At the RoSCA meetings, usually held weekly or monthly, group members make small payments. The full amount collected at each meeting goes to one person. Then, at the next meeting, another person obtains the funds, until each person has a turn. RoSCAs have various names. In Cameroon and other French-speaking countries, they are *tontines*. In India, they are *chitty*, *tandas* in Mexico, and *osusu* in Nigeria.

Think Critically

What factors might influence the types of financial services offered in different countries?

CUSTOMER SERVICE

Each day, millions of customers seek service, all kinds of service. For example, they might want to purchase a computer, return a defective toaster, exchange a gift, schedule a delivery, complain about poor service, request information, apply for a loan, or pay a parking ticket. Employment opportunities in customer service include careers in business, in government, or with a nonprofit organization. Customer service employees work directly with customers in places such as banks, hospitals, and retail stores. They also work in offices and call centers. The specific focus of customer service positions varies widely. For example, there are customer service professionals who help people check into hotels, buy products, make insurance claims, and register for social services. They even offer suggestions for how to cook a turkey.

Related Job Titles

- Customer Service Representative
- Bank Teller
- Catalog Sales Agent
- Computer Support Specialist
- Customer Assistance Coordinator
- Customer Service Specialist
- Financial Service Representative
- Internet Customer Service Representative
- Hotel Desk Clerk
- Receptionist
- Retail Sales Clerk

Analyze Career Opportunities in ...
CUSTOMER SERVICE

Use library and Internet resources to learn more about careers in customer service. Choose one of the job titles listed in the box above and answer the following questions.

1. How would you describe the physical work environment for jobs in this field?

2. Is this a career that interests you? Describe a few things you could do to learn more about this career.

What's it like to work as a . . . Customer Service Specialist?

Before he even takes off his coat, Brian starts his day by checking e-mail messages. Today, several messages request information about identity theft. Yesterday, it was complaints about online auctions. Tomorrow, it could be comments about a proposed consumer protection law.

As a customer service specialist with the state consumer protection office, Brian must be ready for a variety of activities. Research, responding to requests, and report preparation are just a few of his daily responsibilities. Recently, Brian has been collecting information to help the state attorney general develop policies that will help expand protection to consumers.

When talking to people about his job, Brian always mentions the satisfaction he gets from helping others. He also mentions how much he likes having variety in his day. He never knows what he will find in his mailbox.

What about you? Would working in the field of customer service be of interest to you?

15-1 Consumer Buying Decisions

Goals

1 Identify major sources of consumer information.

2 Explain wise buying actions.

3 Describe the main types of shopping locations.

Key Terms

unit price 372

brand 373

impulse buying 374

Focus on REAL LIFE

"I am going on a wilderness retreat with a community service group and I have to buy a sleeping bag," Kristen said to Joshua.

"I don't know much about sleeping bags, but I want to get the best one for my trip. I stopped by the sporting goods store and they had many varieties and prices. I was confused. Can you help?"

"I don't know much either, but I expect your choice depends on where you will use the bag," said Joshua. "Did you gather information before you began looking? There are consumer groups that test products. If you want, I can help you look online, or we can go to the library to find magazine articles."

"That sounds like a good idea," Kristen replied. "A salesperson at the store might be able to help, but researching in advance should help me ask the right questions."

Goal 1

Identify major sources of consumer information.

CONSUMER INFORMATION SOURCES

Consumers have the power to decide to buy or not to buy. Businesses must serve the needs of consumers. Without satisfied consumers, businesses would not make sales, earn profits, or remain in business. Several information sources are available to help consumers with their buying decisions.

Product Testing Organizations

Product testing organizations test products and services for the benefit of consumers and business. Manufacturers pay these organizations to perform safety tests on products. Underwriters Laboratories tests electrical components of products from all over the world for fire and electrical safety. The UL symbol indicates that the product has been tested and judged safe for normal use.

The Association of Home Appliance Manufacturers (AHAM) develops and maintains performance standards for appliances such as refrigerators, air conditioners, and freezers. The AHAM seal indicates that a product has met performance standards. The Carpet and Rug Institute and the Motorist Assurance Program issue other seals of quality.

Consumers Union reports scientific, technical, and educational information about products and services. This non-profit organization performs independent tests on consumer goods. It publishes articles in a monthly magazine called *Consumer Reports*.

Media Sources

Each day, you have access to a range of media sources offering consumer information. Most media exist in both traditional and online formats.

Print-Based Media Many magazines and newspapers provide various types of consumer assistance. General interest magazines such as *Consumers Digest*, *Good Housekeeping,* and *Parents* provide articles and product information. For money management, financial planning, and investment advice, you could read *Money* or *Kiplinger's Personal Finance Magazine*.

Specialty magazines and newspapers also provide information about specific types of products or services. These publications cover topics such as motor vehicles, computers, boats, electronic equipment, travel, and education. Readers can obtain a better understanding of the technical aspects of these products and services.

Broadcast-Based Media Radio and television are valuable sources of up-to-date consumer information. Many stations carry programs or archive information on their websites to inform you about product safety, care and use of products, and shopping tips.

Internet-Only Media Websites with no affiliation to print or broadcast media have become a valuable resource for consumers. The use of a search engine allows you to obtain specific answers for your consumer questions.

Government Agencies

Federal, state, and local governments also inform consumers. The federal government has the Consumer Information Center, which serves as headquarters for consumer information. This agency puts out a quarterly catalog of publications. It also maintains an extensive website to assist consumers.

The United States Department of Agriculture (USDA) offers publications and online information about food buying, meal planning, and nutrition. The USDA also inspects and grades meat and other foods. It makes that information available to consumers.

Other federal government agencies that provide consumer information include the Federal Trade Commission (FTC), Food and Drug Administration

NETBookmark

The U.S. federal government maintains one of the most comprehensive websites with information for consumers. Access the website shown below and click on the link for Chapter 15. Select a specific consumer category. What types of information are available on this topic? What federal agencies provide this information? Describe some specific suggestions for consumers related to this topic.

www.cengage.com/school/genbus/pob

(FDA), Consumer Product Safety Commission (CPSC), National Highway Traffic Safety Administration, Department of Housing and Urban Development, Environmental Protection Agency, and the newly created Bureau of Consumer Financial Protection.

Every state has consumer protection agencies. These agencies have websites to provide information and handle consumer questions. State departments of banking

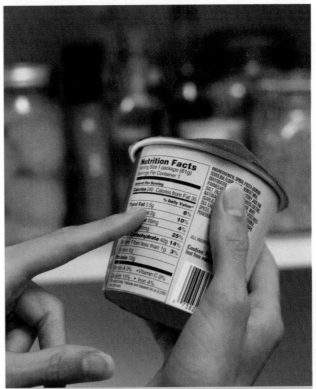

Name some ways in which you are protected on a daily basis by the activities of a government agency.

Photodisc/Getty Images

and insurance are available to assist with those areas. Large cities and counties also have consumer assistance offices.

Business Sources

As a public service and in an effort to sell goods and services, businesses make consumer information available.

Advertising Advertising is widely available. It is a popular source of consumer information. The main purpose of an advertisement is to encourage you to buy. Because of this, you should carefully evaluate this information source.

Advertising can be helpful. Useful advertisements tell you what the product is, how it is made, and what it will do. Advertisements give facts that you can use to compare the product with other competing products. Beware of advertising claims that really tell you nothing about the product. If an advertisement states that a product is better, ask, "Better than what?"

Would you find more reliable information in an advertisement or on a product label? How do you know?

Digital Vision/Getty Images

Product Labels A label, attached to or printed on a product, provides useful information. A label will report the nature or content of a product. The label will also likely tell you what the product is made of, its size, how to care for it, and when and where it was made. Clothing labels must tell you what the product is made of and must give instructions for washing or cleaning.

Customer Service Departments Many businesses have special departments focused on customer service. Some firms provide customers with booklets on a range of consumer topics. For example, banks and insurance companies publish booklets to help consumers manage their money. Some large retail firms provide printed materials to help consumers with their buying problems.

Better Business Bureau The Better Business Bureau (BBB) can provide helpful information. If you plan to buy a used car from a particular dealer, you could call the BBB to find out what experiences others have had with that dealer. If consumers have reported problems with the firm, you could find out about these complaints. BBBs give facts only. They do not recommend products or firms.

Personal Contacts

An often-used information source is "word of mouth." This includes information received from other people. You often trust information provided by others who have bought and used a product. When planning a purchase, you may talk to someone who already owns the product or has used the service. This word-of-mouth consumer information can be a valuable resource when making consumer decisions.

> **checkpoint ✓**
> What are the main sources of consumer information?

WISE BUYING STRATEGIES

Whenever you plan to buy something, think about several key decisions. These include the following. Do you really need the item now or can you wait? Which stores should you consider? What quality do you want? What price are you willing to pay? Should you pay cash or use credit? If you make the purchase, what other important item may you have to do without?

Use Decision-Making Steps

As a consumer, you should follow the decision-making steps when making a purchase.

1. *Identify your needs or wants.* Be able to state clearly why you intend to buy something.

2. *Know the choices available.* These choices include price, quality, location, variety, reputation, and other factors.

3. *Determine your desired satisfaction.* You should develop answers to questions such as, "How much am I willing to pay?" "What quality level do I want?" and "How long am I willing to wait for the item?"

4. *Evaluate alternatives.* At this stage, you will shop for the products and services that could satisfy your needs. You will compare them in terms of the criteria you have identified.

5. *Make the decision.* Decide whether to buy or not. Determine what product or service is most satisfying. Decide from which business you will make the purchase.

Goal 2

Explain wise buying actions.

Business Insight for the 21st Century

Electronic Package Tags

You are walking along and suddenly you receive a text message on your cell phone. You are informed that a certain item is on sale at a store as you walk by that exact store. This message could be both convenient and frightening.

Radio frequency identification devices (RFIDs) in clothing labels and other products allow keeping track of things and people. Currently, RFIDs are being used in highway toll lanes, and for pet identification, library book circulation and retrieval, and baggage tracking by airlines. They are also used in warehouses to monitor the location of inventory. Companies are able to identify the exact location of their products. Using RFID technology reduces theft and misplaced inventory.

Two components make up an RFID system. First, the data-loaded tag (called the transponder) is attached to the item to be tracked. Second, a reader (the transreceiver) captures the tag's data using radio waves. These data are then sent to a computer for processing.

Walmart is tagging clothing items such as underwear and socks to gain greater control over their in-store inventory. Employees use scanners to determine what sizes are missing. In the future, RFIDs could be used in homes to turn on appliances and monitor heating and security.

Think Critically

1. What are possible uses of RFIDs that could benefit consumers?

2. What concerns might be associated with RFIDs?

Good buying skills will make you a better consumer. You can get greater value for your money each time you make a purchase.

Comparison Shopping

Smart consumers are comparison shoppers. They compare price, quality, services, and brands.

Compare Prices A **unit price** is a price per unit of measure. Most stores help consumers compare among various brands and sizes of the same product. Shelf labels show both the total price and the price of one standard measure, or unit, of the product.

If you need to calculate a unit price, divide the price of the item by the number of units per measure. For instance, in the supermarket, you see that a 16-ounce bag of Golden Frozen Corn costs $1.26. An 8-ounce box of Yellow Perfection Corn sells for $0.69 per box. Which is the better buy for the dollar?

If you compare the total prices only, it is not easy to decide. Because stores usually post the cost per ounce, the unit price, you could quickly compare the two package sizes. In this case, the 16-ounce bag would show a unit price of 7.9 cents an ounce ($1.26 ÷ 16). The 8-ounce box would be 8.6 cents per ounce ($0.69 ÷ 8). Unit pricing would quickly tell you that the 16-ounce bag is a better buy per ounce for the dollar.

Prices of products can vary greatly. The cost of the same item often differs from store to store and in different geographic regions. For example, an identical camera may be available with prices ranging from $25 to more than $40. These price differences emphasize the need for comparison shopping.

Compare Quality High-quality products and services often cost more. Buying lower-quality items can sometimes turn out to be more expensive than buying higher-quality items. For example, if you buy a lower-quality pair of shoes, they may wear out in a short time. You will have to replace the lower-quality shoes sooner. You may end up buying two pairs of low-quality shoes in a short span of time.

Compare Services Most businesses try to provide good service, but types of services can differ. Some businesses sell for cash only. Others offer credit. Some businesses provide free delivery. Other services offered may include layaways, repairs, and special orders. Service is important, but be careful not to pay for more service than you need.

Compare Sales The word "sale" is perhaps the most overused, and least trusted, word in marketing. You have probably seen sale signs a thousand times. When an item is really on sale, it is offered at a price lower than its normal selling price. Some "sales" may not really be sales at all.

Name an instance when you spent time comparing prices, quality, and service on an item before making a purchase. How did you determine which item was the best choice?

Promotional sales are used to promote the selling of regular merchandise with short-term price reductions. This type of sale may be used when a new store opens or when new products are introduced. Retailers may use promotional sales in hopes that customers will buy the sale items as well as other products not on sale.

A *clearance sale* is used to clear merchandise that stores no longer wish to carry. This may be end-of-season items, odd sizes and models, or discontinued merchandise. Clearance sales usually offer some bargains. Be sure that you need a sale item before you buy it.

Compare Brands A **brand** is a name given to a product or service to distinguish it from other similar and competitive items. The company that makes the product or service usually creates a *brand name*. Brand names are designed to help build customer loyalty.

National brands are advertised all over the country. They are sold in almost every community. Among these goods are items such as food, clothing, shoes, tools, and cosmetics. Manufacturers of such goods often place brand names on the items they make. Well-known brand names include Kellogg's, JELL-O, Colgate, Gap, and L'Oreal. Recognizing national brand names allows you to expect uniform quality. Buying brand-name goods is especially helpful when it is hard to inspect for quality, such as packaged products.

Some stores have their own brand names, called *store brands* or *private label brands*. For example, Craftsman has long been one of the brand names on tools sold by Sears. Store brands are usually sold at a lower cost than national brands. Buying store brands may save you money and offer good quality at the same time.

Stores may also carry unbranded items at reduced prices, called *generic products*.

Explain why an ability to make wise buying decisions is important for achieving your life-span goals. Do you believe buying skills contribute to your ability to reach your life-span goals? What could you do to improve your buying skills?

Generic products are less expensive because they do not require advertising and fancy packaging. These lower costs result in lower prices. Differences in quality between generic and branded products may be small, making these items a good value.

Wise Buying: A Summary

Skillful consumers are efficient in their shopping activities. They save time, energy, and money by planning.

Take Your Time "I just don't have the time" is something many people say. Spending time planning purchases usually results in savings. Taking your time will allow you to look for the best values. As a good shopper, you should refuse to be hurried. Then, you can avoid buying things that you really do not want or need.

Compare different brands of similar items. Name similarities and differences. Is one better than the other? Why?

Digital Vision/Getty Images

Time Your Purchases For some items, prices are lowest at predictable times. Certain seasons and conditions favor goods and services being sold at reduced prices. Some examples include:

- Fresh fruits are usually lower in price during the local growing season.

- Winter clothing is often on sale in January.

- Firewood often costs less in the summer.

Consumer information sources, including advertisements, can help you identify good times to make certain kinds of purchases.

Avoid Being Impulsive The opposite of spending time and effort is buying too quickly and is called **impulse buying**. Impulse buying should be avoided. It often happens when an item is nicely displayed where customers are likely to see it, such as near the checkout counter.

Some impulse buying is harmless when the cost is small and the item is worth the price. Be aware that buying more expensive items on impulse can be costly. One of the best ways to avoid impulse buying is to use a shopping list. You can save money with a list whether it is for groceries, hardware, or clothing.

checkpoint ✓

What decision-making steps should be taken when making a purchase?

WORK as a TEAM

Today, consumers have more ways to buy than ever before. Using the three main categories of buying locations (tra ditional retailers, contemporary retailers, and non-store shopping), create a list of businesses in your community. Then, discuss the advantages and disadvantages of using each of the three categories.

SHOPPING LOCATIONS

When deciding where to buy, you have many choices. The types of stores and other buying locations expand every day because of competition and technology.

Traditional Retailers

Many of the stores in which you shop have developed over the past 100 years. *Department stores* have an extensive product line and emphasize service. They may have personal shoppers, make deliveries, and wrap gifts.

Discount stores emphasize lower prices on their products. Most discount stores base their success on a high volume of sales and low prices. If service is not important to you, this may be where you should shop.

Specialty stores have a special line of products for sale. They carry a wide variety of products in a narrow line such as sporting goods, jewelry, or women's shoes. Some specialty stores may also be discount stores.

In food retailing, a *supermarket* is the large, full-service store that carries many brands. *Convenience stores* are small stores that emphasize the sale of food items, an accessible location, and long operating hours. These stores usually stock popular items at higher prices.

Contemporary Retailers

Today, *specialty superstores* offer low prices and a wide variety of a limited product line. These include retailers such as OfficeMax, Home Depot, and Best Buy.

Discount stores have expanded to include a wide array of food products. These *superstores* may also include other retail services such as a bakery, restaurant, pharmacy, video rentals, and banking.

The *warehouse club* is a no-frills outlet focusing on the sale of large quantities at reasonable prices. Products are displayed in simple settings resembling a warehouse. These stores target small business owners who are looking to buy various supplies and equipment.

Factory outlets have been popular. These stores have a reputation for selling high-quality merchandise at low prices. Products are direct from the factory and sometimes have minor flaws.

Non-Store Shopping

Shopping at home started with door-to-door sales. Then, *mail order* catalogs became very popular. People sent in their orders by mail and later called by telephone. Now, you can buy using your television, computer, or fax machine.

Non-store shopping also includes *vending machines*. Each year, more and different products are available through these automated devices. In Japan, a person can buy everything from eggs and toys

What are some advantages to shopping in a store rather than using a catalog or shopping online?

to flowers and toilet paper from a vending machine.

> **checkpoint** ✓
> What are the main categories of shopping locations?

15-1 Assessment

Key Concepts

Determine the best answer.

1. The most reliable consumer information source will usually be
   a. advertising
   b. comments from salespeople
   c. comments from other consumers
   d. reports from consumer testing organizations

2. The first step in the buying decision-making process is to
   a. identify product alternatives
   b. evaluate the services at different stores
   c. decide whether to use cash or credit
   d. identify your needs

3. Which of the following is an example of a non-store shopping location?
   a. club warehouse
   b. vending machine
   c. factory outlet
   d. hypermarket

Make Academic Connections

4. **Math** A 12-ounce package of cereal is priced at $3.20. A larger container of the cereal costs $5.20 for 1½ pounds. What is the unit price for each item?

5. **Communication** Select several advertisements. Develop a list of questions to ask when evaluating advertising. Use these guidelines to evaluate the ads you selected. Prepare a one-page summary of your findings.

15-2 Consumer Rights and Responsibilities

Goals

1 Explain the consumer movement.

2 Explain seven consumer rights.

3 Describe consumer responsibilities.

Key Terms

consumer movement 376

fraud 377

guarantee 379

express warranty 379

implied warranty 379

Focus on REAL LIFE

Juan met Michelle after school. "Hi, Michelle. Have you decided which computer to buy?"

"I don't know," replied Michelle. "I looked at the computers at Bayside Computer Store and they have the lowest price. But I got the impression they didn't take me seriously because of my age."

Young people often comment that businesses do not respect them as customers or treat them as well as adults. Successful businesses recognize that teens are a powerful consumer group with purchasing power. They not only choose where they want to spend their money, but they also often influence the buying decisions of family and friends.

Businesses that ignore or disrespect younger customers jeopardize sales. They may also lose long-term customers who don't feel comfortable when shopping in these stores. You can be sure that businesses that are aware of consumer rights and buying power will welcome teen customers.

Goal 1

Explain the consumer movement.

THE CONSUMER MOVEMENT

In the past, some businesses were viewed as often trying to take advantage of consumers. False claims were sometimes made about products. Prices were often too high. Some products were unsafe. To fight against unfair business practices, consumers united to demand fair treatment from businesses, giving rise to what is known as the **consumer movement**.

Because of this movement, public and private agencies, policies, laws, and regulations were developed to protect consumer interests. In 1962, President John F. Kennedy presented his Consumer Bill of Rights and declared that every consumer has the first four rights shown in Figure 15-1. In 1969, President Richard M. Nixon added the

fifth right to the list. In 1975, President Gerald R. Ford added the sixth. In 1994, President William J. Clinton added the seventh.

CONSUMER BILL OF RIGHTS
1. The right to be informed.
2. The right to safety.
3. The right to choose.
4. The right to be heard.
5. The right to a remedy.
6. The right to consumer education.
7. The right to service.

▶ **Figure 15-1**

Give examples of how your rights as a consumer are respected.

YOUR CONSUMER RIGHTS

As a consumer, you have the right to expect honesty and fair treatment from businesses. Few businesses are intentionally dishonest. Being a skilled consumer means that you know the Consumer Bill of Rights and how to exercise these rights.

The Right to Be Informed

Most products and services are described in advertisements, on labels, or by a salesperson. You have a right to know what the product or service is and what it will do for you.

Fraud occurs when consumers are given false information in an effort to make a sale. If a salesperson knowingly sells you a car on which the odometer has been turned back 30,000 miles, fraud has occurred.

Not all product information you receive can be expected to be perfectly accurate. Suppose you were looking for a used car for transportation to and from school. If a salesperson told you she thought the car would get about 20 miles to the gallon but it only got 18, you were not deceived. The salesperson may not have been accurate in estimating gas mileage, but no guarantee was made.

When a salesperson exaggerates the good qualities of a product and says, "It's the best" or "It's a great buy," there is no fraud. On the other hand, if the salesperson tells you a car has new brakes and it does not, this is fraud.

The Right to Safety

Consumers have a right to be safe from harm associated with using products or services. Several agencies work to assure the safety of consumers. The Consumer Product Safety Commission has the authority to set safety standards, ban hazardous products, and recall dangerous products from the market.

The Food and Drug Administration (FDA) makes certain that food, drug, and cosmetic products are not harmful to consumers. This federal agency enforces laws and regulations that prevent the distribution of unsafe or misbranded foods, drugs, and cosmetics.

The FDA also works to ensure that product labels do not mislead consumers. The United States Department of Agriculture (USDA) helps ensure consumer safety by setting quality standards for farm products. The USDA also controls the processing, inspection, and labeling of meat products.

The Right to Choose

The right of consumers to choose from a variety of goods and services has become well established. In fact, one of the main activities of the Federal Trade Commission (FTC) is to prevent one firm from using unfair practices to force competing firms out of business. When a business has no competitors and controls the market for a product or service, it is said to have a *monopoly*. Competing firms encourage customers to buy from them by offering a choice of products and services

Why is it important for consumers to have choices?

at a range of prices. By driving away this competition, monopolies limit the right to choose.

The Right to Be Heard

Most businesses have a customer service department to hear the concerns or complaints of customers. Some smaller businesses have a specific person assigned to that duty. Businesses are usually happy to take care of problems you have with their products or services.

Several federal government agencies, such as the FTC, also assure your right to be heard. As a consumer, you can complain directly to the FTC if you believe that your consumer rights have been violated. The FTC regulates advertising and encourages informative and truthful advertising.

State government agencies, such as the Office of the Attorney General or the Department of Consumer Affairs, have responsibility for protecting the rights of consumers. They can prosecute businesses for breaking state consumer protection laws. These offices also inspect advertising practices. They handle consumer problems related to automobile repairs, credit, and door-to-door sales practices.

Privately funded groups also help to make certain you are heard. Various national and local groups inform and protect consumers in a variety of

A Question of Ethics

©Andreas Prott/iStock

Frauds by Consumers

Most people are familiar with bait-and-switch tactics, work-at-home schemes, and "lose weight fast" scams. These frauds against consumers result in lost money for consumers and are usually illegal. Various actions by consumers can also cause higher prices. People who would not think of shoplifting may be dishonest in other ways. Deceptive actions by consumers include the following.

- Eating items in a store without paying for them

- Buying a book, reading it, and returning it for a full refund

- Copying a DVD and giving it to friends so they can watch a movie without paying

- Making photocopies of sheet music and passing them out to all the members of your chorus

- Buying clothing, wearing the item, and then returning it

- Asking for a cup for water and using it to take a soft drink from a self-serve dispenser

- Switching price tags from lower-priced items and putting them on the more expensive items

While most of these actions are illegal, all affect the operating costs of businesses. Each of these "frauds by consumers" results in higher prices. Many of these practices have become more difficult with technology. While new electronic devices have improved

store security, this equipment has also added to business costs and higher prices.

Think Critically

1. What other actions by consumers can result in higher prices for the things you buy?

2. Describe how businesses and individual consumers might help reduce these actions that result in higher prices for everyone.

purchasing areas. Some groups specialize in auto safety or consumer credit. Others will assist with any consumer problem.

The Better Business Bureau is concerned with problems arising from false advertising or misrepresented products and services. Dues paid by member businesses support BBBs. They work to maintain ethical practices and combat consumer fraud. If you believe your consumer rights have been violated, you can get help from one of 120 Better Business Bureaus around the country. After reporting your concern, the bureau will try to persuade the business to fix the problem. Most businesses willingly carry out the BBB request.

Discuss a time when you had difficulty returning an item. How many people did you speak with? Were you successful, or did you give up? Why?

The Right to a Remedy

The Fair Packaging and Labeling Act, National Traffic and Motor Vehicle Safety Act, Truth in Labeling Act, and Fair Debt Collection Practices Act all protect consumers. These and other laws are designed to provide assurances that consumers can seek a legal remedy when a problem occurs.

Consumers also have protection provided through a guarantee. With some purchases, a consumer can expect a guarantee or a warranty. A **guarantee** is a promise by the manufacturer or dealer, usually in writing, that a product is of a certain quality. A guarantee may apply to the entire item or only to some parts of it. It may promise that defective parts will be replaced only if a problem occurs during a specified period. No guarantee covers damages caused by misuse.

When making a purchase, a skillful consumer asks about a guarantee. A guarantee is frequently in the form of statements like these: "The working parts of this watch are guaranteed for one year." "This sweater will not shrink more than 3 percent." These kinds of guarantees are sometimes called express warranties. An **express warranty** is made orally or in writing and promises a specific quality of performance.

You should review the guarantee before buying an item. You can also require the business to put in writing any other guarantees that have been offered orally. Written guarantees are useful if you need to return a faulty product. Read the guarantee carefully to find out exactly what is covered and for what period.

Some guarantees are not written. They are called implied warranties. An **implied warranty** is imposed by law and is understood to apply even though it has not been stated. In general, the law requires certain standards to be met. For example, it is implied that health care products purchased over the counter at a pharmacy will not harm you when used according to the directions.

The Right to Consumer Education

Although individual buying decisions are important, educated consumers need to understand how their choices affect the economy. Consumer education should take into account how buying actions create an interaction between consumers and producers. Educated consumers are aware that their decisions not only affect their personal situation, but also have economic and social implications.

The Right to Service

This latest right suggests consumers can expect convenience, courtesy, and responsiveness to consumer problems and needs. The right to service encourages businesses to take steps necessary to ensure that products and services meet the quality and performance levels claimed for those products and services.

> **checkpoint** ✓
> How does an express warranty differ from an implied warranty?

What kind of service should you expect from the company that sells you a cell phone?

Cultura/Getty Images

YOUR CONSUMER RESPONSIBILITIES

Just as some businesses have not met their responsibilities to consumers, some consumers try to take advantage of businesses. Even consumers who are not unethical or dishonest may have expectations that businesses cannot meet. Consumers also have responsibilities in business relationships.

Be Honest

Most people are honest, but those who are not cause others to pay higher prices. Shoplifting losses are estimated to be in the billions of dollars each year. Businesses make up losses from shoplifting by charging higher prices.

As a responsible consumer, you must be as honest with a business as you want it to be with you. You should be as quick to tell the cashier that you received too much change at the checkout counter as you are to say that you received too little.

Be Reasonable

As a buyer, you are usually responsible for what you buy if the business has been honest. If you are dissatisfied and wish to complain, you should complain in a reasonable way.

You should first be sure that you have a cause for complaint. Be sure that you have followed the directions for using the product. After you have confirmed the details of your complaint, calmly explain the problem to an employee of the business from which you bought the item. In most cases, the business will be glad to correct the problem because it does not want to lose you as a customer.

Be Active

As a responsible consumer, you should report unethical business practices to prevent other consumers from becoming victims. By reporting the matter to a consumer agency, you might be able to get the shop to keep its word both to you and to future customers.

Be Informed

The most important responsibility you have as a consumer is to be informed. Just having the right to be informed will not make you an informed consumer. You must find and use the information available to you.

You should also keep informed about your rights as a consumer. Learn about the laws and agencies that protect your rights and how to report a violation of your rights. Being an informed consumer is hard work, but the extra effort spent in making your dollars go as far as possible will be worth it.

Be Involved

In the United States, involvement is an important consumer activity. As a citizen, you have a responsibility to participate in government, which starts by being an informed voter.

As a consumer, you also have responsibilities. When the opportunity arises, make your concerns known to government officials or consumer agencies. Only when you become involved as a consumer can agencies do their jobs and legislative bodies pass appropriate laws.

You have an obligation to society to be a wise and efficient consumer. The world has only a limited supply of natural resources such as petroleum, metals, clean air, and clean water. Sometimes, uninformed consumers unnecessarily waste these resources and contribute to damaging the environment.

> **checkpoint** ✓
> What actions can be taken to be an involved consumer?

15-2 Assessment

Key Concepts

Determine the best answer.

1. True or False. The U.S. Consumer Product Safety Commission is responsible for regulating the safety of food.

2. True or False. An implied warranty is usually printed in the owner's manual of a product.

3. A person who compares product information on labels is using the consumer right to
   a. service
   b. be informed
   c. be heard
   d. a remedy

4. If a person returns an item as new for a refund after using it, this violates the consumer responsibility to be
   a. honest
   b. involved
   c. informed
   d. active

Make Academic Connections

5. **Research** Go to the website of your state's office of consumer protection. What services does this government agency provide? How do you and other consumers benefit from the actions of this agency?

6. **Law** The Truth in Labeling Act requires that certain information be presented on food labels. Using a label from a food product in your home, identify some of these required items. How would you make food labels more informative for consumers?

Consumers Union

Imagine 24 different washing machines all operating in the same room. Envision 32 cameras being used by a small group of people. These are scenes you might encounter in one of the 50 testing laboratories of Consumers Union in Yonkers, New York.

Consumers Union was created in 1936 to provide information on products and services to help buyers get the most for their money. Today, Consumers Union continues to sort out low-quality and unsafe products from those items that will give you the best value. Each month, the results of these consumer tests are reported in *Consumer Reports* magazine and on the Consumer Reports website.

Consumers Union also conducts extensive testing on motor vehicles. Each year, the organization buys the vehicles the same way you would buy a car. That is, Consumers Union has shoppers bargain with dealers for the best price. After an inspection of the vehicle's features, road testing occurs on a 195-mile course. Engineers record various performance data. Finally, crash tests are conducted to assess safety and the possibility of a rollover. All of these findings are then published to help consumers make wiser car-buying choices.

In recent years, as consumers spend more of their income on services, Consumers Union has expanded its activities. Every month in the magazine, consumers are provided with information about banking services, health care, insurance, lawyers, and other personal and financial services.

Consumers Union is involved with protecting consumers in other ways. Offices in Washington, DC, California, and Texas promote improved consumer protection laws. The Washington office works to build support for laws related to telecommunications, product safety, food safety, financial services, health care policy, energy, international trade, and other consumer issues.

The advocacy arm of Consumers Union conducts research and offers educational programs on consumer topics. This group also publishes reports, organizes conferences, and testifies at government hearings.

Why would consumers be interested in the results of lab tests conducted on 24 different washing machines before making a purchase?

Think Critically

1. How do the activities of Consumers Union assist consumers?

2. Conduct research to create a list of current consumer issues that are of concern to Consumers Union.

15-3 Consumer Protection Actions

Goals

1 List common consumer concerns.

2 Describe the steps of the consumer complaint process.

3 Explain legal actions available to assist consumers.

Key Terms

mediation 386

arbitration 386

class action suit 386

small claims court 387

Focus on REAL LIFE

Monica was annoyed as she walked into the store, but she knew that getting upset or angry was not a good idea. She took a deep breath, walked up to the counter, and spoke to the sales associate.

"Hi, I bought this about six weeks ago," Monica said calmly as she took an expensive leather purse out of a shopping bag. "I really like the bag, but the zipper broke."

The salesperson smiled warmly, picked up the handbag, and asked, "Do you have your receipt?"

"Here it is," Monica said as she got the receipt out of the bag.

"This will be easy," the salesperson said as she looked at the receipt. "With a receipt you have a choice of a replacement, a store credit, or a refund."

"Oh, a replacement would be terrific, but I didn't see one on the display." Monica said.

"Let me check inventory. Even if we don't have that exact bag, I know I can help you find something you will enjoy. We just got some new things this morning that are still in the stockroom."

"Thanks, you're right—this is easy."

COMMON CONSUMER PROBLEMS

Consumers hope that their purchases will always result in a satisfactory transaction. Still, problems sometimes arise. The item may have been damaged in transit. The wrong size sweater may have been shipped. These types of consumer problems are usually resolved quite easily.

Sometimes, problems that are more serious might occur. Your credit card payment may not be properly recorded to your account. A product you purchased might stop working after just a few days of use.

Sources of Complaints

State attorneys general have the primary responsibility for the enforcement of their state's consumer protection laws.

Figure 15-2 shows the top ten consumer complaints compiled by the National Association of Attorneys General (NAAG).

TOP 10 LIST OF CONSUMER COMPLAINTS	
1	Debt Collection
2	Auto Sales
3	Home Repair and Construction
4 (tie)	Credit Cards
	Internet Goods and Services
6	Predatory Lending and Mortgages
7	Telemarketing and Do-Not-Call
8	Auto Repair
9 (tie)	Auto Warranties
	Telecom, Slamming, and Cramming

Source: National Association of Attorneys General Association

Goal 1

List common consumer concerns.

▶ **Figure 15-2**

What are some examples of specific problems that might cause consumers to complain?

Joel Calheiros/Shutterstock.com

TV shoppers are the same as those that govern purchases made by telephone. The seller must send you the item within 30 days or within another period specifically stated by the company. If there is a delay, the seller must notify you. You then have the right to cancel your order.

If an unreceived or returned item is billed to your credit card, you have 60 days to dispute it. The credit card company then has 30 days to respond. Within 90 days of your letter, the credit card company must investigate the matter and explain why the bill is correct or incorrect.

You do not have to pay the part of your credit card bill under dispute until the matter is resolved. To avoid finance charges, you must pay the rest of your bill on time.

Deceptive Business Activities

Consumer fraud can be discovered in media ads, in the mail, or even on a city street corner. Various scams, cons, and swindles have been around for a long time. When a deal seems like it's too good to be true, it probably is! Each year, federal government agencies report consumers losing billions of dollars on phony investments and other deceptive offers.

The Internet has become the number one source of fraudulent offers. Consumers may not know the identity or location of all online merchants. This makes it difficult to track down the con artist after you have already lost your money.

The most common online scams involve sales of Internet services and general merchandise. Online auctions, non-delivery of products, credit/debit card scams, and work-at-home offers are also common sources of fraud.

Internet scams can also take the form of prizes, sweepstakes, and credit card offers. Consumers have lost as much as $10,000 through Internet fraud. Be cautious when making your online purchases.

Protection for Shoppers

With the increasing popularity of e-commerce comes the concern for consumer rights. Federal laws that protect Internet and

> **checkpoint ✓**
> What are sources of common consumer complaints?

Describe some Internet scams or other suspicious schemes. How do you know that they are probably not legitimate offers?

Digital Vision/Getty Images

THE COMPLAINT PROCESS

While no one wants consumer problems, they do occur. When they happen, a person should be prepared. Consumer protection experts suggest four steps when trying to resolve a purchasing problem.

Step 1 Contact the Place of Purchase

Most consumer complaints are settled by returning to the place of purchase. Calmly explain the situation. Provide evidence of your purchase and the problem. A receipt or other dated documents will help you convince the store to take action in your favor.

Step 2 Contact the Company Headquarters

If communicating with the place of purchase does not bring satisfaction, you should move up in the organization. Contact the customer service department or other office within the company. The address, phone, and e-mail of most organizations can be obtained on the package or through a search.

When contacting the company, once again provide facts about the situation. Tell what happened in a brief letter or e-mail. Include copies of any documents that back up your story. Be specific about what action you would like them to take.

Step 3 Involve a Consumer Agency

If communication with the business fails to satisfy your demands, consider using the services of a consumer agency or public interest organization. Contacting a local, state, or federal government agency can encourage the business to take action.

Some agencies and organizations specialize in specific consumer topics such as consumer credit, health care, motor vehicles, or telecommunications. Other groups, such as state consumer protection offices, will help you with almost any consumer concern.

Step 4 Take Legal Action

When the first three steps do not work, more extreme actions may be required. Several legal actions are available to consumers. These include the use of a third party for dispute resolution, class action suits, small claims court, and hiring a lawyer.

Goal 2

Describe the steps of the consumer complaint process.

> **checkpoint** ✓
> List the steps of the consumer complaint process.

Why might someone decide not to pursue a lawsuit against a company even when the company has been fraudulent?

Digital Vision/Getty Images

Each day, many consumers encounter consumer difficulties. Based on your experiences and observations, prepare an individual list of consumer problems of which you are aware. Then, compare your list with others on your team. How did most people become aware of various consumer problems? What actions were taken to resolve some of these concerns?

If the parties agree to it in advance, another third-party action may be used. **Arbitration** results in a decision that is legally binding. After hearing both sides and considering evidence, the arbitrator makes a decision. Both the consumer and business must abide by the arbitrator's verdict.

Goal 3

Explain legal actions available to assist consumers.

LEGAL ACTIONS FOR CONSUMERS

If contacting the business or a consumer agency does not resolve the problem, various legal actions may be considered.

Third-Party Settlements

A third party may be used to settle consumer differences. **Mediation** involves the use of a third party who tries to resolve the complaint between the consumer and the business. A mediator suggests a compromise between the two parties. This process helps the parties work out their own mutually agreeable solution to the dispute.

Class Action Suits

What would you do if you are overcharged a couple of dollars? Maybe nothing, but what if this same injustice occurred to thousands of consumers?

A **class action suit** is legal action by one party on behalf of a group of people who all have the same grievance. In this type of lawsuit, one person or a small group represents the interests of many others (the *class*). The settlement may result in a refund to all consumers involved. If they cannot all be identified, the funds are sometimes given to public education programs or schools.

Name some benefits of joining a class action suit rather than trying to win a case alone.

Small Claims Court

In every state, a court system exists to resolve cases involving small amounts. These courts are called **small claims court**. In these courts, disputes are resolved quickly and inexpensively.

The rules are simple and informal, and the dispute involves less than a set amount. The limits for cases heard in small claims court vary by state. The amount ranges from less than $1,000 in some states to $10,000 in others.

Most often, lawyers are not involved. Individuals present the facts of the situation and provide written and other evidence. Witnesses may also be used.

Name some types of cases that would be appropriate for small claims court.

dcdebs/iStockphoto.com

Using a Lawyer

If all else fails, a final step might be to hire a lawyer. When a situation involves larger amounts of money or severe injuries from a product, the use of an attorney may be appropriate. Information about potential lawyers may be obtained from advertisements or referrals from other people.

Before using the services of a lawyer, you should ask various questions. Is the lawyer experienced in this type of case? Will you be charged a flat fee or an hourly rate? When will you be required to make payment for services?

checkpoint ✓

How does mediation differ from arbitration?

15-3 Assessment

Key Concepts

Determine the best answer.

1. Most consumer complaints are resolved by
   a. taking legal action
   b. using arbitration
   c. hiring a lawyer with consumer protection experience
   d. returning to the place of purchase

2. A company refused to refund $10 to more than 4,000 customers. This situation might result in the use of
   a. mediation
   b. arbitration
   c. a class action suit
   d. small claims court

Make Academic Connections

3. **Visual Communication** Create a poster or other visual that communicates the four steps in the consumer complaint process. Use a specific consumer problem as the basis for your visual presentation.

4. **Research** Use library materials or an Internet search to determine the small claims court limit amount in your state. Also, obtain information about filing a case in small claims court.

Business Notes

15-1 Consumer Buying Decisions

● The main sources of consumer information are product-testing organizations; media sources such as print publishers, broadcast organizations, and the Internet; government agencies; business sources such as product labels, customer service departments, and Better Business Bureaus; and personal contacts.

● Comparison shoppers will evaluate price, quality, service, sales, and brands when making a purchase. Wise consumers take their time when making purchases, buy when prices are lowest, and avoid impulse buying with shopping lists.

● The main shopping locations used by consumers can be viewed in three categories. Traditional retailers include department stores, discount stores, specialty stores, supermarkets, and convenience stores. Contemporary retailers include specialty superstores, warehouse clubs, and factory outlets. Non-store shopping options include door-to-door, mail order, phone, computer, and vending machines.

15-2 Consumer Rights and Responsibilities

● The consumer movement emerged to fight unfair business practices. Because of this movement, public and private agencies, policies, laws, and regulations were developed to protect consumer interests.

● The Consumer Bill of Rights declares that every consumer has the right to be informed, to safety, to choose, to be heard, to a remedy, to consumer education, and to service. Being a skilled consumer means that you know the Consumer Bill of Rights and how to exercise these rights.

● Consumers also have responsibilities in business relationships. The five basic responsibilities of consumers are to be honest, to be reasonable, to report unethical practices, to be informed, and to be involved.

15-3 Consumer Protection Actions

● The main consumer complaints are related to debt collection; auto sales; home repair and construction; credit cards; Internet goods and services; predatory lending and mortgages; telemarketing and do-not-call; auto repair; auto warranties; and telecom, slamming, and cramming.

● Four steps are suggested when encountering a consumer problem: (1) contact the place of purchase, (2) contact the company headquarters, (3) involve a consumer agency, and (4) take legal action.

● A variety of legal actions is available to help consumers. Mediation and arbitration involve the use of a third party to resolve a consumer complaint. Class action suits allow a small group of consumers to act on behalf of many. Small claims court allows a person to take legal action without the use of a lawyer.

Communicate Business Concepts

1. Why do you think most businesspeople like to have well-informed customers?

2. Do you go through all of the steps of comparison shopping on every purchase you make? Explain.

3. List factors you might consider when evaluating the usefulness of a consumer information source.

4. If you were planning to buy a cell phone, what information sources might be most valuable?

5. One autumn day, a woman and a man appear at Carrie Franklin's door. They introduce themselves as chimney sweeps who would like to clean her chimney before she began using her fireplace. The man says it will be inexpensive and make her home safer, reducing the chances of a chimney fire. Carrie sees the name "Chim Chim Chimney Sweeps" on their truck. What should Carrie do to protect herself from a scam?

6. When would you consider an impulse purchase a harmless activity?

7. What are some factors you might consider when deciding where to shop?

8. Which of the consumer rights have you recently used?

9. Why, with all of the laws and organizations to protect consumers, do you continue to hear of examples of consumer fraud?

10. Which of the following situations would be considered fraud? Why?

    a. A salesperson says the sound system you are looking at is the best on the market. After you buy it, you find it rated in a consumer magazine as second best.
    b. An advertisement for a bookcase cabinet claims it is made of solid walnut. Upon close inspection after buying the bookcase, you see that it is only walnut veneer glued over less expensive plywood.
    c. The person who sells an electric corn popper says it is completely washable. Before using it, you put it into a sink filled with water to wash it. The first time you try to make popcorn, there is a flash and the popper's electrical unit catches fire. When you return the popper to the store, the salesperson tells you that she did not mean the popper could be put under water. She says you should have known that electrical appliances should not be put in water. She refuses to give you either a refund or an exchange.

11. Describe situations in which a person might use (a) a class action suit and (b) small claims court.

12. When might you use a lawyer to resolve a consumer dispute? What are some of the pros and cons of using a lawyer versus other dispute resolution methods?

Develop Your Business Language

Match the terms listed with the definitions.

13. Use of a third party who attempts to resolve the complaint between a consumer and business.

14. Buying too rapidly without much thought.

15. A name given to a product or service to distinguish it from other similar products or services.

16. A legal system for resolving cases involving small monetary amounts.

17. The price per unit of measure of a product.

18. When false information is given to a customer in an effort to make a sale.

19. A lawsuit brought by one party on behalf of a group with the same grievance.

20. Guarantees made orally or in writing that promise a specific quality of performance.

21. Third-party settlement resulting in a decision that is legally binding.

22. A promise by the manufacturer or dealer, usually in writing, that a product is of a certain quality.

23. Guarantees imposed by law that are not stated orally or in writing and that require certain standards to be met.

24. Banding together of consumers to demand fair treatment from businesses.

Key Terms

a. arbitration
b. brand
c. class action suit
d. consumer movement
e. express warranty
f. fraud
g. guarantee
h. implied warranty
i. impulse buying
j. mediation
k. small claims court
l. unit price

Make Academic Connections

25. **Law** Prepare a summary of various federal consumer agencies and laws designed to protect consumers related to product safety, motor vehicles, food, medical products, and consumer credit.

26. **Visual Communications** Select a magazine advertisement. Create a poster describing various elements of the ad. Highlight the sections of the ad that would be useful or deceptive to consumers.

27. **Research** Collect examples of advertisements with the word "sale" included. Group the ads into categories based on the type of sale being displayed. What types of sales are most common?

28. **Art** Design a label for a food product with your own brand, product name, graphics, nutritional information, and other features.

29. **Math** Berri purchased a new cell phone that stopped working one month after the warranty expired. When she returned to the store, she was offered the choice of purchasing a new phone for 5 percent off the list price of $98 or a reconditioned phone that carried the same warranty as a new phone for $75.

a. What would be the price of the new phone with the discount?
b. What percent of the price of a new telephone is the price of the reconditioned phone?
c. How much money would Berri save by purchasing the reconditioned phone?

30. **Technology** Conduct an online search of Internet frauds. What types are most common? How can a person avoid these deceptive online business practices?

31. **Math** The Jones family ordered a new car from Germany. The express warranty said the average driver would get 48.3 kilometers for every 3.85 liters of gasoline used.

a. How many miles per gallon is this?
b. If they traveled 90 miles and used 10.5 liters of gas, did the car perform better or worse than the warranty claimed?

32. **History** Conduct research on the way that people shopped in the 1800s to mid-1900s. Comment on some of the cultural, geographic, economic, and social factors that contributed to these customs.

Decision-Making Strategies

Pierre needs a new digital camera to take on his trip to Mexico as an exchange student. He is not a photography expert, but he has taken some pictures for the school newspaper. He intends to use the camera to take indoor and outdoor pictures of people as well as scenery.

Pierre has about $150 to spend on the camera. He wants the camera to be sturdy, easy to use, and to take good-quality pictures.

33. What sources of information could Pierre use to find out what cameras are in his price range?

34. What two sources of information do you believe are best? Why?

Linking School and Community

Talk to people in your community about the types of consumer problems they have encountered. What was the nature of the situation? What actions did they take to resolve the problem? What suggestions do they have for other consumers? Prepare a short written or oral summary of your findings.

Web Workout

Many websites provide online reviews of products from customers. Reading reviews by satisfied and dissatisfied customers can be helpful when a consumer is researching or planning to purchase a product or service. Past customers can post their positive and negative comments and even, in some cases, photographs. Some websites allow customers to rate products or services using a scale such as one to five stars.

Think Critically

1. Identify two different websites that use customer reviews or ratings to help others with their purchase. Write a brief description of the sites and how their systems work.

2. Explain how the number of opinions offered might influence consumer purchasing decisions. Also address the issue of fraud or manipulation of review and rating systems.

Global Marketing Team Event

American farmers are interested in selling beef, pork, wheat, and corn to international markets. Your team has been hired by your state's agricultural department to market American agricultural products in Japan.

Your team of two will develop an international marketing plan for the agricultural products mentioned above. The marketing plan must not exceed 10 single-spaced pages. Team members will present before a panel of judges (class members) and a timekeeper. The length of the presentation will be no more than 10 minutes.

The completed plan should include the following components:

Title page and table of contents
Synopsis or mini-plan
Company goals
Description of customers and their needs
Description of pricing strategy
Competition
Price selection methods

Performance Indicators Evaluated

● Develop an international marketing plan.

● Identify a customer base, including consumer and organizational markets.

● Illustrate fundamentals of consumer behavior in different cultures.

You will be evaluated for your

● Knowledge of demographics in the international market

● Understanding of the marketing mix

● Understanding of economic, social, legal, and technological trends

● Use of appropriate research and accompanying documentation

● Description of timeline for business success

For more detailed information about performance indicators, go to the BPA website.

Think Critically

1. Why is Japan a good prospective market for American farm products?

2. Why must the culture of Japan be researched before developing the marketing campaign?

3. How do politics affect international business?

4. What demographic and cultural issues must be considered when marketing these products?

5. What characteristics of American products should be emphasized for international trade?

www.bpa.org

CHAPTER

16 Money Management and Financial Planning

aldomurillo/iStockphoto.com

Most people have questions about their finances such as: *How much should I save for retirement? What is the best type of life insurance for my family situation? How can I get out of debt?*

These and many other questions are answered by people who work in personal financial planning. Employment in this field has a wide range of opportunities. If you choose a career in financial planning your work may involve providing financial planning services through a large financial services corporation, a small consulting firm, or a community-based bank. You will likely have a diverse group of clients. Some clients may have little knowledge about financial planning and others might be well-informed and eager to learn even more. In addition, the income and personal wealth of your clients will likely vary.

Related Job Titles

- Credit Counselor
- Certified Financial Planner
- Personal Financial Advisor
- Family Money Management Counselor
- Tax Preparer
- Chartered Financial Analyst
- Insurance Agent
- Stock Broker

As an alternative, you might work for a social service agency or consumer advocacy organization. In these environments you would help people deal with financial difficulties and develop a plan for avoiding future problems.

Analyze Career Opportunities in ...

FINANCIAL PLANNING

Use library and Internet resources to learn more about careers in personal financial planning. Choose one of the job titles listed in the box above and answer the following questions.

1. Identify the minimum educational requirements for this job. Explain other training or education that might be needed for advancement.

2. Is this a career that interests you? Explain how careers in this field match up with your goals and interests.

What's it like to work as a ... Financial Planner?

As the sun comes up, carl leaves his kitchen and heads for work. His office is only seconds away. Carl runs a personal financial planning business out of his home. This morning he is reviewing the files of several clients before advising them about various personal financial decisions. Then it's time to get on the road. At 10 A.M., Carl is scheduled to meet with a client who just retired but does not have enough income to cover current living expenses. At noon, he meets with several small business owners who want to create a retirement fund for their employees.

The afternoon is open so Carl can relax or take care of personal errands. In the evening, things get busy. Right after dinner, Carl meets with a family who wants to create a savings and investment program to set aside funds for their children's college education. His day ends with a phone call from a client who has a question about recent tax law changes.

What about you? What personal financial situations might result in a need for hiring someone trained as a financial planner or budget counselor?

16-1 Personal Financial Statements

Goals

1. Explain the basics of money management.

2. Create a personal balance sheet.

3. Develop a personal cash flow statement.

Key Terms

money management 394

personal assets 395

net worth 396

cash flow statement 396

Focus on REAL LIFE

"My financial situation is just fine—or it is a disaster! It all depends on what day of the week it is."

"Tell me; what's the problem, Yung-su?" asks his neighbor.

"Mr. Liang, I can't seem to get a grip on my finances. I work 10 hours a week and make about $10 per hour. That seems like a lot of money for a part-time job while going to school. But I always seem to run out of money before I get paid."

"I suppose that also means you are not saving any money, but rather spending everything you make. My advice is to get some lessons in money management. I'd be glad to help."

The one thing most people have in common is a desire to use money wisely so that needs, wants, and goals will be satisfied. While no individual, family, or organization is likely to have every desire met, several money management techniques can help you use your financial resources wisely.

Goal 1

Explain the basics of money management.

MONEY MANAGEMENT BASICS

Right now $1,000, or maybe $100, seems like a lot of money to you. Once you graduate from high school, and perhaps college, and have a full-time job, your thinking about what is a large amount of money will change. You will probably earn nearly two million dollars, or more, in your lifetime. As a college graduate, you will likely make even more.

While this may seem like a lot of money, remember that you will be responsible for many living expenses. You will have to pay for food, housing, clothing, and transportation as well as other goods and services you need and want. Upon beginning a career and living on your own, you will face the same problem you face now—having a limited amount of money to pay for all the goods and services you want and need.

Money management refers to the day-to-day financial activities associated

Do you keep track of how you spend your money? What method do you use?

with using limited income to satisfy your unlimited needs and wants. Money management involves getting the most for your money through careful planning, saving, and spending. It involves making and using a plan for spending.

Some people have the wrong idea about money management. They think it means never spending, doing without things, and not having any fun. If you learn to manage your money well, you will be able to buy what you really want. Planning ahead and deciding what is important will help you have money for things you enjoy. If you set goals, make wise decisions, buy wisely, and live within your income, you will be a successful money manager.

The process of good money management should start with knowing your current financial status. When watching a baseball or soccer game, most people want to know the score. In the money management game, score is kept with the use of two financial statements: the balance sheet and the cash flow statement.

PERSONAL BALANCE SHEET

"How much money do you have?" might be the first question many people would ask when measuring your financial situation.

The answer to that question would not give the entire picture because most people have other items of value besides money. A *balance sheet* is a record of assets and liabilities at a point in time. It reports what a person or family owns as well as owes. The main parts of a balance sheet are displayed in Figure 16-1.

Assets

Items of value are **personal assets**. Assets include such things as money in bank accounts, investments, furniture, clothing, automobiles, jewelry, and rare coins. The current value of all assets of an individual or family is the first thing stated on a balance sheet.

Goal 2

Create a personal balance sheet.

> **checkpoint ✓**
> What are some characteristics of a wise money manager?

Personal Balance Sheet

Assets		Liabilities	
Home	$97,000	Home mortgage	$45,000
Automobile	4,600	Education loan	1,800
Household items and furniture	6,200	Credit card balance	230
Personal computer	1,600	*Total liabilities*	$47,030
Jewelry	1,100		
Savings account	2,300		
Checking account	450	**Owner's Equity (Net Worth)**	
Total assets	$113,250	Total assets − Total liabilities	$66,220

▶ **Figure 16-1**

What accounts for the bulk of this family's assets, liabilities, and equity?

Liabilities

Amounts owed to others are *liabilities*. These debts may include credit card balances, car loans, a home mortgage, or personal loans. A listing of your liabilities is the second item on a balance sheet.

Net Worth

The difference between a person's assets and liabilities is your **net worth**. This difference represents the amount of money that could be claimed if all assets were sold for cash and all debts were paid off. For example, if a family has $189,000 in assets (including the value of a home) and has $87,000 in debts (mainly their home mortgage), the family has a net worth of $102,000. Net worth is also referred to as *owner's equity*.

A balance sheet is a helpful way to measure financial strength. Businesses commonly prepare a balance sheet either once a month or quarterly to determine the financial condition of the business. In the same way, a balance sheet can help in measuring financial progress.

checkpoint ✓
What are three main categories of a personal balance sheet?

Goal 3

Develop a personal cash flow statement.

PERSONAL CASH FLOW STATEMENT

A balance sheet reports assets, liabilities, and net worth on a given date. Almost every day, business transactions occur that change these balance sheet items. For example, when you make a loan payment, your liabilities decrease. If you save part of your earnings, your assets and net worth increase by the amount of the savings.

To examine changes in a person's net worth, another financial statement can be helpful. A **cash flow statement** reports net wages and other income along with spending for a period, such as for a month. Figure 16-2 on the next page includes typical items found in a cash flow statement.

Cash Inflows

The first part of a cash flow statement reports cash inflows, or your income. *Cash inflows* is the money you have available to spend as a result of working or from other income, such as interest earned on your savings.

When preparing a cash flow statement, first report your *net pay* or *take-home pay*, which is the amount of a paycheck after taxes and other payroll deductions. These deductions may include retirement contributions, charges for health benefits, and other things, as well as local, state, and federal taxes. Your take-home pay is the amount you actually have available

Daisy-Daisy/iStockphoto.com

Make a list of ways to increase your current cash inflows.

to spend. Be sure to include any other income, such as interest earned.

Cash Outflows

The second part of a cash flow statement reports your *cash outflows*, or your expenditures. Amounts spent for food, clothing, transportation, and other living costs are cash outflows. Keeping track of how much is spent for various living expenses will help you plan and control your spending. Your personal cash flow statement can be used to develop a budget, which can help you avoid cash flow problems.

Compare Inflows and Outflows

The final step in preparing the cash flow statement is to subtract the cash outflows (total spending) from the cash inflows (total income). If you spent less than you had in income, the difference represents an increase in your net worth. Most likely, this amount will be kept in savings for future needs or wants. If you spent more than you had in income, you either had to use some of your savings or had to use credit to pay these additional expenses.

Personal Cash Flow Statement		
Cash Inflows (Income)		
Net income (take-home pay)	$1,300	
Other income (interest)	10	
Total Income		$1,310
Cash Outflows (Expenditures)		
Rent	$300	
Food	400	
Clothing	50	
Utilities	60	
Telephone	30	
Transportation	120	
Personal care	30	
Recreation/entertainment	75	
Total Spending		$1,065
Net Cash Flow		$245

▶ **Figure 16-2**

What percentage of total income did this person spend on basic needs?

checkpoint ✓
What do cash outflows represent?

16-1 Assessment

Key Concepts

Determine the best answer.

1. Savings accounts and a home are examples of
   a. liabilities
   b. assets
   c. net worth
   d. cash outflow

2. A payment for rent represents
   a. a cash inflow
   b. a cash outflow
   c. a liability
   d. an asset

Make Academic Connections

3. **Math** Calculate the missing amount.
   a. Assets $7,000
      Liabilities $1,800
      Net worth __?__
   b. Assets $26,000
      Liabilities __?__
      Net worth $19,000
   c. Assets __?__
      Liabilities $5,600
      Net worth $67,800

4. **Research** What types of liabilities are commonly listed on the personal balance sheets of households in the United States?

Doing Business in... Nigeria

Imagine trying to do business in a country that has more than 250 languages and ethnic groups. In Nigeria, the most populous country in Africa, you are likely to encounter a variety of business situations.

When in Nigeria, you will conduct important business in face-to-face meetings. In these settings, you may see Nigerian businessmen wearing a suit and tie. Or, they might wear traditional clothing such as a buda, a loose-fitting shirt that extends to the knees.

As you greet business associates in Nigeria, remember that formal titles are very important. Be ready to address someone as "Chief," "Prince," or "Alhaji." Respect for older persons is vital. It is offensive in Nigerian society to pass an elderly person without a greeting. Handshakes are the most appropriate greeting.

At the first meeting with a business contact, be patient and expect many ongoing greetings. At first the conversation might seem overly personal, because Nigerians like to know the people with whom they are doing business.

If you are having lunch with a business acquaintance, make sure you always use your right hand (or both hands) to pass and accept dishes. The left hand is taboo and is rarely used for interpersonal transactions. Left-handers are especially advised to practice the use of their right hand. Foods that you will likely encounter include yams, cassava (a starchy root), and rice. Meats you are offered might include beef, chicken, turkey, goat, goose, and fish.

Nigeria is one of the world's largest oil producers. Due to political turmoil and unstable financial conditions, the country has continually faced economic difficulties. The informal economy (also called the underground economy) accounts for more than half of the business activities in Nigeria. Large numbers of workers make their living in unregulated settings. The items they produce and sell create income not reported to the government.

Think Critically

1. How does doing business in Nigeria differ from doing business in other countries?

2. What are the benefits and concerns related to informal economic activities?

3. Conduct library or Internet research to obtain additional information about business and economic activities in Nigeria.

What benefits might result from the oil production in Nigeria?

Photographer's Choice/Getty Images

16-2 Budgeting Techniques

HermanEritou/iStockphoto.com

Goals

1. Identify purposes of a budget.
2. Describe steps for preparing a budget.
3. Describe characteristics of successful budgeting.

Key Terms

fixed expenses 400

variable
  expenses 400

allowance 401

budget variance 402

Focus on REAL LIFE

Brandon Zeng has been practicing his Chinese through written communication with relatives in Hong Kong and conversations with his parents. He also has taken several business courses in high school. Brandon hopes to have a career in international business working in the Pacific Rim countries.

"I can't wait to go to Asia next summer, but the trip is going to cost me a fortune! The air transportation, housing, food, and other living expenses will cost more than $6,000. My parents have agreed to pay half. Fortunately for me, I developed a plan to save money for this trip. By the end of the year I will have the $3,000 I need. It's going to be a great experience. Hey Josh, why don't you go with me?"

"Are you kidding? I'm not as disciplined as you! I would never be able to save enough money. You are a pro at managing money. Maybe you can give me a few tips."

BUDGET ACTIVITIES

A *budget* allows you to meet your personal goals with a system of saving and wise spending. Having a plan for saving will help you do the following:

- Live within your income.

Make a list of items you buy regularly. How might you start spending less on these items?

Brand X Pictures/Getty Images

- Make wise buying decisions.
- Avoid credit problems.
- Plan for financial emergencies.
- Develop money management skills.
- Achieve your financial goals.

Having a written budget is a key part of successful money management. Your budget may be a simple record of how much you make, how much you plan to spend, and how much you want to save. On the other hand, your budget may be a more detailed record with specific amounts to be spent in categories such as food, clothing, and transportation. A good budget should take very little of your time, but it should provide needed information on your spending and savings plans.

> **Goal 1**
>
> Identify purposes of a budget.

> **checkpoint** ✓
> What are the main purposes of a budget?

Make a list of short-term and long-term financial goals. What steps do you need to take to reach these goals?

Goal 2

Describe steps for preparing a budget.

THE BUDGET PROCESS

The process of creating and using a budget involves four main steps.

1. Set financial goals.

2. Plan budget categories.

3. Maintain financial records.

4. Evaluate your budget.

Any individual, family, or organization can use these steps to aid them in using available financial resources.

Set Financial Goals

Setting financial goals is the first step for any financial action. Goals identify results you want to achieve. Your financial goals should take a SMART approach—specific, measurable, action-oriented, realistic, and time-based. Figure 16-3 provides more details about the SMART approach.

Writing down short-term and long-term goals will help you decide how to spend and save your money. If your goals include going to college, your budget will require more for savings. If you are working at a job that requires you to spend a large amount for transportation, you will likely budget more for this item.

Plan Budget Categories

Most financial advisers recommend that an amount be set aside for savings as the first part of a budget. If savings are not considered first, other expenses may use all available income.

After savings, two types of living expenses must be considered: fixed and variable expenses. **Fixed expenses** are costs that occur on a regular basis and are for the same amount each time. Examples of fixed expenses are rent, mortgage payments, and insurance premiums.

Variable expenses involve living costs that differ each time and may not be as easy to estimate. These types of expenses include food, clothing, and utilities. Some variable expenses, such as medical and dental costs, occur less often and may be large when they do occur. Such expenses must be provided for in the budget.

The amount budgeted for savings and other expenditures is referred to as an

SMART Approach to Setting Financial Goals

S	Specific	Make the goals specific so you know exactly what you want to achieve.
M	Measurable	Make the goals measurable so that you know the specific amount to save.
A	Action-oriented	Make the goals action-oriented so that you know what actions you need to take.
R	Realistic	Make the goals realistic based on your income.
T	Time-based	Make the goals time-based so that you have a time frame for achieving them.

▶ **Figure 16-3**

What are some of the advantages to the SMART approach?

allowance. An **allowance** is the amount of money you plan to use for a certain budget category. Although budget categories can vary for different situations, eight main divisions are commonly used.

1. **Savings** Savings accounts, government bonds, stocks, and other investments

2. **Food** Food eaten at home and meals eaten away from home

3. **Clothing** Clothing, shoes, dry cleaning, and repairs

4. **Household** Rent, mortgage, property taxes, insurance, utilities, furnishings, household supplies, and repairs

5. **Transportation** Auto payments, insurance, operating costs, maintenance, repairs, and public transportation

6. **Health and Personal Care** Medical and dental expenses, medications, eyeglasses, health insurance, and personal care costs

7. **Recreation and Education** Books and other reading materials, theater tickets, concerts, vacations, school expenses, hobbies, and club dues

8. **Gifts and Contributions** Charitable contributions and personal gifts

fyi A once-popular system for family budgeting required envelopes marked with labels of different expenses such as "Food," "Housing," and "Automobile." Each envelope contained the budgeted amount of money, and expenses were paid from the money in the envelopes. This system allows a person to see where the money is going. Unfortunately, a danger exists with keeping large amounts of cash at home.

Joel Calheiros/Shutterstock.com

At this point, ask yourself, "How much should I set aside for each category?" Planned spending for various budget categories will depend on income, family size, ages of children, cost of living in your area, and work-related expenses. It will also depend on personal values, needs, and goals. A cash flow statement, similar to Figure 16-2, can help you develop budget categories.

Other help for developing a budget can come from government reports on family spending or from articles in magazines, such as *Kiplinger's Personal Finance* and *Money*. An example of a family budget for one month is shown in Figure 16-4.

Family Budget for One Month

Chung Household					
Monthly Budget					
January, 20--					
ESTIMATED INCOME			**ESTIMATED EXPENSE**		
Manuel's net income	$4,225		Savings		$2,225
Lydia's net income	4,350		Food		1,100
			Clothing		475
			Household		1,825
			Transportation		1,275
			Health & personal care		450
			Recreation & education		800
			Gifts & contributions		425
Total Income	$8,575		Total Expenses		$8,575

▶ **Figure 16-4**

What percentage of income have the Chungs budgeted for savings? How do people decide how much to save?

Maintain Financial Records

After planning a budget, individuals and families should record their income and expenses to find out if the plan is working. An example is shown in Figure 16-5. The first line shows the monthly income available to the family ($8,575 after taxes and other paycheck deductions) and the budget allowances for each category.

During the month, entries for expenditures were recorded. Because the family pays most bills by check, a checkbook is a reference for the information needed to prepare the income and expense summary.

Goal 3

Describe characteristics of successful budgeting.

Evaluate Your Budget

All columns were totaled at the end of the month. Actual spending is compared with the budgeted amounts. Any difference between these amounts is a **budget variance**.

If actual spending is greater than planned spending, such as for the "Household" category, it is referred to as a *deficit*. When actual spending is less than the budgeted amount, as with the "Food" category, a *surplus* occurs.

A category-by-category comparison allows you to find areas where changes in the budget may be appropriate. A variance in the actual amount spent and the budgeted amount does not always mean a change in your spending plan is necessary.

Your budgeted amount may still be appropriate with a slight deficit or surplus occurring every few months in some categories. If you expect necessary higher or lower spending in a certain category, a change in your budget is probably needed.

> **checkpoint** ✓
> What are eight commonly used budget categories?

What kinds of adjustments would you have to make to live within a budget?

SUCCESSFUL BUDGETING

Effective budgeting will be an ongoing learning process for you.

Characteristics of an Effective Budget

The following are common characteristics of a successful budget.

- *Must be realistic.* It should reflect current income and planned spending.

- *Should be flexible.* When unexpected expenses arise, your spending plan should be able to adapt for these living costs.

- *Should be evaluated regularly.* Every few months, evaluate the budget to determine whether it still is appropriate.

- *Must be well planned and clearly communicated.* All family members should discuss financial goals, wants and needs, and plans for spending.

- *Should have a simple format.* If it is too detailed and difficult to understand, family members may not be willing to use the spending plan.

Budgeting Formats

A good budgeting system allows the user to develop a budget, track expenses, and pay bills. Some people prefer to use the latest technology for their budget and others prefer to work with traditional

Family Income and Expense Record

Chung Household

Income and Expense Record

Date		Explanation	Totals		Distribution of Savings and Expenditures							
			Receipts	Payments	Savings	Food	Clothing	Household	Transport.	Health/Per.	Rec./Edu.	Gifts & Con.
		Budget	$8,575.00		$2,225.00	$1,100.00	$475.00	$1,825.00	$1,275.00	$450.00	$800.00	$425.00
January	1	Balance	1,300.00									
		Manuel's net income	2,112.50									
		Lydia's net income	2,175.00									
	2			2,225.00	2,225.00							
	7			1,075.00		210.00	140.00	100.00	100.00	150.00	225.00	150.00
	14			950.00		230.00	90.00	200.00	145.00	125.00	90.00	70.00
	15	Manuel's net income	2,112.50									
		Lydia's net income	2,175.00									
	17	Mortgage payment		1,200.00				1,200.00				
	21	Car payment		850.00					850.00			
	22			925.00		200.00	150.00	190.00	75.00		160.00	150.00
	29			1,055.00		300.00	95.00	220.00	50.00	200.00	90.00	100.00
	31	Totals	$9,875.00	$8,280.00	$2,225.00	$940.00	$475.00	$1,910.00	$1,220.00	475.00	$565.00	$470.00
February	1	Balance*	$1,595.00									

*Balance = January's total receipts - total payments = $9,875.00 - $8,280.00

▲ **Figure 16-5**

In which categories did the Chung's expenditures exceed the amount they had budgeted? In which were they less than the amount budgeted?

WORK
as a
TEAM

For a budget to be successful, it must be followed. Work as a team to identify some situations in which a person or household may not be able to stay within their budget. Then explain actions that might be taken to resolve the situation.

handwritten documents. There are also people who try to keep their budgets in their heads. There are advantages and disadvantages to each format.

Money management software, cell phone applications, and financial websites offer budgeting tools. Although there are wide variations among the tools available, they are generally easy to use, provide guidance and organization, and utilize built-in calculators.

Handwritten budgets have the advantage of being inexpensive. They require nothing more than pencil and paper, although some people use a calculator or spreadsheet to help with calculations. For people with a single source of income and

few expenses, a handwritten budget might be a good choice.

Some people choose to use their checkbook register and bank statements as a substitute for a budget. These documents allow the user to pay bills and monitor deposits and balances, but there is no mechanism for financial planning.

The idea of keeping a budget in your head is appealing to some people because of its simplicity. However the possibility of mistakes is greatly reduced when budget information is documented on paper or in an electronic file.

Your decision for a budgeting system will depend on your personal situation and your personal preferences. Most important is choosing a method that provides accurate and timely information for helping you achieve your financial goals.

> **checkpoint** ✓
> What are five characteristics of an effective budget?

16-2 Assessment

Study Tools

www.cengage.com/school/genbus/pob

Key Concepts

Determine the best answer.

1. True or False. Retirement planning is usually considered a short-term goal.

2. A major purpose of a budget is to
   a. assist with comparison shopping
   b. achieve financial goals
   c. reduce a person's enjoyment of life
   d. gather data for using credit cards

3. The most uncertain aspect of the budgeting process involves
   a. estimating variable expenses
   b. determining net worth
   c. estimating fixed expenses
   d. setting financial goals

Make Academic Connections

4. **Math** Mary and Fred James budgeted $340 a month for groceries. During the month, they spent $87, $93, $38, $61, and $52 at the supermarket.
   a. What was the total amount spent for food?
   b. Did Mary and Fred have a budget deficit or surplus? What was the amount?

5. **Visual Art** Talk to several people about various short-term and long-term goals they have had in their lives. Prepare a poster or computerized presentation summarizing various types of goals, both financial and personal.

16-3 Taxes in Your Life

Goals

1 Identify the types of taxes paid by consumers.

2 Describe the steps when filing a federal income tax return.

3 Explain tax assistance sources.

4 Identify common tax-planning strategies.

Key Terms

tax 405

earned income 407

investment income 407

tax deduction 407

exemption 408

taxable income 408

tax credit 408

Focus on REAL LIFE

"I just got my first paycheck and was I surprised," commented Nick. "I earned more than $200, but my check was for less than $160. What's the deal with that?"

"I guess you didn't pay attention in business class about income taxes and Social Security taxes," suggested Margie.

"Well, I do know that some of my pay has to go for roads, parks, and protecting our country," responded Nick. "And that I must file a tax return to get my refund or to pay an additional amount. Also, my tax return must be filed each year by…"

"OK—it sounds like you did learn a few things about taxes in our business class," acknowledged Margie.

TYPES OF TAXES

Each day, without thinking about it, people pay taxes. Many people pay taxes through paycheck deductions. Depending where you live and shop, you might pay taxes when you make purchases. Wise tax planning starts with knowing the types of taxes you pay.

A **tax** is a charge imposed by a government to finance public services. Federal, state, and local governments levy taxes. Most people pay taxes in four major categories: purchases, property, wealth, and earning. Common taxes on purchases are sales tax and excise tax. Real estate property tax and personal property taxes are examples of taxes on property. Taxes on wealth include estate tax, inheritance tax, and gift tax. Social Security tax and income tax are examples of taxes on earnings. Examples of common taxes are described in Figure 16-6.

Not everyone pays every kind of tax. The types of taxes you pay and how much you pay is related to where you live, how much money you earn, and how you spend and save your money.

When and Where You Pay Taxes

Some taxes are paid as part of everyday living. Other taxes are due on specific dates. And some taxes, such as estate taxes, are triggered by an event—the death of a person.

Sales tax is collected at the time of purchase. If you buy a jacket for $80 you might pay more than $80. If your state has a 5 percent sales tax and you are shopping in a county with a 1 percent sales tax, you will pay the seller $84.80 for your coat. The seller will pay $4 to the state and $0.80 to the county. In recent years, five states did not have a state sales tax: Alaska, Delaware, Montana, New Hampshire, and Oregon.

In addition to paying sales tax at the cash register, you also pay taxes at the pump. The state price of gasoline includes various taxes. The tax may be hidden, but you still pay it.

Real estate taxes are usually due once or twice a year. Some property owners choose to pay the bill when it is due.

Goal 1

Identify the types of taxes paid by consumers.

Common Taxes

CATEGORIES	EXAMPLES	DESCRIPTION
Taxes on purchases	Sales tax	A sales tax is a state or local tax on goods and services that is collected by the seller. Food and prescription drugs are often exempt.
	Excise tax	An excise tax is imposed on specific goods and services. For example, all states impose an excise tax on gasoline.
Taxes on property	Real estate property tax	This tax is based on the value of land and buildings. Most property tax revenue is used to pay for schools and local government services.
	Personal property tax	This tax is based on the value of personal property such as boats, cars, and trucks.
Taxes on wealth	Estate tax	This tax is based on the value of a person's property at death.
	Inheritance tax	This tax is based on the value of items received from a deceased person.
	Gift tax	This tax applies to gifts of any kind of property, including money, when the value of the gift exceeds a certain dollar amount. Generally the donor is responsible for the gift tax.
Taxes on earnings	Social Security tax	This tax is based on earnings and is used to finance retirement and disability benefits.
	Income tax	This tax is based on earnings and other sources of income and is a source of revenue for governments.

▶ **Figure 16-6**

What are some taxes that you and your family pay?

Others choose to add money to their mortgage payments and ask the financial institution that holds the mortgage to set the money aside until it is time to pay the property tax. The financial institution then pays the bill when it is due.

Income Tax Payments

People make payments for federal, state, and local income taxes in two ways: withholding and estimated payments. Withholding is a "pay-as-you-go system" in which an employer deducts income tax from the earnings of workers each pay period. In January, workers receive a W-2 from each employer. A W-2 is a summary of a worker's earnings for the previous year and includes the amounts deducted for taxes.

Some people are required to make estimated payments for income taxes. Examples of income that may require estimated payments include significant income from savings and investments, income from royalties and pensions, and income from self-employment or working as an independent contractor. Estimated payments are made directly to the government and are due quarterly. Estimated payments for federal income tax are due on April 15, June 15, September 15, and January 15 of the next year.

Most states also have an income tax to fund the cost of highways, state parks, and other public services. In recent years, these states did not have a state income tax: Alaska, Florida, Nevada, South Dakota, Texas, Washington, and Wyoming. These states fund services with other types of taxes and fees.

checkpoint ✓
What are the four main categories of taxes?

PREPARING THE FEDERAL INCOME TAX RETURN

The Internal Revenue Service (IRS) is part of the U.S. Treasury. The IRS is the agency responsible for collecting federal income tax. In order to make sure that people pay the taxes they owe, the IRS requires taxpayers to file, or submit, a federal income tax return each year. With some exceptions, the filing deadline is April 15 of the next year.

The main purpose of preparing a federal income tax return is to determine the amount of tax a taxpayer is required to pay for a particular year. Because most people make tax payments throughout the year, the form is also used to determine if you have paid all that you owe, you need to pay more, or you are entitled to a refund or credit. The seven main steps in the preparation of a federal income tax return are presented in Figure 16-7.

Step 1: Determine Gross Income The two main types of income for most people are earned income and investment income. **Earned income** results from wages, salary, commission, fees, tips, and bonuses. **Investment income** is the result of earnings from dividends, interest, and rent. Federal income tax must also be paid on other types of income such as alimony, awards, lottery winnings, and prizes. For example, cash and prizes won on television game shows are subject to both federal and states taxes.

Tax-exempt income is income not subject to tax. Interest earned on most state and city bonds, for example, is exempt from federal income tax. In contrast, *tax-deferred income* will be taxed at a later date.

Step 2: Calculate Adjusted Gross Income Certain items, called *adjustments to income,* are subtracted from gross income to obtain adjusted gross income (AGI). These reductions include deposits in retirement accounts and alimony payments.

Step 3: Subtract Deductions A **tax deduction** is an amount that reduces taxable income. All taxpayers are eligible for a standard deduction, an amount on which no taxes are paid. As an alternative, a taxpayer may choose to itemize deductions. The rules regarding what can be included in itemized deductions are very specific and change to reflect tax policies and laws.

Examples of items that might be included in itemized deductions include the following:

- Certain medical and dental expenses
- Taxes paid for state and local income tax and property taxes
- Interest paid on a home mortgage or home equity loan
- Contributions to charitable organizations
- Casualty and theft losses
- Moving expenses when a new job is more than 50 miles away
- Certain job-related expenses such as union dues, required continuing education, work clothes, and tax preparation fees

The decision to use the standard deduction or to itemize your deductions

Goal 2

Describe the steps when filing a federal income tax return.

FEDERAL INCOME TAX RETURN PREPARATION	
Step 1	Determine gross income
Step 2	Calculate adjusted gross income
Step 3	Subtract deductions
Step 4	Determine exemptions
Step 5	Compute taxable income
Step 6	Calculate tax owed
Step 7	Make tax payments or ask for a refund or credit

▶ Figure 16-7

What are some ways that tax money is used by the federal government?

1. The person must not earn more than a certain amount unless he or she is under age 19 or is a full-time student under age 24.

2. The taxpayer must provide more than half of the dependent's support.

3. The dependent must live with the taxpayer or be a relative.

depends on your income and your expenses for the year. In some cases it is worthwhile to calculate your tax liability both ways and choose the one that is more advantageous.

Step 4: Determine Exemptions An **exemption** is a tax deduction for the taxpayer, a spouse, and each dependent. For each exemption, taxable income is reduced by a set amount. Therefore, the more dependents a taxpayer can claim, the greater the reduction in taxable income.

In most cases dependents are minor children, but specific criteria must be met. For a person to qualify as a dependent, all three of the following conditions are necessary:

Step 5: Compute Taxable Income **Taxable income** is the amount on which taxes are calculated. This amount results from subtracting adjustments to income, deductions, and exemptions from gross income.

Step 6: Taxes Owed Tax rates are the percentages used to compute the amount owed for taxes. In recent years, the federal income tax rates have ranged from 10 to 35 percent, depending on the level of taxable income.

A person's taxes can be reduced by a **tax credit**, an amount subtracted directly from taxes owed. Tax credits may be obtained for child- and dependent-care expenses. Low-income workers may qualify for the earned-income credit (EIC).

Remember that a tax credit differs from a deduction in that a tax credit lowers taxes by the full dollar amount. In contrast, a deduction reduces the amount on which the taxes are calculated.

Step 7: Make Tax Payments or Ask for a Refund or Credit The final step in preparing a tax return is to compare the amount paid with the amount owed for taxes. You may owe an additional amount, or you may receive a refund or credit if you paid more than you owe for taxes. Many people like receiving a refund. However, it is important to remember, your money was being held by the government and you were not able to use it or earn interest on it.

micro 10x/Shutterstock.com

What documents would you need to complete your federal tax return?

Completing the Federal Income Tax Return

The process of completing the federal income tax return requires taxpayers to determine their filing status and which tax form is appropriate for their situation. It is important to provide complete and accurate information and avoid common filing errors. The completed tax return must be filed with the IRS by mailing it to an IRS processing center or submitting it electronically.

Filing Status All U.S. citizens and residents are required to file a federal income tax return if their income exceeds a certain amount. Marital status and the number of dependents determine a taxpayer's filing status. The five options for filing status are explained in Figure 16-8.

Tax Forms Taxpayers use one of three forms to file their federal income tax return. Form 1040 is the basic form and Form 1040A and Form 1040EZ are shorter, less complicated versions.

Form 1040EZ allows a person with a simple tax situation to easily file a federal income tax return. While a little more complicated than the EZ, Form 1040A may be used by people who have less than $50,000 in taxable income from wages,

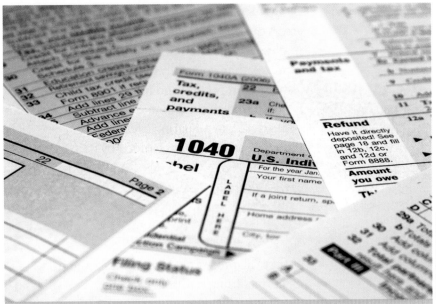

How are Forms 1040A and 1040EZ related to Form 1040?

salaries, tips, unemployment compensation, interest, or dividends and use the standard deduction. The most detailed of the three forms, Form 1040, has sections for all types of income. A person must use this form if income is over $50,000 or if claimed as a dependent by a parent and had interest or dividends over a certain amount. Form 1040 is also used when itemizing deductions. The decision regarding which tax form to use depends on your income level, the amount of your deductions, and other complexities of your tax situation.

INCOME TAX FILING STATUS	
Single	Refers to individuals who are unmarried, divorced, or legally separated with no dependents.
Married filing jointly	Refers to a married couple filing a joint return.
Married filing separately	Is an option available to a married couple when each spouse takes responsibility for his or her own tax return.
Head of household	Refers to an unmarried individual or a surviving spouse who maintains a household (paying for more than half of the costs) for a child or a dependent relative.
Qualifying widow or widower	Refers to an individual whose spouse died within the past two years and who has a qualifying dependent child.

▶ **Figure 16-8**

Why might people who are married choose the filing status *married filing separately*?

Avoiding Common Filing Errors Filing errors can cost time and money. An error might delay a refund or result in paying more tax than you really owe. Errors can also result in penalty and interest charges for not filing on time or underpayment of taxes. When preparing a federal tax return, mistakes can be avoided by doing the following:

- Create a filing system for tax documents, receipts, and tax forms.
- Follow instructions carefully.
- Use the proper tax form, tax table, and correct filing status.
- Check, and recheck, calculations carefully.
- Include all required documents, such as a copy of your W-2 form.
- Sign the tax return.
- Make your check payable to the U.S. Treasury.
- Write your Social Security number and the tax year on your check.
- File online or mail your return before the deadline.
- Use the proper amount of postage.
- Keep a copy of the tax return.

Filing Taxes Online The use of tax preparation software can save 10 or more hours of time. These programs allow taxpayers to use a computer to prepare federal and state tax forms by answering a series of questions or entering information on forms. The tax forms can be printed for filing by mail or the user may choose to file online. Filing online means that the tax return is submitted electronically.

Goal 3

Explain tax assistance sources.

The Internal Revenue Service now makes online filing easier and less expensive than it was a few years ago. The Free File Alliance provides online tax preparation and e-filing free to millions of taxpayers. This program is a partnership between the IRS and the tax software industry.

> **checkpoint** ✓
> What are the seven steps for preparing a federal income tax return?

TAX PREPARATION ASSISTANCE

Many taxpayers prepare their own federal income tax returns by hand or with tax preparation software. Other taxpayers use the services of a tax professional to prepare their returns. While some people like the convenience, others choose a professional because they are not comfortable completing their own tax return. Many resources are available to help taxpayers with the preparation of their federal tax return and tax planning.

IRS Services Tax information and assistance is available directly from the Internal Revenue Service. The IRS website allows you to access needed tax forms and instructions. The IRS also offers:

- Tax forms requested by telephone or fax
- Recorded tax tips from a 24-hour a day toll-free number
- Answers to specific tax questions by calling a toll-free hotline
- Walk-in tax assistance at the 400 local IRS offices around the country

Another IRS service is the Volunteer Income Tax Assistance (VITA), which offers free tax help to low- and moderate-income taxpayers who cannot prepare their own tax returns.

Tax Publications Commercial tax guides are available to assist taxpayers.

WORK *as a* **TEAM**

Many people make mistakes when preparing their tax return, resulting in delays in processing and penalties. As a team, create a list of specific actions that a person might take to avoid common errors when filing an income tax return.

These guides cover a wide range of topics. Some are intended for specific groups such as small businesses, and are updated annually.

Online Sources Many websites focus on tax information. These may be located using an online search.

Tax Preparation Software Many taxpayers use tax preparation software to prepare tax returns. These products allow users to print returns for filing or to file electronically. Data entry is quick and easy. Options allow for updating information from last year's return and accessing income data from employers and financial institutions.

Tax preparation software also has features to help taxpayers organize records, avoid common mistakes, and take advantage of appropriate deductions and credits. Tax planning features offer strategies for making financial decisions.

Tax Preparation Services Many taxpayers pay for professional tax preparation

service. Some might pay as little as $35 and others pay thousands of dollars for these services. The fee varies based on the complexity of the tax return and the level of training of the tax preparer. Professional tax preparation services include:

- Tax services ranging from local, one-person organizations to national companies with hundreds of offices

- Enrolled agents who are government-approved tax preparers with specific training

- Certified public accountants (CPA) with specific tax training to assist with tax planning and preparation of tax returns

Some tax preparation services and other businesses offer *refund anticipation loans*. In most cases the interest rate on this type of loan is very high. In some cases the annual interest rate is more than

What factors might a person consider when selecting a professional tax service?

100 percent of the amount being borrowed. You should be cautious of any loan or special financing that is dependent on a tax refund.

checkpoint ✓

Name the professionals from whom a person can obtain tax assistance.

Goal 4

Identify common tax-planning strategies.

EFFECTIVE TAX STRATEGIES

Tax laws and tax forms change frequently. Using print and online resources, attending classes, and consulting with financial professionals are ways of staying informed about taxes. Being knowledgeable can help you develop strategies and make decisions that limit the amount of taxes you are required to pay. It is also important to understand that your personal and financial situation will change over time and you will need to be aware of how these changes relate to taxes.

Three common ways to limit the amount of income tax you owe are home ownership, tax-exempt investments, and tax-deferred investments.

Home Ownership Home ownership may reduce taxable income if the taxpayer itemizes deductions. Amounts paid for real estate taxes and mortgage interest are itemized deductions that reduce taxable income. Interest on a home-equity loan of up to $100,000 is also an itemized deduction.

Tax-Exempt Investments Interest income from municipal bonds, issued by state and local governments, and other tax-exempt investments is not subject to federal income tax.

Tax-Deferred Investments Income from tax-deferred investments has the advantage of lowering current taxes. A common tax strategy for working people is the use of tax-deferred retirement plans to reduce their current taxes.

checkpoint ✓

What is the main difference between tax-exempt investments and tax-deferred investments?

16-3 ASSESSMENT

Study Tools

www.cengage.com/school/genbus/pob

Key Concepts

Determine the best answer.

1. A tax on earnings would be an _____ tax.
   a. inheritance
   b. estate
   c. income
   d. excise

2. Cami Bartosz calculated that she owed taxes of $254 and had $278 withheld from her pay during the year. This would result in
   a. a refund of $278.
   b. a refund of $24.
   c. additional taxes owed of $254.
   d. additional taxes owed of $24.

Make Academic Connections

3. **Culture** Different types of taxes exist in other countries based on government policies and other factors. Conduct library or online research to determine the taxes people might encounter in European or Asian countries. Prepare a brief written summary of your findings.

4. **Technology** Locate a website that people might use to prepare their federal income tax return. Prepare a poster or computer presentation that illustrates the web address, features of the website, cost of the services, and other information available to taxpayers.

16-4 Your Financial Future

Goals

1 Describe the financial planning process.

2 Explain actions for implementing a financial plan.

3 Identify actions for reviewing a financial plan.

Key Terms

financial plan 413

individual retirement account (IRA) 416

estate planning 418

Focus on REAL LIFE

"Gloria, are you going to the Business Speakers Series monthly luncheon on Friday?"

"I really hadn't given it much thought, Maria. Are you?"

"Yes! The speaker is from the local college and is supposed to be very dynamic and informative. The topic is financial planning, and if I am going to go to college, I need some help in planning right now! Why don't you meet me there?"

"Great idea, Maria. I always thought of financial planning as something for people out of college. But it certainly makes sense to start now! I guess if I start planning early, I can get a head start on my future!"

DEVELOPING A FINANCIAL PLAN

To successfully reach financial goals, you must have a plan. Successful coaches have a game plan. Travel agents refer to vacation plans. Builders must have house plans. Successful consumers and businesspeople must have a financial plan. A **financial plan** is a report that summarizes your current financial condition, acknowledges your financial needs, and sets a direction for your future financial activities.

Financial planning includes evaluating one's financial position, setting financial goals, and guiding activities and resources toward reaching those goals. Everyone should have a carefully developed financial plan.

Your financial plan should include all that you know about good money management. This plan should be developed carefully. It should be evaluated and updated frequently. A well-developed financial plan can make your financial life more satisfying.

Financial planning offers several specific advantages.

- Your financial uncertainties will be reduced.

- You will gain more control of your financial activities.

- Your family and household members will know more about your financial situation in case they need to assume control of your finances.

- Earning, spending, protecting, and saving your resources will be more systematic.

Financial Planning Process

Financial planning experts recommend the following steps.

> ### Goal 1
> Describe the financial planning process.

Describe the role of financial planning in the creation of a person's life-span plan. Do you have a financial plan? Explain why people who fail to create and follow a financial plan often fail to achieve their life-span goals.

1. *Analyze your current financial condition.* You should create a balance sheet and cash flow statement.

2. *Develop financial goals that are responsive to your vision.* What short-term and long-term objectives do you have? How much money will you need, and when?

3. *Create your financial plan.* This activity will require that you plan various actions for your saving and spending goals. This step may require help from a financial planner or other financial specialists.

4. *Implement the plan.* This may involve buying or selling property or investments, moving bank accounts, acquiring insurance, or any number of financial activities.

5. *Revise your financial plan.* As time goes on, you will frequently evaluate and revise your financial plan.

Financial Inventory

Think of a financial inventory as a financial checkup. When you get a medical checkup, the physician assesses your health. A financial inventory is a careful assessment of your finances.

A financial inventory will usually include the creation of a personal balance sheet and cash flow statement. This process will provide information about your current financial position in terms of income, savings, investments, property, living expenses, insurance, and money owed.

Personal Financial Filing System

To keep your financial inventory and other records in order, you should create a personal financial filing system. Well-organized files are key to financial planning. These files should contain all of the documents and records related to such things as contracts, bills, receipts, bank balances, and legal papers. The files will become an invaluable resource to you as you progress with your financial planning. The contents may be organized in categories as shown in Figure 16-9.

A FILING SYSTEM FOR PERSONAL FINANCIAL RECORDS	
Personal records • Birth certificate • Social Security card • Current resume	**Housing records** • Lease • Mortgage papers • Property tax records
Money management records • Current budget • Personal balance sheet • Cash flow statement	**Insurance records** • Insurance policies • Medical information • Claim reports
Financial services and credit records • Bank statements • Certificates of deposit • Monthly credit card statements	**Consumer purchase records** • Warranties • Receipts for major purchases • Motor vehicle registration
Tax records • Pay stubs, W-2 forms • Receipts for tax deductions • Income tax forms	**Investment, retirement, and estate records** • Investment account statements • Pension plan information • Will, trust information

▶ **Figure 16-9**

Name some ways computers have made financial record keeping more efficient.

Financial Life Cycle

Most people's lives follow a predictable pattern called a *life cycle*. Each stage of life is distinguished by unique characteristics, requirements, and expectations. For example, during the teen years, people are exploring career options, developing plans for independence, and evaluating future financial needs. In your twenties, you will likely train for a career, set up a household, and perhaps marry and have children.

Later in life, you may decide to obtain additional career training or make plans for paying for children's education. Then retirement plans, investing, and estate planning will likely become a priority.

Each life stage has financial matters that need attention. That attention can be provided through the development of a good financial plan. Remember, a good plan is one that is flexible and useful throughout several life stages.

Using a Financial Planner

Creating a financial plan is not a simple task. Doing your own financial planning requires time, information, and patience. Financial planners are professionals who can help you. A financial planner should have studied and passed examinations on various topics, including investments, insurance, taxes, real estate, and estate planning.

Questions you might ask when choosing a financial planner include the following:

- What experience and training do you have?

- Are you willing to supply references from past clients?

- How are your fees determined?

WORK *as a* TEAM

Having an organized system of financial records is important for financial planning success. As a team, (1) develop a list of financial records in addition to those in Figure 16-9, (2) discuss where you might keep various documents in addition to a home file, (3) decide how long various documents should be kept.

checkpoint ✓

List five recommended steps for financial planning.

IMPLEMENT A FINANCIAL PLAN

Implementing your plan may involve a wide variety of actions. You may need to move your savings to an account in which you will earn a higher interest rate. You may buy a bond. Maybe you will begin to work more hours at your part-time job to earn more money.

The list of financial planning actions can seem almost endless. For your plan to lead to achieving your financial

Goal 2

Explain actions for implementing a financial plan.

Talk with an older person who started saving when he or she was your age. What can you learn from this person's financial successes or mistakes?

Monkey Business Images/Shutterstock.com

goals, several common areas should be considered.

Insure Current Income

Protecting your income so that it contributes to your goals is a key financial planning action. Insurance is available that will provide an income to those who fear the two most common causes of loss of income: disability and unemployment.

Disability Income Insurance To replace income that is lost when you cannot work because of an illness or injury, you can purchase *disability income insurance.* Many different disability income policies are available. Most disability income insurance will pay 60 to 70 percent of your salary while you are disabled. Before the benefits begin, there is usually a waiting period from one week to 90 days after you are disabled. Many employers provide this type of insurance.

Unemployment Insurance Unemployment is another hazard to a financial plan. To reduce the financial hardship of unemployment, most states have an *unemployment insurance* program, operated in cooperation with the federal government. This coverage provides cash payments for a limited time to people who are out of work for a reason other than illness. A local unemployment office will provide guidance to help find a new job. If no suitable job is found, you may qualify for payments to replace part of your lost wages.

Plan for Future Income

The success of any financial plan also calls for a stream of future income. Once people retire, their salaries stop, but they continue to need money to cover living expenses. Workers can ensure that they will have enough income during their retirement years through Social Security, pensions, individual retirement accounts, and annuities.

Social Security A key form of income protection comes through the federal government's Social Security system called *retirement, survivors, and disability insurance.* This part of Social Security provides pensions to retired workers and their families, death benefits to dependents of workers who die, and benefits to disabled workers and their families.

Social Security benefits are funded by payroll taxes from both workers and employers. The taxes are deducted from employees' paychecks. Employers match the amounts paid by their employees. Self-employed people, such as farmers and small business owners, pay the entire tax themselves.

When a worker retires, becomes disabled, or dies, monthly payments are made from the trust fund. The amount of benefits received depends on how long a worker was employed and how much a worker earned while employed.

Pensions A *pension* is a series of regular payments made to a retired worker under an organized plan. Some employers offer plans that provide monthly payments to retired workers. Unions often establish similar plans. To qualify under most pension plans, you must work for the same organization for a minimum number of years.

Retirement Accounts People can also develop their own retirement income plans. The most popular of these plans is the **individual retirement account (IRA)**. An IRA is a tax-sheltered retirement plan in which people can annually invest earnings up to a certain amount. Contributions to traditional IRAs are tax-deductible. The investment gains are tax-deferred and the funds are taxed when they are withdrawn after age 59½. Contributions to a Roth IRA are not tax-deductible. However, all funds, including any investment gains, are tax-free when withdrawn after age 59½.

Other types of retirement accounts for self-employed workers and people who run their own businesses include the 401(k), Keogh, SIMPLE, and SEP plans. Each of these involves tax-deferred retirement income. *Tax-deferred* means the investment earnings will be taxed later, after retirement. The type of retirement plan for which you qualify will depend on your employment situation and income level.

Annuities An amount of money an insurance company pays to a person who has previously deposited money with the company is called an *annuity*. This financial agreement is an investment plan for retirement income. You pay the insurance company a certain amount of money either in a lump sum or in a series of payments. In return, the company agrees to pay you a regular income beginning at a certain age and continuing for life or for a specified number of years.

How much money per month will you need to live comfortably when you retire? Where will this money come from?

moodboard/Jupiter Images

checkpoint ✓

What are common sources of income during retirement?

REVIEW YOUR FINANCIAL PLAN

A financial plan must be flexible. View your financial plan as a changeable document. Your plan should be evaluated and adjusted on a regular basis to produce the outcomes you desire.

Revise Financial Goals

Once you have an understanding of changes in your financial or personal situation, you should consider changes in your financial goals. These goals may be short-term or long-term. They are usually stated in dollar amounts. An example of a short-term goal is "saving $1,000 in one year." This goal is simple, straightforward, and fairly short-term.

By contrast, long-term financial goals are often more complex and involve a

Goal 3

Identify actions for reviewing a financial plan.

longer period. These might include "owning a home by age 30."

Often, short-term goals may need to be given up in order to achieve long-term ones. For example, you may have to forgo buying a bicycle in order to save for an automobile.

Review Financial Activities

Changes in your goals will require changes in spending and saving habits. Although retirement may be years away, preparing for it is a vital part of financial planning. Chances are very good that you will spend many happy and healthy years in retirement. Those years will be happier and healthier if you have an adequate supply of money.

Estate planning involves the accumulation and management of property during one's lifetime and the distribution of one's property at death. During your life you build your estate through savings, investments, and insurance. You also plan

how you wish your estate to be transferred when you die.

Remember to Save and Share

Money management and financial planning are ongoing activities. Every decision you make will affect both current spending and long-term financial security. The only way to have money in the future is to spend less than you receive. The overuse of credit and other poor spending habits are the basis for long-term financial disaster. Your budget and spending activities should also involve sharing some resources. This may involve religious donations or contributions to local and global organizations that provide food, housing, and other necessities to people in need.

checkpoint ✓
What activities are involved when reviewing a financial plan?

16-4 Assessment

Study Tools
www.cengage.com/school/genbus/pob

Key Concepts

Determine the best answer.

1. A common source of retirement income is
   a. disability income insurance
   b. a mortgage
   c. pensions
   d. unemployment insurance

2. A long-term financial goal usually involves
   a. less than two years
   b. buying with a credit card
   c. using the services of a financial planner
   d. saving over many years

Make Academic Connections

3. **Research** Use library or online research to determine common financial planning activities for different stages of life. Prepare a poster to summarize your findings for people in their 20s, 30s, 40s, 50s, 60s, and older.

4. **Oral Communication** Conduct an interview with another student. Ask that person about her or his financial goals. Suggest actions to help the person achieve those goals.

Social and Cross Cultural Skills

Effective Interviewing

As a job applicant, you will be interviewed. You will be asked questions to determine your experiences and knowledge. In contrast, your ability to interview others can be of value in several ways. Someday you may interview potential employees for a company. Or, you may interview people for information for class assignments or in work situations.

When conducting an interview to make a business decision or to obtain information, follow these guidelines.

1. Create four or five open-ended questions related to the topic to get the person talking.

2. Develop questions that cannot be answered with one or two words.

3. The best interview questions start with *why, what, when, where, how,* and *describe.*

4. Listen for major themes or key ideas. Give the respondent time to answer. Don't interrupt.

5. Use follow-up questions to obtain additional information.

6. Do not ask leading questions—ones that suggest an answer for which you are looking.

Probing and Clarifying

Two valuable interviewing techniques are probing and clarifying. Probing is a technique to obtain additional information from a respondent. Probing starts with careful questioning by the interviewer. Probing can be achieved with repeating a question. Probing phrases include:

- Anything else?
- Please tell me more.
- What do you mean by that?
- Why do you feel that way?

Clarifying is a process to get an explanation about an answer that has already been given. You want to know specifically what is meant by an answer. One clarifying technique is to ask, "What do you mean by..." and then repeat the respondent's exact words. Another way to clarify is to ask the respondent to provide additional information about some response that has already been given.

What are some of the social skills you need to demonstrate when participating in an interview?

Professional Behavior

Whether you are the person being interviewed or you are the person conducting the interview, the situation requires a professional appearance and demeanor. Being well-groomed, dressed appropriately, and punctual are all signs of respect. It is also important to demonstrate the kinds of social skills that will be needed on the job such as shaking hands, maintaining eye contact, sitting up straight, speaking clearly, and not interrupting when someone else is speaking.

An effective interview provides an opportunity for both parties to gain knowledge that relates to the business situation. When an interview is going well it is easy to slip into a personal conversation and provide too much information or say something inappropriate. While you want to be friendly and open, your goal should be to conduct the interview in a professional manner.

Think Critically

1. What are situations in which your ability to interview others would be useful?

2. What actions could you take to improve your interview skills?

3. Conduct an interview to obtain information about a career, company, or country. Write an essay about your experience.

Business Notes

16-1 Personal Financial Statements

- You can manage your money wisely by planning carefully, using information to help you better understand and take action on your money matters, comparing products and prices, and making wise decisions.

- A balance sheet is a record of assets and liabilities at a point in time. Assets are items of value. Liabilities are amounts owed to others. Net worth is the difference between assets and liabilities.

- A cash flow statement is a record of cash inflows (income) and cash outflows (payments for living expenses) for a given period, such as a month.

16-2 Budgeting Techniques

- The main purposes of a budget are to help you live within your income, achieve your financial goals, buy wisely, avoid credit problems, plan for financial emergencies, and develop good money management skills. Having a written budget is an important phase of successful money management.

- The process of creating and using a budget involves setting financial goals, planning budget categories, maintaining financial records, and evaluating your budget.

- A successful budget will be realistic, flexible, evaluated regularly, well planned, clearly communicated to those involved, and in a simple format.

16-3 Taxes in Your Life

- The main taxes people pay are sales tax, excise tax, real estate property tax, personal property tax, estate tax, inheritance tax, gift tax, Social Security tax, and income tax.

- The steps for filing a federal tax return are: (1) determine gross income, (2) calculate adjusted gross income, (3) subtract deductions, (4) determine exemptions, (5) compute taxable income, (6) calculate tax owed, and (7) make tax payments or ask for a refund or credit

- The main sources of tax information and assistance are the IRS, online sources, printed materials, tax preparation software, and tax professionals.

16-4 Your Financial Future

- The five main steps in the financial planning process are to analyze your current financial condition, develop financial goals, create a financial plan, implement the plan, and evaluate and revise the plan over time.

- Two key areas to consider when implementing a financial plan are protecting current income and providing for future income. Current income can be protected by disability income insurance and unemployment insurance. Sources of future income during retirement include Social Security, pensions, individual retirement accounts, and annuities.

- When reviewing your financial plan, view it as a fluid, changeable document that will accommodate opportunity. You should revise financial goals as your financial or personal situation changes. Changes in your goals will require changes in spending and saving habits. Most importantly, remember to save. The only way to have money in the future is to spend less than you receive.

Communicate Business Concepts

1. Identify each of the following items as an asset or a liability:

   a. Money owed to the dentist
   b. An automobile
   c. Clothing
   d. Savings account
   e. Credit card balance
   f. Amount due for a personal loan
   g. 100 shares of stock

2. "Money management means never spending, doing without things, and not having any fun." Do you agree with this statement? Explain your answer.

3. Describe the difference between short-term and long-term goals. Give two examples of each type.

4. What two actions could you take if your expenditures were consistently greater than your income?

5. Every week, Chris Thorson puts any amount he has not spent during the week into a savings account. If he needs more money than he has during a week, he withdraws it from his savings. Is Chris following a good money management plan? Explain.

6. Consider a family of four people: mother, a supermarket manager; father, a department store salesperson; and two children, ages 14 and 11.

   a. List four fixed expenses that this family would likely have each month.
   b. What are some variable expenses that they are likely to have?
   c. How are the family's expenses different from those of other families with younger children or no children?

7. Why might a person want to better understand income tax laws?

8. One financial planner has said, "Doing nothing about financial planning is equivalent to making a decision about financial planning." What do you think she meant by this?

9. How does a budget differ from a financial plan?

10. Give examples of activities that might be involved in implementing a financial plan.

11. Some people claim that living by a budget is too structured and restrictive. That is, they do not like to live such a planned and strict economic life. What would you say to those individuals who have that point of view in order to convince them that budgets can be helpful to everyone?

12. Tell in your own words how people's financial goals change throughout their life cycle.

13. List some items that might be a want for one person but a need for someone else.

Develop Your Business Language

Match the terms listed with the definitions.

14. The amount of money you plan to use for a certain budget category.

15. A tax deduction for the taxpayer, a spouse, and each dependent.

16. Living costs involving differing amounts each time.

17. The financial statement that reports net wages and other income along with spending for a given period.

18. The amount on which taxes are calculated.

19. Accumulation and management of property during one's lifetime and the distribution of one's property at death.

20. Costs that occur regularly and are for the same amount each time.

21. An amount subtracted directly from taxes owed.

22. Items of value.

23. Earnings from dividends, interest, and rent.

24. A tax-sheltered retirement plan in which people can annually invest earnings up to a certain amount. The earnings contributed and interest earned are tax-free until the funds are withdrawn.

25. The day-to-day financial activities associated with using limited income to satisfy your unlimited needs and wants.

26. The difference between a person's or family's assets and liabilities.

27. An amount that reduces taxable income.

28. Money from wages, salary, commission, fees, tips, and bonuses.

29. A difference between actual spending and planned spending.

30. A report that summarizes your current financial condition, acknowledges your financial needs, and sets a direction for your future financial activities.

31. A charge imposed by a government to finance public services.

KEY TERMS

a. allowance
b. budget variance
c. cash flow statement
d. earned income
e. estate planning
f. exemption
g. financial plan
h. fixed expense
i. individual retirement account (IRA)
j. investment income
k. money management
l. net worth
m. personal assets
n. tax
o. tax credit
p. tax deduction
q. taxable income
r. variable expense

Make Academic Connections

25. Economics Use newspaper ads and Web research to determine the current value of various assets such as homes, motor vehicles, jewelry, antiques, and rare coins.

26. Culture Conduct research using personal interviews and other sources to determine the main assets (possessions) of typical households in other countries.

27. Math The Gage family's assets total $268,400. Their total liabilities are $166,300. What is the amount of their owner's equity? What actions could they take to increase their net worth?

28. Technology Conduct an Internet search for budget guidelines suggested for various categories of spending such as food, housing, transportation, clothing, health care, and others.

29. Research Locate in-store or online information about available money management software. Prepare a brief written summary comparing the prices and features of different programs.

30. Visual Art Create a flowchart to communicate the five steps of the financial planning process.

31. Research Conduct research to determine various professionals who might help you with your financial planning in the future. Prepare a summary table reporting the name, title, training and background, area of specialization, and cost of services for various financial planners.

32. Law Obtain information about recent changes in Social Security taxes and benefits. Prepare a two- to three-paragraph summary.

33. Research Locate a copy of a budget or financial report for your school, church, city government, or a public company from at least five years ago, as well as a copy of the current budget for the same entity. Compare the two budgets. Prepare a brief summary comparing assets, liabilities, and net income. Discuss what factors may have caused these differences.

34. Economics Interview fellow students, your parents, or other adults who are employed. Gather information about the deductions that are taken from their paychecks. Prepare a table listing the various deductions. Indicate which deductions are required and which are optional.

35. Personal Finance Assume you have been given a three-year-old car as a gift. Research the monthly costs associated with owning a car. Include items such as insurance, license, local annual use taxes, cost of gasoline based on 10,000 miles per year, and regular maintenance costs. Use a spreadsheet to present your findings.

36. Culture Select one city each in North America, South America, Europe, and Australia. Conduct Web research to determine the per-person cost of an afternoon out with your friends in each city. Use the current exchange rate to convert the costs to U.S. dollars. Include items such as transportation, lunch, a movie, and a new music CD. Present your findings in a table.

Decision-Making Strategies

Joan Leitzel just graduated from college and got her first job as a speech therapist. Joan wants to make sure she manages her income wisely so that she can be independent and eventually buy a house on her own. She lives with her parents now, so her only expenses are payments on a college loan and an auto loan.

37. What advice would you give Joan if she wants to buy a house in the future?

38. When she eventually goes to the bank for a loan, how should Joan organize her financial information?

Linking School and Community

Talk with people in your community about their money management activities. What are their main budgeting concerns? How do they cope with these? What actions do they take to save money for the future? What types of investments do they recommend?

©sweetym/iStock

Web Workout

You can find many sources of information about money management and personal financial planning on the Internet. The websites vary widely in the types and quality of information provided. Choose a topic from this chapter and find two websites offering information or advice related to the topic.

Think Critically

1. Write a short summary of the main ideas from each website.

2. How does the information presented address differences related to age and household situations?

3. What additional information could be added to the site related to your topic?

Presentation Management—Team Event

This event will assess your use of current desktop technologies and software to prepare and deliver an effective multimedia presentation.

You will design a computer-generated multimedia presentation. You have 15 minutes for preparation and setup. The presentation will last a minimum of seven minutes and a maximum of 10 minutes. Up to five minutes will be allowed for questions from the judges. The participants must make effective use of current multimedia technology in the presentation. In preparation for the presentation, participants should use space, color, and text as design factors. No VCR or laserdisc may be used in the presentation. Charts and other graphics should be used in the presentation. Participants are responsible for securing a release form from any individual whose name, photograph, and other information is included in the presentation.

You will prepare a presentation for middle school students that encourages saving money for future purchases. Your presentation should include interactive activities with your middle school audience. The following concepts must be addressed:

- The Rule of 72 and the advantages of saving over using credit for major purchases
- Savings options with different rates of return
- The role of government agencies that insure financial institutions
- The relationship between risk and financial return or reward
- Time commitment for different types of savings and liquidity

Performance Indicators Evaluated

- Demonstrate knowledge of multimedia software and components.
- Demonstrate effective oral communication skills.
- Apply technical skills to create a multimedia presentation that enhances the oral presentation.

You will be evaluated for your

- Knowledge of the topic
- Organized presentation of the topic
- Confidence, quality of voice, and eye contact
- Relationship of the topic to business strategy

For more detailed information about performance indicators, go to the BPA website.

Think Critically

1. What does liquidity of an investment mean?

2. Which investments involve greater risk?

3. Why should middle school students start saving now?

4. How does the Rule of 72 work?

www.bpa.org

CHAPTER

17 Banking and Financial Services

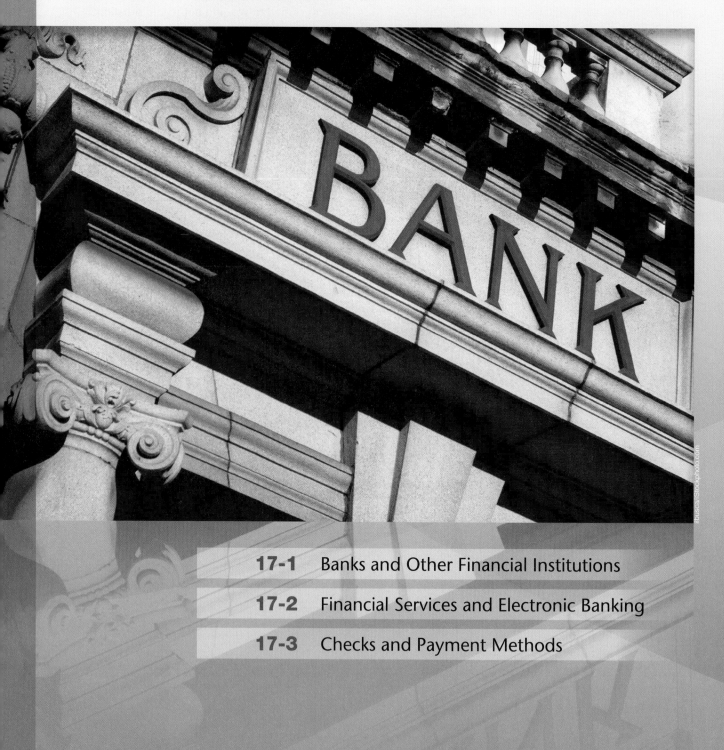

Planning a Career in ...

BANKING

The banking and financial services industry offers many career opportunities. Numerous financial workers are employed in commercial banks, specialized banks, savings and loan associations, credit unions, and finance companies. Work activities in the financial services industry range from serving customers and researching economic trends to planning marketing activities for financial institutions.

When working in the banking industry, you will encounter various tasks depending on your position. Tellers process daily customer transactions such as receiving deposits or loan payments. Bank officers, such as a loan department manager, will meet with people applying for credit. These interactions with borrowers can involve auto loans, education loans, or small business loans.

The marketing department of a bank communicates services available and attempts to expand the customer base. Advertising, personal selling, and other promotional activities are used to maintain and enhance customer satisfaction. When working with various target markets or international banking, you will likely use your foreign language skills.

Related Job Titles

- Branch Manager
- Teller
- Loan Officer
- Customer Service Representative
- Financial Services Sales Agent
- Financial Manager
- Information Processing Manager
- Economist

Analyze Career Opportunities in ...

BANKING

Use library and Internet resources to learn more about careers in banking. Choose one of the job titles listed in the box above and answer the following questions.

1. What is the employment outlook for careers in this field?

2. Is this a career that interests you? Describe how you might use your talents, abilities, and skills in this career.

What's it like to work as a ... Bank Economist?

Each morning, Ken Li goes online to see how various economic factors are affecting interest rates. He knows that when money is more expensive, borrowing by businesses and consumers declines. But if interest rates are lower, the use of credit will likely increase. This additional borrowing can result in higher earnings for banks and economic expansion.

Changing interest rates are just one area of research for Ken, who works for a bank with offices in 23 states. Today, he must also investigate current trends for employment, consumer spending, and retail sales. These economic indicators provide managers with information to better plan strategies for their banking organizations.

Since starting in the banking industry, Ken has observed two important trends. First, technology has improved many aspects of the business. Today, he is able to obtain better and faster data. Second, banks continually encounter changing government regulations.

What about you? What aspects of Ken's job sound interesting to you?

17-1 Banks and Other Financial Institutions

Goals

Key Terms

Federal Reserve System (Fed) 427

commercial bank 428

credit union 429

Federal Deposit Insurance Corporation (FDIC) 430

Focus on REAL LIFE

"I finally got a job for the summer," Gerri told Mike. "I can save money and go on that trip."

"Where are you going to save your money?" asked Mike.

"At home, of course," responded Gerri.

"Are you kidding?" Mike went on to say. "That's dangerous! Your money can get lost, or you might spend it before summer comes."

"Well, what should I do with my money?" asked Gerri.

"Deposit it in a bank," answered Mike.

"Will it be safer?" asked Gerri.

"For sure," said Mike. "Banks and other financial institutions provide safety and growth for your money. Plus they help their customers in many ways with other financial matters."

"You're kidding! I guess it's time I learn about banking," Gerri responded.

Goal 1

Explain the purpose of the Federal Reserve System.

THE BANKING SYSTEM

Some people do not think of a bank as a business. However, banks operate in much the same way as stores, factories, and other companies. As a business, a bank sells services such as checking and payment accounts, savings accounts, loans, and investments.

Banks are regulated more strictly than most other businesses. If a business fails, some people lose money. If a bank fails, thousands of people are affected.

What is the purpose of the Federal Reserve?

Do you believe that people need a safe and reliable banking system to achieve their life-span goals? Describe how you expect to use banks and other financial institutions to reach the goals you set in your life-span plan.

The Federal Reserve System

Most banks attempt to attract the deposits of customers. However, as an individual, you cannot open an account in a Federal Reserve Bank because it is a *bank for banks*.

The federal government set up the **Federal Reserve System (Fed)** to supervise and regulate member banks and to help banks serve the public efficiently. All national banks are required to join the Federal Reserve System, and state banks may join. Banks that join the system are known as *member banks*. The United States is divided into 12 Federal Reserve districts, with a central Federal Reserve Bank in each district, as shown in Figure 17-1.

Federal Reserve Activities

A Federal Reserve Bank serves member banks and the economy in several ways. One service provided by the Fed is the holding of *reserves*. Banks cannot lend all of the money they receive from customers. They are required to keep a part of the money deposited by customers on deposit

WORK
as a
TEAM

Banks are considered one of the most important types of businesses in any economy. Prepare a list of ways in which the banking system affects (1) businesses, (2) consumers, and (3) workers.

with the Federal Reserve System. The Fed holds these deposits in case the banks need additional funds to meet the daily customer demand.

As a result, a bank will lend only a certain percentage of deposited funds. It keeps the rest in reserve. This regulation is designed to help the banking system and the economy operate efficiently and to protect deposits.

For example, suppose a customer deposits $1,000 and the bank is required to hold 15 percent of all deposits in reserve. This means the bank can lend $850, which is 85 percent of the new deposit (85% × $1,000 = $850).

Another service of the Federal Reserve System is clearing checks for member banks. *Clearing* refers to the process of

Federal Reserve Districts

▲ *Federal Branch Cities*
● *Federal Reserve Bank Cities*
✱ *Board of Governors of the Federal Reserve System*

Source: Federal Reserve System

▶ **Figure 17-1**

Which Federal Reserve Regional Bank serves banks in your community?

paying checks and other payments among different banks. The Fed electronically processes millions of payments each day, making sure that the correct amounts are added to and subtracted from the appropriate accounts.

checkpoint ✓

What is the main purpose of the Federal Reserve System?

Banking and the Economy

The actions of the banking system affect you in many ways. Several million people work in banks, savings and loan associations, credit unions, and other financial institutions. The following activities are just some of the ways that individuals, businesses, and governments use banking services.

- Borrow money to build roads
- Borrow money to buy seeds for crops
- Deposit cash from business operations
- Finance a college education
- Invest for retirement
- Obtain a mortgage
- Process credit card transactions
- Save for a vacation

The savings you and others deposit make banking services possible. Deposits do not remain idle in bank vaults. They are put to work. When you and others deposit money in a bank, you are helping to create jobs and economic growth that benefit your community and your society.

TYPES OF FINANCIAL INSTITUTIONS

When someone says, "I'm going to the bank," the person might actually mean a credit union or a cash machine. There are many types of financial institutions that provide a wide range of products and services. Figure 17-2 shows how financial institutions are classified.

Deposit Institutions

Deposit institutions, also called *depository intermediaries*, accept deposits from people and businesses and use them to finance their business.

Commercial Banks The most common way for a bank to be organized is as a **commercial bank**. Commercial banks are often called *full-service banks* because they offer a wide range of financial services. Commercial banks offer checking accounts, provide savings accounts, make loans to individuals and to businesses, and offer other services. In large banks, different departments may handle these services. There may be a loan department, a trust department, a real estate department, and an investment department. Many

FINANCIAL INSTITUTIONS	
DEPOSIT INSTITUTIONS	**NON-DEPOSIT INSTITUTIONS**
• Commercial banks • Savings and loan associations • Mutual savings banks • Credit unions	• Life insurance companies • Investment companies • Consumer finance companies • Mortgage companies • Check cashing outlets • Pawnshops

▶ Figure 17-2

Which of these types of institutions have you done business with?

banks have full-service branch offices in shopping centers and grocery stores.

Savings and Loan Associations
Traditionally, a savings and loan association (S&L) specialized in savings accounts and making loans for home mortgages. Deregulation in the 1980s allowed these institutions to expand the array of services they could offer. They have become more like banks. Today, many S&Ls use the words *savings bank* in their names.

Mutual Savings Banks
A *mutual savings bank* is a savings bank that is owned by, and operated for the benefit of, its depositors. The profits are distributed in proportion to the amount of business each participant does with the company. While a mutual savings bank provides a variety of services, it is organized mainly for savings and home loans. Mutual savings banks are located mainly in the northeastern United States.

Credit Unions A user-owned, not-for-profit, cooperative financial institution is called a **credit union**. People in the same company, government agency, labor union, or profession often form credit unions. Serving members only, credit unions accept savings deposits and make loans for a variety of purposes. When people deposit money in a credit union, they become members because deposits are considered partial ownership in the credit union. Today, credit unions also offer a wide range of financial services. The National Credit Union Administration (NCUA), a federal agency, regulates these financial institutions.

Non-Deposit Financial Institutions

The other major category of financial institutions is *non-deposit institutions* or *non-depository intermediaries*. They

What is unique about a credit union?

Comstock Images/Jupiter Images

do not take or hold deposits. They earn their money selling specific services or policies.

Life Insurance Companies People commonly buy life insurance to provide financial security for their dependents. Besides protection, many life insurance companies also offer financial services such as investments. Through careful investing in new and existing companies, life insurance companies help to expand business in the economy.

Investment Companies People can choose investment opportunities for long-term growth of their money through investment companies. Many investors own shares of one of the more than 60,000 mutual funds worldwide. Investment companies make these mutual funds available.

Consumer Finance Companies A business that specializes in making loans for long-lasting or durable goods, such as cars and refrigerators, and for financial emergencies is a consumer finance company. Because consumer finance companies make loans, they are a part of the financial services industry. Unlike banks and other financial institutions, consumer finance companies do not accept savings deposits.

Mortgage Companies Buying a home is an important activity in society. Mortgage companies, along with other financial institutions, provide loans for buying a home or other real estate.

Check-Cashing Outlets People who do not have bank accounts may use check-cashing outlets (CCOs) to cash paychecks and to obtain other financial services. CCOs offer a wide range of services such as electronic tax filing, money orders, private postal boxes, utility bill payment, and the sale of bus and subway tokens. Often, services provided at a CCO are more expensive than at other businesses.

Pawnshops Pawnshops make loans based on the value of some tangible object, such as jewelry or other valuable items. Pawnshops commonly charge higher fees than other financial institutions and should usually be avoided.

depo881/iStockphoto.com

Why is a bank a safe place for your valuables? Are there any risks?

checkpoint ✓
What are some examples of non-deposit financial institutions?

SELECTING A FINANCIAL INSTITUTION

To obtain the best value for your financial services dollar, comparison shop. You should think about the services offered, safety, convenience, fees and charges, and restrictions.

Services Offered

As financial institutions offer additional financial services, your choices may become confusing. There are four basic types of banking services you will use.

1. Savings accounts
2. Checking and payment accounts
3. Loans and other credit plans
4. Other services, such as safe-deposit boxes and investment advice

As you work through the marketplace maze, it is important for you to determine which banking services meet your needs. Do not be attracted by fancy financial product names or flashy services that you might never need or use.

Safety

The federal agency that helps to regulate banks and other financial institutions is the **Federal Deposit Insurance Corporation (FDIC)**. It protects depositors' money in case of the failure of a bank or financial institution that it regulates. The FDIC insures all accounts in the same name at each bank up to an amount of $250,000. Although the FDIC is a government agency, banks provide money for its operation. Almost 99 percent of all banks are FDIC members.

The National Credit Union Administration (NCUA) regulates credit unions.

Goal 3

Discuss factors for selecting a financial institution.

NCUA insures a depositor's funds, through its National Credit Union Share Insurance Fund. Some state-chartered credit unions use a private insurance program.

Although most banks and financial institutions have federal deposit insurance, do not assume that this is the case at every financial institution. Make sure the institution where you keep your savings is insured.

Convenience

Do you want online banking services? Do you want branch offices near your home or work? These are some of the factors you will need to think about as you decide about convenience. There is usually a trade-off. While more convenience may mean higher costs, in recent years online banking has resulted in lower costs for many consumers.

Fees and Charges

Financial services have costs. Compare your needs with the price you pay.

Remember, seemingly low fees for using an ATM or having a checking account can add up to hundreds of dollars in a short time.

Restrictions

Costs are not always measured in dollars. If you must keep $500 on deposit to get "free" checking you may be losing the chance to earn interest on those funds at another institution.

If you must keep money on deposit for two years to earn a higher rate, you are restricted from using those funds for some unplanned purpose. Always balance your needs with the conditions imposed upon you. When you are not satisfied, shop around to compare the services and costs of other financial institutions.

> **checkpoint** ✓
> What factors should be considered when selecting a financial institution?

17-1 Assessment

www.cengage.com/school/genbus/pob

Key Concepts

Determine the best answer.

1. The financial institution most likely to charge the highest rate for a loan would be a
   a. bank
   b. pawnshop
   c. credit union
   d. mortgage company

2. If deposit insurance is most important to you when selecting a financial institution, you are most concerned with
   a. safety
   b. convenience
   c. services
   d. fees

Make Academic Connections

3. **Research** Conduct library and online research about the Federal Reserve System. When and why did it start? What are the main responsibilities of the Fed?

4. **Technology** Visit the website of the Federal Deposit Insurance Corporation to obtain current information on deposit insurance. What other information on the FDIC website would be of value to consumers?

5. **Math** A person is required to keep a $300 balance for a free checking account. What would be the amount of lost interest over five years if the person could earn 4 percent on savings in another type of account?

17-2 Financial Services and Electronic Banking

Goals

1 Identify the financial services used by consumers.

2 Explain types of checking accounts.

3 Describe electronic banking activities.

Key Terms

safe-deposit box 434

service charge 434

debit card 436

Focus on REAL LIFE

"Sixteen dollars for cash machine fees!" exclaimed Hans George as he opened his bank statement. "I guess the cost of those cash withdrawals adds up fast!"

Hans George has a routine of using his cash card at an automatic teller machine several times a week. He really likes the convenience of obtaining cash.

Hans also finds that when getting cash is easy, he easily overspends. While automatic teller machines are convenient and easy to use, you must also consider fees and the potential for impulse buying. In recent years, cash machine fees have risen from nothing to $1 or $2 per withdrawal.

How much can cash machine transaction fees cost? If you have two $1 transaction fees a week, you will pay $104 in fees over a year.

Goal 1

Identify the financial services used by consumers.

TYPES OF FINANCIAL SERVICES

A financial institution can provide services for various personal and business activities. The services you use depend on your needs.

Savings Services

Safe storage of funds for future use is a common need. One of the main services that financial institutions offer is accepting money from customers for safekeeping. A range of savings plans is available for this purpose.

Payment Services

The ability to transfer money to others is necessary for daily business activities. Types of payment services include checking accounts, debit cards, online payments and automatic withdrawals.

What can you do to reduce or eliminate bank fees?

Lending Services

Most people, businesses, and governments borrow money at some time. A business may want to borrow money to build a new warehouse or buy products to resell. Individuals may borrow to buy a car or pay college tuition. Banks make loans because most of their income is from the interest they charge borrowers.

Banks offer many types of lending services. These include auto loans, business loans, and mortgages. Credit cards allow a person to buy items without having the cash. When paying with a bank credit card, you are borrowing money from the bank.

Electronic Banking

Electronic funds transfer (EFT) refers to the use of computers and other technology for banking activities. Electronic banking services include the use of automated teller machines (ATM), point-of-sale transactions, direct deposit, and automatic bill payment. Online computer banking allows a customer to access many financial services.

Business Insight for the 21st Century

Biometric Banking

"Place your finger on scanner to authorize payment." This is an example of biometry at work in the real world. Biometry is the analysis of biological observations, and its use in identification is not new. For centuries, scars, complexion, eye color, and height have been used to identify people. Today, technology known as biometrics allows banking and other security activities based on physical features.

Fingerprint Verification Bank of America created a program to use a person's fingerprint to give individuals access to their online banking services. Law enforcement agencies have long used fingerprint identification techniques. For banking, a chip is used to store a customer's fingerprint. A payment or funds transfer is authorized

when the customer places a finger on a small scanner.

Iris Scanning The pattern of every person's eyeball is unique. Scanning the characteristics of your eyeball can be used as a bank account "password" or to allow access to your computer. Cameras are available to scan an iris from a distance of two or three feet.

Voice Recognition Customers at the American Savings Bank in Hawaii no longer have to enter a number to access their account. Using a voice-activated response system, customers are able to obtain an account balance or make a money transfer.

Hand Geometry Instead of tapping out a password on a keypad or swiping a card, hand geometry is used to measure physical characteristics of

the hand or fingers. Using a three-dimensional view, this technology allows workers to access a secure area and may be used in the future to permit banking transactions.

Face Recognition The Mr. Payroll face recognition system uses machines to compare two images of the face to authorize check cashing.

Think Critically

1. What concerns might be associated with biometric banking activities?

2. Conduct an Internet search to obtain additional information on new technology currently being used in banking transactions. Choose one technology and write a short report.

Storage of Valuables

Banks offer **safe-deposit boxes** for storage of valuables. Because these safe-deposit boxes are in secured areas, they are very safe places to keep jewelry, rare coins, investment certificates, birth records, a list of insurance policies, and other valuable documents.

Only you or someone to whom you have given the right to open the box may open it. Not even a bank has the right to open your safe-deposit box unless it is ordered to do so by a court. You rent safe-deposit boxes by the year. They come in a variety of sizes.

Investment Advice

Many financial institutions help customers by offering financial advice and investment services. Banks can assist customers with decisions about buying a home, offer tips on money management, and help customers exchange U.S. funds for foreign currency.

Most banks offer advice on investments. This involves savings that are put to work to earn more money. Types of investments include government bonds, stocks, and mutual funds.

Management of Trusts

Many banks manage investments on behalf of customers. When they do this, the money or other property that is turned over for the bank to manage is said to be held in *trust*. This service can be offered through a trust company or through trust departments in banks.

Trusts are used by people of all ages. They are especially useful for very young people and for some elderly people. A young person who inherits money may not have the skill and experience to manage it wisely. Elderly people who are ill may ask the trust department of a bank to manage their money. The bank makes investments and keeps the customers informed about what is happening to their money.

TYPES OF CHECKING ACCOUNTS

While checking accounts vary from one bank to another, three types are most common.

Regular Checking Accounts

If you write a lot of checks each month, consider a regular checking account. A **service charge** is a fee a bank charges for handling a checking account. With most banks, there is no service charge for a regular checking account as long as you maintain a certain minimum balance. This amount varies and is often $300 or higher. A checking account at a credit union may be called a *share draft* account because the members are called *shareholders*.

How does online banking make managing your checking account and paying bills more convenient?

Interest-Earning Checking Accounts

Many financial institutions offer checking accounts that earn interest. These accounts may require a higher monthly balance than regular checking accounts. If the account falls below the required amount, the bank usually pays no interest and may add a service charge.

The rates of interest that banks pay their customers also vary. Usually, a bank will offer a higher rate of interest when a higher balance is kept in the account. Very often, interest rates on checking accounts are quite low. When you are depositing larger amounts of money, consider other savings alternatives.

Special Checking Accounts

If you only write a few checks each month, consider a *special checking account*. Also called an *activity account*, banks charge customers about 10 to 20 cents for each check written. A monthly service charge may also be added.

Comparing Checking Accounts

When selecting a checking account, evaluate the following items.

- Minimum balance
- Interest rate earned, if any
- Monthly service charge
- Fees for other services, such as printing checks and stop payment orders
- Other restrictions

When choosing a checking account, be careful. A bank may attract you with a low minimum balance, but fees can result in a higher total cost.

> **checkpoint** ✓
> What are three main types of checking accounts?

ELECTRONIC BANKING

Each day, more and more people are using electronic banking services. ATMs, personal computers, cell phones, and other electronic devices are processing most bank transactions.

E-Banking Services

Over the years, banks have expanded their hours of operation to meet the demands of their customers. Traditional "banker's hours" of 9 A.M. to 3 P.M. are a thing of the past. Banks have expanded hours, whiles ATMs and online banking

> **Goal 3**
> Describe electronic banking activities.

EXAMPLES OF ELECTRONIC BANKING ACTIVITIES				
	ATM ACTIVITIES	PREAUTHORIZED ACTIVITIES	ONLINE ACTIVITIES	POINT-OF-SALE ACTIVITIES
Check account balances	✓		✓	
Withdraw cash	✓			
Make deposits	✓			
Transfer funds	✓		✓	
View account history			✓	
Pay bills			✓	
Apply for loans			✓	
Manage investments			✓	
Accept direct deposits		✓		
Pay bills automatically		✓	✓	
Make debit card purchases			✓	✓

▶ Figure 17-3

Has electronic banking made it easier for you to manage your finances? Explain your answer.

are available 24 hours a day. Figure 17-3, on page 435, illustrates some common electronic banking services.

Automatic Teller Machines Commonly called a *cash machine*, an automatic teller machine (ATM) allows many banking services. The most common use of an ATM is withdrawing cash from a bank account or getting a cash advance from a credit card. Bank customers also can use ATMs to check account balances, make deposits, or transfer funds from one account to another.

A **debit card**, or *cash card*, is used for ATM transactions. A debit card is different from a *credit card*. With a debit card issued by your bank, you are using money that is in your account. With a credit card, you are borrowing from the bank to pay later.

A lost or stolen debit card can be expensive. If you notify the financial institution within two days of the lost card, your liability for unauthorized use is $50. After that, you can be liable for up to $500 of unauthorized use for up to 60 days.

ATM services have expanded to provide other types of transactions. You can use these machines to buy bus passes, postage stamps, and gift cards.

Be aware that many banks charge fees for ATM usage. To minimize ATM fees, compare rates at several financial institutions. Use your bank's ATMs to avoid surcharges. Withdraw larger amounts to avoid fees on several small transactions.

Payments at the Point-of-Sale In a *point-of-sale transaction*, a merchant accepts a debit card to pay for purchases. Most gas stations, stores, and restaurants accept this type of payment. Vending machines that accept debit cards are also becoming more common.

Direct Deposit A major portion of society uses *direct deposit* of paychecks and government payments. Funds are deposited electronically and available automatically for your use.

Automatic Bill Payments Each month, many people pay their rent, mortgage, loans, utilities, and other bills without doing anything. *Automatic bill payment* requires a bank customer to authorize preset amounts of monthly expenses. The bank deducts the payments from your account and transfers them to the appropriate companies. With automatic bill payments, be sure to check each month that the correct amounts have been deducted.

Electronic Payment Options

The use of cash, checks, and credit cards is declining. These payment methods are being replaced by newer electronic alternatives.

Debit Card Transactions Most stores, restaurants, and other businesses accept debit cards issued by Visa and MasterCard. You may also know these cards as *check cards*. When the debit card transaction is processed, the amount of the purchase is deducted from your checking account.

Online Payments Various Web companies and banks now provide online bill payment services between buyers and sellers. When using these services, be sure to think about the monthly charge as well as online security and customer service availability.

Some online payment services give you a choice of using a credit or a bank account, while others require one or the other. Being linked to your checking account may not give you as much leverage when disputing a transaction.

Stored-Value Cards The gift card your aunt sent you for your birthday is a stored-value card. Prepaid cards for phone service, transit fares, highway tolls, and school lunches are common. Some stored-value cards are disposable. Others can be reloaded with additional funds. Some employers use prepaid cards instead of paper paychecks to help employees avoid check-cashing fees. Employees can use the cards to make purchases and to withdraw cash at ATM machines.

Smart Cards These "electronic wallets" are similar to ATM cards. Their embedded microchip stores prepaid amounts as well as account balances, transaction records, insurance information, and medical history.

Banking in the Future

Your use of banks and money will continue to change. Electronic financial services will be available though wireless technology. You will be able to do almost any banking transaction through your

fyi *Banking apps for your phone allow you to check your account balances, make payments and transfer funds, locate ATMs, and obtain information and assistance with various banking services. These smart phone programs, which range in price from free to a few dollars, are available from banks, financial institutions, and other sources. Banking apps are becoming a "virtual wallet" for many people.*

Joel Calheiros/Shutterstock.com

home computer, cell phone, or access card. Technology will create a personalized system for obtaining, transferring, and using funds.

Even when your bank is not open, touch-screen systems will permit you to apply for, negotiate, and finalize loans. And, *location-based services* will allow financial activities and other business transactions based on your geographic position. You will be able to identify the location of the nearest cash machine or bank branch through a variation of global positioning technology.

> **checkpoint ✓**
> What are common electronic banking services?

17-2 Assessment

Study Tools

www.cengage.com/school/genbus/pob

Key Concepts

Determine the best answer.

1. True or False. Using a debit card is similar to writing a check.

2. True or False. Automatic payments are made through automatic teller machines.

3. True or False. If you write only a few checks each month you should consider a regular checking account.

Make Academic Connections

4. **Visual Communication** Conduct a survey of 20 students to determine the types of financial services they use. Create a table or graph to report your findings.

5. **Technology** Locate examples of online payment services and "cybercash" companies. What services are provided? What concerns might be associated with these services?

Microfinance

How could a loan of $50 result in a life-changing experience? In countries such as Bangladesh, Nepal, the Philippines, and Zimbabwe, microfinance has helped improve the economy and society.

Microfinance, also called microlending and microcredit, involves programs of small loans to people for self-employment projects. The resulting business activities generate enough income to provide for life necessities and family needs. Most microcredit efforts involve nonprofit organizations, which helps avoid political influences.

Most microfinance clients have little income and no access to formal financial institutions. They are usually self-employed, household-based entrepreneurs. In rural areas, clients are small farmers or food-processing workers. In urban areas, microfinance clients include shopkeepers, service providers, artisans, and street vendors.

In southeastern Bangladesh, one of the poorest regions in the world, BRAC (formerly the Bangladesh Rural Advancement Committee) helps women obtain loans. Loans help them farm fish, keep cows for milk production, grow vegetables, raise poultry, buy rickshaws, and sew clothing. The women pay 15 percent simple interest on loans, which is much less than they would have to pay to loan sharks. The banking is done in the village through an agent of the microfinance

How do loans from BRAC change the lives of women in Bangladesh?

institution. Loans are not secured through collateral. Repayment is made in 52 weekly installments in a year's time, and simple interest is used rather than compound interest.

BRAC also works to improve the health of women and children. More than 30,000 volunteers have been trained by BRAC to recognize and treat 10 common illnesses such as anemia, diarrhea, ringworm, and scabies.

The success of microfinance is not limited to Bangladesh. Organizations around the world provide affordable financing to improve the economy in many poor countries. Using a model similar to the one used by BRAC, an organization offers a small inexpensive loan to help an entrepreneur start or grow a small business. Income

generated by the business is then used to cover living expenses, operate the business, and repay the loan.

Over time, many microfinance programs have expanded to include other financial services. In addition to loans, savings accounts and insurance coverage may be provided. These services help borrowers build assets and protect against risks.

Think Critically

1. What are the main benefits of microfinance programs?

2. What are some possible concerns of microfinance?

3. Conduct an Internet search to find other examples of microfinance around the world.

17-3 Checks and Payment Methods

Goals

1 Describe three main types of endorsements.

2 Describe proper check-writing procedures.

3 Explain the bank reconciliation process.

4 Identify other payment methods.

Key Terms

endorsement 440

check register 441

stop payment order 443

bank statement 443

bank reconciliation 445

outstanding checks 445

Focus on REAL LIFE

Alicia Garcia made her first deposit in her new checking account. Her friend Joni asked her, "If I write you a check, could you give me the cash? You can deposit my check in your account later."

"How do I know your check is good?" Alicia asked.

"What? We've been friends for more than 10 years," Joni responded. "Don't you trust me?"

"Of course I trust you," said Alicia. "Just remember that if a check isn't good, it can result in some expensive service fees."

The next day, Laura came up to Alicia and said, "I can't wait to send away for this sweater, but the ad says 'no personal checks.' How can I pay for it?"

"Let me tell you about money orders," responded Alicia.

OPENING A CHECKING ACCOUNT

While fewer checks are being written each year, a checking account is usually the foundation for using a debit card and for your online banking activities.

Traditionally, checks provide convenience, ease, and safety for making payments, while also being used as proof of payment and a record of spending. These benefits of a checking account continue.

The First Deposit

Opening a checking account starts with providing personal data and a sample of your signature. In the past, a *signature card* was used. This document usually requires your legal name, address, phone, Social Security number, driver's license number, and e-mail address. Today, signature cards might not be actual cards. Most financial institutions enter your personal data online and use an electronic capture device to obtain your signature sample.

The electronic image of your signature can then be available to tellers at branch banks

These methods are used to verify your signature. The bank compares the signature on checks to the one on record when the account was opened. Signatures will likely be verified when you are cashing a large check at your bank, or when the bank suspects that a forged check is being presented for payment.

Goal 1

Describe three main types of endorsements.

How does recording your signature when you open a checking account protect you and the bank?

Sometimes two or more people have an account together called a *joint account*. Each person who will write checks on the account must provide a sample signature. Any signer for a joint account can write checks on the account as if he or she were the only owner.

When you deposit money in a checking account, you fill out a *deposit slip*. This form lists all items you are depositing—currency, coins, or checks. The deposit slip shows your name, account number, the date, the items deposited, and the total amount of the deposit.

Types of Endorsements

Before depositing a check, it must be endorsed. This involves writing your name on the back of the left end of the check. An **endorsement** is written evidence that you received payment or that you transferred your right of receiving payment to someone else.

When you endorse a check, your responsibilities are almost as great as if you had written the check yourself. As an endorser, you are actually making this promise: "If this check is not paid by the bank, I will pay it."

Your endorsement must be made in the 1½-inch space on the left side of the check. If you write outside this limit, the bank may return the check. Different endorsements have different purposes. Figure 17-4 shows some examples.

Blank Endorsement An endorsement that consists of only the endorser's name is a *blank endorsement*. To endorse a check, sign your name in ink exactly as it is written on the face of the check. If the name on the check is different from your official signature, you will need to endorse the check twice. First, use the name as given on the check. Then, write your name as it appears on the account.

A blank endorsement makes a check payable to anyone who has the check. While you can use this endorsement to transfer any check, sometimes another type of endorsement is better.

Full Endorsement The use of a *full endorsement*, also called a *special endorsement*, allows you to transfer a check to another person. You write the words "Pay to the order of..." followed by the name of the person or business to which the check is being transferred. This is followed by your signature. This phrasing results in only the specified person being able to sign and cash the check.

Restrictive Endorsement A *restrictive endorsement* limits the use of the check to the purpose given in the endorsement. For example, you may have several checks that you want to mail to the bank. You could write *For deposit only* above your signature, followed by your account number. This endorsement restricts use of the check so it can only be deposited to your account. Often, organizations that receive

Types of Endorsements

Special Endorsement	Two Signatures Required	Restrictive Endorsement
ENDORSE HERE *Pay to the order of* *Kunio Shinoda* Nancy R. Brooks DO NOT WRITE, STAMP, OR SIGN BELOW THIS LINE	ENDORSE HERE A.O. Veras NinaVeras DO NOT WRITE, STAMP, OR SIGN BELOW THIS LINE	ENDORSE HERE For deposit only Nancy R. Brooks DO NOT WRITE, STAMP, OR SIGN BELOW THIS LINE

▶ **Figure 17-4**

Describe the benefits of each type of endorsement.

Why do some businesses use a stamp to endorse checks?

many checks use a rubber stamp with the words *For Deposit Only* followed by the company name and its account number.

> **checkpoint** ✓
> What are the three types if endorsements?

USING A CHECKING ACCOUNT

Checking accounts are an easy way to access funds. Still, to use a checking account correctly, you must understand certain information and follow some simple procedures.

Check-Writing Procedures

Some checks are light blue or green in color. Others have a picture of a forest, a sports team logo, or an inspirational quote. No matter what they look like, all checks contain essentially the same information.

Elements of a Check Figure 17-5 shows some terms that are used to identify the parts of a check. Three parties are shown on each check.

- The *drawer* is the owner of the account who signs the check.

- The *payee* is the person to whom the check is written.

- The *drawee* is the bank or other financial institution that pays the check.

The Check Register Your checkbook will provide one of three formats for recording account activities. The *check stub* is a form attached to the check by a perforated line. A **check register** is a separate book, usually the same size as

Goal 2

Describe proper check-writing procedures.

Parts of a Check

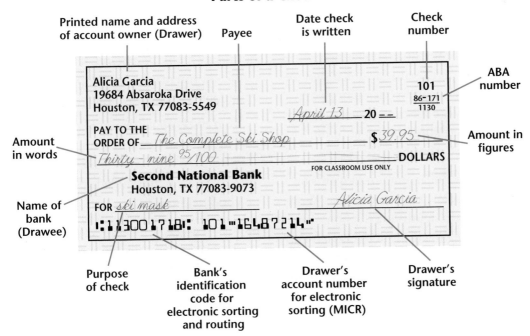

▶ **Figure 17-5**

Why is the amount of this check written twice?

the checkbook, that allows you to maintain a record of the checks written. A *duplicate copy* of the check may also be automatically created when you write the check.

Always fill out the stub or register first. If you write the check first, you may forget to record the information before you transfer the check. Your check register should also be used for maintaining a record of debit card payments and cash withdrawals.

Writing a Check Fill out the check completely and carefully using the following seven steps.

1. Write checks in order by number so you know which checks have been paid.

2. Write the date in the proper space.

3. Write the payee's name on the line following *Pay to the Order of.*

4. Write the amount of the check in figures after the printed dollar sign. Write the amount close to the dollar sign to prevent someone from altering your check. Write the cents figures close to the dollar figures so that additional numbers cannot be inserted.

5. Write the dollar amount in words on the line below the payee's name. Write the cents in figures as a fraction of a dollar. Begin writing at the far left end of the line. Draw a line from the fraction to the printed word *Dollars* to fill all unused space.

6. Write the purpose of the payment on the line at the bottom of the check.

7. Sign checks with the same signature you wrote on your signature card.

Proper Check Writing Poor check writing can cause problems and financial difficulties. Follow these tips to avoid trouble.

1. *Write checks only on the forms provided by your bank.* Checks can be written on just about anything—even a paper bag—but sorting and processing can be delayed when you do not use the proper form.

2. *Write checks in ink.* This prevents someone from altering the amount.

3. *Only write checks if money is available.* Writing a check for more than is in your account can result in an *overdrawn account.* The bank may not pay the check and you will most likely be charged a fee.

4. *Use the current date.* A *postdated* check is one that is dated later than the date on which it is written. This business practice is unwise and can result in additional service charges.

5. *Avoid making checks payable to "Cash" or to "Bearer."* Such a check can be cashed by anyone. Instead, make the check out to yourself or to the bank as payee.

6. *Always fill in the amount.* If you leave it blank, you may be held responsible for amounts filled in by others.

7. *Void checks on which you make errors.* Do not try to erase or retrace your writing. Write "Void" across the check. Make note of the voided check in the check register.

8. *Record every payment from your checking account, whether the payment is by check, debit card, or automatic payment.* Some people carry a few blank checks. When one is used, make a note of it and record it in the register. Also, promptly record all transactions made at an ATM.

Stopping Payment

In certain situations, you may not want your bank to pay a check that you have written. To do so, you will fill out a **stop payment order**, a written notice that tells the bank not to pay a certain check. Because banks charge a high fee for stopping payment on a check, use this process only for good reason. You may learn, for example, that a check you have written to pay a bill was lost in the mail. A check you have written may have been stolen. Before you write a new check, you should stop payment on the one that was lost or stolen.

> **checkpoint** ✓
> What is the purpose of a check register?

THE RECONCILIATION PROCESS

As a depositor, you will need to review the record of your account that the bank keeps. At regular intervals, usually monthly, the bank will send you a report on the status of your account known as a **bank statement**.

Bank Statement Information

While bank statement formats vary, most present the following information.

- The balance at the beginning of the month.
- The deposits made during the month.
- The checks paid by the bank during the month.
- Any automated teller transactions made during the month.
- Any electronic fund transfers (EFT) or special payments the bank has made.
- Service charges for the month, including charges for services such as stopping payment on a check.

- Any interest earned on the account.
- The balance at the end of the month.

Examples of some of these items appear on the bank statement shown in Figure 17-6 on page 444.

Determine Checks Paid

When your bank statement arrives, compare the checks you wrote to those that have been paid by your bank. Banks might not return actual *canceled checks* that have been paid. Instead, banks can use a *substitute check*, which is a digital reproduction of the original paper check. In some cases banks do not return checks or provide substitute checks unless the customer requests them.

There are times when you need to show proof of a payment. In most cases, information on the statement will be sufficient to prove payment. If the check showing the endorsement is needed, a substitute check is considered a legal equivalent of the original check.

> **Goal 3**
> Explain the bank reconciliation process.

How can a computer program help with reconciling your checkbook?

sjlocke/iStockphoto.com

Second National Bank

Checking Account Statement

Account Number:　　　　1648-7214

Alicia Garcia

19684 Absaroka Drive

Houston, TX 77083-5549

Page: 1 of 2

Date: 5/1/20--

Checking Account Summary

Balance Summary

Transaction Summary

Beginning balance	Deposits and other additions	Checks and other deductions	Charges and fees	Ending balance	Withdrawals	Deposits
0.00	926.95	533.89	3.00	390.06	14	2

Activity Detail

Deposits and Other Additions

Date	Description	Amount	Date	Description	Amount
4/10/20--	Deposit	331.85	4/24/20--	Deposit	175.00
4/16/20--	Deposit	150.00	4/29/20--	Direct Deposit	270.10

Checks and Substitute Checks

Date paid	Check number	Amount	Date paid	Check number	Amount
4/13/20--	101	39.95	4/26/20--	*109	65.33
4/15/20--	102	50.00	4/27/20--	110	33.46
4/22/20--	103	32.97	4/27/20--	111	24.33
4/22/20--	104	100.87	4/27/20--	112	5.80
4/24/20--	*106	16.30	4/27/20--	113	12.85
4/24/20--	107	25.78	4/30/20--	114	4.25

Banking/Check Card Withdrawals and Purchases

Date	Description	Amount	Detail
4/23/20--	ATM-W	50.00	ATM withdrawal 3970 Waverly Ave

Online and Electronic Banking Deductions

Date	Description	Amount	Detail
4/30/20--	AP	72.00	TexPower automatic payment

Other Deductions

Date	Description	Amount	
4/30/20--	SC	3.00	Service charge for checking

▶ Figure 17-6

How many checks were paid by the bank and posted to Alicia's account?

Find Differences

You keep your own record of your checking account, usually in a check register. The bank statement is the bank's record of your account.

The document created to show how the two balances were brought into agreement is called the **bank reconciliation**. Bringing the balances into agreement is known as *reconciling the bank balance*. The bank often prints forms for reconciling on the backs of bank statements. Figure 17-7 shows an example of a bank reconciliation.

The balances shown on your records and the bank statement may be different. Following are some of the most common reasons for the difference.

- Some of the checks you wrote may not have *cleared* (been paid). These checks, which have not been deducted from the bank statement balance, are called **outstanding checks**.

- You may have forgotten to record a transaction in your register, such as an ATM deposit or automatic bill payment.

- A service charge may appear on the bank statement.

- You may have mailed a deposit to the bank that has not yet been received.

- Interest earned may have been added.

- You may have recorded the amount of a check incorrectly in the check register. You may have added or subtracted incorrectly.

Sample Bank Reconciliation Form

BANK RECONCILIATION

Directions: You can easily balance your checkbook by following the procedure outlined on this form. Fill in below amounts from your checkbook and bank statement.

BALANCE SHOWN ON BANK STATEMENT $ 390.06

ADD DEPOSITS NOT ON STATEMENT $ _____

A _____

TOTAL $ 390.06

SUBTRACT CHECKS ISSUED BUT NOT ON STATEMENT

B
108 $ 10.00
115   21.00
116   17.50

TOTAL $ 48.50
E
BALANCE $ 341.56

BALANCE SHOWN ON YOUR CHECKBOOK $ 416.56

ADD ANY DEPOSITS NOT ALREADY ENTERED IN CHECKBOOK $ _____

C _____

TOTAL $ 416.56

SUBTRACT SERVICE CHARGES AND OTHER BANK CHARGES NOT IN CHECKBOOK
D
$ 3.00
Tex Power 72.00

TOTAL $ 75.00
E
BALANCE $ 341.56

These totals represent the correct amount of money you have in the bank and should agree. Differences, if any, should be reported to the bank within ten days after the receipt of yours statement.

► **Figure 17-7**

What does the $341.56 balance represent? Is it always less than the balance shown on the statement? Explain your answer.

A You recorded these deposits in your check register, but the bank has not posted them to your account.

B You recorded these checks in your check register when you wrote them, but they have not have not cleared.

C The bank recorded these deposits when they were received, but you have not recorded them in your check register.

D The bank recorded these withdrawals when they occurred, but you have not recorded them in your check register.

E Both the revised bank statement balance and the revised checkbook balance should be equal.

What information is included on your bank statement?

checkpoint ✓
What are causes of differences between the bank statement balance and a person's check register?

OTHER TYPES OF PAYMENTS

Often, you might need to make a payment in a situation when a personal check is not acceptable. Several payment alternatives are available.

Certified Checks

A *certified check* is a personal check for which a bank has guaranteed payment. The certification is stamped on the face of the check and is signed or initialed by a bank officer.

Cashier's Checks

A bank usually keeps funds in an account of its own on which it writes its own checks. A *cashier's check* is a check that a bank draws on its own funds. A cashier's check costs the amount of the check plus a service fee. These banker's checks are more acceptable than the personal checks of an individual whom the payee may not know.

Traveler's Checks

Carrying a large sum of money when you travel is risky. In addition paying traveling expenses with personal checks may be difficult. *Traveler's checks* are special forms designed for making payments when away from home. You can buy them at banks, credit unions, and travel bureaus. Traveler's checks are sold in several denominations such as $10, $20, $50, and $100. In addition to the value of the checks, a fee of 1 percent may be charged. This means that $100 worth of traveler's checks will cost $101.

Goal 4

Identify other payment methods.

Calculate Adjusted Balance

To determine the true balance in your account, take the following steps.

1. Subtract the total of the outstanding checks from the bank statement balance.

2. Add any *deposits in transit* to the balance statement balance.

3. Subtract service charges, fees, and automatic payments from your checkbook balance.

4. Add any interest earned to your check register balance.

   At this point, if the balances do not agree, either you or your bank has made an error. You should check each of the steps again. Then, carefully go over the calculations in your check register. If you do not find an error in your calculations, contact your bank.

   After you have reconciled your bank statement, correct any errors that you made on your register. The new balance now agrees with the bank statement. With your account updated, you can write checks on the new balance.

Traveler's checks require your signature in two places. First, you sign each one when they are bought. Then, when you cash a check or pay for a purchase with it, you sign it again in the presence of the person accepting it. Businesses throughout the world commonly accept traveler's checks.

Money Orders

A person who does not have a checking account and wants to send a payment through the mail may purchase a money order. A *money order* is a form of payment that orders the issuing agency to pay the amount printed on the form to another party.

Several types of organizations commonly sell money orders.

- A *bank money order* is sold by a bank stating that money is to be paid to a specific person or business.

- A *postal money order* purchased from the U.S. Post Office can be sent safely through the mail. It can be cashed only after the payee signs it.

- An *express money order* is issued by various organizations including traveler's check companies, travel agencies, and many supermarkets, pharmacies, and convenience stores.

- A *telegraphic money order* involves buying a message to direct a telegraph office to pay a sum of money to a certain person or business.

If a money order is lost or stolen, the receipt copy that you receive may be used in making a claim.

checkpoint ✓

How does a certified check differ from a cashier's check?

17-3 Assessment

Study Tools

www.cengage.com/school/genbus/pob

Key Concepts

Determine the best answer.

1. The first document that must be completed when opening a checking account is the
   a. deposit slip
   b. reconciliation statement
   c. check register
   d. signature card

2. A personal check with guaranteed payment is a
   a. cashier's check
   b. money order
   c. certified check
   d. traveler's check

Make Academic Connections

3. **Math** Service charges for Tom Harding's regular checking account at Second National Bank are based on the bank's rate schedule:

Minimum Balance	Charge
0–$199	$6
$200–$399	$4
$400 and over	no charge

During a recent six-month period, Tom's balances were: April, $148.00; May, $201.97; June, $101.61; July, $418.53; August, $248.29; and September, $154.36.
   a. How much was Tom's service charge for each month?
   b. What was the total service charge for the six-month period?

Business Notes

17-1 Banks and Other Financial Institutions

- The Federal Reserve System serves member banks by accepting their deposits, lending them money, clearing checks, and providing other services.

- The main deposit-type institutions are commercial banks, savings and loan associations, mutual savings banks, and credit unions. Non-deposit financial institutions include life insurance companies, investment companies, consumer finance companies, mortgage companies, check-cashing outlets, and pawnshops.

- To obtain the best value for your financial services dollar, investigate and compare services offered, safety, convenience, fees and charges, and restrictions.

17-2 Financial Services and Electronic Banking

- The most common services offered by financial institutions are accepting deposits, transferring funds, lending money, electronic banking, storing valuables, providing financial advice, and managing trusts.

- The main types of checking accounts are regular checking accounts, interest-earning checking accounts, and special checking accounts.

- Electronic banking services include the use of automated teller machines (ATM), point-of-sale transactions, direct deposit, automatic bill payment, online payments, stored-value cards and smart cards.

17-3 Checks and Payment Methods

- The purpose of an endorsement is to allow the recipient of the check to cash, deposit, or transfer it to someone else. A blank endorsement consists of only the endorser's name. A full endorsement, also called the special endorsement, allows you to transfer a check to another person. A restrictive endorsement limits the use of the check to the purpose given in the endorsement.

- Reconciling a checking account involves finding the differences between the balance on the bank statement and the balance in your checkbook.

- Other types of payment methods include certified checks, cashier's checks, traveler's checks, and money orders.

Communicate Business Concepts

1. Some people believe that banks need more regulations and control by the government. Others would like fewer regulations for banks. What are some arguments for each point of view?

2. What factors might affect whether you use a commercial bank or a credit union for your banking activities?

3. List the type of banking service that you think each person would be most likely to use. Explain your answer.

   a. A person planning to open a fitness center
   b. A musical group
   c. A wealthy senior citizen
   d. A buyer of a van
   e. A high school recycling club

4. Jake Olsen has decided to put $1,000 in the bank. List several questions Jake might want to ask before choosing whether to put the money in a checking or a savings account.

5. Cher Alonso often makes deposits and withdrawals at the ATM that she passes on her way to work. She frequently forgets to record these banking activities in her check register and never seems to know how much money she has in the bank. In addition, she has overdrawn her account twice and has had to pay a fee each time. Can you suggest a plan for Cher to follow that would allow her to use the automatic teller services and still be sure of having an accurate record?

6. Name items that a person might keep in a safe-deposit box.

7. While using a debit card increases the speed and efficiency of business transactions, what effect can this have on a person's money management skills?

8. Isaac Ahlred has received his bank statement for the month of May. The bank statement shows a balance of $401.19, but his check register shows a balance of only $364.52.

   a. What is the most likely reason that the bank's balance is larger than Isaac's?
   b. What steps should Isaac take to bring his balances into agreement?

9. While on a trip, the Mendoza family decided to buy furniture, which cost $500. The dealer would not accept a personal check or credit cards. What method could be used to pay for the furniture?

10. "You should shop for the best place to open a checking account as carefully as you shop for the best buy in any product or service." Give two reasons to support this statement.

11. Matt Huffman believes that it is a waste of time to record information each time he uses his debit card or writes a check. "The bank sends me a statement each month. That's all I need," he says. How could you convince Matt that he should keep records?

Develop Your Business Language

Match the terms listed with the definitions.

12. A bank that offers a full range of financial services.

13. A nationwide banking plan set up by the federal government to supervise and regulate member banks.

14. A written notice telling the bank not to pay a certain check.

15. A separate form on which the depositor keeps a record of deposits and checks.

16. A device used for cash machine transactions.

17. A container in a secured area in a bank vault for storing valuables.

18. Written evidence that you received payment or that you transferred your right of receiving payment to someone else.

19. A report sent by the bank to a depositor showing the status of his or her account.

20. A federal agency that protects deposited money in case of the failure of a bank or financial institution that it regulates.

21. A fee a bank charges for handling a checking account.

22. Checks that have not been deducted from the bank statement balance.

23. A user-owned, not-for-profit cooperative financial institution.

24. A statement showing how the checkbook balance and the bank statement were brought into agreement.

Key Terms

a. bank reconciliation
b. bank statement
c. commercial bank
d. check register
e. credit union
f. debit card
g. endorsement
h. Federal Deposit Insurance Corporation (FDIC)
i. Federal Reserve System
j. outstanding checks
k. safe-deposit box
l. service charge
m. stop payment order

Make Academic Connections

25. **Geography** Look at several U.S. one dollar bills. Which Federal Reserve Banks are noted on the seal of this currency?

26. **Culture** Research financial services and payment methods commonly used in various countries around the world.

27. **Communication** Collect advertisements, promotions, and online information from several financial institutions. Analyze these materials to determine information that is useful for consumers. Create a poster to highlight and report your findings.

28. **History** Investigate the availability of credit unions in your community. Who may join? What services are offered?

29. **Law** Check-cashing outlets and pawnshops frequently charge fees and rates much higher than other financial institutions. Research laws that regulate these financial institutions. Prepare a one-page summary of your findings.

30. **Economics** Select various economic measurements of the economy, such as interest rates and consumer prices. Describe how changes in these economic factors might affect the use of financial services.

31. **Math** If a person pays $2 in ATM fees each week for 5 years, what would be the total cost of that service?

32. **Communication** Work with a partner to act out situations in which you might use a certified check, a cashier's check, traveler's checks, and a money order.

33. **Math** In October, Tom Jarez received his bank statement that showed a balance of $378.65. The service charge was $3. In examining his statement, he found that the following checks were outstanding: No. 31, $7.16; No. 34, $15.10; and No. 35, $9.95. His checkbook balance at the end of the month was $349.44. Reconcile his bank statement.

34. **Read** Find an online article that relates to the use of location-based services for banking. Read the information and create an illustration that displays a concept, idea, or process discussed in the article. Include a properly formatted citation for your source.

Decision-Making Strategies

Fran and Bill Hamilton recently moved to a new community. They are having trouble deciding whether to use a financial institution near their workplaces or near their home. The Hamiltons have the opportunity to do business with a credit union, a national bank with many branches, a local bank with strong personal service, or a savings and loan association.

35. What factors should the Hamiltons consider when selecting a financial institution?

36. How could Fran and Bill obtain information about the financial institution that would best serve their needs?

Linking School and Community

Talk to people in your community about the financial institutions and financial services they use. Which of these have you learned about in this chapter? Are there other financial services that you need to learn about? Create a two-paragraph summary of your findings.

Web Workout

Most major banks offer many services to meet the needs of various groups in the economy. Banks often organize their services based on three types of customers: consumers, small businesses, and corporations and institutions. Consumer services include checking, saving, and loans. Small business services include lines of credit, SBA loans, retirement plans, and cash management. Banks serve commercial banking customers, including corporations and institutions, by servicing new loans, assisting with fund transfers, documenting legal requirements, and suggesting risk management strategies. Some banks also offer a variety of global financial services, which may include foreign currency exchange services, payment services for importers and exporters, and sending money electronically to international locations.

Think Critically

1. Locate the website of a large bank that offers financial services for several types of customers. Prepare a brief written summary of the features of the bank's website.

2. Make a list of the loan services offered to each type of customer.

3. Identify a service that is only offered to commercial customers. Write a brief statement explaining the service.

Presentation Management Individual Event

This event will assess your ability to use current technology to prepare and deliver an effective multimedia presentation. You will research the assigned topic and design a presentation to deliver your findings. On the day of the event, you will have 15 minutes to set up your presentation. The actual presentation must last a minimum of 7 minutes and a maximum of 10 minutes. Up to 5 minutes will be allowed for questions from the judges.

Effective multimedia presentations use audio and visual elements to complement and enhance the content of the presentation. You will need to decide how to use images, color, text, white space, and other design elements to make your presentation interesting without overwhelming your audience. Selecting the appropriate music, sounds, audio clips, and narration is also part of the process. You will need to secure a signed release from any individual whose name, photograph, and other information is included in the presentation.

For this event you must prepare an electronic multimedia presentation that thoroughly explains debit cards. You must conduct research to learn about the purpose and uses of debit cards and describe the pros and cons associated with using debit cards when making purchases and reservations. The presentation must be objective and cannot emphasize one side of the issue.

Performance Indicators Evaluated

- Demonstrate knowledge of multimedia software and components.
- Demonstrate effective multiple communication skills.
- Apply technical skills to create a multimedia presentation that enhances the oral presentation.

You will be evaluated for your

- Knowledge of the topic
- Organized presentation of the topic
- Confidence, quality of voice, and eye contact

For more detailed information about performance indicators, go to the BPA website.

Think Critically

1. What are some advantages of debit cards? List two specific examples.

2. What are some disadvantages of debit cards? List two specific examples.

3. Why should the record keeping for a debit card be the same as record keeping for a checking account?

www.bpa.org

18 Consumer Credit

Photodisc/Getty Images

Planning a Career in ...

CONSUMER CREDIT

Credit is important in most economies. Many individuals and businesses use credit for various purchases. Consumer credit involves loans for housing, motor vehicles, and college expenses. Business loans are vital for companies to start operations, purchase inventory, and buy equipment.

As a result, many workers employed by banks and credit card companies are involved in approving, processing, servicing, and collecting credit transactions.

People do not always make wise credit and buying choices. Workers in consumer credit also find jobs in credit counseling, helping people regain control of their finances and plan for their financial future.

Workers in consumer credit must combine knowledge of finance and economics with excellent communication skills for interaction with customers. They also must have strong computer and math skills.

Related Job Titles

- Bill and Account Collector
- Credit Clerk
- Loan Officer
- Credit Analyst
- Loan Counselor
- Information and Record Clerk
- Credit Counselor
- Credit Administrator
- Credit and Collections Manager
- Commercial Credit Analyst

Analyze Career Opportunities in ...
CONSUMER CREDIT

Use library and Internet resources to learn more about careers in consumer credit. Choose one of the job titles listed in the box above and answer the following questions.

1. How would you describe the earnings potential for this field?

2. Is this a career that interests you? What can you do now to help prepare yourself for this career?

What's it like to work as a ... Credit Counselor?

"We're not sure where our money goes each month. We just know we owe more than $8,000 in credit card bills," explained Joan Salvatore.

Joan and her husband, Hank, have a monthly income of $3,750, but their expenses are more than $4,400. That's why they came to the community credit counseling service. Joan and Hank were assigned to Bev Gonzalez. Bev worked for a consumer loan company for more than 15 years. Today, instead of granting credit to people, she helps them with credit problems.

Bev recommends that the Salvatores set up a budget to help them plan purchases and reduce spending. For example, Joan and Hank can eat at home more often and make occasional restaurant meals a treat. The extra money the Salvatores will have as a result of following a budget can be used to pay off their debt. In addition to offering a strategy for getting out of debt, Bev will help Joan and Hank learn how to manage their money in the future. No more arguing about money and no more calls about late bill payments.

What about you? What work activities in the consumer credit field appeal to you? What will you have to do to achieve success in this career field?

453

18-1 Credit Fundamentals

Goals

1. Identify the types of consumer credit.

2. Describe the benefits of using credit.

3. Explain some disadvantages of using credit.

Key Terms

credit 454

finance charge 455

down payment 458

installment loan 458

promissory note 458

collateral 458

cosigner 458

credit rating 459

Focus on REAL LIFE

In most economies, consumers, businesses, and governments use credit. For example, a person buys gas with an oil company credit card. A student applies for and receives a government loan to help with college expenses. A business receives a $2 million loan to build a new store. Another company borrows $150,000 to finance the purchase of additional inventory. The state of Louisiana may borrow $35 million through a bond issue to build new college buildings. A county board might borrow $250,000 to make emergency road repairs.

What do these people, businesses, and governmental institutions have in common? They all have wants, but lack the money to satisfy those wants. If they borrow money to satisfy their wants, they will be using credit.

Goal 1

Identify the types of consumer credit.

USING CREDIT

Credit is the privilege of using someone else's money for a period of time. That privilege is based on the belief that the person receiving credit will honor a promise to repay the amount owed at a future date. Two parties are involved in a credit transaction. Anyone who buys on credit or receives a loan is a *debtor*. The one who sells on credit or makes a loan is the *creditor*.

Although the credit system uses forms and legal documents, it also depends on trust between the debtor and creditor. This trust means that the creditor believes that the debtor will honor the promise to pay. Without that trust, the credit system could not operate.

Types of Credit

Businesses use trade credit. *Trade credit* occurs when a company receives goods from a supplier and pays for them later.

Businesses may secure long-term loans for land, equipment, and buildings. They may also borrow money for shorter periods, usually for 30 to 90 days, to meet short-term needs for cash.

Local, state, and federal governments often use credit to provide goods and services that benefit the public. Governments may use credit to buy items such as cars, aircraft, and police uniforms. They may also borrow funds to build highways, parks, and airports.

Most consumers use credit. You may use credit to buy expensive products that will last a long time. You may also use credit for convenience in making smaller purchases.

If you borrow money to use for some special purpose, you are using *loan credit*. Loans are available from several kinds of financial institutions. Loan credit usually involves a written contract. The borrower agrees to repay the loan in specified amounts, called *installments*, over a period of time.

If you charge a purchase at the time you buy the good or service, you are

---

using *sales credit*. Most businesses offer sales credit. Sales credit involves the use of charge accounts and credit cards by consumers.

Charge Accounts

A charge account represents a contract between the firm offering the account and the customer. Three types of charge accounts are generally available: regular, budget, and revolving.

Regular Accounts A regular charge account requires the buyer to make full payment within a stated period—usually 25 to 30 days. The seller may set a limit on the total amount that may be charged during that time. People use regular accounts for everyday needs and small purchases. Service providers, such as doctors, dentists, lawyers, and plumbers, commonly offer this type of credit.

Budget Accounts Some stores and utility companies offer *budget* charge accounts. This credit agreement requires that a customer make payments of a fixed amount over several months. One budget plan that businesses offer is the 90-day, three-payment plan. Under this plan, you pay for your purchase over a 90-day period, usually in three equal monthly payments.

With a utility company budget plan, the company makes an estimate for gas or electricity charges during a certain period, such as a year. You then agree to pay a certain amount each month to cover those charges. This plan avoids large payments during some times of the year. You pay the same amount each month.

Revolving Accounts The most popular form of sales credit is the *revolving* account. You may charge purchases at any time, but only part of the debt must be paid each month. Features of revolving credit include the following.

- A maximum amount may be owed at one time, called a *credit limit*.

fyi *Trade credit terms are often stated "2/10, n/30." This means that the business can take a 2 percent discount if the bill is paid within 10 days from the billing date. The full or net amount must be paid within 30 days.*

- A payment is required once a month, but the total amount owed need not be paid at one time.

- A finance charge is added if the total amount owed is not paid. A **finance charge** is the total dollar cost of credit, including interest and all other charges. You must pay this additional amount for the convenience of using credit.

What are some reasons that a business would borrow funds?

Revolving charge accounts are convenient, but they can make overspending easy. The finance charges on unpaid balances can be quite high, sometimes 1½ percent per month (18 percent per year) or higher. There is rarely a finance charge if balances are paid in full within a specified period, such as within 25 days.

Credit Cards

Charging purchases with credit cards is common. Most credit cards issued today are multipurpose cards. Consumers can use them at thousands of stores, restaurants, and other businesses, as well as to pay for goods and services online.

Bank Cards Bank credit cards have become very popular all over the world. MasterCard and VISA are two of the

best known. Sometimes an annual fee must be paid for the privilege of using these cards.

While banks and various merchants may issue credit cards, most credit card processing is done through *Independent Sales Organizations (ISOs)*. When you use your bank credit card, electronic terminals typically send the transaction data to an ISO which then authorizes payment. At the end of the day, credit sales information is submitted electronically and the banks then pay the business for the sales amount minus a service fee.

This fee covers the bank's expenses of processing the sales receipts and collecting amounts owed from customers. The bank is doing the work that the business' own credit departments would have to do otherwise.

Business owners like bank credit cards because the bank takes on the liability and expense of granting credit. Customers like bank charge cards because they are accepted by many businesses all over the world.

Charge Cards American Express and Diners Club, once called travel and entertainment cards, are widely used charge cards. Subscribers pay a yearly membership fee that is usually higher than the fee for bank cards. Cardholders are not given a spending limit. They are usually expected to pay the full balance each month. Business travelers like to use charge cards because the detailed records they receive are useful for business and tax record keeping. They offer proof of travel expenses.

Affinity Cards Some organizations allow their names to be affiliated with a credit card. These affinity cards are *co-branded* with an issuing bank. They allow an organization, such as a charity, sports team, or oil company to receive a small percentage of credit sales.

Retail Store Cards Many retail stores offer their own credit cards to customers.

Photodisc/Getty Images

What are the different types of credit cards that a person can apply for?

These cards show the name of the store that issues them. Customers can only use these cards at the issuing stores.

Installment Credit

You may want to purchase a new $600 flat screen TV or $500 laptop computer. For these purchases you may use a different type of credit. *Installment sales credit* is a contract issued by the seller that requires periodic payments at specified times. The seller adds finance charges to the cost of the items purchased. The credit agreement shows the total amount to be paid. Consumers often purchase furniture and household appliances with installment sales credit.

Unlike credit cards, installment sales credit is a contractual agreement directly between the buyer and the seller. The following are some features of installment credit.

- Signing a sales contract that shows the terms of the purchase.

- Receiving the purchased item at the time of the sale. Be aware that the seller has the right to *repossess,* or take back, an item if payments are not made on time.

Business Insight for the 21st Century

Marketing Credit Cards to College Students

The economic recession that started in 2008 cut the number of credit card offers sent by mail from an average 7 billion to 2 billion per year. This is still an average of six credit card offers for everyone in the United States. Some of those offers were sent to college-aged young adults because research shows that individuals develop their first brand loyalties between the ages of 18 and 25.

Abusive practices related to credit card offers prompted the passage of the Credit Card Accountability Responsibility and Disclosure Act (Credit CARD Act) of 2009. This act includes new protections for college students. Under the CARD Act, anyone under the age of 21 must apply for a card. Prior to the CARD Act a bank could issue a card without an application. A young person must provide evidence that they can pay their credit

card bill by showing proof of employment or income. They may also need a cosigner who can promise to pay for any debt. A student's line of credit is limited to $500.

Credit card companies used to freely market on college campuses. They would give away coupons, T-shirts, free pizza, and other incentives to get students to sign up for cards. Under the new CARD Act, banks must be 1,000 feet away from a college campus to offer giveaways.

It is important for young people to establish a good credit rating by demonstrating financial responsibility. They can open checking and savings accounts and use their local bank to obtain a student credit card or a prepaid card. Cosigners, such as parents, can help ensure that a student receives a card and that payments are made on time. Using cards

to make small purchases that total less than 30 percent of the credit limit each month and then paying the bill each month will help establish a good credit history.

Think Critically

1. Why are credit card companies interested in college-aged customers? Do you think the CARD Act will force credit card companies to act in a socially responsible way? Are college-aged students better off with the new law?

2. Use Internet and library resources to learn about strategies for selecting a credit card and using it wisely. Create a poster or brochure targeted at college-aged customers that incorporates tips for building a credit score.

- Making a **down payment**, which is a payment of part of the purchase price. It is usually made at the time of the purchase.

- Paying a finance charge on the amount owed.

- Making regular payments at stated times, usually weekly or monthly. For example, if a total of $120 is to be repaid in 12 monthly installments, $10 is paid each month.

In some cases, the seller charges a penalty if a payment is received after the due date. In others, all remaining payments may become due at once if only one payment is missed.

Consumer Loans

A loan is an alternative to charge account buying or installment sales credit. The terms of the loans and the requirements for securing the loans differ.

An **installment loan** is one in which you agree to make monthly payments in specific amounts over a period of time. The payments are installments. The total amount you repay includes the amount you borrowed plus the finance charge on your loan.

Another kind of loan is a *single-payment loan*. With this type of credit, you do not pay anything until the end of the loan period, possibly 60 or 90 days. At that time, you repay the full amount you borrowed plus the finance charge.

A lender needs some assurance that each loan will be repaid. If you are a good credit risk, you may be able to sign a promissory note. A **promissory note** is a written promise to repay based on a debtor's excellent credit history. The amount borrowed, usually with some interest, is due on a certain date. Promissory notes should include the following components:

- **Principal** The amount that is promised to be paid

- **Time** The days or months from the date of the note until it should be paid

- **Date of maturity** The date on which the note is due

- **Payee** The one to whom the note is payable

- **Interest rate** The rate paid for the use of the money

- **Maker** The one who promises to make payment

In some cases, the lender may ask you to offer some property you own, such as a car, a house, or jewelry, as *security*. Property that is used as security is called **collateral**. You give the lender the right to sell this property to get back the amount of the loan if you do not repay it. This type of loan is a *secured loan*.

What if you do not have an established credit history or any property to offer as security? You may be able to get a relative or friend who has property or a good credit history to sign your note. They become the legal **cosigner**. The cosigner of a note is responsible for payment of the note if you do not pay as promised.

> **checkpoint** ✓
> What are the major types of consumer credit?

BENEFITS OF CREDIT

Both businesses and consumers can benefit from credit use. The main advantages of credit for consumers include the following.

- **Convenience** Credit can make it easy for you to buy. You can shop without carrying much cash.

- **Immediate Possession** Credit allows you to have the item now. A family can

Goal 2

Describe the benefits of using credit.

WORK as a TEAM

Most businesses sell on credit. Create a list of situations in which a company may not offer credit to customers. What would be benefits and drawbacks of this action?

buy a dishwasher on credit and begin using it at once.

- **Savings** Sometimes credit allows you to buy an item on sale at a good price. Some stores, especially department and furniture stores, send notices of special sales to credit customers.

- **Credit Rating** A person's reputation for paying bills on time is known as a **credit rating**. If you buy on credit and pay your bills on time, you gain a reputation for being dependable. In that way, you establish a favorable credit rating. A credit rating is valuable when you might need to borrow money or when you want to make a major purchase.

- **Useful for Emergencies** Access to credit can help in unexpected situations. Sometimes you may not have

enough cash and have an urgent need for something. For example, your car might need repairs.

> **checkpoint** ✓
> What are the main advantages of consumer credit?

CREDIT CONCERNS

Buying on credit is convenient and can be beneficial. There are also some disadvantages if you are not careful.

- **Overbuying** A common spending hazard of credit involves buying something that is more expensive than you can afford. Attractive store displays and advertisements invite you to make purchases.

Goal 3

Explain some disadvantages of using credit.

Business Insight for the 21st Century

Databases, Personal Privacy, and Identity Theft

Information about you is readily available to many people. Businesses and governments all over the world use computer databases and electronic networks to store and exchange this information about you.

How is this information obtained? Most databases are created from information given voluntarily. For instance, you offer information when you apply for credit, obtain telephone service, apply for a driver's license, obtain insurance, and answer survey questions.

Privacy is a basic right to have information about you kept confidential. Like most consumers, you are probably concerned about your privacy. While there is some reason

to be concerned about databases and personal privacy, protections exist. Decisions about granting credit or obtaining insurance are most often based on accurate, up-to-date information. The information gathered is used for legitimate business reasons.

Various state and federal privacy laws continue to be under review. Government officials must decide what information is private and when consumers should be asked to give permission before credit or medical reports are released to others. In recent years, stronger privacy protection laws have been enacted.

Identity theft is the fastest-growing financial crime. That's the bad news.

The good news is that the technology that is used to steal a person's identity can also be used to protect it. Each year, credit card companies, retail stores, and online businesses improve their security systems. These efforts help to ensure that your personal information and financial data will not be viewed or used by unauthorized individuals or companies.

Think Critically

1. What dangers are involved with having private information easily accessible to others?

2. Conduct a web search to determine actions you can take to protect your privacy.

- **Careless Buying** If you become impatient or distracted in your shopping, you may not shop carefully. You may fail to make comparisons, causing you to buy at the wrong time or the wrong place. Credit can tempt you not to wait for a better price on an item you want now.

- **Higher Prices** Stores that only accept cash may sell items at lower prices than stores that offer credit. Extending credit is expensive for stores. When customers do not pay as agreed, there are collection costs. Sometimes businesses must write off consumer debts as uncollectible. These increased costs often result in higher prices.

- **Overuse of Credit** Buying now and paying later may sound like a good idea. If too many payments need to be made later, the total amount due can become a problem. Consumers must keep records of the total amount owed so that they do not have monthly payments that exceed their ability to pay.

Questions to Ask

Before making a final decision about whether to buy on credit, think about these important questions.

Why do you think stores offer discounts to consumers?

- How will you benefit from this use of credit?

- Is this the best buy you can make or should you shop around?

- What will be the total cost of your purchase, including the finance charges?

- What would you save if you paid cash?

- Will the payments be too high for your income?

Answering these questions will help you make wise credit decisions.

> **checkpoint** ✓
> What are potential drawbacks of buying on credit?

18-1 Assessment

Study Tools

www.cengage.com/school/genbus/pob

Key Concepts

Determine the best answer.

1. Large purchases (such as motorcycles and automobiles) are commonly bought using
   a. a bank credit card
   b. installment credit
   c. a charge account
   d. trade credit

2. Signing a promissory note occurs when using
   a. a credit card
   b. a charge account
   c. a loan
   d. trade credit

3. Which of the following is an advantage of using credit?
   a. overbuying
   b. convenience
   c. higher prices
   d. lower credit rating

Make Academic Connections

4. **Marketing** Collect advertisements from newspapers, magazines, and websites for companies that offer credit. What types of credit are offered? Is the company selling credit as its primary product or using credit to promote the sale of other goods and services?

5. **Economics** Create a table showing the benefits of credit and credit concerns. For each benefit and each concern, describe the effect consumer credit has on individuals and businesses.

18-2 Cost of Credit

Goals

1 Calculate interest in consumer credit situations.

2 Explain finance charges when using credit.

Key Terms

interest 461

annual percentage rate 464

Focus on REAL LIFE

"Dad, I think I need a credit card," Peter said.

"Really? What are you planning to buy and how are you going to pay the bill?" asked Peter's father.

"Dad, it is almost impossible to buy anything online without a credit card. I want to be able to download music and maybe buy movie tickets. Plus, it would be nice to pay at the pump when I put gas in the car. I have money from my allowance and my job. I'm not planning a big shopping spree, but I think having a credit card would be a good idea," responded Peter.

"I think you're right. Let's look at our bank's website and see what kinds of cards they offer. They might have a credit card with a low credit limit or something else designed for someone your age. Then we can shop around for the best terms—credit is not free."

FINDING INTEREST

Borrowing money has a cost. **Interest**, I, is the cost of using someone else's money. The amount of interest paid on a loan or charge account should be clearly understood. To determine this amount, you need to know the following.

1. Principal, P Amount of the loan.

2. Interest Rate, R Percent of interest charged or earned. Remember that a percent can also be expressed as a decimal or a fraction. The symbol for percent is %.

3. Time, T Length of time for which interest will be charged, usually expressed in years or parts of a year.

Simple Interest

On single-payment loans, interest is usually *simple interest*. The formula for computing simple interest is shown below.

$$\text{Interest} = \text{Principal} \times \text{Rate} \times \text{Time}$$
$$I = P \times R \times T$$

A simple interest rate of 12 percent per year means you are paying 12 cents for each dollar you borrow for a year. At this rate, if you borrow $1, you pay 12 cents in interest. If you borrow $2, you pay 24 cents. If you borrow $10, you pay $1.20, and so on.

Goal 1

Calculate interest in consumer credit situations.

How does time affect the amount of interest that you pay?

Suppose you borrow $100 ($P$) at 12 percent ($R$) for one year ($T$). To calculate the amount of interest, first change 12 percent to a decimal, 0.12. Using the formula, the interest is $12.

$$I = P \times R \times T$$
$$I = \$100 \times 0.12 \times 1 = \$12$$

If you borrow $100 at 12 percent for two years, you pay twice as much interest, or $24.

$$I = \$100 \times 0.12 \times 2 = \$24$$

If you borrow the money for three years, you pay $36, and so on.

Time in Months Your loan may be for one month instead of one year. How is simple interest calculated for less than a year? The amount of interest is based on the portion of the year. There are 12 months in a year, so one month is one-twelfth of a year, regardless of the number of days in the particular month.

If you borrow $100 at 12 percent for one month, the interest is

$$I = P \times R \times T$$
$$I = \$100 \times 0.12 \times \frac{1}{12} = \$1$$

Time in Days A loan may be for a certain number of days such as 30, 60, or 90 days. To make the computation easy, a year is often considered as 360 days. The interest on a loan of $100 at 12 percent for 60 days is $2.

$$I = P \times R \times T$$
$$I = \$100 \times 0.12 \times \frac{60}{360} = \$2$$

Maturity Dates

The date on which a loan must be repaid is the *maturity date*. When the time of the loan is stated in months, the date of maturity is the same day of the month as the date on which the loan was made. A one-month loan made on January 15 will be due February 15. A two-month loan will be due March 15, and so on.

When the time is in days, you must count the exact number of days to find the date of maturity. First, determine the

What happens when you use credit to take on too much debt?

number of days remaining in the month when the loan was made. For example, if the loan was made on January 10, there would be 21 days counted in January, because there are 31 days in January. Then add the days in the following months until the total equals the required number of days.

Suppose you want to find the date of maturity of a 90-day loan made on March 4. First find the number of days remaining in March. Then add the days in the following months until you reach 90 days. In this case, the due date is June 2. Figure 18-1 illustrates the process.

FINDING MATURITY DATE	
March	27 days (31 – 4)
April	30 days
May	31 days
June	2 days
Total	90 days

▶ **Figure 18-1**

What would the due date be for a 60-day loan made on March 4?

Installment Interest

When you borrow money, you usually make several partial payments instead of one large single payment. A loan that you repay in partial payments is an installment loan (or consumer loan). Each payment is an *installment*.

Banks, credit unions, and consumer finance companies all offer installment loans. With an installment loan, the bank gives the borrower a schedule of payments. It shows how much the borrower must pay each month.

With some loans, the lender adds the amount of the interest to the amount you borrow. You sign a *promissory note* for the total amount. You then repay the note in equal monthly installments.

Suppose you borrow $100, sign a note for $110, and agree to repay the loan in 12 monthly installments of $9.17 each. If you had borrowed $100 for one year and paid $110 at maturity, the interest rate would be 10 percent ($10 ÷ $100 = 0.10).

However, you paid off just part of the loan each month. You had the use of the entire $100 for one month and a smaller amount each succeeding month as you repaid the loan. In this case, the true interest rate amounts to 18.5 percent.

Amortization Schedules On some installment loans, interest is calculated on the amount that is unpaid at the end of each month. The payment table of principal and interest over time is called an *amortization schedule*.

Suppose that a person obtained a loan for $1,000 and agreed to repay $100 per month. The lender applies the payment to principal and interest. The borrower makes payments each

Think about how the use of credit can help people achieve their life-span goals. Explain why the excessive use of credit can prevent people from achieving their goals. What are some things you should consider when trying to decide whether or not to borrow funds?

month on a level payment schedule. Figure 18-2, on page 464, shows this amortization schedule.

Amortization schedules show that when loans are first taken, a larger percentage of the payments go to interest.

What large purchases often require an individual to apply for an installment loan?

mangostock/Shutterstock.com

NETBookmark

Consumers need to stay informed about using credit wisely. Access the website shown below and click on the link for Chapter 18. Select two topic areas. Prepare a summary of the main ideas presented for each area. Explain how this information might be valuable to consumers who use credit.

www.cengage.com/school/genbus/pob

Goal 2

Explain finance charges when using credit.

At the end of the schedule, more goes to principal. For example, the second payment includes more than $9 in interest and the tenth payment includes only $1.57 in interest. Only $90.90 from the second loan payment is applied to the principal. The tenth payment includes more than $98 in principal.

checkpoint

What three things are necessary to calculate interest?

FINANCE CHARGES

Before you borrow money or charge a purchase, you should know the exact cost of using credit. Three things to consider are the annual percentage rate, the total dollar charges, and the alternative sources of credit.

Annual Percentage Rate

The **annual percentage rate** (APR) is a disclosure required by law. It states the percentage cost of credit on a yearly basis. All credit agreements, whether for sales credit or loan credit, require disclosure of the APR.

In addition to interest, the APR includes other charges that may be made. *Service fees* involve the time and money it takes a creditor to investigate your credit history, process your loan or charge account application, and keep records of your payments and balances.

The costs of collecting from those who do not pay their accounts may also be passed on to other borrowers. *Uncollectible accounts* are frequently referred to as *bad debts* or *doubtful accounts.*

▶ **Figure 18-2**
Which kind of loan schedule would be best for very large loans paid back over a number of years?

AMORTIZATION SCHEDULE
$1,000 loan, 12% interest rate, monthly payments are $100

PAYMENT	INTEREST	APPLIED TO PRINCIPAL	LOAN BALANCE
			$1,000.00
$100.00	$10.00	$90.00	910.00
100.00	9.10	90.90	819.10
100.00	8.19	91.81	727.29
100.00	7.28	92.72	634.57
100.00	6.35	93.65	540.92
100.00	5.41	94.59	446.33
100.00	4.46	95.54	350.79
100.00	3.51	96.49	254.30
100.00	2.54	97.46	156.84
100.00	1.57	98.43	58.41
58.99	0.58	58.41	-------

Lenders may also add an amount to cover the cost of credit insurance. This coverage repays the balance of the amount owed if the borrower dies or becomes disabled.

Total Dollar Charges

To make you aware of the total cost of credit, federal law requires that the lender must tell you the finance charge. The *finance charge* is the total dollar cost of credit, including interest and all other charges. Either your contract or your charge account statement must state this finance charge.

Compare Credit Costs

If you have to borrow money or buy on credit, be sure to compare the total cost of credit among alternative sources. Check with several lenders and compare the APRs.

If you make a purchase with a credit card, know which card has the lowest APR. If an installment sales contract is required, think about whether an installment loan from a financial institution may be cheaper for you.

WORK *as a* **TEAM**

Various factors affect interest rates. Create two lists: (1) What economic factors can affect interest rates? (2) What personal factors can affect the rate a lender charges a borrower?

When getting a loan, shop around just as carefully as you would for any major purchase. Borrowing money is costly, so make sure that you get the best loan. Some of the things you should check include the annual percentage rate, the amount of the monthly payments, and the finance charge.

Always remember that when you use credit, you are spending future income. If you decide to use credit, the benefits of making the purchase now should outweigh the costs of using credit. Effectively used, credit can help you have more and enjoy more. Misused, credit can result in too much debt, loss of reputation, and even bankruptcy.

checkpoint ✓
What does APR represent?

18-2 Assessment

Study Tools

www.cengage.com/school/genbus/pob

Key Concepts

Determine the best answer.

1. True or False. The principal of a loan is the total amount of interest that will be paid.

2. True or False. Interest rates are stated on the basis of one year even if a loan is for several years.

3. The most valuable number to consider when comparing credit among various borrowing sources is the
   a. total finance charge
   b. maturity date
   c. annual percentage rate
   d. principal

Make Academic Connections

4. **Math** Calculate the amount of interest for each of the following loans.
   a. $6,000 borrowed for 1 year at 7% APR
   b. $2,000 borrowed for 4 months at 8% APR
   c. $1,100 borrowed for 2½ years at 6% APR

5. **Economics** Several types of interest rates exist in every economy. Use library materials or an Internet search to determine common reported interest rates. Which of these rates are related to consumer credit?

18-3 Credit Application and Documents

Goals

1 Explain the credit application process.

2 Describe the activities of a credit bureau.

3 Discuss commonly used credit documents.

Key Terms

credit application 466

credit bureau 469

statement of account 470

Focus on REAL LIFE

"I don't get it. How do you get credit if you never had it? It seems like you have to have a good credit history before you even have credit."

When Amy Compton mentioned her concerns during her business class, a few students said they were already working on establishing good credit. Some students said they had credit union or bank accounts in their own names. Others reported that they had part-time jobs.

Everyone agreed that the first step toward getting credit was opening a bank account and demonstrating your ability to repay a debt.

Goal 1

Explain the credit application process.

CREDIT APPLICATION PROCESS

To obtain a loan or credit card, you must prove that you are a good credit risk. Not everyone who wants credit will receive it. Lenders need certain information in order to make a decision about granting credit. They want to be assured of two things: your ability to repay a debt and your willingness to do so.

The Three Cs of Credit

In deciding whether to grant you credit, businesses consider three main factors, known as the three Cs—character, capacity, and capital.

Character refers to your honesty and willingness to pay a debt when it is due. If you have a history of paying bills on time, creditors believe that you are a good credit risk.

Capacity refers to a person's ability to pay a debt when it is due. The lender or seller must decide if you have enough income to pay your bills. If your income is too small or unsteady, granting you credit may not be wise. In contrast, your income may be high, but if you have other debts, you may not be able to handle more payments.

Capital is the value of the borrower's possessions. Capital includes the money and property you own. Your capital may include a car that is paid for and a house on which a large amount has been paid. A checking account and savings also add to your capital. The amount of capital gives the lender some assurance that you will be able to meet your credit obligations.

Credit Applications

When you apply for credit or a loan, the lender will ask you to fill out an application. A **credit application** is a form on which you provide information needed by a lender to make a decision about granting credit. Figure 18-3 shows an example of a credit card application. In addition to printed applications, some companies take credit card applications online.

One of the most important parts of a credit application is your *credit references*—businesses or individuals who are able and willing to provide information about your creditworthiness. Your

---

CREDIT CARD APPLICATION

S econd
N ational
B ankCorp

Important: Fill in all information requested below.

1. Information About Yourself *(Name of person in whose name card will be issued)*

☐ Mr. ☐ Mrs. ☐ Miss ☐ Ms. First Name   Middle   Last Name

(Courtesy titles are optional)

Home Address	Apt.	City	State	ZIP Code	How Long? Years ____ Mos. ____

Previous Address (if less than 2 years at present address)	Apt.	City	State	ZIP Code

Home Telephone ( )	Business Telephone ( )	Social Security Number	Date of Birth / /	No. of Dependents (Exclude Yourself)

Are You a U.S. Citizen? ☐ Yes ☐ No	If No, Explain Immigration Status	Are You a Permanent Resident? ☐ Yes ☐ No	Do You: ☐ Own ☐ Rent ☐ Other	Monthly Rent or Mortgage $

2. Employment Information *(Your total yearly income from all sources)*

Employer	Address	City	State	ZIP Code

How Long? Years ____ Mos. ____	Occupation	Yearly Gross Salary $	Other Income*	Source

Former Employer (if less than 1 year with present employer)	How Long? Years ____ Mos. ____	*Note: Alimony, child support or separate maintenance income need not be disclosed if you do not wish to have it considered as a basis for paying this obligation.

Nearest Relative Not Living with You	Address	City	State	Relation	Telephone

3. Other Credit

Major Credit Cards (Visa, MasterCard, etc....)	Account Number

Other Credit Cards (Dept. Stores, etc....)	Account Number

Other Credit	Account Number

4. Banking Information

☐ Checking	Name of Bank	City	Account Number

☐ Savings	Name of Bank (if different from above)	City	Account Number

☐ Other (Check here if you have any of the following:)	IRA CD	Money Market Account Stocks/Bonds	Investments Cash Management Account

5. Joint Account Information *(Complete for joint account or if you are relying on the income of another person to qualify for an account)*

First Name	Middle	Last Name	Relation

Home Address	Apt.	City	State	ZIP Code

Home Telephone ( )	Business Telephone ( )	Social Security Number	Date of Birth / /

Employer	Address	City	State	ZIP Code

How Long? Years ____ Mos. ____	Occupation	Yearly Gross Salary $	Other Income*	Source

Former Employer	How Long? Years ____ Mos. ____	*Note: Alimony, child support or separate maintenance income need not be disclosed if you do not wish to have it considered as a basis for paying this obligation.

6. Additional Cards *(Complete this section if you want cards issued to additional buyers on your account.)*

1. Spouse First Name	Middle	Last Name

2. Other First Name	Middle	Last Name

7. Signatures

I authorize the Second National BankCorp to check my credit record and to verify my credit, employment, and income references.
I have read the important information on the reverse side.

X _____   X _____

Applicant's Signature   Joint Applicant's Signature

I understand that Second National BankCorp may amend the account terms and charges specified in the Cardmember Agreement in the future.

▶ **Figure 18-3**

Why is it important to fill in all the blanks and to do so accurately?

Why is good credit important to a landlord? Who else might request a copy of your credit report?

signature on the application gives a lender permission to contact your credit references to inquire about your credit record.

Your signature also indicates that you understand the type of credit and that the information you have provided is true. You need to fill out the credit application completely, accurately, and honestly. You should only sign it when you understand it and have provided the requested information.

Documenting Credit Data

Information provided on credit applications must be verified to assure its accuracy. Present and former employers can verify employment dates and salary figures. Banks and other financial institutions can report whether the applicants have the accounts they listed. Landlords can indicate how long tenants have been renting and if they pay their rent on time. Other creditors can report how an applicant makes payments on accounts.

You may list a personal reference because you do not have sufficient business credit references. The person you list can indicate how he or she feels you conduct your personal business activities. In each case, the reference helps the credit manager to get a better picture of you as a credit risk. The credit manager can then make an accurate appraisal of your creditworthiness.

Actions to Establish Credit

Building a good record of creditworthiness can be important. You can begin while you are still in school. Trust and reliability are important in matters of credit. You can help to establish yourself by having a good record of grades and attendance. Both employers and lenders know that school behavior patterns tend to carry on later in life.

In addition, start a checking and savings account. If you keep a balance in each account, a lender can see that you can handle money. Making regular deposits to your savings account also suggests that you will be a good credit risk.

Some people establish credit records by charging small purchases. You may buy a sweater on credit and make the payments according to the agreement. This action is an important step toward proving you are a good credit risk. You may want to pay off your account within 30 days and avoid an interest charge. Either way, you will be building a good credit record.

Having a good part-time or full-time employment record also helps to start a favorable credit record. Changing jobs often does not look good. Being on a job for two or more years is a positive part of a good credit record.

Other information that lenders will want to know relates to your finances. You will need to report how much you earn, what kinds of savings and investments you have, and whether you have any other sources of income. A lender may also want to know about your reliability. In other words, they will want to know your occupation, how long you have been with your present employer, how long you have lived at the same address, and whether you own or rent your home.

> **checkpoint** ✓
> What are the three Cs of credit?

CREDIT BUREAU

In addition to checking with your credit references, a lender will usually check with a credit bureau. A **credit bureau**, or credit reporting agency, is a company that gathers information on credit users. It sells this information to businesses offering credit. Banks, finance companies, and retail stores are among the customers of credit bureaus.

Credit bureaus keep debt records of consumers. They can record only information that is officially reported to them. For example, mortgage lenders and credit card companies report information about their customers. The information shows if payments are up to date or overdue and if any action has been taken to collect overdue bills. Credit information from other sources such as utility companies, collection agencies, and courts may be added to create a month-by-month credit history for the consumer accounts.

National and local credit bureaus cooperate with each other and share information. If you are new to an area, the local credit bureau can obtain information from the bureau in your previous community.

Joel Calheiros/Shutterstock.com

Credit Report

A credit bureau uses your debt records to grade you as a credit risk. Your credit report shows the debts you owe, how often you use credit, whether you pay your debts on time, and other credit data. All of this information is of interest to credit grantors. Credit bureaus do not make value judgments about any individual. The bureau simply gathers facts as reported to them.

The formats used by credit bureaus vary, but credit reports all contain similar information. Reports are usually divided into six parts: personal information, public records, accounts in good standing, adverse accounts, credit history requests, and personal statement. Figure 18-4 lists the main components of a credit report along with descriptions and examples for each component.

Goal 2

Describe the activities of a credit bureau.

MAIN COMPONENTS OF A CREDIT REPORT		
COMPONENT	**DESCRIPTION**	**EXAMPLES**
Personal Information	Information that helps identify or locate the consumer	Names, aliases, current and former addresses, Social Security number, and telephone numbers
Public Records	Information from public records that might be viewed negatively by creditors	Information about bankruptcy, liens, judgments, and garnishments
Adverse Accounts	Information about accounts that might be viewed negatively by creditors	Accounts that are past due or in dispute as well as accounts that have missed or late payments
Accounts in Good Standing	Information about accounts that have a positive status	Accounts that are current or that have been paid off on time
Credit History Requests	Information about creditors who have requested credit history information	Businesses and lenders where the consumer has applied for a mortgage, loan, credit card, or charge card
Personal Statement	Optional statement provided by the consumer	Information about identity theft, unemployment, and disputed charges

▶ **Figure 18-4**

What kind of information would be on your credit report?

Your credit record is confidential. That is, only you or those who have a legitimate reason for examining it can obtain it. For example, when you fill out an application to rent an apartment, you might be asked to give the landlord or leasing agent permission to check your credit. The same is true when you apply for a loan or a credit card.

> **checkpoint ✓**
> What is the main purpose of a credit bureau? "

CREDIT DOCUMENTS

Credit is important in many ways. Millions of consumers and businesses enjoy this privilege. No matter what kind of credit is involved, both parties have legal responsibilities.

You can help maintain a good credit record by keeping track of your purchases and payments. When you buy on credit, you should keep a copy of the sales slip, credit card receipt, or other documents. As you make payments by check, keep track of the date and check number.

Credit Contracts

"KWYS" are four letters to keep in mind when signing any legal form. These letters stand for "know what

Why is it important to read and understand your credit documents before signing them?

you're signing." This principle applies to all credit contracts. An installment contract is one of the most important forms you may sign. Before signing one, consider the following questions.

- How much are the finance charges? Are they clearly shown on the contract?
- Does the contract include the cost of services you may need, such as repairs to a television or a washing machine?
- Does the contract have an add-on feature so that you can later buy other items?
- If you pay the contract in full before the ending date, will the finance charge be reduced?
- Is the contract completely filled in before you sign? Be sure to draw a line through any blank space before signing.
- Will you be given a copy of the contract?
- Under what conditions can the seller repossess the merchandise if you do not pay on time?

Statement of Account

As a credit card or charge account customer, you will receive a monthly summary of your account. The **statement of account**, or simply the *statement*, is a record of the transactions completed during the billing period. Most statements report the following information:

- The balance that was due when the last statement was mailed
- The amounts charged during the month
- The amounts credited to your account for payments or for returned items
- The current balance, which is the old balance + finance charges + purchases – payments
- The minimum amount of your next payment and when it is due

Figure 18-5 shows a sample of part of a monthly credit card statement.

Photodisc/Getty Images

Second National Bank Credit Card Account Statement
Account Number Ending in 9999
February 21, 20-- to March 22, 20--

Summary of Account Activity	
Previous Balance	$535.07
Payments	−$450.00
Other Credits	−$13.45
Purchases	+$529.57
Balance Transfers	+$785.00
Cash Advances	+$318.00
Past Due Amount	+$0.00
Fees Charged	**+$69.45**
Interest Charged	**+$10.89**
New Balance	$1,784.53
Credit limit	$2,000.00
Available credit	$215.47
Statement closing date	3/22/20--
Days in billing cycle	30

QUESTIONS?

Call Customer Service	1-832-555-0000
Lost or Stolen Credit Card	1-832-555-0000

Please send billing inquiries and correspondence to: PO Box 9073999, Houston, TX, 77083

Payment Information	
New Balance	$1,784.53
Minimum Payment Due	$48.00
Payment Due Date	4/20/20

Late Payment Warning: If we do not receive your minimum payment by the date listed above, you may have to pay a $35 late fee and your APRs may be increased up to the Penalty APR of 28.99%.

Minimum Payment Warning: If you make only the minimum payment each period, you will pay more in interest and it will take you longer to pay off your balance. For example:

If you make no additional charges using this card and each month you pay...	You will pay off the balance shown on this statement in about ...	And you will end up paying an estimated total of...
Only the minimum payment	10 years	$3,284
$62	3 years	$2,232 (Savings = $1,052)

If you would like information about credit counseling services, call 1-800-555-0000.

Transactions				
Reference Number	Trans Date	Post Date	Description of Transaction or Credit	Amount
Payments and Other Credits				
854338203FS8000Z5	2/25	2/25	PAYMENT THANK YOU	$450.00−
045148714518979874	3/4	3/5	BIG BOX CENTRAL 412 HOUSTON TX	$13.45−
Purchases				
5884186PS0388W6YM	2/22	2/23	FOOD COURT 0006 HOUSTON TX	$2.05
55541860705RDYD0X	2/24	2/25	FOOD COURT 0006 HOUSTON TX	$4.63
554328608008W90M0	2/24	2/25	WESTSIDE STORE HOUSTON TX	$114.95
841517877845AKOJIO	2/25	2/26	ONLINE BOOKSELLER ST LOUIS MO 63101	$40.35
895848561561894KOH	2/26	2/27	FIVE STAR DINER KATY TX	$27.68
1871556189456SAMKL	2/26	2/27	BIG BOX CENTRAL 412 HOUSTON TX	$124.76
2564894185189LKDFID	2/27	2/28	CORNER GASOLINE BAYSIDE TX	$32.87

(transactions continued on next page)

Sources: United States Treasury and Federal Reserve Board

▶ **Figure 18-5**

Why would it be better to pay more than the minimum payment on a credit card?

Accuracy of Records

Accurate record keeping is a good personal business practice. Keeping accurate records will help you avoid credit problems.

Many errors are simply honest mistakes. Whatever the source of the error, you need to contact the business, explain the problem, and request a correction. Your creditworthiness may be at stake. Businesses are usually as eager to correct errors as you are. Bad publicity may also hurt the reputation of the business if errors are not corrected.

Avoiding Fraud

The Federal Trade Commission reports that credit card fraud is a major problem. To avoid loss due to fraud, you should check your credit card account statements very carefully for errors.

Each month, you should check the accuracy of your statement by comparing it with your copies of credit card receipts. This includes the receipts you get from merchants and documents you print or save when you make online purchases. Verify payments and other credits, such as amounts subtracted when merchandise is returned. If you discover an error on a statement, you should notify the business as well as the

What safety precautions are in place on the Internet to prevent credit card fraud?

credit card company. Keep checking new statements to ensure the problem is resolved.

In some cases, your credit card company may contact you if fraud is suspected. This happens when charges being made on a card do not match the pattern of past purchases. Unusual product purchases or charges made in new locations often trigger fraud alerts.

To help prevent Internet fraud, online credit card transactions require account numbers, expiration dates, and printed security numbers. The data transfer is also encrypted.

> **checkpoint** ✓
> What are the main items reported on a statement of account?

18-3 Assessment

Key Concepts

Determine the best answer.

1. A reputation for paying bills on time relates to a person's
   a. capacity
   b. collateral
   c. character
   d. capital

2. The main activity of a credit bureau is to
   a. calculate the cost of credit for lenders and borrowers
   b. determine when a person is overusing credit
   c. contact a government agency when lenders overcharge for credit
   d. report information on the use of credit by consumers

Make Academic Connections

3. **Business Math** Don Ghonski received his credit card statement. This report showed $45 in new purchases, a current balance of $178, a payment of $70, and finance charges of $2. What was the amount of Don's beginning balance from the previous month?

4. **Technology** Go to the website of one of the major credit reporting agencies. What services does the agency provide for businesses? What information is available to assist consumers?

5. **Read** Find an online news article that relates to credit card debt. Read the article and write a 140-character review for your classmates that includes the URL and your suggest to read, skim, or ignore the article.

Doing Business in... Mexico

Mexico and the United States share a long history and a long border—more than three thousand kilometers. Much of the southwest United States once belonged to Mexico and is still strongly influenced by the Mexican culture and language. The connection continues today through trade valued at more than $300 billion. Mexico is the third largest U.S. trade partner after Canada and China.

Mexico's main exports are manufactured goods, oil and oil products, silver, and agricultural products such as fruits, vegetables, coffee, and cotton. Imports include metalworking machines, steel mill products, agricultural machinery, electrical equipment, and car and truck parts for assembly and repair.

In Mexico, business meetings are normally conducted in Spanish, the official language. It is likely that business executives will be able to speak English, but to show respect, it is important to learn some Spanish. Any printed information should be in Spanish.

Mexican work days usually start around 8 A.M. and end at 6 P.M. Your business meeting could include lunch, the main meal of the day, which can last for several hours. Business lunches are time to socialize, not a time to present formal business information. In Mexico, relationships are developed first, and business follows.

Mexican business meetings are formal and you should dress conservatively. A dark suit is appropriate. Status is important and individuals should be addressed by their titles. Top executives will want to meet with individuals of similar rank. Always shake hands when you meet and when you leave. Personal contact is important. Negotiations should start with small talk and family is a common topic. When you move on to business, the discussions are likely to be unstructured and not follow a specific agenda.

In Mexico, time is flexible. The concept of *mañana,* or an indefinite time in the future, is the rule. So, don't be surprised if your contact is late. You, however, should arrive on time and ready to work.

Think Critically

1. What cultural facts would you need to take into consideration when doing business in Mexico?

2. Describe how you could develop a relationship with your Mexican business partner.

3. Conduct library or Internet research to find additional information about business activities and economic conditions in Mexico.

Why would an Oregon berry farm be interested in doing business with a raspberry farm in Mexico? How could the raspberry farm benefit from this relationship?

KEVIN G. HALL/MCT/LANDOV

18-4 Protection of Credit Rights

Goals

1. Identify credit application regulations.

2. Explain credit use regulations.

3. Discuss credit problems and available assistance.

Key Terms

credit counselor 477

bankruptcy 478

Focus on REAL LIFE

Ben Khan mistakenly leaves a credit card lying on a counter at a store. After asking at the store and waiting a few weeks, he realizes the card will not be returned. On his next statement, he sees that more than $200 worth of merchandise was charged.

Julie Roma checks her charge account statement and finds several errors on it. One charge is for a purchase she did not make, and this is the third month in a row that this charge has shown up on the statement.

Your friends, Monique and Gary Buckman, had their loan application turned down. The loan officer explained that their credit bureau report was not good. Monique and Gary were shocked. They always pay their bills on time, with only a few minor exceptions. They need this loan for home improvements.

These credit problems can happen to anyone. If consumers know about credit laws and regulations, they can take actions to avoid and correct problems.

Goal 1

Identify credit application regulations.

CREDIT APPLICATION REGULATIONS

Most businesses are honest in their business dealings. Unfortunately, some are not. Because of this, it became necessary for federal and state governments to pass laws to protect credit consumers.

Truth-in-Lending Act

The *Truth-in-Lending Act of 1968* was the first of a series of credit protection laws. Truth-in-Lending requires that you be told the cost of credit before signing an agreement. The lender must clearly state the annual percentage rate (APR) and total finance charge.

The Truth-in-Lending Act also protects consumers against unauthorized use of credit cards. The law limits your liability to $50 for unauthorized credit card purchases made prior to notifying the card issuer. You are not liable for any fraudulent charges made after you have notified the credit card company. You can notify the company by telephone, but you should also put your notification in writing.

Credit Card Act of 2009

The *Credit Card Accountability Responsibility and Disclosure Act of 2009* was designed to establish fair and transparent credit card practices. Among its provisions, the CARD Act keeps credit card companies from changing fees and interest rates without cardholder approval. Cardholders must be notified of changes and they then have the right of refusal. Cardholders can also control their credit limit.

The CARD Act requires a credit card statement to show how long it would take to pay off the balance if the cardholder pays only the minimum due. The act also protects people under 21, college students, and other vulnerable consumers.

Equal Credit Opportunity Act

The *Equal Credit Opportunity Act* prohibits creditors from denying a person credit because of age, race, sex, or marital status. Young people who may have just entered the labor market cannot be denied credit based only on age. Older, possibly retired, people also have special protection under this act.

Married women who previously found it difficult to establish credit in their own names now have a legal right to do so. Under this law, a woman has a right to her own credit if she proves to be creditworthy.

Unless your state still requires a person to be at least 21 to enter into a contract, a creditor cannot deny you credit based on your age alone. A creditor must look into your creditworthiness. Upon request, a creditor must give any person who is denied credit a written statement of the reasons for denial.

> **checkpoint ✓**
> How does the Truth-in-Lending Act assist consumers?

CREDIT USE REGULATIONS

Several laws have been created to protect your rights when using credit.

Fair Credit Billing Act

The *Fair Credit Billing Act* requires prompt correction of billing mistakes. To get a correction of an error, you must notify the creditor in writing within 60 days after your statement was mailed. A good rule is to report errors as soon as you discover them. After you report an error, remember the following points.

- While waiting for an answer, you are not required to pay any amount in question.
- The creditor must acknowledge your complaint within 30 days unless your statement is corrected before that time.
- You do not pay finance charges on any amount in error.
- If no error is found, the creditor must bill you again. The bill may include finance charges that have accumulated plus any minimum payments that were missed while the statement was being questioned.

Goal 2

Explain credit use regulations.

Why is the Equal Credit Opportunity Act so important?

Digital Vision/Getty Images

The Fair Credit Billing Act also provides that you may withhold payment of any balance due on defective merchandise or services purchased with a credit card. Your first step should be to contact the business and try to resolve the problem. You can correct many situations if your complaint is made in a courteous but firm manner. The law protects you if you have made this "good faith" effort to work with the business.

Fair Credit Reporting Act

The *Fair Credit Reporting Act* is the law that gives consumers the right to know what information credit bureaus are giving to potential creditors, employers, and insurers. This law provides that if credit is denied based on information in a credit report, the applicant must be given the name, address, and phone number of the credit bureau that provided the information. In addition, credit records for both a husband and wife are kept if both are responsible for the debt. This allows a credit history to be developed for each spouse.

Prior to the passage of this law, many consumers were unaware that potential lenders had access to reports on their bill-paying habits. This act makes those reports available to the consumer. It provides ways in which consumers can access and correct information.

The Fair Credit Reporting Act also requires that credit bureaus must delete any information dealing with a personal bankruptcy that is more than 10 years old. The credit bureau must also delete any other adverse information if it is more than seven years old.

A Question of Ethics

©Andreas Prott/iStock

Pawnshops, Payday Loans, and Credit Repair

Consumer credit is an area where unfair and deceitful business credit practices thrive. Pawnshops lend money based on the value of property, such as jewelry. These small loans are usually repaid in a month or two, but typically at a high interest rate. Some states allow pawnshops to charge 3 percent a month—that's 36 percent a year.

People in need of a small amount of money for a short time may use a *payday loan*. Nearly 25,000 of these companies now operate in the United States. The interest rate for this cash advance can be more than 600 percent. With a payday loan, a consumer may write a personal check for $230 to borrow $200 for 14 days. The lender agrees to hold the check until the next payday. This $30 finance charge for the 14 days translates into an APR of nearly 400 percent. Often, a customer continues to borrow without paying anything back. Within a few weeks, the finance charge can exceed the amount borrowed.

"Credit Repair—Are you in trouble with past due payments? Is your credit record being ruined? We can fix all problems quickly—come in today." Every day, credit repair companies offer to help consumers with poor credit histories. They promise to improve your credit rating, for a fee. Too often, after paying hundreds of dollars, consumers get nothing. Companies disappear with your money. To protect consumers, the Credit Repair Organizations Act requires that credit repair companies cannot collect their fee until completing the promised services.

Think Critically

1. Why are people attracted to these credit situations?

2. Conduct research to obtain additional information about pawnshops, payday loans, and credit repair companies. Report your findings in a short report.

Consumer Credit Reporting Reform Act

An unfavorable credit report can force you to pay a higher interest rate on a loan or you might be denied a loan. *The Consumer Credit Reporting Reform Act* places the burden of proof for accurate credit information on the credit reporting agency rather than on you. Under this law, the creditor must certify that disputed data is accurate. If a creditor or the credit bureau verifies incorrect data, you can sue for damages. The federal government and state attorneys general can also sue creditors for civil damages.

Fair Debt Collection Practices Act

A *debt collection agency* attempts to obtain money that is past due. The agency may contact people who are overdue with credit payments.

To prevent threats and other inappropriate actions, the *Fair Debt Collection Practices Act* requires that debt collectors treat you fairly. It bans various debt collection actions. This law does not take away the debts that are owed.

A debt collector may contact you in person, by mail, telephone, telegram, or fax. A debt collector may not contact you at inconvenient times or places, such as before 8 A.M. or after 9 P.M. They also may not contact you at work if your employer prohibits such contact.

> **checkpoint ✓**
> What is the purpose of the Fair Credit Reporting Act?

CREDIT PROBLEMS AND ASSISTANCE

A person who cannot pay his or her bills when they are due might take these four steps.

WORK as a TEAM

Many people have financial problems that result from the use of credit. Describe three situations in which people have credit problems. As a team, discuss the actions that might be taken to address these situations.

1. Contact creditors and explain the situation.
2. Make a realistic proposal for when and what you can pay. Don't just say, "I can't pay."
3. Keep any promises you make.
4. Make a written copy of your agreement to avoid problems later.

You may be able to work out a *debt repayment plan.* A creditor and a debtor develop this agreement to reduce payments to a more manageable level and still pay off the debt. This is good for both the creditor and the debtor.

One thing to avoid is being misled by advertisements that tell you, "Erase bad credit! 100% guaranteed." Claims such as these are fraudulent. No one can unconditionally correct a bad credit record—it does not work that way. If you need help with a credit problem, contact a reputable credit counseling organization.

Credit Counseling

Different kinds of help are available to people with credit problems. A **credit counselor** discusses and suggests actions to take to reduce spending and eliminate credit difficulties.

Various nonprofit counseling services are available around the country. The National Foundation of Consumer Credit can direct you to a local credit assistance program. This nonprofit organization has hundreds of member agencies that operate local offices around the country. Many of the member agencies are known as Consumer Credit Counseling Service (CCCS). Consumers are warned to be

Goal 3

Discuss credit problems and available assistance.

Digital Vision/Getty Images

What can a credit counselor do for people with credit problems?

cautious of for-profit credit counseling services.

Bankruptcy

Consumers may take one additional step when facing credit problems. They should use this final option only for extreme situations. **Bankruptcy** is the legal process of reducing or eliminating an amount owed. This process is costly and requires legal assistance. Consumers can usually avoid bankruptcy by using credit wisely and practicing sensible money management.

> **checkpoint ✓**
> What actions can a person take when facing credit problems?

18-4 Assessment

Study Tools

www.cengage.com/school/genbus/pob

Key Concepts

Determine the best answer.

1. A person may be denied credit on the basis of his or her
   a. gender
   b. age
   c. income
   d. type of job

2. The federal law that provides protection when an error occurs on a monthly statement is the
   a. Truth-in-Lending Law
   b. Fair Credit Reporting Act
   c. Fair Credit Billing Act
   d. Equal Credit Opportunity Act

3. The legal process of reducing or eliminating an amount owed is
   a. credit
   b. credit reporting
   c. bankruptcy
   d. financing

Make Academic Connections

4. **Statistics** Obtain current data about the number of people who have declared personal bankruptcy in recent years. Prepare a chart to show the trend of these data. Give an explanation as to why the trend occurred. What are the costs of bankruptcy to a society?

5. **Communication** Create a role-playing situation in which you are denied credit. Have one person explain how he or she encountered credit problems. Have the other person suggest actions to eliminate the credit problems.

Leadership and Responsibility

Time Management—A Leadership Skill

Effective leaders know how to manage their time. They spend time planning how they will use their time to achieve their goals.

Plan and Use Your Time

You need a way to plan your day, your week, your month, and more. There are plenty of tools to help you, but it all starts with a calendar. It might be in your computer, in your pocket, on the wall, or on your phone.

Spend a few minutes at the beginning of the day checking your calendar to see what you will be doing that day and the rest of the week. Spend a few minutes at the end of the day looking at your calendar to ensure that you will be ready for tomorrow.

What are some advantages to using a wall calendar? What are some disadvantages?

Your calendar should reflect the time you have committed to others and yourself. It should include meetings, appointments, social engagements, and other activities. For example, if you have a part-time job, you should block out the times you work as soon as you get your schedule. If you are supposed to be somewhere doing something, it should be on your calendar.

What about your other time commitments? It is easy to record the due date for a project on your calendar, but you also need to carve out time to work on the project. Depending on your current situation, you might need to schedule time to work on projects, read assignments, study for tests, pay bills, balance your checkbook, or practice your golf swing.

Respect Other People's Time

Part of planning and monitoring your own time is learning to respect other people's time. You need to be on time for work, appointments, and meetings. When you are late you send a message that you do not value other people's time. It makes you appear self-absorbed and disrespectful.

Meetings should start and end on time. Waiting for latecomers to arrive is unfair to those who arrived on time. Allowing a meeting to drag on past the planned end time interferes with other plans and puts people in the uncomfortable position of having to decide if they should stay or leave.

Respect Your Own Time

Effective leaders learn how to balance their work with their personal life. Scheduling time for exercise, relaxation, and personal interests are good habits. It is also important to establish routines that allow you to eat well and get adequate sleep. According to the National Sleep Foundation, adults need 7 to 9 hours of sleep each night and teens require 8.5 to 9.25 hours. Adequate sleep helps you pay attention and remember new information.

Knowing when to say "no" is another component of time management. People who demonstrate leadership skills are recognized for their accomplishments and sought after for assignments and committees at work and in the community. Effective leaders learn to work to their capacity without overextending themselves. They also learn to identify the strengths of others and help develop and inspire new leaders.

Think Critically

1. How does being late distract from your ability to lead others?

2. What are some things that you can do right now to improve your time-management skills?

Business Notes

18-1 Credit Fundamentals

- Credit is the privilege of using someone else's money with the obligation to repay it at a future time. The major types of consumer credit are charge accounts, credit cards, installment credit, and consumer loans.

- Credit used wisely makes some buying more convenient, gives the purchaser immediate possession rather than waiting until later, allows buyers to take advantage of special sales, and establishes a person's credit rating.

- Credit is misused if it results in overbuying, careless buying, paying higher prices in stores that grant credit, or incurring excessive debt.

18-2 Cost of Credit

- The amount of interest expense is calculated by multiplying the interest rate times the principal times the number of days or months.

- The annual percentage rate (APR) states the percentage cost of credit on a yearly basis. Costs of credit in addition to interest include service fees, the cost of collecting bad debts, and credit insurance. The finance charge is the total dollar cost of credit including interest and all other charges.

- The cost of credit varies among lenders. You can save money by shopping around to compare the APR, amount of monthly payments, and total finance charge.

18-3 Credit Application and Documents

- A credit application is a document on which you provide information needed by a lender. A business considers a person's character (honesty and willingness to pay debts), capacity (the ability to pay debts), and capital (the value of the person's possessions) in reviewing an applicant for credit.

- A credit bureau gathers information on credit users. A credit record documents your credit history. You can maintain a good credit history by paying your bills on time.

- Two commonly used credit documents are the installment contract and the statement of account. Before signing an installment contract, consider the finance charges and other features of the loan. Credit statements should be checked carefully and errors reported as soon as they are discovered.

18-4 Protection of Credit Rights

- The Truth-in-Lending Law, the CARD Act, and the Equal Credit Opportunity Act provide information and protection when applying for credit.

- The Fair Credit Billing Act, the Fair Credit Reporting Act, the Consumer Credit Reporting Act, and the Fair Debt Collections Act protect consumers when using credit.

- Assistance with credit problems is available from counselors, debt consolidation, and, as a last option, bankruptcy.

Communicate Business Concepts

1. Edward Adiska buys everything he possibly can on credit. If he does not have enough money to cover his monthly payments when they are due, he borrows money to pay them. His sister, Debbie, likes to buy things only after she has saved enough money to pay cash for them.

   a. Whose plan do you think is better? Why?
   b. What suggestions about the use of credit might you make to Edward and Debbie?

2. Gerry Shadle owns and operates a flower shop. She is considering expanding her shop to include home decorating items. At present, Gerry sells for cash only. How might extending credit help or hurt her business?

3. Read the following statements and explain why you agree or disagree.

   a. "A credit card is nice to have. If I'm out of cash, I can still buy what I want."
   b. "I don't believe in using credit for most purchases. I pay cash for everyday items and use credit only for expensive items, such as a new refrigerator."

c. "If I can't pay cash, I can't afford it. I won't buy anything unless I can pay cash."

d. "I often don't pay the full amount of my charge account when it is due; the finance charges are quite reasonable."

4. Les Heddle needed to borrow $15,000 to do some remodeling in his store and has three options:

OPTION 1: The Thrifty Loan Company offered him an APR of 16 percent for a three-year loan. Monthly payments, including finance charges, would be $555.

OPTION 2: The Greenback Bank offered him a five-year loan at 15 percent APR with a total monthly payment of $375.

OPTION 3: The Silk Purse Finance Lending Shop did not quote an APR figure but said, "We have a 'no frills' loan policy, and you can have a four-year loan with monthly payments at the amazingly low figure of $496 per month."

Construct a loan comparison chart showing the lender, APR, loan length, monthly payment, total payment, and cost of credit. Then decide which loan would be the best for Les Heddle. Give reasons for your decision.

5. Suzanne Winters does not believe in buying anything on credit. She says too many people get into trouble with credit and many errors are made in credit transactions. Explain to Suzanne ways in which laws protect consumers who engage in credit transactions and tell her about some of the help that is available for consumers who have credit problems.

Develop Your Business Language

Match the terms listed with the definitions.

6. Your reputation for paying your bills on time.

7. Someone who becomes responsible for payment of a note if you do not pay as promised.

8. The privilege of using someone else's money for a period of time.

9. A loan in which you agree to make monthly payments in specific amounts over a period of time.

10. The legal process of reducing or eliminating an amount owed.

11. A person who suggests actions to reduce spending and eliminate credit difficulties.

12. A payment of part of the purchase price that is made as part of a credit agreement.

13. A written promise to repay based on the debtor's excellent credit rating.

14. Property that is offered as security for some loan agreements.

15. The total dollar cost of credit, including interest and all other charges.

16. The percentage cost of credit on a yearly basis.

17. A company that gathers information on credit users and sells that information in the form of credit reports to credit grantors.

18. A record of the transactions that you have completed with a business during a billing period.

19. A form in which you provide information needed by a lender to make a decision about granting credit.

20. The cost of using someone else's money.

KEY TERMS

a. annual percentage rate (APR)

b. bankruptcy

c. collateral

d. cosigner

e. credit

f. credit application

g. credit bureau

h. credit counselor

i. credit rating

j. down payment

k. finance charge

l. installment loan

m. interest

n. promissory note

o. statement of account

Make Academic Connections

21. **History** Research the use of credit throughout history. When was credit first used in various civilizations? How has credit been used to influence the development of retailing and other business activities in the United States?

22. **Culture** People in different countries have different attitudes toward credit. Based on web searches, library research, and talking with people who know about other countries, prepare a summary of how credit is used around the world.

23. **Research** Collect credit applications, advertisements, and online offers. Create a table to compare the different APRs reported in the various credit information sources.

24. **Communication** Prepare a one-minute oral summary of the activities of a credit bureau. Explain how credit bureaus serve both consumers and businesses.

25. **Math** Find the date of maturity for each of these loans:

DATE OF LOAN	TIME OF LOAN
March 15	4 months
May 26	3 months
July 31	5 months
April 30	30 days
October 5	45 days

26. **Research** Some credit contracts include the "Rule of 78." This condition results in a "prepayment penalty" if a loan is paid off early. Conduct a web search to obtain a basic understanding of the Rule of 78.

27. **Technology** Conduct a web search to locate a sample of a credit contract. What features of the contract provide consumers with clear information about the cost of credit and other terms of the loan agreement?

28. **Law** Several federal agencies, including the Federal Trade Commission and the Federal Reserve Board, administer consumer credit protection laws. Conduct research on the laws discussed in the chapter. Prepare a table with a summary of which agency to contact when your rights are violated.

29. **Math** Before borrowing $200, Laura Demetry visited a small loan company and the loan department of a bank. At the loan company, she found that she could borrow the $200 if she signed a note agreeing to repay the balance in six equal monthly installments of $36.50. At the bank, she could borrow the money by signing a promissory note for $215 and repaying the balance in six equal monthly payments.

    a. What would be the cost of the loan at the small loan company?
    b. What would be the cost of the loan at the bank?

Decision-Making Strategies

Samantha Mae has been out of school for three years and has held four different jobs with different employers. She has been on her present job for two months. Her monthly take-home pay is $1,362. She shares an apartment with two friends to keep expenses down, but she is always in debt. Each month, she is short of the money she needs to pay all of her charge accounts. Her checking account is frequently overdrawn. Samantha has decided it would be better to live by herself. She blames her roommates for her credit spending sprees. She has come to you for a loan of $2,000. Her new apartment will cost $400 a month, and she wants to pay off some of her bills that are past due. She assures you that she will pay you at least $50 each month.

30. What are some criteria you would use to determine whether a personal loan for Samantha would be a good idea? What additional information might you want?

31. Would you loan the money to Samantha? Why or why not?

Linking School and Community

Obtain information on the responsibilities involved with cosigning a loan. Talk to people in your community. What do they know about being a cosigner? What precautions should be taken when cosigning? Talk with a credit counselor to obtain information about problems associated with cosigning a loan.

Web Workout

Individuals should give considerable evaluation to choosing a credit card and not react to free offers, temporary low interest rates, or pre-approved cards. Individuals should choose a credit card offer that meets their needs. Use the Internet to identify a wide variety of card types. Evaluate different card offerings using at least three different credit card sources such as a bank, a credit card company, or other businesses that offer reward cards (airlines, hotels, etc.).

Think Critically

1. Develop a table to evaluate at least three different cards. Choose from this list a card you would like to use and justify your choice.

2. Identify cards that are directed toward students. Compare interest rates for cards directed toward students versus cards for individuals with good credit ratings. Explain why there are differences.

Impromptu Speaking Event

Leaders have the special skill to express their thoughts without prior preparation. Poise, self-confidence, and organization of facts are three valuable skills that are beneficial for articulate leaders.

Participants will draw a current event and will be given 10 minutes to organize their speech. One 4" by 6" index card will be given to the participant and may be used during the preparation and performance of the impromptu speech. Information may be written on both sides of the note card. Your speech should be four minutes in length, and no reference materials may be brought to or used during the preparation or presentation. No microphone will be used for your speech. Participants will receive a five-point deduction for any time under 3:31 or over 4:29 minutes. Some impromptu topics:

- Importance of Credit
- Minding Your Cs of Credit
- Credit Protection and Rights
- Avoiding Credit Disasters

Performance Indicators Evaluated

- Understand the three Cs of credit.
- Differentiate the pros and cons of credit.
- Define the role of credit in the market economy.
- Explain credit concepts in a clear, concise manner.

For more detailed information about performance indicators, go to the FBLA website.

Think Critically

1. List two advantages and two disadvantages of credit.

2. What are the three Cs of credit? How can individuals protect their credit rating?

3. Do you believe that consumers are addicted to credit in a negative way? Explain your answer.

www.fbla-pbl.org

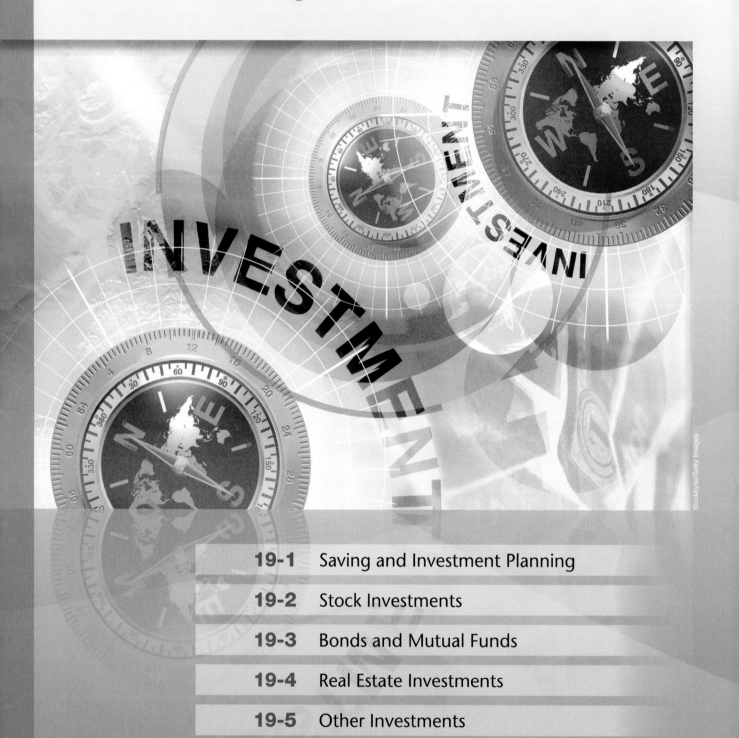

Stockbyte/Getty Images

Planning a Career in ...

INVESTMENTS

People and organizations save and invest money in many ways. Some careers in the investment industry involve working with individual investors, while others revolve around institutional investors, such as banks and pension funds.

Career opportunities exist for workers who want to work directly with clients and those who prefer to work behind the scenes. Positions are located in diverse settings such as retail outlets, call centers, and corporate headquarters. Although some positions are located in major financial centers, career opportunities exist around the country and around the world.

New and different investment products continue to be created. These investment alternatives result in employment opportunities for those interested in helping others plan their financial futures. Changing interest rates, foreign currency fluctuations, and global economic conditions influence these emerging investment vehicles.

Related Job Titles

- Brokerage Account Executive
- Brokerage Clerk
- Economist
- Financial Analyst
- Fund Manager
- Investment Banker
- Real Estate Appraiser
- Real Estate Agent
- Securities Research Analyst
- Securities and Commodities Sales Agent
- Stockbroker

Analyze Career Opportunities in ...

INVESTMENTS

Use library and Internet resources to learn more about careers in investments. Choose one of the job titles listed in the box above and answer the following questions.

1. How would you describe the nature of the work? Include examples of things that might happen in a typical work day.

2. Is this a career that interests you? Describe a few things you could do to learn more about this career.

What's it like to work as an ... Investment Broker?

"Do you think I should sell my health care stocks? Or will they be a good investment for my future? How will changing interest rates affect my investments? Will I have to pay a fee to sell my stocks? How much will it be?"

These questions are commonly asked of Roberto Jiminez, an investment broker. He has found that an understanding of economic conditions and business trends is the foundation of success in this field.

Each day, financial markets around the world process millions of transactions to buy and sell investments. Stocks, bonds, mutual funds, real estate, currencies, commodities, gold, and silver are bought and sold by investors. The people who research, sell, and record these transactions are employed by a variety of investment companies and other financial businesses.

What about you? How could economic conditions affect the demand for investment jobs? What training and knowledge would be important for success in investment careers?

19-1 Saving and Investment Planning

Goals

1 Explain the basics of saving and investing.

2 Identify types of savings and investments.

3 Discuss factors to consider when evaluating savings and investment alternatives.

Key Terms

saving 486

investing 486

yield 489

liquidity 491

Focus on REAL LIFE

"I'd sure like to buy a new phone," said Mel. "I found one that has all the features I want. But it costs about $150. I can't afford it."

"Try saving your money," Hank said in an encouraging voice. "Maybe if you cut back on some of your other spending, you could save enough money to buy it."

"That would take forever," sighed Mel.

"It's easier than you think," responded Hank. "If you put aside just a dollar a day, within six months you'd have more than $150. If you save even more each day, you could buy the phone fairly soon."

"You're kidding!" exclaimed Mel.

"Really," said Hank. "Most people don't realize that saving small amounts of money on a regular basis can result in large amounts in the future, and that doesn't even include the interest you can earn."

Goal 1

Explain the basics of saving and investing.

SAVING AND INVESTMENT BASICS

Creating a personal saving and investing strategy is vital for every financial plan. Putting money aside in a systematic way is the basis for achieving financial goals.

When savings are invested and used, the economy benefits. Individuals, businesses, and governments borrow money from financial institutions. People commonly borrow the savings of others to pay for homes, motor vehicles, and college. When this money is spent, demand for goods and services increases. This results in more jobs and creates more spending by workers.

Businesses borrow funds to operate or expand their operations. Building a new factory, replacing old equipment, or selling a new product are common reasons for business borrowing. These actions create jobs and expand economic activity.

Governments may borrow for highways, schools, or other public services. An economy would be significantly weakened without savings and investments.

Savings and Investment Activities

Saving is the storage of money for future use. How much you save, where you put your savings, and what you save for are important decisions. People save different amounts of money for different reasons and in different ways.

Some people save for years and then use those funds for a down payment to buy a home. Saving is also important to have money available for emergencies. Financial planning experts encourage people to deposit 10 percent of their income into a savings account or other investment each month.

After building up some savings, most people want to earn more. **Investing** means using your savings to earn more money. While a savings plan is a simple type of investing, many other investment choices are available.

Determine Investment Goals

Every saver and investor has one of two major financial goals: income or growth. People who want income for current living expenses desire *current income*. People select various types of savings plans and investments to provide current income.

In contrast, *long-term growth* is the other main investment goal. This goal is for those who desire financial security in the future. Investors who desire long-term growth choose investments that they hope will increase in value over time.

The Growth of Savings

In addition to putting money aside as savings, you should have those savings working for you. *Interest* is money you receive for letting others use your money.

If you save $50 a month, in a year, the savings will amount to $600. Suppose you deposit this money in a savings program that earns 6 percent simple interest, paid quarterly. You will earn $9 every three months. You will earn $36 each year. The interest may not be added to your account, but rather is paid directly to you. At the end of 10 years, you will still have $600 in the account but will have earned $360 in interest.

Compound Interest Earning interest on previously earned interest results in faster growth of savings. *Compound interest* is computed on the amount saved plus the interest previously earned. For example, simple annual interest of 10 percent on $1,000 is $100.

If the interest is compounded, then the interest computed at the end of the next year is based on $1,100 ($1,000 + $100 first-year interest). The 10 percent interest earned in the second year is $110.

Explain why people who have created life-span plans are often more successful in saving than those who have not. Include some specific examples. How might your life-span plan help you save?

Interest the third year is based on $1,210 ($1,100 + $110 second-year interest) and is $121. When interest is compounded, the amount of interest paid increases each time it is calculated. Without compounding, the interest paid would be only $100 each year.

Interest can be compounded daily, monthly, quarterly, semiannually, or annually. The more frequent the compounding, the greater the growth in your savings. Figure 19-1 shows how quickly monthly savings of different amounts increase when interest is compounded quarterly at 6 percent.

> **checkpoint** ✓
> How does saving influence economic activity?

COMPOUND INTEREST (QUARTERLY)					
MONTHLY SAVINGS	END OF FIRST YEAR	END OF SECOND YEAR	END OF THIRD YEAR	END OF FOURTH YEAR	END OF FIFTH YEAR
$ 5.00	$ 61.98	$ 127.76	$ 197.76	$ 271.68	$ 350.32
10.00	123.95	255.52	395.15	543.35	700.47
25.00	309.89	638.79	987.87	1,358.38	1,751.62
30.00	371.86	766.55	1,185.45	1,630.05	2,101.94
35.00	433.84	894.30	1,383.02	1,901.73	2,452.26
50.00	619.77	1,277.58	1,975.74	2,716.75	3,503.24

▶ **Figure 19-1**

What would be the effect if the interest was compounded monthly or weekly?

Savings Account A savings plan with a low balance is a regular savings account. Usually, you may deposit and withdraw money as needed. These accounts pay interest while keeping money safe.

Certificate of Deposit A *certificate of deposit* allows you to earn a higher interest rate than a regular savings account. This savings instrument usually requires a minimum deposit of $100 to $1,000 or more. You must leave the money on deposit for a specified period, from a few days to several years. Penalties, in addition to loss of interest, may be assessed if the money is withdrawn early.

Money Market Account A *money market account* pays a variable interest rate based on various government and corporate securities. Interest paid on money market accounts reflects the current rates of interest being paid in the money markets.

In general, money market accounts do not require long-term deposits. They may have a large minimum balance requirement. The earnings on money market accounts are usually higher than regular savings accounts but slightly less than long-term certificates of deposit.

Goal 2

Identify types of savings and investments.

SAVING AND INVESTMENT CHOICES

Many choices are available for your saving and investing dollars. The choices range from very safe savings accounts to rather risky investments.

Savings Plans

Banks, credit unions, and other financial institutions offer a choice of savings plans. Regular savings accounts, certificates of deposit, and money market accounts all provide a safe location for storage of your money.

Securities

Investments in securities include stocks, bonds, and mutual funds. Corporations and governments sell these securities to raise money.

Stock Investments When you buy a share of stock, you become part owner of a company. A stock purchase, made directly or indirectly through mutual funds, is a very common way of investing. If a stock increases in value and is then sold for more than its original cost, a *capital gain* results. When an investment is sold for less than its original cost, a *capital loss* is the result.

Bond Investments Lending money for use by businesses and governments is another common investment. *Bonds*

AntiGerasim/Shutterstock.com

What savings options are available to young people?

represent debt. When you purchase a bond, you are lending funds to a company or government agency to use for their business activities.

Mutual Funds Instead of buying individual stocks and bonds, people can buy shares in a mutual fund managed by an investment company. Money from many investors is used to invest in a variety of securities. Mutual funds allow investors to spread out their risk among many investments.

Alternative Investments

Other investment choices include real estate, commodities, and collectibles. These choices often carry greater risk than savings or securities choices. As with all investments, you should carefully review your situation and options before investing in these areas.

Real Estate People invest in real estate for numerous reasons. Many people purchase their own home for the sense of security and stability. Some purchase property for rental income. Others buy vacant property in hopes that its value will increase. Housing, farmland, apartment buildings, and shopping malls are some examples of real estate investments.

Commodities Grain, livestock, precious metals, currency, and financial instruments are all commodities. Investors purchase commodity contracts in anticipation of higher market prices for the commodity in the near future. Commodity investing is considered very risky.

Collectibles Old coins, works of art, antique furniture, and other rare items are often bought with the hopes that their value will increase.

> **checkpoint** ✓
> What are the nine main categories of saving and investment alternatives?

fyi To determine how many years it will take your savings to double, use the "Rule of 72." To use this rule, divide 72 by the interest rate on your investment. The result is the number of years it will take you to double your money. For example, if your investment is earning 6 percent interest, you divide 72 by 6. At an interest rate of 6 percent, your money will double in 12 years.

Joel Calheiros/Shutterstock.com

EVALUATING SAVINGS AND INVESTMENTS

As you decide which investments are best for you, four main factors should be considered: safety, return, liquidity, and taxes.

> **Goal 3**
> Discuss factors to consider when evaluating savings and investment alternatives.

Safety and Risk

Today, savings accounts at most financial institutions are insured up to $250,000 by the federal government. This insurance is a promise that your money will be available when you need it. *Safety* is assurance that the money you have invested will be returned to you.

Suppose you lend $100 to someone who promises to pay it back with 10 percent interest at the end of one year. If the loan is paid back, you will receive $110 ($100 + $10 interest). If the borrower has no money at the end of the year, you may get nothing back. You may lose both the $100 you loaned and the $10 interest you should have earned.

Not all investors require the same degree of safety. Someone may have enough money to make 20 different investments. If one of them loses value, the investor still has the other 19. Another person may only have a small amount of money and can make only one investment. One loss would be serious. Most people want to make investments that are relatively safe.

Potential Return

A good savings plan or investment should earn a reasonable return. The **yield** is

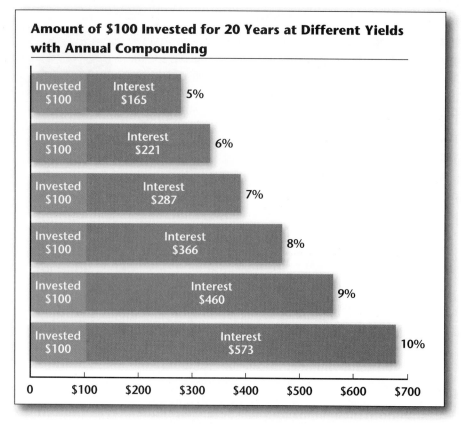

Amount of $100 Invested for 20 Years at Different Yields with Annual Compounding

Invested $100	Interest $165	5%
Invested $100	Interest $221	6%
Invested $100	Interest $287	7%
Invested $100	Interest $366	8%
Invested $100	Interest $460	9%
Invested $100	Interest $573	10%

0   $100 $200 $300 $400 $500 $600 $700

▶ **Figure 19-2**

What is the price of investing in higher-yielding securities?

the percentage of money earned on your savings or investment over a year. Other common names for yield are the *rate of return* or the *annual yield*. Figure 19-2 shows the value of an investment of $100 after 20 years at several different yields.

Usually, higher yields and greater risk of loss go together. Investments you make with the federal government are the safest. When you invest money with individuals or businesses, it usually earns higher interest than that paid by the government because there is less safety. For example, the government may pay 3 percent interest on an investment. At the same time, one business may

pay 5 percent while a business with even greater risk may have to pay 10 percent.

Most investors will not accept higher risk unless the potential yield is greater. However, a low rate of return on an investment does not guarantee safety. Similarly, high rates of interest do not mean that a loss will surely occur. Higher yields mean that investors believe the situation involves a higher risk. Figure 19-3 shows the risk level for various investments.

The Truth in Savings Act (TISA) requires that financial institutions give consumers information to compare savings accounts. The law defines the *annual percentage yield* (APY) as the percentage rate equal to the total amount of interest that a $100 deposit would earn based on a 365-day period. APY helps eliminate confusion caused by different interest calculation methods. Some

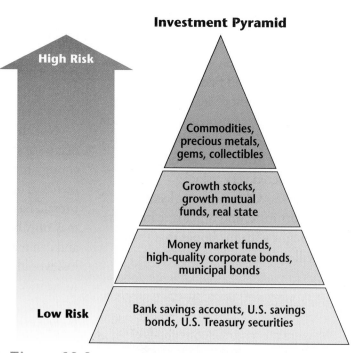

Investment Pyramid

High Risk

Low Risk

- Commodities, precious metals, gems, collectibles
- Growth stocks, growth mutual funds, real state
- Money market funds, high-quality corporate bonds, municipal bonds
- Bank savings accounts, U.S. savings bonds, U.S. Treasury securities

▶ **Figure 19-3**

Why would a person make a high-risk investment?

financial institutions previously used 360- or 366-day years to calculate interest.

Liquidity

Sometimes cash is needed quickly to pay unexpected bills. Investments that can be turned into money quickly are called *liquid*. **Liquidity** is the ease with which an investment can be changed into cash without losing its value.

Suppose you have $5,000 on deposit in a bank. If you need money right away, you usually can go to your bank and withdraw it. On the other hand, suppose you own a piece of land that you bought for $5,000. The land may be a safe investment. However, if you need money immediately, you may find it difficult to sell the land right away. You might even have to sell it for less than $5,000 if you cannot wait for a buyer who is willing to pay your price.

If you have several investments, not all of them need high liquidity. The amount of liquid investments you should have will depend on your expected need for cash in the near future.

Taxes

Earnings from most savings and investments are taxed. Taxes reduce your rate of return. For example, if you earn $100 in interest but 20 percent is taken in taxes, you have only earned $80, $100 − ($100 × 0.20). Some investments have *tax-exempt* earnings, meaning you don't have to pay taxes on that income. These investments are attractive because the tax-free yield may actually be higher than a comparable taxable investment.

> **checkpoint** ✓
> What are four factors to consider when selecting an investment?

19-1 Assessment

Key Concepts

Determine the best answer.

1. Which of the following is investing for current income?
   a. retired person who needs to pay living expenses
   b. business manager planning for retirement
   c. student putting away money for college
   d. family that wants to buy a vacation home

2. The most liquid investment listed here is
   a. rare coins
   b. real estate
   c. a savings account
   d. a house

3. A person who desires high income from an investment would be most concerned with
   a. safety
   b. return
   c. liquidity
   d. risk

Make Academic Connections

4. **Math** To determine the annual yield (rate of return) on an investment, divide the income from the investment for the year by the original amount invested. Look at the example. Then, calculate the annual yield for the other investments.

INVESTMENT	ANNUAL INCOME	AMOUNT INVESTED	ANNUAL YIELD
Example	$80	$800	10%
Savings account	$4	$200	
Bond	$85	$1,000	
Real estate	$6,400	$40,000	

5. **Economics** Prepare a list of benefits of saving and investing for (a) consumers, (b) business, and (c) government.

Goals

1 Compare the two major types of stock.

2 Describe the activities involved with buying or selling stock.

3 Identify factors that affect the value of a stock.

Key Terms

preferred stock 492

common stock 493

stockbroker 493

stock exchange 493

market value 494

Focus on REAL LIFE

Josie's older brother buys stock with part of his wages. He is planning for his retirement years. One day, Josie asked her brother about the benefits of investing in stock.

"You have the opportunity for big growth of your money over the years," he responded, "if you pick the right stocks."

"That's for me," Josie said. "I'm putting all my savings I have earned from babysitting in stock!"

"Wait a minute," warned her brother, "it's not that easy! You have to determine which companies have stocks with the most growth potential. Then you have to contact a broker or open an online account. Next you should..."

"That's enough," was Josie's response. "I'm really not interested in something that complicated."

"Don't give up," encouraged her brother. "While investing in stock may not be best for you right now, it is a topic that you should start learning about."

Goal 1

Compare the two major types of stock.

TYPES OF STOCK

When you buy shares of ownership in a corporation, you become a *stockholder*. If a business is profitable, it may pay out part of the profits in cash to the stockholders. These payments are *dividends*. The opportunity to earn a high rate of return attracts people to invest in stocks. Keep in mind that the risk of losing money on a stock investment also exists.

Before it can pay any dividends to stockholders, a corporation must pay bondholders the rate of interest promised to them. Sometimes there is not enough money left to pay dividends. If the corporation decides to put the money it earns toward business expansion, stockholders receive no dividends. If a corporation goes out of business, a stockholder may get little or nothing back from the investment.

Preferred Stock

The two main classes of stock issued by corporations are preferred stock and common stock. **Preferred stock** has priority over common stock in the payment of dividends. The dividends paid to preferred stockholders are usually limited to a set rate. Investing in preferred stock is less risky than common stock, but preferred stockholders generally have no voting rights.

Describe how a life-span plan can influence the types of investment choices a person makes. How much risk are you willing to take? How may your willingness to accept risk affect the life-span goals you set for yourself?

Common Stock

The second main class of stock is common stock. **Common stock** represents general ownership in a corporation and a right to share in its profits. Common stock has no stated dividend rate. As part owners of the corporation, common stockholders are invited to the annual meeting of the corporation. They are entitled to one vote per share of common stock owned.

Common stockholders receive dividends only after preferred stockholders are paid their dividends. Yet, if the profits of a company are large, the common stockholders may receive higher dividends than preferred stockholders. Suppose that a company has issued $100,000 worth of common stock and $100,000 worth of preferred stock with a dividend rate of 6 percent. The company earns a profit of $20,000 and pays all the profit out as dividends. Preferred stockholders would be paid $6,000 in dividends, $100,000 × 0.06. The remaining $14,000 ($20,000 – $6,000) would be available to pay dividends to the common stockholders. The common stockholders would earn a return of 14 percent.

> **checkpoint** ✓
> How does preferred stock differ from common stock?

STOCK TRANSACTIONS

Each day, people buy and sell billions of shares of stock. Buying a stock that is right for you is an important decision.

Using a Stockbroker

A licensed specialist in the buying and selling of stocks and bonds is a **stockbroker**. Through brokers, stockholders state the price at which they are willing to sell their shares. Interested buyers tell brokers what they would be willing to pay for those shares. The brokers then work out a price

NETBookmark

An extensive amount of information is available online to help investors. Access the website shown below and click on the link for Chapter 19. Select a type of investment. Obtain information from two articles related to this topic. What are the main suggestions offered regarding this type of investment?

www.cengage.com/school/genbus/pob

that is acceptable to both buyers and sellers. For their services, brokers charge a fee called a *commission*.

Two types of brokers are common. A *full-service broker* provides information about securities you may want to buy. Full-service brokers work for brokerage houses with large research staffs.

In contrast, a *discount broker* just places orders and offers limited research and other services. They charge lower commissions than full-service brokers. Investors who do their own research can save money by using a discount broker.

Online Investing

Nearly all brokers provide online services. These services allow investors to access account information as well as buy and sell securities. When investing online, you are serving as your own financial planner.

These transactions are usually less expensive and more convenient than using a financial planner or broker. There are also disadvantages to investing online. Inexperience in making investment trading decisions can result in a large financial loss. Many online investors buy or sell stocks too quickly because making trades is only a click away.

Stock Exchanges

Brokers work through a **stock exchange**, which is a business organization that accommodates the buying and selling of securities. The best-known stock exchange

> **Goal 2**
> Describe the activities involved with buying or selling stock.

is the New York Stock Exchange in New York City. The American Stock Exchange is also in New York City. Regional stock exchanges operate in Boston, Chicago, Philadelphia, and San Francisco. More than 170 stock exchanges are in operation around the world.

Usually, stocks of smaller companies are not traded on a stock exchange. The *over-the-counter* (OTC) market is a network where securities transactions occur using telephones and computers rather than on an exchange. The OTC market in the United States is the NASDAQ, which stands for the National Association of Security Dealers Automated Quotations. Today, the NASDAQ includes many large companies.

Changing Stock Values

The **market value** of a stock is the price at which a share of stock can be bought and sold in the stock market. The market value indicates the current value of a share of stock.

The prices at which stocks are being bought and sold are available through stock market listings in newspapers and online. Figure 19-4 shows a stock market price report.

The market value can change rapidly. If the business is doing well, the market value is likely to go up. If the business has a poor record, the market value usually goes down. The market value also may be affected by current economic conditions as well as national and global politics.

Another measurement of investment values is a *stock index*. These indicators of stock values are commonly reported on websites, television, radio, and in newspapers. The Dow Jones Industrial Average (DJIA) includes 30 of the largest U.S. companies. Another commonly reported stock index is the Standard & Poor's (S&P) 500, which is based on stock values of 500 major companies.

> **checkpoint ✓**
> What is the purpose of a stock exchange?

▶ Figure 19-4

What factors might affect the daily changes in the market value of a company's stock?

Stock Market Price Report

1	2	3	4	5	6	7	8	9	10	11	12
52-Week					Yld.		Vol.				Net
Hi	Lo	Stock	Sym.	Div.	%	PE	100s	Hi	Lo	Close	Chg.
64.99	40.28	Deere	DE	1.20	1.9	28	46125	60.14	59.23	60.02	−0.42
97.75	63.46	FedExCp	FDX	0.48	0.6	22	72259	83.64	82.00	83.39	+2.43
56.00	45.58	Kellogg	K	1.50	2.9	15	27920	51.51	50.67	51.34	−0.24
24.60	17.08	Mattel	MAT	0.75	3.5	13	42107	21.82	21.08	21.79	+0.55
78.55	51.43	Nike	NKE	1.08	1.5	19	37279	73.95	72.48	73.22	+0.48

1 - Highest price paid for stock during past 52 weeks
2 - Lowest price paid for stock during the past 52 weeks
3 - Abbreviated company name
4 - Symbol used to report company
5 - Current dividend per share (in dollars)
6 - Dividend yield based on current selling price
7 - Price-earnings ratio
8 - Number of shares traded, expressed in hundreds, on the trading day
9 - Highest price for a share on the trading day
10 - Lowest price for a share on the trading day
11 - Closing price for the day
12 - Change in closing price compared to previous trading day

STOCK SELECTION

Buying stocks can involve a process similar to the one shown in Figure 19-5. By viewing various economic and social trends in the United States and around the world, you will determine what types of companies would benefit from those trends. For example, as people live longer, they require increased health care. Companies involved in health care products may be a wise investment.

Stock Information Sources

When choosing stocks, you should learn about the company. Several sources are available to assist you. These include *Moody's Handbook of Common Stocks*, *Value Line*, and *Standard and Poor's Encyclopedia of Stocks*. Publications like these provide data about net worth, debt, sales revenue, profits, dividend history, and the future prospects of companies. Many websites are also available to provide valuable information on companies.

The U.S. Securities and Exchange Commission (SEC) oversees the financial markets. It requires all companies that issue publicly traded securities to

WORK as a TEAM

Discuss various business and economic trends. Prepare a list of stocks that your team believes would be good investments. Explain what factors influenced the selection of these companies.

electronically file detailed reports. You can access these reports at the SEC website.

Economic Factors

Many economic conditions affect stock prices. Awareness of these factors will help you make better choices about stock investments. You should consider the following economic factors.

- **Inflation** Higher prices can result in lower spending by consumers, reducing company profits.

- **Interest rates** As the cost of money changes, company profits can increase or decline.

- **Consumer spending** Profits of companies that sell products and services to households are directly affected by buying habits.

Goal 3

Identify factors that affect the value of a stock.

Four-Step Process for Deciding Stock Purchases

1. Observe and analyze economic and social trends.

↓

2. Determine industries that will be affected.

↓

3. Identify companies in those industries.

↓

4. Decide whether to buy, sell, or hold the stock of those companies.

▶ **Figure 19-5**

Name a company or industry that has profited from a trend in recent months.

- **Employment** As people obtain or lose jobs, the amount of money they have for spending will affect company profits.

Company Factors

If you are considering investing in a company, ask the following questions.

- Has the company been profitable over a period of years?

- Have the company's managers made good business decisions?

- Does the company have growth potential in coming years?

- Does the company have an unusually large amount of debt?

- How does the company compare with others in its industry?

Other information about a company should also be considered. The *yield* of a stock is important if your goal is to earn a good return from your investment.

Suppose a company is paying a quarterly dividend of $0.60 a share. The total dividend for the year would be $2.40. If the stock were selling for $40 a share, the current yield (return) would be calculated as

$$\frac{\text{Dividend per share}}{\text{Market price per share}} = \text{Dividend Yield}$$

$$\frac{\$2.40}{\$40} = 0.06 \text{ or } 6\%$$

The price of a stock should also be considered. Many investors look at the stock's *price-earnings (P/E) ratio*, which is the relationship between a stock's selling price and its earnings per share. The P/E ratio gives you an indication of whether the stock is priced high or low in relation to its earnings per share.

> **checkpoint ✓**
> How do various economic factors affect stock prices?

19-2 Assessment

www.cengage.com/school/genbus/pob

Key Concepts

Determine the best answer.

1. Which of these statements best describes preferred stock?
   a. vote at the annual meeting of the company
   b. first priority for receiving dividends
   c. low priority for receiving dividends
   d. no stated dividend rate

2. Higher spending for recreation in the economy would most benefit the stock prices for companies in the __?__ industry.
   a. electronics
   b. health care
   c. office equipment
   d. financial services

Make Academic Connections

3. **Math** Based on Figure 19-4, answer the following questions:
   a. What number of shares was traded for Deere on this day?
   b. What is the highest price of a share of Kellogg's stock during the past year?
   c. What was the closing price of Mattel on the previous trading day?

4. **Communication** Conduct a survey of people about what they believe are the most important factors to consider when selecting a stock. Prepare a summary data table and written analysis of your findings.

19-3 Bonds and Mutual Funds

Goals

1 List types of government bonds.

2 Describe features of corporate bonds.

3 Describe various types of mutual funds.

Key Terms

municipal bond 497

corporate bond 499

mutual fund 499

Focus on REAL LIFE

Barbara Malcolm has decided to invest in bonds. She believes that bonds provide greater security for her investment funds. However, after looking into buying bonds, the process seemed very complicated.

"I'm not sure what to do," Barbara commented to her friend. "I'd like to invest in bonds, but you have to be an expert to pick the right ones."

"Instead, how about investing in a mutual fund?" responded Barbara's friend Mandy.

"What's a mutual fund?" asked Barbara.

Mandy explained, "A mutual fund takes money from many people and buys several investments. This action allows an expert to manage your investment funds."

"That sounds like something I should consider," said Barbara. "Tell me more."

GOVERNMENT BONDS

To raise money for current operations or future expansion, most governments and corporations sell bonds. A *bond* is a certificate representing a promise to pay a definite amount of money at a stated interest rate on a specified due date. The due date is also called the *maturity date*. Bonds are similar to promissory notes issued by individual borrowers. When you buy a bond, you are lending money to the organization selling the bond. You become a *creditor* of the organization. Governments issue bonds to raise money for funding public services. The federal, state, and local governments issue a variety of bonds.

Municipal Bonds

A city may want to build a new park or new school. A state may need funds to build or repair highways and bridges. Bonds issued by local and state governments are called **municipal bonds**, or *munis*.

Why do state and local governments issue bonds?

Goal 1

List types of government bonds.

How do investors keep track of their changing investment values?

bond is held determines the amount of interest. The time it takes for a savings bond to mature will vary depending on the current interest rate being paid.

In addition to paying interest, Series EE bonds have tax advantages. Interest is exempt from state and local taxes, and you do not pay federal income tax on the earnings until the bonds are redeemed. Funds from Series EE bonds may be exempt from federal income tax if the funds are used to pay tuition and fees at a college, university, or qualified technical school. This benefit is designed to assist low- and middle-income households. People with incomes above a certain amount do not qualify.

Another type of savings bond is the *I bond*. These investments pay an interest rate that changes with inflation. I bonds are purchased at face value, a $50 bond costs $50.

Other Federal Securities

The federal government also borrows using Treasury bills and notes. The difference between these debt securities is the length of time to maturity. Treasury bills, or *T-bills*, involve short-term borrowing with maturities from 91 days to one year. Treasury notes, or *T-notes*, have maturities from 1 to 10 years.

The U.S. government also issues treasury bonds, called *T-bonds*. These involve long-term borrowing, with a maturity of up to 30 years.

> **checkpoint ✓**
> List the types of bonds issued by the federal government of the United States.

Municipal bonds often have an advantage over bonds issued by companies. Usually, interest earned on municipal bonds is exempt from federal and most state income taxes. In order to avoid taxes, people buy municipal bonds even though the interest rates usually are not as high as the rates offered on corporate bonds. In general, most municipal bonds are considered safer investments than corporate bonds.

U.S. Savings Bonds

For people with small amounts of money to invest, U.S. savings bonds are a safe investment. Series EE savings bonds come in denominations ranging from $50 to $10,000.

A Series EE bond is bought at half its face value. A $50 bond costs $25. At the end of its full term, it pays at least $50. The difference between the purchase price and the redemption value is the interest earned. The length of time the

Goal 2

Describe features of corporate bonds.

CORPORATE BONDS

Investing in the bonds of a company is quite different from investing in stock. When you invest in stock, you become an owner. When you buy a bond, you are lending money to the company. Bonds issued by corporations are **corporate bonds**.

Bond Components

Each bond has a *face value*, also called the *maturity value*. This is the amount being borrowed by the corporation issuing the bond. Corporate bonds are issued for $1,000 and $25,000, and sometimes higher amounts.

Interest is paid to the investor periodically (usually twice a year) based on the face value and the stated interest rate. On the bond's maturity date, the face value is repaid to the investor.

Bond Values

Bonds are bought and sold in the bond market. The market value of a bond varies based on changing interest rates and the credit rating of the borrowing organization.

Bond values are reported similarly to the way stocks are reported. Corporate bond prices are stated in 100s, but the bonds are sold in $1,000 denominations (10 times the listed amount). For example, a bond reported at 100 is selling at its face value—$1,000. A bond selling at 105 has a market value of $1,050.

The price investors are willing to pay for a bond depends upon the *stated interest rate*. If the bond's stated rate is lower than interest rates on similar bonds, investors will want to buy the bond for less than its face value. If the bond's stated interest rate is higher than interest rates on similar bonds, the seller of the bond will want to receive more than its face value.

> **checkpoint ✓**
> What affects the value of a bond?

MUTUAL FUNDS

Many people who are interested in investing do not have the time or knowledge needed to make wise investment decisions. A **mutual fund** is an investment fund set up and managed by a company that receives money from many investors. The mutual fund is managed by a professional who uses the investors' money to buy and sell a wide variety of stocks or bonds. The value and income of the investments made determine the value of the mutual fund shares.

Types of Mutual Funds

More than 60,000 different mutual funds are available to investors around the world. These funds have many different objectives. For instance, some emphasize investing in growth stocks, some emphasize stocks that pay high dividends, and some emphasize international stocks. The following list includes some of the main types of mutual funds.

> **Goal 3**
>
> Describe various types of mutual funds.

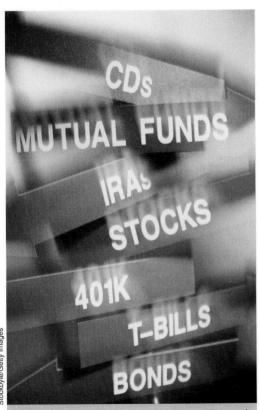

Stockbyte/Getty Images

Make a list of long-term investment options. What are the pros and cons for each type?

Review the list of types of mutual funds. Describe situations in which each type might be appropriate for a particular individual or family. Explain how this type of mutual fund could meet various investment goals.

- Aggressive-growth stock funds seek quick growth, but also have higher risk.

- Income funds specialize in stocks that pay regular dividends.

- International funds invest in stock of companies from around the world.

- Sector funds buy stocks of companies in the same industry such as health care, energy, or telecommunications.

- Bond funds specialize in corporate bonds.

- Balanced funds invest in both stock and bonds.

When selecting a mutual fund in which to invest, match your personal investment goals to the type of mutual fund.

Mutual Fund Values

Mutual fund investors own shares of the mutual fund. The value of each share is based on the total value of all investments made by the mutual fund company. For example, if the investments were worth $400,000 and 80,000 shares existed, each share would be worth $5, $400,000 \div 80,000 = \$5$. This amount is called the *net asset value (NAV)* of a mutual fund.

A part of the dividends and interest received from the fund's investments is used to pay operating expenses of the fund. The major portion of earnings is distributed to the mutual fund shareholders or reinvested in the fund.

> **checkpoint ✓**
> What are the main types of mutual funds?

19-3 Assessment

Key Concepts

Determine the best answer.

1. Municipal bonds are issued by
   a. corporations
   b. the federal government
   c. international companies
   d. state and local governments

2. The price of a mutual fund share is most affected by
   a. current tax rates
   b. the value of investments
   c. current foreign rates
   d. the value of housing

3. True or False. A bondholder is part owner of a company.

4. True or False. Interest rates in an economy affect the value of a bond.

Make Academic Connections

5. **Technology** Go to the website for U.S. savings bonds to obtain information about how to buy savings bonds online. What features are available online to calculate the current value of savings bonds?

6. **Research** With thousands of mutual funds available to investors, how could a person evaluate them? Locate library and online information that could provide assistance when deciding in which mutual funds to invest.

19-4 Real Estate Investments

Goals

1 Describe home-buying activities.

2 Explain the benefits of home ownership.

3 Discuss the costs of home ownership.

Key Terms

real estate 501

mortgage 502

equity 503

assessed value 505

Focus on REAL LIFE

Driving home from their honeymoon, Joshua Moskowitz turned to his bride Carrie. "You know, we have some money that we received as wedding gifts," said Joshua. "We should buy some stocks for our long-term financial future. I have heard of a lot of people who made fortunes with stocks."

"How much do you know about stocks? Are you sure we won't lose our money?" asked Carrie.

"Well, it's true, I don't know much about stocks," responded Joshua. "But I do know baseball cards! Let's invest our money in baseball cards."

"That's kind of risky, isn't it?" was Carrie's next question.

"OK...OK. Then let's buy gold bars. Gold can be a solid investment," replied Joshua. "You can't go wrong with gold."

"Hold on. We both want what's best for our future, but don't you think that first we'd better find a place to live?" responded Carrie.

SELECTING HOUSING

Real estate—land and anything that is attached to it—is one investment that many people eventually acquire. Getting started with real estate usually means finding a place in which to live.

Renting Your Residence

Most people start by renting an apartment. As renters, you are freed from much of the work and expense of property maintenance. Renting also makes it easier for you to move when needed. As a tenant, you must take care of the rented property, but you are not able to call the apartment your own.

Many people want to own a house and yard that they can maintain and fix up just the way they want. To realize this goal, they must save money for a down payment on a house.

What are the pros and cons of renting compared to buying your residence?

Goal 1

Describe home-buying activities.

What are the advantages and disadvantages of owning a mobile home?

Owning a Mobile Home

To become a real estate owner, some people purchase a mobile home. This financial decision provides the opportunity for home ownership. An advantage of owning a mobile home is having a place to call your own. As time passes, a person might consider other types of real estate purchases.

Buying a Home

Unless you have thousands of dollars available, you will need to borrow to buy a house. A **mortgage** is a legal document giving the lender a claim against the property if the principal, interest, or both are not paid as agreed.

Mortgages are long-term loans—for 15, 20, or 30 years—that require monthly payments. These payments are usually higher than rent. A mortgage payment includes a portion of the principal and interest charges. In addition, it often includes money to be used to pay property taxes and insurance. Money used for a down payment reduces the amount of loan needed with the mortgage.

Interest rates on mortgages may be set for the term of the loan. This type of mortgage is called a *fixed-rate mortgage*. Market interest rates generally increase or decrease during the life of a mortgage depending on economic conditions. Therefore, lenders also offer an *adjustable-rate mortgage (ARM)*. The interest rate of an ARM is raised or lowered from time to time depending upon the current interest rate being charged by lenders. Monthly payments for ARMs

Will home ownership be one of your life-span goals? Describe how different family and household situations might affect the housing choice you make. Explain how buying a home is different from other types of investments you may make.

may be lower, especially in the early years of the mortgage, compared with fixed-rate mortgages.

Services of Real Estate Agents

Buying a house is not a simple matter. Most homebuyers use a real estate agent. This person is trained and licensed to help with the buying and selling of real estate. Someone who wants to buy a house contacts a real estate agent. The agent helps the person decide what they want in a house. The agent will also arrange for the prospective buyer to view homes offered for sale.

Sellers of real estate may also use the services of a real estate agent. Someone who wants to sell a house contacts an agent. The real estate professional helps to set the selling price and promotes that the house is for sale.

Other Real Estate Professionals

Legal matters are also a part of the real estate purchase process. A lawyer, working with the real estate agent, will help you with the transaction. A lawyer assures that your property has no claims against it, such as back taxes. Having a lawyer represent you in the transaction can help to avoid legal problems.

When buying a house, an appraiser's report on the home's value is also important. An *appraiser* is someone trained to estimate the value of property and who can give an official report on the value. Factors such as the quality of construction, the location, and the price of similar houses are considered when doing the appraisal.

Buying a Condominium

In some areas, *condominiums*, or *condos*, are popular. This is an individually owned housing unit in an apartment-like complex. The maintenance and yard work are normally taken care of with a service fee paid by condo owners.

What real estate professionals will you need when purchasing real estate?

checkpoint ✓
What are four available housing alternatives?

BENEFITS OF HOME OWNERSHIP

The advantages of home ownership include tax benefits, increased equity, and pride of ownership.

Tax Benefits

Although you may pay both mortgage loan interest and property taxes on real estate you own, these costs can be to your benefit. Reduced income taxes result when the interest paid on a mortgage is included as a deductible expense. Real estate property taxes are usually also deductible when computing your federal income taxes.

Increased Equity

From an investment standpoint, the potential increase in home value is an important aspect of ownership. **Equity** is the difference between the price at which you could currently sell your house

Goal 2

Explain the benefits of home ownership.

Digital Vision/Getty Images

and the amount owed on the mortgage. Equity builds up over the years. It increases rapidly in the last few years of a mortgage.

Because of *appreciation*, a general increase in the value of property that occurs over time, homes increase in value. During the 10 years that one family had lived in their home, its market value had increased to $244,000 and their debt decreased to $165,000. Therefore, their equity was $79,000.

Many factors affect the value of a home. Most important is location. In addition, the quality of schools, maintenance of the property, and home features increase home values. Features that can add to the value of a home include an updated kitchen, remodeled bathrooms, a master bedroom suite, a finished basement, and a large garage.

Goal 3

Discuss the costs of home ownership.

Pride of Ownership

Another advantage of owning real estate is pride of ownership. Many people feel a sense of accomplishment when they buy a home. Having a home to use and decorate as desired is a strong motivation for many home buyers.

> **checkpoint ✓**
> What are the main benefits of home ownership?

COSTS OF HOME OWNERSHIP

While there are important benefits to owning your own property, various costs also exist. Home ownership has costs such as property taxes, interest payments, property insurance, and maintenance.

Business Insight for the 21st Century

Online Home-Buying

Online home-buying activities are expanding. The process starts by viewing homes online. After researching location, features, and price, the homes are visited.

Next, financing involves a Web search of current mortgage rates. When you complete your online application, the lender determines the mortgage you can afford based on income and down payment amount.

Then, the home price is negotiated by e-mail. After the price is established, the final mortgage approval is received from your online lender.

Finally, the closing occurs with documents sent by e-mail to the closing agent. The buyer electronically transfers the required money. The deed is scanned and delivered by computer image. Completed documents are forwarded to the appropriate parties, with the buyer receiving electronic versions of all files.

The Electronic Signature in Global and National Commerce Act permits this online process. This law allows an electronic signature, such as an electronic sound, symbol, or process, to be attached to a contract or other

online record. The time spent for the home-buying process is greatly reduced. The paper-based recording of documents usually takes 45 days. Online, the process can be completed in just a few hours.

Think Critically

1. What benefits and concerns are associated with buying a home online?

2. Conduct an online search to obtain additional information about online home buying. Prepare a report about your findings.

Property Taxes

Property taxes vary greatly from state to state and community to community. Generally, real estate taxes range from 2 to 4 percent of the market value of the property. Taxes are based on the **assessed value**, which is the amount that your local government determines your property to be worth for tax purposes. Assessed values normally are lower than the market value, often the assessed value is only about half.

A home with a market value of $180,000 may be assessed at $90,000. If the tax rate is $60 per $1,000 of assessed value, the annual taxes are $5,400.

$90,000 ÷ $1,000 × $60 = $5,400

The tax rate is 6 percent of the assessed value, but only 3 percent of the market value.

Interest Payments

Interest payments add to the cost of the house. A 30-year mortgage for $100,000 at 8 percent interest would result in more than $164,000 in interest paid over the life of the loan.

Property Insurance

Property insurance is an essential home ownership cost. The value of the house, the construction material, the location in respect to other buildings, and the availability of fire protection are some factors that affect the cost of homeowners insurance. Typical annual home insurance costs are less than 1 percent of the market value of the house. Property insurance provides protection from fire, theft, accident, or other losses of your home or property.

Maintenance

The cost of *upkeep*—maintaining your property in good condition—is important in home ownership. Annual upkeep costs average about 2 percent of the property's value. Postponing repairs or not taking good care of the house and yard through regular maintenance can be very costly in the long run.

WORK as a TEAM

Various factors affect the value of a home. Prepare two lists with your team: (1) situations and actions that could increase the value of a home, and (2) factors that might decrease a home's value.

> **checkpoint ✓**
> What are common costs of home ownership?

19-4 Assessment

Study Tools

www.cengage.com/school/genbus/pob

Key Concepts

Determine the best answer.

1. The person who reports on the value of a home is a(n)
   a. lawyer
   b. real estate agent
   c. appraiser
   d. mortgage broker

2. A common financial benefit of home ownership is
   a. low property insurance costs
   b. tax deduction for your down payment
   c. increased property value
   d. low maintenance costs

Make Academic Connections

3. **Finance** Find the asking price for three different homes that are currently for sale in your community. Use an online mortgage calculator to calculate the monthly payments for each home for a 30-year fixed rate mortgage with a 10 percent down payment and with a 20 percent down payment. Report your findings in a table.

4. **Math** A home worth $123,000 and a mortgage of $72,400 would have equity of $_?_. A home with an assessed value of $178,000 with a tax rate of $52 per $1,000 would have a property tax bill of $_?_.

Doing Business In... Thailand

Known as Siam until 1939, Thailand is the only nation in Southeast Asia that was never colonized. The country's name means "land of the free." Thailand is also known as the "Land of Smiles." A sense of humor, laughter, and a pleasant attitude are highly regarded.

While Thailand guarantees freedom of religion with many religions represented, 95 percent of the population is Buddhist. Traditionally, all young men are expected to become monks for at least three months to study Buddhist principles.

Monks in Thailand are highly respected. The first rows of the theater are reserved for them and for high-ranking officials. People are also expected to give up their seats on a bus or train to a monk who is standing.

Greet others in Thailand with a *wai* (pronounced *why*), in which you place the palms of your hands together at chest level, fingers extended, and bow slightly; women curtsy. A wai communicates respect.

The head is considered very sacred in Thailand. Never touch another person's head or pass an object over it. In contrast, the bottoms of the feet are least sacred. Avoid pointing your feet toward others. Stamping your feet is considered very improper. Removing your shoes is customary when entering a Buddhist temple or private home.

A business lunch may last two hours, from 1 to 3 P.M. The time is used to develop relationships with business associates. You may discuss sports such as soccer, table tennis, badminton, volleyball, and basketball, which are popular in Thailand.

Dinner may extend from 7 to 10 P.M. with an eight- or nine-course meal. Rice is served with nearly every meal. In addition, you will likely have spicy dishes consisting of meat, vegetables, fish, eggs, and fruits.

English is the second most common language after Thai. Remember that speaking loudly or showing anger in public is offensive. During negotiations, Thais will never say "no." Avoiding confrontation is a high priority.

Think Critically

1. What actions might be necessary when doing business in Thailand?

2. How might a person negotiate with business associates in Thailand?

3. Conduct library or Internet research to find additional information about business and economic activities in Thailand.

What type of businesses might be interested in doing business with women who use traditional looms to weave textiles?

19-5 Other Investments

Goals

1 Discuss types of commodity investments.

2 Explain the use of collectibles as an investment.

Key Terms

commodities 507

futures contract 507

collectibles 509

Focus on REAL LIFE

"Take a look at this one! It must be more than 100 years old," said Colin. "Now that's a great investment."

"But how do we know these coins are genuine and whether they will increase in value?" asked Paul.

"Well, we could check on the Internet or get another opinion," responded Colin.

"But that's a lot of money to invest in something with that much risk," cautioned Paul. "I'm not sure that's how I want to invest my college savings."

"Come on," urged Colin. "You have to take a risk to make big bucks."

"But I could also lose big bucks!" noted Paul.

"OK, that's enough. I guess you need to consider other types of investments that match your risk level and investment goals," Colin said.

COMMODITIES AND FUTURES

Another type of investment considered by experienced investors is commodities. **Commodities** include grain, livestock, and precious metals. Generally, commodity investing is considered to be speculative. A *speculative investment* is one with an unusually high risk.

Commodity investors buy and sell futures contracts. An agreement to buy or sell an amount of a commodity at a specified price in the future is a **futures contract**. Futures contracts also involve the buying and selling of currencies and financial instruments.

Commodity Exchanges

Commodities are bought and sold on exchanges similar to stock exchanges. Buyers and sellers are represented by traders on the exchanges.

One of the best known commodities exchanges is the Chicago Board of Trade (CBOT). Established in 1848 to provide a market for agricultural products, CBOT helps to avoid the huge price variances for these products. In 2007, the CBOT merged with the Chicago Mercantile Exchange to create the CME Group.

Other commodity exchanges around the world include the Kansas City Board of Trade, Brazilian Futures Exchange, the African Mercantile Exchange, and the London Metal Exchange.

Agricultural Commodities

Agricultural products, such as corn, soybeans, and wheat, are some of the items traded on commodity exchanges. Agricultural producers sell their crops in advance of a harvest at what they believe is a good price. Farmers will then know in advance how much they will receive for a crop.

> **Goal 1**
>
> Discuss types of commodity investments.

The futures contract buyers hope the price of the crop will go up when harvested so that they can earn a profit. Conditions that affect agricultural commodity prices include weather, international trade agreements, and worldwide demand and supply.

Gold, Silver, and Precious Metals

Precious metals have worldwide importance. Investors have traded gold and silver on commodity markets for centuries. Gold has the longest history as a monetary commodity, going back to gold coins that were circulated as early as 500 BC. Gold is highly prized for both ornamental and industrial reasons. More recently, other metals, such as copper and platinum, have also become valuable commodities.

Prices of these metals are affected by economic conditions as well as supply and demand. Since 1979, the price of an ounce of gold has ranged from more than $1,000 to less than $300. These changing values usually provide investors with protection against inflation.

Precious metals are quoted as *spot prices* per one troy ounce. This is the current price quoted for precious metals in the world markets. You can find the spot price for gold in London and New York in newspapers and online.

Money invested in precious metals does not earn interest. If you hold gold, silver, or platinum, you might profit by selling them later at a price higher than what you paid. Gold and other precious metals have another advantage—many view them as protection against currency becoming worthless. Gold could be used for buying goods and services when paper money might not be accepted.

Currency and Financial Instruments

Currencies, such as the U.S. dollar, euro, and Japanese yen, and financial instruments, such as Treasury bills and notes, are traded on the futures markets. The price of currency and financial instruments is affected by a country's economic outlook and current interest rates. Again, investors buy currency or financial instruments expecting the prices to increase in the future so that they can sell them to others at a profit.

> **checkpoint** ✓
> What types of commodities are commonly used with futures contracts?

Photodisc/Getty Images

Can you think of some collectibles that may be worth more now than when they were acquired? Provide some examples.

COLLECTIBLES

Another form of investment that is popular with many people is collectibles. **Collectibles** are items of personal interest to collectors that can increase in value in the future.

An advantage of collectibles is the personal pleasure of buying, collecting, storing, arranging, and displaying what is collected. Often, collectors even form organizations. For example, stamp clubs around the country bring together stamp collectors who buy, sell, trade, display, and discuss their stamps. Baseball card trading takes place at scheduled events in huge arenas as well as over kitchen tables. Antique dealers and collectors gather for major events at which they buy and sell their items.

Types of Collectibles

A wide variety of collectible items may serve as investments. Commonly obtained items are stamps, coins, sport trading cards, and antiques. In addition, unusual items purchased as an investment include autographs and letters of famous people, Chinese ceramics, movie posters, glassware, rare books, and toys.

WORK as a TEAM

On paper, create three columns. In the first column, list various collectibles that might be used as an investment. In the second column, describe people who might buy these items as investments. Finally, in the third column, describe factors that could affect the value of the collectibles.

Goal 2

Explain the use of collectibles as an investment.

Collectible Values

The possibility of the average buyer of collectibles making a large profit is uncertain. Only rare stamps, coins, art, and antiques—which may cost hundreds or thousands of dollars—tend to be items on which the investor can make a considerable profit. The wise investor in collectibles studies the market, knows the product well, and analyzes the potential risk.

> **checkpoint ✓**
> What are common types of collectibles?

19-5 Assessment

Study Tools

www.cengage.com/school/genbus/pob

Key Concepts

Determine the best answer.

1. The spot price for gold or silver refers to the
   a. interest for borrowing to buy the precious metal.
   b. current market price of the precious metal.
   c. future market price of the precious metal.
   d. global price for the metal set by the World Bank.

2. The value of collectibles is most influenced by
   a. the current tax rate on investments.
   b. government regulations of the market.
   c. the futures market for commodities.
   d. interested buyers and potential sellers.

Make Academic Connections

3. **Research** Go to the website of a commodity exchange. Prepare a summary of the commodities and financial instruments traded on this exchange.

4. **Art** Identify paintings and other works of art that would be considered valuable investments.

5. **Read** Find a news article about the cost of agricultural commodities. Read the article and illustrate the effect of changing farm prices on consumers. Include a properly formatted citation for your source. Possible sources include printed and online versions of newspapers and magazines. You should also consider online sources that produce original content.

Business Notes

19-1 Saving and Investment Planning

- Savings plans help buy needed goods and services as well as prepare for future expenses and emergencies. Savings help the economy by making funds available to individuals, businesses, and governments for borrowing. The main investment goals are current income and long-term growth.

- The major categories of savings and investments are savings accounts, certificates of deposit, money market accounts, stocks, bonds, mutual funds, real estate, commodities, and collectibles.

- When evaluating savings and investments, consider safety, yield, liquidity, and taxes.

19-2 Stock Investments

- Stock is equity and represents ownership. Preferred stock has priority over common stock in the payment of dividends. Preferred stockholders receive dividends paid at a set rate. Common stock represents general ownership in a corporation and a right to share in its profits. Common stockholders vote to elect the officers of the corporation.

- Stockbrokers work through stock exchanges to buy and sell shares of stock for investors.

- When selecting stock investments, consider a company's profitability, debt, growth potential, yield, and price-earnings ratio (P/E). Also consider economic factors such as inflation, interest rates, consumer spending, and employment.

19-3 Bonds and Mutual Funds

- A bond represents a debt owed by an organization. Government and companies sell bonds to raise funds to finance current operations or future expansion. Local and state governments sell municipal bonds. The federal government sells savings bonds, Treasury bills, and Treasury notes.

- Companies issue corporate bonds to raise funds. Investors are paid interest for lending money to the company.

- Mutual funds allow people to combine their funds to buy a variety of securities, which reduces risk and increases potential returns. Types of mutual funds include aggressive-growth stock funds, income funds, international funds, sector funds, bond funds, and balanced funds.

19-4 Real Estate Investments

- A person can get started in real estate by renting a place to live or buying a mobile home. When buying a home, you may need to obtain a mortgage and use the services of a real estate agent and lawyer.

- The advantages of home ownership are tax benefits, increased equity, and pride of ownership.

- The major costs associated with owning a house include property taxes, interest payments, property insurance, and maintenance.

19-5 Other Investments

- Commodities commonly used as investments include corn, soybeans, wheat, gold, silver, copper, platinum, foreign currencies, and Treasury debt instruments.

- Collectibles can combine a hobby with an investment that may increase in value.

Communicate Business Concepts

1. What actions could employers and government take to encourage saving in society?

2. How does inflation increase the risk of an investment?

3. Ella Chapman, a wealthy businessperson, invests $5,000 in a newly organized company. Frank Brokaw earns an average moderate salary and has $5,000 in a savings account. Because Ella has a reputation for being a good investor, Frank decides

to also invest in that company. Does the fact that the investment may be a good one for Ella mean that it is also a good investment for Frank? Explain your answer.

4. What are some reasons people buy stocks even though they are not as safe as other types of investments?

5. Why do municipal bonds usually pay a lower rate of interest than corporate bonds?

6. Susan Haugen bought $5,000 of gold mining stocks a few years ago. Last week, she received a letter saying that the company went out of business. It could not operate profitably, so it closed down. How much of her investment might Susan lose?

7. People who buy and sell land and houses commonly say that the three most important factors to consider when buying real estate are "location, location, and location!" Why do you think this is their belief?

8. Blair Vazquez owns a house that has a value of $180,000. For the past three years, the upkeep has averaged less than $800 a year. Can Blair assume that his expenses will be only $800 in future years?

Develop Your Business Language

Match the terms listed with the definitions.

9. The amount that your local government determines your property to be worth for tax purposes.

10. Licensed specialist in the buying and selling of stocks and bonds.

11. Land and anything that is attached to it.

12. Represents general ownership in a corporation and a right to share in its profits.

13. Investments set up and managed by companies that receive money from many investors.

14. A legal document giving the lender a claim against real estate property.

15. Items of personal interest to collectors that can increase in value in the future.

16. Using your savings to earn more money.

17. The percentage of money earned on your savings or investment over a year, also called the rate of return.

18. Bonds issued by local and state governments.

19. Storage of money for future use.

20. The difference between the price at which you could currently sell your house and the amount owed on the mortgage.

21. Business organizations that accommodate the buying and selling of securities.

22. Bonds issued by corporations.

23. Agreements to buy or sell an amount of a commodity at a specified price in the future.

24. The price at which a share of stock can be bought and sold in the stock market.

25. Grain, livestock, and precious metals.

26. Stock that has first priority in the payment of dividends.

27. The ease with which an investment can be changed into cash without losing its value.

KEY TERMS

a. assessed value
b. collectibles
c. commodities
d. common stock
e. corporate bond
f. equity
g. futures contract
h. investing
i. liquidity
j. market value
k. mortgage
l. municipal bond
m. mutual fund
n. preferred stock
o. real estate
p. saving
q. stock exchange
r. stockbroker
s. yield

Make Academic Connections

28. Law The Truth in Savings Act was created to provide consumers with clear, accurate information on the earnings of savings accounts. Conduct an online search to obtain additional information about this law.

29. Math Small amounts add up to large sums in a short time. How much will each person below save in one year (365 days) if he or she saves the following amounts without interest being added?

    a. Charles Jason: 20 cents a day
    b. Carla Spivak: 95 cents a week
    c. Alice Farney: $10 every two weeks
    d. Nolan Robinson: $20 a month

30. Technology Buying investments online can be convenient and reduce commission costs. Locate a website that allows you to buy and sell stock and other investments online. What services are provided by this e-broker? What costs are involved?

31. Math The price-earnings (P/E) ratio is calculated by dividing the price per share by the earnings per share. If a company has 100,000 shares of stock and earns a net profit of $150,000, (a) what is the earnings per share? (b) If the company's stock is selling for $30 per share, what is the P/E?

32. Geography Research the location of stock exchanges around the world. Identify one in Europe, one in Asia, one in Africa, and one in Latin America. Prepare a map showing the locations of these stock exchanges.

33. Economics Select a company and research its stock price for one day a week for the past eight weeks. Prepare a table showing the changing market value of the stock. Describe situations that may have affected the market value of this stock.

34. Communications Talk to a person who is a member of an investment club. What is the purpose of an investment club? How do these groups help investors earn money while learning about stocks and bonds?

35. Economics Locate current bond prices in the newspaper or online. Select a bond for a company. Identify the following: (a) company name, (b) stated rate of the bond, (c) bond maturity date, (d) current yield, and (e) current market value of the bond. What economic and company trends are likely affecting the current market value of the bond?

36. Research Junk bonds are investments with high risk but also potential for a high return. Conduct library or online research to obtain information about these risky bonds.

37. Business Commodity trading is governed by the Commodity Futures Trading Commission (CFTC) and the National Futures Association (NFA). Conduct library and online research to obtain additional information on these agencies.

Decision-Making Strategies

Jennie Wolfe has inherited $18,000. She graduated from high school three years ago, has an accounting job, is renting a small apartment, and saves regularly.

Jennie understands the need to evaluate stock and bond investments based on safety, liquidity, and rate of return. In addition, she realizes that the investments she selects must be guided by her personal financial needs and goals. Jennie also believes that she will not need any large amounts of cash for the next several years.

38. Jennie wants to invest in stocks that will be very safe, highly liquid, and earn a fair return. Is there anything wrong with this investment goal?

39. What advice would you give Jennie to help her study the companies from which she is considering buying bonds and stocks?

Linking School and Community

Talk to people in your community about their investments. What types of investments do they own? (Do not ask the value of the investments.) How did they decide to obtain these investments? What types of investments do they recommend for people of various ages? Prepare a one-paragraph summary of your findings.

©sweetym/iStock

Web Workout

Investment advice is available from many sources. An investment blog can help you research investments and plan for the future. These web logs provide comments and other information based on experiences of various investors.

It is important to evaluate any information posted on a blog. You should be concerned about the accuracy of postings. It is also important to view postings in light of your specific situation.

Think Critically

1. Locate a blog that discusses investments. Describe several typical postings.

2. What actions might be taken to make sure the information presented on this blog is valid?

3. Write a comment you might post on this blog.

Presentation Management–Team Event

This event will assess your use of current desktop technologies and software to prepare and deliver an effective multimedia presentation.

You will design a computer-generated multimedia presentation. You have 15 minutes for preparation and setup. The presentation will last a minimum of seven minutes and a maximum of 10 minutes. Up to five minutes will be allowed for questions from the judges. Contestants must make effective use of current multimedia technology in the presentation. In preparation for the presentation, contestants should use space, color, and text as design factors. Charts and other graphics should be used in the presentation. Contestants are responsible for securing a release form from any individual whose name, photograph, and other information is included in the presentation.

The topic for this team event is introduction to investing. The presentation should help audience members understand investment options based on the amount of money available to invest, risk factors, and rate of return. Your presentation must cover stocks, bonds, real estate, futures, commodities, and collectibles. You must discuss the safety, liquidity, and possible rate of return for each investment.

Performance Indicators Evaluated

● Demonstrate knowledge of multimedia software and components.

● Demonstrate effective oral communication skills.

● Apply technical skills to create a multimedia presentation that enhances the oral presentation.

You will be evaluated for your

● Knowledge of the topic

● Organized presentation of the topic

● Confidence, quality of voice, and eye contact

For more detailed information about performance indicators, go to the BPA website.

Think Critically

1. What does liquidity of an investment mean?
2. Which investments involve greater risk?
3. What is the advantage of investing in real estate?
4. Why are futures markets and collectibles classified as riskier investments?

www.bpa.org

Planning a Career in ...

INSURANCE

More than two million people work in the insurance industry. The main focus of their work is to determine and satisfy the insurance needs of consumers and business organizations.

Insurance employment opportunities involve diverse positions including sales, management, and technical work, such as underwriting. Your work setting can range from a large office in a major city to a one-person sales agency in a rural area.

Related Job Titles

- Insurance Sales Agent
- Actuary
- Insurance Broker
- Insurance Underwriter
- Claims Examiner
- Auto Damage Appraiser
- Insurance Policy Processing Clerk
- Customer Service Representative
- Insurance Fraud Investigator

Varied types of personal and business insurance creates a need for varied training to work in this industry. Assessing and managing risk requires a diverse knowledge of geographic, economic, political, and social situations.

Working in the insurance business will often require specialized training and continuing professional education. These upgraded skills, obtained through courses offered by insurance organizations, provide workers with an ability to identify and plan for the changing insurance needs of households and companies.

Analyze Career Opportunities in ...

INSURANCE

Use library and Internet resources to learn more about careers in insurance. Choose one of the job titles listed in the box above and answer the following questions.

1. How would you describe the physical work environment for jobs in this field?

2. Is this a career that interests you? Explain how careers in this field match up with your goals and interests.

What's it like to work as an ... Insurance Agent?

"Now that we have your life, car, and home insured, how about considering a portfolio of mutual funds for your retirement plan?" asked Valerie Esposito.

"Wait a minute, I thought you were an insurance agent, not an investment broker," responded Jane Conley.

"Well, we now do a lot more than just sell insurance," responded Valerie. "My company offers all types of insurance for businesses and individuals. In addition, we can help you with various financial services and investment products. We also make car loans and mortgages, and we issue credit cards."

"That's nice to know," commented Jane. "I'll be able to get assistance from you about my insurance needs, but I will also be able to borrow and invest through your company. How convenient!"

What about you? What aspects of the insurance business might interest you for a future career?

Goals

1 Discuss motor vehicle risks.

2 Explain auto insurance coverage.

3 Identify factors that affect auto insurance costs.

Key Terms

bodily injury liability 517

medical payments coverage 518

uninsured motorist coverage 518

property damage liability 518

collision coverage 518

deductible 518

comprehensive coverage 519

Focus on REAL LIFE

"Chris! What a great-looking car! How did you ever afford it?"

"It's not easy, Roberto, to afford a car and still be in school. Not only do I have to make car payments, but I also have to pay for insurance. It's been quite a shock! I did save enough money from a part-time job last summer to buy the car, but I didn't plan on how much insurance would cost. I'm looking for a job right now so I can afford to keep the car."

Purchasing car insurance can be expensive, but not everyone has to pay high premiums. Drivers who insurance companies view as low risks pay significantly less than those in the high-risk category.

Goal 1

Discuss motor vehicle risks.

MOTOR VEHICLE RISKS

Owning a vehicle puts you in a position of high economic risk. You might have an accident and injure yourself or other people. You might damage your vehicle or others' property. Your vehicle might be vandalized or stolen. Someone could sue you because of an accident.

Treating injured people and repairing damaged property resulting from an automobile accident can take all of the assets of a person who does not have insurance. The amount of money paid to injured people and to owners of damaged property has increased dramatically in recent years. Vehicle insurance provides protection from the financial risks involved with owning and driving a car.

Sometimes you cannot avoid an accident. No one may be directly blamed for it. However, in most cases someone is at fault. The person who is legally at fault is liable for damages and financial losses that result from the accident. Although you may

think you are faultless, you can be sued. If you are insured, your insurance company will provide legal defense for the suit. If the court decides that you are legally liable for injuries or damage to property, your insurance company will pay up to the limits stated in your insurance policy.

Individual states regulate laws related to vehicle insurance. Most of these laws benefit responsible drivers. Owners of vehicles

In what ways can automobile insurance protect you?

should know about financial responsibility laws and compulsory insurance laws.

Financial Responsibility

All states have some type of *financial responsibility law*. These laws protect the public from financial loss caused by drivers. If you cause an accident and cannot pay for damages or injuries through insurance, the legal system may take other action. Your savings or property may be taken. Your driver's license will also likely be suspended or taken away. Financial responsibility laws make you legally responsible for any injuries you cause to people. You are also responsible for damage to the property of others.

Compulsory Insurance

Most states require drivers to carry certain types of automobile insurance before they can get a license for their car. In these states, it is compulsory that an automobile owner have insurance for personal injury and property damage. Compulsory insurance laws may not allow a driver to register a car or get a driver's license without proof of the required insurance coverage.

> **checkpoint ✓**
> What are financial responsibility laws?

AUTOMOBILE INSURANCE COVERAGE

Goal 2

Explain auto insurance coverage.

Insurance companies offer several types of auto insurance protection. The two main categories are personal injury coverage and property damage coverage. Figure 20-1 summarizes the types of automobile insurance coverage.

Personal Injury Coverage

Personal injury coverage includes bodily injury liability, medical payments, and uninsured motorist protection. These three types of coverage are the main source of money paid in claims by automobile insurance companies.

Bodily Injury Liability Protection

Insurance that protects a driver from claims resulting from injuries or deaths for which the insured is at fault is **bodily injury liability** coverage. This type of insurance covers people in other cars, passengers riding with the insured, and pedestrians. The insured and, in most cases, the insured's immediate family are not covered.

Dollar amounts of bodily injury coverage are generally expressed as two numbers, such as 100/300. The first number refers to the limit in thousands of dollars that the insurance company will pay for injuries to any one person in an accident.

Automobile Insurance Coverage

TYPES OF COVERAGE	COVERAGE ON	
PERSONAL INJURY COVERAGE	**POLICYHOLDER**	**OTHERS**
Bodily injury liability	No	Yes
Medical payments	Yes	Yes
Uninsured/Underinsured motorist protection	Yes	Yes
PROPERTY DAMAGE COVERAGE	**POLICYHOLDER'S AUTOMOBILE**	**PROPERTY OF OTHERS**
Property damage liability	No	Yes
Collision insurance	Yes	No
Comprehensive physical damage	Yes	No

▶ **Figure 20-1**

Which types of auto insurance coverage do you think might be the most important? Why?

For example, with 100/300 bodily injury liability coverage, the insurance company would pay up to $100,000 for injuries to one person.

The second number, 300, is the maximum amount that the company would pay for injuries to multiple people because of the accident. If more than three people were injured, each person may not receive the full $100,000. The insurance company is only liable for $300,000 in this case. You may obtain larger amounts of bodily injury protection for a slight increase in your premium.

Medical Payments Protection

Policyholders and family members are covered if they are injured while riding in their car or another car through **medical payments coverage**. This protection may also cover them if they are walking and are hit by a car. In addition, the policy protects guests in the insured car.

Medical payments insurance covers the costs of medical, dental, ambulance, hospital, nursing, and funeral services. Payment, up to the limit stated in the policy, is made no matter who is at fault. Car owners usually purchase medical payments insurance along with bodily injury liability coverage.

Uninsured Motorist Protection

In some cases, injuries are caused by hit and-run drivers or by drivers without insurance or money to pay claims. To protect against these drivers, insurance companies offer **uninsured motorist coverage**.

This coverage is available only to those people who carry bodily injury liability insurance. Uninsured motorist protection covers the policyholder and family members. It also covers guests in the policyholder's car. Uninsured motorist protection covers the insured person only if the uninsured motorist is at fault. This is different from medical payments coverage, which pays regardless of who is at fault.

Insurance companies also offer *under-insured motorist* coverage. This insures you for losses caused by another driver whose coverage is insufficient.

Property Damage Coverage

Three types of automobile insurance protect you from economic loss as a result of property damage. The three types of coverage are property damage liability, collision, and comprehensive damage.

Property Damage Liability Insurance that protects a driver against claims if the insured's car damages someone else's property and the insured is at fault is **property damage liability** coverage. The damaged property is often another car, but it may also be property such as telephone poles, fire hydrants, or buildings. Property damage liability insurance does not cover damage to the insured's car.

Collision Insurance Insurance that protects a car owner against financial loss resulting from a collision or rollover is **collision coverage**. This insurance does not cover injuries to people or damage to the property of others.

Collision coverage is usually written with a **deductible** clause. You must pay this amount before the insurance company pays a claim. For example, suppose your car suffers $2,500 damage in an accident and your deductible amount is $500. You would pay $500 and the insurance company would pay a $2,000 claim ($2,500 damages – $500 deductible = $2,000). Deductible amounts are often $200, $500, or more. Deductibles reduce the premium cost.

Why might insurance rates be higher on certain kinds of vehicles?

Collision coverage does not provide for payment of damages greater than the car's value. Suppose the insured's car incurs $6,500 in damages in a collision with another vehicle. If the car has a value of only $6,100, the collision coverage would pay only $6,100, not $6,500.

Collision coverage may not be worthwhile on a car that is of little value. In some situations, the cost of repairing the car may be more than the car is worth.

Comprehensive Coverage Your car can be damaged or destroyed in other ways. Common causes of loss include theft or damage from fire, tornado, flood, vandalism, or falling objects. **Comprehensive coverage** protects the insured against almost all damage losses except those caused from a collision or rollover.

If the insured's car is stolen or destroyed, the amount paid by insurance is not necessarily equal to the amount paid for the car. Rather, it is equal to the car's estimated value at the time of the loss. Suppose the insured's car cost $15,000.

It is stolen soon after it is purchased. The insurance company will probably pay almost as much as the car cost—perhaps $14,500. If the car is stolen two years after it is purchased, the insurance company may pay only $10,500. The car has grown older and has a decreased value.

No-Fault Insurance Laws

In an effort to reduce insurance costs and speed up claim settlements, *no-fault insurance* has been adopted by some states. Under this program, people injured in an automobile accident collect for their financial losses from their own insurance companies no matter who is at fault. These losses include their medical bills, loss of wages, and other related expenses.

> **checkpoint** ✓
> What are the two main categories of automobile insurance coverage?

AUTOMOBILE INSURANCE COSTS

Automobile insurance is expensive. You should spend this money wisely and carefully. It is important to understand how to get the most protection for your insurance dollar.

Insurance Rates

Insurance companies use several factors to determine automobile insurance costs. Examples of these factors include:

- Your age and other characteristics such as accident record, marital status, academic standing, and credit rating

- Purpose for which you use your car

- Number of miles you drive each year

- Value and type of your car

- Community in which you live

- Amount of coverage and deductibles

Because some drivers are more likely to have accidents than others, they pay higher premiums. To determine premium rates, drivers are classified according to age, marital status, driving record, and scholastic achievement.

The lowest rates are reserved for the best risks—those least likely to have an accident. When a driver in the family is under age 25, the cost of insurance is usually higher than if all drivers are over age 25.

The purpose for which a car is driven and the number of miles it is driven in a year also affect insurance rates. Cars used for business purposes are generally driven more miles in a year than are cars driven for pleasure. This increases the chances of an accident.

The value of your car has an important effect on the cost of insurance. Premiums for collision coverage and comprehensive physical damage coverage are higher for a car worth $18,000 than for a car worth only $11,000. The insurance company

What are some actions you can take to increase your driving safety?

runs the risk of paying out much more to the insured if the $18,000 car is destroyed or stolen. The type of car also affects the rate. Drivers of a luxury car or a sports car will pay higher rates.

Rates for automobile insurance vary from state to state. They vary from city to city within a state. The population in a particular area and the number of accidents that occur in the area also affect insurance rates. Insurance companies gather statistics on the amount of claims paid for in an area. They base their rates on this information.

The cost of your automobile insurance will vary according to the coverage you have and the deductibles you choose. The more coverage you carry, the higher the cost.

Reducing Auto Insurance Costs

By planning your automobile insurance purchase carefully, you can save money. For example, insurance companies often decrease the extra amount charged for young drivers if they complete a driver education course. Companies in most states also offer young people a good student discount.

Selecting a Company

Automobile insurance premiums also vary from company to company. Be sure to compare rates. Companies may offer lower rates if the family insures more than one car or if the insured buys other types of insurance from the same company. Also, paying premiums on a monthly basis is usually more expensive than paying a premium for six months or one year.

WORK *as a* **TEAM**

Automobile insurance can be very expensive, but it is necessary. As a team, prepare a list of actions that a person can take to lower automobile insurance costs. Suggest promotional activities that insurance companies might take to inform drivers of ways to lower their rates.

Assigned-Risk Plans

Usually as a result of a poor driving record, some drivers are unable to buy automobile insurance in the normal fashion. Because of this, every state has an *assigned-risk plan*. Every automobile insurance company in the state is assigned a certain number of high-risk drivers, based on the amount of insurance each company sells. Each company has to insure a fair proportion of high-risk drivers. Drivers in high-risk categories pay much higher premiums.

Insurance for Other Vehicles

Insurance on motorcycles, recreational vehicles, and snowmobiles is similar to automobile insurance. Bodily injury liability, property damage liability, collision, and comprehensive physical damage insurance are the most important types of coverage. The engine size and value of the vehicle are the key factors in determining the cost. Generally, the larger and more expensive the vehicle, the higher the insurance cost.

> **checkpoint ✓**
> What factors affect the cost of automobile insurance?

20-1 Assessment

Study Tools

www.cengage.com/school/genbus/pob

Key Concepts

Determine the best answer.

1. Health care costs for a person you hit while driving would be covered by
   a. collision
   b. medical payments
   c. bodily injury liability
   d. uninsured motorist

2. While driving, you damage a fence. The repair costs would be covered by
   a. collision
   b. property damage liability
   c. comprehensive
   d. no-fault insurance

Make Academic Connections

3. **Math** Joan Nordland is a college student who took a driver education course in high school. She has a B + average in her college work. She qualifies for a driver education discount of 20 percent and a good student discount of 15 percent off the premium for her automobile insurance. If the standard premium for her policy is $850 per year, how much will Joan save?

4. **Communication** Research automobile accident rates for various age groups. Create a graph to communicate the data.

Goals

1 Describe property insurance coverage.

2 Explain property insurance policies.

3 Identify factors that affect property insurance costs.

Key Terms

personal liability coverage 523

homeowners policy 523

depreciation 525

Focus on REAL LIFE

"I love our new apartment! We have spent a lot of money getting it ready to move into when school starts, but now I'm broke! Are you sure we really need renters insurance?"

"Trust me, Susan, with three college girls sharing an apartment, we need insurance. If our belongings were stolen or destroyed in a fire, we would be out a lot of money. I couldn't afford to replace all my personal items if they were stolen or destroyed. And with three of us sharing the insurance expense, it really won't cost us that much money."

"I guess you're right, Ashley. I know I couldn't replace all my personal belongings either. Go ahead and call your mom's insurance agent and find out what we need to do to get the process started."

Goal 1

Describe property insurance coverage.

PROPERTY INSURANCE COVERAGE

Insurance that protects you from the financial loss you would incur if some of your property were lost or destroyed due to fire, theft, vandalism, flood, or other hazard is *property insurance*. Property owners also are at risk of being sued by other people who are injured on their property. Because the risks of loss in such situations are high, everyone should carry property insurance.

Home and property insurance protect you against three kinds of economic loss.

1. Damage to your home or property

2. Expenses you must pay to live somewhere else if your home is damaged and must be repaired or rebuilt

3. Liability losses related to your property

Damage to Home or Property

You should insure your home and other expensive property for damage from fire, vandalism, unavoidable accidents, and natural disasters such as lightning, wind, and hail. If your property is damaged and you are insured, the insurance company will pay all or a portion of the cost of repair or replacement.

What kinds of weather might cause property damage in your area?

Additional Living Expenses

If a fire or other disaster strikes your home, one of the first shocks you will experience is that you do not have a place to live. You may have to move into a hotel, motel, or furnished apartment while your home is being repaired.

Property insurance often includes coverage for *additional living expenses*. This insurance feature helps to pay for the living costs you would incur if something happened to your home.

Liability Losses

The third kind of loss, liability loss, is protected by personal liability insurance. **Personal liability coverage** covers claims from injuries to people or damage to property caused by you, your family, or even your pets. Suppose a neighbor slips on your icy sidewalk and it is proven you are at fault. Personal liability coverage will pay for any medical and legal costs up to a stated limit. What if a child damages a car in an adjacent driveway with a tricycle? Claims will be paid through the policy of the child's family. Specifically, the provisions that cover liability for physical damage to the property of others will be used to determine the claim amount.

These kinds of events may seem remote and rather petty. Yet court awards to those who suffer the damage or injury often are neither remote nor petty. In fact, these awards (and therefore premiums) are increasing so quickly that the insurance industry often refers to it as the insurance liability crisis. Awards to injured people for millions of dollars are not uncommon. Everyone should have some form of liability protection from economic loss.

> **checkpoint** ✓
> What are the three main types of property insurance coverage?

PROPERTY INSURANCE POLICIES

> **Goal 2**
>
> Explain property insurance policies.

When purchasing property insurance, you must first decide what you should insure. You must also decide the perils from which you should insure your property. *Perils* are the causes of loss such as fire, wind, or theft.

Property permanently attached to land, such as a house or garage, is *real property*. Property not attached to the land, such as furniture or clothing, is known as *personal property*. You may insure real and personal property with a homeowners policy.

Homeowners Policies

The most common form of home and property insurance policy sold today is a **homeowners policy**. This coverage provides a very convenient package-type insurance policy designed to insure homes and property. Homeowners policies come in several forms.

DanCardiff/iStockphoto.com

What different kinds of perils should a home be insured against?

Home and Property Insurance

Common Perils Related to Home Ownership

- Fire, lightning
- Windstorm, hail
- Explosion
- Riot or civil commotion
- Aircraft
- Vehicles
- Discharge of water
- Freezing
- Smoke
- Vandalism or malicious mischief
- Theft
- Glass breakage
- Volcanic eruption
- Falling objects
- Tearing apart of heating system or appliance
- Weight of ice, snow, or sleet
- Accidental damage from steam or electrical current

Homeowners Insurance Policies

Several types of home insurance policies are available. Each covers the perils listed above, as well as other items noted for each policy type:

HO-3	Special Form (All risk)	Covers all above perils, plus any other perils except exclusions, such as flood, war, earthquake, and nuclear accidents
HO-4	Tenants Form	Covers personal belongings of renters against the perils listed above.
HO-5	Comprehensive Form	Expands HO-3 to include replacement cost coverage for home contents and buildings.
HO-6	Condominium Form	Covers personal belongings for condominium owners.
HO-7	Country Home Form	Provides coverage for agricultural buildings and equipment for non-farm business rural residents.

Other major coverages for each policy type usually include: personal liability, medical payments for visitors and guests on your property, additional living expenses when you are required to live elsewhere due to a home insurance claim.

Note: In the past, insurance companies also offered HO-1 (Basic Form), HO-2 (Broad Form), and HO-8 (Modified Coverage Form for older homes with a high replacement value); these policies are no longer offered by most companies.

All forms of homeowners policies cover the perils listed at the top of Figure 20-2. The *special form* and *comprehensive form* policies have become the most common types of home insurance. These policies insure against most perils except those excluded by the policy. Other home insurance policies are designed for special situations such as condominium owners and renters.

Personal liability coverage is included with all forms of the homeowners policy. With a homeowners policy, you are as protected as you would be if you bought several separate policies.

Renters Policies

Many people rent homes, condominiums, or apartments. Their dwellings are filled with personal property. Renters have many of the same property and liability insurance needs as homeowners. A *renters policy* is a property and liability policy suitable for renters.

This policy covers household goods and personal belongings. This coverage provides protection against the same kinds of perils covered by homeowners policies. A renters policy may include personal liability coverage, but it doesn't protect the actual dwelling. The dwelling should be covered under the owner's policy.

Other Coverage

You can purchase policies for damage caused by flood in a flood-prone area. You can also obtain insurance to protect against economic losses caused by earthquakes. Neither of these two perils is typically covered in other policies.

Making a Claim

If you have to make a claim for a property loss, you will want to be well prepared. You should keep a list, called an *inventory*, of personal property that you have insured. The list should include the following information.

1. The brand name and description of each item

2. The purchase price

3. The date and place of the purchase

In addition to an up-to-date personal property inventory, insurance agents suggest keeping receipts for purchases. Taking photographs or making videos of your furniture and other property can also help to support claims.

Inventory records along with photographs or videos should be stored in a location that cannot be damaged by fire, water, or smoke. If the records are lost or damaged, it will be hard to provide the insurance company with the information it needs to make a payment for your claim. A safe deposit box in a bank or other safe location away from your home is a good storage area for property records.

The age of a personal property item is quite important. Most property becomes old, gradually wears out, and decreases in value. This decrease in value is **depreciation**. It may affect the amount an insurance company will pay if the property is destroyed.

For example, a sofa costing $700 that is expected to last 10 years would depreciate $70 each year ($700 cost ÷ 10 years = $70 depreciation per year). Its value after six years would be $280 (depreciation per year $70 × 6 years = total depreciation $420; original cost $700 − total depreciation $420 = $280).

In recent years, homeowners have begun to purchase *replacement insurance*. With this method, the insurance company actually replaces an item that has been destroyed. No depreciation is deducted. Instead, the item is actually replaced no matter what the current cost may be. A replacement cost policy would pay whatever it cost to replace your property.

checkpoint ✓
How does a renters policy differ from homeowners insurance?

What is the value of homes in your neighborhood? How does this affect insurance rates in your area?

Photodisc/Getty Images

Why is the purchase of property and liability insurance important to all life-span plans? What amounts and types of insurance should you plan to buy in the next few years? What resources might be valuable as you look for information about insurance coverages?

Goal 3

Identify factors that affect property insurance costs.

PROPERTY INSURANCE COSTS

As with any insurance purchase, a wise consumer should seek the proper protection at the lowest cost. This process involves making sure that you insure the property for the correct amount. You should also carefully consider the factors affecting property insurance costs. The value of a home and furnishings represents the largest investment that many people make. The purchase of a carefully selected insurance plan to protect these items makes good sense.

Coverage Selection

Suppose a family had a house built in 2004 for $180,000. They insured it for that amount. If today's cost of building a similar house is $220,000, the current replacement value of the house is $220,000. Yet if the house is destroyed by fire, the insurance company may pay the family only $180,000.

Some insurance companies provide for automatic increases in property coverage as the price level increases. Others will pay the current replacement value if the property is insured for at least 80 percent of that replacement value.

Building costs and property values increase almost every year. Property owners should review the value of their homes and insurance coverage on a regular basis. They should determine the cost of replacing their property. They must make sure that their insurance policies provide enough protection.

Special care should be taken to correctly estimate the value of personal property. Because personal property includes many items, some may be overlooked. Most homeowners policies provide personal property coverage at 50 to

Why is a detailed household inventory helpful if you need to submit an insurance claim?

70 percent of policy value. For example, if your home is insured for $100,000, your personal property is insured for 60 percent of this, or $60,000. The value of personal property that you obtain over the years is often high. In many cases, a homeowner's personal property is worth a great deal more than the coverage provided. Additional coverage is available for a slightly higher premium.

Insurance Premiums

Premiums paid for homeowners insurance have increased over the years. Several factors determine the price that you pay for insurance on a home and furnishings. The most important factor is the estimated danger of loss based on the insurance company's past experiences. In addition to the loss experiences, an insurance company considers the following factors in determining homeowners' insurance premiums.

- Value of the property insured
- Construction of the building: whether it is made of brick, wood, or concrete, and the construction of the roof
- Number of claims on the property
- Type of policy

WORK *as a* **TEAM**

When items are stolen or damaged, insurance companies require that you prove the value of the item. Prepare a list of possessions that are commonly found in a home. Describe actions that might be taken to prove the value of these items.

- Distance to the nearest fire department and water supply
- Amount of deductible (the higher the deductible, the lower the premium)
- Credit rating of the insured

You should consider these items before purchasing or building a home. You should also keep them in mind when you are shopping for insurance on a home you already own. In addition, homeowners insurance discounts are often available for policyholders who are nonsmokers, for installing smoke detectors and burglar alarms, and for buying multiple policies, such as life and auto insurance, from the same company.

checkpoint ✓
What factors affect the cost of home insurance?

20-2 Assessment

Key Concepts

Determine the best answer.

1. True or False. Most property insurance policies will pay for living somewhere else while a damaged home is being repaired.

2. True or False. A garage is an example of personal property.

3. The most coverage is provided by the _?_ form of homeowners insurance.
   a. tenants
   b. special
   c. comprehensive
   d. condominium

4. Renters would not be covered for
   a. living expenses
   b. personal liability
   c. personal property
   d. real property

Make Academic Connections

5. **Visual Art** Use photos, drawings, and other visual images to create a display that communicates the various perils covered by property insurance.

6. **Research** Contact a local insurance agent to obtain information on the costs of renters insurance in your community.

Creativity and Innovation

Enhancing Presentations with Visuals

An audience benefits from the visual presentation of data, ideas, and concepts through improved clarity and stronger recall. A graph can illustrate the importance of sales figures. A map can help participants get their bearings. An interesting graphic can capture people's attention.

Create Effective Visuals

Commonly used visuals include slides, transparencies, posters, videos, models, photographs, flip charts, computer images, chalkboards, dry erase boards, maps, and demonstrations. To create effective visuals, be sure to use the following guidelines.

- Keep the design simple. Include only one major idea per visual.
- Limit how many visuals you use.
- Be concise and accurate. Proofread text and check calculations.
- Choose the visual that is most appropriate for the information or data you are presenting.
- Make sure that data are represented accurately.
- Make visuals large enough to be seen by the entire audience.
- Position yourself so the audience can clearly see the visuals.

Charts and graphs can enhance a presentation by creating a visual representation of data. They are particularly helpful in demonstrating relationships and trends. Commonly used charts and graphs include pie charts, organization charts, bar graphs, flow charts, line graphs, and pictographs.

Use Presentation Software

Presentation software such as PowerPoint® or Keynote® can enhance an oral report. Templates and designs should be selected carefully to create audience appeal and limit distraction. When creating a presentation using software, consider these guidelines.

- Limit the text quantity to six lines per slide and approximately six words per line.
- Choose text and background colors that contrast for easy reading.
- Use a consistent font style with a size that can be read.

Stockbyte/Getty Images

What are some alternatives to the visual shown in this photo?

- Add images, such as photos, maps, graphs, and illustrations, to emphasize key ideas.
- Avoid distracting transitions, animation, and sound effects.

When presenting, do not read from the screen or your notes. Talk to your audience with enthusiasm, expression, and voice projection.

Think Critically

1. How can visuals enhance the effectiveness of a presentation?
2. Create a visual that could be used with a presentation for a class or other situation.

20-3 Life Insurance

Goals

1. Discuss the principles of life insurance.

2. Explain the types of life insurance.

3. Describe the process of buying life insurance.

Key Terms

beneficiary 529

term life insurance 530

permanent life insurance 530

Focus on REAL LIFE

"I was shocked when I heard that one of my fraternity brothers died. He was only 30 and he had young children—just like me. Now, I can't stop worrying about my own family. What would they do if something happened to me?"

"Rafael, I know this is upsetting, but I'm sure you have life insurance. Maybe you need to check to make sure you have enough coverage," replied Steve.

"You probably won't believe this, Steve, but I don't have any life insurance. I have other kinds of insurance, but I thought I was too young to worry about life insurance."

"Everyone needs life insurance to protect their family against economic loss. Julie and I just met with our insurance agent to make sure we had the right kind of coverage. She talked to us about some policies that combine insurance and investments. Do you want her name and phone number?"

This seems like a good time for Rafael to consider purchasing life insurance. He will need to decide what kind of life insurance to buy, how much to buy, and where to buy it.

LIFE INSURANCE PRINCIPLES

Life insurance protects survivors against financial loss associated with death. Specifically, it is designed to replace a loss of income for family members who are financially dependent upon another person. Life insurance can also be considered a means of saving or investing, but its primary purpose is always protection against financial loss.

The Life Insurance Policy

A life insurance policy is a contract between the insurance company and the person buying the insurance, called the *insured*. The following are the major elements of a life insurance policy.

- Name of the insured

- Amount of coverage, also called the face value or death benefit of the policy

- Cost of the insurance, called the premium amount

- Name of the beneficiary

Beneficiary Selection

When you buy life insurance, you must name a beneficiary. A **beneficiary** is the person named in the policy to receive the insurance benefits. The beneficiary is most often a spouse, children, or other dependents. You may insure not only your own life, but also the life of any person in whom you have an insurable interest. To have an *insurable interest* in the life of another person, you must receive some kind of financial benefit from that person's continued life.

> **Goal 1**
>
> Discuss the principles of life insurance.

You have, for example, an insurable interest in the lives of your parents. You do not have an insurable interest in a stranger's life. A partner in a business has an insurable interest in the lives of other partners.

> **checkpoint ✓**
> What is an insurable interest?

Goal 2

Explain the types of life insurance.

TYPES OF LIFE INSURANCE

Insurance companies offer a variety of life insurance plans that meet different needs. The two basic types of life insurance policies are term life and permanent, or cash value, life.

Term Life Insurance

Insurance that provides financial protection from losses resulting from a death during a definite period, or term, is **term life insurance**. This coverage is the least expensive form of life insurance. Term insurance is also the *only* form of life insurance that is purely life insurance. All other forms of insurance also have savings or investment features.

Term policies may run for a period of 1 to 20 years or more. If the insured dies during the period for which the insurance was purchased, the amount of the policy is paid to the beneficiary. If the insured does not die during the period for which the policy was purchased, the insurance company is not required to pay anything. Protection ends when the term expires.

By paying a slightly higher premium, a person can buy *renewable* term insurance. This type of policy allows the policyholder to continue term insurance for one or more terms without taking another physical examination.

Term insurance policies may be level term or decreasing term.

With *level* term insurance, the amount of protection and the premiums remain the same while the insurance is in effect. With *decreasing* term insurance, the amount of protection gradually becomes smaller, but premiums remain the same during the term. This is often appropriate because the need for insurance normally declines as children become independent and other savings and investments grow.

Permanent Life Insurance

The common characteristics of **permanent life insurance** are that it has cash value and an investment feature. Part of the premium you pay for permanent life insurance is used for insurance that provides protection. This feature is just like term insurance. The insurance company invests the remaining part of the premium that is not needed to pay for the coverage. It adds to the cash value of the insurance policy.

Name some of the various types of dependents who might be protected by life insurance.

Cash value refers to the amount of money that the insurance company will pay if the policyholder decides the insurance is no longer needed. The cash value is much less than the death benefit that would be paid to beneficiaries. As long as permanent policies are kept in force, they accumulate cash value in addition to providing life insurance.

The longer you keep your permanent life insurance policy, the higher its cash value will be. If you give up or surrender your policy, you receive the amount of the cash value. If you need money but do not want to cancel your policy, you can borrow an amount up to the cash value from the insurance company. If you should die before the loan is repaid, the insurance company will withhold the unpaid amount from the face value of the policy when it pays your survivors. *Face value* is the amount of insurance coverage that was originally purchased and that will be paid upon the death of the insured.

The cash value of permanent life insurance can be seen as a savings plan. Usually, the return on your money in the cash value portion of permanent life insurance is not large. Nevertheless, permanent insurance plans have a built-in savings feature that encourages people to save for the future. Permanent life insurance comes in the form of whole life, variable life, and universal life policies. Each type builds up cash value.

Whole Life Insurance Permanent insurance that extends over the lifetime, or whole life, of the insured is *whole life insurance*. One type of whole life insurance is an *ordinary life policy*. Premiums for ordinary life insurance remain the same each year as long as the policyholder lives.

Some whole life insurance policies are meant to be paid in full in a certain number of years. *Limited-payment policies* may be designated by the number of years the policyholder agrees to pay on them, such as 20-payment life policies. They are like

Many life-span plans are created to serve a family. Explain why these plans should include life insurance for all adult members. When do you expect to purchase life insurance? How much and what type will you buy?

ordinary life policies except that premiums are paid for a limited number of years or until a person reaches a certain age. Limited-payment policies free the insured from paying premiums during retirement when income may be lower.

Variable Life Insurance An insurance plan that resembles an investment portfolio is *variable life insurance*. This plan lets the policyholder choose among a broad range of investments. These investments include stocks, bonds, and mutual funds. The death benefits and cash values of variable life policies vary according to the yield on the investments that the policyholder selects.

Photodisc/Getty Images

Why do people's insurance needs change at different times in their lives?

The insurance company first designates an amount of the variable life premiums to cover the cost of insurance. It places the remaining amount in an investment account. Both the death benefit and the cash value rise and fall with the success of the investment account.

A variable life policy might guarantee a minimum death benefit. There is no guaranteed cash value. The minimum death benefit, in relation to premiums paid, is well below other types of life insurance. On the positive side, a strong rate of return on the investment account can increase the cash value and the death benefit.

Universal Life Insurance *Universal life insurance* provides both insurance protection and a substantial savings plan. The premium that you pay for universal life insurance is split in three ways. One portion of it pays for insurance protection. The insurance company takes a second portion for its expenses. The third portion goes into interest-earning investments for the policyholder.

The most important feature of universal life insurance is that the investment portion of the policy earns a variable rate of return. This rate is usually higher than is paid on other types of cash value life insurance. This yield on the investment portion tends to rise or fall based on changing economic conditions. Figure 20-3 compares the features of the different types of life insurance.

▶ **Figure 20-3**

Which kind of insurance is least expensive for a given amount of death benefit?

Types of Life Insurance Policies

POLICY FEATURES	TERM LIFE INSURANCE	PERMANENT LIFE INSURANCE			
		Whole Life Insurance			
		Ordinary Life Insurance	Limited Life Insurance	Variable Life Insurance	Universal Life Insurance
Premium	Begins low but increases gradually	High, but usually stays constant	Higher than ordinary life insurance but constant	Fixed and regular	Varies at the discretion of the policyholder
Payment Period	Specified number of years—normally 5, 10, or 15 years	Life of the insured	Specified number of years—normally 20 to 30 years	Specified period	Specified period
Cash Value	None	Some cash value	More cash value than ordinary life but less than variable life	Varies with the rise or fall in the value of the investment account	Varies with the interest rate paid on the cash value
Death Benefit	Fixed	Fixed	Fixed	Death benefit always exceeds cash value	Can vary at the discretion of the policyholder
Purposes	Protection for a specified period of time	Protection for life, some cash value for policyholder	Protection for life, some cash value for policyholder	Life insurance plus an opportunity to select different cash value investment options	Life insurance with a fairly high rate of return on cash value

Group Life Insurance

Some individuals are fortunate to have an employer or some other group offer the opportunity to buy group life insurance. An insurance policy that covers a group of people is called *group life insurance*. The group acts as a single unit in buying the insurance.

The cost of group life insurance is less than the cost of a similar individual policy. This savings results from the insurance company covering many people in one policy.

Most group life insurance plans offer term rather than permanent insurance. The insurance company works with an employer or other organization, such as a union, to develop the insurance plan. Then, each employee or member of the organization may purchase individual life insurance coverage.

> **checkpoint** ✓
> What is the difference between term and permanent life insurance?

Lawrence Wee/Shutterstock.com

Why do people working in dangerous occupations cost more to insure?

BUYING LIFE INSURANCE

Many people need the protection offered by life insurance. Without insurance, few people have the financial resources needed to pay for a funeral and other related expenses when someone close to them dies. For a life insurance program to be effective, it must fit your needs and those of your family.

Coverage Amount

Anyone with dependents should consider life insurance. A *dependent* is a person who must rely on another for financial support. In the future, you will need to ask the question, "What would happen to the people who are financially dependent on me if I die tomorrow?" If they could not live financially in the way in which they lived before your death, you most likely need life insurance.

The following questions will help to determine the need for life insurance.

- How much money is required for your dependents' financial stability if your income is lost?

Goal 3

Describe the process of buying life insurance.

NETBookmark

Insurance can be confusing, but many valuable online information sources are available. Access the website shown below and click on the link of Chapter 20. Select a link for one type of insurance. Explain how this information might be used in your life now or in the future.

www.cengage.com/school/genbus/pob

Life insurance needs vary, and determining how much life insurance to have requires careful consideration. As a team, prepare a list of factors that a person might consider when determining the amount of life insurance to obtain.

- How much income will you need when you retire and what will be the sources of your income?

- What can you afford to pay for your life insurance needs?

Answers to these questions will help you purchase the best life insurance program for you.

Life Insurance Application

To buy individual life insurance coverage, you need to complete a life insurance application. You apply for this coverage through an insurance agent representing an insurance company.

You may be required to take a physical exam to assess your health. If you have no serious health problems, you then pay a premium and receive your life insurance policy.

If you are in poor health or work in a dangerous job, you may be considered a poor risk. Even so, you likely will be able to get insurance. You will probably pay higher premiums than people who are in good health and are employed in less hazardous jobs.

Premium Payments

In addition to the health and occupation of the insured, the type of policy affects the cost of life insurance. The age of the person being insured also affects premiums. In purchasing a whole life policy, for example, the premiums for ordinary life insurance are higher than those for term insurance, but the annual premium stays the same throughout the insured's life. The premiums on limited-payment life insurance are higher than those for ordinary life insurance, but they are payable for only a limited number of years.

> **checkpoint** ✓
> What factors affect the need for life insurance?

20-3 Assessment

www.cengage.com/school/genbus/pob

Key Concepts

Determine the best answer.

1. _____ life insurance is considered temporary coverage.
   a. Whole
   b. Universal
   c. Term
   d. Variable

2. The beneficiary of a life insurance policy
   a. is the cost of insurance
   b. makes the premium payments
   c. receives money when the insured dies
   d. is the period for which the policy is in effect

Make Academic Connections

3. **Technology** Use the Internet to find an insurance company website that includes frequently asked questions about life insurance. Find three questions that interest you. Copy the questions and their answers along with the name of the company and the URL.

4. **Math** The rate of return on the investment portion of a life insurance policy is 6.47 percent for a given year. If the investment portion (cash value) was $17,643 at the beginning of the year, what will it be worth at the end of the year? Round to the nearest cent.

20-4 Health Insurance

Goals

1. Describe health insurance coverage.

2. Discuss health insurance providers.

3. Explain disability and long-term care insurance.

Key Terms

hospital insurance 535

surgical insurance 535

regular medical insurance 536

major medical insurance 536

coinsurance 536

comprehensive medical policy 537

disability income insurance 541

Focus on REAL LIFE

"Carlotta! Welcome back to school! We really missed you. How is your arm?"

"Kendra, my arm is doing great. Thanks for asking. I can't believe that a simple fall put me in the hospital and I had to have surgery," responded Carlotta. "I'm almost feeling normal again, and we were very fortunate that the insurance company paid nearly all of my bills. My mother has very good health insurance at her job. Without that coverage, we would have had to pay more than $40,000."

"Wow! I'm glad you were covered by your mother's insurance. Now, Carlotta, how soon before you can throw again?" asked Kendra.

"Sooner than I would be able to pay my medical bills if I didn't have health insurance!"

HEALTH INSURANCE COVERAGE

Several types of health-related insurance are available to provide different kinds of coverage. One type of health insurance is *medical insurance*. It can be classified as (1) hospital insurance, (2) surgical insurance, (3) regular medical insurance, (4) major medical insurance, and (5) a comprehensive medical policy. Insurance companies also offer combination policies.

Hospital Insurance

An illness or injury may require you to be hospitalized. In this situation, **hospital insurance** usually pays most or all of the charges. These include expenses for your room, food, and medical items such as use of an operating room, anesthesia, X-rays, laboratory tests, and medications. Because of the high cost of hospitalization, people purchase hospital insurance more than any other kind of health insurance.

You can buy hospital insurance from insurance companies or from nonprofit corporations, such as Blue Cross. If expenses are more than the amount covered by the hospital insurance plan, the patient must pay the difference.

Surgical Insurance

Surgery is a major reason for hospitalization. It can be very expensive. **Surgical insurance** covers all or part of the surgeon's fees for an operation. The typical surgical policy lists the types of operations that it covers and the amount allowed for each. Some policies allow larger amounts for operations than others. This, of course, requires that a higher premium be paid. Surgical insurance is often bought in combination with hospital insurance.

Again, you can buy surgical insurance from insurance companies or from nonprofit organizations. Surgical plans cover mainly medical and surgical treatment

> **Goal 1**
> Describe health insurance coverage.

rather than hospital care. These plans list the maximum amounts that they will pay for different types of surgery. They also cover the doctor's charges for care in the hospital. Some plans pay the doctor's charges for office or home care. The coverage generally does not provide for preexisting conditions or for illnesses or injuries that are covered by other insurance.

Regular Medical Insurance

Sometimes normal care provided by a physician can be quite expensive. **Regular medical insurance** covers fees for nonsurgical care given in the doctor's office, the patient's home, or a hospital. The policy states the amount payable for each visit or call. It also lists the maximum number of visits covered. Some plans provide payments for diagnostic and laboratory expenses.

Regular medical insurance is usually combined in one policy with hospital and surgical insurance. The protection provided by regular medical, hospital, and surgical insurance is often referred to as *basic health coverage*.

Major Medical Insurance

Long illnesses and serious injuries can be very expensive. Bills of $50,000 to $100,000 and higher are not unusual. **Major medical insurance** provides protection against the high costs of serious illnesses or injuries. This coverage complements the other forms of medical insurance.

Major medical insurance helps pay for most kinds of extended and specialized health care prescribed by a doctor. It covers the cost of treatment in and out of the hospital, special nursing care, X-rays, psychiatric care, medicine, and many other health care needs. Maximum benefits may be limited, but usually extend to a high amount, such as $500,000 or $1,000,000.

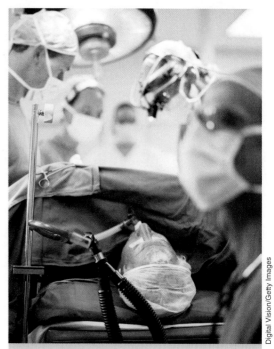

Why is hospital insurance so expensive?

Digital Vision/Getty Images

All major medical policies have a *deductible* clause. The clause is similar to the one found in automobile collision insurance. With this clause, the policyholder agrees to pay the first part of the expense resulting from sickness or injury. The deductible may be $500 or more.

Major medical policies usually contain a *coinsurance* clause. **Coinsurance** is the sharing of expenses by the policyholder and the insurance company. The policyholder typically pays a deductible and then shares the remaining cost with the insurance company.

For example, the insurance company may pay 80 percent of the cost for medical treatment after the deductible is paid. The policyholder will then pay the remaining 20 percent. The policyholder's share is limited to a specific dollar amount stated in the policy. Once the deductible and the coinsurance amounts are met, the insurance company reimburses 100 percent of the cost up to the policy's coverage limits.

The deductible clause discourages the filing of minor claims. The coinsurance clause encourages the policyholder to keep medical expenses as reasonable as possible. Thus, both clauses help to lower premiums because they help to reduce payments of insurance claims.

Comprehensive Medical Policy

Insurance providers have developed a **comprehensive medical policy** that combines the features of hospital, surgical, regular, and major medical insurance. This coverage retains the features of each separate coverage, such as amounts-payable limits. The policy has only one deductible. A combination of coverages will likely be less expensive than the total of the separate coverage.

Dental Insurance

As dental expenses have increased over the years, insurance companies now offer coverage to help pay for normal dental care. Dental insurance usually includes examinations, X-rays, cleaning, and fillings. It may cover part or all of complicated dental work such as crowns or bridges. This policy also covers dental injuries resulting from accidents.

Most dental plans contain deductible and coinsurance provisions to reduce the cost of premiums. Dental insurance is offered mainly through group plans. It continues to grow in popularity.

Vision Care Insurance

In anticipation of eye care expenses, many individual consumers and groups purchase vision care insurance. These policies cover eye examinations, prescription lenses, frames, and contact lenses. Some vision care plans now cover the cost of laser eye surgery, which can eliminate the need for glasses. New medical developments may result in additional vision care coverage.

monkeybusinessimages/iStockphoto.com

Why do most people need some kind of health insurance?

checkpoint ✓
What four types of health insurance would be included in a comprehensive medical policy?

HEALTH INSURANCE PROVIDERS

Health insurance is available from several sources. These options include group health insurance, individual health insurance, health maintenance organizations, preferred provider organizations, and government programs.

Goal 2

Discuss health insurance providers.

Group Health Insurance

The most popular way to buy health insurance is through a group. As with group life insurance, employers, unions and other organizations offer group health insurance policies.

Companies that sponsor group policies often pay part or all of the insurance premiums for their employees. They provide this as an employment benefit. Employees can usually buy coverage for family members as well.

The cost of group health insurance is lower per insured than the cost of a comparable individual policy. The costs are lower because insurance companies can manage group plans more economically.

Individual Health Insurance

Some people are not eligible for group health insurance. They may be self-employed and have no employer to help buy health insurance. One alternative is to buy individual health insurance. These policies are available to individuals and are adapted to individual needs. Individual health insurance policies are usually rather expensive. They may require a physical

Business Insight for the 21st Century

Telemedicine

A physician in a rural hospital learns new surgery techniques by viewing live images of a procedure being performed by a surgeon halfway around the world. A nurse in an emergency room prepares for the arrival of a heart attack patient while receiving real-time data from diagnostic equipment being used by paramedics in the field. While sitting at a home computer, a teenager with cancer participates in a support group with young people from 10 different states.

These are examples of *telemedicine,* which refers to a wide range of activities involving medicine, communication technology, and distance.

Specialist referral services usually involve specialists helping other physicians diagnose a patient's condition. For example, a radiologist, a physician who specializes in the interpretation of diagnostic images, can read a chest X-ray from a remote location across town or in a different country.

Patient consultations are direct interactions between a patient and a health care provider. A common situation may involve a patient in a rural clinic communicating with a physician in another location such as a private medical office or a hospital.

Remote patient monitoring relies on devices to collect data from a patient and transmit it to another location for interpretation. Home health agencies use this technology to monitor chronic conditions such as diabetes and congestive heart failure.

Medical education provides continuing education and special training to health care professionals. Telemedicine is a convenient and cost-effective way to participate in classes, seminars, workshops, and demonstrations.

Consumer medical and health information offers online medical and health resources for the general public as well as specialized service for specific patients or groups. Examples include online chats with midwives, web-based food diaries for nutritional counseling, blogs focused on issues family caregivers face, and e-mail follow-up after an office visit.

The use of telemedicine is growing and changing with the introduction of new technologies and innovations. While concerns exist about cost-effectiveness, insurance coverage, and privacy, it is likely that many telemedicine services will become routine.

Think Critically

1. How might the availability of telemedicine services impact the cost of health care?

2. Use library or Internet resources to find three examples of telemedicine being used in different settings. Write a short summary of your findings.

exam and have a waiting period before the policy takes effect.

Managed Care Plans

Various alternative health insurance plans have grown in popularity. Known as *managed health care* or *managed care*, these programs cover more than two-thirds of Americans who have insurance through their employer. These plans often provide lower-cost, comprehensive health care through networks of medical professionals.

Managed care plans usually have higher monthly premiums. Yet the overall cost of health care may be lower for the consumer because of low or no deductibles, low copayments, and little or no paperwork. A potential drawback is that patients have less control and limited choices of whom they see for health care. Managed care plans have various names, such as HMOs (health maintenance organizations) and PPOs (preferred provider organizations).

The growth of managed care has resulted from large companies trying to control the rising cost of providing health care coverage for employees. Today, many managed care plans are run by insurance companies.

Health Maintenance Organization (HMO)

One managed care choice is a health maintenance organization. A *health maintenance organization (HMO)* commonly consists of a staffed medical clinic to serve members. You join an HMO for a fixed monthly fee. As a member, you are entitled to a wide range of prepaid health care services, including hospitalization. HMOs emphasize preventive health care. Early detection and treatment of illnesses help reduce hospital visits and keep costs down. Generally, HMOs do not cover treatment or care that is not authorized by a physician or procedures that are above the average cost for the area.

WORK *as a* TEAM

Everyone is affected by rising health care costs. As a team, prepare a list of actions that might be taken by (a) individuals, (b) businesses, and (c) government to (1) improve the health of people in society and (2) reduce costs for medical services.

Preferred Provider Organization (PPO)

A popular alternative is the *preferred provider organization (PPO)*. This system involves several health care providers, such as a group of physicians, a clinic, or a hospital. These medical professionals contract with an insurance company to provide services to members. These providers agree to charge set fees for services.

Members are encouraged, but not required, to use the PPO services through financial incentives. Members are able to get medical treatment through the PPO at a significant discount. They may seek medical treatment elsewhere. However, expenses for treatment outside the PPO may be only partially reimbursed.

State Government Assistance

An important health insurance program by state governments is *workers' compensation*. This insurance plan provides medical and survivor benefits for people injured, disabled, or killed on the job. Accidents can occur on almost any job. Employees may suffer injuries or develop some illness because of working conditions. Workers' compensation laws provide medical benefits to employees who are injured on the job or become ill as a direct result of their working conditions. Under these laws, most employers are required to provide and pay for this insurance for their employees.

State governments also administer a form of medical aid to some low-income individuals and families known as *Medicaid*. The federal government shares with states the cost of providing health benefits to eligible individuals and families. The services covered by Medicaid include hospital care, doctor services, X-rays, lab tests, nursing home care, and home health care services. States may also offer a health insurance program for people who have trouble obtaining coverage. Past health conditions can result in a person being turned down by most health insurance providers.

Federal Government Assistance

The nation's Social Security laws provide a national program of health insurance known as *Medicare*. This insurance is designed to help people aged 65 and older and some disabled people pay for health care. Medicare has two basic parts: hospital insurance and medical insurance.

The hospital insurance plan includes coverage for hospital care, service in an approved nursing home, and home health care up to a certain number of visits. No premium payments are required for the hospital insurance. Almost everyone 65 years old and older may qualify.

The medical insurance portion of Medicare is often called supplementary or voluntary medical insurance. The services covered under this plan include doctor services, medical services, supplies, and home health services. The medical insurance requires a monthly premium. The federal government pays an equal amount to help cover the cost of the medical insurance.

Cost Reduction Actions

Health care costs have consistently increased faster than the overall cost of living. The cost of health insurance is determined by four main factors: extent of coverage, number of claims filed, age of the policyholder, and number of dependents. You have no control over your age and little control over the number of people who depend on you. However, you can make sure you buy only the kind and amount of insurance you need. You can also take care of yourself and not use medical benefits unnecessarily.

What can you do to reduce your health insurance costs?

Insurance companies encourage policyholders to play an active role in *cost containment*, or keeping costs down. The most common methods are coinsurance and deductibles. Also, in the health care industry, patients are encouraged to obtain a second opinion to ensure the necessity of a medical procedure.

Another cost-containment strategy is the use of outpatient services for some surgical procedures. In the past, people undergoing some procedures might have been admitted to the hospital for one or two days. Now, the person comes to the hospital or an outpatient center in the morning. After the surgery, the patient returns home the same day. Recent federal government actions attempt to reduce health care costs while maintaining choice and quality of service for patients. This health insurance legislation is also designed to provide affordable coverage for those who do not have access to medical care.

checkpoint ✓
Who are the main providers of health insurance?

DISABILITY AND LONG-TERM CARE INSURANCE

The need for health insurance goes beyond various medical expenses. Disability income and long-term care

Goal 3

Explain disability and long-term care insurance.

insurance programs protect people in other types of situations.

Disability Income Insurance

For most people, income from employment is their single most important economic resource. Protecting your income is very important. One form of health insurance provides periodic payments if the policyholder becomes disabled. **Disability income insurance** protects you against the loss of income caused by a long illness or an accident. The insured receives weekly or monthly payments until they are able to return to work.

Disability income policies often include a waiting period. This requires the policyholder to wait a specified time after the disability occurs before payment begins. Monthly payments under disability insurance plans are usually much smaller than the income people earn from their jobs. The amount may be 40–60 percent of the normal income, but many disability payments are not subject to income taxes.

Long-Term Care Insurance

With people living longer, *long-term care insurance* is the fastest-growing type of protection. This coverage provides *long-term*

What effect does longer lifespan have on the health insurance industry?

Photodisc/Getty Images

care, which is daily assistance needed because of a long-term illness or disability. This assistance may involve a stay in a nursing home. It may cover help that is provided at home for daily activities such as dressing, bathing, and doing household chores.

> **checkpoint** ✓
> What is the purpose of disability income insurance?

20-4   Assessment

Study Tools

www.cengage.com/school/genbus/pob

Key Concepts

Determine the best answer.

1. Health insurance coverage for a long illness is __?__ insurance.
   a. hospital
   b. surgical
   c. regular medical
   d. major medical

2. If you are injured on the job, you are likely to be covered by
   a. Medicare   c. workers' compensation
   b. Medicaid   d. an HMO

Make Academic Connections

3. **Government** Investigate health insurance resources provided by your state government. Write a short report about your findings.

4. **Visual Communication** Create a poster or video that addresses one of the concepts presented in this lesson.

5. **Read** Find a recent article about changes in health insurance. Read the article and create an outline of the main points that are presented. Include a properly formatted citation for your source. Possible sources include printed and online versions of newspapers, magazines, or a website that produces original content.

Business Notes

20-1 Vehicle Insurance

- Motor vehicle risks include having an accident, having your vehicle stolen, injuring yourself or another person, or damaging another's property.

- Personal injury insurance covers bodily injury liability, medical payments, and uninsured motorist protection. Property damage liability protects you against claims if you damage another person's property.

- Automobile insurance rates are affected by age, accidents, marital status, academics, credit rating, car use, number of miles driven a year, value of car, and where you live.

20-2 Property Insurance

- Home and property insurance protect against three economic losses: (1) damage to home or property, (2) expenses to live somewhere else if your home is badly damaged, and (3) liability losses.

- A homeowners insurance policy provides coverage for various perils. Renters insurance is available for those who rent.

- Wise consumers select the most appropriate protection at the lowest cost.

20-3 Life Insurance

- Life insurance protects survivors against the financial loss associated with dying. It replaces a loss of income for a family who is financially dependent upon another person.

- Term life insurance provides financial protection from losses of life during a definite period. Permanent insurance has both cash value and an investment feature.

- To buy individual life insurance coverage, a person applies to an insurance agent. A physical exam may be required to assess the person's health. Life insurance premiums depend on the type of policy and the age and health of the person being insured.

20-4 Health Insurance

- Five common types of medical insurance are hospital insurance, surgical insurance, regular medical insurance, major medical insurance, and a comprehensive policy. Dental and vision care insurance provide specific coverage for these medical needs.

- Health insurance providers include group health insurance, individual health insurance, health maintenance organizations, preferred provider organizations, and government programs.

- Disability income insurance protects against income loss due to illness or accident. The insured receives payments until able to return to work. Long-term care insurance provides daily assistance needed because of a long-term illness or disability.

Communicate Business Concepts

1. Which type of automobile insurance would cover the following situations?

   a. A pedestrian is injured by a driver.
   b. A family member is injured when you run into a parked car.
   c. You, in an attempt to avoid hitting a dog in the street, run into a parked car.
   d. Winds cause a tree branch to break your windshield and dent the hood.

2. A driver was at fault when three passengers were badly hurt. The court awarded two of the people $30,000 each and $45,000 to the third person. The driver had bodily injury liability coverage of 50/100. Was this enough coverage for financial loss? Why or why not?

3. Why is collision coverage on a 10-year-old car less important than on a three-year-old car? Why may a person still want to have collision coverage on a 10-year-old car?

4. What type of property insurance would cover these situations?

   a. Damage to furniture because of a fire
   b. The cost of staying at a hotel after your home was damaged by fire
   c. Injury to a repairperson on your property

5. Recently, homes in an Iowa valley were destroyed when heavy rains caused the Mississippi River to rise above flood level. Do you think those Iowa residents who had homeowners policies suffered any financial losses? Why or why not?

6. What type of life insurance policy would you recommend for these people?

   a. Carlos Medina, age 27, wants a policy with premiums as low as possible for the next 10 years.
   b. Julie Hovel, age 45, wants a policy with no premium payments after she retires.

7. Why is a physical examination not usually required when buying group life insurance coverage?

Develop Your Business Language

Match the terms listed with the definitions.

8. Health insurance that covers all or part of surgeon's fees.

9. The person named in the life insurance policy to receive the benefits.

10. Covers claims for injuries or damage to property caused by you or your family.

11. The amount the insured pays before the insurance company pays a claim.

12. Coverage that provides protection against the high costs of serious illnesses or injuries.

13. Coverage for claims resulting from injuries or deaths for which the insured is at fault.

14. Health coverage for your room, food, and other hospital expenses.

15. The decrease in value of property.

16. Insurance coverage for medical expenses of a policyholder and family members if they are injured while riding in a car.

17. Coverage for injuries caused by hit-and-run drivers or by drivers without insurance.

18. Protection against the loss of income caused by a long illness or an accident.

19. Life insurance coverage with a cash value and an investment feature.

20. Coverage that protects a driver against claims if the insured's car damages someone else's property.

21. Health insurance for non-surgical care in a doctor's office, patient's home, or hospital.

22. A package-type insurance policy designed to insure homes and property.

23. Auto coverage for a loss resulting from a collision with another car or object.

24. A health policy combining hospital, surgical, regular, and major medical insurance.

25. Auto coverage for almost all damage losses except those caused from a collision.

26. Life insurance that provides financial protection during a set period.

27. The sharing of expenses by the policyholder and the insurance company.

KEY TERMS

a. beneficiary
b. bodily injury liability
c. coinsurance
d. collision coverage
e. comprehensive coverage
f. comprehensive medical policy
g. deductible
h. depreciation
i. disability income insurance
j. homeowners policy
k. hospital insurance
l. major medical insurance
m. medical payments coverage
n. permanent life insurance
o. personal liability coverage
p. property damage liability
q. regular medical insurance
r. surgical insurance
s. term life insurance
t. uninsured motorist coverage

Make Academic Connections

28. **Law** Obtain information on the financial responsibility and automobile insurance requirements in your state.

29. **Research** Contact a local insurance agent to obtain information on the costs of automobile insurance for young drivers.

30. **Math** Orien was involved in an automobile accident. The total damage to both vehicles was $3,228. The state in which Orien lives assigns a percentage of fault to each driver involved in an accident. Each driver must pay the percentage of damages based on the percentage of fault assigned. If Orien was assigned 35 percent of the fault in the accident, how much of the damages will he be required to pay? How much must the other driver pay?

31. **Law** Describe in writing or present in class various liability situations that would be covered by a person's homeowners or renters insurance policy.

32. **Accounting** The value of personal property declines due to time and use. Using newspaper advertisements and other information sources, compare the value of various new and used items. What observations can you make about depreciation?

33. **Math** If Ellen Williams owned a home worth $98,000 and wanted to be certain it was insured for at least 80 percent of its value, for how much should it be insured?

34. **Communication** Working with other students, write a script and present a short skit that communicates the need for life insurance in various family situations. Consider using simple props and costumes to help communicate your message.

35. **Research** Conduct library or online research about actions that might be taken to reduce the costs of health care.

36. **Visual Arts** Create a poster to educate and remind classmates about financial and social responsibilities that come with owning or driving a car or truck. Consider including concepts related to insurance, safety, and the environment.

37. **Math** Fran Markowitz had her annual medical examination. According to her insurance plan, she paid a portion of the costs of the services. The total costs and her share of each were as shown in the table.

SERVICE	TOTAL COST	PATIENT SHARE
Doctor visit	$80	$15 deductible
Lab work	$220	20% copay
Prescriptions	$120	$20 copay
Vision exam	$65	$10 deductible
New lenses	$180	5%

a. What was the total cost of the medical examination?

b. How much of the total cost did Fran pay?

c. What percent of the total cost did the insurance company pay?

Linking School and Community

Ask several people in your community about the types of insurance coverage they have. What coverage has been obtained through group policies? What coverage is through individual policies? What suggestions do they have for you when buying various types of insurance?

Decision-Making Strategies

Jane is a rather careless driver. She is a 17-year-old with a late-model compact car that looks sporty and is equipped for speed. Jane loves to drive fast and has a poor traffic record. In only one year, she has had two "fender bender" accidents and received two speeding tickets. Those who care about Jane have suggested that her reckless driving habits are putting her and others at risk.

38. What potential property and liability risks are associated with Jane's driving habits?

39. How is Jane's driving affecting her auto insurance premiums?

40. What suggestions do you have for Jane about her driving?

©sweetym/iStock

Web Workout

The Internet can be a valuable source of information about insurance. Select an insurance topic that you would like to learn more about. Find two websites that offer tips or advice related to the topic you have selected. Use critical thinking skills as you choose the websites and consider the value of the advice offered. For example, the advice from a consumer advocacy group might be different from the advice offered on an insurance company's website.

Think Critically

1. Prepare a summary of the information about your topic for each website. Be sure to clearly identify your topic and provide the URL for each website.

2. What are the similarities and differences of the advice presented on the two websites?

3. How might the information obtained be of value to you in the future?

Entrepreneurship Case Study

This event is composed of two parts: a written objective test and a decision-making problem, also known as a case study. Teams consisting of three participants will present and defend their solution to a business challenge.

Once you receive your business topic, you have 30 minutes to prepare your presentation and argument. Each participant will be given two index cards that may be used during the preparation and presentation to the judges. No reference materials or visual aids may be used during the preparation or performance.

Your team has 10 minutes to present the case and your solutions. One member should introduce the team and describe the case. All team members must participate in the presentation. Note cards may be used to explain decisions and rationales to the judges. After the presentation, five minutes are allowed for questions and answers.

Your case involves the rising cost of insurance. Health insurance is an important fringe benefit that you provide your employees. The cost of health insurance is rising at a rapid rate, and now your company is faced with determining strategies to continue to offer employee health insurance. Why is health insurance so important? How much can the company afford? How much should employees be asked to contribute? What are the alternatives to keeping the current coverage? Which fringe benefits are most important to the company and the employees?

Performance Indicators Evaluated

- Understand the importance of health insurance for employees.
- Prepare a concise plan for funding the rising costs of health insurance.
- Explain the sacrifices that must be made to fund health insurance.
- Explain the importance of shopping around for health insurance.

For more detailed information about performance indicators, go to the FBLA website.

Think Critically

1. Why is health insurance such an important fringe benefit?

2. What can a company do to encourage employees to follow healthy lifestyles?

3. What kinds of communication might be used to introduce changes in health insurance benefits to employees?

www.fbla-pbl.org

Using a Calculator and Computer Keypad

TYPES OF CALCULATORS

Many different models of calculators, both desktop and handheld, are available. All calculators have their own features and particular placement of operation keys. Therefore, it is necessary to refer to the user's manual for specific instructions and locations of the operating keys for the calculator being used.

HANDHELD CALCULATORS

There are many different kinds of handheld or pocket calculators. They come in all shapes and sizes with a variety of keys and functions. All calculators have number keys (0 to 9), operation keys (+, −, ×, ÷), and clear keys (C or CE). Most calculators have a percent key (%). Many handheld calculators come with a memory for storing numbers and calculation results. These are shown as M+, M−, and MR. Others, such as scientific calculators, have many more keys including x^2, $1/x$, and $\sqrt{\ }$.

It is important to read the user's manual to learn how your particular calculator works. Be sure to keep the manual in a safe place so you can refer to it for help in solving various mathematical problems.

© Cengage Learning 2012

DESKTOP CALCULATORS

Several operating switches on a desktop calculator must be engaged before it will produce the desired results.

The *decimal selector* sets the appropriate decimal places for numbers that will be entered. For example, if the decimal selector is set at 2, both the numbers entered and the answer will be displayed with two decimal places. If the decimal selector is set at F, the calculator automatically sets the needed decimal places. The F setting allows the answer to be unrounded and carried out to the maximum number of decimal places possible.

The *decimal rounding selector* rounds the answers. The down arrow position will drop any digits beyond the last digit desired. The up arrow position will drop any digits beyond the last digit desired and round the last digit up. In the 5/4 position, the calculator rounds the last desired digit up only when the following digit is 5 or greater. If the following digit is less than 5, the last desired digit remains unchanged.

The *GT* or *grand total switch* in the on position accumulates totals.

Ten-Key Touch System

Striking the numbers 0 to 9 on a desktop calculator or numeric keypad on a computer without looking at the keyboard is called the *touch system*. Using the touch system develops both speed and accuracy.

The 4, 5, and 6 keys are called the *home row*. If the right hand is used for the keyboard, the index finger is placed on the 4 key, the middle finger on the 5 key, and the ring finger on the 6 key. If the left hand is used, the ring finger is placed on the 4 key, the middle finger on the 5 key, and the index finger on the 6 key.

Place the fingers on the home row keys. Curve the fingers and keep the wrist straight. These keys may feel slightly concave or the 5 key may have a raised dot or bar. The differences in the home row allow the user to recognize the home row by touch rather than by sight.

Maintain the position of the fingers on the home row. The finger used to strike the 4 key will also strike the 7 key and the 1 key. Stretch the finger up to reach the 7 and stretch the finger down to reach the 1 key. Visualize the position of these keys.

Again, place the fingers on the home row. Stretch the finger that strikes the 5 key up to reach the 8 key and down to reach the 2 key. Likewise, stretch the finger that strikes the 6 key up to strike the 9 key and down to strike the 3 key. This same finger will stretch down again to hit the decimal point.

If the right hand is used, the thumb will be used to strike the 0 and 00 keys and the little finger to strike the addition key. If the left hand is used, the little finger will be used to strike the 0 and 00 keys and the thumb to strike the addition key.

Performing Mathematical Operations on Desktop Calculators

Mathematical operations can be performed on any calculator both quickly and efficiently. The basic operations of addition, subtraction, multiplication, and division are used frequently on a calculator. Here is how these operations are completed on a typical desktop calculator.

Addition Each number to be added is called an *addend*. The answer to an addition problem is called the *sum*.

Addition is performed by entering an addend and striking the addition key (+). All numbers are entered on a calculator in the exact order they are given. To enter the number 4,375.68, strike the 4, 3, 7, 5, decimal, 6, and 8 keys in that order, and then strike the addition key. Commas are not entered. Continue in this manner until all addends have been entered. To obtain the sum, strike the total key on the calculator.

Subtraction The top number or first number of a subtraction problem is called the *minuend*. The number to be subtracted from the minuend is called the *subtrahend*. The answer to a subtraction problem is called the *difference*.

Subtraction is performed by first entering the minuend and striking the addition key (+). The subtrahend is then entered, followed by the minus key (−), followed by the total key.

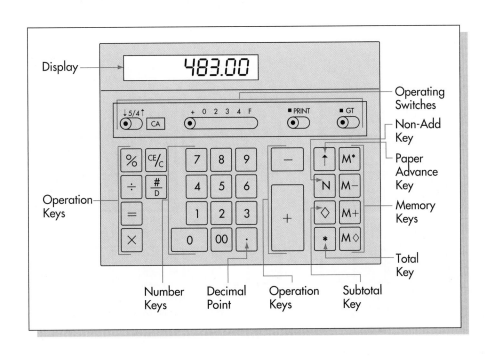

Multiplication The numbers being multiplied together are called *factors*. The answer to a multiplication problem is called the *product*.

Multiplication is performed by entering one factor, striking the multiplication key (×), entering the other factor, and then striking the equals key (=). The calculator will automatically multiply and give the product.

Division The number to be divided is called the *dividend*. The number the dividend will be divided by is called the *divisor*. The answer to a division problem is called the *quotient*.

Division is performed by entering the dividend and striking the division key (÷). The divisor is then entered, following by the equals key (=). The calculator will automatically divide and give the quotient.

Correcting Errors If an error is made while using a calculator, several methods of correction may be used. If an incorrect number has been entered and the addition key or equals key has not yet been struck, strike the clear entry (CE) key one time. This key will clear only the last number that was entered. However, if the clear entry key is depressed more than one time, the entire problem will be cleared on some calculators. If an incorrect number has been entered and the addition key has been struck, strike the minus key one time only. This will automatically subtract the last number added, thus removing it from the total.

the keys on the keypad are pressed. Most computers have a small light that indicates when the Num Lock key is on. When Num Lock is not on, the arrow, Home, Page Up, Page Down, End, Insert, and Delete keys can be used. Enhanced keyboards allow you to keep the Num Lock key activated at all times.

The asterisk (*) on the computer is used for multiplication. The slash key (/) is used for division.

Performing Mathematical Operations on Computers

Calculations with a computer keypad are performed in much the same way as on a desktop calculator. However, after the + key is depressed, the display usually shows the accumulated total. Therefore, the total key is not found on the computer keypad. Some computer programs will not calculate the total until the Enter key is pressed.

Subtraction is performed differently on many computer keypads. The minuend is entered, followed by the minus (−) key. Then the subtrahend is entered. Pressing either the + key, the = key, or the Enter key will display the difference.

Multiplication and division are performed the same way as on a desktop calculator. Keep in mind that computers use the * for multiplication and / for division.

COMPUTER KEYPADS

Most computers have a keypad on the right side of the keyboard called the *numeric keypad*. Even though there are several styles of computer keyboards, there are two basic layouts for the numeric keypad, as shown in the illustration on this page.

The *Num Lock* key, located above the 7 key, is an important feature of the numeric keypad. When the Num Lock key is turned on, numbers are entered when

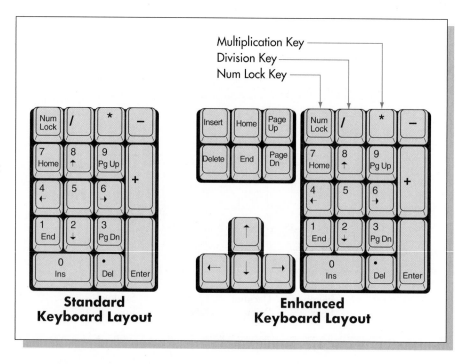

Standard Keyboard Layout

Enhanced Keyboard Layout

Multiplication Key
Division Key
Num Lock Key

Math Review

This arithmetic review will help you solve many of the end-of-chapter problems in this text as well as common arithmetic problems you may encounter in business.

ESTIMATING SUMS AND DIFFERENCES

In some situations, an **estimate** may be useful. Sometimes an exact answer is not needed, so you can estimate. Other times, estimation can be used to check mathematical calculations, especially when using a calculator.

Most people estimate by **rounding** numbers. Rounded numbers are easier to work with. Rounded numbers usually contain one or two nonzero digits followed by all zeros.

Examples

The U.S. Bureau of the Census estimated the 2009 population of Texas at 24,782,302.

- Round 24,782,302 to the nearest ten million.

  24,782,302 ————→ 20,000,000

  Because 4 is less than 5, round down to 20,000,000.

- Round 24,782,302 to the nearest million.

  24,782,302 ————→ 25,000,000

  Because 7 is larger than 5, round up to 25,000,000.

One new car has a list price of $25,209.50.

- Round $25,209.50 to the nearest thousand dollars.

  $25,209.50 ————→ $25,000

  Because 2 is less than 5, round down to $25,000.

- Round $25,209.50 to the nearest dollar.

  $25,209.50 ————→ $25,210

  Because 5 is greater than or equal to 5, round up to $25,210.

Examples

- Estimate the answer to 24,432 + 15,000.

24,432	Option 1:	Option 2:
+ 15,000	Round to the	Round to
	nearest ten	the nearest
	thousand.	thousand.
	20,000	24,000
	+20,000	+15,000
	40,000	39,000

- Estimate the answer to $32.23 − $17.54.

$32.23	Option 1:	Option 2:
−17.54	Round to the	Round to
	nearest ten	the nearest
	dollars.	dollar.
	$30.00	$32.00
	−20.00	−18.00
	$10.00	$14.00

- Estimate how much change you should get if you give the clerk $20 to pay for a bill of $6.98.

$20.00	Round to the
−6.98	nearest dollar.
	$20.00
	−7.00
	$13.00

MULTIPLYING NUMBERS ENDING IN ZEROS

When you multiply numbers that have *final zeros*, you can use this shortcut:

> Multiply the numbers by using only the digits that are not zeros. Then write as many final zeros in the product as there are zeros in the numbers being multiplied.

Examples

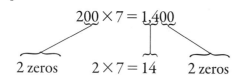

When multiplying larger numbers, use an imaginary line to separate zeros from the rest of the digits.

$36 \times 2,500$

```
 36 |
×25 |00  ◀──────┐
180 |           ├─ 2 zeros
 72 |           │
─────          ◀┘
900 |00         90,000  Answer
```

$3,600 \times 25,000$

```
 36 |00    ◀──── 2 zeros
×25 |000   ◀──── 3 zeros
180 |           2 + 3 = 5 zeros
 72 |
─────
900 |00000  ◀─ 5 zeros
     90,000,000  Answer
```

ESTIMATING PRODUCTS

There are various ways to estimate the answer to a multiplication problem.

- Option 1: Round both numbers **up**. Estimate will be greater than the actual product.

- Option 2: Round both numbers **down**. Estimate will be less than the actual product.

- Option 3: Round each number to the nearest unit with one nonzero digit. The estimate will be close to the actual product.

Examples

Estimate $82,543 \times 653$.
   Option 1: $90,000 \times 700 = 63,000,000$
   Option 2: $80,000 \times 600 = 48,000,000$
   Option 3: $80,000 \times 700 = 56,000,000$

DIVIDING WHOLE NUMBERS

Division is the opposite of multiplication. Division is shown in several ways. To show that 18 divided by 3 is 6, you may use any of these forms:

$$18 \div 3 = 6 \qquad \frac{18}{3} = 6 \qquad 3\overline{)18}^{\,6}$$

In each case, 18 is the dividend, 3 is the divisor, and 6 is the quotient.

$$\text{dividend} \div \text{divisor} = \text{quotient}$$

$$\frac{\text{dividend}}{\text{divisor}} = \text{quotient} \qquad \text{divisor}\overline{)\text{dividend}}^{\,\text{quotient}}$$

DIVIDING NUMBERS ENDING IN ZEROS

When you divide multiples of 10, there are several shortcuts you can use. Try either of the shortcuts discussed below:

- Write the numbers as a fraction. Cross out the same number of zeros in both the numerator and denominator of the fraction.

- Move the decimal point in the dividend to the left the same number of places as there are zeros in the divisor.

Examples

- $1,000,000,000 \div 10,000 = \dfrac{1,000,000,\cancel{000}}{10,\cancel{000}}$
$$= 100,000$$

- $1,000,000,000 \div 10,000$
$$= 100000.0000. \div 1.0000. = 100,000$$

ESTIMATING QUOTIENTS

One way to estimate the answer to a division problem is to start by rounding the divisor to a number with one nonzero number followed by all zeros. Then round the dividend to a multiple of that rounded divisor.

Examples

- Estimate $609 \div 19$.

  Round 19 to 20 and 609 to 600.

  $600 \div 20 = 30$

- Estimate $19{,}876{,}548 \div 650$.

  650 rounds up to 700.

  Multiples of 7 are 7, 14, 21, 28, 35, and so on. Use the closest multiple, 21.

  $$21{,}000{,}000 \div 700 = \frac{21000000}{700}$$
  $$= \frac{210000}{7} = 30{,}000$$

ADDING AND SUBTRACTING DECIMALS

When adding and subtracting decimals, align the decimal points. Then add or subtract as for whole numbers. Place the decimal point in the answer directly below where it is located in the computation. A number like 532 can also be written as 532. or 532.0. When writing decimals less than one, a zero is placed before the decimal point to show that there are no ones.

Examples

- Find the sum of 33.67, 72.84, 0.75, and 43.34.

  $$
  \begin{array}{r}
  33.67 \\
  72.84 \\
  0.75 \\
  + \; 43.34 \\
  \hline
  150.60
  \end{array}
  $$

- Find the sum of 320.5471, 1.4, and 82.352.

  $$
  \begin{array}{r}
  320.5471 \\
  1.4 \\
  + \; 82.352 \\
  \hline
  404.2991
  \end{array}
  $$

- Find the difference between 952.1 and 34.2517.

  $$
  \begin{array}{r}
  952.1 \\
  - \; 34.2517
  \end{array}
  $$

  Add 0s to the **right** after the decimal point.

  $$
  \begin{array}{r}
  952.\mathbf{1000} \\
  - \; 34.2517 \\
  \hline
  917.8483
  \end{array}
  $$

MULTIPLYING DECIMALS

When multiplying decimals, align the numbers at the right. Multiply as if you are multiplying whole numbers. To locate the decimal point in the answer, count all digits to the right of the decimal point in each number being multiplied and place the decimal point so there are that many digits after the decimal point in the answer.

Remember: Estimation can be used to check that your answer is reasonable and that you have correctly located the decimal point in the answer.

Examples

- Multiply 7.46 by 3.2.

  $$
  \begin{array}{r}
  7.46 \quad \longleftarrow \text{2 decimal places} \\
  \times \quad 3.2 \quad \longleftarrow \text{1 decimal place} \\
  \hline
  1492 \qquad 2 + 1 = 3 \\
  2238 \quad\; \\
  \hline
  23.872 \quad \longleftarrow \text{3 decimal places}
  \end{array}
  $$

- Multiply 0.193 by 0.2.

  $$
  \begin{array}{r}
  0.193 \quad \longleftarrow \text{3 decimal places} \\
  \times \quad 0.2 \quad \longleftarrow \; +\text{1 decimal place} \\
  \hline
  0.0386 \quad \longleftarrow \text{4 decimal places}
  \end{array}
  $$

  If needed to get enough decimal places, add a zero before the numeric answer but after the decimal point.

Remember that the zero before the decimal point shows that there are no ones in the product. The answer is less than one.

Estimate to check your answer.

$0.2 \times 0.2 = 0.04$

0.04 is close to 0.0386, so the answer is reasonable.

MULTIPLYING BY POWERS OF 10

Numbers like 100,000,000, 10,000, 100, 0.1, 0.01, and 0.00001 are powers of 10. To multiply by these, simply move the decimal point in the number being multiplied.

When multiplying by a power of 10 greater than one, move the decimal point to the right. The answer is larger than the number you started with.

When multiplying by a power of 10 less than one, move the decimal point to the left. The answer is smaller than the number you started with.

Examples

- Multiply 25,397 by ten thousand.

  $25,397 \times 10,000 = 253,970,000$

  Think: 25397.0000.

- Multiply 0.078 by one hundred.

  $0.078 \times 100 = 7.8$

  Think: = 0.07.8

- Multiply 192,536 by one ten-thousandth.

  $192,536 \times 0.0001 = 19.2536$

  Think: 19.2536.

- Multiply 0.293 by one hundredth.

  $0.293 \times 0.01 = 0.00293$

  Think: 0.00.293

SHORTCUTS WHEN MULTIPLYING WITH MONEY

Businesses price items at amounts such as 49¢, $5.98, or $99.95. A price of $99.95 seems less to the buyer than an even $100. When finding the cost of several such items, you can use a mathematical shortcut.

Examples

- Find the cost of 27 items at 98¢ each.

  normal multiplication

  $$
  \begin{array}{r}
  \$0.98 \\
  \times\ 27 \\
  \hline
  686 \\
  196 \\
  \hline
  \$26.46 \\
  \end{array}
  $$

Shortcut: Think: 98¢ = $1−2¢

$(27 \times \$1) - (27 \times 2¢) = \$27 - 54¢$

$54¢ = \$0.54$

$$
\begin{array}{r}
\$27.00 \\
-0.54 \\
\hline
\$26.46 \\
\end{array}
$$

- Find the cost of 32 items at $6.95 each.

  Shortcut: Think $6.95 = $7 − $0.05

  $(32 \times \$7) - (32 \times \$0.05)$

  $= \$224 - \$1.60 = \$222.40$

- Find the cost of 101 items at $9.99 each.

  Shortcut: Think $9.99 = $10 − $0.01

  $(101 \times \$10) - (101 \times \$0.01)$

  $= \$1,010 - \$1.01 = \$1,008.99$

  Alternate Shortcut:

  Think: 101 = 100 + 1

  $(100 \times \$9.99) + (1 \times \$9.99) =$

  $\$999 + \$9.99 = \$1,008.99$

MULTIPLYING A WHOLE NUMBER BY A FRACTION

To multiply a whole number by a fraction, multiply the whole number by the numerator (top number) and then divide that answer by the denominator (bottom number).

Examples

- $180 \times \dfrac{2}{3} = \dfrac{180 \times 2}{3} = \dfrac{360}{3} = 120$

- $500 \times \dfrac{3}{4} = \dfrac{500 \times 3}{4} = \dfrac{1500}{4} = 375$

- $768 \times \dfrac{1}{8} = \dfrac{768 \times 1}{8} = \dfrac{768}{8} = 96$

- $90 \times \dfrac{4}{5} = \dfrac{90 \times 4}{5} = \dfrac{360}{5} = 72$

Simplifying Fractions

When working with fractions, you can simplify the fractions by dividing the numerator and the denominator by a common factor (a number that will divide into both numbers evenly). Division by such common factors is called **canceling** or **cancellation**.

Examples

- Simplify $\dfrac{10}{12}$. **Think**: 2 is a factor of both 10 and 12.

$$5 \longleftarrow \qquad 10 \div 2 = 5$$
$$\dfrac{\cancel{10}}{\cancel{12}} = \dfrac{5}{6}$$
$$6 \longleftarrow \qquad 12 \div 2 = 6$$

- Simplify $\dfrac{75}{100}$. **Think**: Use 25 as a common factor.

$$3 \longleftarrow \qquad 75 \div 25 = 3$$
$$\dfrac{\cancel{75}}{\cancel{100}} = \dfrac{3}{4}$$
$$4 \longleftarrow \qquad 100 \div 25 = 4$$

- Simplify $\dfrac{280}{60}$. **Think**: Use 20 as a common factor.

$$14 \longleftarrow \qquad 280 \div 20 = 14$$
$$\dfrac{\cancel{280}}{\cancel{60}} = \dfrac{14}{3}$$
$$3 \longleftarrow \qquad 60 \div 20 = 3$$

Using Fractional Parts of $1.00 in Multiplying Mentally

While goods and services may be priced at any amount, prices are frequently expressed in fractional parts of $1, $10, or $100. For instance, 2 items for $1 is the same as $\dfrac{1}{2}$ of 100¢, or 50¢ per item, and 3 items for $10 is the same as $\dfrac{1}{3}$ of $10, or 3.33\dfrac{1}{3}$ per item.

You can also use fractional parts of $1.00 to find the cost of multiple items mentally.

24 items selling for $1.00 would cost $24.00

24 items at 50¢ each = $\dfrac{1}{2}$ of $24 or $12.00

24 items at 25¢ each = $\dfrac{1}{4}$ of $24 or $6.00

24 items at 33$\dfrac{1}{3}$¢ each = $\dfrac{1}{3}$ of $24 or $8

Many similar calculations can be made mentally. While there are many fractional parts of $1.00, a chart of those most commonly used follows.

FRACTION	PART OF $1.00
$\dfrac{1}{8}$	0.12\dfrac{1}{2}$
$\dfrac{1}{6}$	0.16\dfrac{2}{3}$
$\dfrac{1}{5}$	$0.20
$\dfrac{1}{4}$	$0.25
$\dfrac{1}{3}$	0.33\dfrac{1}{3}$
$\dfrac{3}{8}$	0.37\dfrac{1}{2}$
$\dfrac{2}{5}$	$0.40
$\dfrac{1}{2}$	$0.50
$\dfrac{3}{5}$	$0.60
$\dfrac{5}{8}$	0.62\dfrac{1}{2}$
$\dfrac{2}{3}$	0.66\dfrac{2}{3}$
$\dfrac{3}{4}$	$0.75
$\dfrac{4}{5}$	$0.80
$\dfrac{5}{6}$	0.83\dfrac{1}{3}$
$\dfrac{7}{8}$	0.87\dfrac{1}{2}$

Examples

- Find the cost of 16 items at 12$\dfrac{1}{2}$¢ each.

  Think: $12\dfrac{1}{2}$¢ $= \dfrac{1}{8}$ of $1

  $16 \times \dfrac{1}{8} = 2$

  16 items at 12$\dfrac{1}{2}$¢ each will cost $2.

- Find the cost of 33 items at 25¢ each.

  Think: 25¢ $= \dfrac{1}{4}$ of $1

  $33 \times \dfrac{1}{4} = \dfrac{33}{4}$, or $8\dfrac{1}{4}$

  33 items at 25¢ each will cost 8\dfrac{1}{4}$, or $8.25.

- Find the cost of 48 items at 75¢ each.

  Think: $75¢ = \frac{3}{4}$ of $1

  $$48 \times \frac{3}{4} = \frac{\overset{12}{\cancel{48}} \times 3}{\underset{1}{\cancel{4}}} = \frac{12 \times 3}{1} = \frac{36}{1} = 36$$

  48 items at 75¢ each is $36.

- Find the cost of 34 items at $62\frac{1}{2}$¢ each.

  Think: $62\frac{1}{2}¢ = \frac{5}{8}$ of $1

  $$34 \times \frac{5}{8} = \frac{\overset{17}{\cancel{34}} \times 5}{\underset{4}{\cancel{8}}} = \frac{17 \times 5}{4} = \frac{85}{4} = 21\frac{1}{4}$$

  34 items at $62\frac{1}{2}$¢ each is $21\frac{1}{4}$, or $21.25.

Fractional Parts of Other Amounts

You can use the table on the previous page to find fractional parts of multiples of 10.

Examples

- Find $\frac{5}{6}$ of $1,000.

  $$\frac{5}{6} \text{ of } \$1,000 = 1000 \times \frac{5}{6} \text{ of } \$1$$
  $$= 1000 \times \$0.83\frac{1}{3}$$
  $$= \$833.33\frac{1}{3}$$

  So, $\frac{5}{6}$ of $1,000 is $833.33.

  ($\frac{1}{3}$ dollar = $0.33\frac{1}{3}$, which is $0.33 when rounded to the nearest cent.)

- Find $\frac{3}{4}$ of $100.

  $$\frac{3}{4} \text{ of } \$100 = 100 \times \frac{3}{4} \text{ of } \$1$$
  $$= 100 \times \$0.75$$
  $$= \$75$$

  So, $\frac{3}{4}$ of $100 is $75.

- Find $\frac{7}{8}$ of $10.

  $$\frac{7}{8} \text{ of } \$10 = 10 \times \frac{7}{8} \text{ of } \$1$$
  $$= 10 \times \$0.875$$
  $$= \$8.75$$

  So, $\frac{7}{8}$ of $10 is $8.75.

Dividing Decimals

Division involving decimals is completed like division of whole numbers, except for dealing with the decimal point. When you divide a decimal by a whole number, you divide as for whole numbers and place the decimal point directly above the location of the decimal point in the dividend.

Examples

- Divide 12.944 by 8.

  ```
      1.618
  8) 12.944
      8
      ‾‾
      49
      48
      ‾‾
      14
       8
      ‾‾
      64
      64
      ‾‾
       0
  ```

  To check division, multiply your quotient by the divisor. The result should be the dividend.

  ```
      1.618
  ×       8
  ‾‾‾‾‾‾‾‾‾
   12.944  ✓
  ```

- Divide 37 by 4.

  ```
      9.25
  4) 37.00
     36
     ‾‾
      1 0
        8
      ‾‾‾
      20
      20
      ‾‾
       0
  ```

  Add zeros as needed.

  ```
  Check:    9.25
          ×    4
          ‾‾‾‾‾‾
          37.00  ✓
  ```

To divide by a decimal, move the decimal point to the right the same number of places in both the divisor and the dividend so you are dividing by a whole number.

Examples

- Divide 12.944 by 0.8.

    Think: 0.8 has one decimal place, move the decimal points in the divisor and the dividend right one place.

    $$
    \begin{array}{r}
    1\,6.18 \\
    0.8.\overline{)12.9.44} \\
    \underline{8} \\
    49 \\
    \underline{48} \\
    14 \\
    \underline{8} \\
    64 \\
    \underline{64} \\
    0
    \end{array}
    $$

- Divide 37 by 0.004.

    $$
    \begin{array}{r}
    9\,250. \\
    0.004.\overline{)37.000.} \\
    \underline{36} \\
    1\,0 \\
    \underline{8} \\
    20 \\
    \underline{20} \\
    0
    \end{array}
    $$

    Add zeros as needed.

    Remember: Estimation can be used to check that your answer is reasonable and that you have correctly located the decimal point in the answer.

Determining Percentages and Interest in Business

Two frequently used mathematical functions in business are determining percentages and calculating simple interest. If you are preparing for a business career you need to be comfortable with these calculations. Using a calculator simplifies the work but you also need to understand how the calculations are completed to check the accuracy of answers.

MEANING OF PERCENT

Percent is derived from two Latin words, "per centum," meaning "by the hundred." You can express a percent as a common fraction or a decimal fraction. When the percent involves a fraction, such as $7\frac{1}{4}\%$, change the mixed number to a decimal and move the decimal point two places to the left.

$$7\frac{1}{4}\% = 7.25\% = 0.725$$

Examples

- Write 19% as a fraction and a decimal.

  Percent means *per one hundred*, so write it as a fraction with a denominator of 100.

  $$19\% = \frac{19}{100} = 0.19$$

- Write 0.98 as a fraction and a percent.

  $$0.98 = \frac{98}{100} = 98\%$$

- Write $\frac{3}{100}$ as a decimal and a percent.

  $$\frac{3}{100} = 0.03 = 3\%$$

- Write $8\frac{1}{2}\%$ as a decimal and a fraction.

  $$8\frac{1}{2}\% = 8.5\% = 0.085 = \frac{85}{1000}$$

  Notice that 0.085 is 85 *thousandths*, so the fraction has a denominator of 1000.

FINDING A PERCENT OF A NUMBER

To find the percent of a number, change the percent to a fraction or decimal and multiply.

Examples

- Find 18% of 117,334.

  With fractions:

  $$117,334 \times \frac{18}{100} = \frac{117334 \times 18}{100}$$
  $$= \frac{2112012}{100} = 21,120.12$$

- Find 18% of 117,334.

  With decimals:

  $$\begin{array}{r} 117,334 \\ \times \quad 0.18 \\ \hline 938672 \\ 117334 \quad \\ \hline 21,120.12 \end{array}$$

- Find 10% of 359.

  $$359 \times 0.10 = 35.9$$

CALCULATING SIMPLE INTEREST

Interest is the fee paid to a lender for the use of borrowed money. Interest is always expressed as a percent. The *principal* is the amount of money borrowed. Simple interest (I) is calculated by multiplying the principal (P) times the annual interest rate (R) times the length of time in years (T). The formula is written as:

$$I = P \times R \times T$$

Examples

- Find the amount of simple interest due on $400 borrowed for 2 years at 8%.

  $I = \$400 \times 0.08 \times 2 = \$64$

- Find the amount of simple interest due on $600 borrowed for 1 month at 18%.

  Think: 1 month is $\frac{1}{12}$ of a year.

  $I = \$600 \times 0.18 \times \frac{1}{12} = \$9$

- Find the amount of simple interest due on $3,000 borrowed for 6 months at $9\frac{3}{4}$%.

  $I = \$3,000 \times 0.0975 \times \frac{6}{12} = \$146.25$

COMPOUND INTEREST

Compound interest is used more frequently than simple interest. Compound interest calculates interest not only on the amount borrowed but on the interest accumulated in prior periods. For example, a credit card may say that it charges 1.5% interest per month. It then seems that you are paying 12 × 1.5%, or 18% interest per year. However, in reality you are charged more than 18% interest per year because you are paying interest on the interest accumulated each month.

Example

Suppose that you owe $100 on your credit card and do not make any payments for one year. Assuming there are no late fees, your balance at the end of each month would be the amount shown in the last column of the following table. When the interest is calculated, all amounts are rounded up to the next cent. For example, the ending balance for May is $107.74225, which has been round up to $107.75.

FINDING WHAT PERCENT A NUMBER IS OF ANOTHER

To find what percent a number is of another, divide the one number (the part) by the other number (the whole). Then show the result as a percent.

Example

- 50 is what percent of 200?

  Divide 50 by 200.

  $$\begin{array}{r} 0.25 \\ 200\overline{)50.00} \\ \underline{40\,0} \\ 10\,00 \\ 10\,00 \end{array}$$

  $0.25 = 25\%$

  50 is 25% of 200.

MONTH	BEGINNING BALANCE	INTEREST (1.5% PER MONTH)	ENDING BALANCE
Jan.	$100.00	$1.50	$101.50
Feb.	$101.50	$1.53	$103.03
Mar.	$103.03	$1.55	$104.58
Apr.	$104.58	$1.57	$106.15
May	$106.15	$1.60	$107.75
June	$107.75	$1.62	$109.37
July	$109.37	$1.65	$111.02
Aug.	$111.02	$1.67	$112.69
Sept.	$112.69	$1.70	$114.39
Oct.	$114.39	$1.72	$116.11
Nov.	$116.11	$1.75	$117.86
Dec.	$117.86	$1.77	$119.63

After 12 months you must pay $19.63 in interest on $100. This means that the interest rate is really 19.63%, not 18%.

Using Measurements in Business

The metric system of measurement is used in business by most nations in the world. Because of extensive trade with other countries, the United States has taken some steps toward conversion to the metric system. Most U.S. companies have already made the change, so you should be familiar with the metric system.

There are some things about the metric system that may already be familiar to you. For example, if you have been to a track meet or swimming meet or have seen one on television, you know that distances can be measured in meters, not just in feet, yards, or miles. Food is often labeled to show amounts in grams as well as pounds or ounces. Meters, kilometers, and grams are examples of metric units of measurement.

BASIC METRIC UNITS

The basic metric units are the meter (length), the liter (capacity), and the gram (mass or weight). All measurements can be expressed in terms of these three basic units. However, prefixes are used with the basic units to avoid dealing with very large and very small numbers. The most common prefixes used in the metric system are:

Kilo- ⟶ one thousand times
Centi- ⟶ one one-hundredth of
Milli- ⟶ one one-thousandth of

Look at the chart below. The same prefixes are used for length, capacity, and mass or weight.

LENGTH
1 kilometer = 1000 meters
1 meter = 100 centimeters
1 meter = 1000 millimeters
1 centimeter = 10 millimeters
1 centimeter = 0.01 meter
1 millimeter = 0.001 meter

CAPACITY
1 kiloliter = 1000 liters
1 liter = 100 centiliters
1 liter = 1000 milliliters
1 centiliter = 10 milliliters
1 centiliter = 0.01 liter
1 milliliter = 0.001 liter

MASS (WEIGHT)
1 kilogram = 1000 grams
1 gram = 100 centigrams
1 gram = 1000 milligrams
1 centigram = 10 milligrams
1 centigram = 0.01 gram
1 milligram = 0.001 gram

The abbreviations, or symbols, for metric measurements are also uniform, changing only to show whether you are measuring length, capacity, or mass. This is illustrated in the chart at the top of the next page.

LENGTH	
kilometer	km
meter	m
centimeter	cm
millimeter	mm
CAPACITY	
kiloliter	kL
liter	L
centiliter	cL
milliliter	mL
MASS (WEIGHT)	
kilogram	kg
gram	g
centigram	cg
milligram	mg

CONVERTING UNITS WITHIN THE METRIC SYSTEM

Using the tables above, you can see that one kilometer is 1000 times as long as a meter and that one millimeter is one-thousandth of a meter. Because the relationships between the prefixes are multiples of 10, you can change from one unit to another by multiplying by a power of ten, which can be done by moving the decimal point.

Examples

- Change 0.36 meters to centimeters.

  Think: 1 meter = 100 centimeters

  To get from 1 to 100, move the decimal point to the right 2 spaces.   0.36.

  So 0.36 meters = 36 centimeters

- Change 5000 grams to kilograms.

  Think: 1000 grams = 1 kilogram

  To get from 1000 to 1, move the decimal point to the left 3 spaces.   5.000.

  So 5000 grams = 5 kilograms

- Change 4.5 liters to milliliters.

  Think: 1 liter = 1000 milliliters

  To get from 1 to 1000, move the decimal point to the right 3 spaces.

4.500. Notice how zeros are added so the decimal can be moved the needed number of spaces to the right.

So 4.5 liters = 4500 milliliters

- Change 0.86 millimeters to centimeters.

  Think: 10 millimeters = 1 centimeter

  To get from 10 to 1, move the decimal point to the left 1 space.

0.0.86 Notice that a zero is added so the decimal can be moved the needed number of spaces to the left.

So 0.86 millimeters = 0.086 centimeters

CUSTOMARY MEASUREMENT

In the United States feet, pounds, and gallons are still common units of measure. Below is a list of common customary measurements and their equivalents.

LENGTH
1 foot = 12 inches
1 yard = 3 feet
1,760 yards = 1 mile
5,280 feet = 1 mile
CAPACITY
1 pint = 2 cups
1 quart = 2 pints
1 gallon = 4 quarts
WEIGHT
1 pound = 16 ounces
1 ton = 2,000 pounds

MEASURING TEMPERATURE

Thermometers that measure temperature are marked in degrees Celsius (°C) or in degrees Fahrenheit (°F). The Celsius scale is a metric scale. The Fahrenheit scale is nonmetric.

CELSIUS	EVENT	FAHRENHEIT
100°C	Water boils	212°F
37°C	Normal body temperature	98.6°F
0°C	Water freezes	32°F

CONVERTING BETWEEN SYSTEMS

Once in a while it may be necessary to convert from the metric system to the customary system or vice versa. You can use the charts on this page when you need to change metric measurements to customary or vice versa.

Examples

- You are in a 440-yard race. How many meters long is the race?

  To change from yards to meters, multiply by 0.91.

  $440 \times 0.91 = 400.4$

  The race is 400.4 meters long.

- A store shelf has a weight limit of 250 kilograms. What is that limit in pounds?

  To change kilograms to pounds, multiply by 2.20.

  $250 \times 2.20 = 550$

  The weight limit is 550 pounds.

- It is 10°C outside. What is the temperature in degrees Fahrenheit?

  To change from °C to °F, multiply by 9, divide by 5, then add 32.

  $10 \times 9 = 90; 90 \div 5 = 18; 18 + 32 = 50$

  The temperature is 50°F.

- It is 95°F outside. What is the temperature in degrees Celsius?

  To change from °F to °C, subtract 32, multiply by 5, then divide by 9.

  $95 - 32 = 63; 63 \times 5 = 315; 315 \div 9 = 35$

  The temperature is 35°C.

LENGTH/DISTANCE

When you know:	You can find:	If you multiply by:
inches	millimeters	25.40
inches	centimeters	2.54
feet	meters	0.305
yards	meters	0.91
miles	kilometers	1.61
millimeters	inches	0.04
centimeters	inches	0.39
meters	inches	39.37
meters	feet	3.28
meters	yards	1.09
kilometers	miles	0.62

WEIGHT/MASS

When you know:	You can find:	If you multiply by:
ounces	grams	28.35
pounds	kilograms	0.45
grams	ounces	0.035
kilograms	pounds	2.20

CAPACITY/VOLUME

When you know:	You can find:	If you multiply by:
pints	liters	0.47
quarts	liters	0.95
gallons	liters	3.78
liters	pints	2.11
liters	quarts	1.06
liters	gallons	0.26

TEMPERATURE

When you know:	You can find:	If you:
°F (degrees Fahrenheit)	°C (degrees Celsius)	subtract 32, multiply by 5, then divide by 9
°C (degrees Celsius)	°F (degrees Fahrenheit)	multiply by 9, divide by 5, then add 32

Glossary

A

Ability the quality of being able to perform a mental or physical task.

Absolute advantage a situation where a country can produce a good or service at a lower cost than other countries.

Accountability taking responsibility for the results achieved.

Accounts payable record a financial document that identifies the companies from which credit purchases were made and the amount purchased, paid, and owed.

Accounts receivable record a financial document that identifies customers that made purchases using credit and the status of each account.

Adjustable-rate mortgage (ARM) a mortgage in which the interest rate is raised or lowered from time to time depending on the current interest rate being charged by lenders.

Advertising any paid form of communication through mass media directed at identified consumers to provide information and influence their actions.

Agricultural products crops and animals raised by farmers.

AI See **Artificial intelligence**

Allowance the amount of money you plan to use for a certain budget category.

All-risk policy See **Special form**

Annual percentage rate (APR) the percentage cost of credit on a yearly basis.

Annual percentage yield (APY) the percentage rate equal to the total amount of interest that a $100 deposit would earn based on a 365-day period.

Annuity an amount of money an insurance company pays (usually monthly) to a person who has previously deposited money with the company.

Antitrust laws laws that prevent monopolies and promote competition and fairness.

Application form a document used by employers that asks for information related to employment. It gives the employer standard information about each job applicant.

Application software computer programs that perform specific tasks such as word processing, database management, or accounting.

Applied research marketing research that studies existing products to develop design improvements or new product uses.

Appraiser someone trained to estimate the value of property and who can give an official report on the value.

Appreciation a general increase in the value of property that occurs over time.

APR See **Annual percentage rate**

APY See **Annual percentage yield**

Arbitration a third-party action resulting in a decision that is legally binding.

ARM See **Adjustable-rate mortgage**

Articles of incorporation a written legal document that defines ownership and operating procedures and conditions for the business.

Artificial intelligence (AI) software that enables computers to reason, learn, and make decisions using logical methods similar to the methods humans use.

Assessed value the amount that your local government determines your property to be worth for tax purposes.

Asset record a financial document used to name the buildings and equipment owned by the business, their original and current value, and the amount owed if money was borrowed to purchase the assets.

Assets what a company owns; anything of value owned by a business.

Assigned risk plan a plan in which every automobile insurance company in the state is assigned a certain number of high-risk drivers based on the amount of insurance each company sells.

Authority the right to make decisions about how responsibilities should be accomplished.

Automatic bill payment a service by which a bank deducts a payment from your account and transfers the funds to the appropriate companies. This service requires a bank customer to authorize preset amounts of monthly expenses.

Automatic teller machine a computerized device that allows customers to make bank transactions including withdrawing cash.

B

Baby boomers people born between 1946 and 1964.

Balance of payments the difference between the amount of money that comes into a country and the amount that goes out of a country.

Balance of trade   the difference between a country's total exports and total imports.

Balance sheet   a report that lists a company's assets, liabilities, and owner's equity at a specific point in time.

Bank money order   a form sold by a bank stating that money is to be paid to a specific person or business.

Bank reconciliation   the document created to show how your own record of your checking account and the bank's record of your account were brought into agreement.

Bankruptcy   the legal process of reducing or eliminating an amount owed.

Bank statement   a report on the status of a bank account.

Base plus incentive   a compensation system which combines a wage or salary with an additional amount based on the employee's performance.

Basic economic problem   the mismatch of unlimited wants and needs and limited economic resources.

Basic health coverage   protection provided by regular medical, hospital, and surgical insurance.

Basic product   the simplest form of a product. It is not unique and is usually available from several companies.

Behavioral interviewing   an interview that evaluates an applicant's on-the-job potential. Questions typically begin with "describe" or "tell me about."

Benchmark   the best practices among all competitors.

Beneficiary   the person named in an insurance policy to receive the insurance benefits.

Benefits   compensation in forms other than direct payment.

Blank endorsement   an endorsement of a check that consists of only the endorser's name.

Blue-collar workers   workers who are involved in physical work, including the operation of machinery and equipment or other production activities.

Board of directors   the people who make the major policy and financial decisions for the business.

Bodily injury liability   insurance that protects a driver from claims resulting from injuries or deaths for which the insured is at fault.

Bond   a certificate representing a promise to pay a definite amount of money at a stated interest rate on a specified due date.

Brand   a name given to a product or service to distinguish it from other similar and competitive items.

Brand name   a unique identification for a company's products.

Budget   detailed plans for the financial needs of individuals, families, and businesses.

Budget charge account   a credit agreement that requires a customer to make payments of a fixed amount over several months.

Budget deficit   a financial situation that occurs when a government spends more than it takes in.

Budget surplus   a financial situation that occurs when a government spends less than it takes in.

Budget variance   any difference between actual spending and budgeted amounts.

Business consumers   persons, companies, and organizations that buy products for the operation of a business, for incorporation into other products and services, or for resale to their customers.

Business cycle   the movement of the economy from one condition to another and back again. It has four phases including prosperity, recession, depression, and recovery.

Business ethics   rules about how businesses and their employees ought to behave.

Business interruption insurance   compensation for ongoing business expenses that occur if a business has a temporary shutdown due to a fire, flood, or other major problem.

Business plan   a written description of the business idea and how it will be carried out, including all major business activities.

Buying motives   the reasons consumers decide what products and services to purchase.

C

CAD   See **Computer-aided design**

Cafeteria plan   an employee benefit program that allocates a certain amount of money to each employee that can be spent on benefits.

CAI   See **Computer-assisted instruction**

Capacity   a person's ability to pay a debt when it is due.

Capital   the value of the borrower's possessions, including money and the property owned.

Capital gain   the result of a stock increasing in value and then being sold for more than its original cost.

Capitalism   the private ownership of economic resources by individuals rather than by the government.

Capital loss   the result of an investment being sold for less than its original cost.

Capital projects   spending by businesses for items such as land, buildings, equipment, and new products.

Capital resources   products and money used to produce goods and services.

Career   a goal for work that is fulfilled through an occupation or series of occupations.

Career planning   the process of studying careers, assessing yourself in terms of careers, and making decisions about a future career.

Career portfolio   tangible evidence of your ability and skills.

Cash budget   an estimate of the actual money received and paid out for a specific period of time.

Cash card   See **Debit card**

Cash flow statement   a financial statement that reports net wages and other income along with spending for a period, such as for a month.

Cashier's check   a check that a bank draws on its own funds.

Cash inflow   the money you have available to spend as a result of working or from other income, such as interest earned on your savings.

Cash machine   See **Automated teller machine**

Cash outflow   your expenditures including amounts spent for food, clothing, transportation, and other living costs.

Cash record   a financial document that lists all cash received and spent by the business.

Cash value   the amount of money that the insurance company will pay if the policyholder decides the insurance is no longer needed.

Cell   the location where a column and row intersect.

Central processing unit (CPU)   the control center of the computer.

Certificate of deposit   a savings instrument that requires a minimum deposit for a specified period of time.

Certificate of deposit rate   the rate for six-month time deposits at savings institutions.

Certified check   a personal check for which a bank has guaranteed payment.

Channel members   businesses that take part in a channel of distribution.

Channel of distribution   the route a product follows and the businesses involved in moving a product from the producer to the final consumer.

Character   a person's honesty and willingness to pay a debt when it is due.

Check cards   See **Debit cards**

Check register   a separate book form on which the depositor keeps a record of checking account activities.

Check stub   a form attached to the check by a perforated line.

Civil case   a legal action in which a plaintiff asks the court to take action against a defendant.

Claim   a policyholder's request for payment for a loss that the insurance policy covers.

Class action suit   a legal action by one party on behalf of a group of people who all have the same grievance.

Clearance sale   sale used to clear merchandise that stores no longer wish to carry.

Clearing   paying of checks among different banks in different cities.

Cloud computing   using software, resources, and work files that are maintained on a common server.

Co-branded credit card   a company credit card that is affiliated with a bank card company.

Code of ethics   a set of rules for guiding the action of employees or members of an organization.

Coinsurance   the sharing of expenses by the policyholder and the insurance company.

Collaboration software (groupware)   software that provides real-time communications capabilities by voice, text, and video.

Collateral   property that is offered as security for some loan agreements.

Collectibles   items of personal interest to collectors that can increase in value in the future.

Collective bargaining   formal negotiation between members of unions and management to resolve issues.

Collision coverage   insurance that protects a car owner against financial loss resulting from a collision with another car or object.

Command economy   an economy in which resources are owned and controlled by the government.

Commercial bank   a bank that offers a full range of financial services.

Commercial property insurance   coverage of property losses resulting from fire, storms, accidents, theft, and vandalism.

Commission   the amount of money an employee is paid based on a percentage of sales for which he or she is responsible; the fee stockbrokers charge for their services.

Commodities   grain, livestock, and precious metals.

Common market (economic community)   a market in which members do away with duties and other trade barriers.

Common stock   stock that represents general ownership in a corporation and a right to share in its profits.

Communication channel   the way the information being communicated from a sender is being transmitted to the receiver.

Comparative advantage a situation in which a country specializes in the production of a good or service at which it is relatively more efficient.

Compensation the amount of money paid to an employee for work performed, including salary and wages.

Compensation and benefits the human resource activity involving planning and managing payroll, personnel records, and benefits programs.

Competition the rivalry among businesses to sell their goods and services.

Competitors businesses offering very similar products to the same customers.

Compound interest the interest computed on the amount saved plus the interest previously earned.

Comprehensive coverage insurance that protects the insured against almost all damage losses except those caused from a collision or rollover.

Comprehensive form homeowners insurance that expands special form policy to include replacement cost coverage for home contents and buildings.

Comprehensive medical policy a policy that combines the features of hospital, surgical, regular, and major medical insurance.

Computer-aided design (CAD) the use of technology to create product styles and designs.

Computer-assisted instruction (CAI) the use of computers to help people learn or improve skills at their own pace.

Computer language a system of letters, words, numbers, and symbols used to communicate with a computer.

Computer literacy the ability to use computers to process information or solve problems.

Computer network a group of computers such as those in businesses and schools that are linked together so users can share hardware, software, and data.

Computer system all functional components of a computer, including an input device, processing unit, memory and storage, and an output device.

Computer virus a program code hidden in a system that can later do damage to software or stored data.

Conditions of work clauses related to employee well-being while on the job that are often included in labor contracts and company policy manuals.

Condominium (condo) an individually owned housing unit in an apartment-like complex.

Conflict of interest a situation in which an action by a company or individual results in an unfair benefit.

Conservation saving scarce natural resources.

Consumer a person who buys and uses goods and services.

Consumer decision-making process the specific sequence of steps consumers follow to make a purchase.

Consumer movement consumers united to demand fair treatment from businesses and to fight against unfair business practices.

Contingent worker one who has no explicit or implicit contract for long-term employment.

Continuous process improvement (CPI) a way to increase the quality of work by reducing errors, inefficiencies, and waste. Rather than waiting for a problem to occur, processes are continuously reviewed with the goal of finding ways to improve them.

Continuous processing changing the form of raw materials into a specific product useable for consumption or for further manufacturing by constantly moving the materials through specially designed equipment.

Contract an agreement to exchange goods or services for something of value, usually money.

Controllable risk a risk that you can reduce or eliminate by actions you take.

Controlling determines to what extent the business is accomplishing the goals it set out to reach in the planning stage.

Convenience stores small stores that emphasize the sale of food items, an accessible location, and long operating hours.

Cooperative a business formed to market products produced by members or to purchase products needed by the members. It is owned by members, serves their needs, and is managed in their interest.

Copyright the protection of the creative work of authors, composers, and artists.

Core values the important principles that guide decisions and actions in the company.

Corporate bond rate the cost of borrowing for large U.S. corporations.

Corporate bonds bonds issued by corporations.

Corporate bylaws the operating procedures for the corporation.

Corporation a separate legal entity formed by documents filed with a state. It is owned by one or more shareholders and managed by a board of directors.

Cosigner the party responsible for payment of a note if the borrower does not pay as promised.

Cost containment keeping costs down.

Counterfeiting illegal uses of intellectual property, patents, trademarks, and copyrights.

Cover letter a letter expressing your interest in a specific job.

Credit the privilege of using someone else's money for a period of time.

Credit application a form on which you provide information needed by a lender to make a decision about granting credit.

Credit bureau a company that gathers information on credit users and sells that information in the form of credit reports to businesses offering credit.

Credit counselor a person who suggests actions to reduce spending and eliminate credit difficulties.

Credit limit a maximum amount that may be owed at one time.

Creditor one who sells on credit or makes a loan; the purchaser of a corporate or government bond.

Credit rating a person's reputation for paying bills on time.

Credit references businesses or individuals who are able and willing to provide information about your creditworthiness.

Credit report a document that shows the debts a person owes, how often credit is used, and whether he or she pays debts on time.

Credit union a user-owned, not-for-profit, cooperative financial institution.

Criminal case a legal action brought for violations of criminal laws.

Culture the accepted behaviors, customs, and values of a society.

Current assets cash and those items that can be readily converted to cash such as inventory and accounts receivable.

Current income income for current living expenses.

Current liabilities amounts owed by the business that will be paid within a year.

Current ratio current assets compared to the current liabilities.

Custom manufacturing building a specific and unique product to meet the needs of one customer.

D

Database an organized collection of information with data items related to one another in some way.

Database marketing using information about customers to increase sales.

Database software software that allows you to maintain, analyze, and combine a collection of information.

Debit card (cash card) a bank-issued card used for ATM transactions.

Debt collection agency a company that attempts to obtain money that is past due.

Debt repayment plan an agreement between a creditor and a debtor to reduce payments to a more manageable level and still pay off the debt.

Debt to equity ratio the company's liabilities divided by the owners' equity.

Debtor anyone who buys on credit or receives a loan.

Decoding interpreting information for understanding.

Decreasing term insurance the amount of protection gradually becomes smaller, but premiums remain the same while the insurance is in effect.

Deductible the amount the insured must pay before the insurance company pays a claim.

Deficit a financial situation in which actual spending is greater than planned spending.

Deflation a decrease in the general level of prices.

Demand the quantity of a good or service that consumers are willing and able to buy.

Demand curve the graphic view of the demand for a product or service. The demand curve for a product, for example, illustrates the relationship between the price of the product and the quantity demanded by consumers.

Department stores stores that have an extensive product line and emphasize service.

Dependent a person who must rely on another for financial support.

Depository institution a financial institution that accepts deposits from individuals and businesses and uses the money to finance its business.

Depreciation the decrease in value of a property as it becomes old and gradually wears out.

Depreciation record a financial document used to identify the amount assets have decreased in value due to their age and use.

Depression the phase of the business cycle that is marked by a prolonged period of high unemployment, weak consumer sales, and business failures.

Direct channel of distribution a channel in which products move from the producer straight to the consumer with no other organizations participating.

Direct deposit the process by which funds are deposited electronically and available automatically for your use.

Disability income insurance insurance that replaces income that is lost when the insured cannot work because of an illness or injury.

Discharge a type of termination that ends employment due to inappropriate work behavior.

Discount broker a stockbroker who places orders and offers limited research and other services.

Discounting the process in which savings bonds pay interest.

Discount rate the rate financial institutions are charged to borrow funds from the Federal Reserve banks.

Discount stores stores that emphasize lower prices on their products.

Discrepancies differences between actual and budgeted performance.

Displaced workers workers who are unemployed because of changing job conditions.

Display a device used by retailers to exhibit a product at the point of sale.

Distribution the locations and methods used to make a product or service available to the target market; determining the best ways for customers to locate, obtain, and use the products and services of an organization.

Diversity the comprehensive inclusion of people with differences in personal characteristics and attributes.

Dividends payments of profits in cash to stockholders.

Domestic business the making, buying, and selling of goods and services within a country.

Down payment a payment of part of the purchase price that is made as part of a credit agreement.

Downsizing a planned reduction in the number of employees needed in a firm in order to reduce costs and make the business more efficient.

Drawee the bank or other financial institution that pays the check.

Drawer the owner of the account who signs the check.

E

Earned income money from wages, salary, commission, fees, tips, and bonuses.

Earnings report a report, usually included with the employee's paycheck, which includes information for the current pay period as well as the cumulative amounts for the year.

E-commerce conducting business transactions using the Internet or other technology.

Economic community See **Common market**

Economic decision-making the process of choosing which needs and wants will be satisfied.

Economic resources things available to be used to produce goods and services.

Economic risk a risk that can result in financial loss, including personal risk, property risk, and liability risk.

Economic system the method a country uses to answer the three economic questions.

Effective communication the exchange of information so there is common understanding by all participants.

EFT See **Electronic funds transfer**

Electronic funds transfer (EFT) the use of computers and other technology for banking activities, including the use of automated teller machines (ATM), point-of-sale transactions, direct deposit, and automatic bill payment.

Emerging markets places where consumer incomes and buying power are increasing because of economic expansion.

Embargo an action imposed by the government to stop the export or import of a product completely.

Emotional buying motives reasons consumers decide what products and services to purchase based on feelings, beliefs, and attitudes.

Employee benefits compensation in forms other than direct payment such as vacation time, insurance coverage, and retirement programs.

Employee relations responsible for maintaining a safe, healthy, and productive work environment for all employees.

Employment interview a two-way conversation in which the interviewer learns about you and you learn about the job and the company.

Encoding preparing the information to be communicated.

Endorsement written evidence that a person received payment or transferred the right to receive payment to someone else.

Entrepreneur someone who takes a risk in starting a business to earn a profit.

Entrepreneurship the process of starting, organizing, managing, and assuming the responsibility for a business.

Equity stock ownership; the difference between the price at which you could currently sell your house and the amount owed on the mortgage.

Estate planning planning for the accumulation and management of property during one's lifetime and the distribution of one's property at death.

Ethical business practices practices that ensure the appropriate standards of conduct are observed in a company's relationships with everyone who is a part of the business or affected by the business' activities.

Ethics principles of morality or rules of conduct.

Exchange rate the value of a currency in one country compared with the value in another.

Executives top-level managers with responsibilities for the direction and success of the entire business.

Exemption a tax deduction for the taxpayer, a spouse, and each dependent.

Exit interview an interview in which your employer asks questions about your work upon your leaving the company.

Expenses costs of operating a business.

Experienced-based resume a resume in which experiences are listed in order of work history.

Experiment a method of marketing research which presents two carefully controlled alternatives to subjects in order to determine which is preferred or has better results.

Expert influence influence that arises when group members recognize that the leader has special expertise in the area.

Expert systems computer programs that help people solve technical problems.

Exports goods and services sold to other countries.

Express money order a form issued by various organizations including traveler's check companies, travel agencies, and many supermarkets, pharmacies, and convenience stores.

Express warranty a warranty that is made orally or in writing and promises a specific quality of performance.

External communication communication that occurs between those inside the organization and outsiders such as customers, suppliers, and other businesses.

External data sources input provided to the management information system from outside an organization, such as financial institutions, government agencies, and customers.

Extraction and cultivation a form of production in which products are obtained from nature or grown using natural resources.

Extractor a business that takes resources from nature for direct consumption or for use in developing other products.

F

Face value the amount of insurance coverage that was originally purchased and that will be paid upon the death of the insured.

Factors of production economic resources, including natural resources, human resources, and capital resources.

Family leave policy a policy that allows employees to take a leave of absence for the birth or adoption of a child, to care for a sick family member, or for other personal emergencies.

Farmers people who cultivate land and use other natural resources to grow crops and raise livestock for consumption.

Federal Deposit Insurance Corporation (FDIC) the federal agency that helps to regulate banks and other financial institutions.

Federal Reserve System (Fed) a system set up by the federal government to supervise and regulate member banks and to help banks serve the public efficiently. All national banks are required to join the Federal Reserve System, and state banks may join.

Feedback a response to the sender from the receiver.

Final consumers persons who buy products and services mostly for their own use.

Finance charge the total dollar cost of credit including interest and all other charges.

Financial analysis budgeting for marketing activities, obtaining the necessary funds needed for operations, and providing financial assistance to customers so they can purchase the business' products and services.

Financial performance ratios comparisons of a company's financial elements that indicate how well the business is performing.

Financial plan a report that summarizes your current financial condition, acknowledges your financial needs, and sets a direction for your future financial activities.

Financial records financial documents that are used to record and analyze the financial performance of a business.

Financial responsibility law a law that protects the public from financial loss caused by drivers.

Financial statements reports that sum up the financial performance of a business.

Fixed expenses costs that occur on a regular basis and are for the same amount each time.

Fixed-rate mortgage interest rates on mortgages that are set for the term of the loan.

Flexspace a program that allows some employees to complete part or all of their work away from the business site.

Flextime a program that allows employees some choice in how their work days and work hours are arranged.

Focus group a marketing research study that gathers the ideas, experiences, and opinions from a small number of consumers who take part in a group discussion.

Foreign debt the amount a country owes to other countries.

Foreign exchange market banks that buy and sell different currencies.

Foreign trade See **International business**

Formal communications communication methods that have been established and approved by the organization.

Formal influence power based on a leader's position within the formal structure.

Franchise a written contract granting permission to operate a business to sell products and services in a set way.

Franchisee the company purchasing the rights to run the business.

Franchiser the company that owns the product or service and grants the rights to another business.

Fraud deception of consumers by providing false information in an effort to make a sale.

Freedom of choice   the freedom to make decisions independently while accepting the consequences of those decisions.

Free-trade agreement   an agreement between member countries to remove duties and trade barriers on products traded among them.

Free-trade zone   a selected area where products can be imported duty-free and then stored, assembled, and/or used in manufacturing.

Full endorsement (special endorsement)   an endorsement that allows you to transfer a check to another person.

Full-service broker   a broker who provides information about securities you may want to buy. They work for brokerage houses with large research staffs.

Full-time employee   one who regularly works a schedule of 30 hours or more a week.

Futures contract   agreement to buy or sell an amount of a commodity at a specified price in the future; contract involving the buying and selling of currencies and financial instruments.

G

GDP per capita   the output per person, calculated by dividing gross domestic product (GDP) by the total production.

GDP   See **Gross domestic product**

Generic products   unbranded items at reduced prices because they do not require advertising and fancy packaging.

Glass ceiling   an artificial limit placed on minority groups moving into positions of authority and decision-making.

Global strategy   a strategy that uses the same product and marketing strategy worldwide.

Goal   a precise statement of results the business expects to achieve.

Goods   things you can see and touch; they are products you can purchase to meet your wants and needs.

Goods-producing industries   businesses that produce or manufacture products used by other businesses or purchased by final consumers.

Green management   facilities management using the practice of protecting the environment through conservation of natural resources, wise energy use, and reduction of emissions, waste, and pollution.

Gross domestic product (GDP)   the total value of all final goods and services produced in a country during one year.

Gross margin   the difference between the selling price and the product costs.

Group insurance   health insurance coverage offered to a large number of employees and their family members.

Group life insurance   an insurance policy that covers a group of people. The group acts as single unit in buying the insurance.

Guarantee   a promise by the manufacturer or dealer, usually in writing, that a product is of a certain quality.

H

Hardware   the physical elements of a computer system.

Health insurance   protection against the high costs of individual health care. It covers routine costs of medical care and may also cover costs of hospitalization or other needed medical treatments.

Health maintenance organization (HMO)   a managed care plan whose members are entitled to a wide range of prepaid health care services, including hospitalization.

Heterogeneous   characterized by the differences in the type and quality of service provided.

HMO   See **Health maintenance organization**

Homeowners policy   a package-type insurance policy designed to insure homes and property.

Horizontal communications   communications that move across the organization at the same level—employee to employee or manager to manager.

Hospital insurance   insurance that usually pays most or all hospital charges if an illness or injury requires the insured to be hospitalized.

Host country   the country in which the multinational company (MNC) places business activities.

Human relations   the way people get along with each other.

Human resources   people producing goods and services; people who work for a business.

I

I bond   bond that pays an interest rate that is lower than the rate of other savings bonds, but it is a variable rate that increases with inflation.

Identity influence   influence that stems from the personal trust and respect members have for the leader.

Identity theft   stealing information about a person from online sources to obtain money.

Implementing   a manager's effort to direct and lead people to accomplish the planned work of the organization.

Implied warranty   a guarantee imposed by law and is understood to apply even though it has not been written or stated.

Imports   goods and services bought from other countries.

Improvement   a designed change that increases the usefulness of a product, service, or process.

Impulse buying   buying quickly without much thought.

Incentive systems   compensation systems connected to the quality or quantity of an employee's performance.

Income statement   a report of revenue, expenses, and net income or loss from operations for a specific period.

Income tax   taxes levied on the income of individuals.

Indirect channel of distribution   a channel in which products move from the producer to the consumer through one or more other businesses.

Individual retirement account (IRA)   a tax-sheltered retirement plan in which people can annually invest earnings up to a certain amount.

Inflation   an increase in the general level of prices.

Influence   power enabling a person to affect the actions of others.

Informal communications   common but unofficial ways that information moves in an organization.

Informal influence   power resulting from the personal characteristics of a leader rather than the formal structure of an organization.

Informational interview   a planned discussion with a worker who is willing to help you find out about the work that a person does, the preparation needed for that career, and the person's feelings about the career.

Information management   using technology to access and exchange information to complete the work of an organization.

Infrastructure   a factor that supports international trade in industrialized countries, including a nation's transportation, communication, and utility systems.

Innovation   an invention or creation that is brand new.

Inseparable   something that is consumed at the same time it is produced.

Installment loan   a loan in which you agree to make monthly payments in specific amounts over a period of time.

Installments   a specified amount a borrower agrees to repay for a loan.

Installment sales credit   a type of credit contract issued by the seller that requires periodic payments at specified times. The seller adds finance charges to the cost of the items purchased.

Insurable interest   a financial benefit from an insured person's continued life.

Insurable risk   when a large number of people face a given risk and the cost of the possible losses can be predicted.

Insurance   a form of risk protection that exchanges the uncertainty of a possible large financial loss for a certain smaller payment.

Insurance agent   an agent who represents the insurance company and sells insurance policies to individuals and businesses.

Insurance policy   a policy stating the conditions to which the insurance company and the policyholder have agreed.

Insured   the person or business for which the insurer assumes the risk.

Insurer   a company that agrees to take on certain economic risks and to pay for losses if they occur.

Intangible   something that has no physical form.

Intellectual property   technical knowledge or creative work. It includes software, clothing designs, music, books, and movies.

Interest   the money you receive for letting others use your money; the money you pay for using someone else's money.

Interest rates   the cost of using someone else's money.

Interests   activities that give you satisfaction and that can provide a basis for your employment goals and possible career paths.

Intermediaries   businesses involved in selling the goods and services of producers to consumers and other businesses.

Intermittent processing   using short production runs to produce a precise amount of a variation of a product.

Internal communications   communications that occur between managers, employees, and work groups.

Internal data sources   input provided to the management information system from within the organization, such as accounting records, inventory information, and company sales figures.

International business   business activities needed for creating, shipping, and selling goods and services across national borders.

Internship   work experience in organizations while learning about a career field.

Interstate commerce   business dealings involving companies in more than one state.

Intranet   a local computer network based on the same communication standards as the Internet. It looks like and functions just like a typical website, but it is private and only accessible to authorized users.

Intrastate commerce   business dealings involving companies that do business in only one state.

Inventory   a detailed account of a company's materials, supplies, and finished products.

Inventory management   maintains the supply of all resources needed for production and the products produced.

Inventory records   a financial document used to identify the type and number of products on hand for sale.

Investing   using your savings to earn more money.

Investment income   earnings from dividends, interest, and rent.

IRA   See **Individual retirement account**

J

Job analysis   a specific study of a job to identify in detail the job duties and skill requirements.

Job shadow   a person who spends time with a worker for a day or a week to learn about that person's occupation.

Job sharing   an arrangement in which one job is offered to two people. Each person works a part-time schedule. They share the work space and duties of the job.

Joint account   when two or more people have an account together.

Joint venture   a unique business organized by two or more other businesses to operate for a limited time and for a specific project. It is a type of partnership.

Just-in-time   a logistics process in which goods arrive when needed for production, use, or sale rather than sitting in storage.

L

Labor force   all people above age 16 who are actively working or seeking work.

Labor union   an organized group of employees who negotiate with employers about issues, such as wages and working conditions.

Layoff   a type of termination which is a temporary or permanent reduction in the number of employees due to changing business conditions.

Leadership   the ability to motivate individuals and groups to accomplish important goals.

Level term insurance   the amount of protection and the premiums remain the same while the insurance is in effect.

Liabilities   what a company owes.

Liability insurance   protection against losses from injury to people or property resulting from the products, services, or actions of a business.

Liability risk   a risk that relates to harm or injury to other people or their property because of your actions.

Licensing   selling the right to use some intangible property (production process, trademark, or brand name) for a fee or royalty.

Life cycle   predictable pattern of life stages that are distinguished by unique characteristics, requirements, and expectations.

Life insurance   insurance that pays the amount of the insurance policy upon the death of the insured. The payment is made to people named in the policy known as beneficiaries.

Limited liability company (LLC)   form of business ownership that provides liability protection for owners. It has a simpler set of organizing and operating requirements than a corporation. No articles of incorporation or bylaws are needed. A simple document much like a partnership agreement must be developed.

Limited liability partnership (LLP)   a partnership that identifies some investors who cannot lose more than the amount of their investment, but they are not allowed to participate in the day-to-day management of the business.

Limited-payment policies   a whole life insurance policy that is designated by the number of years the policyholder agrees to pay on it, such as a 20-payment life policy.

Liquidity   the ease with which an investment can be changed into cash without losing its value.

Loan credit   borrowed money for special use. It usually involves a written contract.

Locational unemployment   unemployment that occurs when jobs are available in one place but go unfilled because those who are qualified to fill those jobs live elsewhere and are not willing to relocate.

Logistics   managing the acquisition, movement, and storage of supplies, materials, and finished products in a business.

Long-term assets (fixed assets)   the assets with a lifespan of more than a year, such as land, buildings, equipment, and expensive technology.

Long-term care insurance   insurance that provides long-term care including daily assistance needed because of a long-term illness or disability.

Long-term financing   money needed for the main resources of a business (such as land, buildings, and equipment) that will last for many years.

Long-term liabilities   business debts that will continue for longer than a year.

M

Mail order catalogs   catalogs whereby customers can shop and send in their orders by mail and by telephone.

Major medical insurance   protection against the high costs of serious illness or injuries. It complements other forms of medical insurance.

Management   the process of accomplishing the goals of an organization through the effective use of people and other resources.

Management information system (MIS)   a coordinated system of processing and reporting information in an organization.

Management style the way a manager treats and involves employees.

Manufacturers businesses that get supplies from other producers and convert them into products. They sell their products to consumers and other businesses.

Manufacturing combining raw materials and processed goods into finished products.

Markdown a reduction from the original selling price.

Market economy an economy in which the resources are owned and controlled by the people of the country.

Marketing The activity, set of institutions, and processes for creating, communicating, delivering, and exchanging offerings that have value for customers, clients, partners, and society at large.

Marketing-information management obtaining, managing, and using market information to improve business decision-making and the performance of marketing activities.

Marketing mix the blending of four marketing elements—products, distribution, price, and promotion.

Marketing orientation an approach that considers the needs of customers when developing a marketing mix.

Marketing research finding solutions to problems through carefully designed studies involving customers.

Marketing strategy a company's plan that identifies how it will use marketing to achieve its goals.

Marketplace anywhere that goods and services are exchanged.

Market price the point where supply and demand are equal.

Market value the price at which a share of stock can be bought and sold in the stock market.

Markup the amount added to the cost of a product to set the selling price.

Mass production an assembly process that makes a large number of identical products using a continuous efficient procedure.

Mass promotion communication to many people at the same time with a common message.

Materials processing changing the form of raw materials so they can be consumed or used to make other products.

Maturity date the date on which a loan must be repaid.

Maturity value (face value) the amount being borrowed by the corporation issuing the bond.

Mediation use of a third party who tries to resolve the complaint between the consumer and the business.

Medicaid a form of medical aid to low-income individuals and families administered by state governments. The federal government shares the cost of providing health benefits to eligible individuals and families.

Medical payments coverage insurance that covers policyholders and family members if they are injured while riding in their car or another car.

Medicare a national health insurance program for people aged 65 and older and some disabled people.

Memory a component of a computer system that stores a computer program.

Mentor an experienced employee who serves as counselor to a person with less experience.

Merchandising a set of promotional activities designed to obtain sales in the retail setting.

Middle managers specialists with responsibilities for specific parts of a company's operations.

MIS See **Management information system**

Mission statement short, specific written statement of the reason a business exists and what it wants to achieve.

Mixed economy an economy that combines elements of the command and market economies.

Mixed management the combined use of tactical and strategic management styles.

MNC See **Multinational company**

Mobility the willingness and ability of a person to move to where jobs are located.

Money management the day-to-day financial activities associated with using limited income to satisfy your unlimited needs and wants.

Money market account an account that pays a variable interest rate based on various government and corporate securities.

Money order a form of payment that orders the issuing agency to pay the amount printed on the form to another party.

Monopoly when a business has control of the market for a product or service.

Mortgage a legal document giving the lender a claim against the property if the principal, interest, or both are not paid as agreed.

Mortgage rate the amount individuals pay to borrow for the purchase of a home.

Multinational company (MNC) an organization that does business in several countries. It usually consists of a home country and divisions or separate companies in one or more host countries.

Multinational strategy a strategy that treats each country market differently. Firms develop products and marketing strategies that adapt to the customs, tastes, and buying habits of a distinct national market.

Municipal bonds bonds issued by local and state governments.

Mutual fund an investment fund set up and managed by companies that receive money from many investors.

Mutual savings bank a savings bank that is owned by, and operated for the benefit of, its depositors.

N

National brands brands that are advertised all over the country.

National debt the total amount owed by the federal government.

Natural resources raw materials supplied by nature.

Needs things that are required in order to live.

Negative or unfavorable balance of payments the result of a country sending more money out than it brings in.

Net asset value (NAV) the market share price of a mutual fund based on the total current worth of all stocks and bonds owned by the investment company.

Net income the result of revenue being greater than expenses.

Net income ratio the total sales compared to the net income for a period such as six months or a year.

Net loss the result of expenses being greater than income.

Net pay the amount of a paycheck after taxes and other payroll deductions; take-home pay.

Networking the process of talking to other people about their jobs.

Net worth the difference between a person's assets and liabilities.

No-fault insurance insurance allowing people who are injured in an automobile accident to collect for their financial losses from their own insurance companies no matter who is at fault. Those losses include their medical bills, loss of wages, and other related expenses.

Non-depository intermediaries a category of financial institutions that does not take or hold deposits. They earn their money selling specific services or policies.

Non-economic risks may result in inconvenience or discomfort but do not have a financial impact.

Nonprofit corporation a group of people who join to do some activity that benefits the public.

Non-renewable resource a natural resource that cannot be replaced when used up.

O

Observations a marketing research study that collects information by recording the actions of consumers rather than asking them questions.

Occupation a task or series of tasks that is performed to provide a good or service.

Operating budget describes the financial plan for ongoing operations of the business for a specific period of time.

Operating expenses all of the expenses of operating the business that are associated with the product.

Operating system software a computer program that translates commands and allows application programs to interact with the computer's hardware.

Operational plan identifies how work will be done, who will do it, and what resources will be needed.

Opportunity cost the value of the next-best alternative that you were not able to choose.

Options choices of product features.

Oral communications communications that are spoken.

Ordinary life policy a type of whole life insurance in which premiums remain the same each year as long as the policy-holder lives.

Organizational culture the environment in which people work, made up of the atmosphere, behaviors, beliefs, and relationships.

Organization chart a diagram that shows the structure of an organization, classifications of work and jobs, and the relationships among those classifications.

Organizing the function of a manager involving identifying and arranging the work and resources needed to achieve the goals that have been set.

Output a component of a computer system that presents data in a form that can be retrieved later or may be communicated immediately.

Outsourcing removing work from one company and sending it to another company that can complete it at a lower cost.

Outstanding checks checks that have not been deducted from the bank statement balance.

Over-the-counter (OTC) market a network where securities transactions occur using telephones and computers rather than on an exchange.

Owner's equity the value of the business after liabilities are subtracted from assets; the value of the owner's investment in the business.

P

Packaging protection and security for the product before it is used.

Partnership a business owned and controlled by two or more people who have entered into a written agreement.

Partnership agreement a written agreement among all owners detailing the rules and procedures that guide ownership and operations.

Part-time employee one who works a schedule with either fewer hours each day or fewer than 30 hours each week.

Patent the exclusive right of an inventor to make, sell, and use a product or process.

Payee the person to whom the check is written.

Payroll the financial record of employee compensation, deductions, and net pay.

Payroll records documentation used to process earnings payments and record each employee's pay history.

Payroll system maintains information on each employee to be able to calculate the company's payroll and to make the necessary payments to each employee.

Payroll taxes required federal and state payments for each employee, consisting of income taxes, Social Security, Medicare, and unemployment taxes.

Pension a series of regular payments made to a retired worker under an organized plan.

Performance management evaluating the work of employees and improving performance through training and development.

Perils the causes of loss, such as fire, wind, or theft.

Perishable the availability of a service to match the demand for that service at a specific time.

Permanent employee one to whom the company makes a long-term commitment. It is expected that the employee will work for the business as long as the business is profitable and the employee's performance is satisfactory.

Permanent life insurance life insurance that has cash value and an investment feature.

Personal assets items of value.

Personal data sheet a summary of your important job-related information.

Personal income salaries and wages as well as investment income and government payments to individuals.

Personalized promotion communication directly with each customer using information tailored to that person.

Personal liability coverage insurance that covers claims for injuries to people or damage to property caused by you or your family.

Personal property property not attached to the land, such as furniture or clothing.

Personal risk a risk that can result in personal losses such as health and personal well-being.

Personal selling direct, individualized communication with prospective customers to assess their needs and assist them in satisfying those needs with appropriate products and services.

Personal time a few hours each month that can be scheduled for non-job activities.

Piece rate a pay-for-performance plan in which an employee receives a specific amount for each unit of work produced.

Piracy stealing or illegally copying software packages or information.

Planning the function of a manager involving analyzing information, setting goals, and making decisions about what needs to be done.

Planning and staffing activities activities directed at identifying and filling all of the jobs in the company with qualified people.

Point-of-sale transaction a transaction in which a merchant accepts debit cards to pay for purchases.

Policies guidelines used in making consistent decisions.

Policyholder the person or company buying the policy.

Pollution occurs when the environment is tainted with the by-products of human actions.

Position influence the ability to get others to accomplish tasks because of the position the leader holds.

Positive or favorable balance of payments occurs when a nation receives more money in a year than it pays out.

Postal money order a form of payment purchased from the U.S. Post Office that can be sent safely through the mail.

Postdated check a check that is dated later than the date on which it is written.

Preferred provider organization (PPO) a managed care plan that involves several health care providers, such as a group of physicians, a clinic, or a hospital.

Preferred stock stock that has priority over common stock in the payment of dividends.

Premium the amount a policyholder must pay for insurance coverage.

Presentation software a program that allows a speaker to show text, data, photos, and other visuals. The images may be accompanied by sound effects, music, or other audio.

Price money customer must pay for a product or service.

Price-earnings (P/E) ratio the relationship between a stock's selling price and its earnings per share.

Price index a number that compares prices in one year with some earlier base year.

Pricing setting and communicating the value of products and services.

Primary research studies carried out to gather new information specifically directed at a current problem.

Prime rate the rate banks make available to their best business customers, such as large corporations.

Procedure a list of steps to be followed for performing a particular work activity; a description of the way work is to be done.

Processed goods products that have been changed in form to increase their value and usefulness.

Processing changing and improving the form of another product.

Producers individuals and organizations that determine what products and services will be available for sale.

Product everything a business offers to satisfy a customer's needs.

Product and service management designing, developing, maintaining, improving, and acquiring products and services that meet consumer needs.

Product costs costs to the manufacturer of producing the product or the price paid by other businesses to buy the product.

Product features additions and improvements to the basic product.

Production process the activities, equipment, and resources needed to manufacture a product.

Productivity the production output in relation to a unit of input, such as a worker.

Profit the amount of money available to the business after all costs and expenses have been paid.

Program a series of detailed, step-by-step instructions that tell the computer what functions to complete.

Promissory note a written promise to repay based on a debtor's excellent credit history.

Promotion any form of communication used to inform, persuade, or remind; communicating information about products and services to potential customers; the advancement of an employee to a position with greater responsibility.

Promotional sales sales used to promote the selling of regular merchandise with short-term price reductions.

Property damage liability insurance that protects a driver against claims if the insured's car damages someone else's property and the insured is at fault.

Property insurance insurance that protects you from the financial loss you would incur if some of your property were lost or destroyed due to fire, theft, vandalism, flood, or other hazard.

Property rights the exclusive rights to possess and use property and its profits.

Property risk a risk that can lead to loss of personal or business property including money, vehicles, and buildings.

Property tax a major source of revenue for local governments based on the value of land and buildings.

Proprietorship a business owned and run by just one person.

Prosperity the peak of the business cycle, it is a period in which most people who want to work are working, businesses produce goods and services in record numbers, wages are good, and the rate of gross domestic product (GDP) growth increases.

Publicity non-paid promotional communication presented by the media rather than by the business or organization that is being promoted.

Public relations an ongoing program of non-paid and paid communications intended to favorably influence public opinion about an organization, marketing effort, idea, or issue.

Public utility an organization that supplies a service or product vital to all people including companies that provide local telephone service, water, and electricity.

Pure research research done without a specific product in mind with the goal of discovering new solutions to problems.

Pure risk a risk that presents the chance of loss but no opportunity for gain.

Q

Qualifications-based resume a resume in which your abilities and experiences related to the job for which you are applying are highlighted.

Quota a government-set limit on the quantity of a product that may be imported or exported within a given period.

R

Rational buying motives reasons consumers decide what products and services to purchase based on facts and logic.

Real estate land and anything that is attached to it.

Real property property permanently attached to land, such as a house or garage.

Receiver a person or organization that is being communicated to by another person or organization.

Recession the phase of the business cycle in which demand begins to decrease, businesses lower production, unemployment begins to rise, and gross domestic product (GDP) growth slows for two or more quarters of the calendar year.

Records of account a financial document used to identify all purchases and sales made using credit.

Recovery the phase in the business cycle in which unemployment begins to decrease, demand for goods and services increases, and gross domestic product (GDP) begins to rise again.

References people who can give a report about your character, education, and work habits. These individuals may be teachers, previous employers, supervisors, or coworkers.

Refund anticipation loan a short-term loan based on the expected amount of a tax refund.

Regular medical insurance insurance that covers fees for nonsurgical care given in the doctor's office, the patient's home, or a hospital. The policy states the amount payable for each visit or call. It also lists the maximum number of visits covered.

Renewable term insurance an insurance policy that allows the policyholder to continue term insurance for one or more terms without taking another physical examination.

Renters policy a property and liability insurance policy suitable for renters. It covers household goods and personal belongings and protects against the same kinds of perils covered by homeowners policies.

Replacement insurance insurance in which the insurance company actually replaces an item that has been destroyed. No depreciation is deducted.

Responsibility the obligation to complete specific work.

Restrictive endorsement an endorsement that limits the use of the check to the purpose given in the endorsement.

Resume a tool that provides information about you to a potential employer.

Retailers the final business organization in an indirect channel of distribution for consumer products.

Retail sales the sales of durable and nondurable goods bought by consumers.

Return on equity ratio the net profit of the business compared to the amount of owners' equity.

Revenue all income that a business receives over a period of time; government income.

Revolving account allows account holder to charge purchases at any time, but only part of the debt must be paid each month.

Reward influence influence that results from a leader's ability to give or withhold rewards.

Risk the possibility of incurring a loss.

Robotics mechanical devices programmed to do routine tasks, such as those in many factories.

S

Safe-deposit box a container for storage of valuables offered by banks.

Salary and wages direct payment of money to an employee for work completed.

Sales credit involves the use of charge accounts and credit cards by consumers purchasing goods and services.

Sales promotion activities and materials designed to reinforce a company's brand and image. It is also a direct incentive to take an action likely to immediately increase sales of a product or service.

Sales tax a state or local tax on goods and services that is collected by the seller.

Saving the storage of money for future use.

SBA See **Small Business Administration**

Scanners input devices that translate words and photos into computer-readable formats.

Scarcity not having enough resources to satisfy every need.

Schedule a time plan for completing activities. It matches people with resources to make sure activities are finished on time.

S corporation a corporate form of business that offers the limited liability of a corporation.

Secondary research analyzing existing information gathered for another purpose but used to solve a current problem.

Secured loan a loan in which you must put up property or collateral as security for repayment.

Selling communicating directly with potential customers to determine and satisfy their needs.

Selling price the price paid by the customer for the product.

Sender a person or organization that has information to communicate to another person or organization.

Service business a business that carries out activities that are consumed by its customers.

Service charge the fee a bank charges for handling a checking account.

Service fee a charge involving the time and money it takes a creditor to investigate your credit history, process your loan or charge account application, and keep records of your payments and balances.

Service-providing industries businesses that perform services that satisfy the needs of other businesses and consumers.

Services activities provided for the satisfaction of others that are consumed at the same time they are produced.

Share draft account a checking account at a credit union.

Shareholders members of credit unions.

Short-term financing the money needed to pay for the current operating activities of a business.

Signature card a document used to verify your signature.

Simple interest the interest on single-payment loans.

Single-payment loan   a loan in which you do not pay anything until the end of the loan period, possibly 60 or 90 days. At that time, you pay the full amount you borrowed plus the finance charge.

Small business   an independent business with fewer than 500 employees.

Small Business Administration (SBA)   a government agency that helps small business owners develop business plans and obtain financing and other support for their companies.

Small claims court   a court system in every state that exists to resolve cases involving small amounts.

Smart cards   plastic cards with silicon chips that are used to store information. The chip within the card stores such data as a cardholder's current account balance, credit history, or medical information.

Social responsibility   the duty of a business to contribute to the well-being of a community.

Software   the instructions that run the computer system.

Span of control   the number of employees who are assigned to a particular work task and manager.

Special checking account   checking accounts for people who only write a few checks each month. Banks charge customers about 10 to 20 cents for each check written.

Special form   a form of a homeowners policy that insures property against all perils except earthquakes, flood, war, nuclear accidents, and certain others.

Specialty stores   stores that have a special line of products for sale.

Specialty superstores   stores that offer low prices and a wide variety of a limited product line.

Speculative risk   the chance either to gain or to lose.

Spreadsheet software   a program that formats data in columns and rows in order to do calculations.

Staffing   the function of a manager including all of the activities involved in obtaining, preparing, and compensating the employees of a business.

Standard   a specific measurement against which an activity or result is judged.

Start-up budget   a budget that plans income and expenses from the beginning of a new business or a major business expansion until it becomes profitable.

Start-up financing   the amount of money needed to open the business.

Statement of account   a record of the transactions completed during the billing period.

Stock   ownership in a corporation.

Stockbroker   a licensed specialist in the buying and selling of stocks and bonds.

Stock exchange   a business organization that accommodates the buying and selling of securities.

Stock index   a measurement of investment values.

Stop payment order   a written notice that tells the bank not to pay a certain check.

Store brands (private label brands)   brands owned by stores. For example, Craftsman is one of the brand names on tools sold by Sears.

Straight salary   a specific amount of money paid to an employee for each week or month worked.

Strategic management   a style in which managers are less directive and involve employees in decision-making.

Substitute check   a digital reproduction of the original paper check.

Supermarket   in food retailing, it is the large, full-service store that carries name brands.

Superstores   discount stores that have expanded to include a wide variety of food products. They may also include other retail services such as a bakery, restaurant, pharmacy, video rentals, and banking.

Supervisors   the first level of management in a business, responsible for the work of a group of employees and some non-management duties.

Supply   the quantity of a good or service that businesses are willing and able to provide.

Supply chain management   See **Logistics**

Supply chain management software   software that allows cooperating companies to share ordering, production, and shipping information.

Supply curve   the graphic view of the supply for a product or service. The supply curve for a product, for example, illustrates the relationship between the price of the product and the quantity businesses will supply.

Surgical insurance   insurance that covers all or part of the surgeon's fees for an operation.

Surplus   a financial situation in which actual spending is less than the budgeted amount.

Surveys   a marketing research study that gathers information from people using a carefully planned set of questions.

T

Tactical management   a style in which the manager is directive and controlling.

Take-home pay   the amount of a paycheck after taxes and other payroll deductions.

Talent   a natural, inborn aptitude to do certain things.

Targeted application letter a letter that provides a quick summary of your ability to meet the needs of an organization. It usually includes a list of major skills and competencies.

Target market a specific group of customers that have similar wants and needs.

Tariff a tax that a government places on certain imported products.

Tax a charge imposed by a government to finance public services.

Taxable income the amount on which taxes are calculated.

Tax credit an amount subtracted directly from taxes owed.

Tax deduction an amount that reduces taxable income.

Tax-deferred earnings the investment earnings on a retirement plan that will be taxed later, after retirement.

Tax-deferred income income will be taxed at a later date.

Tax-exempt earnings earnings on which the recipient is not required to pay taxes.

Tax-exempt income income not subject to tax. Interest earned on most state and city bonds, for example, is exempt from federal income tax.

Tax record a financial document that shows all taxes collected, owed, and paid.

T-bill rate the yield on short-term (13-week) U.S. government debt obligations.

T-bills See **Treasury bills**

T-bonds See **Treasury bonds**

Technology the use of automated machines, electronic equipment, and integrated computer systems to help increase the efficiency of producing goods and services.

Telecommuting allows employees who primarily use personal computers and other technology to work from home. They communicate with managers, coworkers, and customers using the Internet, telephone, and fax machines.

Temporary employee one hired for a specific time or to complete a specific assignment.

Tentative career decision a decision that is subject to change as new information is received.

Termination the end of an employment relationship between a company and an employee.

Term life insurance insurance that provides financial protection from losses resulting from a death during a definite period or term.

Time wage a specific amount of money paid to an employee for each hour worked.

Title ownership of goods.

T-notes See **Treasury notes**

Trade barriers restrictions to free trade.

Trade credit occurs when a company receives goods from a supplier and pays for them later.

Trade deficit a situation in which a country imports (buys) more than it exports (sells).

Trademark a distinctive name, symbol, word, picture, or combination of these that a company uses to identify products or services.

Trade-off what you make when you give something up to have something else.

Trade surplus a situation in which a country exports (sells) more than it imports (buys).

Traditional economy an economy in which goods and services are produced the way they have always been produced. It is used in countries that are less developed and are not yet participating in the global economy.

Transfer the assignment of an employee to another job in the company with a similar level of responsibility.

Traveler's checks special forms designed for making payments when away from home.

Treasury bills (T-bills) bills that involve short-term borrowing with maturities from 91 days to one year.

Treasury bond rate the yield on long-term (20-year) U.S. government debt obligations.

Treasury bonds (T-bonds) bonds that involve long-term borrowing, with maturities ranging from 10 to 30 years.

Treasury notes (T-notes) note that involve borrowing with maturities from 1 to 10 years.

U

Uncollectible accounts bad debts or doubtful accounts.

Uncontrollable risk a risk that cannot be reduced by your actions.

Unemployment insurance insurance to reduce financial hardship of unemployment.

Unemployment rate the portion of people in the labor force who are not working.

Uninsurable risk when a risk is not common or if it is impossible to predict the amount of loss that could be suffered.

Uninsured motorist coverage protection against hit-and-run drivers or drivers without insurance money to pay claims.

Unit price a price per unit of measure.

Unity of command a clear reporting relationship for all staff of a business.

Universal life insurance insurance that provides both insurance protection and a substantial savings plan.

Upkeep maintaining your property in good condition.

V

Values things that are important to you.

Variable expenses living costs that differ each time and may not be as easy to estimate.

Variable life insurance an insurance plan that resembles an investment portfolio. It lets the policyholder choose among a broad range of investments.

Vehicle insurance coverage of automobiles, trucks, and other business vehicles.

Vending machines non-store shopping where customers can shop for items by putting money into machines.

Venture capital money provided by large investors to finance new products and new businesses that have a good chance to be very profitable.

Vertical communications communications that move up or down in an organization between management and employees.

Videoconferencing allows people in different geographic locations to meet "face-to-face" by satellite.

Visual merchandising visual signals used to communicate information in a retail setting.

Voice-activated systems input devices that allow words spoken into a microphone to be entered as data or to be translated into instructions or commands.

W

Wants things that add comfort and pleasure to your life.

Warehouse club a no-frills outlet focusing on the sale of large quantities at reasonable prices.

White-collar crime illegal acts carried out by office or professional workers while at work.

White-collar worker one whose work is more mental than physical and involves the handling and processing of information.

Whole life insurance permanent insurance that extends over the lifetime, or whole life, of the insured.

Wholesalers intermediaries between manufacturers and retailers.

Work environment the physical conditions and the psychological atmosphere in which employees work.

Workers' compensation an insurance plan that provides medical and survivor benefits for people injured, disabled, or killed on the job.

Workforce all of the people 16 years or older who are employed or who are looking for a job.

World trade See **International business**

Written communication communication that includes notes, letters, reports, and e-mail messages.

Y

Yield the percentage of money earned on savings or investment over a year.

Index